DATE DUE

BRITISH CIVIL AIRCRAFT
SINCE 1919

Prototype, G-AVDF, and three early production Beagle Pups near Shoreham power station in March 1968, G-AVLM flown by Beagle chief test pilot J. W. C. 'Pee Wee' Judge to whose dedicated development flying and inspired showmanship the Pup owed so much.

BRITISH
CIVIL AIRCRAFT
SINCE 1919
VOLUME ONE

A. J. JACKSON

PUTNAM

LONDON

BY THE SAME AUTHOR
De Havilland Aircraft since 1915
Avro Aircraft since 1908
Blackburn Aircraft since 1909

TL
526
.G7
J32
V. 1

ISBN 0 370 10006 9
Filmset in Photon Times 10 pt. by
Richard Clay (The Chaucer Press), Ltd.,
Bungay, Suffolk
and printed in Great Britain by
Fletcher & Son, Ltd., Norwich
for
Putnam & Company Limited
9 Bow Street, London WC2E 7AL
First Published 1959
Second Edition 1973

Contents

5

Foreword

The aircraft described in this series of books reflect the progress made in sport and transport flying during the first half century of civil aviation in Britain. This began in February 1919 when a Civil Aviation Department of the Air Ministry was formed, and the Air Navigation Act 1911–19 passed which empowered the Secretary of State for Air to prepare air traffic regulations which included the first airworthiness and registration requirements ever formulated. They were issued on 30 April 1919 and civil flying began on the next day.

Surplus 1914–18 military aircraft, hastily adapted, served their purpose until gradually replaced by the classic commercial and light aeroplanes of the 'golden age' between the wars, and this pattern was repeated after the 1939–45 conflict. Unhappily the next quarter century witnessed the influx of sophisticated foreign light aircraft in such numbers that large scale production of British light aeroplanes was brought to an end. Some commercial success was enjoyed in the field of jet executive and short range utility aircraft but main effort was centred on the development of advanced intercontinental transports which culminated in the mighty, supersonic Anglo-French Concorde.

During the first decade, control of Civil Aviation remained under military influence but from 1929 the British Corporation Register and Lloyd's Register of Shipping were permitted to renew, on behalf of the Air Ministry, the Certificates of Airworthiness for light aircraft. The Air Navigation Act of 1936 then paved the way for the founding of the Air Registration Board, an independent body which, from 1937, brought British airworthiness and maintenance requirements to standards unequalled anywhere in the world.

In the 1960s, when amateur construction established itself as a hobby, structural integrity of such projects became the responsibility of the Popular Flying Association, an amateur organisation whose engineering inspectors were entrusted with clearing the final product with the A.R.B. By 1972 at least 30 home-built aircraft had already flown in Britain, and over 300 additional machines of more than 20 different types were under construction.

Despite its title the A.R.B. had little to do with the registration of aircraft, this traditionally being the responsibility of variously-titled civil aviation ministries and lately of the Department of Trade and Industry. Records maintained by these bodies, by manufacturers, by the author and other historians, make it possible to trace in these three books the evolution of aircraft types, to recall epic flights and famous pilots, and to mention individually not only every civil aeroplane and helicopter produced by Britain's aircraft industry since 1919 but also to enumerate the multiplicity of imported foreign types, all military aircraft flown with civil markings, and such one-off home-builts as have been registered to date. Each main chapter ends with a list of exported aircraft which, if integrated with the British-owned examples set down in the British Civil Register appendix, gives the complete production run.

7

Space limitations prevent the inclusion of unregistered machines, gliders, balloons or airships but to meet the needs of readers wishing to compile complete British civil registers, markings issued to a small number of gliders and lighter-than-air craft, together with registrations which, for various reasons, could not be allotted, form the subjects of separate appendixes.

The author acknowledges with gratitude the advice and encouragement received from many individuals and organisations during the preparation of these volumes, particularly from E. B. Morgan and C. H. Barnes, technical librarians of the British Aircraft Corporation at Weybridge and Filton respectively; Frank Parker, chairman of the Popular Flying Association; the Airworthiness section of the Department of Trade and Industry; and the staff of *Lloyds List and Shipping Gazette*. My sincere thanks go also to Ann Tilbury, photographic librarian of *Flight International*; David Dorrell, editor of *Air Pictorial*; and John W. R. Taylor, editor of *Jane's All the World's Aircraft* who dug deep and enthusiastically into ancient photographic files and without whose ever-willing assistance the record could not have been completed. The excellence of other illustrations is testimony to the skill of photographers Richard Riding, W. L. Lewis and P. J. Bish; L. E. Bradford's three view drawings being, as ever, unmatched in artistry and accuracy. John Goring has assisted expertly with the revision of chapters on transport aircraft, David Roberts has again double-checked and indexed all factual data, and the text has been typed by my wife Marjorie whose enormous grasp of obscure aeronautical phraseology, designations and aviation company styling has made dictation so easy.

Contributions from the personal archives of the following long term associates has enriched the text and served as a constant check on accuracy: J. A. Bagley, D. K. Fox, M. J. Hooks and B. Martin, Air-Britain; F. G. Swanborough, editor of *Air Enthusiast*; B. N. Stainer, Aviation Photo News, M. J. Vines, Air Portraits; P. M. Jarrett and J. D. Gillies, Royal Aeronautical Society; K. M. Molson, J. R. Ellis and J. A. Griffin, Canadian Aviation Historical Society; C. Feldwick and D. P. Woodhall, Aviation Historical Society of New Zealand; K. R. Meggs, D. L. Mackenzie and N. M. Parnell, Aviation Historical Society of Australia; J. R. Batt, Aviation Traders Ltd.; J. M. Bruce, R.A.F. Museum, Hendon; M. D. N. Fisher; J. S. Havers; Leslie Hunt; H. Kofoed; T. Leigh; I. Macfarlane; W. R. Matthews; A. W. J. G. Ord-Hume; E. Ritaranta; Bruce Robertson; K. F. Smy; and John Stroud, editor of the Putnam aeronautical series.

Thanks are also extended to Air-Britain for the use of material which originated in its publications; to P. W. Moss for data extracted from *Impressments Log*; to N. H. Ellison and R. O. MacDemetria for the use of their Auster Production List; to M. R. Cain and C. Frost for providing space in *Anglia Aeronews*, and to all those kind friends who have assisted in other ways.

Leigh-on-Sea,   A. J. J.
January 1972

The British-built Aeronca 100 G-AEXD at Blackbushe in October 1969. (*Tony Leigh*)

Aeronca 100

Bearing an abbreviation of its maker's name, the near-ultra-light Aeronca was first produced in America in 1928 and two years later an open-cockpit single-seat model C-2, G-ABHE, was imported by Col. M. O. Darby. This machine was powered by a 26 h.p. twin-cylinder air-cooled engine and after erection in the A.D.C. factory at Croydon made its first flight in February 1931 piloted by S. A. Thorn. In November 1931 it was sold to R. G. T. Denman, and was based at Heston until acquired by Major H. J. Parham, who was later to become the pioneer of A.O.P. flying. Nine months of enthusiastic daily use ended the life of the small engine, and the machine was then converted into a glider. Its first motorless flight took place on 15 May 1937, and, still carrying its civil registration, it was given to the Dorset Gliding Club.

Col. M. O. Darby also imported an open-cockpit, side-by-side two-seater (likewise designated C-2) which was erected at Croydon alongside G-ABHE and registered G-ABKX in April 1931. It was predecessor of the well known C-3 cabin type built in Britain by the Aeronautical Corporation of Great Britain Ltd. at Peterborough. As an interim measure 16 American-built aircraft were erected at Hanworth, the first two, G-ADSO and 'SP, obtained via the Murray Aeronautical Corporation of Canada, being convincingly demonstrated there in high wind on 19 September 1935. A number of these C-3s were sold to private owners at £395 each, one, G-AEAC, being delivered by air to Johannesburg by David Llewellyn in a solo flight lasting from 7 February to 1 March 1936. Others were sold abroad and to the flying clubs; the Cinque Ports Flying Club and the Bedford School of Flying respectively owning G-AEFT and G-ADYS, which are today the sole survivors. G-AEFT, in 1956–58 the personal mount of Mr. B. F. Collins, M.B.E., Commandant of Southend Airport, was fitted with a second door and additional cabin windows by Paul Simpson in 1952. Chief pre-war user of the C-3 was the London Air Park Flying Club at Hanworth, which in September 1936 had five (G-ADSO, 'SP, 'YP, G-AELX and 'LY), low maintenance and operating costs enabling A Licences to be offered for under £20. This period saw the Aeronca C-3 at the height of its popularity, boosted by Richard Grubb's spectacular victory in the 1936 Folkestone Trophy Race at 84·75 m.p.h. flying G-ADYR. He lost his life when crossing the Irish Sea in G-AEXB, the last British-built specimen, on 8 July 1937.

The Aeronca E.113C engine fitted to the C-3 was manufactured under licence in this country by J. A. Prestwich Ltd. as the Aeronca JAP J-99, but differed from the original by virtue of its dual ignition. Peterborough-built aircraft fitted with these motors were known as the Aeronca 100, many of which were merely test flown and then stored through lack of orders. This state of affairs brought production to an end in six months, after only some two dozen, including one improved Aeronca 300 and two known as Ely 700s, had been built. The latter were G-AFLT and 'LU, which had two doors and fuselages 10 in. wider than standard. Eventually they were all taken over by Aircraft Exchange and Mart Ltd., which, after some difficulty, succeeded in disposing of three to Australia, six (G-AETG, 'TR, 'VT, 'WU, 'WV and 'XD) to the London Air Park Flying Club and four (G-AEVR, 'XA, 'VE and G-AFLU) to the Peterborough Flying Club.

Four were exported to Australia in November 1936, three becoming VH-UYZ (Light Aeroplanes Pty. Ltd., Brisbane) and VH-UXU and 'XV (Aerial Transport Ltd., Sydney). The latter were first flown in January 1937 before sale to private owners W. H. Colville and A. R. Clancy but in June 1940 'XU and 'YZ were both delivered to the Northern Aero Club at Cairns, Queensland.

The other, VH-UXV, sold to I. F. Sparrow, was stored at Ardlethan, N.S.W. during the 1939–45 war and afterwards flew regularly at Sydney until shipped to Fiji aboard R.M.V. *Mootah* and first flown at Nadi Airport, Suva, as VQ-FAJ by G. J. Webster and J. P. Meehan on 30 October 1949. On 28 October 1965 the old Aeronca 100 left for New Zealand on the M.V. *Argentinian Reefer*, consigned to Mr. Colin Feldwick for restoration as ZK-AYW.

Not being suitable for impressment in a military role in 1939, most of the 20 or so surviving Aeroncas were stored, some to be handed over to the A.T.C. for ground instruction but many merely to corrode away. Sixteen were found in various parts of the country after the war, of which 11 flew again, and the little aircraft later enjoyed a popularity denied it in earlier days. In July 1949 Peter Gooch flew G-AEWU all the way to Barcelona and back to participate in the Spanish Rally, after which it flew with the Brookside Group. Two of the former L.A.P. Flying Club machines, G-AETR and 'LX, were less fortunate. The former, stored with G-AETG and 'VT at Tattersall's Garages, Gisburn, Lancs. during

S. A. 'Bill' Thorn in the open cockpit Aeronca C-2 at Heston in February 1931. (*Flight Photo 10399*)

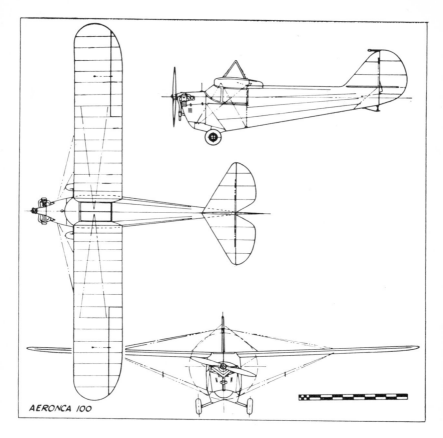

AERONCA 100

the war, was overhauled by Shorts at Belfast in August 1946, but crashed into Strangford Lough, Co. Down, soon afterwards, killing the pilot, W. S. S. Henry. G-AELX was lost with its pilot, R. R. Ward, in the Irish Sea in 1951 in identical circumstances to those in which Grubb was killed 14 years earlier.

The Aeronca 300, G-AEVE, flown during the war in camouflage and rediscovered in good condition behind a hedge opposite Warton Aerodrome, Lancs. in September 1949, donated its wings to A. W. J. G. Ord-Hume and P. Simpson who were rebuilding G-AEVT at Pinner. Twenty years later the four Aeronca 100s surviving in Britain also owed their existence to the inspired interchange of serviceable components.

SPECIFICATION

Manufacturers: (Aeronca C-2 The Aeronautical Corporation of America Inc., Lunken
and C-3)   Airport, Cincinnati, Ohio, U.S.A.
      (Aeronca 100) The Aeronautical Corporation of Great Britain Ltd.,
        Walton Aerodrome, Peterborough, Northants.

The sole Aeronca 300, G-AEVE, inscribed 'Ely' on the rudder, which John Kirwan demonstrated at the Hatfield S.B.A.C. Show on 29 June 1936. (*via Colin Feldwick*)

Power Plants: (Aeronca C-2) One 26 h.p. Aeronca E.107A.
(Aeronca C-3) One 36 h.p. Aeronca E.113C.
(Aeronca 100) One 40 h.p. Aeronca JAP J-99.

	Aeronca C-2	Aeronca C-3	Aeronca 100
Span	36 ft. 0 in.	36 ft. 0 in.	36 ft. 0 in.
Length	20 ft. 0 in.	20 ft. 0 in.	20 ft. 0 in.
Height	7 ft. 10 in.	7 ft. 10 in.	7 ft. 10 in.
Wing area	142·2 sq. ft.	142·2 sq. ft.	142·2 sq. ft.
Tare weight	426 lb.	569 lb.	569 lb.
All-up weight	700 lb.	1,005 lb.	1,005 lb.
Maximum speed	75 m.p.h.	95 m.p.h.	95 m.p.h.
Cruising speed	60 m.p.h.	87 m.p.h.	87 m.p.h.
Initial climb	450 ft./min.	450 ft./min.	450 ft./min.
Ceiling	16,500 ft.	12,000 ft.	12,000 ft.
Range	200 miles	200 miles	200 miles

Production: (a) Aeronca 100

Twenty-one aircraft: (c/n AB.101) G-AENW; (AB.102) VH-UYZ; (AB.103) Lyons Bros., Sydney; (AB.104) VH-UXU; (AB.105) VH-UXV/VQ-FAJ; (AB.106) G-AESX; (AB.107) untraced; (AB.108) G-AEUW; (AB.109) G-AESP; (AB.110) G-AETG; (AB.111) G-AEVR; (AB.112) G-AETR; (AB.113) G-AEXA; (AB.114) G-AEVS; (AB.115) G-AEVT; (AB.116) G-AEWU; (AB.117) G-AEWV; (AB.118) G-AEWW; (AB.119) G-AEWX; (AB.124) G-AEXD; (AB.134) G-AEXB.

(b) Aeronca 300

One aircraft only: (c/n AB.120) G-AEVE; (AB.121–AB.123) and (AB.125–AB.129) not completed.

(c) Ely 700

Two aircraft only: (c/n AB.130) G-AFLU; (AB.131) G-AFLT; (AB.132 and AB.133) not completed.

(d) Ely Type F.C.1

One aircraft only: (c/n F.C.1) G-AFXC, project abandoned.

The prototype Airspeed Ferry, G-ABSI, showing the original upright Gipsy II outboard engines. (*Flight Photo 11531*)

Airspeed A.S.4 Ferry

Pleasure flying in the 1920s was confined mainly to the activities of itinerant Avro 504Ks belonging to small firms using farm fields and flying for the masses did not, in fact, begin until Sir Alan Cobham's genius devised the National Aviation Day Displays. He assembled a small fleet of aircraft at Hanworth on 12 April 1932, to give a never-to-be-forgotten inaugural air display which was followed by large scale pleasure flying in any of the participating machines but his newest, most interesting and unorthodox aeroplane, Airspeed Ferry prototype G-ABSI 'Youth of Britain II', still on test at Martlesham, did not reach Hanworth until 23 April, and was separately demonstrated on 4 May. It was a large three-engined biplane of wooden construction with plywood-covered fuselage and fabric wings, built to Sir Alan's specification by Messrs. A. H. Tiltman and N. S. Norway in the newly established Airspeed factory at York, and first flew at Sherburn-in-Elmet piloted by H. V. Worrall.

Although a biplane specifically designed for short range pleasure flying and having an outstanding small field performance, its three engines and roomy cabin for 10 passengers made it virtually an airliner in miniature. No more suitable aircraft could have been designed for firmly establishing in the minds of those making their first flights the safety, comfort and speed of the airlines and this form of propaganda was, of course, the underlying motive of National Aviation Day's activities.

The display went on tour, and later in the year was joined by a second Ferry, G-ABSJ, 'Youth of Britain III', and thereafter their silver and green became a familiar sight at no fewer than 200 towns and villages visited in all parts of the United Kingdom. The 1933 tour was no less popular than the first, and with 'SJ renamed 'Youth of Africa' the Ferries continued faithfully to carry their 11-man loads out of little fields. Total power was 360 h.p. (or only 36 h.p. per paying passenger) given by one Gipsy III inverted engine in the top centre section and two upright Gipsy IIs mounted on the lower mainplanes. The second Ferry, 'SJ, was eventually disposed of in favour of the Handley Page Clive G-ABYX, and was sold by R. K. Dundas Ltd. to the Himalaya Air Transport and Survey Co. Ltd. and ferried out to India by Flt. Lt. Bremridge. On arrival it was christened 'Dragoman' and during the period 25 April to 21 October 1934, flew a 70 mile shuttle from Hardwar to Gauchar with pilgrims en route to a holy shrine at Badinrath, high in the Himalayas. Said to have been ravaged by termites, it was, in fact, burned out in a hangar at Delhi on 5 October 1936 by vandals who clubbed the watchman.

In 1933 a second and final pair of these aeroplanes, G-ACBT and 'FB, had been acquired by John Sword, a bus operator of wide experience and managing director of Midland and Scottish Air Ferries Ltd. The two white Ferries, with their smart red trimmings, flew for two seasons on the company's services from Renfrew to Campbeltown, to Belfast and to Speke. Here, by mutual arrangement, they connected with Hillman's Dragons, thus giving a through trunk service to the South of England. In the face of increasing competition, the firm closed down at the end of 1934 and the Ferries were put up for sale. In 1939 'BT still languished at Renfrew, its stable-mate having been sold in April 1936 to C. W. A. Scott's Air Display and sent to Hanworth for overhaul. Here it joined the prototype, acquired when National Aviation Day Displays came to an end in 1935. After a season in a new all-red colour scheme, 'SI and 'FB became the property in the following November of Air Publicity Ltd. of Heston, and during the winter the varied assortment of ageing Gipsies was removed, and in 1937 the Ferries reappeared with three new inverted Gipsy Major engines apiece, in which form they continued their joyriding careers until the end of the following season. In 1939 the prototype was bought by Portsmouth, Southsea and Isle of Wight Aviation Ltd., but saw little service on their I.O.W. shuttle, as the annual C. of A. overhaul did not take place until December 1939, well after the outbreak of war. It was then impressed into the R.A.F. as AV968, served with the Halton Station Flt., July–November 1940, and spent a year in store at No. 51 M.U., Lichfield before

The prototype Ferry in its final form with three 120 h.p. Gipsy Major inverted engines.

disposal to No. 474 A.T.C. Squadron, Long Eaton, Derbyshire as instructional airframe 2758M.

The other Ferry, G-ACFB, was allowed to lapse into disuse after the C. of A. expired on 21 November 1938 and remained picketed at Heston until dismantled and transferred by road to No. 1037 A.T.C. Squadron, Meir, Stoke-on-Trent, in 1941.

SPECIFICATION

Manufacturers: Airspeed Ltd., Piccadilly, York.

Power Plants: One 120 h.p. de Havilland Gipsy III and two 120 h.p. de Havilland Gipsy II.

Three 130 h.p. de Havilland Gipsy Major.

Dimensions: Span, 55 ft. 0 in. Length, 39 ft. 8 in. Height, 14 ft. 3 in. Wing area, 610·5 sq. ft.

Weights: Tare weight, 3,300 lb. All-up weight, 5,400 lb.

Performance: Maximum speed, 112 m.p.h. Cruising speed, 100 m.p.h. Initial climb, 800 ft./min. Ceiling, 15,500 ft. Range, 340 miles.

Production: Four aircraft only: (c/n 4) G-ABSI; (5) G-ABSJ; (6) G-ACBT; (9) G-ACFB.

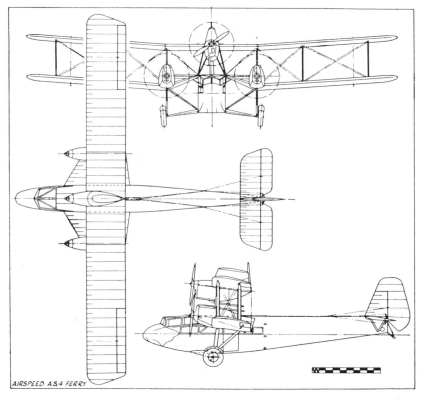

AIRSPEED A.S.4 FERRY

15

G. H. Stainforth at the controls of the prototype Courier on one of its early test flights.
(Aeroplane)

Airspeed A.S.5 Courier

The all-wood, six-seat Courier, designed by A. H. Tiltman, was notable for being the first British type with a retractable undercarriage to go into production. This was hydraulically operated by means of a hand pump, the maximum speed being increased by 13 m.p.h. for a weight penalty of but 30 lb. The prototype, designated A.S.5 and registered G-ABXN, was built at York in 1932 for Sir Alan Cobham's non-stop refuelling flight to India but was taken south by road when Airspeed moved to more spacious premises at Portsmouth and made its first flight there, piloted by G. H. Stainforth on 10 April 1933. Powered by a 240 h.p. Lynx IVC radial, it was equipped with overload tanks of 275 gallons capacity in the cabin, with a circular trap in the roof for handling the tanker hose.

More than a year was spent in perfecting airborne refuelling techniques and on 24 September 1934 it took off lightly loaded from Portsmouth en route to India piloted by Sir Alan with Sqn. Ldr. Helmore as co-pilot and hose operator. The cabin tanks were then filled over the Channel from the Handley Page W.10 tanker G-EBMM, after which all went well until south of Malta when throttle linkage failure necessitated a wheels-up landing at Hal Far. The attempt was then abandoned and the machine shipped home.

Courier production began with a batch of 15 A.S.5s having increased normal tankage and tail wheels, the first, G-ACJL, being completed in August 1933. Specially painted up in the two tone blue livery of Aircraft Exchange and Mart Ltd., it was flown by Sqn. Ldr. D. E. Stodart and K. G. Stodart into fourth place in the handicap section of the immortal MacRobertson Race from Mildenhall to Melbourne in October 1934. The third production Courier was the green and gold G-ACLF, fitted with the more powerful Cheetah V motor, which gave a cruising speed of 152 m.p.h. This was the A.S.5B, demonstration in India resulting in an order for G-ACVG, the only other A.S.5B built. At home the first serious operators of the Courier were Portsmouth, Southsea and Isle of Wight Aviation Ltd., who flew the fawn and blue G-ACLR and 'LT on their Portsmouth–Ryde–Sandown ferry. Croydon-based Air Taxis Ltd. also took delivery of the all-red G-ACLS.

In 1934 the Courier, with its clean lines, represented the advanced aerodynamic

16

thought of the period, the R.A.E. Farnborough and D. Napier and Son Ltd., the engine manufacturers, each acquiring one for research purposes. Napier's machine was used as a testbed for the new Rapier IV 16-cylinder air-cooled 'H' engine of 325 h.p., and was designated the A.S.5C. Of unusually small frontal area, the Rapier with four-bladed airscrew sensationally increased performance and in the 1934 King's Cup Race, Air Vice-Marshal A. E. Borton averaged 166 m.p.h. before being eliminated in the heats. The R.A.E. Courier K4047, delivered in February 1934, was returned to the makers a year later for modifications calculated to steepen the glide and reduce the landing float of so clean an airframe. To this end a large Schrenk flap was fitted under the fuselage and coupled to Handley Page slotted wing flaps and to ailerons which were also capable of being lowered as flaps. It was used also for testing de-icing equipment and, at a later date, automatic controls. In 1938 it was re-engined with a 360 h.p. Armstrong Siddeley Cheetah IX and served as the R.A.E. communications aircraft until written off in 1943.

London, Scottish and Provincial Airways Ltd., founded in 1934, adopted the Courier and operated for a limited period through the Midlands to Heston and Paris with G-ACSY and 'SZ. In 1936 financial interests acquired a number of Couriers with a view to selling them for military purposes in the Spanish Civil War. The scheme fell through after the spectacular crash at Portsmouth of G-ACVE,

The Air Ministry's Courier K4047 awaiting delivery in May 1937. (*Flight Photo 10299S*)

The Rapier Courier G-ACNZ showing the four bladed airscrew. (*Flight Photo 10468S*)

17

Sqn. Ldr. R. J. Jones and the author in Courier G-ACVF (fixed undercarriage) over Southend on 30 March 1947. (*E. J. Riding*)

which was stolen by ground staff, who, without flying experience, intended taking it themselves to Spain. North Eastern Airways Ltd. bought the remainder, and in 1937 were running G-ABXN, 'CLF, 'LT and 'VF from Edinburgh to Woolsington, Doncaster and Croydon, a route on which they flew in conjunction with Envoys. P.S. & I.O.W. Aviation Ltd. eventually bought all the remaining Couriers and not only converted the Cheetah and Rapier variants to take Lynx IVCs, but also fitted them all with fixed undercarriages for the very short Ryde ferry. Their 1939 fleet consisted of G-ACLF, 'LR, 'LT, 'NZ, 'VF and G-ADAY, all of which were impressed as taxi machines for National Air Communications. In camouflage with yellow undersides but retaining their civil marks for a time, they were based initially at White Waltham but in March 1940 received R.A.F. serials and flew to Hawarden for similar duties with Air Transport Auxiliary and were joined there by G-ABXN, G-ACZL and G-ADAX. An exception was G-ACLF which remained at A.T.A. headquarters, White Waltham.

Three detached to communications flights were X9343/G-ADAY to No. 48 M.U., Hawarden (Oct. 1940–Mar. 1941); X9346/G-ACNZ to Airspeed Ltd., Portsmouth (Mar. 1941–Jan. 1944); and X9347/G-ACVF to Boulton Paul Ltd., Wolverhampton (Feb. 1942–Jul. 1943). The prototype, G-ABXN, was scrapped at Hawarden in September 1940; three were broken up at Portsmouth as beyond economical repair in 1941; X9394/G-ACLT was damaged beyond repair by enemy action there in April 1942; X9344/G-ACLR crashed on take-off from Bolt Head, Devon on 1 August 1942 while attached to the Station Flt., Exeter; and the remainder were dismantled at No. 5 M.U., Kemble 1943–44.

After the war only G-ACVF survived for disposal at the famous Kemble sale and, following complete overhaul by the makers, was flown to Southend by Sqn. Ldr. R. J. Jones on 2 January 1947. One season of gruelling seaside joyriding with East Anglian Flying Services Ltd., brought the last of the breed to the scrap heap through lack of spares.

SPECIFICATION

Manufacturers: Airspeed (1934) Ltd., City Airport, Portsmouth, Hants.

Power Plants: (A.S.5, 5A) One 240 h.p. Armstrong Siddeley Lynx IVC.

(A.S.5B) One 277 h.p. Armstrong Siddeley Cheetah V.

(A.S.5C) One 325 h.p. Napier Rapier IV.

(K4047) One 350 h.p. Armstrong Siddeley Cheetah IX.

Dimensions: Span, 47 ft. 0 in. Length, 28 ft. 6 in. Height, 8 ft. 9 in.
Wing area, 250 sq. ft.

Weights: Tare weight, 2,344 lb. All-up weight, 3,900 lb.

Performance: Maximum speed, 153 m.p.h. Cruising speed, 132 m.p.h. Initial climb, 730 ft./min. Ceiling, 13,500 ft. Range, 635 miles.

Production: (a) A.S.5 and A.S.5A Courier

Thirteen aircraft: (c/n 7) G-ABXN; (10) G-ACJL; (11) G-ACLR; (13) G-ACLS; (14) G-ACLT; (15) K4047; (16) G-ACSY; (19) G-ACSZ; (22) G-ACVE; (23) G-ACVF; (25) G-ACZL; (26) G-ADAX; (27) G-ADAY.

(b) A.S.5B Courier

Two aircraft only: (c/n 12) G-ACLF; (24) G-ACVG.

(c) A.S.5C Courier

One aircraft only: (c/n 20) G-ACNZ.

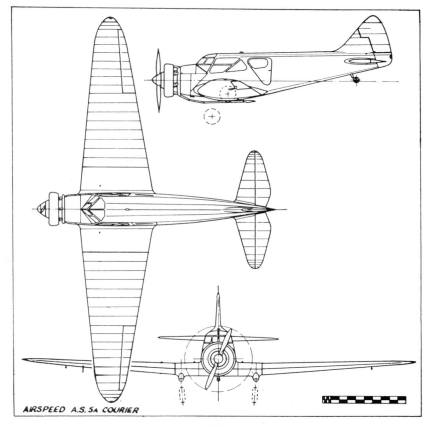

AIRSPEED A.S. 5A COURIER

The first production Envoy I showing the twin Wolseley A.R.9 Mk.I radial engines.
(*Aeroplane*)

Airspeed A.S.6 Envoy

The Envoy was a six/eight-passenger medium range feeder liner designed by N. S. Norway and A. H. Tiltman as the logical twin-engined development of the Courier. It not only embodied the same form of wooden construction, but also used the same outer wing panels and, like its predecessor, was fitted with a backward retracting undercarriage. The silver and green prototype G-ACMT made its first public appearance at the Hendon S.B.A.C. Show on 1 July 1934, after which preparations went ahead at Portsmouth for small scale production. The first Envoy Series I G-ACVH was, like the prototype, fitted with Wolseley A.R.9 motors and mainly used for demonstration flying, but the second production machine, 'VI, went to Castle Bromwich for the personal use of Lord Nuffield. Named 'Miss Wolseley' and equipped with the new Wolseley Aries III radials, it was to have been flown in the great MacRobertson Race to Australia by George Lowdell, but was withdrawn following damage sustained in a forced landing at St. Neots on the eve of the race. Two years later, however, it became the property of Ansett Airways Ltd. and went into airline service in Australia. By 1945, when the machine had flown over 10,000 hours, exhaustion of spares for the Aries brought about its modification to take two Wright Whirlwind radial engines.

A special windowless long-range version, G-ACMU, fitted with Cheetah VI supercharged engines, and with a large fuel tank in the cabin, was designated the A.S.8 Viceroy. This aircraft was built to the order of T. Neville Stack and flown by him, with the assistance of S. L. Turner, in the Australia Race, but they were dogged by ill luck through minor faults and gave up at Athens. The Viceroy then returned to Portsmouth where it remained at the back of a hangar until July 1936 when it left for France en route to the Spanish War.

Like its predecessor, the Courier, the Envoy was also offered with the Lynx IVC or the Cheetah V, the first Lynx Envoy being the R.K. Dundas demonstrator G-ACVJ. The first Cheetah model was VH-UXY, a special machine with cabin tanks built for the Australian long distance pioneer Charles Ulm and shipped to Canada in readiness for his trans-Pacific flight. This aircraft was lost at sea with its distinguished crew between Oakland, California, and Honolulu on 4 December 1934 on the first stage of the flight.

North Eastern Airways Ltd. also acquired three Cheetah engined Envoys G-ADAZ named 'Tynedale', G-ADBB 'Wharfedale' and G-ADBZ 'Swaledale', which from Easter 1935 became familiar sights on the Edinburgh–Heston run. Croydon was the operating base of the Olley Air Service G-ADBA, later sold to Cobham Air Routes Ltd. for the Bournemouth service. During the holiday months of the same year the Lynx Envoy G-ADCA was employed on the Ryde shuttle of Portsmouth, Southsea and I.O.W. Aviation Ltd.

Six Envoy Series I machines delivered in the summer of 1935 for services linking Japan with Manchuria, were joined later by others built under licence at Nagoya by Mitsubishi Shoji Kaisha under the type name Hina-Zuru or Young Crane. Three were used by the Japanese Air Transportation Co., and four by Manchurian Air Transport. It is believed the rest went to the Japanese Navy.

In 1936, in the light of flight experience with the early Envoys and the experimental Courier K4047, the prototype Envoy G-ACMT was modified to Series II with flaps and more powerful engines. In this form it followed the Viceroy to the Spanish War, became a communications machine and was destroyed with the loss of Gen. Mola and crew when it struck a mountain in bad weather. First production Series IIs were seven ordered for joint use by the South African Air Force and South African Airways, three serialled 251 to 253 being delivered in military form with guns and bomb racks, and four as civil transports ZS-AGA to 'GD for a weekly Johannesburg–Port Elizabeth service which began on 12 October 1936. All were convertible to either configuration and in 1937 the civil machines were, in fact, taken over by the S.A.A.F. as 254 to 257 and the military trio became civil as ZS-ALD to 'LF temporarily in 1937.

An order placed by British Scandinavian Airways Ltd. in 1936 for two Cheetah IX engined Envoy Series IIIs, G-AEGF and 'GG, was subsequently cancelled, the aircraft being diverted to another operator, E. Hoffman of Vienna, only to be impounded en route. They are believed to have remained crated in Rotterdam Docks until taken over by D. V. Reinders of The Hague as PH-ARK and 'RL and to have been destroyed by enemy action at Ypenburg on 10 May 1940.

In September 1936 another tanked Envoy, G-AENA, made its appearance for participation in the historic Schlesinger Race from Portsmouth to Johannesburg. Named 'Gabrielle', it was owned and flown by two Brooklands School of Flying instructors, Max Findlay and Ken Waller, and was the first A.S.6J or Envoy III fitted with Cheetah IXs in helmeted cowlings. It was no luckier than previous

The Viceroy at Mildenhall in October 1934 with long chord cowlings, enlarged nacelles and windowless fuselage. (*Aeroplane*)

The first convertible Envoy II for the South African Air Force on test near Portsmouth in 1936. (*Flight Photo 12892S*)

OK-BAL, first of four Envoy IIIs with which Ceskoslovenské Statni Aerolinie inaugurated a Prague–Moscow service in 1935. (*Aeroplane*)

Envoy III P5629 in use by the Royal Navy as an admiral's barge 1939–40. (*Imperial War Museum A.8386*)

special Envoys, Max Findlay being killed when it crashed on take-off from Abercorn, Northern Rhodesia. The most illustrious of all Envoy IIIs was delivered to the King's Flight in 1937. Resplendent in the red and blue livery of the Guards, and registered G-AEXX, it was used by the Royal Household until handed over to the R.A.F. in 1939. Together with the Brevet Flying Club's G-AHAC, formerly P5626 and one of a batch of five Envoy IIIs built for R.A.F. and Royal Navy communications under Contract 967114/38 in 1939, 'XX reappeared at Hanworth in 1946 and later flew in Sweden as SE-ASN.

Designation A.S.6E was given to Envoy IIIs OK-BAL to 'AO with Walter Castor radials delivered to Ceskoslovenske Statni Aerolinie in July 1935 for the 1,200 mile Prague–Moscow route which opened on 1 August. Wolseley Scorpio III versions, known as A.S.6K, included OK-VIT for the Victorise Mill and Steel Co. of Prague; VT-AHR and VT-AIC for the Maharajahs of Jaipur and Indore respectively; and six of French registry for Air Pyrénées, one of which, F-AQAA, was shown at the Hatfield S.B.A.C. Show on 29 June 1937. Flt. Lt. C. H. A. Coleman and G. B. S. Errington made outstanding long distance delivery flights later in 1937 in G-AERT and 'XE respectively from Portsmouth to Lui Chow in the Kwangsi Province of South China and in 1939 VT-AIC returned to the U.K.

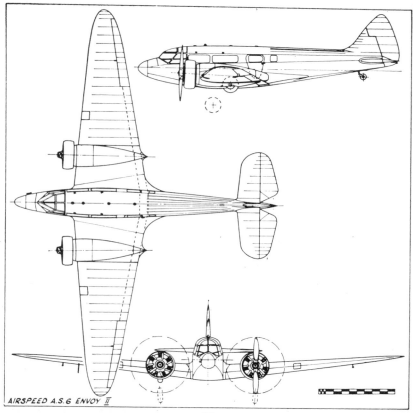

AIRSPEED A.S.6 ENVOY III

23

where, with G-ADAZ, then the property of Air Service Training Ltd., Hamble, it was impressed for R.A.F. use.

SPECIFICATION

Manufacturers: Airspeed (1934) Ltd., City Airport, Portsmouth, Hants.
Power Plants: (Envoy I)   Two 185 h.p. Wolseley A.R.9 Mk. 1.
                           Two 220 h.p. Armstrong Siddeley Lynx IVC.
                           Two 277 h.p. Armstrong Siddeley Cheetah V.
          (Envoy II) Two 220 h.p. Armstrong Siddeley Lynx IVC.
          (Envoy III) Two 350 h.p. Armstrong Siddeley Cheetah IX.
                           Two 260 h.p. Walter Castor.
                           Two 290 h.p. Wolseley Scorpio III.
        (Viceroy)   Two 290 h.p. Armstrong Siddeley Cheetah VI.

	Envoy I	Envoy II	Envoy III	Viceroy
Span	52 ft. 4 in.	52 ft. 4 in.	52 ft. 4 in.	51 ft. 0 in.
Length	34 ft. 6 in.	34 ft. 6 in.	34 ft. 6 in.	34 ft. 6 in.
Height	9 ft. 6 in.	9 ft. 6 in.	9 ft. 6 in.	9 ft. 6 in.
Wing area	339 sq. ft.	339 sq. ft.	339 sq. ft.	299 sq. ft.
Tare weight	3,442 lb.	3,780 lb.	4,340 lb.	3,900 lb.
All-up weight	5,300 lb.	5,830 lb.	6,600 lb.	6,300 lb.
Maximum speed	170 m.p.h.	174 m.p.h.	203 m.p.h.	210 m.p.h.
Cruising speed	150 m.p.h.	153 m.p.h.	170 m.p.h.	190 m.p.h.
Initial climb	850 ft./min.	1,070 ft./min.	—	1,000 ft./min.
Ceiling	17,000 ft.	16,500 ft.	22,000 ft.	—
Range	400 miles	650 miles	620 miles	1,400 miles

Production: (a) A.S.6 and A.S.6A Envoy I
Sixteen aircraft: (c/n 17) G-ACMT; (28–38) G-ACVH, 'VI, 'VJ, G-ACYJ/VH-UXY, G-ADAZ, 'BA, 'BB, 'BZ, 'CA, 'CB and 'CC; (40–43) G-ADCE, J-BAOH, J-BAOI, J-BDCO.

       (b) A.S.6D Envoy II
Eight aircraft: (c/n 39) ZS-AGA; (44–46) 251, ZS-AGD 'Alex Biggar', ZS-AGC; (49–52) 252, 253, ZS-AGB 'Sir Hercules Robinson', G-AEBV.

       (c) A.S.6E Envoy III
Four aircraft: (c/n 47) OK-BAL; (48) OK-BAM; (53) OK-BAN; (54) OK-BAO.

       (d) A.S.6J Envoy III
Nineteen aircraft: (c/n 55) G-AEGF; (56) G-AEGG; (60) G-AENA; (66–74) G-AEXX, 'XE, 'RT, F-APPQ, F-AQAA, 'AB, 'CR, 'CS, 'CT; (76–82) G-AFJD, 'JE, P5625–P5629.

       (e) A.S.6K Envoy III
Three aircraft: (c/n 57–59) VT-AHR, OK-VIT, VT-AℾC.

       (f) A.S.8 Viceroy
One aircraft only: (c/n 18) G-ACMU.

       (g) Mitsubishi Hina-Zuru
Ten aircraft: J-BAOD, 'OF, 'OK, 'OL, 'OP, 'OQ, 'OR, 'OS, 'OV, 'OW.

Ambassador 2 G-ALZS R.M.A. 'William Shakespeare' flying in the red, white and polished metal livery of the B.E.A. Elizabethan fleet. (*B.E.A. Photo*)

Airspeed A.S.57 Ambassador

The Airspeed A.S.57 was originally conceived as a Dakota replacement powered by two Bristol Hercules motors and conforming to the Brabazon IIA specification of 1943 but the design team led by A. E. Hagg, foresaw that post-war medium-haul types, staging between the principal European capitals, would carry twice the payload of a Dakota. A large two-motor high-wing cantilever monoplane of all-metal construction, with split flaps and nose wheel undercarriage was therefore envisaged, with the twin operational economies of high cruising speed through aerodynamic purity and long inter-overhaul periods for the engines. To provide the higher power now required, Bristols produced a commercial version of the two-row Centaurus, development flying of which was done by Airspeeds at Christchurch in a Vickers Warwick.

Orders were placed by the Ministry of Aircraft Production in September 1945 for two prototypes to be known by the type name Ambassador. The first,G-AGUA, fitted with Centaurus 130 engines, made its initial flight at Christchurch on 10 July 1947, piloted by Airspeed's chief test pilot G. B. S. Errington, and impressed everyone with its grace and effortless performance when shown to the public for the first time at the Radlett S.B.A.C. Show on 9 September 1947. The second prototype, G-AKRD, differed from the first by virtue of its fully pressurized fuselage permitting a maximum cabin differential of $4\frac{1}{2}$ lb./sq. in. giving conditions equivalent to 8,000 ft. when flying at 20,000 ft. Fitted with later Centaurus 630 engines, it made its maiden flight on 26 August 1948.

A substantial order for 20 production aircraft, value £3 million, was secured from B.E.A. on 22 September 1948, after delays which, in 1951, cost Airspeed a number of small orders from overseas operators and the larger charter companies. The Corporation thus became the sole operator of the type and specified the higher-powered Centaurus 661 with two-stage supercharger for all production aircraft which were also to have slotted instead of split flaps to improve short runway take off. By the end of 1949 the prototypes had amassed an impressive number of hours of development flying in the hands of G. B. S. Errington and R. E. Clear, the fuselage had passed its pressurization tests under water in Portsmouth Docks and the wing had passed 100 per cent. of its design strength in the test frame at Farnborough. The first prototype aircraft was then fitted with the first of the Centaurus 661 power plants, externally identifiable by the chin-type air intakes, driving 16 ft. diameter de Havilland constant-speed and braking airscrews. The third, or production prototype, G-ALFR, was soon complete, and also the fourth, or first production Mk. 2 machine G-AMAD, which underwent intensive B.E.A. and A.R.B. proving trials in May 1951. These resulted in the issue of a normal category C. of A. to G-ALFR for temporate zones enabling it to fly out to Khartoum, piloted by R. E. Clear, on 14 August 1951 for tropical trials.

With production now in full swing, G-ALZN, flagship of the newly named 'Elizabethan' Class, fitted to carry 47 passengers and three crew, was delivered to B.E.A. at London Airport on 22 August 1951. It was used on crew training and proving flights to Paris with passengers, under the direction of Capt. C. E. F. Riley. The first scheduled service to Paris was flown on 13 March 1952, by which time seven Ambassadors had been delivered for proving flights to all the European capitals. By the following August, load factors of over 80 per cent. on most services were resulting in a really useful profit and the Centaurus 661s had been cleared for 600 hours between overhauls. The largest and last of the B.E.A. piston engined airliners was thus fairly and squarely in service and three and a half years later, in December 1955, the Ambassador fleet had reached the highest utilization rate of any B.E.A. aircraft at 2,230 hours per annum per aircraft.

Their initial work done, the prototypes were again used for experimental purposes. In 1951 G-AGUA was partially dismantled at Christchurch and remained there for radio aerial tests until removed to Filton in 1952 for use as a Bristol engine test rig. G-AKRD was employed in 1952 for tests with D.H. hollow steel airscrews for the Bristol Britannia and in the following year was fitted with Bristol Proteus 705 propeller-turbine engines, again for Britannia development. G-ALFR was loaned to Napiers in 1955 and went to Luton as a flying testbed during A.R.B. acceptance tests on the Eland El.1 propeller-turbine engine and, in October 1959, was registered in their name. Rolls-Royce Ltd. also used Ambassadors for this purpose and took delivery of G-ALZR at Hucknall on 30 August 1957 as testbed for the new Tyne engine. In March 1958 G-AKRD was similarly equipped and operating under Class B marks as G-37-4 and G-37-3 respectively, the two aircraft were then flown intensively on 2,000 hours of simulated airline operations as a contribution to Vickers Vanguard development. G-37-3/G-AKRD later flew

The second prototype Ambassador, G-AKRD, fitted with Proteus 705 engines during the Britannia development programme in 1953.

26

G-37-3/G-AKRD flying with two different marks of Rolls-Royce Dart engines as the Ambassador P. Special. (*Rolls-Royce*)

with Dart engines (201P port and 525 starboard) under the designation Ambassador P. Special.

Early in 1957 a number of Ambassadors at last became redundant on being ousted from B.E.A. routes by the Viscount. G-ALZX, G-AMAE and 'AH were sold to the Australian firm Butler Air Transport Ltd., and caused a mild stir by appearing over Sydney in formation on 18 June 1957, at the end of their long delivery flight.

The last scheduled B.E.A. Ambassador service was flown from Cologne to London by Capt. J. W. Cooke in 'Lord Howard of Effingham' on 30 July 1958. Thus ended the B.E.A. Elizabethan era which had lasted almost $6\frac{1}{2}$ years.

Butler's aircraft began N.S.W. feeder services on 5 August 1957 but were little used, returned to Heathrow a year later and in 1959 were sold to Dan-Air Services Ltd. They were the first of eight which the company maintained at Lasham for scheduled, charter and inclusive tour operations from Gatwick 1959–1968 which included G-AMAG, one of two earlier refurbished as executive aircraft for Shell. In July 1957 G-AMAD was commissioned as a 55 seater by B.K.S. Air Transport Ltd. for its Newcastle–Dublin route, which on 4 June 1958 was extended to Bergen following the acquisition of G-ALZT and 'ZW. G-AMAC was added in 1960 and on 20 May 1963 the Tyne-powered G-ALZR was delivered to the company at Southend where it reverted to standard with Centaurus 661s and re-entered service on 26 November 1964 with a large rear freight door for horse charter work. G-AMAD, which first flew at Southend on 10 June 1968 after a similar conversion, suffered fatigue failure of part of the flap mechanism when landing at Heathrow on 3 July and crashed in the central terminal area with the loss of eight horses and crew.

Autair International Airways Ltd. of Luton used three Ambassadors, G-ALZS, 'ZV and 'ZZ 1963–68, all of which saw service in Switzerland with Globe Air as HB-IEK to 'EM 1960–63. Two of these, 'ZS and 'ZZ, had been painted up as LN-BWE and LN-BWF for the Norwegian operator Norrønafly at Southend and Cambridge respectively in 1960 but were never delivered. The other foreign user, the Royal Jordanian Air Force, bought G-ALZY, 'ZO and 'ZP as Amman-based V.I.P. transports 107, 108 and 109 respectively 1959–1963. Two then returned for Dan-Air but 109/G-ALZP was never delivered, being sold instead to the Sultan of Morocco as CN-MAK. It too returned in November 1963 and was

G-ALZS in the blue and white livery of Autair International Airways Ltd., Luton, with whom it served from 1964 to 1967. (*John Goring*)

G-ALZT in the red, white and silver colour scheme of B.K.S. Air Transport Ltd. (*John Goring*)

G-AMAE at Gatwick in the dark blue, white and silver livery of Dan-Air Services Ltd., 1964. (*Aviation Photo News*)

employed by the Decca Navigator Co. Ltd. as a flying laboratory until retired at West Malling in 1971 and sold to South Seas Airways of Wellington, N.Z. as ZK-DFC.

SPECIFICATION

Manufacturers: Airspeed Ltd., later the Airspeed Division of the de Havilland Aircraft Co. Ltd., Christchurch Aerodrome, Hants.

Power Plants: Two 2,625 h.p. Bristol Centaurus 661.

Dimensions: Span, 115 ft. 0 in. Length, 82 ft. 0 in. Height, 18 ft. 10 in. Wing area, 1,200 sq. ft.

Weights: Tare weight, 35,377 lb. All-up weight, 52,500 lb.

Performance (with 11,650 lb. payload): Maximum speed (75 per cent. power), 312 m.p.h. Cruising speed, 260 m.p.h. Initial climb, 1,250 ft./min. Range, 550 miles.

Production: (a) A.S.57 Ambassador 1

Two aircraft only: (c/n 61) G-AGUA; (62) G-AKRD.

(b) A.S.57 Ambassador 2

Twenty-one aircraft: (c/n 5210) G-ALFR; (5211) G-AMAD; (5212) G-ALZN; (5213–5222) G-ALZP to G-ALZZ; (5223–5226) G-AMAA to G-AMAC; (5227–5230) G-AMAE to G-AMAH.

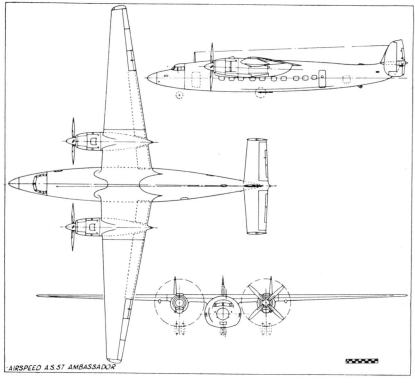

AIRSPEED A.S.57 AMBASSADOR

29

Apart from the stretcher door in the port side, the ambulance Consul G-AJWR was externally identical with standard models.

Airspeed A.S.65 Consul

In the years 1946–48 the Airspeed factory at Portsmouth converted over 150 surplus Oxford airframes into light civil transports designated the A.S. 65 Consul. During the immediate post-war years these gave sterling service and satisfied the demand for charter class aircraft at a time when more modern designs were not yet available. All the main Oxford components were retained, but the cabin was redesigned to accommodate six passengers. Double doors were fitted to the cockpit bulkhead, extra windows installed and luggage space provided at the rear of the cabin. The prototype, G-AGVY, converted from the de Havilland built Oxford V3679, received its Certificate of Airworthiness on 15 March 1946, and in the standard dark blue and gold Consul colour scheme was delivered to the Bata Shoe Co. Ltd. for communications between its European factories.

All subsequent Consuls carried passengers' baggage in an elongated nose which not only released cabin space and extended the C.G. range, but also provided a useful recognition feature. Airwork Ltd. were appointed official distributors, their demonstration machine G-AHEG, formerly Oxford T1206, being delivered to Heston in April 1946. The type suited the embryo post-war charter industry very well, and during the following 12 months 70 were delivered to British firms alone. The machine sold well, and very little demonstration was necessary, but Atlas Aviation Ltd.'s first machine, G-AHJY, took part in the Victory Air Pageant at Eastleigh on 22 June 1946, and Westminster Airways Ltd. of Gatwick lent their third machine, G-AICZ, for exhibition at the Radlett S.B.A.C. Show in the following September.

The largest Consul fleets were those owned by Morton Air Services Ltd. (8), British Air Transport Ltd. (5), Chartair Ltd., Thame (9), Atlas Aviation Ltd., Elstree (4), Westminster Airways Ltd., Blackbushe (7), Lancashire Aircraft Corporation Ltd., Yeadon (6), International Airways Ltd., Croydon (5), Air

Enterprises Ltd., Croydon (7), British Aviation Services Ltd., Blackbushe (4), Hornton Airways Ltd., Gatwick (3), Steiner's Air Service, Speke (6) and Transair Ltd., Croydon (5). Their rugged serviceability was used to good advantage on short haul work and on long-distance charters which took them to all parts of Europe, the Near and Middle East and to Central and South Africa. Two of the earliest Consuls, G-AHEF and 'JZ, were employed for many years on the de Havilland inter-factory air service, and another, G-AIDX, flew for 10 years with the Esso Group. 1947 was a great Consul year, G-AIKP, owned by O. H. Simpson, made several return trips to the Cape, Butlins bought G-AIKU for executive flights between their various holiday camps, Prince Aly Khan acquired G-AJLP for his personal use and Wg. Cdr. H. C. Kennard flew G-AIUS, belonging to Air Kruise (Kent) Ltd., in the Folkestone Trophy Race.

The type was also in considerable demand in the Near East, French Indo-China, and French Colonial Africa, a demand which largely contributed to its eventual disappearance from British skies. A number were leased by Mortons, Chartair, International Airways and Air Enterprises in 1947–49 to the United Nations Commission in Israel. They were painted white and bore the large letters UN and a numeral in the 95–105 range. While engaged on this work, the prototype was lost in a crash in a remote part of the Lebanon on 11 February 1949. Several of the British Aviation Services and Chartair Consuls were based in Malta and flew on Air Malta services to Cairo, Catania and Tunis, while nine others

Consul TJ-ABE awaiting restoration to G-AIKO after its return from Jordan in 1953.

Consul EC-ACZ, specially converted for Real Aero Club Espana from Oxford NJ309 in 1948.

31

Consul VX587 equipped for test flying Alvis Leonides radial engines driving three-bladed variable-pitch metal airscrews.

were sold outright to Air Jordan and for two years were used on short haul routes radiating from Amman.

Three were put into service by Malayan Airways Ltd., Singapore, on 1 May 1947; four by Union of Burma Airways Ltd., Rangoon; two by Airways (India) Ltd., Delhi; three by United Air Services Ltd., Dar-es-Salaam; five each by the Belgian Congo Police and the Spanish airline Iberia; and two by Aer Lingus, Dublin, whose first, EI-ADB, was later sold to B.S.A.A. as G-ALTZ and second, EI-ADC, to the Karachi Aero Club as AP-AGK.

One of the last home orders was for five special models, G-AJXE to 'XI, delivered to the M.C.A. Flying Unit at the end of 1947 for use in training and testing commercial pilots in instrument flying and blind approach techniques and also for calibrating airport radio installations. Two others, G-AIUX 'Star Master' and G-ALTZ, 'Star Monitor', were used for a similar purpose by B.O.A.C., both, as their names suggest, inherited from the old British South American Airways Corporation.

Consul variants were few, the prototype ambulance version, G-AJWR, with enlarged door, was exhibited at the 1947 Radlett S.B.A.C. Show, but, like many others, was exported immediately to French Indo-China. Two standard Consuls, G-AIEA and G-AJXI, were refitted with Oxford noses and went to French West Africa as F-OAHJ and F-BHVY respectively for aerial survey work. Following the original flight testing of the Alvis Leonides engine in an Oxford, Consul G-AKCW, formerly Oxford NJ318, was acquired by the Ministry of Supply and renumbered VX587. It was then handed over to Alvis Ltd. at Baginton for further work in this direction, later averaging 188·5 m.p.h. in the *Daily Express* Race from Hurn to Herne Bay on 16 September 1950 piloted by R. E. M. B. Milne.

One of the last serviceable Consuls in Britain, G-AIKR of the Rapid Flying Group, Baginton, when finally grounded in May 1965, was put on show at Woburn Abbey but was later packed for shipment at R.A.F. Bicester and left Southampton Docks in the following November, en route to R.C.A.F. Rockcliffe for reconversion and preservation as an Oxford. G-AJLR received similar treatment at Henlow for the R.A.F. Museum, Hendon.

SPECIFICATION

Manufacturers: Airspeed Ltd., City Airport, Portsmouth, Hants.

Power Plants: Two 395 h.p. Armstrong Siddeley Cheetah 10.
Dimensions: Span, 53 ft. 4 in. Length, 35 ft. 4 in. Height, 11 ft. 1 in. Wing area, 348 sq. ft.
Weights: Tare weight, 6,047 lb. All-up weight, 8,250 lb.
Performance: Maximum speed, 190 m.p.h. Cruising speed, 156 m.p.h. Initial climb, 1,180 ft./min. Service ceiling, 19,000 ft. Range, 900 miles.
Production:

At least 147 aircraft comprising 119 British registered Consuls and the following exported direct from the works: (c/n 910) Airways (India) Ltd. VT-CJA; (4031) Malayan Airways Ltd. VR-SCE 'Pipit', later F-OAER; (5096) VR-SCF 'Layang Layang'; (5108) VT-CJB; (5118) Aero Technique, Algiers F-BCJK; (5140–5144) unregistered to the Argentine 1947; (5147) F-BCJL; (5149) M. Wauthier, Tangiers F-BDPS, later F-DABL; (5151) Aer Lingus EI-ADC, later AP-AGK, HB-LAU and EC-ARU; (5152–5156) unregistered to the Argentine 1947; (5163) Union of Burma Airways Ltd. XY-ABC; (5171) Sté. Indochinoise de Transports Aériens F-BDPU; (5181) Real Aero Club Espana EC-ACZ; (5189) Belgian Congo C-33; (5190) C-31; (5191) C-35; (5192) Aero Technique, Algiers F-BECD; (5193) C-36; (5202–5203) unregistered to Sté. Indochinoise de Ravitillement 1950.

Note: c/n 5182–5187, 5194–5201, 5204–5209, 5231–5241 were allotted to military conversions exported to Turkey (12), New Zealand (6), Mexico and elsewhere.

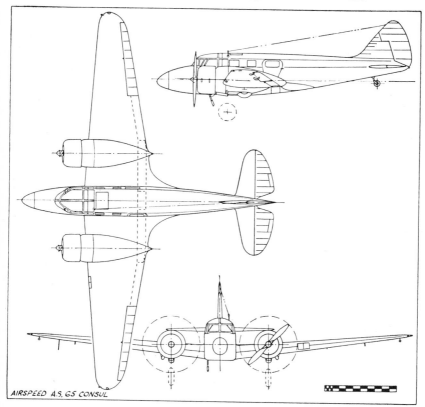

AIRSPEED A.S. G5 CONSUL

George Reynolds starting the clipped wing ANEC IA, numbered 15, in the Grosvenor Trophy Race at Lympne, 3 August 1925. (*Flight*)

ANEC I, IA, II and IV Missel Thrush

The ANEC monoplanes were designed by W. S. Shackleton and built at Addlestone, Surrey, by the Air Navigation and Engineering Co. Ltd., successors to the war-time Blériot and Spad Manufacturing Co. Three in number, and with the firm's initials forming their name, they were among the earliest ultra-light aircraft designed in Britain, but the temperamental engines of the period prevented them from showing their true paces. All were built of wood and were made as small as possible, the pilot's restricted forward view being improved by their common recognition feature: the hollow top decking which faired into the inverted V two-cylinder engine.

ANEC I G-EBHR first flew at Brooklands on 21 August 1923 piloted by J. H. James, powered by the first inverted engine to fly in the U.K., the 696 c.c. Blackburne Tomtit modified motor cycle engine built by Burney and Blackburne Engines Ltd. of Bookham, Surrey. A week or two later an exactly similar machine, G-EBIL, made its appearance, and both were flown in the *Daily Mail* performance trials for light single-seaters held at Lympne in September 1923. Maurice Pearcy flew G-EBHR, but his performance was eclipsed by test pilot J. H. James, who achieved fame by flying G-EBIL for 87·5 miles on a gallon of petrol and by later reaching the amazing altitude of 14,400 ft. Making play with the war-time name of the company and masquerading as a Blériot type, it was entered in the Tour de France reliability trial at Buc, Paris, in July 1924, but was eliminated when the French pilot Rabatel was forced to land it at Nevers on the first day.

The first ANEC I, G-EBHR, was eventually sold to A. G. Simpson of Perth, Western Australia, where it first flew as G-AUEQ in October 1924 but in August that year the Air Ministry purchased G-EBIL and the unregistered Raynham monoplane against which it had competed at Lympne and evaluated them at Martlesham. For this purpose 'IL was fitted with a ·1,100 c.c. Anzani engine and repainted as J7506. Later it returned to the makers for modification and reverted to civil status with greatly reduced wing span for entry in the 1925 Lympne August Bank Holiday Races as the ANEC IA. Although an unsuitable airscrew prevented the engine from giving its full take-off power, once in the air the aircraft proved fast enough to win the prize for speed over a 50 km. course at 83·76 m.p.h., but had no other successes.

A third ANEC 1, built for Air Travel (Australia) Ltd. and issued with a British C. of A. on 25 January 1925, arrived at Rockhampton, Queensland, in the following May and was flown briefly by Messrs. Church and Boehm as G-AUET. It was withdrawn from use in May 1926.

W. S. Shackleton's final design before leaving to join Wm. Beardmore Ltd. was the little ANEC II G-EBJO, built for the Air Ministry's 1924 competition for two-seaters fitted with engines of up to 1,100 c.c. It emerged as a scaled-up version

Running up the prototype ANEC I, G-EBHR, at Brooklands in August 1923. (*Leonard Bridgman*)

The two-seat ANEC II in its original condition with Anzani inverted V twin-cylinder engine.

Guy Warwick taking off from Hendon in the Genet engined ANEC IV at the start of the fatal 1928 King's Cup Race. (*Flight Photo 6664*)

The award-winning ANEC I, G-EBIL, at Martlesham as J7506 in 1924.

of the single-seaters, even to the characteristic one-piece elevator, but after erection at Lympne, broken valve springs eliminated the machine both from the competition and from the Grosvenor Trophy Race. As Major J. C. Savage's entry in the 1925 King's Cup Race, it failed to reach the starting line due to an engine change.

Last of the ANECs was G-EBPI, the two-seat ANEC IV Missel Thrush, a biplane designed by J. Bewsher, who had been responsible for the large ANEC III transport biplane built for use in Australia. The Missel Thrush was built for the 1926 *Daily Mail* competition for two seaters fitted with engines of less than 170 lb. weight. Although a complete departure from previous ANEC designs, it shared the same bad luck when G. L. P. Henderson broke the undercarriage in a taxying accident at Brooklands on the eve of the trials. In April 1927 it was sold to a private owner, G. N. Warwick, for whom the original 35 h.p. three cylinder Blackburne Thrush radial was removed and an 80 h.p. Armstrong Siddeley Genet II substituted. He was killed when it flew into Broad Law, near Peebles, while flying on the Newcastle to Renfrew leg of the 1928 King's Cup Race.

Sole survivor of these four historic aeroplanes is the ANEC II, which was fitted with a 32 h.p. Bristol Cherub III engine and a strutted undercarriage by G. L. P. Henderson, thus heightening its resemblance to a similar Shackleton design, the Beardmore Wee Bee. It then took part in both the 1926 Bournemouth Meetings and the races at the Hampshire Air Pageant, Hamble, flown by its new owner, Norman Jones. On 16 July 1927 he flew it to victory in the Air League Challenge Cup Race, covering the 116 miles course from Castle Bromwich to Woodford and back at an average speed of 73·5 m.p.h., but after averaging 74·7 m.p.h. on the first lap of the King's Cup course a fortnight later, had the misfortune to hit a bird, and withdrew. The machine was later sold to A. H. Wheeler and flew continuously at Heston and elsewhere until the C. of A. expired at West Malling in 1937. Today its remains are in the possession of the Shuttleworth Trust at Old Warden, but it is unlikely to fly again.

SPECIFICATION

Manufacturers: The Air Navigation and Engineering Co. Ltd., Addlestone, Surrey.

36

Power Plants: (ANEC I) One 696 c.c. Blackburne Tomtit.
One 1,100 c.c. Anzani.
(ANEC IA) One 1,100 c.c. Anzani.
(ANEC II) One 1,100 c.c. Anzani.
One 32 h.p. Bristol Cherub III.
(ANEC IV) One 35 h.p. Blackburne Thrush.
One 80 h.p. Armstrong Siddeley Genet II.

	ANEC I	ANEC IA	ANEC II	ANEC IV
Span	32 ft. 0 in.	18 ft. 4 in.	38 ft. 0 in.	28 ft. 0 in.
Length	15 ft. 7 in.	15 ft. 7 in.	20 ft. 8 in.	21 ft. 6 in.
Height	3 ft. 0 in.	3 ft. 0 in.	3 ft. 0 in.	8 ft. 0 in.
Wing area	145 sq. ft.	82 sq. ft.	185 sq. ft.	210 sq. ft.
Tare weight	290 lb.	—	420 lb.	—
All-up weight	470 lb.	530 lb.	730 lb.	1,150 lb.
Maximum speed	74 m.p.h.	83·75 m.p.h.	85 m.p.h.	80 m.p.h.

Production:

Three ANEC I: (nil c/n) Lympne No. 18/G-EBHR/G-AUEQ; (c/n 1) Lympne No. 17/G-EBIL/J7506; (3) G-AUET. One ANEC II: (2) Lympne No. 7/G-EBJO. One ANEC IV: (1) G-EBPI.

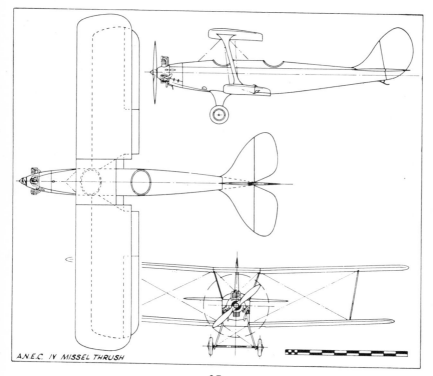

A.N.E.C. IV MISSEL THRUSH

ANEC III G-AUEZ 'Diamond Bird' outside the hangars at the Coode Island, Melbourne, base of Australian Aerial Services Ltd. in October 1928

ANEC III

Following the award on 1 November 1921 of an Australian Government contract for passenger and mail services between Adelaide and Sydney, the Larkin Aircraft Supply Co. Ltd. sought a suitable modern aircraft in England and to meet their requirement G. H. Handasyde of the Handasyde Aircraft Co. Ltd. produced designs for a commercial monoplane in two variants, a 10-seater powered by one 450 h.p. Napier Lion and a 6-seater with 300 h.p. Hispano-Suiza. Larkin chose the smaller version but stipulated the 400 h.p. Rolls-Royce Eagle IX water-cooled engine and Handasyde, having no factory of his own, placed an order with the Air Navigation and Engineering Co. Ltd. for the construction of four aircraft at Addlestone.

Known as the Handasyde H.2, the new type was a high-wing cantilever monoplane of radical design, its plywood covered wing, fuselage and tail surfaces representing a great advance over contemporary fabric-covered biplanes. The sharply tapered, thick section mainplane was bolted directly on top of the fuselage with the main legs of the wide track undercarriage attached to the main spar and to prevent nosing over on unprepared strips in the Australian outback, two smaller wheels were provided under the front fuselage. Passengers sat in a small cabin and the pilot in an open cockpit ahead of the mainplane.

Non-availability of new 400 h.p. Rolls-Royce Eagle IX engines caused delays which eventually made it necessary to install the 350 h.p. Government surplus Eagle VIII so that the first Handasyde H.2 was not erected at Brooklands until November 1922. F. T. Courtney made the first taxying trials there on 6 December and the first flight on the 9th. Although unregistered, a second flight was made on 5 February 1923 and during the month performance measurement flights by F. P. Raynham revealed a need for greater fin area. Eventually, when poor performance by the Vickers Vulcan (a biplane of similar specification to the H.2), during demonstrations to QANTAS in the heat of the 1923 Australian summer, made it

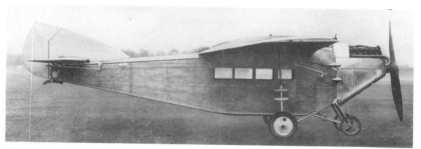

The unregistered Handasyde H.2 monoplane (350 h.p. Rolls Royce Eagle VIII), ready for test flight at Brooklands in December 1923.

evident that the monoplane might fare no better, all work on the H.2 ceased. The inaugural Larkin service between Adelaide and Sydney was consequently flown on 2 June 1924 by Capt. F. L. Roberts in the veteran Sopwith Wallaby G-AUDU formerly G-EAKS.

The Larkin contract was later transferred to the Air Navigation and Engineering Co. Ltd. itself and three Eagle VIII powered ANEC III unequal span biplanes were built to the designs of their chief engineer John Bewsher. Engine mountings and cabin sections were taken from the Handasyde H.2s and it is possible that, in the case of the second and third aircraft, these were the only items constructed for Handasyde. The rear fuselage was fabric covered and, as before, the pilot sat in the open above the mail compartment with six passengers behind.

The first ANEC III was taken by road to Brooklands on 19 March 1926, erected in the hangar of T. B. André and Co. Ltd., and first flown by J. R. King on 23 March. Although not registered in Britain, all three aircraft were issued with British Cs. of A. in the name of the Larkin Aircraft Supply Co. Ltd. before being crated for shipment, and on arrival at Melbourne received Australian marks G-AUEZ, 'FC and 'GF. They then went into service with Larkin's operating subsidiary, Australian Aerial Services, as 'Diamond Bird', 'Satin Bird' and 'Love Bird' respectively. In his book 'The Wandering Years', Capt. A. H. Affleck recalls how he made the first post-erection flights in 'EZ and that its C. of A. was suspended

VH-UEZ 'Diamond Bird' and 'GF 'Love Bird', converted to Lascowls, preparing to leave Melbourne at the start of the Mackay Expedition to Central Australia, 22 May 1930.
(*D. L. Mackenzie*)

39

because it cruised at only 55 m.p.h., was tail heavy with full load, and needed considerable external assistance when taxying or manoeuvring on the ground. After modification and re-rigging however, and heavy duty wheels and tyres had been fitted, the ANEC IIIs gave good service and made a number of important pioneering flights into the outback.

In 1927 'Satin Bird' conveyed explorer W. Oliver into Central Australia and on 4 July 1928 Capt. F. Neale left Melbourne in 'Diamond Bird' accompanied by Capt. H. J. Larkin flying D.H.50 G-AUEK on a similar expedition for the Australian railways. Flying via Mildura, Oodnadatta, Charlotte Waters and Hermannsburg, they were the first aircraft ever to land in that remote area. Typical of the many shorter trips which would have taken days by ground transport was one by Capt. F. S. Briggs who left Melbourne one day before dawn in 'Diamond Bird' and flew a doctor 170 miles to Deniquilin to perform an urgent operation.

The ANEC IIIs were transferred to Australian Aerial Services' new aerodrome at Coode Island, Melbourne, when it opened on 20 October 1928 but when

Larkin Lascowl VH-UGF 'Love Bird' in May 1930 after landing two miles from Ayers Rock, a vast monolith rising 1,143 ft. above the Central Australian plain.

regular services ceased at the end of the year they were withdrawn for modernisation. Two were then rebuilt as 11-seaters to the design of W. S. Shackleton with lengthened front fuselages carrying 485 h.p. Armstrong Siddeley Jaguar supercharged radial engines but the third is believed to have been used as spares. In final form they were known as Lasco Lascowls, becoming VH-UEZ and 'GF but retaining their original names for daily flights over a new route between Camooweal and Daly Waters opened on 19 February 1930.

Both Lascowls were chartered by the Mackay Aerial Survey Expedition and left Canberra on 25 May 1930 for Ilbilla, 400 miles west of Alice Springs and base for a 67,000 square mile survey of Central Australia in the course of which they landed near Ayers Rock. They returned to Coode Island without mishap in mid-July, each having exceeded 300 hours of flying since conversion to Lascowl, and returned to service on the Melbourne–Sydney run until 'Love Bird' crashed and burned at Temora with the loss of pilot J. A. S. Geddes and engineer Rust on 14 July 1931. 'Diamond Bird', last of the trio, retired in June 1932 and was broken up at Coode Island.

SPECIFICATION

Manufacturers: The Air Navigation and Engineering Co. Ltd., Addlestone, Surrey.
Power Plants: (Handasyde H.2) One 350 h.p. Rolls-Royce Eagle VIII.
          (ANEC III)   One 350 h.p. Rolls-Royce Eagle VIII.
          (Lascowl)   One 485 h.p. Armstrong Siddeley Jaguar.

	Handasyde H.2	ANEC III	Lascowl
Span upper	47 ft. 6 in.	60 ft. 6 in.	60 ft. 6 in.
Span lower	—	52 ft. 0 in.	52 ft. 0 in.
Length	35 ft. 0 in.	45 ft. 0 in.	—
Height	10 ft. 2 in.	—	—
Wing Area	380 sq. ft.	740 sq. ft.	740 sq. ft.
Tare weight	—	3,470 lb.	—
All-up Weight	5,000 lb.	5,600 lb.	—
Maximum speed	115 m.p.h.	105 m.p.h.	—
Cruising speed	95 m.p.h.	90 m.p.h.	—

Production:

Three aircraft only: (c/n 1), C. of A. 23.4.26, G-AUEZ 'Diamond Bird', converted 1929 to Larkin Lascowl VH-UEZ, scrapped at Coode Island 6.32; (2), 20.7.26, G-AUFC 'Satin Bird', reduced to spares 5.29; (3) 13.8.26, G-AUGF 'Love Bird', converted 1929 to Larkin Lascowl VH-UGF, crashed at Temora, N.S.W. 14.7.31.

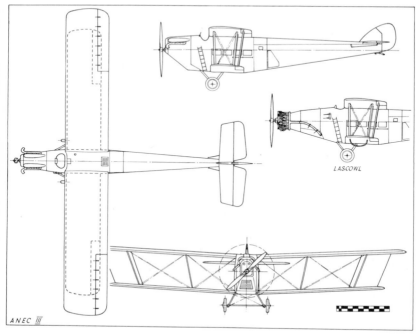

LASCOWL

ANEC III

41

E. D. C. Herne's Armstrong Whitworth F.K.3 B9629/G-EABY 'Porthcawl' at Filton in May 1919. (*W. K. Kilsby*)

Armstrong Whitworth F.K.3 and F.K.8

The F.K.3 was a two-seat reconnaissance and training biplane of wood and fabric construction designed in 1915 by Frederick Koolhoven, chief designer of Sir W. G. Armstrong Whitworth and Co. Ltd., and powered by one 90 h.p. R.A.F.1A air-cooled engine. It was built in quantity by A.W. at Newcastle and by the sub-contractors, Hewlett and Blondeau Ltd. at Luton. The F.K.8, a larger machine of similar outline powered by various engines and capable of carrying a useful bomb load, followed in 1916 and was also built in considerable numbers so that when batches of surplus aircraft were auctioned at Hendon after the war, it was inevitable that a number of F.K.3s and F.K.8s were included.

Four Luton-built F.K.3s became civil in this way. B9629, first of two bought by E. D. C. Herne in May 1919, was lettered 'Porthcawl' on the fuselage and flown to Filton en route to South Wales where the owner was to give pleasure flights in the Avro Transport Co.'s 504Ks. The F.K.3 accompanied the Avro 'circus' on a tour of South Coast resorts and was last heard of at West Blatchington Farm, Brighton, on 25 October 1919. B9612 was used for joyriding and tuition by the Kingsbury Aviation Co. at Stag Lane, Edgware, for a few months in 1919 but B9603, acquired by L. G. Lowe of London, seems not to have been used. There is no evidence that their respective civil markings G-EABY, 'BZ, 'EU and 'LK were ever carried.

Eleven recorded civil examples of the large F.K.8, all but one built by Angus Sanderson Ltd. and fitted with 160 h.p. Beardmore engines, include D5150 purchased by the London and Provincial Aviation Co. Ltd. on 1 June 1919 for £260. In R.A.F. markings and daubed with *Evening Standard* in whitewash, it carried newspapers from Stag Lane to Southsea daily from 23–30 June piloted by T. Neville Stack who then flew it to Great Yarmouth to give free flights near Burgh Castle on behalf of the *Daily Sketch*. At this stage it bore 'L. and P.' in whitewash below the cockpits and was suitably inscribed but evidently came to grief without ever carrying registration G-EAET because Stack continued the free flight programme at Mousehold Aerodrome, Norwich, in his own F.K.8, G-EAIC, on 4, 7, 11 and 14 September.

The third machine, G-EAJS, left Hounslow for Copenhagen on 11 November piloted by Lt. Col. G. L. P. Henderson on delivery to P.O. Flygkompani at Barkaby, Sweden, with whom it flew unmarked apart from a large S on the fuselage. The fourth, G-EALW, belonged to By Air Ltd., a small Coventry-based joyriding concern, but lasted only a month as a civil machine, pilot J. G. Riley being killed when it crashed near Bedford on 16 August 1920. G-EATO, purchased at Hendon for £260 by a Lt. Howard, was registered to commercial pilot R. E. Duke and is believed to have gone to the Netherlands on a pleasure flying venture in 1920. Its near-neighbour, G-EATP, was registered to Swedish explorer Maj. Tryggve Gran who flew it from Hounslow to Skagen, Denmark, on 24 June 1920 and continued to Kristiania (Oslo) next day. He covered the 750 miles in 9 hours flying time but later crashed during a European tour.

The final British civil F.K.8s, G-EAVQ and 'VT, registered to Handley Page Ltd. at the end of 1920, were probably sold in the Argentine. Three others, registered in Australia in June 1921, were bought up by Queensland and Northern Territory Aerial Services Ltd. in September 1922 for their Charleville-Cloncurry route, G-AUCF and 'DE, acquired from Simpson Tregilles Aircraft and Transport Ltd. of Perth, W.A. and pioneer pilot H. Miller of Melbourne respectively, being sent by rail to Longreach for erection. They were joined later by G-AUCS. G-AUDE, formerly F4231, was constructed originally from serviceable components by No. 3 (Western) Aircraft Repair Depot at Yate, Gloucestershire.

The inaugural flight with 166 letters was made by P. J. McGuinness and W. A. Baird from Charleville to Longreach in G-AUDE on 2 November and the second stage to Cloncurry was flown next day by Hudson Fysh with the company's first passenger, 87 year old Alexander Kennedy, in the rear seat. F.K.8s could not maintain altitude in tropical conditions when fully loaded and frequent forced landings occurred when engines boiled. Larger radiators were fitted but engine lives were short and even the Beardmore engine from the defunct Avro 547 Triplane G-AUCR was pressed into service. G-AUCF crashed during a sluggish take-off from a small fair ground at Jericho on 25 February 1923 and 'DE was wrecked at Blackall on 13 September but 'CS kept the route open until new D.H.9Cs were delivered at the end of the year and was then dismantled at Longreach.

Armstrong Whitworth F.K.8 G-AUDE at Longreach, 2 November 1922, on arrival from Charleville with the first Queensland air mail. (*Q.A.N.T.A.S.*)

SPECIFICATION

Manufacturers: Sir W. G. Armstrong Whitworth and Co. Ltd., Elswick Works, Gosforth, Newcastle-upon-Tyne and subcontractors.

Power Plants: (F.K.3) One 90 h.p. R.A.F. 1A.
(F.K.8) One 160 h.p. Beardmore.

	F.K.3	F.K.8
Span	40 ft. 0 in.	43 ft. 6 in.
Length	29 ft. 0 in.	31 ft. 0 in.
Height	11 ft. $10\frac{1}{4}$ in.	11 ft. 0 in.
Wing area	442 sq. ft.	540 sq. ft.
Tare weight	1,386 lb.	1,916 lb.
All-up weight	2,056 lb.	2,811 lb.
Maximum speed	87 m.p.h.	98 m.p.h.
Service ceiling	12,000 ft.	12,000 ft.
Endurance	3 hr.	3 hr.

Known civil conversions: (a) F.K.3
   B9629/G-EABY; B9518/G-EABZ; B9612/G-EAEU; B9603/G-EALK.

(b) F.K.8
   D5150/G-EAET;   H4473/G-EAIC;   H4612/G-EAJS;   F7484/G-EALW;
F7384/G-EATO;   H4600/G-EATP;   H4585/G-EAVQ;   H4573/G-EAVT;
H4561/G-AUCF; F4231/G-AUDE; unidentified/G-AUCS.

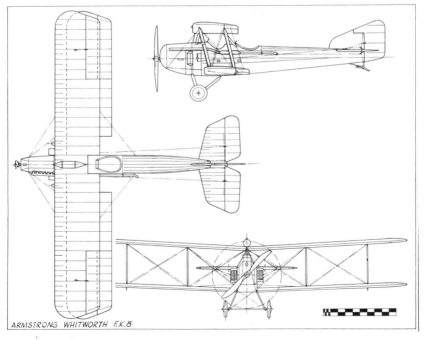

ARMSTRONG WHITWORTH F.K.8

Frank Courtney contemplating the two-seat Siskin II at Croydon prior to the 1922 King's Cup Race. (*Flight Photo 2105*)

Armstrong Whitworth Siskin

Although the diminutive Siskin was designed as a fighter biplane, most of the prototypes had distinguished civil careers in the development field and as demonstrators and racing machines. The prototype Siskin I, C4541, appeared in 1921, and was a product of the Siddeley Deasy Car Co. Ltd. of Parkside, Coventry, who in that year acquired the name and goodwill of Sir W. G. Armstrong Whitworth & Co. Ltd. after that company shut down its aviation department at Newcastle-upon-Tyne. It conformed to contemporary practice and was a fabric-covered wooden structure with single-bay, wire-braced, sesquiplane wings and parallel interplane struts. The fuselage was of good streamlined shape, to take full advantage of the small frontal area of the new Jaguar engine, which was only 43 in. in diameter. This had 14 cylinders, developed 325 h.p. and was one of the earliest two-row radials.

The Siskin II was built as a two-seater and given civil status as G-EBEU for participation in the very first King's Cup Race, which started at Croydon on 8 September 1922. It averaged 127·2 m.p.h. on the round Britain course until a broken centre section fitting compelled test pilot F. T. Courtney to land it at Manchester. This machine was again entered in 1923, this time modified as a single-seater with an increase in performance sufficient to give Frank Courtney a handsome win at an average speed of 149 m.p.h. Meanwhile a second Siskin II single-seater had been constructed and given civil marking G-EBHY to enable it to fly over foreign soil en route to demonstrations in all quarters of Europe. It was finally fitted with skis and sold to the Royal Swedish Air Force in 1925. G-EBEU also showed the flag overseas, and in December 1924 was exhibited at the Prague Aero Show.

Maj. F. M. Green, its designer, was also a pioneer of the high tensile steel construction used on later marks of Siskin, the fuselages of which were of steel tube throughout. The wing spars were also of metal. Jaguar development kept pace with that of the airframe, the two Siskin IIIs entered in the 1924 King's Cup Race being fitted with the 350 h.p. Jaguar II. Long stages between Martlesham and Leith and between Dumbarton and Falmouth necessitated the fitting of large overload fuel tanks to the underside of the top wings in what is now regarded as the modern manner. G-EBJQ, piloted by Flt. Lt. H. W. G. Jones, finished fourth to make fastest time of the day at 126 m.p.h., but 'JS, piloted by Courtney, was forced down at Brough with spinner trouble.

With their V-shaped interplane struts, the Siskin III and IIIA single-seaters and the two-seat Siskin III were the only variants put into R.A.F. service, but the type

The single-seat Siskin II which was evaluated in Sweden in 1925.

The single-seat Siskin III showing the V interplane struts and the long-range tanks fitted for the 1924 King's Cup Race. (*Leonard Bridgman*)

46

Parallel interplane struts were again used on the Siskin V. It was not fitted with the lower fin.

G-ABHT, first of two Siskin III two-seat trainers, used by Air Service Training Ltd. in 1931.

was developed still further via the Siskin IV, first considered in 1923–24, as the unfinished G-EBIK with Jaguar II. It also reverted to parallel interplane struts and, like the Siskin IIIA, was not fitted with the small fin under the tail. The Siskin V was generally similar, but had additional wing area. Together with two Siskin Vs, the sole Siskin IV to fly, G-EBLL, was entered in the 1925 King's Cup Race and flown from scratch into second place by Flt. Lt. H. W. G. Jones. The Mk. V machines, G-EBLN and 'LQ, were given five minutes start and took off together, but although J. L. N. Bennett Baggs wrecked his undercarriage in a ditch when landing for fuel at Town Moor, Newcastle, Imperial Airways' chief pilot, F. L. Barnard, flew G-EBLQ to victory in poor visibility at an average round Britain speed of 151·43 m.p.h. This machine was destroyed in a crash in the following year, after which the others were gradually taken out of commission. Four years later a pair of two-seat Siskin IIIs, G-ABHT and 'HU fitted with Jaguar IV motors, were built for advanced instruction at the A.W. Reserve Flying School at

Whitley, but with the formation of Air Service Training Ltd. were transferred to Hamble in May 1931. Here, 'HT had a very short life, but its sister machine became a familiar sight in the Southampton area for many years.

SPECIFICATION

Manufacturers: Sir W. G. Armstrong Whitworth Aircraft Ltd., Parkside, Coventry.
Power Plants: (Siskin II) One 320 h.p. Armstrong Siddeley Jaguar I.
(Siskin III) One 350 h.p. Armstrong Siddeley Jaguar II.
(Siskin IV) One 385 h.p. Armstrong Siddeley Jaguar III.
(Siskin V) One 385 h.p. Armstrong Siddeley Jaguar III.

	Siskin II	Siskin III	Siskin V
Span	28 ft. 4 in.	33 ft. 1 in.	28 ft. 4 in.
Length	21 ft. 6 in.	22 ft. 6 in.	21 ft. 6 in.
Height	9 ft. 6 in.	9 ft. 9 in.	9 ft. 6 in.
Wing area	253 sq. ft.	298 sq. ft.	253 sq. ft.
All-up weight	2,250 lb.	2,735 lb.	2,460 lb.
Maximum speed	148 m.p.h.	134 m.p.h.	155 m.p.h.
Initial climb	1,250 ft./min.	1,300 ft./min.	1,650 ft./min.
Ceiling	26,000 ft.	20,500 ft.	25,000 ft.

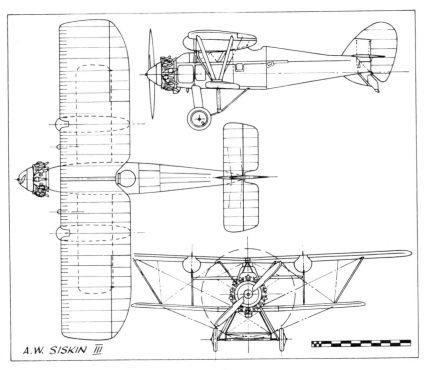

A.W. SISKIN III

Argosy I G-EBLF 'City of Glasgow' flying near Croydon in 1927. (*B.O.A.C.*)

Armstrong Whitworth Argosy

At its formation in April 1924, Imperial Airways Ltd. took over from its pre-decessors 13 aircraft of four different types, more than half of which were single-engined D.H.34s. Of the seven additions to the fleet in the first two years of operation, only two multi-engined aircraft were obtainable from an infant aircraft industry. Realizing that both its own survival and the popularity of air travel depended on the creation of a reputation for safety, Imperial Airways decided that all its future aircraft must be multi-engined and the number of types reduced for spares economy. Orders were thereupon placed with Handley Page, de Havilland and Armstrong Whitworth, who in 1926 delivered a total of 12 two- and three-engined airliners.

The Armstrong Whitworth design, known as the Argosy, was a large three-engined biplane seating 20 passengers in a long, parallel sided, square section fuselage with captain and first officer seated side by side in an open cockpit in the nose. Baggage was housed in a special compartment in the tail, reached by a door in the starboard side. It was the first airliner produced by the company and, as might be expected, owed a great deal to the Siskin, having a steel tube fuselage, all-steel wings and using the direct drive Jaguar engine, one of which was mounted in the nose with two others in flat-sided tapering nacelles on the inboard interplane struts. The contract was for three machines, the first, G-EBLF, making its initial public appearance at the Hendon R.A.F. Display on 3 July 1926. The second Argosy, G-EBLO, was delivered to Imperial Airways Ltd. in the following week and flew the first Argosy service to Paris piloted by the company's air super-intendent, H. G. Brackley, on 5 August 1926. The fuselage was painted in the former Instone Air Line royal blue, which at that time was still in use. The prototype, similarly decorated, was retained for further test flying until delivered to Croydon in the following September, the third machine, G-EBOZ, arriving in April 1927 after a period under Air Council ownership as a potential troop-carrier. Blue fuselages were short lived, the Argosies being redoped in the now

49

familiar silver and black colour scheme at their first C. of A. overhaul. They were then named, like all subsequent Argosies, after famous cities, as shown in Appendix E, and put into regular service to Paris ($2\frac{1}{2}$ hrs.), Basle ($5\frac{3}{4}$ hrs.), Brussels ($2\frac{1}{2}$ hrs.) and Cologne (4 hrs.).

Passenger accommodation was much roomier than in any of the company's earlier airliners, and on 1 May 1927 G-EBLF left Croydon on the world's first luxury 'named' air route, the London–Paris 'Silver Wing' lunch service. The flagship was on this occasion flown by Capt. G. P. Olley and carried a buffet and steward in place of the two rear seats. Deviations from regular airline schedules were few for these trustworthy craft, but on 15 June 1928 G. P. Olley flew G-EBLF from Croydon to Turnhouse via the East Coast in a race against the 'Flying Scotsman' crack express train, and won by 15 minutes.

Three additional Argosies, G-AACH to 'CJ, were put into service on the European routes in 1929, including the Croydon–Basle stage (later extended to Salonika) of the newly introduced England–India service. These Argosy IIs were 20 seaters with an improved performance given by Jaguar IVA geared radials in Townend rings and were distinguishable from the Mk. I by their Handley Page slots and conical engine nacelles. They also had large vertical servo tabs on the trailing edge of the lower mainplane, which gave finger-light aileron control and automatically applied bank in a flat turn or sideslip, thus relieving pilot fatigue on long journeys. The fleet was joined by a seventh Argosy, G-AAEJ, on 9 July 1929 and gave stalwart, uneventful service until G-AACH was destroyed by fire in a crash at Croydon on 22 April 1931 while a pilot was qualifying for a three-engine endorsement.

Shortage of aircraft on the South African route in 1931 resulted in Jaguar IVAs being fitted in the Argosy Is and the transfer of G-EBLO and 'OZ to Almaza. The former crashed at Aswan soon afterwards and was replaced by 'LF which returned to European duty with 'OZ when the Handley Page 42s were commissioned at the end of the year. G-AACI was lost in a mysterious mid-air fire in Belgium while flying on the Cologne–Croydon route in 1933 but the surviving pair continued on scheduled services until 1935 when 'CJ was sold to United

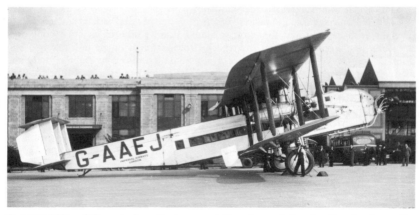

G-AAEJ 'City of Coventry' on the tarmac at Croydon and showing the circular section nacelles and aileron servo tabs of the Argosy II.

50

Airways Ltd. of Stanley Park Aerodrome, Blackpool, for pleasure flights round Blackpool Tower. It was taken over by British Airways Ltd. in the following year but G-AAEJ was broken up at Croydon, not, it is alleged, without protest, so strong was the structure, but its metal maker's plate inscribed 'Argosy No. 7 G-AAEJ', suitably mounted, lives on in the B.E.A. offices at Heathrow.

SPECIFICATION

Manufacturers: Sir W. G. Armstrong Whitworth Aircraft Ltd., Parkside, Coventry.

Power Plants: (Argosy I)   Three 385 h.p. Armstrong Siddeley Jaguar III.

              (Argosy II)   Three 420 h.p. Armstrong Siddeley Jaguar IVA.

Dimensions: (Both Marks) Span, 90 ft. 0 in. Length, 64 ft. 6 in. Height, 19 ft. 0 in. Wing area, 1,890 sq. ft.

Weights: (Argosy I)   Tare weight, 12,000 lb. All-up weight, 18,000 lb.

              (Argosy II)   Tare weight, 12,090 lb. All-up weight, 19,200 lb.

Performance: (Both Marks) Maximum speed, 110 m.p.h. Cruising speed, 90 m.p.h. Range, 405 miles.

Production: (a) Argosy I

  Three aircraft: (c/n A.W.154) G-EBLF; (155) G-EBLO; (156) G-EBOZ.

        (b) Argosy II

  Four aircraft: (c/n A.W.362) G-AACH; (363) G-AACI; (364) G-AACJ; (400) G-AAEJ.

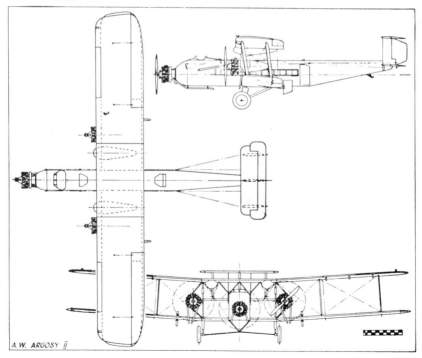

A.W. ARGOSY II

51

The prototype A.W.15 on an early test flight and carrying its original name 'Atalanta'. The spats were not fitted to production machines.

Armstrong Whitworth A.W.15 Atalanta

The second A.W. airliner type, the Atalanta, was, like the Argosy, a product of chief designer J. Lloyd and chief engineer Maj. F. M. Green, eight machines being built in 1931–32 to the order of Imperial Airways Ltd., solely for use on the Nairobi–Cape Town and Karachi–Singapore sections of their trunk routes to South Africa and Australia. The main requirements were for high cruising speed coupled with sufficient reserve power for operation from the high-altitude aerodromes south of Nairobi, and generous passenger space to alleviate the discomforts of tropical flying. It was of plywood-covered steel construction, and in a biplane age its cantilever wing and streamlined fuselage were a great step forward in design. With four Serval (formerly known as Double Mongoose) two-row radials mounted along the leading edge of the wing and with the oleo legs and divided axle of the undercarriage housed entirely within the fuselage, it was one of the cleanest British aeroplanes produced up to that time. Captain and first officer sat side by side in an enclosed cabin in the nose and were separated from the nine passengers, in their unusually spacious saloon, by the main mail and freight compartment, the payload being equally divided between passengers and cargo.

The prototype, G-ABPI, which carried the type name 'Atalanta', made its first public appearance at the first of all the S.B.A.C. Shows at Hendon on 28 June 1932, having been flown down from Whitley by test pilot A. C. Campbell Orde in the then remarkably short time of 40 minutes. It went to Croydon early in September for acceptance trials and some crew training, later returning to the makers for slight modifications. During the course of subsequent tests it made a forced landing near Whitley on 20 October 1932 and suffered considerable damage. In order to minimize any unwarranted adverse publicity for a new and untried type and to cause no further production delays, after repair the prototype was renamed 'Arethusa'. The name 'Atalanta' was switched to the newly completed fourth aircraft, G-ABTI, delivered to Croydon on 24 December 1932. A week later this machine left on the first proving flight to the Cape, piloted by H. G. Brackley. Cape Town was reached on 14 February 1933 after delays at Cairo with engine trouble and at Kisumu and elsewhere with familiarization flights for northbound Imperial pilots.

On his return to England H. G. Brackley organized a similar proving flight to Australia and on 29 May 1933 left in 'Astraea', the seventh of the type, flown by J. V. Prendergast. Although it was intended that Imperial's A.W.15s should connect at Singapore with QANTAS D.H.86s, Brackley took 'Astraea' right through to Australia. Overload fuel-tanks fitted at Croydon proved their worth when adverse winds over the Timor Sea prevented the aircraft from reaching Darwin, a forced landing being made in a jungle clearing on Bathurst Island off the north coast of Australia. The 14,000 mile flight to Melbourne was completed on 30 June at an average speed of over 100 m.p.h., after which the machine was

'Amalthea' running up at Croydon in September 1932 prior to its Middle East delivery flight.

Indian Trans-Continental Airways A.W.15 VT-AEF 'Arethusa' at Willingdon Airport, Delhi, India in 1934. (*Imperial Airways*)

'Aurora', last of the eight A.W.15s, flying in India as DG454 in 1942 with additional front windows. (*Air Ministry*)

53

ferried back to its operational base at Karachi, arriving on 19 July. Meanwhile the final machine, 'Aurora', had been delivered and shown at the S.B.A.C. Show at Hendon on 24 June 1933, and the rebuilt prototype G-ABPI had left Karachi on 7 July on the first service to Singapore. Both these machines were taken over a month later by Indian Trans-Continental Airways Ltd., a subsidiary company formed to manage this section of the route, and spent their entire careers in Indian markings.

For eight years the Atalantas continued to operate their tropical schedules in the unobtrusive way common to efficient aeroplanes, although three were unfortunately lost in accidents. In March 1941 the two Indian and three surviving Imperial Airways Atalantas were impressed for service with the Indian Air Force.

SPECIFICATION

Manufacturers: Sir W. G. Armstrong Whitworth Aircraft Ltd., Parkside, Coventry.

Power Plants: Four 340 h.p. Armstrong Siddeley Serval III.

Dimensions: Span, 90 ft. 0 in. Length, 71 ft. 6 in. Height, 15 ft. 0 in. Wing area, 1,285 sq. ft.

Weights: Tare weight, 13,940 lb. All-up weight, 21,000 lb.

Performance: Maximum speed, 156 m.p.h. Cruising speed, 130 m.p.h. Initial climb, 700 ft./min. Ceiling on three engines, 7,000 ft. Range. 400 miles.

Production:

Eight aircraft: (c/n A.W.740) G-ABPI; (785) G-ABTG; (741) G-ABTH; (742) G-ABTI; (743) G-ABTJ; (744) G-ABTK; (784) G-ABTL; (786) G-ABTM.

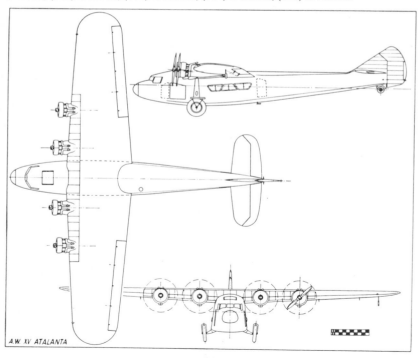

A.W. XV ATALANTA

'Ensign', flagship of the Imperial Airways fleet of A.W.27s, in its original Mk. 1 condition.
(*Flight Photo 15633S*)

Armstrong Whitworth A.W.27 Ensign

Armstrong Whitworth's third airliner type, the Ensign, was the largest landplane built in pre-war days for Imperial Airways Ltd. and, like the Atalanta, was a four motor high-wing cantilever monoplane designed by Mr. John Lloyd. There the similarity ended, the newcomer being of almost twice the physical size, three times the all-up weight, of all-metal stressed skin construction, and fitted with an enormous retractable undercarriage. The need for the Ensign followed a Government decision in 1934 to carry all first-class Empire mail by air, and an order for 12 machines, later increased to 14, was placed in 1935. The Whitley factory was working to capacity on the bomber to which it gave its name, with the result that all Ensign construction took place at Hamble, in the hangars of Air Service Training Ltd., another member of the Hawker Siddeley Group.

Relays of minor modifications called for by Imperial Airways during the construction of the prototype, G-ADSR, delayed its first flight until 24 January 1938, the initial test being carried out by test pilots C. K. Turner-Hughes and E. S. Greenwood. After flight trials during which fuel starvation brought about a lucky forced landing at Bicester, the machine qualified for its C. of A., and flew its first service to Paris on 20 October 1938 piloted by C. K. Turner-Hughes. It carried 27 passengers in three cabins and was intended for the distant Empire routes, sleeping accommodation being alternatively provided for 20. Four machines, 'Eddystone', 'Ettrick', 'Empyrean' and 'Elysian', differed internally, having seats for 40 passengers, and were known as the European model. They were preceded on the production line by the Empire models 'Egeria', 'Elsinore', 'Euterpe' and 'Explorer', the first three of which were used to fly the 1938 Christmas mail to Australia, but, falling by the wayside with engine and other defects, were returned to the makers. More powerful Tiger IXC engines driving constant-speed propellers were then fitted but the delay prevented any further pre-war flying by Ensigns on Empire routes, and four destined for Indian Trans-Continental Airways Ltd., to supplement the two Indian-registered Atalantas on the central section of the Australia air route, never flew with the Indian markings and names allotted in 1937, although 'Euryalus' did appear briefly as VT-AJG before first flight.

By the outbreak of war in 1939 all but one of the first 12 Ensigns had been

55

G-ADTB 'Echo' in Mk. 2 form with Cyclone engines and Lancaster tail wheel, after its repatriation flight from Cairo to Hurn in February 1946. (*Aeroplane*)

delivered, and after evacuation from Croydon to Baginton a few were used under the aegis of National Air Communications for carrying food, ammunition and other stores to British Forces in France. Many and varied were the flight experiences of the camouflaged Ensign fleet in confused, war-torn Europe during 1939–40. Inevitably three machines were lost by enemy action, 'Elysian' destroyed by Me 109s at Merville, 'Ettrick' damaged by bomb blast and abandoned at Le Bourget, and 'Endymion' destroyed by fire in an air raid on Whitchurch Aerodrome, Bristol.

Arduous service flying again proved the Ensign to be underpowered, and in 1941–42 the eight survivors, now in B.O.A.C. service, were re-engined with Wright Cyclone G102A motors, and their designation amended to A.W.27 Mk. 2. The final pair of machines, 'Everest' and 'Enterprise', on which work had stopped in 1939, were completed with the new engines in 1941, and in the following year the fleet was ferried through Portreath to the Near East. Here it was used on a shuttle service linking East and West African ports. In the course of these ferry flights, 'Everest' was shot up by a Heinkel 111 over the Bay of Biscay and was forced to return to England for repairs and 'Enterprise' was forced down 300 miles north of Bathurst on the West African coast by engine trouble and abandoned. 'Enterprise' was later repaired by the French and flown to Vichy France, eventually falling into German hands. Together with 'Ettrick', which had been abandoned at Le Bourget two years earlier, it was re-engined with Daimler-Benz motors, both subsequently being used as German V.I.P. transports.

The final assignment allotted to the nine survivors was the operation of the Cairo–Calcutta section of the Australia route, a task faithfully carried out until

'Everest' at Bramcote in wartime camouflage, 1941, showing the narrow chord cowlings typical of the Mk. 2. (*Aeroplane*)

their retirement in 1945. With the exception of the prototype, grounded in 1944 to become an instructional airframe, and 'Euterpe' cannibalized at Almaza to make their return possible, all the remaining machines were flown home. The last passengers to fly in an Ensign left Almaza on 3 June 1946 in 'Eddystone', piloted by Capt. O. Pritchard on the ferry flight to the British terminal, Hurn.

SPECIFICATION

Manufacturers: Sir W. G. Armstrong Whitworth Aircraft Ltd., Parkside, Coventry.
Power Plants: (Ensign 1) Four 850 h.p. Armstrong Siddeley Tiger IXC.
  (Ensign 2) Four 950 h.p. Wright Cyclone GR-1820-G102A.
Dimensions: (Both Marks) Span, 123 ft. 0 in. Length, 114 ft. 0 in. Height, 23 ft. 0 in. Wing area, 2,450 sq. ft.
Weights: (Ensign 1) Tare weight, 32,920 lb. All-up weight, 49,000 lb.
  (Ensign 2) Tare weight, 36,586 lb. All-up weight, 55,500 lb.
Performance: (Ensign 1) Maximum speed, 205 m.p.h. Cruising speed, 170 m.p.h. Initial climb, 600 ft./min. Ceiling, 18,000 ft. Range, 800 miles.
  (Ensign 2) Maximum speed, 210 m.p.h. Cruising speed, 180 m.p.h. Initial climb, 900 ft./min. Ceiling, 24,000 ft. Range, 1,370 miles.
Production: (a) Ensign 1
  Twelve aircraft (c/n A.W.1156–1167) G-ADSR to G-ADTC inclusive.
  (b) Ensign 2
  Two aircraft: (c/n A.W.1821–1822) G-AFZU and G-AFZV.

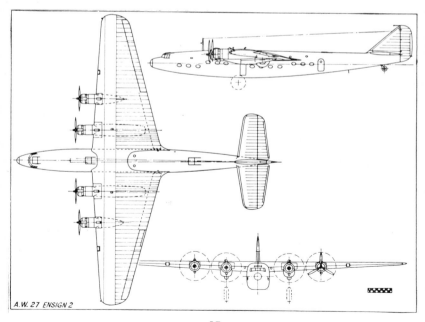

A.W. 27 ENSIGN 2

The Laarbruch Flying Club's ex-Dutch Auster 3 G-ATAX photographed in Germany in 1968. (*M. J. Hooks*)

Auster 3, 4 and 5

Auster A.O.P. monoplanes built for the 1939–45 war survived in large numbers to make a very considerable contribution to post-war light aviation, chief of these being the Auster 5 or Model J, a three-seater of fabric-covered, wood and metal construction fitted with the 130 h.p. Lycoming flat-four engine. For over 14 years only two specimens of the Gipsy Major powered two-seat Auster 3 or Model E were used for civilian purposes in Great Britain, viz. G-AHLI and 'LK, formerly NJ911 and NJ889, with which Vickers-Armstrongs (Aircraft) Ltd. maintained inter-factory communications. They parted in April 1958 when 'LI went to the Vickers flying club at White Waltham and 'LK was acquired by J. W. C. Judge at Shoreham.

The total of British civil Auster 3s rose to three when 9M-ALB landed at Middle Wallop on 15 November 1960 after an outstanding 8,000 mile flight from Ipoh, Malaya, piloted by Capt. M. Somerton-Rayner with his wife as passenger. After overhaul at Eastleigh the all-yellow machine was re-registered G-AREI but also carried its former military serial MT438 on the fuselage. Fitted with extensive radio navigation equipment it was later based in Germany and in the John Morgan Trophy Race at Baginton on 5 August 1963 averaged 111·5 m.p.h. A fourth Auster 3, G-ATAX, which originated in the Netherlands as PH-UFP, was also used in Germany by the R.A.F. flying clubs at Geilenkirchen and Laarbruch. In addition to the four British, at least 44 Auster 3s were civilianised overseas, as shown in the table on page 61.

Earmarked as the first two civil Auster 5s, RT475 and RT476 were taken straight from the Thurmaston production line in August 1944 for use by the embryo M.C.A. and, while still camouflaged, became G-AGLK and 'LL. At the end of hostilities they were painted royal blue to continue their commercial licence testing at Gatwick. From time to time during the next few years small batches of Auster 5s became surplus to R.A.F. requirements and were put up for civilian tender, to be overhauled subsequently for private ownership, joyriding, aerial photography, banner and glider towing and, to a lesser extent, club flying. A number were repurchased by Auster Aircraft Ltd. and after rejuvenation at Rearsby soon found a ready market, a high proportion assisting in the export drive. In November 1953 the R.A.F. declared obsolete all its remaining Auster 5s, R. K. Dundas Ltd. acquiring the last 40 or so, to bring the British civil total to 148. As in the case of aircraft civilianised earlier, some of these proved to be of the Auster 4 or Model G variety, externally recognizable by the small auxiliary trimming surface below the port tailplane and the external venturi. A number were raised to Mk. 5 standard both before and after demobilization by fitting a new elevator incorporating a conventional trailing-edge trim tab, installing a blind-flying panel and modifying the engine to take a Pesco vacuum pump.

Including those registered in Great Britain, at least 17 Auster 4s and 250 Auster 5s flew in civil marks in various parts of the world.

The Auster 5 story is one of faithful service in a number of arduous and often unspectacular roles, and few attempts have been made to modify it for abnormal usage. Several have been converted temporarily into the four-seat Mk. 5A by fitting a bench-type rear seat, one of the first being G-AJJH, formerly NJ617, modified at Fairoaks in 1950 for its owner, the Count de Malet Rochfort. G-AJAK, Elstree-based, was well known as a banner-towing machine over London and elsewhere in the days when this form of advertising was legal. G-AJCH and 'CI supplied with interchangeable wheel and ski undercarriages for use by the Falkland Islands Survey in 1948–49, and later re-registered in the Colony as VP-FAA and 'AB, were joined by VP-FAC fitted with twin floats and evaluated at Beaumaris in September 1949.

T. W. Hayhow starting in the race for the Yorkshire Aeroplane Club Trophy at Sherburn-in-Elmet on 22 July 1950. The external trim tab of the Auster 4 is visible under the port tailplane.

Auster 5 seaplane VP-FAC undergoing trials at Beaumaris, 7 September 1949, prior to shipment to the Falkland Islands.

The sole Auster 5C (Gipsy Major, curved windscreen, small fin and rudder) at Wolverhampton for the King's Cup Race, 17 June 1950. (*A. J. Jackson*)

G-ANHX, the Rochford Hundred Flying Group's Auster 5D, Southend-based 1963–69 (Gipsy Major, flat windscreen, enlarged fin and rudder). (*A. J. Jackson*)

In 1945 Taylorcraft Aeroplanes (England) Ltd. produced a 'one-off' communications aircraft TJ187 with Gipsy Major 1 for its own use but sold it in 1949 to Grp. Capt. A. H. Wheeler who civilianised it at Farnborough as the sole Auster 5C, G-ALKI, and flew it into third place in the 1950 King's Cup Race at Wolverhampton at the remarkable speed of 132·5 m.p.h. After its departure for New Zealand in 1951 to become ZK-AZF, several others, including the original G-AGLK, based at Shoreham in 1969 by W. C. E. Tazewell, had their Lycomings removed in favour of Gipsy Majors but because they also had the enlarged fin and rudder of the Auster J-1N, which they closely resembled, were redesignated Auster 5D. The prototype, G-AJYU, was not a conversion but factory-built as a 5D (c/n 2666) using the fuselage frame of TW453 (c/n 1793).

At least 29 Auster 5D conversions were made for, or in, Italy, Pakistan, Australia and the Far East. These included 11 in Great Britain where, in 1969, those remaining were G-ANHW and 'IJ in private ownership, British United's club machine G-AOCR in Jersey and the Rochford Hundred Flying Group's well known Southend-based G-ANHX.

The only other notable re-designated variant was the Croydon-based Auster 5M G-ANDU fitted in December 1953 with a system of strut-braced underwing neon tubes to the order of Sky Neon Aviation Ltd. for night advertising. Like its forebear the Auster 5C, it went overseas, ending its days in Sweden as SE-CAO. Similar equipment was fitted to G-AOSL, used for night advertising over the Netherlands by Overseas Aviation Ltd. 1957–58 and to G-AJYP which patrolled Nairobi, Kenya, in 1951 and continued in Singapore as VR-SDQ in 1952. There were also two remarkable rebuilds: VH-SEB (previously TW522 and VR-SDY) of Blacker Motors Ltd., Lincoln, S.A. which, in 1961, received an Auster J-4 cabin and 28 ft. Aiglet Trainer mainplane; and G-ALXZ, retrieved from a German barn and converted to Auster 5/150 by Capt. M. Somerton-Rayner who installed a 150 h.p. Lycoming O-320-A2B in 1966.

The 13-year-old design was given a new lease of life in 1956 when Auster Aircraft Ltd. returned to limited production as a purely civil aeroplane without the enlarged A.O.P. rear perspex. In this form it was marketed as the Alpha 5, Lycoming-engined counterpart of the Autocrat, the total production run being fourteen. Three of these were ferried in British marks to Swedish owners, one each to Germany and Austria, and G-APRF spent a year in Sierra Leone as VR-LAF. G-APBE, originally awarded as prize in a newspaper competition, eventually passed into the hands of the Experimental Flying Group, Croydon and Biggin Hill, being joined later by G-APRF. Once the resident joyride machine at Great Yarmouth, G-APTU went to Exeter in private ownership in 1965.

SPECIFICATION

Manufacturers: Taylorcraft Aeroplanes (England) Ltd., Britannia Works, Thurmaston, Leicester. Name changed to Auster Aircraft Ltd. and works transferred to Rearsby Aerodrome, Leicester on 7 March 1946.

Power Plants:

(Auster 3)	One 130 h.p. de Havilland Gipsy Major.
(Auster 4)	One 130 h.p. Lycoming O-290-3.
(Auster 5 and 5M)	One 130 h.p. Lycoming O-290-3/1.
(Auster 5C and 5D)	One 130 h.p. de Havilland Gipsy Major 1 or 1F.
(Auster 5/150)	One 150 h.p. Lycoming O-320-A2B.

	Auster 3	Auster 4	Auster 5
Span	36 ft. 0 in.	36 ft. 0 in.	36 ft. 0 in.
Length	22 ft. 10 in.	22 ft. 5 in.	22 ft. 5 in.
Height	8 ft. 0 in.	8 ft. 0 in.	8 ft. 0 in.
Wing area	185 sq. ft.	185 sq. ft.	185 sq. ft.
Tare weight	1,100 lb.	1,100 lb.	1,160 lb.
All-up weight	1,700 lb.	1,900 lb.	1,900 lb.
Maximum speed	130 m.p.h.	130 m.p.h.	130 m.p.h.
Cruising speed	108 m.p.h.	108 m.p.h.	108 m.p.h.
Initial climb	950 ft./min.	950 ft./min.	950 ft./min.
Ceiling	15,000 ft.	15,000 ft.	15,000 ft.
Range	250 miles	250 miles	250 miles

Conversion list (first allotted registrations only): (a) Auster 3

At least 48 aircraft comprising 4 British registered Auster 3s listed in Appendix E and the following converted overseas: (c/n 238) VH-SNI; (258) VH-GCV; (268) PH-NIN; (271) VH-SNS; (274) PH-POL; (291) PH-NGF; (293) VH-ALS; (295) PH-NGI; (304) PH-NGL; (320) VH-RCT; (321) VT-CGF; (330) VH-WAJ; (333) VH-BCK; (344)

PH-NGK; (348) PH-NGG; (350) PH-NGH; (363) VH-BGU; (365) VH-BGI; (373) VH-BKK; (403) TF-FSR; (413) VH-CYH; (430) VH-BDL; (431) VT-CEU; (436) VH-MBA; (455) VH-BVX; (483) VH-WAI; (492) VH-BBS; (499) I-ULLA; (508) I-ROBY; (531) VH-RKA; (577) PH-UFM; (601) VH-BCF; (613) VH-BCQ; (615) VH-BCG; (635) VH-MHT; (639) VH-BDM; (644) VH-GAE; (654) VH-BHA; (660) VH-PRW; (662) VT-CFZ; (671) VR-SCL; (678) VR-SCK; (721) VT-CHQ; (origin untraced) VT-CIU.

(b) Auster 4

At least 17 aircraft comprising 15 British registered Auster 4s listed in Appendix E and the following converted for Italy: (c/n 945) I-ALLO; (972) I-TONE.

(c) Auster 5

At least 250 aircraft comprising 148 British registered Auster 5s listed in Appendix E and the following converted overseas or exported direct from Rearsby: (c/n 735) F-BFXH; (803) HB-EOK; (863) F-BAVT; (992) HB-EOE; (996) VH-BYN; (997) HB-EOH; (1004) HB-EOW; (1012) HB-EOI; (1016) HB-EOA; (1028) F-OAMT; (1077) HB-EOD; (1102) VT-CKB; (1122) I-AULA; (1171) HB-EOV; (1177) I-METI; (1184) I-METO; (1236) HB-EOC; (1253) I-DOGE; (1262) HB-EOG; (1285) CS-ACK; (1307) VR-SDG; (1321) VT-CMC; (1326) F-OADM; (1333) VT-CKQ; (1337) AP-ACS; (1347) AP-ACR; (1349) VH-AHQ; (1358) VT-COG; (1362) AP-ADF; (1364) VR-RCA; (1371) VT-CLO; (1374) F-OAHF; (1377) VT-CON; (1378) VT-COM; (1382) VT-CKR; (1385) VR-RBR; (1389) VR-RBX; (1410) SE-CDL; (1415) D-ELEG; (1427) SU-AHD; (1440) F-OAOD; (1446) F-OAMX; (1505) EC-AJR; (1517) I-AUKA; (1518) ZS-DXA; (1526) HB-EOB; (1547) F-OAHE; (1551) F-BGXQ; (1552) SE-BZR; (1577) TF-LBP; (1594) CX-AOQ; (1607) F-OADJ; (1622) VR-SDE; (1631) VP-CBC; (1643) AP-ACT; (1644) AP-AEC; (1645) VT-CNA; (1665) EC-AJT; (1666) F-OADP; (1667) YI-ABS; (1669) VT-CLQ; (1670) VT-CLP; (1671) VT-CUB; (1672) F-OABS; (1676) F-OADO; (1682) VT-CMB; (1684) VT-CUC; (1690) F-OADK; (1693) VT-DFX; (1694) AP-ACU; (1696) VR-SDN; (1699) VT-CSH; (1709) F-OADD; (1720) VT-COF; (1725) VT-CSI; (1727) VT-DCU; (1733) AP-ADD; (1736) VH-AZV; (1745) VT-DJR; (1746) VT-CRH; (1763) AP-ADE; (1767) AP-ADG; (1771) AP-ADB; (1773) F-OADL; (1788) SE-BZL; (1798) F-OAJN; (1803) VP-GAM; (1808) OO-GAN; (1812) D-ENIS; (1813) VP-FAC; (1821) F-BBTJ; (1916) VR-SDY; (2060) F-BGXG; (2063) F-OAXO; (origin untraced) LV-NXS; PI-C297; SU-AHA; SU-AHB; SU-AHC; VT-CLN; ZS-DWO; ZS-DWP.

(d) Auster 5C

One aircraft only: (c/n 1272) G-ALKI.

(e) Auster 5D

At least 29 aircraft comprising 11 British registered Auster 5Ds listed in Appendix E and the following converted overseas: (c/n 954) I-OPEZ; (1332) AP-ALG; (1338) AP-AKW; (1348) VH-AGQ; (1360) AP-ALA; (1365) AP-ALB; (1367) AP-AKV; (1376) VR-RCC; (1379) AP-AKU; (1390) AP-AKZ; (1766) AP-ALF; (1772) VH-BYM; (1774) AP-AKX; (1785) VR-HFB; (1814) F-OAJP; (2984 spare airframe) F-OAJO; (origin untraced) AP-AKY; AP-ALC.

(f) Auster 5M

Two aircraft only: (c/n 1510) G-ANDU; (1815) G-AOSL.

(g) Alpha 5

Fourteen newly constructed aircraft: (c/n 3401–3414) G-AOFJ; G-APAH, 'BE, 'AF, 'BW, D-ECUR, G-APHU, D-EHYS; G-APNM, 'NN, 'RE, 'RF, 'TU, 'UL.

An early production Autocrat being flown by C. A. Nepean Bishop in the vicinity of Elstree Aerodrome in 1946.

Auster J-1 Autocrat

During the later stages of the war, the Taylorcraft design team was already assessing the probable post-war light aeroplane requirement and by 1945 a decision had been made to market an economical, lower-powered version of the war-proven Auster 5. Choice of engine fell on the 100 h.p. Blackburn Cirrus Minor 2 and in April 1945 an Auster 5 was modified to take the new engine. Registered G-AGOH to Blackburn Aircraft Ltd. at Brough, it became the flight test and installation development vehicle. Concurrently with the engine trials, work was proceeding at Leicester on a prototype to be known as the Taylorcraft Auster 5 Series J-1 Autocrat. This machine was actually the crashed prototype Taylorcraft Plus D, G-AFWN, built in 1939, taken out of storage at Rearsby and rebuilt with the larger Auster 5 fuselage. The resulting aeroplane was thus externally identical with G-AGOH, but without the extended rear window. In spite of this difference, the erstwhile testbed was officially regarded as an Autocrat, and after 30 years was still flying at Leicester East.

Symbolic of the role it was to play as light aviation's maid-of-all-work, the prototype made the first post-war charter flight on 1 January 1946, the day civil flying was again officially permitted, a token consignment of aircraft spares being flown from Cardiff to Filton by Cambrian Airways Ltd. At the Thurmaston works, manufacture was already in full swing, the first production machine, G-AGTO, having been delivered to T. W. Shipside Ltd. at Tollerton in December 1945, but on 7 March 1946 the firm changed its name to Auster Aircraft Ltd., soon afterwards transferring the works to Rearsby Aerodrome and abbreviating the machine's designation to Auster J-1 Autocrat. Production aircraft had mass balanced rudders, thus differing from the prototype, which was fitted with the horn balanced type. It can with truth claim to be the only light aeroplane to be produced in large numbers in Britain after the war, and when series production ceased at the end of 1947, over 400 had been built. Since then a number have been constructed to special order, raising the final total to approximately 420, many of which went overseas.

A modification introduced in November 1949 made possible its conversion to a four seater known as the J-1A, a small number being so fitted for joyriding. Most of these quickly reverted to three-seaters. Other modifications not affecting the designation were the fitting of glider towing gear, the equipping of G-AIBI with skis, the loudspeakers under G-AIBY, the insecticide spray-bars under the wings of G-AIPU and, most famous of all, the Goodyear castoring undercarriage on G-AJIZ. Flown by test pilot Ranald Porteous at air displays, it was well known in its day for the sheer comedy of its grotesque cross-wind landings on one wheel.

Probably the most spectacular Autocrat performance occurred when G-AERO, owned by Temple Press Ltd., made the first visit of a civilian aeroplane to an aircraft carrier, H.M.S. *Illustrious*, in the English Channel in October 1946. The type will chiefly be remembered, however, as the ancestor of famous Auster types which were to follow. The enlarged vertical tail surfaces of the Autocar and Aiglet were test flown on Autocrat G-AGXC in 1949, and in the following year G-AJER was fitted with a Gipsy Major 1 engine to become the J-5A prototype. Many Gipsy Autocrats had the small J-1 rudder and were known simply as J-5s, the majority being for export to Australia where they were known as Adventurers. Four went to the Southern Rhodesian Air Force as communications machines and six (NZ1701–NZ1706) with large rudders were shipped to the R.N.Z.A.F. for forestry fire patrol duties. Following floatplane trials with Auster's own J-5A, G-AJYL, at Beaumaris in February 1951, NZ1701 was similarly equipped and was first flown as a seaplane by Air Vice-Marshal D. V. Carnegie in September 1952. In 1957 NZ1705 went to Sydney, becoming successively VH-PMG and VH-ADS, and in 1968 was also fitted with floats for operation from Lake McQuarie.

Only G-AMPJ saw lengthy service in the United Kingdom, since the balance of the 12 registered there carried their British marks for ferrying overseas. After

Auster J-1N G-ARGT 'Pegasus' at Gatwick on 18 December 1969 just before take-off in the London–Sydney Air Race piloted by M. Clarke and Flg. Off. Willis.
(*J. M. G. Gradidge*)

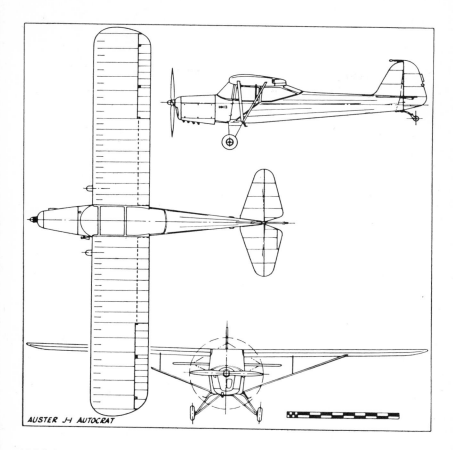

AUSTER J-1 AUTOCRAT

1956 the 1,500-hour overhaul life of the Gipsy Major and the lively performance it imparted, led to its installation in a number of Autocrats which were then known as the J-1N Alpha. These had the enlarged fin and rudder to compensate for the increased nose length and therefore differed from the J-5 which had the engine set far enough back to make standard tail surfaces adequate. A case is also on record of an Auster 5 being converted to J-1N standard as G-AKJU for J. D. H. Radford at Tollerton. As a final development, new Alphas were made available ex works and the Autocrat embarked on a new lease of life.

The last Rearsby-built J-1s, G-AMTM and 'VN, appeared in 1952, the first destined for a long career as a trainer with Brooklands Aviation Ltd., Sywell, and the second for use in Kenya as VP-KKG. It returned to Stapleford ten years later on 6 July 1962 powered by a 145 h.p. Gipsy Major 10 Mk. 2-2 taken from a Kenyan Chipmunk and with this engine was unique as the sole Auster J-1S. In August 1953 it reverted to G-AMVN and was based on a farm strip at Fyfield, Essex, by owner H. R. Montefiore who was killed there when it was in air collision with Forney F-1A G-AROP on 24 April 1969.

Other operators also obtained improved performance by fitting modern

G-AGVI, flying testbed for the Rover TP.90 gas turbine engine, photographed at Fairoaks in 1965. (*A. J. Jackson*)

engines, notably the Elstree Flying Club in 1960 with their 145 h.p. Gipsy Major 1C powered, 1,000 ft./min. climb, G-AGXT; the Royal Victorian Aero Club who converted VH-BOJ to two-seat trainer at Melbourne with 120 h.p. Lycoming; and Kingsford Smith Aviation's 'Kingsmith' conversion of VH-AYJ, ex G-AJPX, at Sydney in 1959 to take the 150 h.p. Lycoming. This engine, as well as J-1N tail surfaces, was fitted to VP-YJG in Southern Rhodesia, and a 135 h.p. Lycoming powered HB-EOP at Ascona, Switzerland. Brazilian registered J-1s PP-DEW and 'EX were fitted with Continental and Franklin engines respectively.

The most impressive J-1 was unquestionably the paraffin-burning G-AGVI which the author flew in 1965 after it had been converted by Mr. V. H. Bellamy at Blackbushe as flying testbed for the 118 h.p. Rover TP.90 gas turbine engine.

In response to a demand for agricultural machines, Auster Aircraft Ltd. produced 44 factory-built J-1Ns, initially to the order of Crop Culture (Aerial)

Auster J-5 (c/n 2806), originally VH-KSG (later VH DDX) crashed at Talwood, Queensland on 29 August 1959 and was rebuilt for crop spraying as VH-SCO 'Prairie Flower' with all-metal fuselage and 200 h.p. Lycoming O-435. (*C. H. O'Neill*)

Ltd. of Bembridge who fitted Britten-Norman rotary atomisers on under-wing pylons before the aircraft went to West Africa on crop spraying contracts. Last of these, G-ARUY, which appeared in February 1962, went to Shoreham for the Beagle Group Flying Club and later to a fashion house at Roborough.

Three 1945–46 export models, brought back from Germany, Rhodesia and Kenya in 1959, became G-APUK, G-ARGT and 'RL respectively, the last being modified to J-1N at Portsmouth in February 1962, but the final British registered Auster J-1 derivative was the J-1N I-AGRI, supplied to Air Agricola in 1957 for crop spraying in Italy, which returned to Lympne on 25 November 1961 en route to Squires Gate for school work as G-ASEE.

SPECIFICATION

Manufacturers: Auster Aircraft Ltd., Rearsby Aerodrome, Leicester.

Power Plants: (Autocrat) One 100 h.p. Blackburn Cirrus Minor 2.
One 118 h.p. Rover TP.90.
One 120 h.p. Lycoming O-235-C1.
One 120 h.p. Franklin 6AC.
One 135 h.p. Lycoming O-290-D2.
One 145 h.p. de Havilland Gipsy Major 1C.
One 145 h.p. Continental C-145.
One 150 h.p. Lycoming O-320-A1A or A2A.
(J-1N)   One 120 h.p. de Havilland Gipsy Major 1.
(J-1S)   One 145 h.p. de Havilland Gipsy Major 10 Mk. 2-2.

Dimensions: Span, 36 ft. 0 in. Height, 6 ft. 6 in. Length (Autocrat), 23 ft. 5 in. (J-1N), 23 ft. 8¼ in. Wing area, 185 sq. ft.

Weights: (Autocrat) Tare weight, 1,052 lb. All-up weight, 1,850 lb.
(J-1N)   Tare weight, 1,219 lb. All-up weight, 2,000 lb.

Performance: (Autocrat) Maximum speed, 120 m.p.h. Cruising speed, 100 m.p.h. Initial climb, 568 ft./min. Ceiling, 14,000 ft. Range, 320 miles.
(J-1N)   Maximum speed, 126 m.p.h. Cruising speed, 105 m.p.h. Initial climb, 710 ft./min. Ceiling, 15,000 ft. Range, 200 miles.

Production: (a) Auster J-1 Autocrat

Prototypes G-AFWN and G-AGOH (c/n 124 and 1442), 297 British registered production aircraft and the following built for export: (c/n 1842) HB-EOS; (1845) PH-NAA; (1846) OY-DGA; (1847) SE-ARB; (1848) SE-ARC; (1851) LV-NBV; (1852) LV-NBY; (1853) LV-NBU; (1854) LV-NBW; (1855) LV-NCD; (1856) LV-NBZ; (1864) SE-ARU; (1867) SE-ARD; (1868) SE-ARE; (1869) SE-ARF; (1882) SE-ARG; (1883) SE-ARH; (1884) OO-ATY; (1890) OY-DGE; (1891) LN-DAO; (1952) SE-ARI; (1953) SE-ARK; (1954) SE-ARL; (1958) LN-DAP; (1959) SE-ARV; (1974) HB-EOP; (1975) OO-AMI; (1978) VP-UAA; (1981) HB-EOF; (1996) OO-AVE; (1997) VP-TAS; (1998) PP-RXO; (1999) VP-UAB; (2000) VP-TAR; (2001) VP-UAC; (2025) OY-DGY; (2026) OO-ABB; (2027) LN-DAR; (2030) OO-ABF; (2031) OY-DGU; (2032) OY-DNA; (2033) OO-ABG; (2034) OO-ABH; (2035) SE-ARS; (2036) SU-ADW; (2037) VP-UAD; (2038) VP-UAE; (2039) VP-UAF; (2040) PP-DAF; (2041) OO-ABK; (2042) OO-ABL; (2043) VP-UAG; (2044) SE-ARM; (2045) SE-ARN; (2046) OO-ABM; (2047) OO-ABN; (2048) VP-UAH; (2049) VP-UAI; (2100) OO-ABO; (2101) SE-ARO; (2102) OY-DNU; (2103) OY-DNE; (2106) Uruguay later LV-FSM; (2108) OY-DPU; (2109) OO-ABQ; (2110) OY-DNO; (2111) OY-DNY; (2114) VP-UAJ; (2116) LN-HAP; (2117) LN-HAR; (2118) OY-DPA; (2119) OY-DPE; (2121) OY-DPY; (2124) VP-CAO; (2125) ZK-AKZ; (2126)

VP-UAN; (2127) VP-UAM; (2128) VP-CAP; (2129) OY-DPI; (2130) LN-HAS; (2131)
LN-NAF; (2132) ZK-ALW; (2142) OY-DRA; (2143) VP-YFL; (2144) VP-YFM; (2152)
VP-YFN; (2162) LN-NAG; (2166) ZK-AOB; (2169) LN-NAH; (2170) SE-ARP; (2171)
OO-CCX; (2178) LN-NAL; (2179) LN-NAM; (2181) HB-EOT; (2196) VP-YGA; (2197)
ZS-BKX; (2198) ZS-BKW; (2201) ZS-BKY; (2210) ZS-BML; (2211) ZS-BMM; (2212)
ZK-APO; (2213) VP-YHG; (2220) PP-DEW; (2221) PP-DEX; (2222) PP-DEY; (2223)
PP-DEZ; (2224) LV-NTQ; (2225) LV-NUJ; (2227) VP-YGR; (2245) ZK-AQL; (2246)
VP-UAQ; (2326) ZK-AQE; (2344) VP-UAR; (2610) YI-ABT; (2641) VP-TAY; (2647)
YI-ABU; (2649) ZK-ATH; (2652) TJ-AAS; (2653) TJ-AAR; (2656) AP-ADY; (2658)
AP-ADX; (2715) F-OAKP; (2749) F-BFYT.

> (b) Auster J-1N Alpha
Forty-four Rearsby-built aircraft, c/n 3351–3394, comprising 21 British registered
aircraft and the following for export: (c/n 3351) VH-RQK; (3353) VH-KCM; (3354)
VH-KCI; (3355) VH-SAF; (3356) VH-KCJ; (3357) F-BFUT; (3358) VH-SAG; (3360)
I-AGRA; (3361) VH-KAW; (3362) VH-KCR; (3363) VH-BTJ; (3364) VH-BTK; (3365)
VH-KCP; (3366) VH-KCT; (3367) VH-KCV; (3368) VH-KCU; (3369) VH-UEB; (3371)
VH-KCH; (3373) VH-KCW; (3374) VH-KCX; (3376) VH-KCZ; (3378) VH-KDC;
(3379) VH-KDA.

The McQuarie Air Service Auster J-5A seaplane 'Andy Capp' (formerly NZ1705) moored
on Lake McQuarie, near Newcastle, N.S.W., in 1968 (*N. M. Parnell*)

> (c) Auster J-5
Twelve British registered aircraft and the following for export: (c/n 2094) NZ1701;
(2095) NZ1702; (2096) NZ1703; (2097) VH-KSC; (2098) VH-KSD; (2099) VH-KSF;
(2801) NZ1704; (2802) NZ1705; (2803) NZ1706; (2804) VH-KSE; (2805) VH-KSH;
(2806) VH-KSG; (2807) VH-KSI; (2808) VH-KSJ; (2809) VH-KSK; (2810) VH-KSL;
(2811) VH-KSN; (2812) VH-KSM; (2813) VH-KSP; (2814) VH-KSQ; (2871) AP-AJU;
(2872) VH-KSR; (2873) VH-KSS; (2875) VH-KST; (2877) VH-KSU; (2878) SR-54;
(2879) SR-53; (2880) SR-55; (2881) SR-56; (2882) VH-KSA; (2883) VH-CAM; (2884)
VH-KSV; (2885) VT-DCF; (2886) VH-KSW; (2887) VH-KSX; (2888) VH-KSY; (2890)
VH-KSZ; (2891) VH-KAR; (2892) VH-KAD; (2893) VH-KAP; (2894) VH-KAV;
(2895) VH-KBA; (2896) VH-KBD; (2897) VH-KBH; (2898) VH-KBL; (2899)
VH-KBM; (2900) PT-ADJ.

Auster J-1B Aiglet VH-KAZ after completion at Sydney, Australia, by Kingsford Smith Aviation Ltd. in 1951.

Auster J-1B Aiglet

The prototype Aiglet of 1950 was a straight conversion of G-AJUW, a stored Autocrat airframe, to take the Gipsy Major 1 engine and the larger horn balanced rudder. Apart from a minor difference in the fuel system, it was thus an identical aeroplane to the later Autocrat conversion known as the J-1N Alpha. The Aiglet was conceived as an agricultural aircraft, and as a crop sprayer was fitted with a wind driven pump for forcing insecticide through a spray bar strutted 4 ft. below the leading edge of the wing. This equipment was, however, quickly removable to permit the use of the machine for more normal purposes. Although the twelfth production Aiglet, G-AJYW, was demonstrated at the 1950 S.B.A.C. Show at Farnborough by Ranald Porteous, chief test pilot of Auster Aircraft Ltd., and excited a great deal of interest, the vast majority of the 86 J-1B Aiglets built were exported engineless to the Antipodes, where they were completed and distributed by Kingsford Smith Aviation Service Pty. Ltd. Seven of the 14 registered in the United Kingdom were employed in the Sudan by Aerial Spraying Contractors Ltd. of Boston, Lincs. In the autumn of 1950 the first three, G-AJUW, 'YR and 'YT, made the 3,200-mile ferrying flight to the banks of the Nile, 100 miles south of Khartoum, in an airborne time of 34 hours, and by the end of a month they had rid some 17,000 acres of insects and, with British pilots and under British ownership, dealt decisively with the insect hordes until the work was taken over by Autocars in 1954. Under extremely arduous conditions, operating in tropical heat from primitive airstrips, only one Aiglet, G-AMJE, was lost in an accident, and one other, G-ALAB, fell out of a formation of three returning home and was lost in the Mediterranean with its pilot and one passenger. When the firm closed down, the Aiglets were transferred to Skegness Air Taxis Ltd., which, despite its name, was also engaged in agricultural aviation.

In 1958 the prototype, G-AJUW, was modified to J-1N standard and in March 1963 went to Ireland for the Meath Flying Group at Kells, and five more of the original British registered batch also went overseas, including G-AMIH 'Lady Lady' in which T. W. Hayhow came second at 135·5 m.p.h. in the *Daily Express* Race at Shoreham on 22 September 1951.

69

Some years later, export models VP-KKS and VP-KKR, delivered to Kenya in 1952, were repurchased for British registry but the first, re-registered G-APMU for a private owner at Fairoaks, was lost in the Mediterranean during its flight back to England. The second returned successfully to Elstree with the intermediate Somali registration VP-SZZ and became G-ARBM in July 1960 for a period in private ownership before being sold for aerial photography work in Ireland.

SPECIFICATION

Manufacturers: Auster Aircraft Ltd., Rearsby Aerodrome, Leicester.
Power Plant: One 130 h.p. de Havilland Gipsy Major 1.
Dimensions: Span, 36 ft. 0 in. Length, 23 ft. $8\frac{1}{4}$ in. Height, 6 ft. 6 in.
Wing area, 185 sq. ft.
Weights: Tare weight, 1,223 lb. All-up weight, 2,000 lb.
Performance: Maximum speed, 126 m.p.h. Cruising speed, 105 m.p.h. Initial climb, 900 ft./min. Ceiling, 18,000 ft. Range, 220 miles.

Production:
Fourteen British registered aircraft and 72 built for export: (c/n 2640) ZK-ATO; (2643) VH-KAC; (2644) VH-KAB; (2648) VT-DEN; (2650) ZK-ATP; (2651) VH-KAI; (2654) VH-KAH; (2661) VH-KAJ; (2662) VH-KAK; (2664) VH-KAO; (2665) VH-KAQ; (2667) ZK-AWS; (2668) ZK-AWY; (2669) ZK-AWZ; (2670) VH-KAU; (2671) VH-KAW; (2672) VH-KAZ; (2673) ZK-AXE; (2674) ZK-AXF; (2675) VT-DFQ; (2676) ZK-AXM; (2677) ZK-AXL; (2678) VH-KBJ; (2679) CS-ADY; (2680) VH-AAE; (2681) VH-KBC; (2682) VH-KBE; (2683) VH-KBG; (2684) VH-KBI; (2685) VH-KBK; (2686) VH-KBO; (2687) VH-KBN; (2688) VH-KBS; (2689) VH-KBQ; (2690) VH-KBV; (2691) AP-AFC; (2692) VR-RBP; (2693) VH-ABE; (2694) VH-KBU; (2695) VH-KBX; (2696) VH-ABD; (2697) VH-KBY; (2698) VH-ABI; (2699) VH-ABS; (2700) F-OAKC; (2701) VH-ADQ; (2702) VH-ABQ; (2703) VH-ABP; (2704) VR-WAB; (2705) VH-ACY; (2710) ZK-AYO; (2711) ZK-AYP; (2730) ZK-AYU; (2746) VH-BYB; (2747) VH-ASQ; (2748) ZK-AZE; (2750) ZK-AZD; (2751) ZK-AZT; (2752) ZK-AZU; (2753) F-OAKZ; (2754) VT-DGH; (2755) OO-CER; (2794) VP-KKT; (3103) ZK-BBY; (3105) ZK-BCJ; (3112) ZK-BCS; (3116) ZK-BDL; (3117) ZK-BDM; (3118) ZK-BDT; (3119) ZK-BDQ; (3121) OH-AUI; (3129) F-OASA.

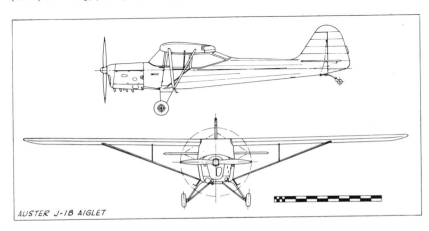

AUSTER J-1B AIGLET

Auster Arrow G-AJXZ of the Kent Coast Flying Club flying over Hythe in 1950 piloted by A. S. Mackenzie-Lowe. (*Skyfotos*)

Auster J-2 Arrow and Auster J-4

In 1945 Taylorcraft Aeroplanes (England) Ltd., later known as Auster Aircraft Ltd., built G-AGPS, an unnamed post-war successor to their prewar series of Taylorcraft Plus C monoplanes. This unique aeroplane, devoid of maker's designation, was a side-by-side two-seater fitted with a 65 h.p. Lycoming O-145-B3 flat-four air-cooled engine and primarily used as a works 'hack'. It may be regarded as the prototype of the Auster J-2 Arrow, which made its first flight at Rearsby in the summer of 1946 under B conditions as Z-1. This machine was powered by a 75 h.p. Continental C-75-12 flat-four and was exhibited as G-AICA at the Radlett S.B.A.C. Show in the following September. At this difficult period in our financial history, import restrictions on American engines intended for installation in British-owned aircraft resulted in the sale of only six Arrows on the home market, although seven others received British markings under manufacturer's ownership. G-AIGN was owned by R. Burton at Tollerton in 1947, G-AIJU by Kenning Aviation Ltd. and later by Wolverhampton Flying School Ltd., G-AJPS by Somerton Airways Ltd. at Cowes, and G-AJXZ was based at Pebsham Aerodrome, Hastings, owned first by A. S. Mackenzie-Lowe and later by R. Allerton-Austin. All but two subsequently followed the balance of the 44 production machines overseas. The surviving pair, G-AJAM, well known in flying-club circles in the London area for over a decade, and G-AJPU, kept at Perth for many years by the Scottish private owner J. M. Rollo, gave long and faithful service. In 1956 'PU went to Southend, where it was flown for a season by C. W. Morley until returned to the makers in May 1957 in part exchange for the Alpha 5 G-APAH.

Most of the export Arrows went to Australia where several were the subject of interesting conversions by Kingsford Smith Aviation Pty. Ltd., Bankstown, Sydney; the Royal Queensland Aero Club, Archerfield, Brisbane; and private owners. The former Somerton Airways machine, G-AJPS, exported in July 1951 as VH-ABF, was re-engined in 1955 with a Cirrus Minor 2 in-line engine and, as VH-BYL, then provided the sole instance of the conversion of an Arrow to Auster J-4 standard, although boasting 10 more horse-power than a standard J-4 with Cirrus Minor 1. Another changeling was the one-time Wolverhampton-based G-AIJU, which, as VH-BNQ, crashed on take-off from a field 50 miles south-west

71

of Bundaberg, Queensland, on 26 March 1951, and after years in storage emerged with a tricycle undercarriage in 1957. This modification was not approved and the machine reverted to standard and was converted to Auster J-4 with Cirrus Minor 1 engine in 1960 as VH-KFF. At Archerfield, where three J-2s were re-equipped with 108 h.p. Lycoming engines by the R.Q.A.C., C. G. Henderson added 23 m.p.h. to the top speed of VH-ACD, formerly G-AJPT, by fitting a 125 h.p. Continental C-125-2 flat-four engine.

An attempt in 1946 to re-create the equivalent of the lower-powered and economical G-AGPS by fitting a 65 h.p. Continental C-65-12 engine to an Arrow airframe, and christening it the J-3A Atom, came to naught. Only one prototype, G-AHSY, was built, and although a production version, the J-3 G-AJIJ, was registered, its construction was almost certainly not completed.

In order to defeat import restrictions on American-built engines, Auster Aircraft Ltd. fitted a British engine, the 90 h.p. Blackburn Cirrus Minor 1, into an Arrow airframe to create the prototype J-4, G-AIGZ. This two-seat, flapless and nameless aircraft made its first flight towards the end of 1946, but failed to achieve the popularity of its more sociable three-seat relative, the Autocrat. Although all 27 production machines were registered in the United Kingdom, by 1951 the majority had followed their Continental powered brethren overseas. They included the prototype which had been owned by H. F. Fulford at Doncaster, the Yorkshire Aeroplane Club's G-AIJL, R. E. Harrington's Elstree-based G-AIPG, T. W. Shipside's G-AIPI, the Southend Flying School's G-AIPJ, the Warwickshire Aero Club's G-AIPK and Inter-City Air Service's Hereford-based G-AIPL. Three were also registered to the manufacturers purely for ferrying abroad. Seven found their way to Australia, where they were allotted the type name Archer. One of these was the seventh production machine, VH-AET, originally operated by the Auster-sponsored Rearsby Flying School as G-AIJP, in the years 1947–1949, became the property of the Kingsford Smith Aviation Service Pty. Ltd., and on 30 August 1955 successfully demonstrated its inherent stability by taking-off from Bankstown unpiloted and flying out over the sea until stalked and shot down by Hawker Sea Furies of the Royal Australian Navy. Its sacrifice was, however, in vain because the feat had already been performed by another Rearsby School Auster J-4, G-AJYX. Watched by the pilot who had attempted to start it unaided, it took off from Rearsby on 22 April 1951, and after circling for two hours and, it is said, reaching a height of 8,000 ft., ran out of fuel and was destroyed in the subsequent crash.

The unnamed Auster prototype G-AGPS differed from production J-2 Arrows by virtue of its low powered Lycoming and horn balanced rudder. (*E. J. Riding*)

G-APJM, the last Auster J-4, flying near Elstree in 1960. (*Richard Riding*)

Auster J-2 VH-PUL, c/n 2384 ex VH-KAY, after the installation of a 108 h.p. Lycoming in Piper Colt-type cowlings. (*L. McIver*)

The last Auster J-4, G-APJM, constructed at Rearsby from major components of Auster J-2 G-AJPU, first flew early in 1958, seven years after series production ceased. In 1969 the five Auster J-4s still airworthy in the United Kingdom included G-AIJT and 'PH operated by the Merlin Flying Club at Hucknall, Notts., where 'PH first flew on 6 January 1966 as a J-4/100 with 100 h.p. Rolls-Royce Continental O-200-A for test flying and communications under Rolls-Royce Class B marking G-37-5. The club's second J-4/100 conversion, G-AIJT, first flew on 10 March 1970.

SPECIFICATION

Manufacturers: Auster Aircraft Ltd., Rearsby Aerodrome, Leicester.

Power Plants: (J-2) One 75 h.p. Continental C-75-12.
One 108 h.p. Lycoming O-235-C1.
One 125 h.p. Continental C-125-2.
(J-3) One 65 h.p. Continental C-65-12.
(J-4) One 90 h.p. Blackburn Cirrus Minor 1.
One 100 h.p. Rolls-Royce Continental O-200-A.

Dimensions: Span, 36 ft. 0 in. Length (J-2), 22 ft. 9 in. (J-4), 23 ft. 5¾ in. Height, 6 ft. 6 in. Wing area, 185 sq. ft.

Weights: (J-2) Tare weight, 872 lb. All-up weight, 1,450 lb.
(J-4) Tare weight, 955 lb. All-up weight, 1,600 lb.

Performance: (J-2) Maximum speed, 98 m.p.h. Cruising speed, 87 m.p.h. Initial climb, 430 ft./min. Range, 320 miles.

(J-4) Maximum speed, 108 m.p.h. Cruising speed, 92 m.p.h. Initial climb, 746 ft./min. Range, 320 miles.

Production (a) Auster J-2 Arrow

Fifteen British registered aircraft and the following built for export: (c/n 2353) VP-YFX; (2354) OO-ABP; (2355) OY-ABY; (2356) LN-NAN; (2357) Uruguay; (2358) SE-ARR; (2359) CS-ACJ; (2360) OO-ABR; (2363) VP-UAP; (2364) EI-ACU; (2366) OO-ABS; (2367) LV-NUH; (2368) LV-NUI; (2369) OO-AXH; (2370) VP-UAO; (2373) ZS-BNO; (2374) OO-ABT; (2375) OO-ABU; (2376) VP-YGO; (2377) OO-ABV; (2379) VH-KAM; (2380) OO-ABX; (2381) PT-AED; (2382) OO-AXA; (2383) OO-AXB; (2384) VH-KAY; (2385) PT-AEE; (2387) OO-AXC; (2388) VH-KAF; (2391) EI-ADN.

(b) Auster J-3 Atom

One prototype only: (c/n 2250) G-AHSY. Production machine (2401) G-AJIJ not completed.

(c) Auster J-4

Twenty-seven British registered aircraft listed in Appendix E.

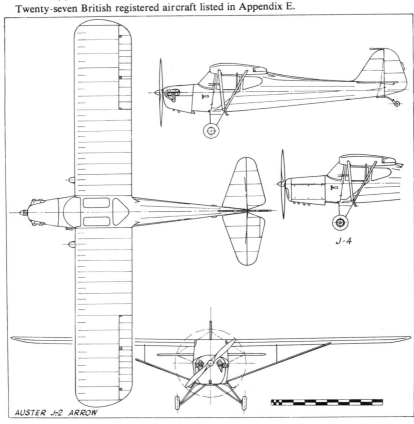

J-4

AUSTER J-2 ARROW

The Rochford Hundred Flying Group's J-5B Autocar G-AMFP, in 1972 the oldest inhabitant at Southend where it has spent 18 of its first 20 years. (*Tony Leigh*)

Auster J-5B Autocar

Following the success of the three-seat Autocrat, a four-seater of similar construction, known as the Auster model P Avis, appeared under B conditions as Z-2 at the Radlett S.B.A.C. Show in September 1947. Chief points of interest were its four doors, slimmer and rounder rear fuselage, underslung wing flaps and Gipsy Major 10-3 engine. Although with modified rear cabin it was granted a certificate of airworthiness in the following year as G-AJXW, it was not a success and was dismantled at Rearsby. The solitary Mk. 2 Avis, G-AJYF, an ambulance version carrying an Army field stretcher and nurse, was built from major components of its predecessor but was written off in a forced landing near Rearsby when the airscrew flew off.

Meanwhile, G-AJYK, prototype of another four-seater known as the J-5B Autocar, had been constructed on more traditional Auster lines and had first flown in August 1949 in time to qualify for inclusion in that year's Farnborough S.B.A.C. Show. It featured the 130 h.p. Gipsy Major 1 engine, the enlarged horn balanced rudder, a domed cabin roof and fuel tanks in the wing roots. The majority of the 80 production J-5Bs were exported to 16 countries and resold in five others as tourers and taxis. VH-WBA, originally delivered in 1953 to an oil company in Singapore as VR-SDO, won the 1,250 mile Brisbane–Adelaide race in March 1964 piloted by owner K. Bassett. Of the 15 sold in Britain, G-AMFO and 'MZ went to Hunting Aerosurveys Ltd. for aerial photography, G-AMNC to the Bristol Aeroplane Co. Ltd. as a communications aircraft, G-AMNB to the Royal Artillery Flying Club and five to private owners. One executive Autocar, G-AJYY, based at Bognor Regis by L.E.C. Refrigerators Ltd., was flown into third place in the Goodyear Trophy Race at Wolverhampton on 17 May 1952 by G. A. Farley at 121·5 m.p.h. Best known of all Autocars were of course G-AMFP and G-AMPW, with which the Southend Flying School and Bees Flight Ltd. gave pleasure flights to thousands of holiday makers at Southend and Sandown respectively. The final pair of British registered J-5Bs, G-ANNX and 'NY, were ferried to the Kuwait Aero Club in March 1954.

Although a lively enough mount in temperate zones, more power, provided by

The Auster model P Avis G-AJXW in its final form.

the 155 h.p. Blackburn Cirrus Major 3 engine, was needed for crop-dusting and tropical bush flying. On 12 September 1950 a special category C. of A. was issued to an experimental J-5E Autocar, G-AJYS, fitted with this engine as a mount for test pilot Ranald Porteous in the *Daily Express* Race four days later. Although it retired from the race, it was the forerunner of the prototype J-5G Cirrus Autocar, G-AMKG, which was successfully flown in July 1951. A year later Pest Control Ltd. of Bourn, Cambridge, took delivery of five, registered G-AMOY to 'PC, which were painted in their distinctive yellow colour-scheme and fitted with 70-gallon insecticide tanks in the cabin for crop-spraying in the Sudan. Altogether some 90 Cirrus Autocars were built, mainly for the overseas market, but G-AMZV was delivered to Saunders-Roe Ltd. at Bembridge, I.O.W. This was fitted with a remarkable experimental hydro-ski undercarriage with which the aircraft could remain almost stationary on the water. Another, G-ANVN, was sent to the Colonial Insecticides Research Unit at Porton Down, Wilts., before going to Malaya with spray-bar attachments and R.A.F. colours as XJ941. In

One of the fleet of all-yellow Auster J-5G Cirrus Autocars operated in the Sudan by Pest Control Ltd. (*A. J. Jackson*)

Auster J-5G Cirrus Autocar G-AMZV alighting on the Solent in 1958 when equipped with Saunders-Roe experimental hydro-ski undercarriage. (*Saunders-Roe Ltd.*)

1957 it returned to civilian guise, this time going to Colonial Pesticides Research Ltd. in Tanganyika as VR-TBR. Two were used privately: G-AMYR, kept on an airstrip by the Ouse at Renhold, Beds., by N. A. Rogers, and G-AOIY, fitted for glider towing, based at Turnhouse by Parkers Stores Ltd. of Edinburgh.

Designation J-5H applied to J-5B VH-KCO after Kingsford Smith Aviation replaced the Gipsy Major by a 145 h.p. Cirrus Major 2, and J-5GL to ZK-CXA, a rebuild of ZK-BDJ with Lycoming engine. A variant with the Gipsy Major 10 Mk. 1 was developed for the Kuwait Aero Club, which was already operating the Gipsy engined J-5B. The first of these, G-ANXZ, known as the J-5P Autocar, was built in 1955, and about 20 others were constructed later. The Bristol Aircraft Ltd. communications J-5B G-AMNC was re-engined to J-5P standard in July 1956, and one more, G-ANYE, was delivered to Kuwait. Several others were registered in Britain, including G-AOBV and G-APKI for executive use by Ferranti and Dunlop respectively, G-AOGM equipped for aerial survey work by Hunting, and G-AOCY and 'HF as communications machines for Bristol Aero Engines Ltd. and Gloster Aircraft Ltd.

Seven Autocars exported in the 1950s were later repatriated, including three unsold airframes from a batch sent to Australia in 1956. These were completed at Rearsby 1961–63 as the J-5P G-ARLY and J-5Gs G-ARUG and G-ASFK respectively for the Portsmouth Aero Club and Anglian Air Charter. G-ARUG was flown initially as G-25-9 to test a new glass plastics wing covering.

SPECIFICATION

Manufacturers: Auster Aircraft Ltd., Rearsby Aerodrome, Leicester.
Power Plants: (J-5B) One 130 h.p. de Havilland Gipsy Major 1.
            (J-5G) One 155 h.p. Blackburn Cirrus Major 3.
            (J-5H) One 145 h.p. Blackburn Cirrus Major 2.
            (J-5P) One 145 h.p. de Havilland Gipsy Major 10 Mk. 1 or 2.
Dimensions: Span, 36 ft. 0 in. Length, (J-5B) 23 ft. 4 in. (Others) 23 ft. 2 in. Height, 6 ft. 6 in. Wing area, 185 sq. ft.

Weights: (J-5B) Tare weight, 1,334 lb. All-up weight, 2,400 lb.

(J-5G) Tare weight, 1,367 lb. All-up weight, 2,450 lb.

Performance: (J-5B) Maximum speed, 117 m.p.h. Cruising speed, 106 m.p.h. Initial climb, 525 ft./min. Range, 260 miles.

(J-5G) Maximum speed, 127 m.p.h. Cruising speed, 110 m.p.h. Initial climb, 710 ft./min. Range, 485 miles.

Production: (a) Auster J-5B Autocar

Fifteen British registered aircraft and the following for export: (c/n 2911) VT-DEL; (2912) HB-EOU; (2914) VH-KAL; (2915) ZK-AVN; (2916) VP-YIJ; (2918) VH-KAS; (2919) VH-KAN; (2920) VH-KAT; (2921) CR-SAF; (2922) VH-KAX; (2924) PT-ADL; (2925) PT-ADK; (2926) F-BFLR; (2929) YI-ACA; (2930) YI-ACB; (2931) VT-DFP; (2932) PH-NEH; (2934) F-OAJH; (2935) CC-PAZ; (2936) VH-ASD; (2937) VH-KBF; (2938) VH-KBP; (2939) VH-KBT; (2940) VH-KBW; (2942) VH-KBB; (2943) ZK-AYN; (2944) ZK-AYQ; (2946) VH-ACL; (2947) VH-ADS later J-5H VH-KCO; (2949) VP-TBD; (2951) VH-ADU; (2952) VT-DGF; (2956) VH-BYC; (2959) F-OALO; (2960) YI-ACE; (2962) F-BGPN; (2963) F-DAAP; (2964) F-OALF; (2965) PT-ANH; (2966) PT-ANI; (2967) EC-AHC; (2968) PT-ANJ; (2969) PT-ANK; (2970) PT-ANL; (2971) VR-SDO; (2972) YI-ACG; (2978) YI-ACH; (2979) YI-ACI; (3056) F-OAOX; (3057) F-OAKA; (3058) F-OAOC; (3063) VT-DGY; (3097) VH-BPB; (3154) VH-BPC; (3162) VH-BYS; (3164) VH-STB; (3166) VH-RNB; (3167) VH-RNA; (3170) VH-DNN; (3186) VH-BYQ; (3190) VH-BPD; (3260) AP-AJM; (3261) VH-KCL; (3264) VH-KCN; (3266) VH-KDB; (3268) VH-BGU; (3269) VH-SNA.

(b) Auster J-5E

One aircraft only for experimental use: (c/n 2917) G-AJYS.

The ex-Pakistani J-5G Cirrus Autocar G-ARUT at Biggin Hill May 1963 with glass plastics skin material, Beagle Terrier spats and strut fairings. (*A. J. Jackson*)

(c) Auster J-5G Autocar

Twenty-one British registered aircraft and the following for export: (c/n 2945) VH-KBZ; (2955) VH-BYD; (2957) VH-BYI; (2958) VH-BYH; (2973) VP-KJN; (2975) JA-3022; (2976) JA-3027; (2977) JA-3023; (2980) VP-GAL; (2981) VH-ADY; (3051) OO-CVH; (3053) JA-3028; (3054) JA-3029; (3055) VP-KKP; (3059) R. Australian

Navy A11-300; (3060) SN-AAF; (3062) VP-KKO; (3064) A11-301; (3066) VP-RCT; (3067) VP-RCU; (3069) ZK-BDJ; (3070) ZK-BDK; (3071) F-DABM; (3072) F-DABN; (3073) F-OAPK; (3074) F-OAPL; (3077) ZS-DJG; (3078) ZS-DJH; (3079) VH-BTH; (3080) LV-FGJ; (3081) LV-FFY; (3082) LN-BDA; (3083) SE-BYT; (3084) LV-FGB; (3085) LV-FGC; (3086) LV-FFZ; (3087) LV-FGH; (3088) LV-FGL; (3089) LV-FGM; (3090) LV-FGN; (3092) LV-FGO; (3093) F-OARL; (3094) VH-CAM; (3098) VH-BSX; (3099) VH-BTA; (3156) VR-NBC; (3160) VH-API; (3163) VH-BYV; (3168) VH-BSZ; (3172) VH-BTB; (3173) VH-RAD; (3174) LV-FGZ; (3175) LV-FHH; (3176) LV-FHB; (3177) LV-FHI; (3179) LV-FHC; (3180) LV-FHM; (3181) LV-FHN; (3182) LV-FHO; (3183) LV-FHP; (3184) LV-FHR; (3185) LV-FHS; (3188) VH-KCG; (3189) VH-KCD; (3194) VR-NBD; (3195) VR-NBE; (3196) VH-KCF; (3253) CS-ADV; (3254) VH-RDL; (3262) ZK-BDN; (3263) VH-WED; (3267) VH-KCY; (3270) VT-DJM.

(d) Auster J-5P Autocar

Twelve British registered aircraft and the following for export: (c/n 3155) VH-BYU; (3192) VH-RES; (3198) VH-KCB; (3200) VH-BTE; (3251) VH-KCC; (3255) OE-DBC; (3256) YI-ADB; (3257) VH-BTG; (3259) VH-BPE; (3265) VT-DIW; (3275) D-EJUX.

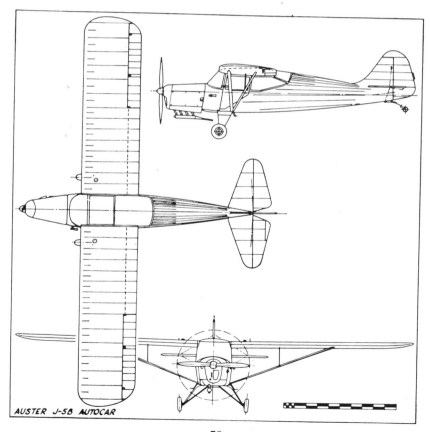

AUSTER J-5B AUTOCAR

G-AMMS flying as a standard Aiglet Trainer. In July 1953 it was modified to J-5L and a year later to J-5K.

Auster J-5F Aiglet Trainer

In spite of its name, the J-5F Aiglet Trainer owed nothing to the Aiglet. Its fuselage was basically that of the J-5, slightly widened and stressed up to permit the Aiglet Trainer to become Auster's first fully aerobatic aeroplane. The rate of roll was improved by fitting an entirely new mainplane 4 ft. 0 in. shorter in span, and the machine would carry four on non-aerobatic flights. Some 70 were built, the majority going to overseas buyers, only 28 flying under British registry, many of these merely for export ferrying. Following the demonstration of the prototype G-25-1 at the Auster Rally at Rearsby on 2 June 1951 and its appearance at the S.B.A.C. Show as G-AMKF, the Airways Aero Association Ltd. of Croydon acquired five, G-AMTA to 'TE; Air Service Training Ltd. of Hamble two, G-AMUI and 'UJ; and the College of Aeronautics of Cranfield three, G-AMYD, 'ZT and 'ZU. Best remembered of the Aiglet Trainers will always be Tom Hayhow's G-AMOS 'Liege Lady', in which he set up no less than 28 point-to-point records for aeroplanes in the C.1B international weight class, between Elstree, Fairoaks and Denham and the principal European capitals. He died from exposure after being forced down in the Austrian Alps 20 miles south of Salzburg while attempting the Belgrade record on 10 April 1953. The second most famous J-5F was G-AMRL, in which the veteran private owner H. B. Showell made an unpublicized return flight from Cambridge to Australia and back, between October 1953 and January 1954, occupying 26 days in each direction.

Several Aiglet Trainer variants were built. The J-5K G-AMYI had a 155 h.p. Cirrus Major engine; a J-5F G-AMMS was fitted with a Gipsy Major 10 of similar power to become the J-5L; and when the J-8L appeared, it proved to be the J-5K G-AMYI re-engined with a Gipsy Major 10 and provided with a centrally placed flap lever within reach of both pilots. Construction of a J-8F, G-ANVJ, with central lever and a Gipsy Major 1, was begun but was not completed. A modest number of J-5L Aiglet Trainers were then built, including three—G-ANXW to 'XY—for the Kuwait Aero Club, but only one other variant got past the prototype stage. This was the Auster J-5R Alpine, which combined the Aiglet

Trainer fuselage and tail unit with Autocar wings fitted with the improved Aiglet Trainer aileron system. The prototype was a demonstration J-5L, G-ANXC, temporarily fitted with the new wings in October 1955, after which six were built to special order including the appropriately lettered G-APAA with which the Automobile Association conducted traffic reconnaissance during 1951; and G-APFW in which Dermot Boyle, son of the former C.A.S. and two friends made a 14,000 mile, five-week return trip to Katmandu in the Himalayas in 1960.

A lower powered Alpine with Gipsy Major 1 in place of the Gipsy Major 10 was also offered under the designation J-5Q but only four were completed.

Production ceased in 1958 with the delivery of 15 J-5L aircraft to the Iranian National Aviation Club, one of which, EP-AIJ, was flown by Ranald Porteous at that year's Farnborough S.B.A.C. Show. The 1959 exhibit, G-APVG, was a frustrated export intended originally for New Zealand as a J-5R Alpine but completed as a J-5L Aiglet Trainer and sold to the College of Aeronautics, Cranfield, in 1961. Two J-5Fs first delivered to the Arab Legion Air Force, Amman, in 1952, arrived at Biggin Hill on 27 August 1963 bearing the colourful cedar tree motif of the Lebanese Aero Club and were subsequently registered to the Marquis of Headfort as G-ASLS and 'LT.

SPECIFICATION

Manufacturers: Auster Aircraft Ltd., Rearsby Aerodrome, Leicester.
Power Plants: (J-5F and J-5Q) One 130 h.p. de Havilland Gipsy Major 1 or 1F.
           (J-5K)   One 155 h.p. Blackburn Cirrus Major 3.
           (J-5L and J-5R) One 145 h.p. de Havilland Gipsy Major 10 Mk. 2-1.
           (J-8L)   One 145 h.p. de Havilland Gipsy Major 10 Mk. 1-3.

	Auster J-5F	Auster J-5L	Auster J-5R
Span	32 ft. 0 in.	32 ft. 0 in.	36 ft. 0 in.
Length	23 ft. 6 in.	23 ft. 2 in.	23 ft. 6 in.
Height	6 ft. 6 in.	6 ft. 6 in.	6 ft. 6 in.
Wing area	164 sq. ft.	164 sq. ft.	185 sq. ft.
Tare weight	1,323 lb.	1,323 lb.	1,464 lb.
All-up weight	1,950 lb.	2,200 lb.	2,250 lb.
Maximum speed	132 m.p.h.	129 m.p.h.	128 m.p.h.
Cruising speed	112 m.p.h.	117 m.p.h.	112 m.p.h.
Initial climb	705 ft./min.	840 ft./min.	1,025 ft./min.
Ceiling	12,500 ft.	13,700 ft.	22,000 ft.
Range	270 miles	440 miles	460 miles

Production: (a) Auster J-5F Aiglet Trainer

Twenty-eight British registered aircraft and the following for export: (c/n 2712) VH-AFT; (2713) VH-ADT; (2714) VH-AFK; (2717) VH-AGM; (2722) VT-DGE; (2723) JA-3012; (2724) Pakistan Air Force W4102; (2725) W4109; (2726) W4100; (2727) W4101; (2728) W4108; (2729) JA-3032; (2732) VH-BWJ; (2733) VH-BYE; (2734) JA-3020; (2735) VH-BYF; (2736) VH-BYG; (2737) JA-3021; (2738) W4103; (2739) W4104; (2740) W4107; (2741) W4106; (2742) W4105; (2743) VP-TBH; (2756) ZK-BBT; (2759) ZK-BBU; (2760–2764) W4110–W4114; (2765) AP-AFV; (2766) AP-AFW; (2769) YI-ACC; (2770) YI-ACD; (2772) ZK-BBZ;

(2774) YV-T-FTA; (2776) F-BGKZ; (2777) YI-ACF; (2778) VP-YJF; (2785–2788) PK-AAA to PK-AAD; (2795) AP-AFU; (2796) AP-AFX; (2797) AP-AFY; (2798) AP-AFZ; (2799) W4115; (2800) W4116; (3106) ZK-BCK; (3111) ZK-BCQ; (3115) F-OARJ; (3125) AP-AHH; (3127) AP-AHE; (3130) AP-AHF; (3137) VH-BYX; (3138) VH-MPW; (3140) SU-AIK; (3142) SU-AIL; (3145) AP-AJN; (3146) AP-AJO.

(b) Auster J-5K Aiglet Trainer

Two aircraft only: (c/n 2745) G-AMMS; (3151) G-AMYI. See Appendix E.

(c) Auster J-5L Aiglet Trainer

Ten British registered aircraft and the following for export: (c/n 3126) VP-XAA; (3136) VH-BYW; (3139) AP-AHB; (3149) EP-AIA; (3150) EP-AIB; (3547–3553) EP-AIC to EP-AII; (3554–3558) EP-AIK to EP-AIO; (3559) EP-AIJ.

(d) Auster J-5Q Alpine

Four aircraft only: (c/n 3201) ZK-BLW; (3202) G-AOZL; (303) VH-UED; (3204) G-APCB.

(e) Auster J-5R Alpine

Six aircraft only: (c/n 3301) G-AOGN; (3302) G-AOGV; (3303) G-APAA; (3304) G-APCX; (3305) VH-KCK; (3307) G-APFW.

(f) Auster J-8F Aiglet Trainer

One aircraft only: (c/n 3152) G-ANVJ construction abandoned.

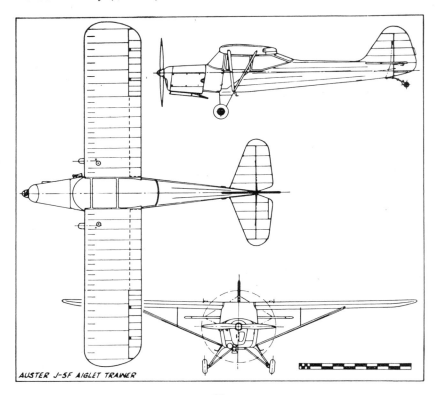

AUSTER J-5F AIGLET TRAINER

The prototype Auster B.8 Agricola on flight test near Rearsby in 1956.

Auster B.8 Agricola

In 1954 R. E. Bird, chief designer of Auster Aircraft Ltd., toured New Zealand for discussions with local top-dressing companies and drew up a specification for an aircraft to meet their future needs. Two design studies resulted, the Auster B.6 high-wing project with Blackburn Bombardier engine and the Auster B.8 Agricola low-wing equivalent which was eventually chosen because it gave the pilot—seated over the leading edge—the best possible view when flying low. Downwash from the mainplane could also be put to good use for spreading the chemical discharge.

Traditional Auster welded structure was carefully protected against corrosion from agricultural chemicals, and the pilot's cockpit (placed high enough to keep his legs clear of the engine in a crash landing) was sealed against toxic fumes. Below and behind the pilot was a 'quick-fill' hopper holding $\frac{3}{4}$ ton of dry fertiliser (or, in the spraying version, a tank holding 144 gallons of insecticide) and in the rear was a compartment, with portholes, to accommodate two passengers when flying light, but with its humped fuselage, flattened nose enclosing the 240 h.p. Continental O-470-B flat six engine, its fang-like exhaust extractor tubes and angular tail, the Agricola was scarcely a thing of beauty.

Piloted by Ranald Porteous the prototype first flew at Rearsby as G-25-3 on 8 December 1955; its British marks G-ANYG were not used and it was certificated in June 1956 as ZK-BMI. A batch of 14 more was then laid down for New Zealand but the prototype remained at Rearsby as European demonstrator and in this role left via Southend on 9 June 1957 to attend the ILSY display at Ypenburg, Holland, but the type did not sell as well as expected and 'MI was dismantled at Rearsby and stored in 1959.

Excluded from the flying programme by its American engine, the third Agricola, ZK-BMK, was a static exhibit at the Farnborough S.B.A.C. Show in September 1956 before shipment to Air Contracts Ltd., Hood Aerodrome, Masterton, New Zealand, along with ZK-BMN. ZK-BMJ went to Airlift (N.Z.) Ltd., 'MM to Associated Farmers' Aerial Work Ltd. and 'ML to Rangitikei Air Services Ltd., Taihape, who fitted internal spray bars (with 48 projecting nozzles) supplied by Austers. The rest of the order was then cancelled; a proposed Auster

G-APFZ, only British operated Agricola, was fitted with a special tank and underwing nozzles for Crop Culture (Aerial) Ltd. (*A. W. J. G. Ord-Hume*)

ZK-BXO, built from spares at Hastings, New Zealand, by Airepair Ltd. in 1966, showing the improved glazing to the rear cockpit. (*K. Morris*)

B.8A abandoned; and only two more were built, viz. the prospective ZK-BMO and 'MP which materialised in 1958 respectively as G-APFZ for Crop Culture (Aerial) Ltd., Bembridge, and VP-GAZ for Bookers Sugar Estates Ltd., Georgetown, British Guiana. These were also spraying versions but, unlike ZK-BML, had external spray bars.

G-APFZ became 'Unit No. 1' of Aerial Agriculture Ltd. at Lasham in May 1959 but was eventually re-registered to Auster Aircraft Ltd. for a demonstration of the 'Oilsink' process in which detergents were dropped on an oil slick off Southend Pier on 29 August 1960. It had then flown 300 hours but was later stored at Leicester East until sold to Air Contracts Ltd. and flown at Masterton as ZK-CCV in September 1962. VP-GAZ was damaged beyond repair at the owner's Skeldon Estate in British Guiana on 27 June 1959 but within three months was back at Rearsby and stored with the prototype.

The Agricola's New Zealand operations were centred in the southern part of North Island where 'MK, 'ML, 'MM and 'CCV were lost in crashes 1957–63. In April 1964 ZK-BMJ and 'MN were acquired by Associated Farmers' Aerial Work Ltd. and moved to Martinborough but 'MN crashed in the wooded Tararua Ranges on 11 March 1965, leaving 'MJ as the only serviceable Agricola in the world at that time. Later it was joined by ZK-CCU and ZK-BXO built at Hastings from the remains of ZK-BMK, 'MM and 'MN. Nearly five years later another Agricola was constructed from spares by Associated Farmers and first flew at Martinborough on 1 March 1971 as ZK-DEU.

SPECIFICATION

Manufacturers: Auster Aircraft Ltd., Rearsby Aerodrome, Leicester.

Power Plant: One 240 h.p. Continental O-470-B.

Dimensions: Span, 42 ft. 0 in. Length, 28 ft. 1 in. Height, 8 ft. 4 in. Wing area, 254·7 sq. ft.

Weights: Tare weight, 1,920 lb. All-up weight, 3,840 lb.

Performance: Maximum speed, 127 m.p.h. Cruising speed, 101 m.p.h. Initial climb, 610 ft./min. Range, 220 miles.

Production:

Eight aircraft only completed initially: (c/n B.101) G-25-3/G-ANYG/ZK-BMI, dismantled at Rearsby 1959; (B.102) ZK-BMJ; (B.103) ZK-BMK crashed at Masterton 11.5.57, rebuilt as ZK-CCU, first flown 11.6.65; (B.104) ZK-BML crashed at Taihape 22.1.59; (B.105) ZK-BMM crashed at Martinborough 7.6.62; (B.106) ZK-BMN crashed 5 miles north of Paraparaumu 11.3.65, rebuilt as ZK-BXO, first flown 15.10.66; (B.107) ZK-BMO completed as G-APFZ/ZK-CCV; (B.108) ZK-BMP completed as B.117/VP-GAZ, crashed in British Guiana 27.6.59; (B.109–B.110) ZK-BMQ and 'MS stored incomplete; (B.111–B.115) ZK-BMT to 'MX not completed: (B.116) Auster B.8A prototype not completed; (AF.001R) ZK-DEU built from spares in New Zealand, first flown 1.3.71.

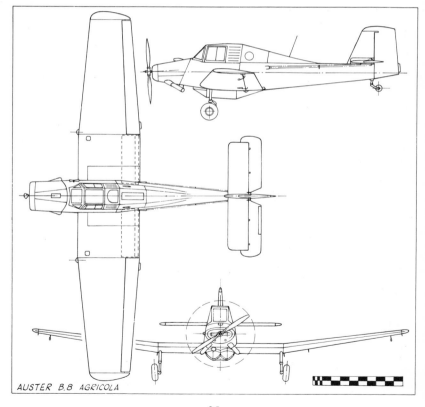

AUSTER B.8 AGRICOLA

Auster 6A G-ASIP, initially converted at Heathrow for glider towing at Booker, was later used by the Bristol Gliding Club at Nympsfield. (*Richard Riding*)

Auster 6A Tugmaster

The A.O.P. Mk. 6 or Auster Model K was a development of the Mk. 5 with 145 h.p. D.H. Gipsy Major 7, wing tanks, longer undercarriage legs and a half-span aerofoil flap to improve the already impressive short field performance. The prototype was a converted Auster 5, TJ707, which first flew at Rearsby on 1 May 1945 and became well known in later years both at Hamble and Perth as an instructional airframe with the registration G-ABBY properly belonging to a pre-war Avro Five. Production 1947–53 comprised 304 aircraft for the R.A.F., Arab Legion, South African, Australian, and Belgian Air Forces, as well as 36 of a special variant with an even taller undercarriage for ski operations in Canada by the R.C.A.F.

First of the type released for civil conversion was TW562 on which some work was done at Croydon in February 1949, but it failed to become G-ALGW and the only standard Auster 6 actually to become a private aeroplane was Egyptian campaign veteran WJ370 which was converted to G-APRO for Air Commodore A. H. Wheeler at Old Warden in 1961.

When the new Auster A.O.P. Mk. 9 was introduced in 1959, all surplus Mk. 6s and near-identical T.Mk. 7 trainers were repurchased by Auster Aircraft Ltd. for conversion and resale. The majority, stripped and completely rebuilt to full Terrier standard for clubs and private owners after the company's style was changed in 1962, are described in the Beagle-Auster section of this book, but a small number, with engines brought up to civil Gipsy Major 10 Mk. 1-1 standard, were fitted with enlarged tail surfaces for glider-towing under the designation Auster 6A. Seating was unusual because the pilot had a space on his right where the A.O.P. radio had been and the second occupant sat in a sideways facing seat in the rear.

The prototype, G-ARCY, produced at Lasham in collaboration with Mr. F. Horridge and equipped with an electrically driven winch under the rear fuselage, first flew as G-25-9 early in August 1960 and was followed within the month by G-ARDX, a Rearsby conversion with a standard Auster towing hook. Both aircraft towed Slingsby and Elliott sailplanes in pairs at that year's Farnborough S.B.A.C. Show, but 'CY stalled when turning finals at Lasham after towing a glider back from Farnborough on 9 September and was destroyed.

Rearsby conversions were given the type name Tugmaster, the first of which, 'DX, replaced 'CY at Lasham, where Mr. F. Horridge formed Air Tows Ltd. and subsequently produced four others for local use, bringing the full total to 29, including 21 at Rearsby, G-ASIP by B.E.A. employees at London Airport for their Silver Wing gliding club at Booker, and G-ASEF and 'EG by Airgineers Ltd., Staverton.

A. H. Wheeler's G-APRO was raised to Auster 6A standard in 1964, and VF512, later to become G-ARRX, was Auster's test vehicle for the new Terrier exhaust system. Tugmasters were powerful workhorses and soon ousted the ageing Tiger Moths from major gliding clubs, G-ARHM for instance, regularly performed the Herculean task of towing the Midland Gliding Club's Eagle off the top of the Long Mynd. They were in considerable demand at the National Gliding Championships and foregathered annually at Lasham for this purpose from 1961 onwards. G-ASEF, first of the Staverton conversions, spent a season joyriding at Great Yarmouth with Anglian Air Charter's Auster J-1N G-APTU and J-5G G-ASFK, but was acquired later by the R.A.F. Bicester gliding club which added R.A.F. roundels and despatched it to Prague via Southend with Beagle Terrier 2 G-ASBU on 5 September 1963. A week later they returned towing Czech-built Blanik sailplanes G-ASKX and 'KY respectively, the latter for permanent use at Bicester.

Auster 6As G-ARIH, 'GB and 'KC were unusual in having two front seats and full dual control, the first being used by Mr. H. Britten at Poddington until it was flown to Haverfordwest in May 1962 for instructional use by the West Wales Flying Group. The other two were sold to the Three Counties Aero Club, Blackbushe in March 1964 and the last eleven Rearsby Tugmasters were ferried to Scandinavia in foreign marks for school work and aerotowing later the same year.

When declared obsolete in 1957–58, the 28 machines surviving from the R.C.A.F. batch and at least three Auster T.Mk. 7s were disposed of by the Crown Assets Disposal Corporation, three as glider tugs to the Soaring Association of Canada at Gimli, Manitoba, and one each to the Queen's University Gliding Club, Kingston, Ontario; the Edmonton Soaring Club; and the Cu Nim Gliding Club, Calgary. Five sold to the Brampton Flying Club, Ontario, were fitted with Auster J-1 Autocrat-type rear cabin glazing in the club's workshops. Secondhand ex military Auster 6s were also flown in civil marks in Belgium, Australia and South Africa.

SPECIFICATION

Manufacturers: Auster Aircraft Ltd., Rearsby Aerodrome, Leicester. Style changed to Beagle-Auster Aircraft Ltd. in June 1961.

Power plants: (Auster 6) One 145 h.p. de Havilland Gipsy Major 7.

(Auster 6A) One 145 h.p. de Havilland Gipsy Major 10 Mk. 1-1.

Dimensions: Span, 36 ft. 0 in. Length, 23 ft. 9 in. Height, 8 ft. 4½ in. (Canadian) 8 ft. 8 in. Wing area, 187 sq. ft. including flaps.

Weights and performance (Auster 6A):

Tare weight, 1,400 lb. All-up weight, 2,200 lb. Maximum speed, 123 m.p.h. Cruising speed, 108 m.p.h. Initial climb, 810 ft./min. Service ceiling, 14,000 ft.

Production: (a) Auster 6

Two British registered aircraft and the following converted overseas:

In Canada: (c/n 2558) R.C.A.F. 16651/CF-MMY; (2576) 16652/CF-KBV; (2577) 16653/CF-NQC; (2578) 16654/CF-FJM; (2579) 16655/CF-KBW; (2580) 16656/CF-LGM; (2587) 16663/CF-KJP; (2589) 16665/CF-KGZ; (2590) 16666/CF-LXT; (2591) 16667/CF-LIC; (2596) 16668/CF-MOE; (2598) 16670/CF-LWK; (2599) 16671/CF-LWA; (2600) 16672/CF-LOE; (2853) 16675/CF-LPA; (2855) 16677/CF-LSU; (2857) 16679/CF-KFN; (2862) 16684/CF-OMW.

In Belgium: (c/n 2817) VT978/Belgian A/F A9/OO-FDD; (2818) VT979/A3/OO-FDA; (2820) VT981/A7/OO-FDB; (2821) VT982/OO-OVL; (2824) VT988/A8/OO-FDC; (2825) VT989/OO-FDG; (2826) VT990/A11/OO-FDE; (2827) VT991/A12/OO-FDF; (2831) VT992/A18/OO-FDK; (2832) VT993/A17/OO-FDJ; (2834) VT995/A15/OO-FDH; (2835) VT996/A16/OO-FDI; (2836) VT997/A22/OO-FDL.

In Australia: VX127/Royal Australian Navy A11-201/VH-RCT.

In South Africa: South African Air Force 5408/ZS-ECW.

(b) Auster 6A Tugmaster

Twenty-nine aircraft comprising 18 British registered machines and the following for export: (c/n 3727) TW529/SE-ELI; (3728) TW578/SE-ELC; (3731) TW577/OH-AUK; (3732) TW538/SE-ELB; (3734) WJ373/SE-ELE; (3735) TW571/SE-ELF; (3736) VF600/SE-ELG; (3737) SE-ELH; (3738) TW537/SE-ELP; (3743) VF514/SE-ELM; (3744) LN-AEV; (SAAF. 5409) ZS-EFL.

(c) Auster 7

One British registered aircraft and the following conversions in Canada: R.C.A.F. 16689/CF-KPM; 16690/CF-KLD; 16691/CF-KYB; 16692/CF-KPL.

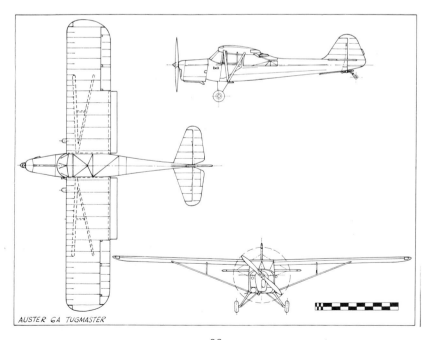

AUSTER 6A TUGMASTER

Flt. Lt. F. O. Soden running up Whippet G-EAPF at Gosport on King's Cup day, 12 August 1924, with Westland Walrus biplane in the background. (*Leonard Bridgman*)

Austin Whippet

The Whippet was a diminutive single-seat biplane designed by J. W. Kenworthy and built by the Austin Motor Co. Ltd. in 1919. Powered by a 45 h.p. Anzani six-cylinder air-cooled radial and intended for the pioneer private owner, it was of robust construction with fabric-covered steel tube fuselage, and wooden folding wings from which all bracing wires were eliminated by using N-type interplane struts and streamlined steel lift struts.

In common with several contemporaries the Whippet was before its time and fell victim of the post-war depression. Only five were built and the first, K-158, was registered to the manufacturers in July 1919. Although underpowered it reached 5,000 ft. in 9 minutes and cruised at 80 m.p.h., the C. of A. being issued in the following December, by which time the aircraft had received permanent registration G-EAGS.

The second and third Whippets were exhibited at the Olympia Aero Show, London, 9–20 July 1920, the former, which had been registered G-EAPF in the previous November, was in plain silver without markings but the other was only a skeleton airframe. Ten days after the Show the third Whippet was sold to A. J. Greenshields as G-EAUZ and shipped to the Argentine for his personal use. It was still flying without markings in 1928.

The fourth and fifth Whippets were shipped to New Zealand to the order of R. A. Dexter, a director of the New Zealand Flying School, Kohimarama. After erection, pioneer pilot John Seabrook flew one of these (unregistered) off the beach at Mission Bay, Auckland, on 4 June 1921 and completed the first Auckland–Hamilton flight when he landed on the Ruakuru State Farm to deliver it to New Zealand's first private owner, H. H. Shaw. Next day demonstration flights were made over Hamilton by Sqn. Ldr. M. C. McGregor and the machine was also exhibited at the local Winter Show. At a later date one of these Whippets was sold to racing driver Percy Coleman who struck high tension cables and crashed at Palmerston North on 22 January 1925. The damaged machine was stored at Wanganui until 1928 and then disposed of to a touring theatre company as stage property. In 1931 it was acquired by W. R. Bennett, registered ZK-ACR and flown briefly by Capt. L. H. Brake. It was said to be extant at Kai-Iwi in the 1940s.

When the Austin company relinquished its aviation interests, the first and second Whippets were disposed of to aircraft dealer C. P. B. Ogilvie at Hendon. G-EAGS seems not to have flown again after C. of A. expiry in November 1921 but G-EAPF was flown at Stag Lane Aerodrome, Edgware, by H. H. Sykes in May 1923. In the following year it was overhauled at Brooklands for initial issue of C. of A. and sold to Flt. Lt. F. O. Soden who flew it at Gosport until he delivered it by air to the Midland Aero Club, Castle Bromwich, on 15 July 1926. It was little used, made a forced landing without damage on 26 September, and club member E. R. King bought it to fly at the Blackpool Air Pageant 6–7 July 1928. It later passed into the hands of H. M. Pearson, Hamble, but the C. of A. was not renewed after April 1929 and it passed away at Shoreham in 1931.

SPECIFICATION

Manufacturers: The Austin Motor Co. Ltd., Northfield Works, Birmingham.
Power Plant: One 45 h.p. Anzani.
Dimensions: Span, 21 ft. 6 in. Length, 16 ft. 3 in. Height, 7 ft. 6 in. Wing area, 134 sq. ft.
Weights: Tare weight, 580 lb. All-up weight, 810 lb.
Performance: Maximum speed, 95 m.p.h. Cruising speed, 80 m.p.h. Initial climb, 5,000 ft. in 9 min. Endurance, 2 hr.
Production:

Five aircraft only: (c/n AU.1) K-158/G-EAGS; (AU.2) G-EAPF; (AU.3) G-EAUZ; (AU.4 and AU.5) New Zealand, one became ZK-ACR in 1931.

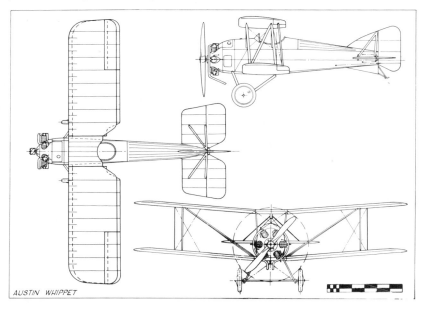

AUSTIN WHIPPET

The prototype Carvair, G-ANYB, on test in Channel Air Bridge colours in 1961.
(Aviation Traders Ltd.)

Aviation Traders A.T.L.98 Carvair

In January 1959 Mr. A. C. Leftley, chief designer of Aviation Traders Ltd., investigated the suitability of existing aircraft for conversion into car ferries to supplement and eventually replace the Bristol Freighter 32s of Channel Air Bridge Ltd. Choice fell on the Douglas DC-4, 20 years old, cheap, reliable and possessing a vast spares backing. The nose was replaced by a new bulbous unit 8 ft. 8 in. longer than the original, entirely designed and built at Southend by Aviation Traders Ltd., using Douglas constructional methods. Direct entry for vehicles through a hydraulically operated, sideways opening nose door was obtained by raising the flight deck 6 ft. 10 in. above its original position and retracting the nosewheel into an externàl blister. Wing and power plants were untouched but DC-6 brakes were fitted and an enlarged DC-7 tail unit built to compensate for extra keel surface forward. Known as A.T.L.98, the conversion imposed a weight penalty of only 2,300 lb. and the aircraft cruised at 190 m.p.h. with five cars forward and 25 passengers in the rear cabin.

Prototype conversion of G-ANYB 'Atalanta', a former World Airways C-54B which Air Charter Ltd. had acquired in 1955 for services in Germany and for Stansted—Cyprus trooping runs, began at Southend on 1 October 1960 and following a local naming competition, was known henceforth as the Carvair, a contraction of 'car-via-air'. After first flight by D. B. Cartlidge on 21 June 1961 and some 155 hr. of test flying, mainly by Capt. R. Langley, the C. of A. was issued on 30 January 1962. Named 'Golden Gate Bridge' its first overseas flight, to Ostend, took place on 16 February, first proving flights to Basle and Geneva on 22 February and 11 March respectively and the Strasbourg inaugural flight on 1 June.

Carvair production began at Stansted using two Resort Airlines Douglas C-54s which were completed as G-ARSD 'Chelsea Bridge' and 'SF 'Pont de l'Europe'.

The latter flew its first Southend–Geneva service on 7 July 1962, but struck a snow covered dyke when landing at Rotterdam on 28 December, the pilot, Capt. J. Toothill being killed. A third Resort machine and one from the German Lufttransport Union were temporarily G-ARSH and 'EK before Carvair conversion as N9758F and N9757F for heavy transport work in the Congo by the Luxembourg operator Intercontinental/Interocean. They were pure freighters with enlarged nose bulkheads to admit military vehicles and had nine seats for slip crews in the bulge behind the flight deck.

N9758F was delivered Southend–Frankfurt for F.A.A. certification trials on 20 September 1962 before both went to Brazzaville, and in March 1963 they conveyed an entire Indian mechanised division from Leopoldville to Mombasa, completing 5,000 flying hours before returning to Southend for overhaul. Thereafter they operated out of Luxembourg as LX-IOG and 'OH respectively until modified to car-ferry standard at Stansted and delivered to the Le Touquet-based Cie Air Transport in May 1965 as F-BMHU 'Cdt. Henri de Montal' and F-BMHV 'Cdt. Max Guedt'.

EI-AMP 'St. Albert/Ailbhe' (which had first flown as G-ARZV on 21 December 1962) and EI-AMR 'St. Jarlaith/Larflaith', fitted out as 55-seaters but quickly convertible to 22-seaters with 5 cars, were handed over to Aer Lingus at Southend on 14 March and 29 April 1963 respectively and inaugurated Dublin–Liverpool, Dublin–Bristol and Cork–Bristol car ferries in the following month, and a Dublin–Cherbourg route in June 1963. At the end of the season they had carried 4,100 cars and 11,000 passengers. A third Carvair, EI-ANJ 'St. Seanan', modified for horse charters, with control runs in the roof of the hold, was delivered on 24 April 1964, and, by way of variety in outsize loads, in it the Pfalz replica G-ATIF was carried from Heathrow to Casement for filming in July 1965. By 1966 however Irish Carvairs were no longer paying their way and were stored until Eastern Provincial Airways of Newfoundland bought them in February 1968 for heavy freighting in Arctic Canada.

In 1962, when British United Air Ferries (a merger of Channel Air Bridge with Silver City Airways) began deep penetration services, two DC-4s from Luxembourg, two from the U.S.A. and one each from Germany and the Lebanon, were fed into the Stansted conversion line, three becoming G-ASDC, 'HZ and 'KN to supplement conversions of the company's own DC-4s G-AOFW and G-APNH. The last was specially converted at Southend for long-range freighting. G-ASDC 'Pont du Rhin' flew its first Southend–Rotterdam service on 26 March 1963; 'HZ flew to Rotterdam to be named 'Maasbrug' on 15 June and 'KN 'Pont d'Avignon' joined the fleet on 26 March 1964. The last two accommodated 55 passengers (with three cars) for the high density Ostend tourist traffic, and B.U.A.F. also extended its network to include Southend–Liége, Lydd–Liége and Baginton–Calais using G-ANYB and two Lydd-based Carvairs, G-ARSD and G-ASDC. The last, which had made the first Carvair landing at Lydd on 13 December 1963, also flew the first Jersey–Hurn service on 31 October 1964.

G-ASKG 'Channel Bridge', which left Southend on 8 August 1963 on four months lease to Compagnia Aerea Meridionale (Alisud), inaugurated the Tirrenian Air Bridge, 450 miles across the Straits of Messina between Naples and Palermo on 15 August and carried 175 cars and 546 passengers in the first month. It rejoined the B.U.A.F. fleet at Southend on 25 February 1964.

Repainted as EC-AVD and inscribed 'Puente Aereo Aviaco', G-AOFW left

Carvair No. 11, G-APNH 'Menai Bridge', taking off from Southend in British United livery 1967. (*John Goring*)

No. 4, LX-IOG, in Interocean colours 1963. (*John Goring*)

No. 14, Aer Lingus EI-ANJ 'St. Seanan' prior to sale in Canada, February 1968. (*John Goring*)

No. 19, VH-INJ, first for the Australian operator Ansett-A.N.A., at Stansted, 1965, (*Richard Riding*)

Stansted on 18 April 1964 on five months lease to the Spanish airline Aviacion y Comercio (Aviaco) to begin vehicle ferries between Valencia, Barcelona and Palma, Majorca. Two Iberia DC-4s, EC-AEP and 'EO, were also converted at Stansted for Aviaco, becoming Carvairs EC-AXI and 'ZA, delivered on 20 June 1964 and 26 March 1965 respectively. EC-AVD rejoined B.U.A.F. at Southend in November 1964 but the others remained in use until sold to Dominicana in 1969.

The final overseas contract was signed by Australia's Ansett-A.N.A. on 26 April 1965 for the conversion of its own DC-4s VH-INJ and 'NK, first flown at Stansted as Carvairs on 14 September and 27 October 1965 respectively. Two years later VH-INM was flown to England for the same purpose, becoming the 21st. and last Carvair, although the 17th., LX-IOF, still lay semi-cocooned, minus engines and instrumentation at Stansted.

Long distance charters included an outsize Admiralty load which left for Singapore in G-ANYB on 19 October 1962, and a Government freight flight by G-APNH 'Menai Bridge' which left Lyneham on 11 January 1965 but got no further than San Francisco. Carrying a heavy computer, the same aircraft left Southend on 16 October for trial operation between the North and South Islands of New Zealand by B.U.A.F.'s associated company, Straits Air Freight Express. Unsuitable for short routes, 'NH returned to Southend on 1 December and positioned at Lyneham next day to carry radio transmitters to Zambia. Later in the month when the airlift of bulk oil commenced between Dar-es-Salaam and Lusaka, G-APNH and G-ASKG were repainted in Air Ferry colours and left Southend with spares for B.U.A.'s Britannia freighters.

Flown home in March 1966 they rejoined the ferry fleet to which was added Carvair G-ATRV, the former OD-ADW which had been 18 months dormant at Stansted. When extensive losses forced the closure of deep penetration routes on 28 February 1967, G-ANYB and G-AOFW were stored at Lydd and the remainder put to work on shorter routes when the Freighter 32s were withdrawn from Southend on 30 March. On the 8th of the same month Cie Air Transport lost F-BMHU in a take-off crash at Karachi during a freight flight to the Far East, and replaced it with G-ATRV, which left Southend on 7 May as F-BOSU for use on the Nice–Corsica car ferry. At the end of the season G-ARSD also went to Lydd for storage, the remainder being painted in new British Air Ferries styling. Finally, on 3 March 1969, G-ASKG was delivered to Cie Air Transport and was replaced on 17 March by G-AXAI, formerly LX-IOF which had been cocooned at Stansted since 1962.

SPECIFICATION

Conversions by: Aviation Traders (Engineering) Ltd., Southend and Stansted Airports, Essex.

Power Plants: Four 1,450 h.p. Pratt & Whitney Twin Wasp R-2000-7M2.

Dimensions: Span, 117 ft. 6 in. Length, 102 ft. 7 in. Height, 29 ft. 10 in. Wing area, 1,457 sq. ft.

Weights: Tare weight, (25 seats) 40,855 lb., (55 seats) 41,300 lb. All-up weight, (B.A.F.) 73,800 lb., (Aer Lingus) 72,700 lb.

Performance: Maximum speed, 250 m.p.h. Cruising speed at 71,250 lb. A.U.W. at 5,000 ft., 195 m.p.h. Initial climb, 650 ft./min. Range (max. payload) 1,700 miles.

Production: Twenty-one aircraft only:

Carvair	First flown	Converted from		Douglas serial	Operator	Disposal
No. 1 G-ANYB	21.6.61	Air Charter	G-ANYB	10528	Channel Air Br.	Scr. 1970
No. 2 G-ARSD	25.3.62	Resort A/L	N57670	10311	Channel Air Br.	Scr. 1970
No. 3 G-ARSF	28.6.62	Resort A/L	N88709	18339	Channel Air Br.	Cr. 1962
No. 4 N9758F	5.9.62	Av. Traders	G-ARSH	10338	Intercontinental	LX-IOG F-BMHU
No. 5 N9757F	2.11.62	Av. Traders	G-AREK	10365	Interocean	LX-IOH F-BMHV
No. 6 EI-AMP	21.12.62	Av. Traders	G-ARZV	7480	Aer Lingus	CF-EPX
No. 7 G-ASDC	19.3.63	Interocean	LX-BNG	10273	British U.A.F.	
No. 8 EI-AMR	18.4.63	World A/W	N88819	10448	Aer Lingus	CF-EPV
No. 9 G-ASHZ	8.6.63	Remmert W.	N9326R	27249	British U.A.F.	
No. 10 G-ASKG	29.7.63	Interocean	LX-BBP	10382	British U.A.F.	F-BRPT
No. 11 G-APNH	4.1.65	Air Charter	G-APNH	18333	British U.A.F.	Scr. 1971
No. 12 G-AOFW	11.2.64	Air Charter	G-AOFW	10351	British U.A.F.	
No. 13 G-ASKN	8.2.64	Continentale	D-ADAM	3058	British U.A.F.	
No. 14 EI-ANJ	17.4.64	Av. Traders	G-ASKD	10458	Aer Lingus	CF-EPW
No. 15 G-ATRV	25.3.66	Trans Med.	OD-ADW	27311	British U.A.F.	F-BOSU
No. 16 EC-AXI	4.6.64	Iberia	EC-AEP	10845	Aviaco	HI-168
No. 17 G-AXAI	2.4.69	Interocean	LX-IOF	18342	British Air F.	
No. 18 EC-AZA	12.3.65	Iberia	EC-AEO	18340	Aviaco	HI-172
No. 19 VH-INJ	14.9.65	Ansett-ANA	VH-INJ	42927	Ansett-ANA	
No. 20 VH-INK	27.10.65	Ansett-ANA	VH-INK	42994	Ansett-ANA	
No. 21 VH-INM	12.7.68	Ansett-ANA	VH-INM	27314	Ansett-ANA	

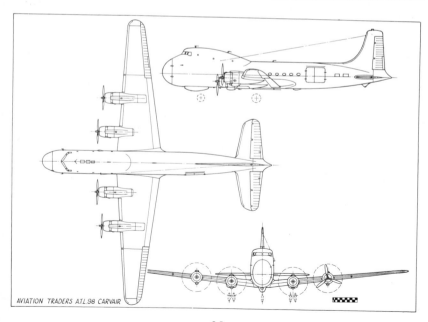

AVIATION TRADERS A.T.L 98 CARVAIR

Northern Air Transport's Avro 504K G-ABLL, formerly R.A.F. trainer J8333, flying over Liverpool in 1933.

Avro 504K

By the end of the First World War, A. V. Roe's immortal 504 design of 1913 had emerged as the Avro 504K, most famous wooden trainer of all time. Its cheapness of operation and ease of maintenance made it the only surplus military aircraft of 1919 to find lasting favour as a civil type. Although used in small numbers for tuition, as at the Beardmore School at Renfrew, which had four, the Avro 504K as a civil machine is synonymous with itinerant joyriding, and up to the advent of the Moth in 1926 was the most common British aeroplane. No less than 319 were converted for civil use by removing the dual controls and cutting away the decking to accommodate a third seat, although this number included several ferried in 'sheep's clothing' to foreign air forces in 1919–20.

When civil flying was officially sanctioned at Easter 1919, the Avro firm was first in the field with a small fleet of 504Ks which carried 30,000 passengers from the beaches of Southport, Blackpool, Weston-super-Mare and elsewhere during the summer. A regular and well patronized service was also flown between Alexandra Park Aerodrome, Manchester, Birkdale Sands, Southport, and Blackpool. In the north-east the North Sea Aerial Navigation Co. Ltd. (a Blackburn subsidiary) ran a similar service during the season from Scarborough to Harrogate, via Hull, with G-EAGV. Airframes, engines and spares existed in vast quantities, and an 'Avro' could be purchased at low cost from the Aircraft Disposal Company at Croydon by any ex R.A.F. pilot bent on trying to earn a living in the air. Records show that over 50 such enterprises were launched, passengers being carried at a guinea a head from little fields all over the country, but the slump of 1921 put an end to easy money and to most of these 'mushroom' concerns. The notable exception was the Berkshire Aviation Co., founded by F. J. V. and J. D. V. Holmes with Le Rhône-engined G-EACL, formerly D9298. In 1920 they were joined by A. J. Cobham and O. P. Jones, two little-known pilots, who brought with them G-EAKX and 'SF, destined to be the longest-lived of all 'old Avros'. Joyriding took place all over the Midlands and the Home Counties, and the machines were overhauled in a barn at East Hanney, near Wantage, during the winter. Another typical joyriding firm was the Cornwall Aviation Co. Ltd., founded at St. Austell in 1924 by Capt. Percival Phillips, who also serviced his 504Ks in a barn during the winter, and carried out passenger flying at Margate and other resorts every summer. By 1930 the fleet consisted of G-EBIZ, 'NR, 'SE, G-AAAF and 'YI. A similar firm, the North British Aviation Co. Ltd., founded at Hooton in 1929 by E. E. Fresson and L. J. Rimmer, covered Lancashire, Cheshire and the Lake District. When, however, Sir Alan Cobham's National Aviation Day displays went on tour in 1932, the red Cornwall Avros went with it, and in the following year the North British fleet, consisting of G-EASF, 'KX, G-EBGZ, 'HE, 'KX, 'SJ, G-AAEZ, G-ABHJ, 'HK and 'LL, was also enlisted, and the heyday of the lone Avro in a field was over.

During its civil career a number of major variants of the Avro 504K appeared. First came the float-equipped 504L, 10 of which augmented the Avro fleet at seaside resorts and on Lake Windermere. Howard Pixton, manager of the Windermere floatplanes, flew a regular and successful newspaper service to the Isle of Man during the summer of 1919. Five others were flown on the south coast that season by the Eastbourne Aviation Co. Ltd. The Avro Company persuaded

First of two dissimilar cabin variants, the Avro 504M K-134/G-EACX made the first recorded British charter flights in 1919.

An Avro 504L, G-EADK, formerly H2582, giving passenger flights from Folkstone beach with J. P. B. Ferrand in 1920. (*Leonard Bridgman*)

four passengers into the rear cockpit of some land machines by increasing the width of the fuselage by 9 in. to create a variant known as the Avro 536. A prototype, K-114, and 20 'production' 536s were made at Alexandra Park in 1919, while four others—G-EBOF, 'OY, 'RB and 'TF—were converted by Surrey Flying Services Ltd. in 1926–27. This firm, founded at Croydon by A. F. Muir and W. J. Grant with two Avro 504Ks, G-EAWI and 'WJ, in 1919, carried thousands of passengers in its famous blue machines until the last of the large fleet, G-AAGB, was written off in 1934. The manufacturers also produced two cabin versions, the first of which was fitted with a 100 h.p. Gnome and designated 504M. This aircraft, K-134, later G-EACX, seated two behind the pilot in a cabin provided with portholes above the top longerons and did a great deal of pleasure flying from Hounslow Heath in 1919–20. Taking off from a grass strip outside Chorley Wood Church in June 1919, it took a newly married couple to Fowey, Cornwall, on what was probably the first post-war British internal charter. The other cabin version, the Avro 546, was a three-seater converted from an Avro 536,

The Avro 536 K-137 joyriding at Southsea in 1919 with four passengers in the enlarged rear cockpit. The extra fin was also fitted to the Avro 504L and M. (*C. A. Nepean Bishop*)

The Avro 504K used by the Aircraft Disposal Co. Ltd., Croydon, in 1923–24 as a Lucifer engine testbed. (*Bristol Photo.*)

Avro Gosport G-EBNF with tapered ailerons. The full stop after the registration was common to all newly built Avro aircraft of the period. (*Flight Photo. 3875*)

The sole example of an Avro 504K powered by an Anzani radial was G-EBWO, in service with the Phillips and Powis School of Flying in 1929.

G-EAOM, in October 1919. The Triplex windows were below the top longeron on this variant, and a 150 h.p. Bentley B.R.1 was fitted. Only one Avro 546 was produced, and only two other variants are worthy of note. First was the Avro Company's experimental machine G-EAPR, which in October 1919 had 504K wings and a 90 h.p. Curtiss OX-5 engine. In this form it was designated the Avro 545. The other was the Avro 504K G-EAGI, built as a fighter variant with long-legged V-strut, skidless undercarriage, and used with seven other standard machines at the Central Aircraft Company's flying school, Northolt.

The final rotary engined variant of the 504 family was the Avro 504R Gosport, a cleaned-up two-seat version with tapered ailerons, powered by a 100 h.p. Gnome. The prototype, G-EBNE, received its C. of A. on 15 June 1926, and five

The Dyak-engined Avro 504K at Mascot, Sydney, in November 1965 in bottle green with varnished struts, brass radiator and silver wings for the projected Q.A.N.T.A.S. museum.
(*N. M. Parnell*)

others—G-EBNF, 'OX, 'PH, 'UY and G-AACT—were built. G-EBPH was experimentally fitted with a 100 h.p. Avro Alpha five-cylinder radial, and used in December 1926 for a landing on the summit of Helvellyn by Messrs. Hinkler and Leeming. The prototype was used for instruction by the Lancashire Aero Club until it crashed near Woodford on 21 October 1928, and G-EBUY was fitted with a 150 h.p. Armstrong Siddeley Mongoose radial to become a 504N/504R hybrid.

During 1919–20 each Dominion received an Imperial Gift of Avro 504Ks, and in the next 12 years 504K and 504L aircraft reconditioned by Avro, Vickers and the Aircraft Disposal Co. Ltd. were exported in very large numbers. Detailed histories of these and licence-built examples are beyond the scope of this book, occupying some 20 pages of the author's *Avro Aircraft since 1908*. In 1921, G-AUBG with 100 h.p. water-cooled Sunbeam Dyak, was the first Q.A.N.T.A.S. aeroplane and 45 years later on 10 December 1966 its former pilot, company chairman Sir Hudson Fysh, taxied a replica (modified from a preserved R.A.A.F. machine, A3-4) among the Boeings at Sydney Airport to mark the 32nd. anniversary of the Australia–England air mail.

Three Le Rhône 504Ks restored at Trenton, Ontario, 1966–67 were given 1919-style markings G-CYCK, 'EI and 'FG for their part in Canadian centennial year celebrations. G-CYFG, restored some years before by Cole Palen at Old Rhinebeck, N.Y., as N8736R was non-flying but the others flew across Canada (dis-assembled inside a Hercules) to give flying displays at each port of call of the R.C.A.F. 'Golden Centennaires' Tutor aerobatic team. G-CAFG and 'CK (the latter ex D8971 and airfreighted from California in a Hercules) later formed exhibits at the Aircraft Museum, Rockliffe.

The several 504Ks preserved in Britain in military marks were joined by G-ATXL, a full size replica constructed for film purposes and first flown by V. H. Bellamy at Blackbushe on 17 August 1966. The film was never made, and after more than four years in the hangar at Kings Somborne, Hants., 'XL was crated at Land's End Airport and shipped to the Cole Palen collection at Old Rhinebeck, N.Y. In May 1969 another Avro, E449, made its appearance at the Biggin Air Fair, built at Henlow for the R.A.F. Museum from the remains of 504K G-EBJE and Avro 548A prototype G-EBKN.

SPECIFICATION

Manufacturers: A. V. Roe and Co. Ltd., Newton Heath, Manchester. Widely sub-
contracted.

Power Plants: One 100 h.p. Gnome.
One 100 h.p. Sunbeam Dyak.
One 110 h.p. Le Rhône.
One 130 h.p. Clerget.
One 150 h.p. Bentley B.R.1.

Dimensions: Length, 29 ft. 5 in. Height, 10 ft. 5 in.

	Avro 504K and 504M	Avro 504L	Avro 536 and 546
Span	36 ft. 0 in.	36 ft. 0 in.	36 ft. 9 in.
Wing area	330 sq. ft.	330 sq. ft.	335 sq. ft.
Tare weight	1,231 lb.	1,408 lb.	1,431 lb.
All-up weight	1,829 lb.	2,006 lb.	2,226 lb.
Maximum speed	95 m.p.h.	80 m.p.h.	90 m.p.h.
Cruising speed	75 m.p.h.	65 m.p.h.	70 m.p.h.
Initial climb	700 ft./min.	600 ft./min.	550 ft./min.
Ceiling	16,000 ft.	15,000 ft.	12,000 ft.
Range	225 miles	160 miles	200 miles

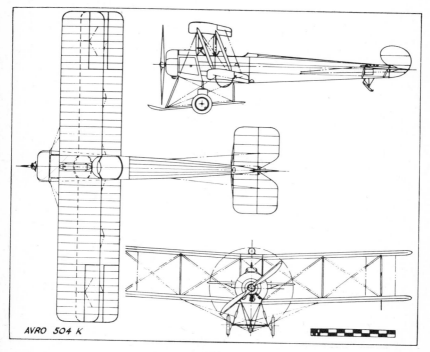

AVRO 504 K

Avro 548 G-EAFH (80 h.p. Renault eight-cylinder air-cooled engine) at Hamble in June 1920

Avro 548

By 1918 the successful development of the in-line and radial air-cooled engines heralded the approaching end of the faithful rotary, and at the end of 1919 trials began at Hamble with a prototype three seater for private owners, powered by an air-cooled 80 h.p. Renault and known as the Avro 548. It was exhibited at the Olympia Aero Show, London, in July 1920 and afterwards went to Croydon for joyriding as G-EAPQ. Three other Hamble conversions were G-EAFH (formerly K-147, testbed 504K for the 170 h.p. A.B.C. Wasp I radial), 'LF and 'VH (for Uruguay).

A total of thirty such aircraft existed in the United Kingdom during the following fourteen years, of which only G-EBIT, 'IU and 'IV, built in 1924 to the order of the North Sea Aerial and General Transport Co. Ltd. for instructional work at Brough, were genuine factory-made 548s. The remainder were ex R.A.F. Avro 504Ks converted by Avros, the Aircraft Disposal Co. Ltd., the de Havilland Aircraft Co. Ltd. and the Henderson School of Flying Ltd.

One of the first conversions was G-EAAL, formerly 504K E4154, owned by Vickers in 1923, by the de Havilland Aircraft Co. Ltd. in 1925, and by Stag Lane private owner, T. H. Richardson, till it crashed in 1928. The type was mainly used for instructional work, the Newcastle Aero Club having G-EBPO ex E3387 in 1926, the Norfolk and Norwich Aero Club G-EBPJ ex E9337 for a few months in 1928, while Surrey Flying Services usually earmarked one machine for this purpose, successively owning G-EBBC, 'IV and G-AABW. It was Brooklands, however, that became the traditional home of the 548, the variegated and fluctuating collection G-EAJB, G-EBAJ, 'FM, 'RD, 'SC, 'VE, 'WH, 'WJ and G-AADT being used by Col. G. L. P. Henderson for tuition and pleasure flying from 1926, until 'RD and 'SC went joyriding in South Africa and the survivors were taken over by the new Brooklands School of Flying in 1928. Most famous of all Avro 548s, however, was the ancient G-EAFH, which, piloted by F. G. M. Sparkes,

102

won all three races at the Croydon Race Meeting on 17 September 1921, subsequently giving pleasure flights with the Welsh Aviation Co. In 1922 it went to Bekesbourne and became the property of the pioneer private owner Dr. E. D. Whitehead Reid until 1927. It finished its days joyriding on Southport Sands and it finally crashed there on 31 May 1935 during a low altitude aerobatic display. It was operated by the Giro Aviation Co. Ltd. for whom the last two British 548s, G-ABMB and 'SV, were built at Barton by Berkshire Aviation Tours Ltd. in 1931.

In 1925 the Aircraft Disposal Co. Ltd. produced its 120 h.p. Airdisco engine of similar layout and design to the Renault. This was fitted into an Avro 504K airframe, E449, to become the first Avro 548A, G-EBKN. This rather lively Avro was well known along the South Coast in the early 'thirties, flown by Shoreham private owner A. G. Head, A.T.A. pilot of later days. The three factory-built 548s at Brough were also re-engined with Airdiscos, bringing the final total of Avro 548As to four.

Four overseas Avro 548 conversions have also been traced, viz. G-CACD, 'CI and 'CN by the Canadian Aircraft Co. Ltd. at Winnipeg in 1921 and G-AUBK in Australia in the same year.

The search for a rotary replacement also embraced the water-cooled engine, and another experimental Hamble-based 504K, G-EAPR, which had been flying with a 90 h.p. Curtiss OX-5 as the Avro 545, was re-engined with a 180-h.p. Wolseley Viper to take part in the 1921 Hendon Aerial Derby. Flown by L. R. Tait-Cox, it came fifth at 102·5 m.p.h. In this guise it was designated the Avro 552, and was used as a test vehicle for the twin float and N type oleo undercarriages and the Frise type ailerons of the later Avro 504N. Subsequently it was converted into the Cierva Autogiro C. 8V G-EBTX in 1927, and three years later emerged as a 552 once more, and, as G-ABGO, flew a great deal at Hanworth with the Inca Aviation Co. Three others also appeared, having been converted into 552s by C. B. Field at Kingswood Knoll, Surrey. These were G-ACAW, 'AX and

The Avro guinea pig G-EAPR as an Avro 552 floatplane in 1924, with Wolseley Viper engine, front radiator and tapered ailerons.

'RP, which in truly gaudy red and yellow colour schemes infested Hanworth on banner towing sorties until written off in 1936.

Fourteen 'Viper Avros' were also built by Canadian Vickers Ltd. at Montreal in 1924, including at least two-long range single-seat 552As and one 552B mounted on a central wooden float designed by the Philadelphia Navy Yard in 1925.

SPECIFICATION

Manufacturers: A. V. Roe and Co. Ltd., Newton Heath, Manchester. Conversions from existing Avro 504Ks by the firms stated.

Power Plants: (Avro 548) One 80 h.p. Renault.
(Avro 548A) One 120 h.p. Airdisco.
(Avro 552) One 180 h.p. Wolseley Viper.

Dimensions: Span, 36 ft. 0 in. Height, 10 ft. 5 in. Length (Avro 548), 29 ft. 5 in. (Avro 552), 28 ft. 0 in. Wing area, 330 sq. ft.

Weights: (Avro 548) Tare weight, 1,338 lb. All-up weight, 1,943 lb.
(Avro 548A) Tare weight, 1,460 lb. All-up weight, 2,150 lb.
(Avro 552) All-up weight, 2,260 lb.

Performance: (Avro 548) Maximum speed, 80 m.p.h. Cruising speed, 65 m.p.h. Initial climb, 350 ft./min. Range, 175 miles.
(Avro 548A) Maximum speed, 91 m.p.h. Cruising speed, 84 m.p.h. Initial climb, 400 ft./min. Range, 300 miles.

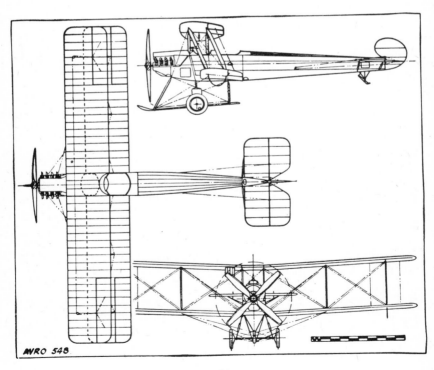

AVRO 548

Avro 504N G-ADBO, formerly K2354, at Bridgewater in 1935, showing the seven-cylinder Lynx engine and underwing banner rollers. (*A. J. Jackson*)

Avro 504N

The front fuselage of the Avro 504K invited the installation of the air-cooled radial rather than the in-line V engine, and as early as October 1919 a Clerget 504K, E4348, had been converted into G-EADL by the Cosmos Engineering Co. and equipped as a testbed for their new 100 h.p. Lucifer three-cylinder radial. This engine, later known as the Bristol Lucifer, was also fitted for test purposes to 504Ks G-EBFB and G-EAJB. In 1923, G-EADA, which had been in use as an Avro 504K since 1919, was also re-engined with the Lucifer, and at the same time fitted with tapered ailerons and the skidless undercarriage later to become standard on Avro 504Ns. In this form it was flown by H. A. Hamersley into fourth place at 71·2 m.p.h. in the 1923 Grosvenor Trophy Race at Lympne. Years later Lympne was the home of the fourth and last Lucifer Avro, G-ABVC, erected there from spares by H. C. Chater in 1932. In 1924 a special floatplane, G-EBJD, was built at Hamble for the Oxford University Arctic Expedition, and fitted with a 160 h.p. Armstrong Siddeley Lynx radial. Designated the Avro 504Q, it showed a close relationship to the Avro 546, and had the widened fuselage, dorsal fin and rear cabin. In addition, an inverted sledge was built into the fuselage decking. After shipment on the S.S. *Polarbjørn*, it was erected and flown, well inside the Arctic Circle, at Green Harbour, Spitzbergen, by Gibb Ellis and J. C. C. Taylor. During the course of the survey flying the aircraft reached latitude 80 deg. 15 min. N., the farthest north ever reached by an aeroplane at that time. The engine was brought home, but the airframe was abandoned at Green Harbour, where it was rediscovered in 1932, partly eaten by bears.

Modification of 504Ks G-EBHC, 'HD, 'HE and 'HT with Lynx radials and oleo compression struts in their undercarriages for Armstrong Whitworth in 1923 made them into hybrids loosely referred to as Avro 504Ns. They were used for tuition at the A.W. Flying School at Whitley until such activities were transferred to Air Service Training Ltd. at Hamble in 1931. Two survivors, G-EBHD and 'HE, were then sold to R. O. Roch and the North British Aviation Co. Ltd.,

G-EBHE, one of the original batch of four Avro 504Ns built in 1923, was nothing more than a Lynx-engined 504K with oleo undercarriage.

The second stage in civil 504N evolution was the fitting of Siskin type undercarriage to G-EADA, here seen taking off at Lympne, 1923. (*Flight*)

respectively, for joyriding, G-EBHE being fitted with a 130 h.p. Clerget to become a 504K once more. The first true Avro 504N, with Frise ailerons and Siskin-type undercarriage, to bear civil markings was G-EBKQ, flown in the 1925 King's Cup Race by Avro test pilot H. J. 'Bert' Hinkler. During its career as an Avro experimental machine it was fitted in March 1926 with very thick R.A.F. 30 aerofoil section wings, single interplane struts and a simplified undercarriage, in which form it was known as the Avro 582. At another stage in its life it was loaned to the Bristol Aeroplane Co. Ltd. for airtesting the 250 h.p. Titan radial engine, and ended its days with Air Service Training Ltd. as a floatplane fitted with a 150 h.p. Armstrong Siddeley Mongoose engine. On such low power it was intended as a 'penguin' for seaplane training, but under favourable conditions could be coaxed off the water by experienced pilots. It was referred to as an Avro 504O, although this designation properly belonged to the Lynx engined floatplane.

In its original form, G-EBKQ was the forerunner of the large batch of Avro 504N ab initio trainers built as 504K replacements for the R.A.F. in 1928–31. These were in no sense conversions, but a major redesign for Service use, incorporating the oleo undercarriage, tapered ailerons, thin centre section, twin gravity tanks under the top mainplane and the Armstrong Siddeley Lynx radial. These were, in turn, replaced by Avro Tutors, and when declared obsolete in 1933 were

106

disposed of by public tender. The civilian life of the 504N followed the familiar lines of its illustrious forebear, the 504K, a large number being employed for pleasure-flying with organized air circuses and for aerial advertising by specialist firms. Two main types of modification took place for banner-towing, winding rollers being fitted under the wings or a simple release gear housed in a box under the tail. The brothers L. J. and L. G. Anderson converted G-ADBO, 'BP and 'BR to the former type at Hanworth, and these will be remembered for their exhortations concerning various brands of tea in 1935. Air Publicity Ltd. favoured the second method, and had a considerable fleet of Avro 504Ns at Heston, consisting of G-ACPV, G-ADDA, 'ET and a number of others. The Earl of Cardigan was for many years unique as the enthusiastic owner of G-ACZC, flying it from his private field at Marlborough. Four other Avro 504Ns reverted to their ancestral 130 h.p. Clerget rotaries as G-ADGB, 'GC, 'GM and 'GN, two of which flew with Zenith Airways on Camber Sands, Sussex, during the summer of 1935. These

The Avro 504N G-EBKQ was rebuilt in 1926 as the Avro 582, with thick section wings without upper ailerons, simplified undercarriage and single interplane struts.

The Avro 504N G-EBKQ as a testbed for the 210 h.p. Bristol Titan engine at Filton, 1928. (*Bristol Photo*)

The solitary Avro 504Q, G-EBJD, which the Oxford University Expedition took to the Arctic in 1924–25. (*J. C. C. Taylor*)

Air Service Training's Mongoose-engined Avro 504O K-8/G-EBKQ taking off near Hamble slipway in 1932. (*Flight Photo 12327*)

One of the Clerget-engined Avro 504K Mk. IIs at Croydon, Easter 1935, before its delivery flight to Zenith Airways at Camber Sands.

were the sole examples of the 504K Mk. II. A number of 504Ns were, however, fitted with the 150 h.p. Armstrong Siddeley Mongoose IIIA engine, a combination which, on reduced fuel load, proved very suitable for short joy flights. To complete all the possibilities, the ingenious C. B. Field revived the original 504N alternative by fitting a Lucifer engine into G-AEAA at Kingswood, Surrey, in 1936.

The sturdy Avro 504N was a very common sight in British skies right up to the outbreak of war, when several of the Air Publicity aircraft were impressed, G-ADBM, 'BP, 'ET and 'EV becoming AX871, AX874, AX875 and BK892 respectively, for experimental glider and radar work along the South Coast.

SPECIFICATION

Manufacturers: A. V. Roe and Co. Ltd., Newton Heath, Manchester.
Power Plants: One 100 h.p. Bristol Lucifer.
  One 150 h.p. Armstrong Siddeley Mongoose IIIA.
  One 215 h.p. Armstrong Siddeley Lynx IVC.
Dimensions: Span, 36 ft. 0 in. Length, 28 ft. 6 in. Height, 10 ft. 11 in. Wing area, 320 sq. ft.
Weights: Tare weight, 1,584 lb. All-up weight, 2,240 lb.
Performance: Maximum speed, 100 m.p.h. Cruising speed, 85 m.p.h. Initial climb, 770 ft./min. Ceiling, 14,600 ft. Range, 250 miles.

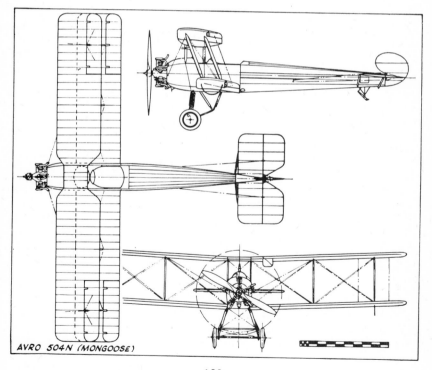

AVRO 504N (MONGOOSE)

H. J. Hinkler's Avro 534 Baby with the original 1911 Green engine.

Avro 534 Baby

The Baby, first practical light aeroplane produced in Great Britain after the First World War, was a conventional single-seat biplane featuring the traditional Avro circular rudder. Nine of these machines were built in the Avro works at Hamble, each and every one playing its part in laying sure foundations for the light aeroplane movement which came in later years. The unregistered prototype, powered by the identical 35 h.p. water-cooled Green engine fitted in the Avro Type D biplane in 1911, crashed immediately after first take-off at Hamble by Capt. Hicks on 10 May 1919. The engine was salvaged and fitted into the second aircraft, K-131, and, despite its age, brought the Baby to victory in the handicap section of the Aerial Derby in June 1919, followed a month later by an outright win in the Victory Trophy Race. To emphasize that it was no low powered freak, Avro test pilot H. A. Hamersley flew it non-stop from Hounslow Heath to Brussels in 2 hours 50 minutes in August 1919, afterwards going on to demonstrate it at the Amsterdam Exhibition. During a stunt flying session with the Avro joyriding campaign at seaside resorts later in the year, the markings were changed to G-EACQ, and on the last day of the following May, H. J. Hinkler flew it non-stop from Croydon, over the Alps, to Turin in $9\frac{1}{2}$ hours. After exhibition at the 1920 Olympia Aero Show and participation in the Aerial Derby, Hinkler shipped it to Australia, and on 11 April 1921 flew 800 miles non-stop from Sydney to Bundaberg in 9 hours to set up an Australian long distance record.

Two weeks later, on 27 April, after a forced landing on a beach in tropical rain, it was towed 16 miles to Newcastle by horse team and remained active as VH-UCQ until 1937. The Baby then remained in store until the last owner, J. J. Smith, presented it to the Queensland Museum and its last flight was as airfreight from Melbourne to Brisbane on 18 March 1970 for exhibition beside Hinkler's Avro Avian G-EBOV.

The close proximity of Hamble to Southampton Water invited seaplane operations, and it is not therefore surprising that the third machine was a floatplane with extra fin area and orthodox rudder. This was the Avro 534A Water Baby, and, despite teething troubles with water soakage, flew quite successfully until it crashed on 7 September 1921. The fourth Baby, G-EAUG, built with plywood fuselage, also had tapered ailerons, and was termed the Avro 534B. It was flown by H. A. Hamersley in the 1920 Aerial Derby, the slight reduction in wing area making it a trifle faster than G-EACQ, and in the event they carried off first and second places. They were followed in July 1920 by the Avro 543 Baby G-EAUM, which carried pilot and passenger in an enlarged cockpit, but was otherwise a standard Baby with the fuselage lengthened by 2 ft. 6 in. Flown by Capt. T. Tulley, it lapped the 1921 Aerial Derby course at 73·67 m.p.h. until forced down at Brooklands, and the following year was raced with a fairing over the rear seat. In 1926 it went to Shoreham, where it lost its superannuated Green and attendant plumbing in favour of the more modern 60 h.p. Cirrus I, and in 1927 was jointly owned by L. E. R. Bellairs and F. G. Miles, in whom it inspired the idea of building the Southern Martlet. After changing hands several times it was acquired by Roper Brown who flew it at Southend from 1932 until the C. of A. expired in 1934. The new owner then flew it to Cambridge on a one flight permit for overhaul but it was not heard of again.

All the remaining Babies were equally remarkable; the Avro 534C G-EAXL had lower wings of reduced span for racing purposes, and after making its initial flight at Hamble in June 1921, was entered in the Aerial Derby of 16 July but Hinkler had trouble with it, and forced landed at Sidcup. Then in September came G-EAYM, the Avro 534D Baby, which had steel engine bearers, a larger radiator and very ample cooling louvres in the cowlings. This machine was built for service

The clipped wing Avro 534C Baby which met a watery end in Southampton Water.

Maj. C. R. Carr taxying the Avro 554 Antarctic Baby on Southampton Water in 1921.

The tropicalised Avro 534D Baby built for India.

The two-seat Avro 543 Baby at Shoreham in 1926 with 60 h.p. A.D.C. Cirrus I air-cooled engine.

in India to the order of E. Villiers. The next two Babies, however, went to vastly cooler climes, G-EBDA completing in May 1922 the first flight ever made between London and Moscow. The pilot was a Russian named Gwaiter, who had considerable difficulty in crossing Germany, where a Russian subject flying a British aeroplane caused international complications. Last of the breed was the Avro 554 Antarctic Baby built in 1921 as a photo reconnaissance aircraft for use by Sir Ernest Shackleton's South Polar Expedition. Limited shipboard stowage space called for swift dismantling and erection by gloved hands and without rigging worries. Steel tube struts therefore replaced the flying wires. N-type interplane struts were fitted and all bolts were extra large. Low air temperatures precluded water cooling and an 80 h.p. Le Rhône rotary was fitted. After trials on Southampton Water by its pilot, Major C. R. Carr, it was embarked in the *Quest* at Tower Bridge and left for the far south. It was never used and arrived back aboard the *Quest* on 16 September 1922.

In 1923 the Antarctic Baby was bought by Bowring Bros. of St. John's and registered to the Aerial Survey Co. as G-EBFE for test flying at Hamble before shipment to Newfoundland to operate on skis as spotter for Bowring's sealing fleet. It was flown initially by R. S. Grandy but mainly by C. S. Caldwell until replaced by an Avro Avian in 1927.

SPECIFICATION

Manufacturers: A. V. Roe and Co. Ltd., Hamble Aerodrome, near Southampton, Hants.
Power Plants: (Avro 534 and 543) One 35 h.p. Green.
(Avro 543)   One 60 h.p. A.D.C. Cirrus I.
(Avro 554)   One 80 h.p. Le Rhône.

	Avro 534	Avro 543	Avro 554
Span	25 ft. 0 in.	25 ft. 0 in.	26 ft. 3 in.
Length	17 ft. 6 in.	20 ft. 0 in.	22 ft. 5 in.
Height	7 ft. 6 in.	7 ft. 6 in.	—
Wing area	176½ sq. ft.	176½ sq. ft.	184½ sq. ft.
Tare weight	607 lb.	630 lb.	980 lb.
All-up weight	860 lb.	970 lb.	1,569 lb.
Maximum speed	78 m.p.h.	82 m.p.h.	90 m.p.h.
Cruising speed	70 m.p.h.	70 m.p.h.	70 m.p.h.
Initial climb	325 ft./min.	450 ft./min.	330 ft./min.
Ceiling	12,000 ft.	12,000 ft.	—
Range	240 miles	225 miles	190 miles

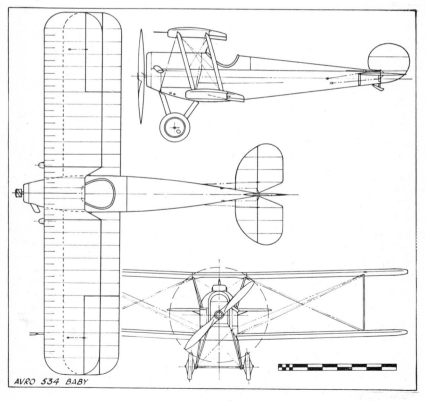

AVRO 534 BABY

Avro Avian IV c/n 226 at Croydon in March 1929 with Spanish ferry markings for delivery to the Marquis di Cordoba. (*Aeroplane*)

Avro 594 Avian

The prototype Avro 581 Avian, G-EBOV, built for the *Daily Mail* two-seat light aeroplane trials held at Lympne in September 1926, was an orthodox biplane fitted with a 75 h.p. Armstrong Siddeley Genet engine, the characteristic circular Avro rudder and square cut wing tips. Although a promising entry in which H. J. Hinkler gained second place in three of the six trials, it was eliminated with magneto drive trouble. After repairs, however, it won the £200 prize in the race sponsored by the motor industry. In modified form as the Avro 581E Avian with an 80 h.p. A.D.C. Cirrus I, additional centre section struts and a triangular fin, the machine was again successfully raced by Hinkler at the Bournemouth Easter Meeting. In the following September he made headline news by flying it non-stop from Croydon to Riga in Latvia. Rounded wing tips were then fitted, and between 7 and 22 February 1928 H. J. Hinkler made his now historic flight from Croydon to Darwin, Australia, in $15\frac{1}{2}$ days. His machine rests today in Brisbane Museum, monument to its immortal owner and to Roy Chadwick's design genius.

Two Avro 594 Avian Is were then built: G-EBQN for the R.A.E. Aero Club at Farnborough, and 'QL for the Lancashire Aero Club, Woodford. A small batch of production Avians IIs was built in 1927 with split-axle undercarriages and lower engine mountings, the fourth machine being fitted with the second of the hand-made Avro Alpha 90 h.p. radials and designated the Avro 594A. In this aircraft, G-EBSD, Mrs. Elliott Lynn took off from Woodford on 8 October 1927 to reach 19,200 ft. and set up a new light aeroplane altitude record. One Avian II with Cirrus II was supplied to the Cape Town Flying Club as G-UAAC and three with 75 h.p. Armstrong Siddeley Genet II radials went to Australia as G-AUFY to 'GA, but Avian development moved swiftly and by September 1927 the first Mk. III had already flown with an A.D.C. Cirrus II and narrow chord metal interplane and centre section struts. Registered G-EBTU and named 'Red Rose', it made a leisurely trip to Australia between October 1927 and March 1928 in 32 flying days, flown by W. N. Lancaster and Mrs. Keith Miller. Less than a month later Lady Heath (formerly Mrs. Elliott Lynn) flew another Avian III, G-EBUG, all the way from the Cape to Croydon, while in 1930 yet another lady pilot, Miss

Winifred Brown, won the King's Cup with Avian III G-EBVZ. The Croydon–Cape record was also broken by an Avian III when Lt. Murdoch ferried G-EBVU out to the *Cape Argus* in 13½ days, arriving on 12 August 1928. At £600 ex-works, they were good value, and were used by several clubs and private owners, but overseas operations demanded internal strengthening, which soon resulted in the Mk. IIIA. The first of these, G-EBYM and 'YN, were sold in Spain, the former leaving Croydon as M-CAAE on 7 September 1928. Another, G-EBYR, was flown in the 1928 King's Cup Race by Edgar Percival. In 1930 this aircraft went to Australia, where it became G-AUJY. Two more, fitted with Armstrong Siddeley Genet II radials went to Ireland as EI-AAA and 'AB but returned to British ownership as G-ABPU and G-ACGT a few years later. In common with all Genet Avians, whatever the mark, they were designated Avro 594B.

The 58 Avian IIIAs built included 16 for the American distributors, Air Associates Inc., N.Y.; one for S.A.A.F. evaluation; one for aerial survey in Tanganyika and a seaplane designated Avro 605 for American round-the-world

The   prototype   Avro   581   Avian   as   flown   at   the   1926   Lympne   Trials.
(*Royal Aeronautical Society*)

The Avro 605 Avian floatplane with Cirrus III engine. (*P. T. Capon*)

115

flier G. H. Storck. This was NX6663 'Seattle Spirit' which left Hamble on 15 September 1928 but capsized taking off from Bastia, Corsica, a few days later. One other Avian IIIA, G-EBVA, was also temporarily a seaplane at Hamble in 1928.

Later that year, when the Avian appeared with forward sloping undercarriage radius rods and horn balanced ailerons as the Mk. IV, it had reached the limit of its development as a wooden aeroplane. The first of some 90 production machines were G-AAAT with Cirrus III for A.D.C. Aircraft Ltd.; G-AADL with 80 h.p. Genet II for J. D. Siddeley; and G-AABX 'Comète' with Cirrus III for P. T. Eckersley. The first of these, re-engined with the prototype 105 h.p. Cirrus Hermes I, flew from Croydon to Berlin in 4 hr. 52 min. non-stop on 19 October 1928 piloted by T. Neville Stack.

The majority of Avian IVs were exported, notably to the U.S.A. via Air Associates Inc. and the Whittlesey Manufacturing Co. of Bridgeport, Conn. Two with Genet IIs went to the Ottawa Flying Club as CF-CAQ and 'AR and others were sold in Argentina, Australia, Brazil, Mexico, Norway, South Africa and Spain. X-CRIA, one of 14 for the Chinese Naval Air Service, was flown from Croydon to Shanghai by Messrs. Johannesen and Wen Lin Chen between 2 March and 28 May 1928. Another, N-38, flown to Norway by Alf Gunnestad in June 1929, operated as LN-ABF with the 1933–34 Norwegian Antarctic Expedition.

The last Avian of all, G-ADEO, was built as a private project by A.S.T. ground engineers at Hamble in 1935, and comprised the fuselage, engine and other major components of the Alpha engined Cierva C. 17 Mk. II Autogiro G-AAGJ. It was thus equivalent to an Avro 594A Avian II, and, as a tribute to its engine, the joint owners flew as the Alpha Club.

Most surviving Avians were impressed as instructional airframes in 1939, and only four survived the war. The Mk. IVM G-ACKE flew at Baginton for a time, but donated its fuselage to the Sports Avian G-ABEE after an argument with a Tiger Moth in 1950. The Giro Aviation Co.'s Avian IIIA G-EBZM, stored since 1939, left Southport in 1958 after a stay of 19 years and in 1972 was in the hands of the Northern Aircraft Preservation Society at Stockport along with G-ABEE. Another Avian IIIA, G-ACGT, Genet powered, was also intact in store at Linthwaite near Huddersfield, Yorks.

Avro 594B Avian II G-ABPU with Genet II engine being tuned at Brooklands by J. F. Legard in readiness for the 1932 King's Cup Race. (*Flight*)

The Alpha Club's rebuilt Avro 594A Avian II flying near Hamble in 1935.

SPECIFICATION

Manufacturers: A. V. Roe and Co. Ltd., Newton Heath, Manchester, and Hamble Aerodrome, near Southampton, Hants.

	581	594 Mk. II	594 Mk. IIIA	605
Engine	Genet	Cirrus II	Cirrus III	Cirrus III
Horse power	75	85	95	95
Span	32 ft. 0 in.	28 ft. 0 in.	28 ft. 0 in.	28 ft. 0 in.
Length	24 ft. 6 in.	24 ft. 3 in.	24 ft. 3 in.	25 ft. 0 in.
Height	—	8 ft. 6 in.	8 ft. 6 in.	—
Wing area	294 sq. ft.	245 sq. ft.	245 sq. ft.	245 sq. ft.
Tare weight	750 lb.	907 lb.	935 lb.	1,053 lb.
All-up weight	1,580 lb.	1,467 lb.	1,435 lb.	1,600 lb.
Maximum speed	70 m.p.h.	98 m.p.h.	102 m.p.h.	97 m.p.h.
Cruising speed	—	82 m.p.h.	87 m.p.h.	82 m.p.h.
Initial climb	—	—	750 ft./min.	480 ft./min.
Ceiling	—	15,000 ft.	18,000 ft.	13,000 ft.
Range	—	325 miles	400 miles	400 miles

Production: (a) Avro 581 Avian prototype
One aircraft only: G-EBOV (c/n 5116).

      (b) Avro 594 Avian I
Two aircraft only: G-EBQL and 'QN, (c/n R3/AV/117 and 100 respectively).

      (c) Avro 594 Avian II
Nine aircraft comprising five British registered machines and the following exported: (c/n R3/AV/122) G-UAAC; (123) G-AUGA; (126) G-AUFY; (127) G-AUFZ.

      (d) Avro 594 Avian III and IIIA
Thirty-three British registered aircraft and the following for export or the R.A.F.: (c/n R3/CN/102) G-AUHC; (103) Senor Juan Acuna; (105) G-CAWI; (106)

117

Argentine; (108) M-CCAC; (109) G-UAAS; (110) G-IAAX; (115) G-CAUH; (119) J. F. Costa; (120) G-AUHK; (122) M-CDAA; (125) J9182; (127–132) G-CANL to 'NQ; (135) NC6881; (136) NC6882; (137) NC7012; (138) NC7013; (139) NC7154; (140) NC7155; (141) NC7289; (142) NC7290; (143) NC7625; (144) G-AUHZ; (145) G-AUIK; (146) G-AUIL; (147) NC7869; (148) NC392; (149) G-CAQA; (150) CF-AFQ; (156) M-CDAD; (157) NC7626; (158) Argentine; (159) G-UAAZ; (162) G-NZEE; (163) G-CAVB; (164) G-AUHY; (165) S.A.A.F.; (166) NC7900; (167) G-UAAT; (168) G-UAAU; (174) G-NZAV; (175) G-UABB; (176) South Africa; (184) G-AUJF; (185) G-AUJG; (186) NC10075; (187) NC10076; (188) NC367; (189) NC362; (192) G-AUIU; (193) G-AUIV; (198) M-CPAA; (199) ZK-AAN; (200) G-UAAK.

(e) Avro 594 Avian IV

Sixteen British registered aircraft and the following exported: (c/n 190) NC540E; (191) PP-TCB; (194) NC502E; (195) NC503E; (196) NC541E; (197) NC549E; (201) G-AUKD; (202) G-AUJZ; (203) Argentine; (205) G-AUKR; (206) Argentine; (207–219) 13 for China; (220) X-CRIA; (221) CF-CAQ; (222) CF-CAR; (224) Argentine; (225) G-UAAV; (226) M-W111; (227) Aero Club of Yucatan, Mexico; (242) NC550E; (243–246) NC600E to NC603E; (247) NC648E; (248) NC649E; (249–251) NC671E to NC673E; (252) NC11048; (253–255) NC674E to NC676E; (256–259) NC818E to NC821E; (260–262) NC833E to NC835E; (263) NC221H; (264) NC836E; (265–267) NC222H to NC224H; (268) NC321H; (269) NC632E; (270) NC524K; (271) NC525K; (272) NC710K; (273) NC711K; (274–277) NC550K to NC553K; (278) NC712K; (279) NC713K; (280) NC577K; (281) NC737K; (303) ZS-AAG; (323) N-38; (327) VH-UMW; (328) VH-URM.

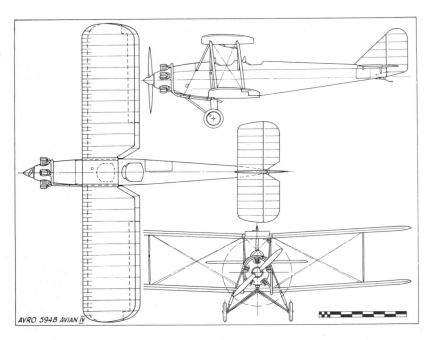

AVRO 594B AVIAN IV

The A.D.C. Aircraft Co.'s Avian IVM, Hermes I, in which S. A. Thorn averaged 117·9 m.p.h. in the 1930 King's Cup Race.

Avro 616 Avian IVM

The Avian IV with steel tube fuselage, identified by its prominent stringers, was known as the Avro 616 Avian IVM, but Martlesham trials with G-AACV (90 h.p. Cirrus III) in March 1929 showed the need for more power so that early deliveries had either the 105 h.p. Cirrus Hermes I or the 100 h.p. (five-cylinder) Genet Major radial. J9783 was supplied to the Air Ministry for competitive trials with the Hawker Tomtit, and large batches were despatched to Canada 1929–30 for erection by the Ottawa Car Mfg. Co. who also built 18 with 135 h.p. (seven-cylinder) Genet Major Is for the R.C.A.F. The Whittlesey Co. also built a few. Others were built at Woodford for civil or military use in Argentina, Australia, Estonia, Mexico, New Zealand, Singapore, South Africa and Spain.

Henlys Ltd. of Heston popularised the type in the U.K. with demonstrator G-AATL (Hermes I), and Air Service Training Ltd. used four, G-ABKA, 'KB, 'SC and 'UN, for instruction at Hamble where, each summer, 'KB was fitted with floats for seaplane training. The Shell Company's Cairo-based G-AATV (Genet Major) was the first of four metal Avians used by the petroleum industry, the others being British Petroleum's G-ABIB 'Peri' and two belonging to Anglo American, G-ABDN and 'IE 'High Test', the last being a Sports Avian (see below) in which Flt. Lt. T. Rose left Lympne on 11 February 1931 in an unsuccessful attempt to lower the England–Cape record. G-ABIC/VR-TAD 'Tanganyika' took part, with other Avro types, in mapping the territory and Gösta Andree delivered SE-ACP (Hermes II) to the Gothenburg Aero Club in June 1931. The largest purchaser of the Hermes model was China for whom sales were handled by the Far East Aviation Co. Ltd. in Hong Kong.

A Hermes I version with straight-axle undercarriage, cut-away top decking and racing windscreens for the 1930 King's Cup Race was known as the Sports Avian. Two examples, G-AAWI and 'YU took part, and another, VH-UQE 'Dabs' (Gipsy II) piloted by H. F. Broadbent, completed a 7,600 mile round-Australia flight on 6 September 1931. A fourth, G-AAXH, flew at Hanworth in 1936 with an experimental reversed tricycle undercarriage designed by British Landing Gears Ltd.

G-AABS, one of three pre-production Genet Major powered Avian IVMs used by A. V. Roe and Co. Ltd. for trial installation work, was fitted with a Sports Avian undercarriage and flew with Class B marking K-2 to test the special 30 ft. span wings built for the long range, single-seat, Gipsy II powered Avian IVA G-ABCF 'Southern Cross Junior' in which Sir Charles Kingsford Smith lowered the England–Australia record to 9 days 21 hours in October 1930. It was used later by Guy Menzies for the first solo crossing of the Tasman Sea to New Zealand but crashed at Sydney on 12 April 1931 after shipment back.

A second long-range single seater VH-UQG 'Southern Cross Minor' was basically a standard Avian with 28 ft. wings, thus differing from 'CF which was a

Manchester-built Avian IVM seaplane CF-AHV, 100 h.p. five-cylinder Genet Major radial, on the Ottawa River in 1931.

Sir Charles Kingsford Smith's long-range Avian IVA 'Southern Cross Junior'.

120

H. F. 'Jim' Broadbent flying the record breaking Sports Avian VH-UQE 'Dabs' near Melbourne in 1931.

G-AAYV, the first Avian Monoplane, Genet Major I radial, at Hanworth before the 1930 King's Cup Race. (*Aeroplane*)

Sports Avian variant. 'Smithy' left Melbourne in 'QG on 21 September 1931 to attempt a record trip to England but gave up in Turkey. Re-registered G-ABLK it was then used for an attack on the England–Cape record by W. N. Lancaster who left Lympne on 11 April 1933 but was not seen again after landing next day at In Salah on the trans-Saharan motor track and it was not until 29 years later, in March 1962, that the wreck was located 170 miles south of Reggane.

British Landing Gears Ltd. were responsible for the tricycle undercarriage on G-AAXH. The humped decking of the Sports Avian should be noted.

Also competing in the 1930 King's Cup Race were two special Sports Avian monoplanes, (Avro 625) G-AAYV with Genet Major flown by F. Tomkins and 'YW with Hermes I flown by T. Neville Stack. G-AAYV was later reconstructed as a biplane but 'YW remained a monoplane first with Sqn. Ldr. R. L. R. Atcherley at Market Drayton and in 1940 with W. L. Handley at Elmdon.

The last three Avians, built for the Liverpool Aero Club in 1933, were Sports Avian G-ACGV (Gipsy III) and Avian IVMs G-ACIF (Gipsy I) and 'KE (Gipsy II), the last of which survived until destroyed in collision with a Tiger Moth at Baginton in 1950. Several others, surviving in 1972, included CF-CDQ in the National Museum, Ottawa; CF-CDV in the Pioneer Museum, Wetaskiwin, Alberta; Sports Avian G-ABEE stored at Stockport by the Northern Aircraft

The Liverpool Aero Club's unique D.H. Gipsy III powered Sports Avian G-ACGV at Hooton in 1935. (*E. J. Riding*)

Preservation Society; ZK-ACM flying in New Zealand; and G-ABLF/VH-UVX restored and flying at Penola, S.A., as VH-UQE, marks originally carried by H. F. Broadbent's record breaking 'Dabs'.

SPECIFICATION

Manufacturers: A. V. Roe and Co. Ltd., Newton Heath, Manchester.
The Ottawa Car Manufacturing Co., Ltd., Ottawa, Canada.
The Whittlesey Body Co. Inc., Bridgeport, Connecticut.

Power Plants: One 90 h.p. A.D.C. Cirrus III.
One 100 h.p. de Havilland Gipsy I.
One 100 h.p. Armstrong Siddeley Genet Major (5-cylinder).
One 105 h.p. A.D.C. Cirrus Hermes I.
One 115 h.p. A.D.C. Cirrus Hermes II.
One 120 h.p. de Havilland Gipsy II.
One 120 h.p. de Havilland Gipsy III.
One 135 h.p. Armstrong Siddeley Genet Major (7-cylinder).

	616 Mk. IV/IVM	616 Sports	616 Mk. IVA
Engine	Hermes I*	Hermes I	Gipsy II
Horse-power	105	105	120
Span	28 ft. 0 in.	28 ft. 0 in.	30 ft. 0 in.
Length	24 ft. 3 in.	24 ft. 3 in.	24 ft. 3 in.
Height	8 ft. 6 in.	8 ft. 6 in.	8 ft. 6 in.
Wing area	245 sq. ft.	245 sq. ft.	262 sq. ft.
Tare weight	1,005 lb.	1,005 lb.	1,100 lb.
All-up weight	1,523 lb.	1,600 lb.	2,225 lb.
Maximum speed	105 m.p.h.	120 m.p.h.	115 m.p.h.
Cruising speed	90 m.p.h.	105 m.p.h.	94 m.p.h.
Initial climb	—	—	485 ft./min.
Ceiling	—	—	12,500 ft.
Range	360 miles	420 miles	1,700 miles

* Alternatively 100 h.p. Genet Major.

Production: (a) By A. V. Roe and Co. Ltd., Manchester; thirty-one British registered aircraft and the following for export: (c/n 240) Mexico; (282–283) R.C.A.F. 92–93; (284) R.C.A.F. 94/CF-CAZ; (285) 95/CF-CAY; (286–287) 96–97; (288) 98/CF-AEZ; (289) 99/CF-CAJ; (290–291) 100–101; (292) Canada; (293) CF-CBA; (294–295) Canada; (296–297) 132, 125; (298) CF-CBD; (299) CF-AHV; (300) CF-CBC; (301) CF-CBB; (302) CF-CBJ; (305) Mexico; (306) Canada; (307) 126/CF-CDG; (308) 127/CF-CDU; (309) 128/CF-CDH; (310) 129/CF-CDE; (311) Canada; (313) CF-CDJ; (314) CF-CDQ; (315) CF-CDR; (329) Mexico; (332) VT-ABD; (334–353) S.A.A.F 504–523; (361) VR-HAA; (362) VR-HAB; (363–368) Estonian Air Force; (369) VH-UMX; (372) VH-UOE; (385) ZS-ABQ; (387) airframe to Hamble; (414) VH-UOB; (425–434) Canada; (443–452) Canada; (453) airframe to Brooklands; (465) VR-HAD; (466) VR-HAF; (469–471) China; (475) VR-HAE; (494) VR-HAG; (495) VR-HAH; (496) ZK-ACM; (530) SE-ACP; (533) airframe to Hamble; (534–535) China; (554)

VR-HAI; (555) VR-HAJ; (556) VR-HAL; (557) VR-HAK; (559) VR-HAM; (560) VR-HAN; (563–568) China; (577) VR-HAO; (578) VR-HAP; (579) VR-HAS; (580) VR-HAT; (590) VR-HBB; (591) VR-HBC; (598) VR-HBJ; (599) VR-HBI; (600) VR-HBO; (601) VR-HBL; (602) VR-HBS; (603) VR-HBT; (604) VR-HBM; (605) VR-HBP; (608) VR-HBV; (609) VR-HBW; (610) VR-HBY; (611) VR-HBU; (612) VR-HBR; (613) China; (614) VR-HCG; (615) VR-HCF; (616) VR-HCB; (617) VR-HCC; (618) VR-HCK; (619) VR-HCJ.

(b) By the Ottawa Car Manufacturing Co. Ltd.

(c/n 316) CF-CDV; (317) CF-CDT; (318) R.C.A.F.141/CF-CDW; (319) 142; (320) 143/CF-CDX; (321) 144/CF-CDL; (65249) CF-CFC; (65250) CF-CFH; (65251) CF-CFI; (65252) CF-CEW; (65253–65254) untraced; (65255–65258) CF-CEY to 'FB; (65259) CF-CEV.

(c) By the Whittlesey Body Co. Inc.

At least (c/n 100) NC530M; (101) NC199N; (102) NC804N; (103) NC805N; (104) NC806N; (105) NC47V; (106) NC48V.

(d) Avro 616 Sports Avian

Fourteen British registered aircraft and three for export: (c/n 455) Mexico; (499) ZK-ACM; (531) VH-UQE.

(e) Avro 616 Avian IVA and Avian V

Two British registered aircraft, G-ABCF and G-ABLK, detailed in Appendix E.

(f) Avro 625 Avian Monoplane

Two British registered aircraft, G-AAYV and G-AAYW, detailed in Appendix E.

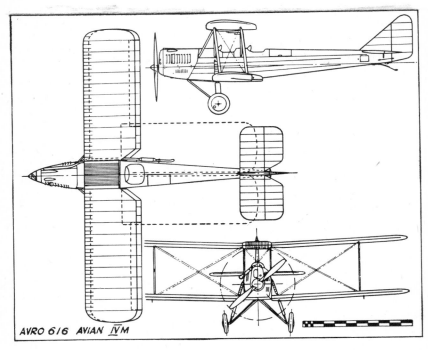

AVRO 616 AVIAN IVM

The Avro Ten which Midland and Scottish Air Ferries Ltd. used on their internal services in 1933–34.

Avro Ten, Five, Six and 642

In 1928 A. V. Roe and Co. Ltd. acquired a licence to build the highly successful Fokker F.VIIB/3m for sale throughout the British Empire, excluding Canada. It was a three-engined high-wing transport featuring a unique welded steel tube fuselage and a one-piece, plywood-covered cantilever wing. The British model was known as the Avro 618 Ten, so named because it carried eight passengers and two crew. It was externally similar to its Dutch prototype, but differed slightly in detail to meet British airworthiness requirements, notably in the downward tilted thrust line of the centre engine. Total production was 14 and five of them were supplied to Air Commodore Sir Charles Kingsford Smith for use by Australian National Airways. The first of these was exhibited at the 1929 Olympia Aero Show, and later carried British markings G-AADM for test flying. It then went to Australia, and as VH-UMF 'Southern Cloud' was the flagship of the A.N.A. fleet, making headline news on 21 March 1931, when it disappeared without trace over the Strathbozie Mountains while being flown on the Sydney–Melbourne service by Capt. W. T. Shortridge. The wreck was not located until 26 October 1958.

Among the others were VH-UMG 'Southern Star' in which Kingsford Smith flew the Christmas mail to Croydon in December 1931; and VH-UMH 'Southern Sky' taken over by New England Airways in 1934 and renamed 'City of Grafton' (together with the Avro Tens VH-UNJ and 'PI supplied originally to the Queensland Air Navigation Co. Ltd.) for the Brisbane–Narromine section of the Empire air route. VH-UMI 'Southern Moon' was re-engined with 330 h.p. Wright Whirlwinds as VH-UXX 'Faith in Australia' for Charles Ulm's long distance flights and in 1941 Stephens Aviation Ltd. used it for casualty evacuation from New Guinea, but it eventually rotted away behind a hangar at Townsville, Queensland.

Imperial Airways Ltd. added the Avro Ten G-AASP 'Achilles' to its fleet early in 1930 for general charter work. It was despatched to Cairo in April 1931, and employed by the Iraq Petroleum Co. Ltd. on its desert pipeline patrol, its place at

125

Croydon being taken by a second machine, G-ABLU 'Apollo'. The latter followed its sister machine to the Near East in October 1932, where both remained until replaced by D.H. Dragons in June 1933. They then continued on European charter work for Imperial Airways Ltd., and were based at Le Bourget, also operating the Paris–Zurich run. In 1938 'Apollo' was destroyed by fire after striking a wireless mast in fog between Ghent and Bruges while flying on the Brussels–Croydon scheduled service.

One of four Avro Tens built for the Indian State Airways in 1931 was diverted for the use of the Viceroy as VT-ACT, and two others left Heston on 11 January 1932 with British ferry markings G-ABSP and 'SR flown by Flt. Lt. Christopher Clarkson and Mr. Dan Cameron who handed them over to the Egyptian Government at Almaza a week later. The first crashed at Assiut while in service with the Egyptian Army Air Force but the other was sold to Indian National Airways in 1935 as VT-AFX. The last machine of the quartet, G-ACGF, was completed to the order of John Sword to supplement the Airspeed Ferries on the internal services of Midland and Scottish Air Ferries Ltd. and was commissioned in 1933.

Last of all the Avro Tens was K2682, delivered to the Wireless and Equipment Flight at the R.A.E., Farnborough, on 27 July 1936.

Wilson Airways' Avro 619 Five VP-KAE with original cockpit canopy.

Avro 624 Six prototype, G-AAYR, with flat windscreen and high mounted nacelles.
(*Flight Photo 8874*)

Avro 642/2m G-ACFV/VH-UXD at Brisbane during the delivery flight to New Guinea in 1936.

The Viceroy's Avro 642/4m VT-AFM 'Star of India' at Croydon in December 1934.
(*Flight Photo 11097S*)

The Avro 619 Five was a scaled down version for pilot and four passengers, and an entirely new design by Roy Chadwick. Like its larger forebear, it was initially supplied to overseas order, two being delivered in 1929 to Wilson Airways Ltd. at Nairobi, Kenya, and a third to Australia. The first of two Avro Fives to see service in this country was the Avro demonstrator G-AASO, entered in the King's Cup Race on 5 July 1930 by Sir Philip Sassoon and flown by Flt. Lt. S. L. G. Pope. It was not a spectacular racer, and conveniently retired at its home base, Woodford. In September 1930 'SO was taken over by Wilson Airways Ltd. to replace their first machine, VP-KAE 'Knight of the Grail', and although allotted the Kenya marks VP-KAH, these were never used. It flew as G-AASO on the African services until 18 January 1932, when it was damaged beyond repair in a forced landing 12 miles from its destination while en route from Salisbury to Broken Hill.

A slightly larger version with cockpit for two pilots side by side appeared in May 1930 as the Avro 624 Six with engine nacelles fitted directly to the underside of the wing. After test flights at Woodford, the outboard engines of the first machine, K-5/G-AAYR, were refitted in underslung nacelles in the manner of the

Avro Five, and after extensive demonstrations at Heston in 1931 it was sold to the Far East Aviation Co. Ltd., Hong Kong, who eventually disposed of it to the Chinese Government together with the third Avro Six, VR-HBF. The second machine, G-ABBY, remodelled in 1933 as a navigation trainer for Air Service Training Ltd., remained at Hamble until taken over by No. 11 Air Observers' Navigation School in the early days of the 1939–45 war.

The final high-wing development, not outwardly recognizable as a Fokker derivative, was the twin-engined Avro 642/2m initially named the Avro Eighteen, which used the Avro Ten wing lowered to the shoulder position with the engines mounted directly on it. The resultant aircraft was much cleaner aerodynamically, and when first built had a semi-circular glazed front to the pilot's compartment which was also immediately replaced by a conventional stepped windscreen. The 16-seat prototype, G-ACFV, was delivered to Midland and Scottish Air Ferries Ltd. at Renfrew in April 1934, and was followed by one four engined Avro 642/4m, VT-AFM 'Star of India', which replaced the Viceroy's Avro Ten VT-ACT. When M. & S.A.F. Ltd. ceased operations later in 1934. 'FV was sold to Commercial Air Hire Ltd. at Croydon for use during 1935–36 on early morning newspaper deliveries to the Continent. Late in 1936 W. R. Carpenter and Co. Ltd. bought it for mail services in New Guinea where it continued in service with Mandated Airlines Ltd. until the Japanese destroyed it in 1942.

SPECIFICATION

Manufacturers: A. V. Roe and Co. Ltd., Newton Heath, Manchester.
Power Plants: (Avro 618) Three 240 h.p. Armstrong Siddeley Lynx IVC.
(Avro 619) Three 105 h.p. Armstrong Siddeley Genet Major 1.
(Avro 624) Three 105 h.p. Armstrong Siddeley Genet Major 1.
(Avro 642/2m) Two 460 h.p. Armstrong Siddeley Jaguar VID.
(Avro 642/4m) Four 240 h.p. Armstrong Siddeley Lynx IVC.

	Avro 618	Avro 619	Avro 624	Avro 642/2m
Span	71 ft. 3 in.	47 ft. 0 in.	51 ft. 0 in.	71 ft. 3 in.
Length	47 ft. 6 in.	35 ft. 9 in.	36 ft. 0 in.	54 ft. 6 in.
Height	12 ft. 9 in.	9 ft. 6 in.	9 ft. 6 in.	11 ft. 6 in.
Wing area	772 sq. ft.	333 sq. ft.	360 sq. ft.	728 sq. ft.
Tare weight	6,020 lb.	2,790 lb.	3,000 lb.	7,360 lb.
All-up weight	10,600 lb.	4,420 lb.	5,000 lb.	11,800 lb.
Maximum speed	115 m.p.h.	118 m.p.h.	113 m.p.h.	160 m.p.h.
Cruising speed	100 m.p.h.	95 m.p.h.	95 m.p.h.	135 m.p.h.
Initial climb	675 ft./min.	750 ft./min.	6000 ft./min.	970 ft./min.
Ceiling	16,000 ft.	15,000 ft.	14,000 ft.	15,500 ft.
Range	400 miles	400 miles	—	600 miles

Production: (a) Avro 618 Ten

Fourteen aircraft comprising five British registered examples and the following: (c/n 229) VH-UMH 'Southern Sky', later 'City of Grafton'; (230) VH-UMG 'Southern Star'; (231) VH-UMI 'Southern Moon', rebuilt as (c/n 1A) VH-UXX 'Faith in Australia'; (371) VH-UNJ 'City of Brisbane'; (388) VH-UNA 'Southern Sun'; (468) VH-UPI 'City of Sydney'; (524) VT-ACT; (Works Order 3302) K2682 to Contract 164779/32.

(b) Avro 619 Five

Four aircraft comprising one British registered machine (c/n 383) G-AASO and three for export: (288) VP-KAE 'Knight of the Grail'; (370) VH-UNK; (436) VP-KAD 'Knight Errant'.

(c) Avro 624 Six

Three aircraft: (c/n 457) G-AAYR; (458) G-ABBY; (575) VR-HBF.

(d) Avro 642

One 642/2m (c/n 642) G-ACFV and one 642/4m (773) VT-AFM 'Star of India'.

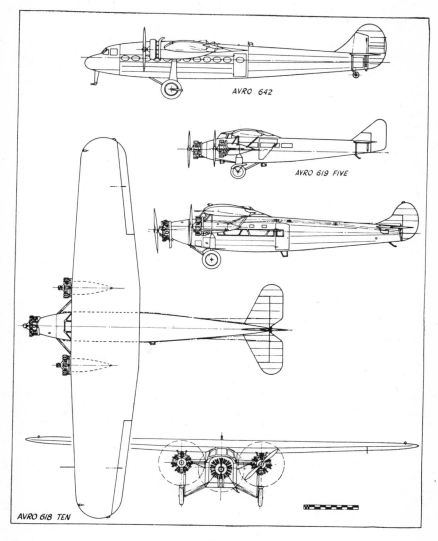

AVRO 642

AVRO 619 FIVE

AVRO 618 TEN

Air Service Training Ltd.'s Avro 626 advanced trainer flying over Southampton Water in 1932. (*Flight Photo 13035*)

Avro 621 Tutor and Avro 626

The Tutor two-seat basic trainer was of fabric-covered metal construction and designed to replace the immortal 504 in R.A.F. service, the prototype, G-AAKT, fitted with a 155 h.p. Mongoose IIIA radial, being exhibited in the New Types Park at the 1930 Hendon R.A.F. Display. A second prototype, G-AATU, appeared soon afterwards, followed by G-AARZ, but this, like the majority of production Tutors, had the 240 h.p. Siddeley Lynx motor. A small batch, K1230 to K1240, was commissioned towards the end of 1930, and although the type had a predominantly military career, a number did leave their mark on civil aviation. Three of the earliest production Tutors, G-ABAP, 'AR and 'HA, were equipped with cameras and mapped wide areas of territory for the Tanganyika Government, while G-ABFL and 'GH were built for demonstration at home. The first of these was tested to destruction; but 'GH was flown on floats at Hamble, finally going to the R.A.F. at Felixstowe in 1932 as the first Avro 646 Sea Tutor. To Hamble also went that well-known pair, G-ABIR and 'IS, with which Air Service Training Ltd. gave advanced instruction from 1931 until the outbreak of war, G-ABIR operating as a seaplane during the summer of 1932.

Main production was for the R.A.F. and foreign air forces, but three exported Tutors acquired civil markings in July 1930: VH-UOL delivered to Australian National Airways Ltd., Sydney; CF-ANQ supplied via Armstrong Siddeley Motors Ltd., Ottawa for evaluation at Rockcliffe with R.C.A.F. serial 224; and VR-HAF used by the Far East Aviation Co. Ltd., Hong Kong, for demonstrations in China.

The winter of 1932–33 found the prototype G-AARZ and two newcomers, G-ABZP and 'ZR, touring South Africa with Sir Alan Cobham's Circus, giving aerobatic joyrides, piloted by Martin Hearn, C. W. Bebb and others. G-ABZR was destroyed in a fatal crash at the Cape but the others participated in the following season's activities until 'RZ crashed on 10 June 1934. Another Tutor, the red-and-white G-ACOV, then appeared on the scene, having been reconditioned by Air Pageants Ltd. for itinerant aerobatic and joyriding work. In the following year the R.A.F. began to declare obsolete small numbers of Tutors, and K1231, one of the original batch, was converted into G-ADYW for T. C. S. Westbrook of Eastleigh. This, together with A.S.T.'s pair, was impressed at the beginning of 1940. This fate also befell K3237, which became G-AFZW in November 1939, was civilianised by Portsmouth, Southsea and I.O.W. Aviation Ltd. and went to the R.A.F. as AV980 in April 1940. Three other redundant Tutors did not become civil until after the war, the first, G-AHSA, formerly K3215, being converted at Weston-super-Mare and delivered to John Neasham at the Darlington and District Aero Club in 1947. Some years later it took part in flying sequences at Kenley for the film *Reach for the Sky* and in 1959 was acquired by the Shuttleworth Trust, overhauled and restored to flying condition in trainer yellow and original serial K3215. K3363, the machine used in the comic event at the 1935 R.A.F. Display, appeared at Croydon in 1947 for conversion to G-AIYM, but languished untouched for some years until scrapped. The final production batch of 1936 also provided the last civil Tutor, K6105, which was converted into G-AKFJ by W. Sturrock, A. V. Roe's manager at Bracebridge Heath, near Lincoln. Raffled on Battle of Britain Day in 1948, it went to Don-caster with the Ultra Light Group, but was written off after the motor cut on take-off on 30 July 1949.

When equipped with a third cockpit and provision for gun ring, the basic Tutor airframe became the unnamed Avro 626 advanced trainer, an early demonstrator, G-ABFM being the machine taken to the British Empire Trade Exhibition at Buenos Aires in the aircraft carrier *Eagle* in March 1931. It was sold on the spot, and heralded the sale of a large number of 626s to overseas buyers. Other demonstrators were K-7/G-ABGG, 'JG and G-ACFW, the last of which could constantly be seen in the early 'thirties, clearing Customs at Heston and elsewhere, en route to foreign sales tours. Air Service Training Ltd. added G-ABYM to its

The prototype Avro 621 with five-cylinder Mongoose, ailerons on the lower wing only, and straight edged rudder. (*Air Ministry*)

131

fleet in July 1932 as a radio trainer, and apart from a visit to Cairo in December 1933 to be flown in the Circuit of the Oases Rally by the C.F.I. Flt. Lt. R. P. P. Pope, was in constant use until 1939. A 626 floatplane demonstrator, G-ACFZ, was also built and based at Hamble, eventually being sold abroad in 1937, by which time thirteen production Avro 626s had received civil registrations for delivery to overseas buyers, including four registered in Hong Kong which were destined for China.

In 1933 the demonstration Avro 626 G-ABJG was re-engined with a 260 h.p. Cheetah and fitted with a new 'high-speed' gun ring as a prototype which led to the Avro 637. This was a lightly armed frontier patrol aircraft built for China, four of which were civil registered in Hong Kong by the Far East Aviation Co. Ltd. Although eventually modified to full 637 standard with long-travel undercarriage and flown under B conditions as K-10, it always retained the top centre section trailing-edge gap of the 626. Seven other Avro 626s were fitted with the more powerful Cheetah radials and delivered to the R.A.F. in 1936 as Avro Prefects. Two of these, K5069 and K5066, were converted into two seaters by Southern Aircraft (Gatwick) Ltd. in June 1946 and became G-AHRZ and 'VO respectively. They saw little service, however, the former being broken up at Gatwick and the latter, owned by A. G. Harding, faded away at Pebsham Aerodrome, Hastings, in 1950. In New Zealand the Prefect NZ203 was converted for J. Frogley at Havelock North in 1947 as ZK-APC and was still in storage there in 1970.

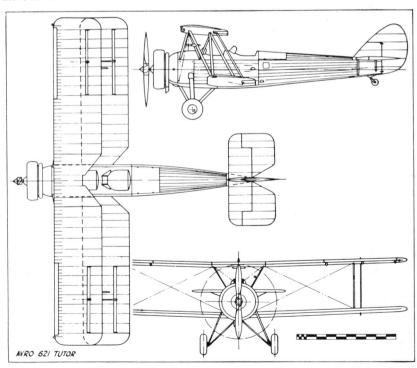

AVRO 621 TUTOR

The Avro 626/637 prototype, G-ABJG, in an intermediate stage, with Avro type 637 gun mounting but still flown from the front seat. (*Air Ministry*)

SPECIFICATION

Manufacturers: A. V. Roe and Co. Ltd., Newton Heath, Manchester.
Power Plants: (Avro 621) One 155 h.p. Armstrong Siddeley Mongoose IIIA.
              (Avro 621) One 240 h.p. Armstrong Siddeley Lynx IVC.
              (Avro 626) One 277 h.p. Armstrong Siddeley Cheetah V.

	Avro 621 (Mongoose)	Avro 621 (Lynx)	Avro 626
Span	34 ft. 0 in.	34 ft. 0 in.	34 ft. 0 in.
Length	26 ft. 7½ in.	26 ft. 4½ in.	26 ft. 6 in.
Height	9 ft. 7 in.	9 ft. 7 in.	9 ft. 9 in.
Wing area	300 sq. ft.	300 sq. ft.	300 sq. ft.
Tare weight	1,560 lb.	1,722 lb.	2,010 lb.
All-up weight	2,218 lb.	2,380 lb.	2,667 lb.
Maximum speed	110 m.p.h.	116 m.p.h.	130 m.p.h.
Cruising speed	95 m.p.h.	100 m.p.h.	108 m.p.h.
Initial climb	675 ft./min.	1,000 ft./min.	1,000 ft./min.
Ceiling	12,400 ft.	18,500 ft.	16,800 ft.
Range	375 miles	300 miles	200 miles

Production: (a) Avro 621 Tutor
Large military production batches, 19 registered as British civil aircraft, and the following civil exports: (c/n 413) VH-UOL; (463) CF-ANQ; (464) China.

      (b) Avro 626
Large military production batches, 17 registered as British civil aircraft, and the following for Hong Kong: (c/n 569) VR-HAU; (570) VR-HAW; (571) VR-HBX; (573) VR-HCO; (620) VR-HBZ; (634) VR-HCA.

      (c) Avro 637
Eight military aircraft for China including four with Hong Kong civil registrations: (c/n 635) VR-HCH; (636) VR-HCI; (637) VR-HCE; (665) VR-HCP.

G-ADTY, one of Air Service Training Ltd.'s long nosed Avro 643 Mk. II Cadets, flying over Southampton Water in 1936. (*Aeroplane*)

Avro 631 Cadet and variants

The Cadet was produced in 1931 as a scaled down version of the Tutor, retaining metal construction for the fuselage but differing from its larger forebear because wood was used for the internals of mainplanes and all control surfaces. The prototype, G-ABRS, registered to A. V. Roe and Co. Ltd. in October 1931, was used as a demonstrator, making its first public appearance at the opening of Skegness Aerodrome on 14 May 1932, when it was aerobatted by test pilot H. A. Brown and later flown into fourth place at 114 m.p.h. in a local race by Roy Dobson. It eventually faded into obscurity and was sold to the Far East Flying School at Hong Kong in October 1934. Although the smart blue G-ABVV was delivered to Major J. E. D. Shaw at Heston, and G-ABYC was acquired by Gardners, the pre-war racing family, by far the largest user of the Cadet was Air Service Training Ltd. at Hamble. Two early production models, G-ABWS and 'XU, were delivered to them in June 1932 and proved to have outstanding aerobatic qualities. Seven more, G-ACCH to 'CN, were therefore acquired in March 1933. During the next two years the final total of A.S.T. Cadets reached 17 with the arrival of G-ACNE, 'NF, 'RY, 'RZ, 'UH, G-ADAU, 'AV and 'CX. Although 'CM, 'RY and 'UH were short-lived, the remainder withstood all the hard knocks of ab initio instruction for over six years.

A.S.T.'s associate, the Far East Aviation School at Hong Kong, which had acquired the prototype Cadet, G-ABRS, later bought VR-HCL, 'CM, 'CN and an unregistered example for sale in China. C.7, last of seven purchased by the Irish Army Air Corps, survived to become a private aircraft, EI-AGO, in the 1950s and one was supplied to Portugal, but the only other user was the Lancashire Aero Club whose second Cadet G-ACMG, lost in a crash, was replaced by Gardner's G-ABYC.

Introduced in September 1934, the Avro 643 Cadet was an improved type 631 with raised rear seat, but very few 643 Cadets were built. The prototype, G-ACXJ, finished its days with the Tollerton Aero Club, G-ADEG was supplied to the York County Aviation Club Ltd. at Sherburn-in-Elmet to join their Club Cadet G-ADEH, G-ADFD went to the Bristol and Wessex Club at Whitchurch, G-ADEX to the Hon. R. F. Watson and G-ADIE to Sir William Firth. The 643 was, in fact, merely the forerunner of the final Cadet development, the Avro 643 Mk. II Cadet which was built in quantity for Air Service Training Ltd. and the Royal Australian Air Force. This had the more powerful 150 h.p. Genet Major 1A mounted 6 in. further forward, stouter wing spars, an inverted fuel system, and bracing wires taken to the front wing root fittings for ease of parachute escape from the front cockpit. The prototype, G-ADJT, was sold in France in 1938 as F-AQMX, the sole British user, A.S.T., operating an extensive fleet at Hamble and at Ansty near Coventry. This included G-ADTF to 'TZ, G-AEAR, 'IR and 'NL, the greater majority of which were impressed as instructional airframes 1941–42. One Avro 631, G-ACIH, and one Avro 643, G-ADIE, survived the 1939–45 war and were sold in Ireland as EI-ALU and 'LP respectively.

Sixteen of the 34 R.A.A.F. Avro 643 Mk. II Cadets became civil in 1946, one, VH-BJB, being fitted with the sliding hood from a Wackett Trainer, but in 1969 the only serviceable example was VH-AFY based at St. George, Queensland by C. H. Parsons. This machine and VH-AFX were rebuilt in 1963 as crop sprayers with 220 h.p. Jacobs R-755 radials.

In 1933, a year after the debut of the Avro 631 Cadet, a version with unstaggered, folding wings, known as the Avro 638 Club Cadet, was introduced for clubs and private owners, the prototype of which was G-ACAY. A small number of these was built, the first, G-ACGY, for the Lancashire Aero Club, which already had two 631s, G-ABVU and the ex-Gardner 'YC. The Airwork School at

Major J. E. Durrant Shaw's Cadet, showing the characteristic staggered wings of the 631 and 643 trainer variants. (*Flight*)

Airwork's second white and green Club Cadet, showing the unstaggered wings and Genet Major radial. (*Aeroplane*)

The Cabin Cadet did not go into production and the second aircraft, G-ACNY, was completed as a standard Club Cadet. (*Flight*)

Avro 643 Mk. II Cadet VH-AFY at Coolangatta, Queensland, in January 1971, equipped for crop spraying as a single-seater with trailing edge nozzles and 220 h.p. Jacobs R-755 engine. (*G. P. Challinor*)

G-ACFH, the first Avro 640 Cadet three-seater, flying in Scottish Motor Traction Co. colours 1933. (*Flight*)

Heston bought three—G-ACHN, 'HO and 'HP—which were delivered from Woodford in formation on 21 June 1933, followed a month later by G-ACTX and 'TZ. Several went to private owners, including G-ACHW to S. P. Tyzack and G-ACNY to Lord Londonderry, but most of these eventually found their way to the clubs, one of the largest of which, Southend Flying Club, had G-ACAY, 'HW, 'JZ, 'TB and 'TX at the outbreak of war. A cabin version, the Avro 639, was flown under B conditions as K-14 and later as G-ACGA during 1933–34, but did not go into production, the Club Cadet being followed into service by the Avro 640 Cadet three seater. Both the 639 and 640 were fitted with the unstaggered wings of the Club Cadet. The Cabin Cadet seated three, with the pilot in front, but the 640 reversed this and was intended for joyriding with two passengers side by side in the front cockpit of a widened fuselage. Like the Club Cadet G-ACIL, built to the order of Douglas and the Hon. Mrs. Fairweather of Renfrew, the prototype Avro 640, G-ACFH, was fitted with an in-line Cirrus Hermes IV engine. It was delivered to the Scottish Motor Traction Co. Ltd. at Renfrew in April 1933 together with G-ACFS, 'FT and 'FU. They were used for joyriding all over Scotland, while the Genet Major 640s G-ACLU, 'OZ and 'PB toured the country giving formation flights with the National Aviation Day Displays. When S.M.T. flying ceased in 1935, 'FU went on tour with Scott's Circus, and the other three joined the ex-Cobham 'PB at Hooton, carrying out joyriding with Utility Airways Ltd. until 1939. Both 'FS and 'FT were destroyed in the Hooton fire of 8 July 1940.

After the war the sole airworthy specimen of these Cadet variants was the Avro 638 Club Cadet G-ACHP, which was at first used as a communications machine by Saunders-Roe Ltd. Later it became the well-known mount of the Vintage Aeroplane Club until wrecked at Denham on 1 January 1956. In common with several others of the former Airwork Club Cadet fleet, 'HP was fitted pre-war with a Gipsy Major 1 engine, which, being of smaller frontal area than the Genet Major, imparted a much-improved performance with attendant fuel economy.

137

SPECIFICATION

Manufacturers: A. V. Roe and Co. Ltd., Newton Heath, Manchester.

Power Plants: (Avro 631)   One 135 h.p. Armstrong Siddeley Genet Major.

              (Avro 638)   One 130 h.p. de Havilland Gipsy Major I.

                                   One 135 h.p. Armstrong Siddeley Genet Major I.

                                   One 140 h.p. Cirrus Hermes IVA.

              (Avro 639)   One 135 h.p. Armstrong Siddeley Genet Major I.

              (Avro 640)   One 135 h.p. Armstrong Siddeley Genet Major I.

                                   One 140 h.p. Cirrus Hermes IV.

              (Avro 643)   One 135 h.p. Armstrong Siddeley Genet Major.

              (Avro 643 Mk. II) One 150 h.p. Armstrong Siddeley Genet Major 1A.

	Avro 631	Avro 643	Avro 643 Mk. II
Span	30 ft. 0 in.	30 ft. 2 in.	30 ft. 2 in.
Length	24 ft. 9 in.	24 ft. 9 in.	24 ft. 9 in.
Height	8 ft. 9 in.	8 ft. 9 in.	8 ft. 10 in.
Wing area	261·25 sq. ft.	262 sq. ft.	262 sq. ft.
Tare weight	1,166 lb.	—	1,286 lb.
All-up weight	1,793 lb.	—	2,000 lb.
Maximum speed	118 m.p.h.	—	116 m.p.h.
Cruising speed	100 m.p.h.	—	100 m.p.h.
Initial climb	750 ft./min.	—	700 ft./min.
Ceiling	13,000 ft.	—	12,000 ft.
Range	350 miles	—	325 miles

	Avro 638	Avro 639	Avro 640
Span	30 ft. 2 in.	30 ft. 2 in.	30 ft. 0 in.
Length	24 ft. 9 in.	24 ft. 9 in.	24 ft. 9 in.
Height	8 ft. 9 in.	8 ft. 9 in.	8 ft. 9 in.
Wing area	262 sq. ft.	262 sq. ft.	261·25 sq. ft.
Tare weight	1,222 lb.	—	1,140 lb.
All-up weight	1,757 lb.	—	1,855 lb.
Maximum speed	115 m.p.h.	—	110 m.p.h.
Cruising speed	100 m.p.h.	—	95 m.p.h.
Initial climb	—	—	700 ft./min.
Ceiling	—	—	13,500 ft.

Production: (a) Avro 631 Cadet

Twenty-three British registered aircraft and the following for export; (c/n 581–586) Irish Army Air Corps C.1 to C.6; (678) Far East Aviation Co. Ltd.; (683) VR-HCL; (684) VR-HCM; (685) VR-HCN; (727) Portugal; (730) Irish C.7/EI-AFO/EI-AGO.

(b) Avro 638 Club Cadet

Seventeen British registered aircraft only.

(c) Avro 639 Cabin Cadet

One British registered aircraft only.

(d) Avro 640 Cadet three-seater

Nine British registered aircraft only.

(e) Avro 643 Cadet

Seven British registered aircraft and one machine for export: (c/n 778) EC-W26.

(f) Avro 643 Mk. II Cadet

i) Twenty-four British registered aircraft and the following for export: (c/n 850–861) R.A.A.F. A6-1 to A6-12; (867) PP-TAF*; (920) VR-RAK; (921) VR-RAL; (986-995) A6-13 to A6-22; (1058–1069) A6-23 to A6-34.

ii) Civil conversions of R.A.A.F. Avro 643 Mk. II Cadets: (c/n 851) VH-APV; (854) VH-AEG; (857) VH-AEJ; (859) VH-AMM; (860) VH-AFW; (861) VH-AFX; (990) VH-AGH; (991) VH-AEH/VH-PRV; (994) VH-AFZ/VH-RAC; (1058) VH-AHH; (1060) VH-AEI/VH-PRU; (1062) VH-AHW; (1063) VH-APW; (1066) VH-AFY; (1067) VH-AGC/VH-BPS/VH-PRT; (1068) VH-AEL; (1069) VH-BJB.

* Duplicating registration of Avro 671 Cierva C.30A c/n 738.

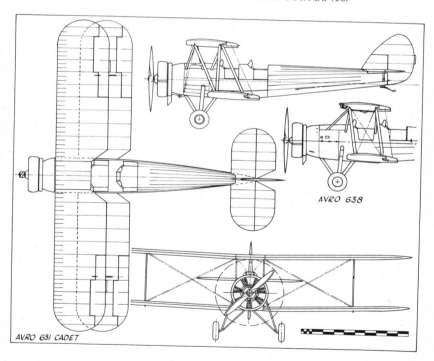

AVRO 638

AVRO 631 CADET

Nanyang Airways' Anson 1 VR-SDK at Singapore in 1952. It had been converted from EG436 to G-ALXF with Rapide-style windows at Squires Gate earlier in the year.
(P. R. Keating)

Avro 652A Anson 1

When the Americans set the fashion for the twin-motor, low-wing monoplane with retractable undercarriage, A. V. Roe and Co. Ltd. adapted their Fokker style airframe to the new configuration by simply putting the wing underneath. The result was the Avro 652, two examples only of which were built and delivered to Imperial Airways Ltd. in March 1935 as G-ACRM 'Avalon' and G-ACRN 'Ava' (originally 'Avatar'). With a crew of two and four passengers, they cruised at the then unprecedented speed of 165 m.p.h. on two 290 h.p. Cheetah VI engines. They flew with monotonous regularity on the long Croydon–Brindisi route for a number of years until sold to Air Service Training Ltd. as navigational trainers, ending their days in impressment during the 1939–45 war. The Avro 660 G-ACUN, a smaller version with fixed undercarriage and 135 h.p. Genet Major engines, was not completed.

A military counterpart, K4771, known as the Avro 652A Anson, made its first flight in March 1935 and was the forerunner of some 11,000 Ansons built during the next 17 years. Production Anson 1s differed from the 652 by virtue of their Cheetah IXs, immense cabin windows and dorsal turret. Twelve of these with registrations between G-AFTU and 'UT became civil only for their ferrying flights to the Greek Air Force in May 1939, and one more, SU-AAO, went turretless to the Egyptian Government for transport work. Egypt was also the destination of the legendary flight of 20 'civilian' Anson 1s, G-AGGJ to 'HD, from Croydon via Lisbon and Takoradi for delivery to the R.A.F. at Aboukir disguised as B.O.A.C. aircraft. The Anson 10 was the nearest derivative of the Mk. 1, merely having a strengthened floor for A.T.A. freighting, both marks having a reputation for ease of handling and maintenance which later resulted in the disposal of large numbers for civil use all over the world, over 100 being civil registered in the U.K. and some 140 in Australia alone. Similarly, Anson Vs with smooth contour Vidal-moulded plywood fuselages served with Spartan Air Services Ltd., Ottawa, and other Canadian concerns for more than two decades, and one, OY-DZI, was used as an ambulance in Denmark by Zone Redningskorpset. Others were ferried to Central and South America for civilian purposes.

The first British civil Anson 1 was G-AHBN, formerly NK271, personal mount of Gerard d'Erlanger, Commodore of the A.T.A. which went with him to become the first B.O.A.C. communications aircraft at Northolt in 1946. Conversions were usually primitive and consisted of fitting six or eight seats in the cabin and in most cases fitting new windows according to taste. The serious Anson users were mainly Air Service Training Ltd. with G-AHNS and 'NT for twin training, the Fairey Aviation Co. Ltd. and Hunting Aerosurveys Ltd. with G-AHXS and G-AKFM for aerial photography, the College of Aeronautics, Cranfield, with G-AIPA, 'PC and 'PD as flying laboratories, and the Straight Corporation with 10 used at first for navigation training and later on scheduled services in the West Country. A number of mushroom concerns tried to make the Anson earn its keep on charter or on tourist routes to Jersey and elsewhere, but only Blue Line Airways of Tollerton with five, G-AJBA, 'FX, 'KFK, 'FL and 'FM; British Air Transport, Redhill, with six, G-AHKH, 'IWV, 'WW, 'WX, 'XU and 'KVW; and Transair Ltd., Croydon, achieved real success. Transair owned and operated 11 Ansons at one time or another, mainly windowless freighters used on the early-morning continental mail and newspaper contract until replaced by Dakota 4s in 1953–54. Several Anson fleets operated overseas, but under British registry, notably C.L. Air Surveys Ltd. in Kenya with six, Gulf Aviation Ltd. at Bahrein with six, Nanyang Airways Ltd. at Singapore with three, Trans Arabian Airways

The prototype Avro 652, G-ACRM, ancestor of approximately 11,000 Ansons built 1935–52. (*B.O.A.C.*)

Avro 652 Mk. II SU-AAO built for the Egyptian Government in 1936 had the entry door on the port side, thus differing from production Anson 1s.

G-AGGY, one of the 20 wartime Anson 1 aircraft ferried to Egypt by B.O.A.C., parked at Almaza on arrival, July 1943. (*Flt. Lt. D. A. S. McKay*)

Ltd. at Amman with two, and Airwork Ltd. in Kenya with three. The last mentioned were fitted with underwing spray-bars and used as crop sprayers and were eventually registered locally and did not return home.

In 1950 the A.R.B. decided it could grant Cs. of A. to no more Anson 1s and the last ever was Derby Aviation's G-AMDA used for geophysical survey work over Southern England with a towed magnetometer, 1954–55, and as a twin trainer by the London School of Flying at Elstree before going to the Skyfame Museum at Staverton in 1963, camouflaged and re-serialled N4877.

In Australia, where the Anson had an even more complex commercial history than in the U.K., the ban came at midnight on 30 June 1962, and on the final day Brain and Brown Ltd.'s VH-BSF, VH-FIA and VH-FIC made a farewell formation flight over Melbourne, while at Perth, W.A., Woods Airways' VH-BEL and VH-MMH circled together for the last time. All these Ansons had for years provided essential links with important off-shore islands.

SPECIFICATION

Manufacturers: A. V. Roe and Co. Ltd., Manchester. Aircraft built at the Newton Heath, Chadderton and Yeadon factories.

Power Plants: (Avro 652) Two 290 h.p. Armstrong Siddeley Cheetah VI.

(Anson 1) Two 350 h.p. Armstrong Siddeley Cheetah IX.

Dimensions: Span, 56 ft. 6 in. Length, 42 ft. 3 in. Height, 9 ft. 6 in. Wing area, 410 sq. ft.

Weights: (Avro 652) Tare weight, 5,100 lb. All-up weight, 7,500 lb.

(Anson 1) Tare weight, 5,375 lb. All-up weight, 9,540 lb.

Performance: (Avro 652) Maximum speed, 195 m.p.h. Cruising speed, 165 m.p.h. Initial climb, 900 ft./min. Ceiling, 21,500 ft. Range, 790 miles.

(Anson 1) Maximum speed, 188 m.p.h. Cruising speed, 158 m.p.h. Initial climb, 720 ft./min. Ceiling, 19,000 ft. Range, 660 miles.

Production: (a) Avro 652

Two aircraft only: (c/n 698) G-ACRM and (699) G-ACRN.

(b) Avro 652 Mk. II

One aircraft only: (c/n 891) SU-AAO.

(c) Avro 652A Anson 1

Large military production batches, including the following for export: (c/n 939–941) Finnish AN101–AN103 ex R.A.F. K8738–K8740; (951) Estonian 158; (967–978) R.A.A.F. A4-1 to A4-12 ex K6212–K6223; (980–981) Irish A.19 and A.20; (1008–1028) A4-13 to A4-33 ex K8792–K8812; (1033–1034) Irish, A.21 and A.22; (1053–1057) A4-34 to A4-38 ex K8840–K8844; (1079–1088) A4-39 to A4-48 ex L7913–L7922; (1111–1122) Greek TT51–TT62, flown out as G-AFTU to G-AFTW, G-AFUH to G-AFUJ, G-AFUM to G-AFUO, and G-AFUR to G-AFUT, Cs. of A. issued between 12.5.39 and 15.6.39; (1127–1132) Turkish Air Force ex N9947–N9952; (1334–1339) Portuguese 213–218 reconditioned 5.47 ex NK182, NK437, NK444, NK476, NK483 and NK484, and (1370–1373) 219–222 ex MG690, MG692, MG696 and MG221.

(d) B.O.A.C. aircraft ferried to Egypt in 1943

G-AGGJ to G-AGGP and G-AGGR to G-AGHD, temporarily demilitarised and allotted constructors' numbers 1152–1171, Cs. of A. issued to British Overseas Airways Corporation 3.6.43. On arrival at Aboukir the aircraft reverted to R.A.F. markings as LT191, LT192, LT203, LT204, LT236, LT255, LT256, LT257, LT307, LT340, EG677, LS985, LT279, LT115, LT176, LT234, LT276, LT281, EG651 and LS989 respectively.

(e) Avro 660

One aircraft only: (c/n 723) G-ACUN registered to A. V. Roe and Co. Ltd., Woodford, 14.6.34, construction abandoned when half complete.

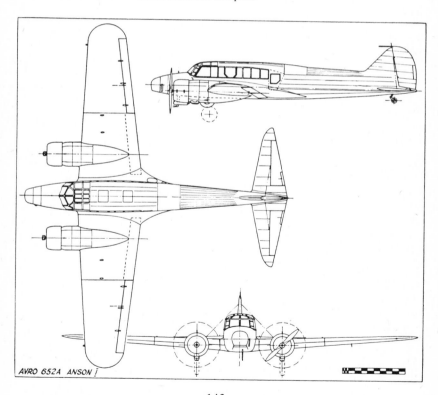

AVRO 652A ANSON 1

'Mancunia' G-AHXK, one of a small fleet of Avro 19 Series 1 aircraft operated by Sivewright Airways Ltd. in 1948.

Avro 652A Nineteen

Major modifications to the basic Anson airframe came in 1944 with the appearance of Mks. 11 and 12. Internal headroom was increased by raising the cabin roof, three square windows were fitted and flaps and undercarriage were hydraulically operated for the first time. Both marks forsook the time-honoured helmetted engine cowlings for the smooth type used on the original Avro 652, but whereas the Anson 11 was powered by two 395 h.p. Cheetah 19 radials, the Anson 12 had Cheetah 15s of 425 h.p. each. They were easily distinguishable, because the Rotol c.s. propellers of the Mk. 12 were fitted with spinners and the fixed-pitch Fairey Reeds of the Mk. 11 were not.

The prototype Anson 12, NL152, first flown at Woodford on 5 September 1944, and the last production Anson 11, NL246, became civil in the autumn of 1944 as G-AGLB and 'LM for use by Air Attachés in Madrid and London respectively. The latter, in full camouflage, was non-standard, having Cheetah 14s and Fairey Reed propellers, but was nevertheless registered as a Mk. 11, returning to the R.A.F. after two years' service to be broken up at Waddington in 1948. Eight other Anson 11s were acquired by R. L. Whyham when the R.A.F. declared them obsolete in 1948, but with the exception of G-ALIH they all became derelict at Kingstown Aerodrome, Carlisle. This same 'IH became the well-known bulbous-nosed Ekco cloud-warning and navigational radar demonstrator which was based at Southend until replaced by the former Avro works 'hack' G-AGPG in 1967. The only other noteworthy Anson 11 was B.K.S. Air Survey's G-ALXH, an Anson 1 converted from major components of PH808 in 1957. The only other recorded civil Anson 12s were SU-ADJ converted from PH806 at Woodford for Misr Airwork Ltd. and ZK-AXY/PH599 used in New Zealand by Southern Scenic Air Services Ltd.

In 1945 A. V. Roe and Co. Ltd. modified an Anson 12, MG159, to take nine seats in a cabin fitted with five oval windows, in which form it satisfied the Brabazon XIX feeder-liner specification of 1943 and was thus dubbed the Avro 652A Nineteen. In civil guise as G-AGNI it was handed over to the internal airlines, at that time run by the wartime Associated Airways Joint Committee and evaluated under normal service conditions. Following the resultant modification programme it was sold for charter work, and met a watery end off the Isle of Man on 11 June 1948. The Anson 12 G-AGLB was recalled from Madrid for similar modification, returning there in October 1945, but retained its square windows.

A total of 48 Avro 19s were registered for civil use in the U.K., the largest fleet being that of Railway Air Services Ltd., which numbered 14 and was used on the routes from Croydon to the North, to Dublin, to the Isle of Man and Belfast, until taken over by B.E.A.C. in February 1947. They were then progressively withdrawn from service and replaced by Dakota 3s. The M.C.A. also kept six at Gatwick for calibrating airport radio installations and for pilots' licence testing. Others were supplied to the Emperor of Ethiopia (G-AGUH and 'UI), Hunting Air Travel Ltd., Sivewright Airways Ltd. and Westminster Airways Ltd. Eventually these proud fleets were dispersed to the four winds, but individual aircraft were used in the Industry as communications machines. G-AGUH, one of the Abyssinians, came back for use by Armstrong Siddeley Motors Ltd., the ex M.C.A. machine G-AGWE as the Decca Navigator demonstrator, the ex B.E.A.C. liner G-AHIC as a flying classroom with the College of Aeronautics at Cranfield, the one-time Hunting charter machine G-AHXK to Hawker Aircraft

Avro 19 Series 2 (tapered wing) G-AKDU at Heany, Southern Rhodesia, in 1947 with pest control spray gear under the fuselage.

Anson Mk. 11 G-ALIH which Ekco Electronics Ltd. operated as a flying radar laboratory at Southend 1954–1967. (*A. J. Jackson*)

Indian Government Anson Mk. 18C civil aircrew trainer VT-CXZ.

Ltd., and the former Sivewright Airways G-AHYN saw service with Armstrong Whitworth Aircraft Ltd.

Chief overseas deliveries were OO-ANT, 'PG, 'PN and 'PX to John Mahieu Aviation, Brussels, 1946–47, and SU-ADO, 'DP and 'DQ (previously British registered) to Misr Airwork Ltd. (Misrair) for internal services in Egypt.

Tapered mainplanes of metal construction and one foot greater span were fitted to six aircraft designated the Avro 19 Series 2, the first being the Smith's Instruments demonstrator G-AHKX. Two others, G-AKDU and 'DV, were based at R.A.F. Heany and used by the Colonial Office for pest control in East Africa. Six others were R.A.F. Anson 19 Series 2 aircraft which acquired temporary civil status for use by Government Officials in foreign countries where British military aircraft were not permitted. These were G-AGPU to Lisbon 1945; G-AIIA and 'RV ex PH858 and PH830 in 1946; G-AJDH ex VL336 in Malta 1950; G-AKFE ex VP512 in Vienna and Belgrade 1947–55; G-AKUO ex VM373 based at Boscombe Down 1948; G-ALFN ex VM336 in Teheran 1948; and G-AMNA ex VL298 in Egypt 1952. All returned after a time to the R.A.F. The final Service developments of the Avro 19 were the T. Mk. 20, 21 and 22 trainers, one of which, the T. Mk. 20 VS512, complete with identifying transparent nose, was acquired by the Fairey Aviation Co. Ltd. in 1954 for aerial survey work. It was equivalent in nearly all respects to the civil Avro 19, and was registered as such, being ferried to Central Africa as G-ANWW to carry on its aerial photography there as VP-YOF. This aircraft returned to White Waltham in January 1958 and reverted to British civil status. One other, G-APTL ex VM305, registered to Air Couriers (Transport) Ltd., was delivered to Biggin Hill in May 1959 before sale in Iran as EP-CAA.

Export production of the Avro 19 Series 2 comprised three for transport work with the Irish Air Corps; OO-CFA and 'FB for Cie Chemins de Fer du Congo Supérieure; CF-FEQ for communications duties with A. V. Roe Canada Ltd.; VT-CLI for Indian Air Survey and Transport Ltd.; VT-CJZ and 'KA for Bharat Airways Ltd., Calcutta; and LV-FBR, test flown as G-11-50 for the Argentine.

Designation Anson Mk. 18 applied to 12 police patrol machines supplied to Afghanistan, 1948–56, and a custom-built version with opaque nose caps was

146

delivered to the Indian Government as aircrew trainers VT-CXT to 'CYE in 1949. Despite their earlier mark numbers, both these types were, in fact, later derivatives of the Mk. 19.

When declared obsolescent, a few R.A.F. Anson 19s and T.Mk. 21 trainers were released to civilian operators as Avro 19 Series 2s and the first batch of six was flown to Croydon as G-APCF to 'CK in July 1957 for overhaul before sale in French West Africa. Ten more registered in 1967 were never used commercially, and one, flown to Southend from Shawbury on 14 March 1967 as G-AVHU, was repainted in its former Service marks as TX211 for the local Historic Aircraft Museum. The final six included G-AWMG and 'MH which Mercy Missions acquired for relief flights between the island of Fernando Po and Biafra where the first one crashed on 6 September 1968. The last one of British registry, G-AWSB, one of two sold to J. R. Hawke, was flown from Bovingdon to America, with U.S. marks N7522, via Prestwick and Stornoway, on 28 November 1968.

SPECIFICATION

Manufacturers: A. V. Roe and Co. Ltd., Greengate, Middleton, Manchester.
Power Plants: Two 420 h.p. Armstrong Siddeley Cheetah 15.

	Avro 19 Series 1	Avro 19 Series 2
Span	56 ft. 6 in.	57 ft. 6 in.
Length	42 ft. 3 in.	42 ft. 3 in.
Height	13 ft. 10 in.	13 ft. 10 in.
Wing area	463 sq. ft.	440 sq. ft.
Tare weight	7,419 lb.	6,576 lb.
All-up weight	10,400 lb.	10,400 lb.
Maximum speed	190 m.p.h.	171 m.p.h.
Cruising speed	174 m.p.h.	149 m.p.h.
Initial climb	730 ft./min.	700 ft./min.
Ceiling	15,000 ft.	16,000 ft.
Range with six passengers	610 miles	660 miles

Production: (a) Anson Mk. 11

Seven ex R.A.F. aircraft allotted British civil markings.

(b) Anson Mk. 12

Three ex R.A.F. aircraft converted at Woodford: (c/n 1205) G-AGLB; (1214) G-AGNI; (1272) PH806/SU-ADJ. Also PH599/ZK-AXY converted in New Zealand.

(c) Anson C.Mk. 19 Series 1

Six ex R.A.F. aircraft converted at Woodford: (c/n 1285) G-AGWD; (1286) G-AGWE; (1287) G-AGWF; (1327) G-AHKC; (1328) G-AHKD; (1329) G-AHKE. Private conversions: PH830/G-AIRV; PH858/G-AIIA. Also eight conversions of Series 1 aircraft which had been converted to Series 2. (G-AVCK, 'GR, 'HU, 'IJ, 'TA; G-AWMH, 'ML, 'RS).

(d) Anson C.Mk. 19 Series 2

Two ex R.A.F. aircraft converted at Woodford: (c/n 1449) G-AKUD; (1508) G-ALFN. Also ten others listed in Appendix E. (G-AJDH, G-AKFE, G-AMNA, G-APHV, G-AVPP, 'VO, 'VP, 'VR, 'SA, 'SB).

(e) Anson Mk. 18

Thirteen for Afghanistan: (c/n 1465–1476) YA-A.251 to YA-A.262; also (1509) YA-A.251 to replace c/n 1465.

(f) Anson Mk. 18C

Twelve built at Yeadon for the Director of Civil Aviation, India: (c/n 1477–1488) VT-CXT to VT-CYE.

(g) Avro 19 Series 1

Main production to British order (see Appendix E) and the following for export: (c/n 1312) OO-ANT; (1357) OO-APN; (1358) OO-APX; (1363) OO-APG.

(h) Avro 19 Series 2

Six for British use and the following for export: (c/n 1313–1315) Irish 141–143; (1361) OO-CFA; (1362) OO-CFB; (1369) CF-FEQ; (1377) VT-CLI; (1383) VT-CKA; (1384) VT-CJZ; (1507) LV-FBR.

(i) Anson T. Mk. 20

Two ex R.A.F. aircraft converted for civil use: VM305/G-APTL; VS512/G-ANWW.

(j) Anson T. Mk. 21

Eight ex R.A.F. aircraft converted as G-APCF to 'CK, G-AVEV and 'MG.

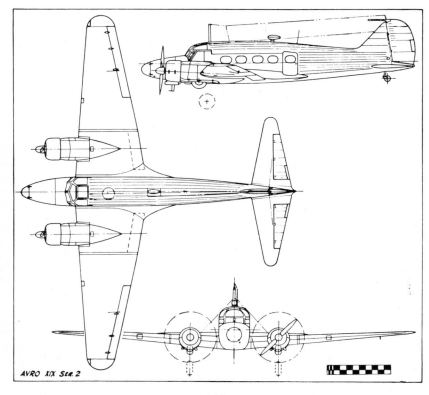

AVRO XIX SER. 2

The Flight Refuelling Lancaster tanker G-AHJW, showing the ventral hatch for the fuel hose. (*Flight Refuelling Ltd.*)

Avro 683 Lancaster

Shorn of its armament, the Lancaster bomber of the Second World War was a viceless and well proven vehicle eminently suitable for experimental civil use, a capacity in which it served for several years. The first was a Lancaster 1 handed over to the newly created B.O.A.C. Development Flight at Hurn as G-AGJI on 20 January 1944. As a camouflaged civil aeroplane with neat fairings in place of front and rear turrets, it was employed as a testbed for a variety of airborne equipment earmarked for post-war airliners under construction. Its most important contribution was the proving of Merlin 102 and annular radiator installations under Atlantic conditions in readiness for the Tudor 1.

Early in 1946 the British South American Airways Corporation took delivery of six Lancaster 1s from the Ministry of Supply. Four of these were commissioned as freighters, the conversions being carried out at the works of A. V. Roe and Co. Ltd. at Bracebridge Heath, Lincoln. They resembled Lancastrians, having the elongated freight nose, but had none of the Lancastrian's fuselage windows, nor was the tail cone fitted, the rear turret merely being silvered over. After a year's freighting with perishable goods and South American cotton crop samples, they proved uneconomical and were pensioned off. G-AGUM was reprieved, however, and handed over to Airtech Ltd. at Thame for development work on an outsize pannier for carrying awkward loads and vehicles on the Berlin airlift. The two unconverted Lancasters were handed back to the R.A.F., but later in the year one of them was sent to the B.O.A.C. Development Flight as G-AHVN to replace G-AGJI.

Flight Refuelling Ltd. was an employer of the Lancaster 3 in an experimental role, acquiring four former R.A.F. machines G-AHJT to 'JW in August 1946. These were converted into two pairs of tanker and receiver aircraft at Staverton, and from their base at Ford were used in perfecting the company's refuelling techniques. Although at first in their natal black with large yellow lettering, they soon followed the example of G-AGJI, and in their later years were silver.

The Lancaster 1 testbed G-AGJI in its original form with Merlin 22 engines.

Between May and August 1947 they were used in co-operation with B.S.A.A.C. on a series of flight refuelling trials over the Atlantic, 22 weekly flights being accomplished. The first trip, typical of the whole series, took place on 28 May 1947, when a Lancaster flown by Air Vice-Marshal D. C. T. Bennett left London Airport, was refuelled in mid-Atlantic with 1,700 gallons of petrol by an Azores-based Lancaster tanker, and completed the 3,355 mile flight to Bermuda non-stop. Two of these machines, together with G-AHVN acquired from B.O.A.C., were flown to Germany in 1948 and in their year's service on the Berlin airlift made a total of 757 tanker sorties.

Seven other Lancasters, with one exception, contributed nothing to British civil aviation. The first, a Lancaster 1, was flown into White Waltham aerodrome in July 1947 complete with nose, tail and mid upper turrets and was unique in having double curvature doors to the 22,000 lb. bomb space. A month later it received the white markings G-AJWM and the legend 'Alitalia-Roma' and was ferried under British European Airways Corporation ownership to Italy for training Alitalia Lancastrian crews. Skyways Ltd. operated a Lancaster 1, G-AKAB 'Sky Trainer', for the same purpose and with good effect at Dunsfold. This, like its Italian equivalent, also retained the three gun turrets of its former life. The remainder were all cannibalized, the Lancaster 1s G-AKAJ to 'AM at Tarrant Rushton to provide spares for Flight Refuelling's tankers in 1948–49 and a Lancaster 7 G-ALVC at Luton to service Eagle Aviation Ltd.'s Yorks in 1950.

'Star Ward,' one of the long nosed Lancaster freighters used by the British South American Airways Corporation in 1946–47.

150

Surplus R.C.A.F. Lancaster Xs FM222, KB907 and KB909 were acquired by Spartan Air Services, Ottawa, in 1956 for survey work as CF-IMF to 'MH but the conversion of 'MH was never completed. FM208 'Polaris' was converted for the bulk transport of diesel fuel by World Wide Airways, Dorval, as CF-KHH but the last civil Lancaster was a B. Mk. VII which saw service as WU-15 in New Caledonia with the French Navy who presented it to the Historic Aircraft Preservation Society when it was withdrawn from use in 1964. Registered G-ASXX it was flown from Sydney to Biggin Hill by John Hampshire and crew, 25 April–13 May 1965, and there restored to wartime appearance as NX611.

SPECIFICATION

Manufacturers: A. V. Roe and Co. Ltd., Greengate, Middleton, Manchester and sub-contractors.

Power Plants: Four 1,640 h.p. Rolls-Royce Merlin T.24.

Dimensions: Span, 102 ft. 0 in. Length, 69 ft. 6 in. Height, 20 ft. 0 in. Wing area, 1,297 sq. ft.

Weights: Tare weight, 36,900 lb. All-up weight, 65,000 lb.

Performance: Maximum speed, 287 m.p.h. Cruising speed, 210 m.p.h. Initial climb, 500 ft./min. Ceiling, 24,500 ft. Range, 1,660 miles.

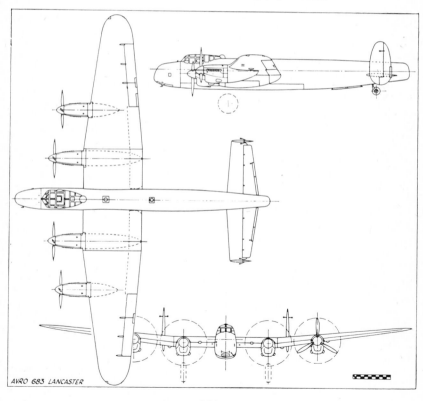

AVRO 683 LANCASTER

York G-ANTK in the red, white and blue Dan-Air livery at Gatwick in 1962. (*Richard Riding*)

Avro 685 York

The York was a military transport designed and built in six months, the prototype, LV626, making its maiden flight on 5 July 1942 at Ringway. It was largely a private venture produced under difficulties imposed by an Anglo-American agreement compelling British firms to build only combat aircraft. For economy in design and jigging, the York made use of several major Lancaster assemblies, such as the mainplane, power units and empennage, although prototype trials resulted in the addition of the third fin. Few materials were available for its construction, and only three were built in 1943. Full quantity production began in 1945, culminating in the departure of the final Avro York, PE108, from Woodford in April 1948. This total included five, numbered MW103, 108, 113, 121 and 129, allotted to B.O.A.C. as G-AGJA to 'JE. These seated 12 passengers in a rear cabin, carried freight in the forward compartment and were used to inaugurate the first U.K.–Cairo route via Morocco on 22 April 1944. Twenty-five were serialled TS789 to TS813 for R.A.F. Transport Command in 1945–46 and G-AHFI 'Skyway', G-AHLV 'Sky Courier' and G-AIUP 'Sky Consul' were built for Skyways Ltd. Twelve were registered G-AHEW to 'FH for the British South American Airways Corporation and the flagship G-AHEW 'Star Leader' was the first aircraft ever to land at London Airport non-stop from North America, chief pilot David Brice having overflown Shannon on charter from Gander on 11 June 1946.

Five 24-passenger machines delivered to Flota Aerea Mercante Argentina (FAMA) in 1946 for operation between Buenos Aires and London brought total York production in Britain to 256.

Yorks were operated as passenger airliners on many of the world's major air routes with such frequency that it was difficult to believe that so few were in use. The machines in the large Transport Command batch eventually left the joint B.O.A.C./R.A.F. services and assumed their civil mantles as G-AGNL to 'OF and G-AGSL to 'SP, the entire fleet bearing the M Class names given in Appendix E. Thirteen were fitted as passenger sleepers with 12 berths for use on the U.K.–Johannesburg 'Springbok' service, five being loaned to South African Airways in 1946–47 pending the delivery of their Douglas DC-4s. The remaining B.O.A.C.

Yorks were fitted out as 18-seaters, a standard to which each of the sleeper Yorks was also converted at a later date. When B.S.A.A.C. was wound up in 1949, the nine surviving Star Class Yorks were absorbed by B.O.A.C., the entire fleet being withdrawn from passenger carrying operations on 7 October 1950. The last passenger service they operated for B.O.A.C. was between Santiago, Chile, and Nassau, Bahamas, but about half a dozen were retained for freighting between London and Singapore, for navigation training at Gibraltar and for flying spare engines to stranded B.O.A.C. airliners. They were redecorated in the modern manner with white top, but the bulk of the fleet was sold to independent operators. Thirteen years of faithful service came to an end on 22 November 1957, when the last two B.O.A.C. Yorks, G-AGJC and 'SO, left London Airport on delivery to Skyways Ltd. at Stansted, 13 years during which they had flown 44 million miles in 226,996 hours and had carried 90,000 passengers.

The veteran transport had meanwhile continued its distinguished career as a long distance charter machine. Operated on behalf of the War Office by the Lancashire Aircraft Corporation Ltd., Eagle Aviation Ltd., Skyways Ltd., Air Charter Ltd., and Scottish Airlines Ltd., they carried troops and their families from Stansted, Blackbushe, London Airport and elsewhere to the Far East. For this purpose they were disguised as R.A.F. machines with new serials in the WW range. Most of the remaining Yorks eventually passed into the hands of Skyways Ltd., themselves pioneer York operators who had achieved a 12-hours-a-day utilization on the Anglo-Iranian Oil Company's Basra–London shuttle in 1946–47.

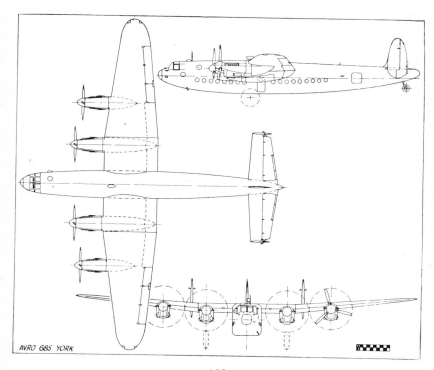

AVRO 685 YORK

The same aircraft were also used on the Berlin airlift, G-AHFI making 147 sorties before crashing at Gatow on 16 March 1949 and G-AHLV no fewer than 467 sorties. They were joined by G-ALBX 'Sky Dominion', which was a solitary York built by Victory Aircraft Ltd. at Malton, Ontario, as FM400 for the R.A.F. in 1945, with a built-up level floor. It was therefore unlike any other York, as all the cabin windows were at the same level. Up to the time of its crash at Wunsdorf on 19 June 1949 this York had also completed the immense total of 467 sorties. These figures were surpassed by many of the R.A.F. Yorks on the airlift, and when they were superseded by the Hastings in 1951–52, about 30 were acquired by civilian operators to augment existing fleets. About half of these were made serviceable by cannibalization, and Hunting-Clan Air Transport Ltd. and Dan-Air Services Ltd. joined the ranks of the York operators. The noise level in the York left much to be desired, and by 1963 only three airworthy examples remained in the United Kingdom.

The last R.A.F. York, MW295 'Ascalon II', was sold to Trans Mediterranean Airways in March 1957 and flew to Beirut as G-APCA to join several other ex-British Yorks then in operation by Persian Air Services, Air Liban and Middle East Airlines on local services or the pilgrim traffic. These included OD-ACN, formerly Gen. Smuts' S.A.A.F.4999 'Oubaas' acquired from Tropic Airways who had used it on their Johannesburg–Amsterdam run as ZS-DGN since 1952.

Twelve Yorks overhauled by the makers in 1955, flown to Canada via Prestwick for the DEW-line airlift, were afterwards sold to Maritime Central Airways and other Canadian operators. The last complete example in existence however is the former B.O.A.C. G-AGNV 'Morville', repainted as Sir Winston Churchill's wartime LV633 'Ascalon' and preserved by the Skyfame Museum at Staverton.

SPECIFICATION

Manufacturers: A. V. Roe and Co. Ltd., Newton Heath, Manchester.
Victory Aircraft Ltd., Malton, Ontario, Canada.
Power Plants: Four 1,620 h.p. Rolls-Royce Merlin T.24.
Four 1,620 h.p. Rolls-Royce Merlin 502.
Dimensions: Span, 102 ft. 0 in. Length, 78 ft. 6 in. Height, 16 ft. 6 in. Wing area, 1,205 sq. ft.
Weights: Tare weight, 42,040 lb. All-up weight, 68,000 lb.
Performance: Maximum speed, 298 m.p.h. Cruising speed, 233 m.p.h. Initial climb, 1,500 ft./min. Ceiling, 26,000 ft. Range, 2,700 miles.
Production:
A total of 265 by A. V. Roe and Co. Ltd. and one by Victory Aircraft Ltd.

(a) For the R.A.F., many of which were later converted for civil use and appear among 84 British registered Yorks listed in Appendix E.

(b) The following conversions for overseas: MW107/SAAF.4999/ZS-DGN/OD-ACN; MW135/CF-HMV; MW136/CF-HMW; MW147/CF-HMZ; MW167/CF-HMX; MW203/CF-HMU; MW237/CF-HMY; MW287/CF-HIP; MW290/CF-HAS; MW294/CF-HIQ; MW233/CF-HFP; MW291/CF-HFQ.

(c) Civil production for British and Argentinian operators including (c/n 1354) LV-XGN/LV-AFV; (1355) LV-XGO/LV-AFY; (1356) LV-XGP/LV-AFZ; (1365) LV-XIG; (1366) LV-XIH.

The first production Tudor 1, G-ARGC, on an early test flight with the original fin and rudder. (*B.O.A.C.*)

Avro 688 and Avro 689 Tudor

The idea of a Lincoln development as a post-war transatlantic airliner was conceived in 1943, but after work started in June 1944 it emerged as an entirely new design, known as the Tudor. It retained the four Merlin layout, but a single fin was used in place of the twin arrangement, the fuselage being of a circular section and pressurized. The Tudor was thus the first pressurized British transport, with heights of up to 25,000 ft. reduced to 8,000 ft. in the 12-seat cabin. The prototype, G-AGPF, first flew at Ringway on 14 June 1945 in the hands of test pilots S. A. Thorn and J. Orrell, and after development went to Boscombe Down as TT176 a year later. Trials with this and the second and third production models, G-AGRD and 'RE, revealed a number of aerodynamic snags which resulted in the fitting of larger fins, rudders and tailplanes, modification of wing root fillets, lengthening the inboard motor nacelles, fitting shorter oleo legs, installing Merlin 621 engines and generally cleaning up the airframe. The unhappy Tudor was not only subjected to two years of protracted modification, but also fell prey to the extremely high ideals set by B.O.A.C. for this, the first new civil airliner of the post-war period. At the final design conference on 12 March 1946 no fewer than 343 modifications were called for by the Corporation, in spite of the fact that two years had already been spent in ever-changing decisions which had seriously retarded the production programme. Then, as a result of tropical trials carried out on the fully modified second production aircraft, G-AGRD, at Nairobi in December 1946, the Tudor was judged incapable of operating on the transatlantic route and was finally rejected by the Corporation on 11 April 1947.

The remainder of the 21 aircraft ordered in April 1945 were meanwhile taking

The British South American Airways Corporation's Tudor 4 G-AHNN 'Star Leopard'.

shape at Woodford, two being sent to Armstrong Whitworth Aircraft Ltd. at Baginton for conversion to nine-seat V.I.P. Mk. 3s for Ministerial use and the remainder modified into two variants of the Tudor 4 for B.S.A.A.C. This involved lengthening the fuselage by 6 ft. and deleting the flight engineer's position to provide accommodation for 32 passengers. The 4B was similar, but retained the flight engineer. The second prototype, G-AGST, also took part in the original test programme as TT181, and after modification was converted to Mk. 4 and eventually to the Mk. 8 prototype VX195, which first flew on 6 September 1948. Four Mk. 4s, G-AHNJ, 'NK, 'NN and 'NP, together with two Mk. 4Bs, G-AGRE and 'RF, were eventually delivered to B.S.A.A.C. for use on their London to Bermuda route, but following the unexplained loss of G-AHNP 'Star Tiger' north-east of Bermuda on the night of 29–30 January 1948 and of G-AGRE 'Star Ariel' between Bermuda and Jamaica on 17 January 1949, the remainder were relegated to freighting duties and those awaiting delivery were sold as scrap and broken up in R. J. Coley's yard at Dukinfield, Cheshire. All were finally withdrawn from use after the Berlin airlift of 1949, in which G-AGRH and 'RJ made a total of 261 successful sorties.

In 1952 Aviation Traders Ltd. felt that the Tudors then in storage under M.C.A. ownership at Tarrant Rushton and Ringway would make suitable replacements for the York on long-range charter. Prolonged negotiations resulted in the purchase of the entire fleet, together with 88 new Merlin power units, on 2 September 1953. They comprised four Tudor Freighter 1s G-AGRG to 'RJ, five Tudor Freighter 4Bs G-AHNI, 'NJ, 'NL, 'NM and 'NO and two Tudor Freighter 3s G-AIYA and 'JKC, all of which were flown to Southend. There they were joined by components of G-AGRF, 'HNK and 'NN, which had been broken up for spares. The drastic modification of G-AGRI by upgrading the engines to Merlin 623, re-routing hydraulic and pneumatic lines, fitting Shackleton-type wheels and providing 42 rearward facing seats in a cabin bereft of its pressurization, resulted in the award of an unrestricted passenger carrying C. of A. in

February 1954. In the following year G-AGRG 'El Alamein' and G-AIYA were similarly modified, and joined 'RI on the Colonial coach service from Stansted to Idris and Lagos.

The Mk. 4Bs G-AGRH 'Zephyr', G-AHNI, 'NJ, 'NM and 'NO were further modified at Southend as Super Trader 4Bs with large freight doors in the port side and then made a number of outstanding long distance charter flights, notably to Christmas Island in the Pacific. In August 1958 G-AHNM 'Cirrus' flew to New Zealand to collect Bristol Freighter spares. Super Traders remained in use until 1959 when 'RG swung on take-off from Brindisi and was burned out, and 'RH struck the 14,547 ft. summit of Mt. Suphan Dag, Turkey, while en route to Woomera.

Unlike the Tudor 1, which was designed as a long range transport carrying a relatively small payload, the Tudor 2 was capable of carrying up to 60 passengers over the comparatively short refuelling stages on the Empire Air Routes. Its flying surfaces, power plants and undercarriage were identical with those of the Tudor 1, but the Mk. 2 was designed with a fuselage 25 ft. longer and 1 ft. greater in diameter. By May 1945 aerodynamic considerations and B.O.A.C. requirements had increased the length to 105 ft. 7 in., making it the largest airliner produced in this country up to that time. Thirty Tudor 2s were ordered by B.O.A.C. in

The prototype Tudor 2 flying near Woodford in 1946 with the original fin and rudder.
(*B.O.A.C.*)

November 1944, but after consultations with Qantas and South African Airways it was decided to standardize it on all the Empire routes and the order was increased to 79.

The prototype, G-AGSU, made its first flight at Woodford on 10 March 1946 piloted by S. A. Thorn and J. Orrell, and after four months of test flying was sent to Boscombe Down for official trials, during which the Merlin 102s were changed for Merlin 600 Specials. The same aerodynamic troubles were encountered

The Hercules engined Tudor 7 prototype.

as on the Mk. 1, and the machine returned to Woodford in September 1946 for modifications, which included the extension of the inner nacelles and fitting the enlarged fin and rudder. It was then evident that the gross weight was in excess of the desired figure due to the increase in fuselage length and changes in the furnishings, engines and tankage. This resulted in a loss of performance serious enough to ban it from aerodromes east of Calcutta and south of Nairobi. Empire interest thereupon waned and Qantas and S.A.A. re-equipped with Constellations and Skymasters respectively, resulting in the order being reduced to 50. During further test flying at Woodford the prototype was totally destroyed on 23 August 1947 in a take-off crash caused by the incorrect assembly of the aileron circuit. This cost the lives of four of the occupants, including Avro's chief designer Roy Chadwick and chief test pilot S. A. 'Bill' Thorn.

In an effort to improve performance, the first production Tudor 2, G-AGRX, was fitted with Bristol Hercules 120 radials of 1,715 h.p., and became the prototype Tudor 7. It made its first flight on 17 April 1947 and was shown at that year's Radlett S.B.A.C. Show, but did not go into production, and 'RX went to the Telecommunications Research Establishment as VX199 in March 1949. Further development of the Mk. 2 was continued with the second production model G-AGRY, which as VX202 went to Nairobi in June 1948 for tropical trials, which, proving unsatisfactory, further reduced the order to 18. These were planned as two Mk. 2s, G-AGRZ and 'SA, for experimental work; six registered G-AKBY to 'CD and modified for B.S.A.A.C as Mk. 5s and 10 freighters with tricycle undercarriages, to be known as the Avro 711A Trader. Registrations G-AGSB to 'SG, 'SV, G-AJJS, 'JT and 'JU were allotted to the Traders, but they were never built.

The Tudor 2s were delivered at the beginning of 1949, 'RZ going to the R.A.E. at Farnborough as VZ366 for airscrew and pressurization research and 'SA to Rolls-Royce, Hucknall, as VZ720 for engine development. All six Mk. 5s were delivered, but the first, G-AKBY, was sold to Air Vice-Marshal D. C. T. Bennett's Airflight Ltd. and left Blackbushe on 3 September 1948 en route to Wunsdorf and the Berlin airlift. The other five, in B.S.A.A.C. livery, were delivered to the firm's base at Langley, but, far from carrying their planned loads of 44 passengers over the South Atlantic, were converted into tanker aircraft and followed G-AKBY to

Germany. Here they joined G-AGRY, now of Airflight Ltd., which, after 85 sorties, each time carrying $9\frac{3}{4}$ tons from Wunsdorf to Gatow, had also become a tanker. The impressive total of 3,167 sorties, with nine ton loads, was flown by the seven 'large' Tudors in just over a year, during one of which G-AKBY took-off with the elevator locked, but was successfully landed by Air Vice-Marshal D. C. T. Bennett on the trimmers.

On their return, 'RY made 13 trooping flights to the Canal Zone as XF537, but 'KBY crashed while making an approach to land at R.A.F. Llandow after a charter flight from Dublin on 12 March 1950, 80 of the occupants being killed. Tudor 5s G-AKCC and 'CD were sold to William Dempster Ltd. and used during 1951 as 52-seaters on tourist flights to Johannesburg. After 'CC overshot on arrival at Bovingdon on 26 October 1951, 'CD joined the remaining Mk. 5s at Stansted, where, as the property of Air Charter Ltd., they were gradually broken up to provide spares for the Super Traders.

Designation Tudor 6 was reserved for six aircraft ordered by the Argentine company FAMA but although airframe numbers were allotted and application made for Cs. of A., they were not completed.

SPECIFICATION

Manufacturers: A. V. Roe and Co. Ltd., Greengate, Middleton, Manchester.
Power Plants: (Mks. 1–4B) Four 1,770 h.p. Rolls-Royce Merlin 621.
        (Tudor 7)   Four 1,715 h.p. Bristol Hercules 120.
        (Tudor 8)   Four 5,000 lb. s.t. Rolls-Royce Nene 5.
Dimensions: Span, 120 ft. 0 in. Length (Tudor 1), 79 ft. 6 in. (Tudor 2), 105 ft. 7 in.
        (Tudor 4), 85 ft. 3 in. Height (Tudor 1 and 4), 20 ft. 11 in. (Tudor 2)
        24 ft. 3 in. Wing area, 1,421 sq. ft.
Weights: (Tudor 1) Tare weight, 47,960 lb. All-up weight, 71,000 lb.
        (Tudor 2) Tare weight, 46,300 lb. All-up weight, 80,000 lb.
        (Tudor 4) Tare weight, 49,441 lb. All-up weight, 80,000 lb.
        (Tudor 7) Tare weight, 51,625 lb. All-up weight, 80,000 lb.
Performance: (Tudor 1) Maximum speed, 260 m.p.h. Cruising speed, 210 m.p.h. Initial
        climb, 700 ft./min. Ceiling, 26,000 ft. Range, 3,630 miles.
        (Tudor 2) Maximum speed, 295 m.p.h. Cruising speed, 235 m.p.h. Initial
        climb, 740 ft./min. Ceiling, 25,550 ft. Range, 2,330 miles.
        (Tudor 4) Maximum speed, 282 m.p.h. Cruising speed, 210 m.p.h. Initial
        climb, 800 ft./min. Ceiling, 27,400 ft. Range, 4,000 miles.
        (Tudor 7) Maximum speed, 270 m.p.h. Cruising speed, 200 m.p.h. Initial
        climb, 750 ft./min. Ceiling, 25,100 ft. Range, 2,800 miles.

Production: (a) Avro 688 Tudor 1
Twelve British registered aircraft (c/n 1234, 1249 and 1251–1260) listed in detail in Appendix E.

      (b) Avro 689 Tudor 2
Five British registered aircraft (c/n 1235, 1250 and 1262–1264) and the following reservations not taken up due to cancelled contracts: (c/n 1395–1401) G-AJJV to G-AJKB; (1425–1436) G-AKTH to G-AKTT; (1437–1448) G-AKUE to G-AKUP.

(c) Avro 688 Tudor 3

Two aircraft only (c/n 1367–1368) G-AIYA and G-AJKC.

(d) Avro 688 Tudor 4 and 4B

Fourteen British registered aircraft (c/n 1253–1256 and 1341–1350) listed in Appendix E.

(e) Avro 689 Tudor 5

Six British registered aircraft (c/n 1417–1422) listed in Appendix E.

(f) Avro 689 Tudor 6

Six aircraft (c/n 1386–1391) ordered by Flota Aerea Mercante Argentina (FAMA) but not built following cancellation of contract.

(g) Avro 689 Tudor 7

One aircraft only (c/n 1261) G-AGRX.

(h) Avro 711A Trader

Prototype (c/n 1250) G-AGSV and nine production aircraft comprising (1265–1270) G-AGSB to G-AGSG registered to the Ministry of Supply and Aircraft Production 9.45 and (1392–1394) G-AJJS to G-AJJU registered to the Ministry of Supply 3.47. None of these was completed.

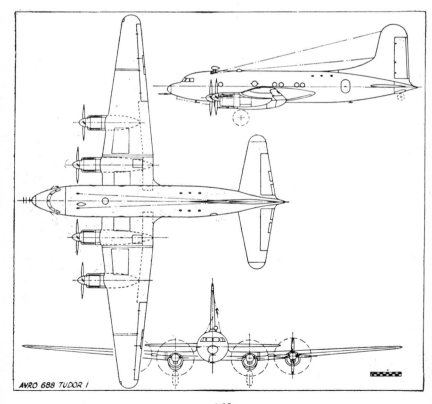

AVRO 688 TUDOR 1

The Lancastrian 1 G-AGLS leaving on 28 May 1946 to fly on the first B.O.A.C. Australian service to start from London Airport. (*B.O.A.C.*)

Avro 691 Lancastrian

Unlike the York, which had a spacious fuselage of new design, the Lancastrian was simply a demilitarized Lancaster fitted with nose and tail cones in place of the turrets. The first conversion was made to the Lancaster III R5727, flown to Canada in 1941 to assist the tooling for production at Malton, Ontario, by Victory Aircraft Ltd. who later made and fitted the original nose and tail fairings. Registered CF-CMS, this machine inaugurated Trans-Canada Air Lines' transatlantic service on 22 July 1943 by carrying four tons of Canadian Forces' mail non-stop from Dorval to Prestwick in a record time of 12 hours 26 minutes. This record was broken repeatedly by the T.C.A. fleet of eight Canadian Lancaster X conversions CF-CMT to CF-CNA known as Lancaster XPPs.

The first of 63 British civil Lancastrian Mk. 1 aircraft was G-AGLF converted from Lancaster VB673 and handed over to the B.O.A.C. Development Flight at Hurn with a C. of A. issued on 7 February 1945. The record-breaking flight two months later by Capt. R. G. Buck in this machine to New Zealand in three and a half days, heavily underlined the end of the leisurely pre-war Empire Air Route schedules. During its relatively short service life the Lancastrian created an entirely new conception of this subject. Thirty-two aircraft from the tail end of Lancaster production were earmarked for B.O.A.C., but only 20 were converted, the last being delivered in October 1945. Their markings were G-AGLS to 'MM (less 'MI). They were for joint use with Qantas on the Kangaroo service, British crews being relieved by Australians at Karachi. The inaugural service left Hurn on 31 May 1945 piloted by Capt. E. Palmer in G-AGLV, the Qantas service leaving Sydney in G-AGLS on 2 June. Lancastrians were far from economical in operation, only nine passengers being carried in a row of seats facing inwards along the port side, but they were an acknowledged post-war interim type and against the estimated £1,400,000 annual loss on the Kangaroo service could be offset the prestige value of their fast three-day schedule to Sydney.

It had long been a British ambition to operate to South America, but no British commercial type prior to the Lancastrian had enough range for the South Atlantic crossing. The honour of making the first survey flight fell to Capt. O. P. Jones, who left Hurn in G-AGMG on 9 October 1945 en route to Buenos Aires and over the Andes to Santiago and Lima. Regular services were opened with a fleet of six

Alitalia's Lancastrian 3 I-AHBY 'Libeccio' at Rome Airport in 1948.

13-passenger Lancastrian 3s, G-AGWG to 'WL, by British South American Airways Corporation in the following year. Twelve more Mk. 3s, G-AHBT to 'CE, built at Woodford, were delivered at the end of 1946, three for the newly formed Silver City Airways and four for Skyways Ltd. The remaining five were sold by B.E.A.C. to the Italian airline Alitalia for a weekly Rome–Montevideo South Atlantic service which began on 2 June 1948. The others were employed on long distance charter work to South Africa, Australia and the Far East. Eight former R.A.F. Mk. 4s, distinguished by their extra windows, were acquired by Skyways Ltd. in 1947–48, two of these being sold to B.S.A.A.C., and three more helping B.O.A.C. over the fleet shortage caused by the withdrawal of the Tudors. Four of the earlier Lancastrians were sold to Qantas, and in 1949 Skyways operated the Nairobi–Mauritius–Réunion shuttle on behalf of B.O.A.C. with G-AGLV re-registered VP-KGT for the purpose.

Three additional ex R.A.F. Lancastrian C. Mk. 4s were overhauled by A. V. Roe and Co. Ltd. for Flota Aerea Mercante Argentina but in 1949 these were taken over by the Argentine Air Force as V.I.P. transports.

In its declining years the Lancastrian gave outstanding service in emergency as a carrier of liquids in bulk, first during the milk shortage of 1947 and secondly on the Berlin airlift. The miscellaneous collection of aircraft used for carrying milk churns from Nutts Corner to Speke included four Skyways Lancastrians. On the Berlin airlift, however, Flight Refuelling Ltd., leading exponents of the bulk carriage of petrol by air, acquired five former B.O.A.C. and B.S.A.A.C. machines and equipped them with large fuselage tanks enabling each aircraft to carry 2,500 gallons of petrol or diesel oil. Four of the surviving T.C.A. Lancastrians were also ferried from Canada for this purpose and became G-AKDO to 'DS, the entire fleet making a total of 3,600 sorties. They were joined in the task by five others belonging to Skyways Ltd., which made nearly 2,000 additional sorties. Their mission completed, the ageing Lancastrians were flown back to their bases at Hurn, Dunsfold and Tarrant Rushton and scrapped in 1951.

SPECIFICATION

Manufacturers: A. V. Roe and Co. Ltd., Greengate, Middleton, Manchester.
Power Plants: Four 1,635 h.p. Rolls-Royce Merlin T.24/4.
              Four 1,635 h.p. Rolls-Royce Merlin 500.

Dimensions: Span, 102 ft. 0 in. Length, 76 ft. 10 in. Height, 19 ft. 6 in. Wing area, 1,297 sq. ft.

Weights: Tare weight, 30,426 lb. All-up weight, 65,000 lb.

Performance: Maximum speed, 315 m.p.h. Cruising speed, 230 m.p.h. Initial climb, 950 ft./min. Ceiling, 25,500 ft. Range, 4,150 miles.

Production: (a) Lancaster XPP conversions by Victory Aircraft Ltd.

Nine aircraft for Trans-Canada Air Lines: CF-CMS to CF-CNA, four of which were later registered in the United Kingdom (see Appendix E).

(b) Lancastrian C. Mk. 1

Twenty-three aircraft for the R.A.F., all but two transferred to B.O.A.C.

(c) Lancastrian C. Mk. 2

Thirty-three aircraft for the R.A.F., ten later converted for civil use.

(d) Lancastrian 3

Eighteen aircraft (c/n 1279–1284 and 1288–1299) detailed in Appendix E.

(e) Lancastrian C. Mk. 4

Eight aircraft for the R.A.F. from which TX288, 287 and 289 were later converted for FAMA by A. V. Roe and Co. Ltd. as (c/n 1382, 1402 and 1403) LV-ACS, LV-ACU and LV-ACV. Four others were converted by Skyways Ltd. (see Appendix E).

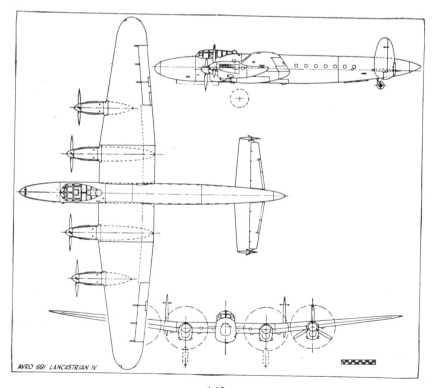

AVRO 691 LANCASTRIAN IV

The second production B.K. Swallow flying near Hanworth in 1934. (*Aeroplane*)

B.A. Swallow

Klemm L.25 two-seaters, first flown in Germany in 1927, soon made a name for themselves despite their low power. Their rugged all-wood construction, cantilever wing and reliable Salmson radials made them most attractive private owners' machines. Inevitably they reached Britain, the first arriving in March 1929, and by 1933 twenty-seven Klemm aeroplanes had been purchased through Major E. F. Stephen of S. T. Lea Ltd., who had secured the selling rights in the United Kingdom. The last two, L.25s G-ABTE and G-ABZO, owned by A. B. Gibbons of Stag Lane and Sir John Carden of Heston, were fitted with 75 h.p. Pobjoy R radials, which improved their already exceptional performance. Encouraged by the popularity born of their comfort and slow-flying characteristics, Major Stephen founded the British Klemm Aeroplane Co. Ltd. with a factory at Hanworth. His works manager was the pioneer designer G. H. Handasyde, and the test pilot E. G. Hordern.

The Hanworth-built version was structurally similar to the German original, but locally strengthened to meet British airworthiness requirements and available with either the Pobjoy or the Salmson A.D. 9 radials. In the event, only the prototype, G-ACMK, first flown in November 1933, and five others had the Salmson, and only the demonstrator G-ACOW had the Pobjoy R. All others were fitted with the improved Pobjoy Cataract motor. Irrespective of the engine fitted, they were known as the British Klemm L.25C 1A Swallow, or. in short, the B.K. Swallow. With its low wing loading it was persuaded on one occasion to soar, engine off, over Dunstable Downs for some 20 minutes, and fully lived up to the claim that it was the safest aeroplane in the world. Even in the worst recorded crash, in which G-ACUM was destroyed by fire, A. S. Montefiore and his passenger escaped unhurt. G-ACVW had the most adventurous career of all, going to Kenya with John Carberry in July 1934 and being the only B.K. Swallow with a coupé top. It returned to Brooklands in 1936 and two years later was sold to B. M. Groves, who, bent on gaining first-hand news of his Russian wife, left Heston in G-ACVW on 4 November 1938 en route to the U.S.S.R. He left Stockholm for Moscow on 13 November but iced up and made a forced landing 100 miles from his destination. The Russians then seized 'VW and imprisoned its pilot.

Twenty-eight B.K. Swallows were built, including six for export, but in 1970 only one remained, G-ACXE, stored at Sandown by D. G. Ellis.

The Royal Aeronautical Society Garden Party at Heathrow on 5 May 1935 witnessed the first public appearance of a much-modified Swallow, G-ADDB, flown by Flt. Lt. J. B. Wilson. Although powered in the normal way by a Cataract II, the curved wing tips, rudder and tailplane had been made straight and the fuselage top decking had been made flat sided. These revisions effectively speeded production, and, with new finance, the firm changed its name to the British Aircraft Manufacturing Co. Ltd., and the designation of the machine to B.A. Swallow 2. One hundred and five were built, all but seven being sold to private owners and flying schools in the United Kingdom. In 1936 the still more powerful Cataract III was installed in G-AECY, the twentieth production airframe, and in all subsequent Swallows except D. R. Pobjoy's personal aircraft G-AEFM, which had the 95 h.p. Niagara. The forty-second airframe, G-AEIB, was the first to have the 90 h.p. Cirrus Minor 1 in-line engine, both variants being produced in almost equal quantities until G-AFGE, the seventy-first, which was the last Pobjoy Swallow. As usual in pre-war practice, changes of engine did not affect the designation.

The Cataract engined B.K. Swallow Coupé which was seized by the Russians, photographed at Shoreham in 1937.

The 101st production B.A. Swallow, showing the Cirrus engine, angular lines, folding wings and generous windscreens.

The sole example of a Swallow 2 fitted with a coupé top was G-AEMW.

In 1938 the principal operator of the Cirrus Swallow was Blackburn's No. 4 E.R.F.T.S. at Brough, which had 15 (G-AFHK–'HP, 'HU–'HW, 'IG–'IL), 12 of which were transferred to the London Air Park Flying Club at Hanworth in 1939 for Civil Air Guard duties. With the coming of war many Swallows were impressed and mainly went to A.T.C. Squadrons as instructional airframes. One of these was the Cirrus-engined G-AEVC, which had survived a pilotless take-off from the Cinque Ports Flying Club, only to be destroyed when a tip-and-run raider bombed the H.Q. of No. 304 (Hastings) A.T.C. Sqn. in 1943. Some became the unofficial mounts of Station C.O.s, and only a few gained R.A.F. serial status, as for instance BK 897, formerly G-AFGD of the Cardiff Aeroplane Club, which was converted into a glider at Farnborough and made a number of towed flights. One, G-AEZM, personal mount of Airspeed test pilot G. B. S. Errington, remained civil in full camouflage throughout the war.

Some 37 of these machines still existed after the war, but many were semi-derelict, and only the prototype, G-ACMK, owned by C. E. Berens of Farnborough, and 17 Swallow 2s flew again. Several were acquired by T. L. McDonald Ltd. and overhauled at Balado prior to export to Eire, and one, G-AECA, was flown from Greatham to South Africa by emigrants R. Redman and C. Brownlow in 39 days in 1946. Another Cataract Swallow 2, G-AELG, was flown in the 1946 and 1947 Folkestone Trophy Races by Paul Godfrey, who won the 1947 event at 96 m.p.h. One of the few Cirrus Swallows then surviving, G-AEMW, was rebuilt with a coupé top but was subsequently lost in an accident, so that by 1970 the only Swallow 2s in existence were VH-UUM and VH-AAB in Australia, G-ADPS in the U.K. and three preserved as static exhibits. These were G-AEVZ by the Northern Aircraft Preservation Society at Stockport and G-AFCL and 'GE at Old Warden.

SPECIFICATION

Manufacturers: The British Klemm Aeroplane Co. Ltd., Victoria Road, Hanworth, Middlesex; name changed to The British Aircraft Manufacturing Co. Ltd. in 1935.

Power Plants: (B.K. Swallow) One 75 h.p. British Salmson A.D. 9 or one 85 h.p. Pobjoy Cataract II.

(B.A. Swallow) One 90 h.p. Pobjoy Cataract III or one 90 h.p. Blackburn Cirrus Minor 1.

Dimensions: Span, 42 ft. 8½ in. Length, 26 ft. 3 in. Height, 7 ft. 0 in. Wing area, 219½ sq. ft. (B.A. Swallow): Length, 26 ft. 0 in. Wing area, 215 sq. ft.

Weights: (B.K. Swallow) Tare weight, 960 lb. All-up weight, 1,500 lb.
                (B.A. Swallow) Tare weight, 990 lb. All-up weight, 1,500 lb.

Performance: (B.K. Swallow) Maximum speed, 104 m.p.h. Cruising speed, 90 m.p.h.
                               Initial climb, 800 ft./min. Ceiling, 17,000 ft. Range
                               420 miles.

                (B.A. Swallow) Maximum speed, 112 m.p.h. Cruising speed, 98 m.p.h.

Production: (a) B.K. Swallow 1

Twenty-eight aircraft (c/n 1–12, 14–24, 26–29 and 31) comprising (c/n 4) VP-KBB;
(19) VP-KBK; (24) VH-USH; (27) VT-AGA; (29) VH-URZ; (31) VH-UTA and twenty-
two British registered machines listed in Appendix E.

       (b) B.A. Swallow 2 (Pobjoy)

Prototype (c/n 32) G-ADDB and 59 production aircraft commencing c/n 400 and
comprising (c/n 403) VH-UTQ; (407) VH-UUH; (409) VH-UUM; (412) VH-UUJ; (414)
VH-UUN; (420) VR-SAL; (422) OE-SSC; (423) OE-SSD; (432) SU-AAQ; (435)
ZK-AEN; (439) VT-AHP; (440) VT-AHS; (450) VT-AIA; (451) VT-AHX; (459)
VT-AIM; (463) VT-AIH and 42 British registered aircraft listed in Appendix E.

       (c) B.A. Swallow 2 (Cirrus)

Forty-seven British registered aircraft listed in Appendix E.

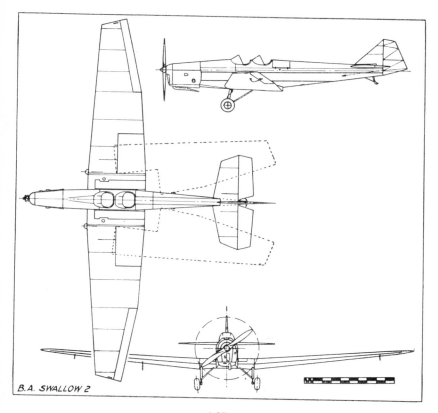

B.A. SWALLOW 2

The prototype B.K. Eagle flying near Hanworth in 1934. (*Flight Photo 10635S*)

B.A. Eagle

The British Klemm B.K.1 Eagle was a low-wing cabin monoplane of wooden construction, seating two passengers side by side behind the pilot and fitted with a manually operated outward retracting undercarriage. Like the Swallow, the Eagle was utterly viceless, and although it bore a superficial resemblance to the Klemm L.32, the machine was in fact an entirely new design by the firm's chief designer, G. H. Handasyde.

The prototype, G-ACRG, first flew at Hanworth early in 1934, and its clean lines and exceptional performance attracted a great deal of attention from racing and long-distance pilots. The first production model G-ACPU, built for E. L. Gandar Dower, was itself a racing version fitted with a 200 h.p. Gipsy VI and flown in the 1934 King's Cup Race by A. C. S. Irwin. The union with this heavy power unit was not exactly a happy one, and the machine afterwards reverted to standard. Another Eagle, G-ACVU, also a racing special, was built with a large cabin fuel tank as Flt. Lt. G. Shaw's entry in the MacRobertson Race to Australia in October 1934 and ponderously named 'The Spirit of Wm. Shaw & Co. Ltd.' It was eventually withdrawn with a damaged undercarriage at Bushire.

Three export orders, CR-MAI for Señor Arocando Torre do Valle in Portuguese East Africa, and VH-USI (ex G-ACTR) and 'SP for the agents, Adastra Airways Ltd. of Sydney, brought B.K.1 Eagle production to an end at the sixth aircraft. VH-USP was sold later to M. W. 'Pat' O'Hara who named it 'Zeelandia' and flew it solo across the Tasman Sea from Richmond, N.S.W., to Mangere, N.Z. in 12 hr. 47 min. on 18 October 1935. It was re-registered ZK-AEA in March 1936 but was shipped back to Sydney a month later and O'Hara was killed when it crashed at Eumangerie, N.S.W., on 24 May 1936.

Constructor's numbers which began normally at 1 and 2, continued with 25 and 30 in the Swallow series but the system was stabilised at the fifth aircraft, CR-MAI, which became 105.

Simultaneously with the reorganization of the company as the British Aircraft Manufacturing Co. Ltd., a new de-luxe version, the B.A. Eagle 2, appeared. As in the case of the Swallow, the tall, rounded rudder was replaced with a more angular unit, the rear fuselage deepened and the doors modified to eliminate the centre roof member. G-ACZT was the first of 37 production Eagle 2s and, in addition, the B.K.1s G-ACRG and 'PU were re-worked to this standard for the King's Cup Race. On one Gipsy Major the speeds were astonishing, 'PU clocking 134·58 m.p.h. and 'RG fitted with a high compression motor came second at 143·02 m.p.h. The prototype 'RG had a notable racing career, the firm's chief test pilot, J. B. Wilson, won the 1935 Heston–Woolsington Race in it, came second in the Folkestone Trophy Race at 139·75 m.p.h. and on 21 September 1935 came a sensational second in the Heston–Cardiff Race at 152·5 m.p.h. It was the unsuccessful King's Cup mount of Amy Johnson in 1936 and of W. L. Hope in 1937.

Señor Juan Pombo, who left Hanworth on 3 May 1935 in the long-range, single-seat Eagle 2 'Santander' (c/n 108), crashed at Port Natal on 26 May but the Spanish Government presented him with a replacement (c/n 115) in which he made a record crossing of the South Atlantic and completed a 9,000 mile flight to Mexico City with his bride as passenger. A similar aircraft, G-ADFB named 'Seikai' ('Blue Seas'), left Hanworth on 12 May 1935 piloted by Katsutaro Ano, who reached Tokyo after a completely uneventful flight. The Schlesinger Race from Portsmouth to Johannesburg in 1936 inevitably included an Eagle. C. G. M. Alington's G-ADID 'Frobisher' carried two passengers, but was eliminated with a damaged undercarriage caused by an unsuccessful take-off after a forced landing in Bavaria. With the attention of the handicappers always on them, the Eagles never won another race. 'ID was flown in the 1937 King's Cup Race, and later in the year competed in the Isle of Man Races, piloted by Tommy Rose. G-ADJO, sold to Major J. C. Hargreaves and based at Alexandria, was no luckier and failed to gain a place in the Egyptian Oases Rally of February 1937. The last few production Eagles also included their quota of unsuccessful racers: G-AERB, flown in the 1937 Isle of Man Races by Hanworth instructor H. J. Wilson,

Katsutaro Ano seated in the long-range B.A. Eagle 2 in which he flew from Hanworth to Tokyo in 1935. (*Flight Photo 11406S*)

The fixed undercarriage B.A. Eagle 2 G-AFAX waiting to start in the Folkestone Trophy Race on 28 August 1937. (*A. J. Jackson*)

G-AFIC, owned and flown in the 1937 King's Cup Race by Flg. Off. A. E. Clouston and G-AFKH, flown by Luis Fontes in the very last pre-war air race, to the Isle of Man on 27 May 1939. G-ACPU eventually passed under feminine ownership, with the Misses Mabel and Sheila Glass. Other private owners were Lord Willoughby de Broke, who kept G-ADES at his private airfield at Kineton, Northants.; G-ADVT, based at Heston by the Marquess of Donegal, and G-AEGO, owned by F. S. Cotton late in 1939. In commercial use G-ACZT was with the Border Flying Club at Carlisle in 1936, G-ADYY was executive transport for the Vacuum Oil Co. Ltd. from 1935 to 1938, G-ADPO flew with Air Hire Ltd. at Heston, and G-AEKI with the Yorkshire Aviation Services Country Club Ltd. at York.

There were also 13 others built to overseas order and comprising three for Australia (two of which were still in existence in 1972); two for Canada including CF-AYH which flew until 1948; two each for Kenya and France; one each for Spain and Singapore; and two for India viz. VT-AKO for R. B. Singh, Partab Garh, and 'KP for the Nawab of Sachur.

The first of the main variants was G-ADJS, used by the Villiers-Hay Development Co. Ltd. in 1936 as a flying testbed for the Villiers Maya 1 four cylinder 125 h.p. engine. The other was the solitary fixed undercarriage model G-AFAX, built in 1937 for H. O. Hamilton of Shoreham who sold it in 1939 to J. D. Hodder who took it to Rangoon and, to escape the Japanese invasion, to Australia where he still flew it as VH-ACN at Parkes, N.S.W., thirty years later.

Eagle 2 G-ADJS was evaluated by No. 16 Sqn., R.A.F. at Old Sarum in 1937 and in 1941 seven were impressed for communications duties in the United Kingdom but in nearly every case were written off when their undercarriages collapsed, so that none survived the war. VP-KCI was impressed in Kenya and those in India, VT-AKO and 'KP, flew as MA945 and AW183 respectively, one at least with the New Delhi Communications Flight.

SPECIFICATION

Manufacturers: The British Klemm Aeroplane Co. Ltd., Victoria Road, Hanworth, Middlesex; renamed The British Aircraft Manufacturing Co. Ltd. in 1935.

Power Plant: One 130 h.p. de Havilland Gipsy Major.
Dimensions: Span, 39 ft. 3 in. Length, 26 ft. 0 in. Height, 6 ft. 9 in.
　　　　　　Wing area, 200 sq. ft.
Weights: Tare weight, 1,450 lb. All-up weight, 2,400 lb.
Performance: Maximum speed, 148 m.p.h. Cruising speed, 130 m.p.h. Initial climb,
　　　　　　700 ft./min. Ceiling, 16,000 ft. Range, 650 miles.

Production: (a) B.K.1 Eagle 1

Four British registered aircraft and two for export: (c/n 105) CR-MAI; (106)
VH-USP/ZK-AEA.

(b) B.A. Eagle 2

Twenty-two British registered aircraft and the following for export: (c/n 108) 'Santan-
der', J. Pombo; (109) VH-UTI, Hannan Bros.; (113) VH-UTG, Adastra Airways Ltd.;
(114) EC-CBC, Lineas Aereos Postales Espanoles; (115) J. Pombo; (117) F-AQDA,
N. Naninesco; (120) untraced; (123) VP-KBS, G. Blowers, Nairobi; (128) VH-UUY,
Adastra Airways Ltd.; (129) VR-SAP, Penang Flying Club; (134) CF-AYH, G. Priestley,
Toronto; (135) Maharajah of Cochin; (136) F-APDG, P. W. Constantine; (139)
CF-BBF, A. Graydon, Montreal; (140) VP-KCI.

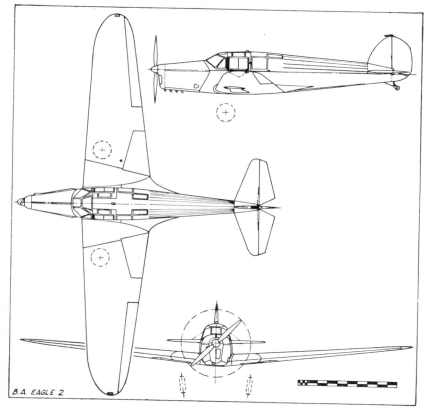

B.A. EAGLE 2

171

Drone G-ADUA (Douglas Sprite) with enclosed cockpit, airborne at Hanworth in the spring of 1936. (*Aeroplane Photo 9609*)

B.A.C. Drone

During the early 1930s the British Aircraft Co. of Maidstone built a series of gliders culminating in the B.A.C. VII tandem two-seater. In 1932 C. H. Lowe Wylde, designer and managing director of the firm, fitted B.A.C. VII BGA.186 with an undercarriage and a 600 c.c. Douglas flat-twin motor cycle engine mounted above the wing on a steel tube pylon. This additional equipment approximately equalled the weight of the second occupant. The single-seat prototype, known as the Planette, proved both docile and manoeuvrable with a speed range of 15–40 m.p.h., and, following this initial success, three more were constructed. These were numbered 2 to 4, but were actually BGA.196 to 198, the prototype being later sold as a glider and re-certificated as BGA.194. Planettes Nos. 1 and 2 made the first of a number of public demonstrations at Hanworth on 27 November 1932 piloted by C. H. Lowe Wylde and E. D. Ayre, but at a similar display at West Malling on 13 May 1933 their designer, allegedly taken ill in the air, sideslipped No. 1 into the ground from 400 ft. and was killed. The firm was then taken over by the Austrian sailplane pilot Robert Kronfeld, who demonstrated No. 2, fitted with a streamlined engine pylon and renamed the Drone, at the opening of Speke Airport in July 1933. Premises nearer London were acquired at Hanworth, and before the firm closed down in 1937, 33 Drones had been built. In addition, the original No. 3 became G-ADSB in September 1935, owned by A. Carpmael at Denham, but grotesquely painted as a fish, was normally crazy flown at air displays by B. F. Collins, one of the firm's pilots. In 1939 this machine was given to the London Gliding Club, and finished up as the B.A.C. VII BGA.609 at Blackbushe in 1951. No. 4 appeared as G-AENZ at Middleton in September 1936 and was flown at Dyce in 1939 by T. J. Thomason.

Production Drones were fitted with the specially developed 23 h.p. Douglas Sprite engine, the four built in 1935 for A. E. H. Coltman, Braunstone; Anglian Air Services, Maylands; Cdr. J. S. Dove, R.N., Hanworth, and a demonstrator, were registered G-ADMU, 'SA, 'PJ and 'UA respectively. Col. the Master of (later Lord) Sempill startled the aviation world by flying 'PJ from Croydon to Berlin and back on 25s. worth of petrol in 11 hours on 2 April 1936, and in the following week 'PJ was exhibited at Selfridges to publicize the event. The latter machine crashed at Huddersfield a year later and was thereafter stored in a

Leicester garage until slowly rebuilt by the proprietor, A. C. Waterhouse. It eventually flew again at Desford in October 1950 powered by a 32 h.p. Bristol Cherub III, and after making a great name for itself at post-war gatherings, was again seriously damaged following engine failure at Leicester East on 3 April 1955.

In 1936, during which 20 machines were built, the firm was renamed Kronfeld Ltd. and the Sprite-powered model became the Kronfeld Super Drone. Two of these, G-AEAN and G-AEEO, flew over 400 hours, or 20,000 miles, with C. W. A. Scott's Air Display, piloted by Idwal Jones and L. J. Rimmer. G-AEDB, originally supplied to Perth private owner G. Scott Pearce, was sold in October 1936 to H. R. Dimock, proprietor of the Ely Aero Club, which later acquired G-ADSA, 'UA and G-AEEP. He remodelled 'DB with a Cherub III and fitted a tricycle undercarriage but the original undercarriage was eventually refitted and in 1972 the aircraft was under reconstruction at Woodley by R. E. Ogden. An alternative version introduced later in 1936 was fitted with a 30 h.p. Carden Ford converted car engine, the prototype being the red, dragon's-tooth-decorated G-AEEN flown at Ramsgate by A. Batchelor and W. M. C. Peatfield and fatally crashed there by a visiting pilot on 24 August 1937. Although a delight to fly, even in low visibility, they could be heard for miles, and in an attempt to reduce the incredible noise created by the close proximity of the propeller tips to the structure, Kronfeld fitted slightly swept-back wings to all later Drones, brought the propeller 6 in. aft of the trailing edge and fitted slotted ailerons. This model was known as the Drone de Luxe, two machines, G-AEJK and 'KN, going north to the Scottish Flying Club at Renfrew. Another, G-AEKU, had a Perspex canopy.

During the war a Drone de Luxe was camouflaged, coded PR-? and flown by the pilots of No. 609 (Fighter) Squadron on duck-shooting sorties using a 12 bore shot gun and a ring-and-bead sight. Eight Drones survived the war and three flew again, including G-AEJS, which crashed at Gerrards Cross on 27 April 1947. Following a rebuild at Upper Heyford in 1950, G-AEKV flew many hours with J. E. Fricker at Southend, E. H. Gould at Christchurch, R. T. Vigors at Kidlington and J. R. Garood at Denham and was rebuilt at Colerne 1971–72. Excluding an interesting penguin trainer which used some Drone components, 'KV was one of the last three Drones built, the others being G-AESF based at Eastleigh by Unwin Williams in 1937 and a special model G-AFBZ built for Lord Sempill with a 35 h.p. Ava 4A-02 flat-four motor.

The red Drone de Luxe G-AEEN was the first to be fitted with the Carden Ford water-cooled engine. (*A. J. Jackson*)

173

SPECIFICATION

Manufacturers: The British Aircraft Co. (1935) Ltd., London Air Park, Feltham, Middlesex, renamed Kronfeld Ltd. in 1936.

Power Plants: (Super Drone)   One 23 h.p. Douglas Sprite.
(Drone de Luxe) One 30 h.p. Carden Ford.

Dimensions: Span, 39 ft. 8 in. Length, 21 ft. 2 in. Height, 7 ft. 0 in. Wing area, 172 sq. ft.

Weights: (Super Drone)   Tare weight, 390 lb. All-up weight, 460 lb.
(Drone de Luxe) Tare weight, 640 lb. All-up weight, 720 lb.

Performance: (Super Drone)   Maximum speed, 70 m.p.h. Cruising speed, 60 m.p.h. Initial climb, 380 ft./min. Ceiling, 12,500 ft. Range, 300 miles.
(Drone de Luxe) Maximum speed, 73 m.p.h. Cruising speed, 65 m.p.h. Initial climb, 480 ft./min. Ceiling, 12,500 ft. Range, 340 miles.

Production:

Thirty-three aircraft: (c/n 1) unregistered; (2) VT-AEU; (3–26) British registered; (27) VT-AHM; (28–31 and 35) British registered; (32) unregistered flyable ground trainer.

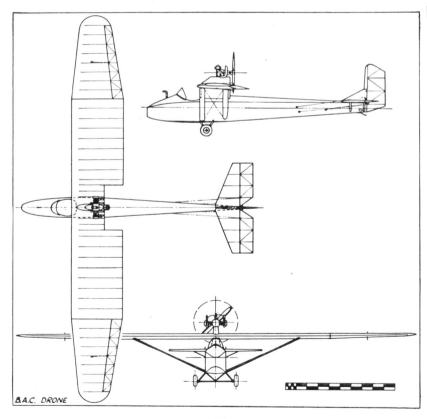

B.A.C. DRONE

One-Eleven 301 G-ATPJ landing at Wisley after first flight, 20 May 1966. Laid down as 9K-ACI for Kuwait Airways, it was delivered to British Eagle on 8 June 1966.

B.A.C. One-Eleven

In 1956 Hunting Aircraft Ltd. designed a 32-seat, short field turbojet transport designated H.107 and powered by two Bristol Orpheus 12Bs mounted externally on the rear fuselage. Registration G-APOH was allotted in July 1958 but the project was then shelved for two years to await the newly developing turbofan engine. An enlarged 48–56-seat version was then offered with two Bristol BE.61 or Rolls-Royce RB.149 and later with two Bristol Siddeley BS.75s but it aroused little interest and lay dormant until Hunting became part of the British Aircraft Corporation Ltd. in 1960.

It was then re-activated as the 59-seat B.A.C.107 but market research revealed sufficient airline interest in a larger, Viscount-size version to warrant construction of three static test airframes and a 79-seat prototype, (180 m.p.h. faster than the Viscount), powered by two Rolls-Royce Spey Mk. 506s. Designated B.A.C.111, it had a circular section, semi-monocoque fuselage mounted on a clean swept wing with Fowler flaps. The variable-incidence tailplane was mounted on top of the fin clear of jet efflux and an auxiliary power unit was mounted in the tail cone for engine starting at ill-equipped airfields.

The first order, 10 aircraft for British United Airways Ltd., was announced in May 1961 and in the following October Braniff International Airways became the first U.S. airline to order foreign equipment 'off the drawing board' by placing an order for six. In due course the B.A.C.111 became known as the One-Eleven and in May 1963 three variants were announced—a basic Series 200; a longer range/greater payload Series 300 with Spey Mk. 511s; and a similar Series 400 meeting U.S. requirements. Further orders to a total of 60 machines were placed before the first flight, each customer-variant being allotted a sub-series number, e.g. ten Series 201s (G-ASJA to 'JJ) for B.U.A.; six Series 203s (N1541–N1546) for Braniff International; two Series 207s (VP-YXA and 'XB) for Central African Airways; and four Series 208s (EI-ANE to 'NH) for Aer Lingus.

The Series 200 prototype, G-ASHG, first flew at Hurn on 20 August 1963 but crashed near Cricklade, Wilts., on 22 October with the loss of test pilot M. J. Lithgow and six crew, victims of a phenomenon known as deep stall. Modification to leading-edge shape, first tried as a wooden addition to G-ASJB, and the introduction of powered elevators, first fitted to G-ASJC, overcame the problem but during certification trials G-ASJB was severely damaged landing at Wisley on 18 March 1964 and replaced in the B.U.A. order by G-ASTJ. Plans to rebuild it as G-ASVT were ultimately abandoned. The programme was then joined by G-ASJF and the first Braniff, N1541, which briefly became G-ASUF (and the first One-Eleven to visit Heathrow) when it collected Minister of Aviation, Mr. Julian Amery, and his advisers from the B.A.C.-Sud Concorde talks at Melun Villaroche on 6 July 1964.

'Hot and high' trials by G-ASJC at Torrejon, Spain, in May 1964 and by G-ASJA at Dakar and Johannesburg 1964–65, followed by 200 hr. of route proving by G-ASJI on B.U.A.'s European, Mediterranean and West African routes, and final A.R.B. trials with G-ASJG, culminated in a full C. of A. on 5 April 1965. The first delivery, G-ASJJ, was made to B.U.A. next day and on 9 April this aircraft flew the world's first commercial One-Eleven service, from Gatwick to Genoa. F.A.A. certification was obtained on 16 April and Braniff's first One-Eleven service from Corpus Christi, Texas, to Minneapolis was flown on 25 April.

Series 400 development aircraft G-ASYD and 'YE first flew at Hurn on 13 July and 16 September 1965 respectively while N5015, first Series 401 for American Airlines, flew on 4 November. G-ASYD was retained for Elliott autoland trials but 'YE left Wisley on 17 November for a worldwide sales tour which led to a repeat order for 15 One-Elevens from American Airlines and small quantity sales in the Philippines, Central and South America, Canada, Spain and West Germany. In 1968 a 'behind the Iron Curtain' order for Series 424s came from TAROM of Rumania. Several aircraft had British markings solely for trials and demonstrations—American Airlines' N5032 was briefly G-ATVU in June 1966; Austral's LV-IZR was G-AVTF in August 1967; and Mohawk's N1124J was G-AWDF in March 1968. Long leases were Philippine Air Line's PI-C1141 to Bavaria Flug, Munich, as G-AVEJ in 1967; and B.A.C.'s G-16-6 to Quebecair as G-AXBB and to TAROM as YR-BCP during 1969.

B.U.A. inaugurated Britain's first domestic 'Interjet' routes from Gatwick to Glasgow, Edinburgh and Belfast with 74-seat Series 201s in January 1966 and British Eagle International Airways Ltd. leased two Central African 207s and three Kuwaiti 301s which were introduced in May of that year on its domestic and European network as G-ATTP, 'VH, 'PJ, 'PK and 'PL respectively. British Eagle was also the first firm to order the Series 300 variant, G-ATPH and 'PI being delivered early in 1967, and in the next two years several were leased abroad— G-ATPJ and 'PL to Scandinavian Airlines; G-ATPK and 'VH to Swissair; and 'PJ to K.L.M., giving an opportunity of comparison with its immediate competitor, the Douglas DC-9.

Later British users were Laker Airways Ltd. to whom Series 320s G-AVBW to 'BY were delivered at Gatwick in 1967, the last being leased to Air Congo and a fourth, G-AVYZ, added. Southend-based Channel Airways Ltd. ordered six Series 408s but only two, G-AVGP and G-AWEJ, were delivered 1967–68. The third, G-AWGG, was sold to Bavaria Flug as D-ALLI, and the fourth, G-AWKJ, was delivered to B.U.A. on 3 April 1969, replacing G-ASJJ written off in a take-off accident at Milan in the previous January. Autair commissioned G-AVOE, 'OF, G-AWBL and 'XJ in 1968–69 and gave them the 'Zephyr' names.

A small number sold as executive and military transports comprised Helmut Horten's D-ABHH, delivered on 29 January 1966; the Tennessee Gas Co.'s N502T, delivered on 4 April 1966 (with N503T to follow in 1969); Victor Comptometer of Chicago's N3939V, formerly the Series 400 development

Airline service—N2111J, first of 16 Series 204s for Mohawk Airlines, Utica, N.Y., on test prior to delivery on 15 May 1965; EI-ANE 'St. Mel', first of four Series 208s for Aer Lingus, Dublin, was delivered 16 May 1965; N11181, first of three Series 215s for Aloha Airlines, leaving Hurn for Honolulu 15 April 1966; YR-BCA, first of four Series 424s for TAROM, after its first Bucharest–Gatwick service 22 June 1968.

Aviateca's first 99-seat, yellow and orange One Eleven 516FP, TG-AZA 'Quetzal', leaving Hurn for the delivery flight to Guatemala 25 March 1971.

G-AYUW, first production One-Eleven 475, taking off at Wisley. It was delivered to Faucett, Peru, on 23 July 1971 as OB-R-953, Type 476FM.

machine G-ASYE; Englehard Industries' N270E; A12-124 and A12-125 for the R.A.A.F.; and two, VC92-2110 and VC92-2111, for Brazil in 1968.

The One-Eleven Series 500 was a 97–109 seat stretched version for British European Airways with a 100 inch fuselage extension forward of the wing and 62 inches aft, strengthened undercarriage, increased span and uprated Spey Mk. 512 engines. On 27 January 1967 B.E.A. ordered 18 (G-AVMH to 'MZ) and the Series 400 prototype G-ASYD was flown to Hurn on 6 February for conversion as the aerodynamic prototype, in which form it flew again on 30 June. Series 510 G-AVMH, first B.E.A. aircraft, flew on 7 February 1968, ten weeks ahead of schedule; 'MI began route proving from Heathrow on 20 July and deliveries began with 'MJ on 29 August.

Other users of the stretched version were B.U.A. with eight 501s (G-AWYR to 'YV and G-AXJK to 'JM); Gatwick-based British Caledonian Airways Ltd. (which absorbed B.U.A. in 1970) with three 509s (G-AWWX to 'WZ) named after Scottish isles; Court Line (formerly Autair) to whom seven brightly hued Halcyon named 518s were delivered in 1970; and British Midland Airways Ltd., Castle Donington with three 523s (G-AXLL to 'LN).

The One-Eleven 500 development aircraft, G-ASYD, made its 1,000th flight in April 1970 piloted by Roy Radford and then went to Hurn to be reworked once more as aerodynamic prototype of the 475 variant intended for operation from the smaller provincial airports. G-AYUW, first production 475 for Faucett, Peru, flew at Hurn on 5 April 1971.

SPECIFICATION

Manufacturers: The British Aircraft Corporation Ltd., Hurn Airport, Bournemouth, Hants. (component construction at Filton, Luton and Weybridge).

Power Plants: (Hunting H.107) Two 7,000 lb. s.t. Bristol Siddeley BE.61.
(Series 200) Two 10,410 lb. s.t. Rolls-Royce Spey Mk. 506.
(Series 300/400) Two 11,400 lb. s.t. Rolls-Royce Spey Mk. 511.
(Series 475) Two 12,550 lb. s.t. Rolls-Royce Spey Mk. 521.
(Series 500) Two 12,000 lb. s.t. Rolls-Royce Spey Mk. 512.

	Hunting H.107	Series 200	Series 300/400	Series 475	Series 500
Span	80 ft. 0 in.	88 ft. 6 in.	88 ft. 6 in.	93 ft. 6 in.	93 ft. 6 in.
Length	85 ft. 2 in.	93 ft. 6 in.	93 ft. 6 in.	93 ft. 6 in.	107 ft. 0 in.
Height	24 ft. 0 in.	24 ft. 6 in.	24 ft. 6 in.	24 ft. 6 in.	24 ft. 6 in.
Wing area	800 sq. ft.	1,003 sq. ft.	1,003 sq. ft.	1,031 sq. ft.	1,031 sq. ft.
Seating capacity	48–56	63–80	89	74–89	97–109
Basic operational wt.	21,892 lb.	45,134 lb.	49,587 lb.	51,814 lb.	54,595 lb.
Maximum take-off wt.	42,400 lb.	74,500 lb.	87,000 lb.	92,000 lb.	98,000 lb.
*Cruising speed	460 m.p.h.	500 m.p.h.	540 m.p.h.	507 m.p.h.	540 m.p.h.
*Range	1,150 miles	1,050 miles	1,420 miles	2,095 miles	1,420 miles

* With maximum payload and 2 hr. fuel reserve.

Production: (a) Hunting/B.A.C.107

One projected aircraft G-APOH (c/n H.107), registered 7.58, not built and registration cancelled 1.64.

(b) One-Eleven Series 200

Thirteen British registered aircraft and the following for export: (c/n 015–020) Braniff N1541–N1546; (021–028) cancelled order; (029–032) Mohawk N2111J and N1112J–N1114J; (036–038) cancelled order; (039) Central African VP-YXA, later G-ATTP; (040) VP-YXB, later G-ATVH; (041–046) Braniff N1547–N1552; (047–048) cancelled order; (049–052) Aer Lingus EI-ANE to 'NH; (070–071) Braniff N1553 and N1554; (082) Mohawk N1115J; (083) Tennessee Gas N502T; (084) Helmut Horten D-ABHH; (096–097) Aloha Airlines N11181 and N11182; (098–102) Mohawk N1116J–N1120J; (103–104) N1122J and N1123J; (105) Aloha N11183; (124–125) R.A.A.F. A12-124 and A12-125; (134) Mohawk N1124J, temporarily G-AWDF; (135) N1125J; (179–182) N1126J–N1129J; (183) Tenneco N503T.

(c) One-Eleven Series 300

Nine British registered aircraft listed in Appendix E.

(d) One-Eleven Series 400

British registered aircraft listed in Appendix E and the following for export: (c/n 055–069, 072–081 and 086–090) American Airlines N5015–N5044; (091–092) Philippine Air Lines PI-C1121 and PI-C1131; (093) T.A.C.A. YS-17C; (094) Philippine PI-C1141; (106) T.A.C.A. YS-18C; (108) L.A.C.S.A. TI-1056C; (111) L.A.N.I.C.A. AN-BBI; (117) Austral LV-PKB/LV-JGX; (118) Brazilian Air Force G-16-2/VC92-2111; (119) V.A.S.P.

PP-SRT; (120) Page/Engelhard N270E; (121) Bahamas Airways G-16-5/VP-BCY, later
G-AXOX; (122) Austral LV-PID/LV-IZR, later G-AVTF; (123) LV-PIF/LV-IZS; (126)
V.A.S.P. PP-SRU; (127) Bavaria Flug G-16-3/D-ANDY, later G-AZED; (130) TAROM
G-16-4/YR-BCA; (154) Brazilian VC92-2110; (155) Austral LV-PKA/LV-JGY; (156)
TAROM YR-BCB; (157) Bahamas VP-BCZ, later G-AXMU; (158) Bavaria D-AISY;
(159) TAROM YR-BCD; (160) Bavaria D-ANNO; (161) Philippine PI-C1151/T.A.E.
EC-BQF, later G-AYHM; (163) Bavaria D-AILY; (164) not built; (165, 167 and 168)
TAROM YR-BCE, 'CC and 'CF; (169–173) not built.

(e) One-Eleven Series 475
British registered aircraft listed in Appendix E and the following early export production: (c/n 238 and 240) not allotted by 12.71; (241) Faucett G-16-16; (242) not allotted by
12.71; (243) Air Malawi 7Q-YKF; (245) Air Pacific DQ-FBQ.

(f) One-Eleven Series 500
British registered aircraft listed in Appendix E and the following for export: (c/n 187)
Paninternational D-ALAT; (188) Bahamas Airways VP-BCN, later G-AZEB; (189)
VP-BCO, late G-AZEC; (190) Germanair D-AMIE; (192) Austral G-16-7/LV-JNR,
leased Sadia 9.70 as PP-SDP, later G-AYXB; (196) Austral G-16-10/LV-JNT; (198)
Bahamas G-16-12/VP-BCQ, not delivered; (207) Paninternational D-ALAR; (208) Pan-
international D-ALAS; (212) Phoenix G-16-13/HB-ITL; (213) Philippine PI-C1161,
later G-AYOS; (216–225) not built; (226) Philippine PI-C1181; (227) Bavaria
D-AMUC; (228) Sadia PP-SDQ; (229) Paninternational D-ALAQ; (230) Sadia
PP-SDR; (231) Aviateca TG-AZA; (234) Bavaria D-ALFA; (236) G-16-15; (238)
Bavaria D-ANUE.

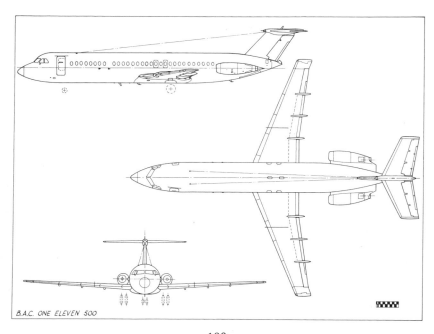

B.A.C. ONE ELEVEN 500

The first of the civil Bantams at Hendon in 1919 bearing the now classic temporary registration K-123. (*Leonard Bridgman*)

B.A.T. F.K.23 Bantam

The Bantam was a small single-seat fighter designed by Frederick Koolhoven and built at Willesden by the British Aerial Transport Co. Ltd. founded in 1917 by Samuel (afterwards Lord) Waring. In its production form it was of mixed wood and metal construction with a monocoque plywood fuselage in which the pilot sat with his head through a hole in the upper mainplane. Only nine production Bantams, F1653–F1661, were built, because the 170 h.p. A.B.C. Wasp I radial with which it was fitted paid the penalty of uncertain behaviour and went out of production.

The Bantam saw no war service and only the first, F1653, which Flg. Off. G. Bulman flew in the Headquarters Race at the Hendon R.A.F. Display on 2 July 1921, was taken on R.A.F. charge, but seven of the remaining eight production machines were registered to the manufacturers for sporting purposes in 1919–21. The first four, civilianised in May–June 1919, were used for Saturday afternoon and Bank Holiday racing which drew the crowds at Hendon in those days. First to compete was B.A.T. test pilot Cyril Turner who won the Whitsun cross country event on 26 May 1919 flying F1657 which carried racing number 5 above which was stencilled '155', identifying it as K-155/G-EAFN.

Bantam K-123/G-EACN was flown in the Aerial Derby by the American pilot Clifford Prodger at Hendon on 21 June 1919 and at the First Air Traffic Exhibition (ELTA) at Amsterdam in the following month by the well known Maj. Christopher Draper. K-125/G-EACP was a racing special with the lower mainplane clipped halfway along the outer bay and the upper-wing overhang braced by slanting struts, a truly frightening vehicle in which Draper came second in the Aerial Derby sealed handicap and fourth in the speed section at 116·78 m.p.h. An all-white Bantam devoid of markings and statically displayed at ELTA was, in fact, K-154/G-EAFM in which Maj. Draper spun in at Hendon Aerodrome from 3,500 ft. in March 1920 after he had become ill in the air.

The clipped-wing Bantam K-125 being prepared for the 1919 Aerial Derby. (*Flight*)

The side-by-side two-seat F.K.27 at Hendon in 1919.

The last Bantam, F1661, was powered by a 200 h.p. A.B.C. Wasp II which imparted a top speed of 146 m.p.h. at 10,000 ft. After trials by L. R. Tait-Cox it was exhibited at the Olympia Aero Show in July 1920 and registered G-EAYA in 1921, but when the B.A.T. concern closed down it was disposed of, with K-123, to C. P. B. Ogilvie and was stored at Willesden until designer Frederick Koolhoven took it to Holland in 1924. Registered H-NACH, fitted with an Armstrong Siddeley Lynx radial and enlarged rudder, it is said to have bettered 154 m.p.h.

Subsequent identities for the remaining three Bantams (F1658–F1660) are not positively proven but it is evident that they became G-EAJW flown to Holland in August 1921; G-EAMM about which little is known; and A.S.94111/P-167 evaluated at Wright Field, U.S.A., in 1922.

The F.K.27 side-by-side two-seat aerobatic and racing variant, K-143/G-EAFA, built in June 1919 with sesquiplane wings and 200 h.p. A.B.C. Wasp II, flew only once at Hendon (with the designer's reluctant consent) in 1920.

The only surviving Bantam relics are the derelict remains of K-123, preserved by the Shuttleworth Trust at Old Warden Aerodrome, Beds.

SPECIFICATION

Manufacturers: The British Aerial Transport Co. Ltd., Willesden, London, N.W.

Power Plants: One 170 h.p. A.B.C. Wasp I or 200 h.p. Wasp II.

Dimensions: (F.K.23) Span, 25 ft. 0 in. Length, 18 ft. 5 in. Height, 6 ft. 9 in. Wing area, 185 sq. ft.

(F.K.27) Span, 26 ft. 0 in. Length, 20 ft. 7 in. Height, 7 ft. 10 in. Wing area, 200 sq. ft.

Weights: (F.K.23) Tare weight, 833 lb. All-up weight, 1,618 lb.

Performance: (F.K.23) Maximum speed, 128 m.p.h. Initial climb, 1,250 ft./min. Ceiling, 20,000 ft. Range, 250 miles.

(F.K.27) Maximum speed, 142 m.p.h. Initial climb, 2,500 ft./min.

Production: Nine F.K.23 Bantams F1653–F1661 (c/n 14–22) and one F.K.27 (33).

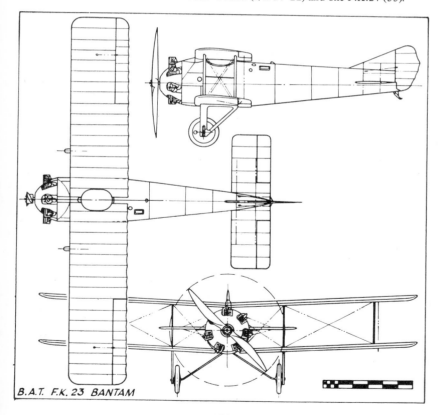

B.A.T. F.K. 23 BANTAM

The prototype F.K.26 about to leave Hounslow with mails for Newcastle during the railway strike of October 1919. (*Flight*)

B.A.T. F.K.26

The unnamed F.K.26, designed by Frederick Koolhoven and built by the British Aerial Transport Co. Ltd., was the first purely civil transport aeroplane built after the First World War and the designs are said to have been put in hand on Armistice Day 1918. It was of orthodox appearance and construction, with a wooden, fabric-covered airframe, two-bay wings and a single Rolls-Royce Eagle VIII water-cooled engine. Four passengers were carried in a glazed cabin 8 ft. long and the pilot sat in an open cockpit in the rear fuselage. The prototype, K-102/G-EAAI, was built at Hythe Road, Willesden, flown at Hendon in April 1919 and later used experimentally on the Hounslow–Paris route. Probably the most discussed detail of the new aircraft was the placing of the pilot's cockpit aft of the cabin, and Koolhoven's intention was, it is said, to give the pilot a good chance of surviving a crash, as he was the only occupant likely to give an intelligent account of it. The second aircraft, K-167/G-EAHN, was flown to the First Air Traffic Exhibition at Amsterdam in July 1919 by Christopher Draper. A third, G-EANI, appeared in the October, was exhibited at the Olympia Aero Show as the 'B.A.T. Commercial Mk. I' in July 1920, and during the rest of the summer was used for passenger flights at Hendon in place of 'HN, which had crashed. The

The Instone Air Line F.K.26 'City of Newcastle'.

reduction in Lord Waring's aviation interests forced the closure of the B.A.T. concern, and G-EAPK, built in November 1919, was the firm's last product. It was sold to S. Instone and Co. Ltd. in August 1920, and went to Croydon for continental charter work and scheduled services to Paris.

When the British Aerial Transport Co. Ltd. closed down, Koolhoven returned to Holland, and a number of machines, including the F.K.26s G-EAAI and 'NI, were sold to Ogilvie Aircraft. They were stored in the company's works at 437 High Road, Willesden, for many years, during which their markings were obliterated. In April 1937 Koolhoven purchased 'AI for £300 and shipped it to Holland, where it was erected and exhibited without markings at that year's Netherlands Aero Show.

SPECIFICATION

Manufacturers: The British Aerial Transport Co. Ltd., Willesden, London, N.W.
Power Plant: One 350 h.p. Rolls-Royce Eagle VIII.
Dimensions: Span, 46 ft. 0 in. Length, 34 ft. 8 in. Height, 11 ft. 3 in.
Weights: All-up weight, 4,500 lb.
Performance: Maximum speed, 122 m.p.h. Initial climb, 1,000 ft./min. Ceiling, 8,000 ft. Range, 600 miles.
Production: Four aircraft (c/n 29) K-102/G-EAAI; (30) K-167/G-EAHN; (31) G-EANI; (32) G-EAPK. See also Appendix E.

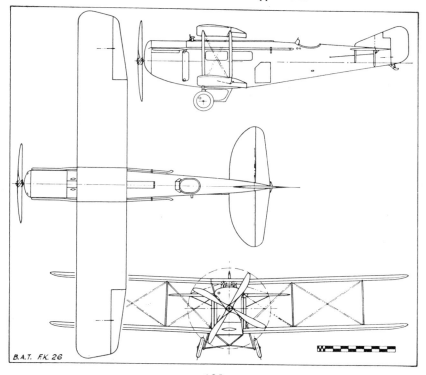

B.A.T. F.K. 26

OE-DEW, last production Beagle Husky, at Shoreham prior to delivery in March 1969. (*G. J. Davies*)

Beagle D.5/180 Husky

In 1960 Auster Aircraft Ltd. introduced the Auster D.4, D.5 and D.6 two-, three- and four-seaters with Workmaster tail units and powered by 108 h.p., 160 h.p. or 180 h.p. Lycoming engines. They were, in fact, modernised versions of the J-2 Arrow, J-1N Alpha and J-5B Autocar developed in 1959 via the J-5T prototype G-25-4, the experimental J-1W flown at Rearsby as G-25-6, and the J-5V Autocar with 160 h.p. Lycoming which became the development prototype for all the D series aircraft from which it differed mainly because it had wooden instead of metal mainspars.

The whole programme originated from a Portuguese Air Force requirement for a two/three seat liaison and training aircraft powered by this American flat-four, light-weight power plant and which could be built under licence by O.G.M.A., the Government-owned aircraft factory near Lisbon. Choice fell on variants of the Auster and a contract was signed on 4 November 1959 for 20 complete aero- planes together with a licence agreement for the manufacture of 150 machines in Portugal from kits of parts supplied by Rearsby. The complete aircraft included five D.4/108 two-seaters, CS-AMA to 'ME, the first of which, G-25-8 (later CS-AME), first flew at Rearsby on 12 February 1960, the second (CS-AMA) being statically exhibited at the Farnborough S.B.A.C. Show in the following September. These and 15 three seat D.5/160s serialled 3501–3515, (the first of which, actually 3512, flew at Rearsby in April 1960 as G-25-7), were crated and shipped but Portuguese Air Force Douglas C-54Es airfreighted early consign- ments of the construction kits out of Langar, Notts. The first O.G.M.A.-built D.5/160, CS-LEI, flew early in 1962 and by 1967 all 150 had been delivered to the Air Force or to flying clubs in Portugal or Angola but production at Rearsby ended in 1961 following the delivery of four D.5/160s (CS-LEA to 'ED) to the Aero Club of Angola; three to the Congolese Air Force, N'Dolo; CR-LEF to 'EH also for Angola but delivered initially to a company at Sutabal, Portugal; and G-ARLG, a D.4/108 constructed without dorsal fin for the Rearsby-based Auster Flying Club.

Also statically exhibited at the 1960 S.B.A.C. Show was G-ARDJ, third and last of a disappointingly small production total of three Rearsby-built D.6/180s, the first of which, OY-ABV, flew on 9 May that year prior to delivery to S. Larsen at Kastrup, Copenhagen. The only D.6/160 built, G-25-10, was later sold to Telemark Flyselskap, Oslo, as LN-BWB.

Operational experience showed that the extra power of the 180 h.p. Lycoming would be an advantage for agricultural flying and O.G.M.A. completed five of its 170 machines as D.5/180s using this engine. Towards the end of 1960 however Auster Aircraft Ltd. had been absorbed by British Executive and General Aircraft Ltd. (BEAGLE) and re-styled Beagle-Auster Aircraft Ltd. Its products were consequently renamed Beagle-Auster also, but following the formation of Beagle Aircraft Ltd. in 1962, the time-honoured name of Auster was dropped so that the only two 180 h.p. aircraft built at Rearsby, CS-LEE for Radio Club Portugal and a demonstrator G-ASBV, were known as Beagle D.5/180s. Carrying French data plates, the latter left Shoreham on 6 December 1962 for a sales tour of Switzerland, accompanying the delivery flight of Beagle Airedale HB-EUE.

On its return 'BV was reworked as a rugged, multi-purpose four seater with oversize tyres for landing on rough strips and presented at the Biggin Air Fair of May 1963 under the designation Beagle A.113, or more familiarly, D.5/180

The Auster J-5V Autocar with 160 h.p. Lycoming, fibre-glass spats and wing strut cuff-fairings. (*A. J. Jackson*)

LN-BWB, the only Beagle D.6/160 completed, was delivered in Norway in June 1960 but was later re-engined as a D.6/180.

Husky, but crashed during demonstrations, on skis, to the Swiss Army near Fribourg, Switzerland, on 20 October. It was replaced by G-ASNC but only 13 production Huskies were sold during the next six years, beginning with glider tug 9G-ABR for the Ghana National Gliding School and including 5H-MMU and 'MV for Tanzania in 1966; four for Burma in 1967; G-ATCD and G-AVOD for the executive use of D. Ancil Ltd., Middleton Stoney, and the Turriff Construction Corp. Ltd., Baginton, respectively; and G-AVSR which was ferried to Teheran by Hon. James Baring in 1968 for communications work during the erection of a power line. Best known examples were the Tiger Club's G-ATMH based at Fyfield strip, Essex, from 1966 for glider towing at nearby North Weald; and G-AWSW which was raffled at a London club and later presented to the A.T.C. by Sir Billy Butlin. This was delivered to Northolt on 14 June 1969 en route to Boscombe Down for handling trials and thence to No. 5 Air Experience Flt., Cambridge, with R.A.F. markings as XW635 'Spirit of Butlins'.

SPECIFICATION

Manufacturers: Auster Aircraft Ltd., Rearsby Aerodrome, Leicester (restyled Beagle-Auster Aircraft Ltd. 1961 and Beagle Aircraft Ltd. 1962). Oficinas Gerais de Material Aeronáutico (O.G.M.A.), Alverca do Ribatejo, Portugal.

Power Plants:
- (J-5V) One 160 h.p. Lycoming O-320-B2B.
- (D.4) One 108 h.p. Lycoming O-235-Cl.
- (D.5) One 160 h.p. Lycoming O-320-A2A.
- (D.6) One 180 h.p. Lycoming O-360-A1A.
- (Husky) One 180 h.p. Lycoming O-360-A2A.

	J-5V	D.4/108	D.5/160	Husky
Span	36 ft. 0 in.	36 ft. 0 in.	36 ft. 0 in.	36 ft. 0 in.
Length	22 ft. 11 in.	23 ft. 4½ in.	23 ft. 4½ in.	23 ft. 2 in.
Height	8 ft. 2 in.	7 ft. 11 in.	7 ft. 11 in.	8 ft. 8 in.
Wing area	185 sq. ft.	185 sq. ft.	185 sq. ft.	185 sq. ft.
Tare weight	1,360 lb.	1,232 lb.	1,450 lb.	1,416 lb.
All-up weight	2,450 lb.	1,900 lb.	2,450 lb.	2,400 lb.
Maximum speed	132 m.p.h.	110 m.p.h.	125 m.p.h.	125 m.p.h.
Cruising speed	112 m.p.h.	92 m.p.h.	108 m.p.h.	109 m.p.h.
Initial climb	780 ft./min.	620 ft./min.	640 ft./min.	800 ft./min.
Ceiling	15,000 ft.	13,200 ft.	12,800 ft.	14,500 ft.
Range	—	500 miles	460 miles	580 miles

Production: (a) Prototypes

Three dissimilar aircraft: Auster J-5T (c/n 3421) G-25-4; J-1W (3600) G-25-5; J-5V (3273) G-APUW.

(b) Beagle-Auster D.4/108

At Rearsby: (c/n 3601–3606) G-25-8/CS-AME; CS-AMA to 'MD; G-ARLG. By O.G.M.A.: (c/n 34–42) CS-AMH to 'MQ less 'MM.

(c) Beagle-Auster D.5/160

At Rearsby: (c/n 3651) G-25-7/Portuguese Air Force 3512; (3652–3661) P.A.F.3501–3510; (3662) 3513; (3663) 3511; (3664–3665) 3514–3515; (3666–3669)

CS-LEA to 'ED; (3671–3673) Congolese WL-05 to WL-07; (3674–3676) CR-LEG, 'EF and 'EH. By O.G.M.A.: 165 aircraft including (c/n 1) CS-LEI; (9) CS-AMF; (10) CS-AMG; (51) CS-AMR; (62–65) CS-AMS to 'MV; (79) CR-LFM; (81) CS-AMX; (94) CS-AMW; (95) CS-AMY; (99) CS-AMZ; (101) CS-ANB; (102) CS-ANC; (108) CS-AND; (109) CS-ANE; (110) CS-DGG; (111–113) CS-ANG to 'NI; (118–130) CS-ANJ to 'NV; (131) CS-ANF; (133) CS-DGF; and P.A.F. serial blocks commencing 3316 and 3501.

(d) Beagle D.5/180

At Rearsby: (c/n 3670) CS-LEE; (3677) G-ASBV. By O.G.M.A.: five aircraft including (c/n 100) CS-ANA; (131) CS-ANF; (132) CS-DGE.

(e) Beagle D.5/180 Husky

Fourteen aircraft at Rearsby: (c/n 3678–3691) G-ASNC; 9G-ABR; 5H-MMV; Burma: G-ATKB/5H-MMU; G-ATCD; G-ATMH; three for Burma; G-AVOD; G-AVSR; G-AWSW; OE-DEW.

(f) Beagle D.6/160* and D.6/180

Four aircraft at Rearsby: (c/n 3701–3704) G-25-10/LN-BWB*; OY-ABV; G-ARCS; G-ARDJ.

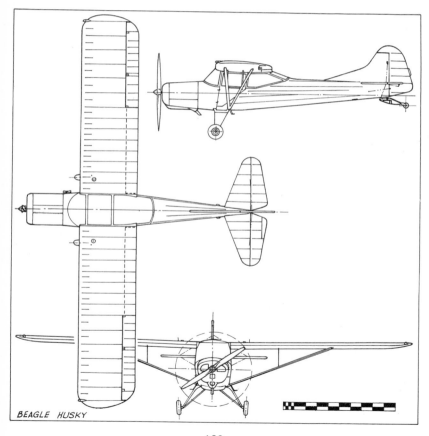

BEAGLE HUSKY

R. G. Cooper's Terrier 2 G-ASAN at Redhill in August 1965. (*A. J. Jackson*)

Beagle A.61 Terrier

In 1959–60 all surplus British Army Auster Mks. 6, 7 and 10 were repurchased by the manufacturers and at one time there were at least 105 stored at Kidlington and Rearsby including TW562 which almost became G-ALGW at Croydon in 1950. They were completely stripped and remanufactured on the Rearsby production line, fitted with enlarged vertical tail surfaces, and offered in two variants —as the Auster 6A Tugmaster utility two-seat glider tug described in an earlier section or as the more sophisticated Auster 6B, a smartly finished three-seater with improved ailerons and car-type upholstery.

The prototype Auster 6B conversion, G-ARLH, which first flew at Rearsby on 13 April 1961, was shown in public at Baginton later in the month but due to changes in company styling had already been redesignated Beagle-Auster A.61 Terrier and eventually became the Beagle A.61 Terrier 1. Although an ageing design, the low initial cost with 145 h.p. Gipsy Major 10 engine attracted numerous orders, notably from the Airways, West London, Southern and Lincoln Aero Clubs. G-ARNO, supplied to Sprague and Price Ltd. at Speke had in its Service days been VX113, the Auster 6 which Capt. N. Baldwick flew into 5th. place in the King's Cup Race at Baginton on 11 July 1959 at an average speed of 126 m.p.h.

Whereas G-ARLH had the extended rear cabin glazing of the original military Auster, subsequent aircraft had J-1 Autocrat-style rear windows. Total production was 18 aircraft including four flown out via Shoreham to Swedish flying clubs; G-ASKJ and 'ZX, frustrated exports originally intended for Ireland and Sweden respectively; and four Mk. 7s, G-ATHU, G-AVCR, 'CS and 'YU, converted locally at Lasham and Bicester as glider tugs 1966–68.

Two early 'production' Terriers G-ARLR and 'RN were earmarked as development aircraft for a much improved version to be known as the Terrier 2 and the second of these flew on 21 June 1961 with luxury interior, Fairey Reed metal airscrew, fibre glass spats and long exhaust pipe with ventral silencer, and on 31 August the original Terrier 'LH flew at Rearsby with similar modifications but still retained the military rear windows. Further modernisation led to an increase in maximum flap angle and a 32 in. increase in tailplane span, features flown experimentally on G-ARRN at Shoreham in January 1962 and incorporated in production Terrier 2s commencing with G-ARLR first flown on 25 April 1962. External refurbishing made many Terrier 1s almost indistinguishable from the Terrier 2 but the latter was easily identified by its hydraulically damped tail wheel spring.

The 13th machine, G-ASBU, was shown at the Farnborough S.B.A.C. Show in September 1962 and production continued steadily until the delivery of the 44th and final Terrier 2, D-EEBN, to the Ebern Flugsport Club in West Germany in December 1967. Small numbers were exported also to Holland, Ireland, New Zealand, Sweden and Switzerland, but the majority were used by private owners, clubs and co-ownership groups in the U.K., notably the Airways Aero Club which had seven; the Casair-operated clubs at Crosby-on-Eden (Carlisle) and Woolsington (Newcastle); the Lapwing Flying Group, Denham (G-ASAD); the Roding Valley Flying Group, Stapleford (G-ASAK); and the Enstone Eagles Flying Group, Enstone (G-ASCH).

Auster 6 VF544 which averaged 123·5 m.p.h. in the 1960 King's Cup Race piloted by Sgt. R. W. Bowles, became a Terrier 2, G-ASPD, in 1964 for executive use at Carlisle but in civil guise the type was seldom raced. In 1968 however Terrier 2s completed quite remarkable long-distance flights, the first by Mr. P. Hewartson who flew G-ASRL solo from Leavesden to Johannesburg in a flight time of 71 hr. 4 min. during May and the other by Mr. and Mrs. G. Wright who left Turnhouse in G-ASCG on 19 June en route to Australia. They arrived at Darwin, like the pioneers of old, on 16 October.

One Terrier was completed at Heathrow by B.E.A. engineering apprentices, under the direction of Mr. K. G. Wilkinson, who installed a 160 h.p. Lycoming flat-four engine of the type which powered the Auster J-5V. This unique aircraft was flown successfully as G-AVYK, the sole Terrier 3, in 1969.

SPECIFICATION

Manufacturers: Auster Aircraft Ltd., Rearsby Aerodrome, Leicester (restyled Beagle-Auster Aircraft Ltd. 1961 and Beagle Aircraft Ltd. 1962).

Power Plants: One 145 h.p. de Havilland Gipsy Major 10 Mk. 1-1.
One 160 h.p. Lycoming O-320-B2B.

Dimensions: Span 36 ft. 0 in. Length 23 ft. 3 in. Height 8 ft. 11 in. Wing area 184 sq. ft.

Weights: (Terrier 2) Tare weight 1,600 lb. All-up weight 2,400 lb.

Performance: Maximum speed 120 m.p.h. Cruising speed 107 m.p.h. Initial climb 530 ft./min. Range 320 miles.

Production: (a) Beagle A.61 Terrier 1
Fourteen British registered aircraft and the following exported to Sweden: (c/n 3733) SE-ELD; (3739) SE-ELK; (3740) SE-ELL; (3741) SE-ELN.

(b) Beagle A.61 Terrier 2
Forty-one British registered aircraft and the following for export: (c/n B.614) D-ECKO; (B.625) ZK-CDG; (B.630) D-EDTU; (B.644) D-EEBN.

(c) Beagle A.61 Terrier 3
One aircraft only: (c/n B.642) G-AVYK.

Beagle Airedale G-ARZP flying at Rearsby before delivery to Belfast in May 1962.

Beagle A.109 Airedale

The Airedale four-seat touring aircraft was a heavier structural derivative of the Auster powered by a 180 h.p. Lycoming and featuring a swept fin, tricycle undercarriage, wheel-type controls and airways instrumentation. The first prototype flew at Rearsby as G-25-11 on 16 April 1961 before assuming Beagle bronze as G-ARKE, but to qualify for participation in the 1961 Farnborough S.B.A.C. Show it was re-engined with a British-built 175 h.p. Rolls-Royce Continental by Marshalls at Cambridge where it first flew as the sole Beagle A.111 on 18 August.

The performance of production models was improved by weight reductions in cabin furnishing and equipment, one of the first sold being G-ARNS, shown on the Beagle stand at Farnborough, minus wings, in 1961 and ferried to Montreux as HB-EUE in September 1962. Another early export was G-ASBX, flown to Lahore, Pakistan, for the use of French civil engineers working on the Mangla Dam. G-ASBZ and 'CA which arrived at Adelaide for Aviation Services Pty. aboard the S.S. *Hector* on 1 November, became VH-UEP and 'EH, while a third, G-ASBI, joined them at Parafield at dusk on 17 July 1963 after being flown from England by Charles Masefield and Lord Trefgarne who were later to operate G-AROJ out of Castle Donington on charter. The Australian total reached six with the arrival of VH-DCP, 'CR and 'CS at Sydney by sea for Allied Aviation Pty., Bankstown. In May 1963 G-ASEL and 'EM were flown to Milan where the latter came 4th in the Giro di Lombardia piloted by Letterio Meli before delivery to a private owner in Sicily. Single examples were also exported to the Perak Flying Club and to Canada, New Zealand, Denmark, Holland, Portugal, Sweden and West Germany.

Home sales included G-ARXD, delivered to *Flight International* at Fairoaks on 28 April 1962, which, in the course of its duties, was present at Baginton on 5 August 1963 when J. W. C. Judge and P. G. Masefield came 9th and 14th respectively in the King's Cup Race in G-ASAI and G-ARNP. At the same meeting Ranald Porteous and J. W. C. Judge were 3rd and 4th respectively in 'NP and 'AI in the John Morgan Trophy Race.

The Airedale failed to achieve real popularity and production ended with the

43rd aircraft in August 1964, but interest revived in 1967 when SE-EGA, originally delivered to Sverigeflyg, Stockholm, from Gatwick on 3 September 1963, returned to become G-AVKP for a private owner in Cornwall. In 1968–69 Shannon Aircraft Holdings Ltd. acquired two of Beagle's own machines as well as D-ENRU (re-imported from Germany) for resale in Ireland as EI-ATE, 'TD and 'TA respectively.

SPECIFICATION

Manufacturers: Beagle Aircraft Ltd., Rearsby Aerodrome, Leicester.
Power Plants: (A.109) One 180 h.p. Lycoming O-360-A1A.
     (A.111) One 175 h.p. Rolls-Royce Continental GO-300.
Dimensions: Span, 36 ft. 4 in. Length, 26 ft. 4 in. Height, 10 ft. 0 in. Wing area, 185 sq. ft.
Weights: Tare weight, 1,630 lb. All-up weight, 2,750 lb.
Performance: Maximum speed, 140 m.p.h. Cruising speed, 133 m.p.h. Initial climb, 650 ft./min. Range, 940 miles.
Production:

 Thirty-six British registered aircraft and the following exported: (c/n B.528) ZK-CCW; (B.529) CS-ALV; (B.530–B.532) VH-DCP, 'CR and 'CS; (B.533) PH-SFA; (B.539) OY-DCN.

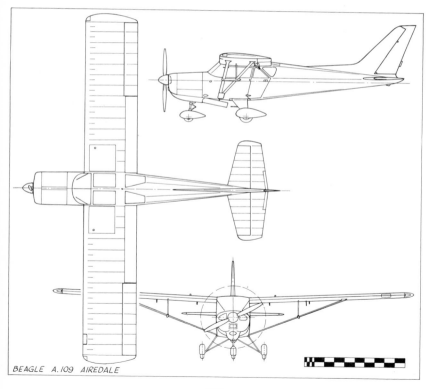

BEAGLE A.109 AIREDALE

Ranald Porteous demonstrating Pup Series 1 G-AVZM at the Farnborough S.B.A.C. Show in September 1968. (*Richard Riding*)

Beagle B.121 Pup

When designing the Pup, Beagle Aircraft Ltd. set itself the difficult task of producing an all-metal aerobatic machine which combined the appearance and comfort of contemporary American types with the handling qualities of matchless British trainers such as the Avro 504K, Tutor or D.H. Tiger Moth. Comments by Beagle chief test pilot J. W. C. Judge after the first flight of the prototype, G-AVDF, at Shoreham on 8 April 1967 made it evident that they had succeeded handsomely and on 17 May 'DF was ranged alongside the Shuttleworth Trust's Sopwith Pup to be officially named by Sir Thomas and Lady Sopwith.

The airframe was designed for completion with two seats and 100 h.p. Rolls-Royce Continental, similar to G-AVDF, as the Pup Series 1 (or Pup 100) for training and aerobatics; or with four seats and 150 h.p. Lycoming as the Pup Series 2 (or Pup 150) for touring purposes. The second and third aircraft, G-AVLM and 'LN, first flown at Shoreham on 4 October 1967 and 17 January 1968 respectively, were Series 2 prototypes fitted with the enlarged rudder which became standard on all production machines.

The second production Ser.1, delivered to the Shoreham School of Flying on 12 April 1968, was the first of four (G-AVZN, 'ZP, G-AWDZ and 'EC) operated by the school until it re-equipped in September 1969. The second purchaser, the Flairavia Flying Club at Biggin Hill, received G-AVZO 'The Guinea Pig' on 23 May 1968 and G-AWDX two months later, but the first production Ser.2, one of several for the Swiss Aero Club, was flown to Lausanne as HB-NAA on 9 August 1968.

An intense sales drive which began when G-AVDF appeared at the Paris Aero Show in May 1967, continued with G-AVZM at Hanover in April 1968 and at the Farnborough S.B.A.C. Show in the following September where this machine was demonstrated by Ranald Porteous in his own masterly and inimitable manner. On static display were G-AVLM which had flown a few days earlier on 5 September with 160 h.p. Lycoming as the prototype Series 3 (or Pup 160); and a Ser.2 which flew up from Shoreham on 18 September. This carried registration

G-AWKK on fabric panels which were stripped on arrival, revealing it to be N557MA, second of two demonstrators for the U.S. agents Miami Aviation. It was ferried with long rang range tanks, via Shannon by R. Bass Jnr. on 12 October, the first, Ser.1 G-AWEB/N556MA, having been delivered over the same route by H. R. 'Slim' Byrd on 11 September.

The Ser.3 four-seater was evolved for the Iranian Civil Air Training Organisation, Teheran, which placed an order for this variant commencing with the 30th. Pup G-AWRR/EP-BAD, delivered via Gatwick on 19 May 1969. Production had then accelerated to one Pup per day, with growing exports to Australia, Austria, Finland, Holland, Iraq, Ireland, Luxembourg, Malaysia and Sweden, in addition to deliveries to flying schools and distributors in the U.K., the majority being ferried to Rearsby or Cambridge, for painting and furnishing, in Class B markings which usefully included the constructor's number. The ill-fated 20th Pup, G-AWRA, was shipped to Adsel Ltd., Wellington, N.Z. to become ZK-CYP but arrived at Ardmore with serious transit damage on 24 February 1969 and was replaced by the 44th aircraft, G-AXCV, which was delivered to R.N.Z.A.F. Wigram for evaluation on 18 August. On 23 September, just 17 months after the first flight of the first production Pup, the 100th aircraft, SE-FGY, was handed over at Shoreham to Swedair, Stockholm, for the Ystad Flying Club, but in December 1969, when 121 Pups had been delivered and another 276 had been ordered, the Government withdrew financial support. Beagle was put in the hands of a Receiver and the final Pups were the 151st and 152nd, first flown on 7 and 12 January 1970 respectively.

The Pup prototype, G-AVDF, flew on 1 April 1969 with a 200 h.p. Lycoming engine for early trials for the development of a military trainer version with upgraded +6g and −3g aerobatic structure, 33 ft. mainplane and sliding canopy. Designated Beagle B.125 Ser. 1 Bulldog, the prototype trainer, G-AXEH, first flew at Shoreham on 19 May 1969 in time for the Paris Air Show where the Royal Swedish Air Force ordered 58, with an option on a further 45, Zambia 8 and Kenya 5. Thus in January 1970 G-AXEH went to Stockholm for Service trials under winter conditions and was there repainted in Swedish colours, as 71-FC and fitted with Finnish-built skis for operation from a frozen lake at Grünträsket.

When Beagle shut down, Bulldog production was undertaken by Scottish Aviation (Bulldog) Ltd., Prestwick, who completed the second prototype,

The first prototype Pup, G-AVDF, flying near Shoreham in May 1967.

Bulldog prototype, G-AXEH, flying near Farnborough in Scottish Aviation colours, September 1970. (*Flight Photo 70-6578*)

G-AXIG, first flown on 14 February 1971 in Swedish military colours. The Zambian order was cancelled but the Royal Malaysian Air Force ordered 15, and production aircraft, civil registered for ferrying, then began with G-AYWN (Swedish 61001, coded 5) first flown on 22 June 1971.

SPECIFICATION

Manufacturers: Beagle Aircraft Ltd., Shoreham Aerodrome, Sussex, and Rearsby Aerodrome, Leicester. Bulldog production by Scottish Aviation (Bulldog) Ltd., Prestwick Airport, Scotland.

Power Plants: (Pup Ser.1)   One 100 h.p. Rolls-Royce Continental O-200-A.
              (Pup Ser.2)   One 150 h.p. Lycoming O-320-A2B.
              (Pup Ser.3)   One 160 h.p. Lycoming O-360-A.
              (Bulldog Ser.100)   One 200 h.p. Lycoming IO-360-A1B6.

	Pup Ser.1	Pup Ser.2	Bulldog Ser.1
Span	31 ft. 0 in.	31 ft. 0 in.	33 ft. 0 in.
Length	22 ft. 11 in.	23 ft. 2 in.	23 ft. 2½ in.
Wing area	119½ sq. ft.	119½ sq. ft.	128½ sq. ft.
Tare weight	1,063 lb.	1,090 lb.	1,398 lb.
All-up weight	1,600 lb.	1,925 lb.	2,350 lb.
Maximum speed	127 m.p.h.	138 m.p.h.	160 m.p.h.
Cruising speed	118 m.p.h.	131 m.p.h.	147 m.p.h.
Initial climb	575 ft./min.	800 ft./min.	1,100 ft./min.
Maximum range	570 miles	440 miles	628 miles

Production: (a) Pup Series 1 (also known as Pup 100)

A large number of British registered aircraft and the following for export: (c/n 029) EI-ATJ; (037) OE-CUP; (051) OH-BGA; (059) OH-BGB; (069) OH-BGC; (079) SE-FGV; (098) OH-BGE; (100) SE-FGY; (102) SE-FGZ; (120) PH-VRV; (140) PH-VRT; (141) PH-VRU; (149) SE-FOC; (151) OY-DVC.

(b) Pup Series 2 (also known as Pup 150)

A large number of British registered aircraft and the following for export: (c/n 036) HB-NAC; (043) HB-NAB; (047) SE-FGR; (050) YI-AEL; (054) HB-NAL; (055)

SE-FGT; (066) HB-NAE; (067) HB-NAO; (068) SE-FGU; (075) VH-EPB; (076) PH-KUF, later G-AZGF; (079) SE-FGV; (081) D-EETH; (083) 9V-BBX; (084) VH-EPC; (085) VH-EPD; (093) VH-EPE; (096) VH-EPF; (097) SE-FGX; (107) SE-FOB; (111) ZS-FZP; (112) ZS-GVZ, later ZS-IGY; (118) D-EDHD; (126) VH-EPI; (128) OE-COP; (130) VH-EPL, later G-AZEU; (131) VH-EPM, later G-AZEV; (132) VH-EPN, later G-AZEW; (134) VH-EPO, later G-AZEX; (136) VH-EPP, later G-AZEY; (137) VH-EPQ, later G-AZEZ; (140) PH-VRT; (141) PH-VRU; (143) VH-EPR, later G-AZFA; (144) HB-NAP; (145) HB-NAM; (146) HB-NAF; (147) SE-FOE.

(c) Pup Series 3 (also known as Pup 160)

Eight for the Iranian Civil Air Training Organisation: (c/n 030) G-AWRR/EP-BAD; (031) EP-BAE; (040) EP-BAF; (042) EP-BAG; (052) EP-BAH; (058) EP-BAI; (060) EP-BAJ; (064) EP-BAK. One for Miami Aviation: (c/n 129) N670MA.

(d) Bulldog Series 1

Two prototype aircraft: (c/n 001) G-AXEH; (002) G-AXIG. Production by Scottish Aviation (Bulldog) Ltd.: Series 101 for Sweden (c/n 101–103) G-AYWN to 'WP; (104) G-AYZL; (105) G-AYZM; (106–114) G-AZAK to 'AT; (117–119) G-AZEN to 'EP; (121) G-AZES; (122) G-AZET; (124–126) G-AZHV to 'HX; (128–130) G-AZHY, 'HZ and 'IS; (132–135) G-AZIT to 'IW; (137–139) G-AZJO to 'JR; (141–143) G-AZJS to 'JU; (145–149) G-AZMP to 'MT; (151) G-AZMU. Series 102 for Malaysia (c/n 115) FM1220; (116) FM1221; (120) FM1222; (123) FM1223; (127) FM1224; (131) FM1225; (136) FM1226; (140) FM1227. Series 103 for Kenya (c/n 144) 701. See also Volume 3, Appendix E, Scottish Aviation Bulldog.

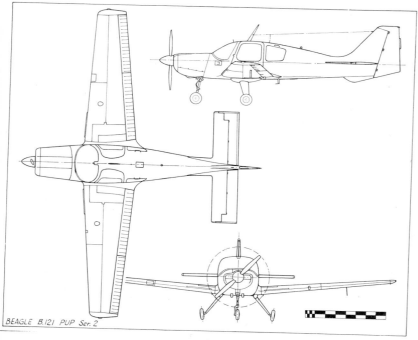

BEAGLE B.121 PUP Ser. 2

G-ATLF, first production Beagle 206 Series 2, showing the extra rear window.

Beagle B.206

Drawings for the Beagle B.206 light transport were begun on 11 November 1960 and the prototype, G-ARRM, designated B.206X, was first flown at Shoreham by John Nicholson on 15 August 1961 with managing director P. G. Masefield flying chase in his special Chipmunk G-AOTM accompanied by the Miles Student G-APLK. Powered by two 260 h.p. Continental flat-six engines the B.206X was a five-seat all metal low-wing monoplane which excited favourable comment at the Farnborough S.B.A.C. Show in the following month.

A second, enlarged prototype G-ARXM designated B.206Y and first flown as G-35-5 by J. W. C. Judge on 12 August 1962, was an elegant seven seater with slim lines disguising an unusually spacious cabin which featured a wider-than-Viscount sized instrument panel. Span was increased by nearly 8 ft., fuel from 166 to 200 gallons, and geared Continentals replaced the direct-drive version. Two B.206Z pre-production aircraft XS742 and XS743 built for Ministry of Aviation evaluation by Boscombe Down were followed by the first Rearsby-built, Rolls-Royce Continental powered, Beagle B.206 Series 1, G-ASMK, which first flew on 17 July 1964. The first of 20 B.206R Basset C.C.1 aircraft for R.A.F. Northern and Southern Communications Squadrons, Topcliffe and Northolt, was delivered in May 1965 and the first civil sales were G-ASWJ flown to Hucknall for Rolls-Royce Ltd. on 13 May 1965; G-ATHO to Maidenhead Organ Studios Ltd., Booker, for transporting electronic organs; and G-ATKO to the Imperial Tobacco Co. Ltd., Lulsgate.

To improve all-round performance the first production machine was modified to take 340 h.p. Rolls-Royce Continental supercharged engines in redesigned nacelles and first flew as the prototype B.206S (or Series 2) on 23 June 1965. Production Series 2s were built with large 42 in. by 38 in. freight doors and extra cabin windows and the first of these, G-ATLF, left Gatwick on 1 May 1966 en route to Beagle Australasia to continue the vigorous sales drive begun in 1965 when Series 1s G-ASOF and G-ATDD were flown out by C. Masefield and H. Dawes respectively.

Shortly after, R. L. Porteous departed westward to deliver G-ATTL to an air taxi company in Buenos Aires, a quite remarkable ferry flight via Iceland, Canada, U.S.A., the Leeward Islands and the east coast of South America.

A 'mass attack' by Series 1 G-ASOF, Series 2s G-ATUK, 'VT, 'YD, 'YE and Basset XS777 at the September 1966 Farnborough S.B.A.C. Show resulted in sales to air taxi companies in Ireland, Spain and South Africa, and of the exhibition aircraft G-ATUK to the Mahdi of the Sudan as ST-ADA. Taking advantage of the exceptionally big door, Maidenhead Organ Studios and the Imperial Tobacco Company re-equipped with Series 2s G-ATYE and G-AVCJ respectively in 1967, while G-AVAL, 'AM, 'CI and 'HO were sold as executive transports to G.K.N. Group Services Ltd., Baginton; Boulay Investments Ltd., Jersey; British Ropes Ltd., Yeadon; and the British Aircraft Corporation Ltd. at Wisley.

Sales abroad in 1967 comprised two aircraft equipped to carry doctor, attendant and two stretcher cases, which were ferried to Australia in quick succession for the Royal Flying Doctor Service by Miss Janet Ferguson; G-ATZR to Beagle Australasia (demonstrated in New Zealand in May 1968 as VH-UNL); G-AVLL to the Federal Military Government of Nigeria, Lagos; and two to America, forerunners of 12 others flown across the Atlantic to Miami Aviation, the U.S. distributors, 1968–69.

Airline equipment in spacious cabins made B.206s very suitable for instrument training. G-ATKP, 'YC and 'ZO were used in this role by Airways Training Ltd. at Gatwick from 1966; G-ATHO by the Shoreham School of Flying; and the one-time Australian demonstrators G-ASOF and G-ATDD by Cumberland Aviation Services Ltd., Carlisle, 1968–69.

Special versions included Series 2 G-AVCG equipped with cameras for an arduous aerial mapping operation in Libya by Hunting Surveys Ltd. in 1968, and the 67th machine, similarly equipped was flown to Damascus for the Syrian Air Force in 1969. Other long-distance deliveries were G-AXCB and VH-KCA flown Gatwick–Sydney by Miss Janet Ferguson in April 1969 and January 1970 for the R.F.D.S. and Groupair respectively; and G-ATZP to Ndola in June 1969 for the Zambian Flying Doctor Service. Three special Series 3 aircraft, G-AWLN, G-35-28 and the unregistered 37th production aircraft, all had built-up rear fuselages to accommodate ten passengers.

Three B.206s originally intended for export to Aero Comahue, Buenos Aires, as LV-PLE to 'LG, remained at Rearsby as G-AWRM to 'RO and the first of these was registered to Executive Flights Ltd. and delivered to Kode International, Colerne, in June 1969. By this time the jigs had been removed from the Rearsby factory to make way for the growing flood of Beagle Pups, and Beagle 206 production ended with the 85th aircraft.

Beagle 206X prototype, G-ARRM, in an early configuration. (*A. J. Jackson*)

The second production B.206R Basset C.C.1 prior to delivery to R.A.F. Andover on 2 June 1965.

The ten-seat Beagle 206 Series 3 G-AWLN at Shoreham in September 1971 showing the deepened rear fuselage and ventral fin. (*A. J. Jackson*)

SPECIFICATION

Manufacturers: Beagle Aircraft Ltd., Shoreham Aerodrome, Sussex, and Rearsby Aerodrome, Leicester.

Power Plants: (B.206X) Two 260 h.p. Continental IO-470D.
(B.206Y) Two 310 h.p. Continental GIO-470A.
(Series 1) Two 310 h.p. Rolls-Royce Continental GIO-470A.
(Series 2) Two 340 h.p. Rolls-Royce Continental GTSIO-520C.

	B.206X	Series 1	Series 2
Span	38 ft. 0 in.	45 ft. $9\frac{1}{2}$ in.	45 ft. $9\frac{1}{2}$ in.
Length	32 ft. 7 in.	33 ft. 8 in.	33 ft. 8 in.
Height	12 ft. 3 in.	11 ft. 4 in.	11 ft. 4 in.
Wing area	190 sq. ft.	214 sq. ft.	214 sq. ft.
Tare weight	4,003 lb.	4,440 lb.	4,800 lb.
All-up weight	6,310 lb.	7,500 lb.	7,499 lb.
Cruising speed	228 m.p.h.	210 m.p.h.	218 m.p.h.
Initial climb	1,840 ft./min.	1,500 ft./min.	1,340 ft./min.
Range (max. fuel)	1,720 miles	1,890 miles	1,620 miles
Range (max. load)	1,150 miles	990 miles	1,020 miles

Production: (a) Prototype and pre-production aircraft

Four only: (c/n B.001) 206X/G-ARRM; (B.002) 206Y/G-ARXM; (B.003) 206Z-1/XS742; (B.004) 206Z-2/XS743.

(b) Beagle B.206 Series 1

Eleven British registered aircraft listed in Appendix E.

(c) Beagle B.206R Basset C.C.1

Twenty aircraft for the R.A.F.: (c/n B.006) XS765; (B.008) XS766; (B.010–B.012) XS767–XS769; (B.014) XS770; (B.016–B.018) XS771–XS773; (B.020–B.021) XS774–XS775; (B.024–B.025) XS776–XS777; (B.030–B.031) XS778 and XS780; (B.033–B.034) XS781 and XS779; (B.036) XS782; (B.042) XS783; (B.045) XS784.

(d) Beagle B.206 Series 2

Twenty-eight British registered aircraft and the following for export: (c/n B.062) G-35-16/PT-DIP; (B.063) N592MA; (B.064) N552MA; (B.065) N539MA; (B.066) N568MA; (B.067) YK-AMA; (B.068) N477EC; (B.069) N569MA; (B.073) N584MA; (B.075) VH-KCA, later PK-OAS; (B.076) N587MA/XB-MAL; (B.077) N662MA; (B.078) N663MA, later PT-DYX; (B.079) N664MA; (B.081–B.085) in storage at Castle Donington and Tollerton 1970.

(e) Beagle B.206 Series 3

Three aircraft only: (c/n B.037) unregistered; (B.074) G-35-28/G-AXPV; (B.080) G-AWLN.

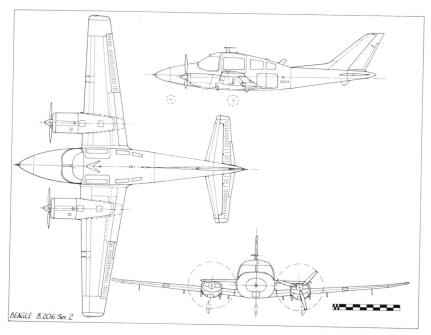

BEAGLE B.206 Ser. 2

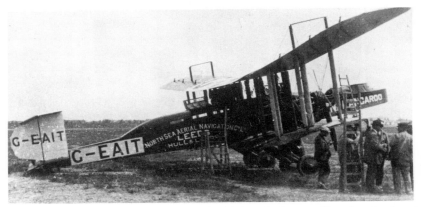

The cabin Kangaroo G-EAIT used on the scheduled service between Hounslow, Leeds and Amsterdam in 1920.

Blackburn Kangaroo

The Kangaroo was a long-range bomber designed towards the end of the First World War, most of the 20 produced being based at Seaton Carew on the North Yorkshire coast and flown with some success on anti-submarine patrols in 1918. It was a large biplane remarkable for its long, slender fuselage and the overhang of the upper mainplane, which amounted to 11 ft. at each wing-tip. Construction was orthodox with a rectangular section fabric-covered fuselage of wire braced spruce internal members, two-spar fabric-covered wings and a large twin-ruddered biplane empennage. The R.A.F. serials allocated were B9970 to '89 (ex N1720–N1739) the first five at least having twin 250 h.p. Rolls-Royce Falcon II engines and the remainder 270 h.p. Falcon IIIs. All but three of the existing Kangaroos were repurchased by the manufacturers in May 1919 and eventually 11 were used for civilian purposes.

Four types of conversion were devised, the most primitive being that of the three Kangaroos, G-EADE, 'DF and 'DG, bought direct from the Air Ministry by the Grahame-White Aviation Co. Ltd. in June 1919 for joyriding at Hendon. They were merely stripped of their gun mountings, and enough fabric removed from the top of the rear fuselage to accommodate seven passengers in two large cockpits, with an eighth in the extreme nose, drab green camouflage and military serials being retained. The first two were lost in accidents within a few weeks but the third was painted-up as G-EADG in September 1919 and carried hundreds of passengers during the two year currency of its C. of A.

Meanwhile a much more ambitious conversion programme was being undertaken by Blackburns at Brough. Two Kangaroos registered G-EAIT and 'MJ were each equipped with a large glazed cabin seating seven passengers, with the eighth occupant in the extreme nose; two others, G-EAIU and 'KQ, had open rear fuselages for freighting or pleasure flying; but whereas 'IU had the ugly enclosure in the nose, 'KQ had tandem cockpits with dual control. In August 1919 G-EAIT

202

and the two open models flew to the First Air Traffic Exhibition at Amsterdam where they carried more than 1,000 passengers and after the Show were used by a Blackburn subsidiary, the North Sea Aerial Navigation Co. Ltd., on a Leeds–Hounslow service at a single fare of £10. The Kangaroos were maintained at Brough and picked up passengers at Roundhay Park, Leeds, but on 5 March 1920 the route was extended to Amsterdam when R. W. Kenworthy flew out a load of ladies' garments in G-EAKQ. The project failed financially and the service ceased later in 1920 after 20,000 miles had been flown, 'KQ being sold to the Peruvian Army Flying Service at Las Palmas near Lima.

One of the four aircraft competing for the Australian Government's £10,000 prize offered in 1919 for the first flight from England to Australia was Kangaroo G-EAOW—the original performance trials machine B9970—entered by the Blackburn Aeroplane Co. Ltd. It took off from Hounslow on 21 November 1919, nine days after the departure of Ross and Keith Smith in the victorious Vimy G-EAOU. It was flown by Lts. Val Rendle and D. R. Williams with the explorer Sir Hubert Wilkins as navigator and Lt. G. H. Potts as engineer. After suspected sabotage en route, they finally developed a serious oil leak in the port motor when 80 miles out from Crete on 8 December. A successful return was made on one engine, and only slight damage resulted from a downwind landing and burst tyre on the aerodrome at Suda Bay, but cables to England for a spare engine were so mutilated that no engine arrived and the flight was abandoned. The machine still lay at Suda Bay in July 1921.

The greatest day in the Kangaroo's history was probably 8 September 1922, when the cabin model G-EAMJ and the standard conversion G-EAIU faced the starter's flag in the King's Cup Race at Croydon. The first, entered by the Rt. Hon. Winston Churchill, M.P., and flown by the well known Lt. Col. Spenser Grey, got away 10 minutes ahead of its sleeker brother flown by Blackburn's test pilot R. W. Kenworthy. Both ran out of daylight between Newcastle and Renfrew, returned to Newcastle and retired but not until Spenser Grey had landed 'MJ at Jarrow to inquire the way!

The Kangaroos finished their careers as twin-engined trainers at the R.A.F. Reserve School at Brough, where a pilot named Macdonald was killed in the crash

G-EBMD, one of the Brough Reserve Flying School tandem cockpit Kangaroo trainers.

of G-EAIT on 5 May 1925. Existing machines were supplemented by three of the first four Kangaroos built, taken out of storage and converted into tandem-cockpit trainers G-EBMD, 'OM and 'PK. In this fourth and final form they were a common sight in the North of England until withdrawn from use in 1928. By March 1929 they had all been flown to Sherburn-in-Elmet and were stored there until taken out one at a time and broken up.

SPECIFICATION

Manufacturers: The Blackburn Aeroplane and Motor Co. Ltd., Olympia, Leeds.

Power Plants: Two 250 h.p. Rolls Royce Falcon II or two 270 h.p. Rolls-Royce Falcon III.

Dimensions: Span, 74 ft. $10\frac{1}{4}$ in. Length, 46 ft. 0 in. Height, 16 ft. 10 in. Wing area, 880 sq. ft.

Weights: Tare weight (cabin model), 5,300 lb. All-up weight, 8,100 lb. Tare weight (freighter/trainer), 5,150 lb.

Performance: Maximum speed, 98 m.p.h. Initial climb, 500 ft./min. Ceiling, 10,500 ft. Range (cabin model), 410 miles; (freighter/trainer), 580 miles.

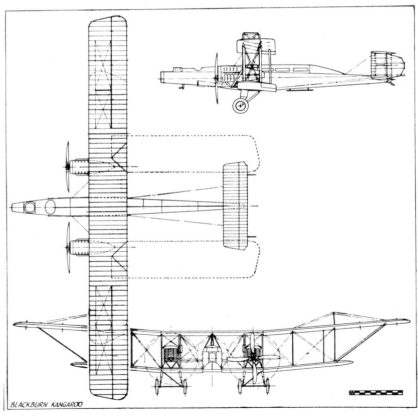

BLACKBURN KANGAROO

The first civil Dart, standing on its retractable beaching wheels at Brough in 1924.

Blackburn Swift, Dart and Velos

By the end of the First World War the Blackburn Aeroplane and Motor Co. Ltd. was entirely engaged on the development of naval aircraft, and continued as leading builders of deck-landing torpedo-bombers for many years afterwards. In so doing they were instrumental in providing Great Britain with most of its pitiful handful of civil twin-float seaplanes. The first post-war design by Major F. A. Bumpus was the private venture Swift which made its first appearance at the Aero Show at Olympia, London, during July 1920. It was a single-seat biplane of truly massive proportions powered by a single 450 h.p. Napier Lion and proved almost uncontrollable when R. W. Kenworthy made the first flight at Brough later in 1920. A few degrees of sweepback cured the trouble and the aircraft flew to Martlesham as N139 on 23 December 1920 without using its civil registration G-EAVN. Its performance was such that five improved Swift Mk. II aircraft were exported, including M-NTBA, 'BB and 'BC to the Spanish Navy.

Development continued, and by 1924 an improved version known as the Dart was in production at Olympia, Leeds, whence the finished machines were taken by road to Brough for erection and delivery to the Fleet Air Arm. In October 1924 Blackburn's subsidiary, the North Sea Aerial and General Transport Co. Ltd., operators of the R.A.F. Reserve and civilian training school at Brough, put three demilitarized ex R.A.F. Darts—G-EBKF, 'KG and 'KH—into commission. These were equipped with large volume, boat-built mahogany floats able to withstand the uncertain seamanship of the trainee and had pilot-operated retractable beaching wheels between the floats. They were extremely docile in the air and would unstick from the Humber 'hands off' in 20 seconds. Thus Brough became the only British seaplane flying school.

A final variant, the two seat, Lion V powered Velos torpedo-bomber, was built for the Greek Navy, the second aircraft being flown before foreign air attachés by Capt. N. H. Woodhead on 28 October 1925. In 1928 four of this type, G-AAAW to 'AZ, joined the flying school and, like the Darts, were converted into trainers

205

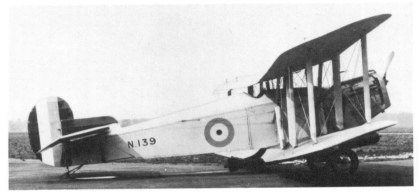

The prototype Swift, G-EAVN, after purchase by the Air Council as N139.

The privately owned Velos G-AAAW at Brooklands on 20 May 1933.

and provided with interchangeable wheel and float undercarriages. They were supplemented by G-EBWB (a floatplane in which H. V. Worrall had toured South America in 1927) and in 1930 by G-AAUM, a cancelled Greek order (Lion IIB) once used for Blackburn's first metal float trials. The Dart/Velos fleet continued in service until the requirement for Reserve floatplane training terminated, whereupon they were fitted with wheeled undercarriages until finally withdrawn from service early in 1933. They were so uneconomical in operation as to rule out their use for any other purpose and were sold as scrap, making their final journeys by road to a number of breakers' yards in the district. Here their decaying hulks disgraced the skyline like so many prehistoric skeletons for a great many years. As late as 1950 the bare bones of Dart G-EBKH were still outside a garage at Hatfield, near Doncaster, where the proprietor, R. Fowler, still preserved the journey log books. The only one of these giants temporarily to avert its fate was G-AAAW, which made the only recorded Velos cross-country flight to the South.

In April 1933 it was acquired for £15 by a private owner, Ian Parker, who flew it home to Hooton, and on 19 May 1933 it hove in sight near Heston, lumbered into the circuit and landed. On the following day the proud owner of this, the largest and noisiest of all contemporary private aircraft, flew it to Brooklands, where it became the star attraction at the display organized by the Guild of Air Pilots. Having used 63 gallons of petrol on the flight down from Hooton and its swan song over, it was flown to Northolt and, on 30 December 1933, to Old Warden where it was broken up to provide aircraft grade timber for rebuilding vintage aircraft of the Shuttleworth Collection.

SPECIFICATION

Manufacturers: The Blackburn Aeroplane and Motor Co. Ltd., Olympia, Leeds.
Power Plants: (Swift) One 450 h.p. Napier Lion IB.
                (Dart) One 450 h.p. Napier Lion IIB.
                (Velos) One 450 h.p. Napier Lion V.
Dimensions: (Velos) Span, 48 ft. 6 in. Length, 35 ft. 6 in. Height, 12 ft. 3 in. Wing area, 654 sq. ft.
Weights: Tare weight, 2,750 lb. All-up weight, 6,300 lb. (Velos) 6,450 lb.
Performance: Maximum speed, 106 m.p.h. Cruising speed, 102·5 m.p.h. Initial climb, 750 ft./min. (Velos), 650 ft./min. Ceiling, 15,000 ft. Range, 350 miles.

BLACKBURN DART

The Suffolk Aero Club Bluebird II G-EBRE flying near Ipswich in 1928.
(*Flight Photo 7789*)

Blackburn Bluebird I, II and III

The wooden Bluebird was well known as the first British side-by-side two-seater to go into production, but its deeds were largely unheeded because it existed only in small numbers, the majority of which enjoyed but four short years of life. The design originated as entry No. 12 in the Air Ministry trials for low-powered two-seaters held at Lympne in September 1924, the prototype being fitted with a 1,100 c.c. Blackburne Thrush three-cylinder radial, product of Burney and Blackburne Engines Ltd. of Bookham, Surrey. With commendable foresight, the machine was not designed purely as a competition freak, but was a genuine attempt to anticipate the layout of the cheap instructional machine of the future. To this end it was stressed to take a more powerful engine and had folding wings. Deep doors admitted the occupants to the cockpit, in which they sat side by side to facilitate instruction or to make private flying more sociable than was possible with tandem cockpits. Unfortunately the Bluebird was not finished in time for the Brough C.F.I., Sqn. Ldr. A. G. Loton, to take it to Lympne.

As the 1924 machines could hardly be considered satisfactory for touring or instruction, the *Daily Mail* sponsored a similar competition at Lympne in September 1926, imposing a weight limitation of 170 lb. on the engine, but otherwise encouraging the construction of more robust aircraft. As entry No. 1, the Bluebird appeared in modified form with a Genet I five-cylinder radial giving a healthy 60 h.p., with the decking which formerly bisected the cockpit removed and full dual control replacing the central shared control column. Sqn. Ldr. W. H. Longton, D.F.C., A.F.C., had the misfortune to slightly damage the undercarriage, and the Bluebird was eliminated, but on 18 September 1926, he succeeded in winning the Grosvenor Cup Race at an average speed of 84·95 m.p.h. In those days the only real way of publicizing a new type was through air racing, and the

208

machine went on to win the Yorkshire Aeroplane Club's Open Handicap at Sherburn-in-Elmet and to come second in a similar event organized by the Lancashire Aero Club at Woodford. As G-EBKD, in 1927, it achieved fame at the Bournemouth Easter Meeting at Ensbury Park, not only by winning Heat 2 of the Business Houses' Handicap, but also for being perforated by anti-aircraft fire from the shotgun of an irate farmer. Later it was used as a honeymoon taxi by an R.A.F. officer quick to realize the potentialities of side-by-side seating. Its career was drawing to a close, however, and during the Bournemouth Whitsun Meeting on 6 June 1927 it was burnt out following an air collision with the Westland Widgeon G-EBPW, both the Westland test pilot, L. P. Openshaw, and Longton being killed.

Interest in the machine resulted in a batch of 14 being laid down at Brough, the production model having the 80 h.p. Genet II, but otherwise generally similar to the revised prototype, and known as the Bluebird II. The fourteenth machine, G-EBWE, built in February 1928 and named 'The Friendship', private mount of Capt. T. A. Gladstone, manager of the N.S.Ae. & G.T. Co. Ltd. overseas air routes, was a structural improvement internally and designated Mk. III. A final batch of six of these was built in 1929. G-EBWE was later used for the trial installation of the in-line Cirrus III engine in readiness for the Bluebird IV. The main Bluebird users were the Suffolk and Eastern Counties Aeroplane Club at Hadleigh, near Ipswich, which had G-EBRE, 'SZ, 'UH, G-AABE and 'BF; the Yorkshire Aeroplane Club with G-EBRF, 'RG, 'SV and G-AABD; and the N.S.Ae. & G.T. Co. Ltd. with G-EBTA and 'TC. The enterprising Suffolk Club had a branch at Conington, near Cambridge, and carried passengers in the Bluebirds on the so-called Ipswich–Cambridge Airway at 30s. single or 50s. return in the course of their bi-weekly positioning flights. These were extended to Grantham on Tuesdays in order to catch the *Flying Scotsman* express.

The leading Bluebird exponent was Col. the Master of (later Lord) Sempill, for whom G-EBSW was fitted with a float undercarriage in July 1928. He flew it non-

The Bluebird II floatplane G-EBSW which made the Round Britain and German flights in 1928.

The Bluebird III G-EBWE after the trial installation of the 90 h.p. A.D.C. Cirrus III.

stop from the Humber to the Welsh Harp, Hendon, in $4\frac{3}{4}$ hours, to indulge, on arrival, in impromptu races with the local speed-boats. On 1 August he alighted on the Thames at Westminster alongside the Imperial Airways Short Calcutta G-EBVG moored there for parliamentary inspection. During the ensuing month the Bluebird seaplane gave a magnificent exhibition of reliability and toughness, carrying its distinguished pilot round the entire coastline of Great Britain, to the Scottish lochs, Cape Wrath, Belfast, Wexford, Land's End, and finally to a night landing on the Welsh Harp by the light of a few flickering matches. In December 1928 he flew it across the North Sea to attend the Berlin Aero Show, landing on the Wansee and returning in the most appalling weather, forced down on the Elbe by fog, held up at Amsterdam by gales and finally making a non-stop crossing to Felixstowe in four hours.

The first production Bluebird III, G-AABB, shown on the Blackburn stand at the Berlin Aero Show, was afterwards shipped to New Zealand and arrived at Auckland in February 1929. It was first used by Southern Cross Airways Ltd. of Mangere, became ZK-AAQ, and was flown on floats by S. J. Blackmore, a later owner who went solo on it after only 2 hr. 20 min. dual instruction. This aircraft finally crashed near Te Rapa Aerodrome, Hamilton, on 2 April 1933 while in service as a landplane with the Waikato Aero Club.

Although King's Cup and similar honours did not fall to the wooden Bluebirds, they gave faithful service in their intended role as club and private aircraft, but only three lasted more than four years. These were G-EBRF, privately owned by L. J. C. Mitchell at Chard in 1930–31 and later kept at Gravesend by the Hon. A. B. Mildmay; G-EBSZ, belonging to R. D. Gerrans of Bishops Stortford; and G-AABE, first light aeroplane of the Southend Flying Club, which was sold to G. H. Charlton at Chilworth in 1936, only to crash a few days later. The last survivor, 'RF, was eventually burned in a fire-fighting display at Gravesend in 1937.

SPECIFICATION

Manufacturers: The Blackburn Aeroplane and Motor Co. Ltd., Olympia, Leeds.

Power Plants: (Bluebird I) One 1,100 c.c. Blackburne Thrush.
One 60 h.p. Armstrong Siddeley Genet I.
(Bluebird II and III) One 80 h.p. Armstrong Siddeley Genet II.
One 90 h.p. A.D.C. Cirrus III.

	Bluebird I	Bluebird II and III
Span	28 ft. 0 in.	28 ft. 0 in.
Length	21 ft. 8 in.	22 ft. 6 in.
Height	7 ft. 11 in.	8 ft. 4 in.
Wing area	243 sq. ft.	237·5 sq. ft.
Tare weight	495 lb.	793 lb.
All-up weight	875 lb.	1,385 lb.
Maximum speed	74 m.p.h.	88 m.p.h.
Cruising speed	—	70 m.p.h.

Production:

One prototype Bluebird I G-EBKD and 13 production Bluebird II (Works Orders 9803/1 to 9803/14).

One Bluebird II G-EBWE (9803/15) completed as prototype Bluebird III (629/1) and six production aircraft (1450/1 to 1450/6).

The entire production was registered in Britain and appears in Appendix E.

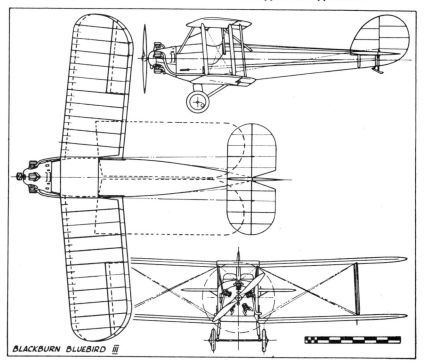

BLACKBURN BLUEBIRD III

The Bluebird IV G-AASU, Gipsy I engine, used by the Airwork Flying School at Heston during the first half of 1930. (*Aeroplane*)

Blackburn Bluebird IV

In 1929 the Blackburn company completely redesigned the Bluebird as an all-metal aeroplane using steel longerons and wing-spars with duralumin formers, stringers and wing ribs. Fabric covering was retained, but the cross-axle undercarriage was abandoned in favour of the divided type, a large aerodynamically balanced rudder without fin replaced the rounded type, and Gipsy I, Cirrus III or Hermes I in-line engines were fitted as standard. The prototype, G-AABV, fitted with a Gipsy I engine, was bought by Sqn. Ldr. L. Slatter, who flew it home to South Africa on leave, departing from Croydon on 7 March 1929 and reaching Durban on 15 April. On its return it was exhibited at the July 1929 Aero Show at Olympia, London, alongside G-AAIR, a Cirrus III version. Only two more metal Bluebirds, G-AACB and 'CC, were Blackburn-built, military commitments compelling them to sub-contract production to Saunders-Roe Ltd. at Cowes. G-AAIR was the first completed Saro airframe, and between the end of 1929 and May 1931 they built at least 55 Bluebird IVs, sales being handled by Auto Auctions Ltd at Heston. The thirtieth Saro Bluebird, G-AAUX, was on show at their Burlington Gardens, London showrooms during November 1930.

The second Brough-built machine, G-AACB, was a floatplane sold in Norway as N-40 in October 1929, but the third and last, G-AACC, had a long career as a private aeroplane. It was raced unsuccessfully for the 1929 King's Cup by Col. the Master of Sempill, but in the following year it was re-engined with a Hermes I and was flown into sixth place at 109·82 m.p.h. by Tommy Rose. The 1930 King's Cup Race was one of the highlights of Bluebird IV history, 'CC being only one of the 13 entered. The others, flown by many famous pilots of the day, were: G-AABV, Norman Blackburn; G-AATO, Flt. Lt. G. G. H. du Boulay; G-AAVG, Sqn. Ldr. L. Slatter; G-AAIR, Col. the Master of Sempill; G-AAOI, Flg. Off. J. W. Gillan; G-AAUV, the Hon. Loel Guinness; G-AATN, Flt. Lt. H. R. D. Waghorn; G-AAUW, Flt. Lt. H. V. Rowley; G-AATS, H. J. Andrews; G-AAUU, Harald Peake; G-AASV, Flt. Lt. F. J. Fogarty; and G-AAVF, Sqn. Ldr. J. W. Woodhouse. The best performance was that of G-AATN, which came third, but in the following year G-AACC was completely victorious at an average speed of 117·80 m.p.h. powered by a Hermes II and flown by Flg. Off. E. C. T. Edwards.

Hanworth, newly opened in 1929, became the H.Q. of National Flying Services Ltd., which ordered 25 Cirrus III Bluebird IVs for instructional purposes, the first six of which, G-AAOA to 'OF, resplendent in N.F.S. orange and black, were delivered in formation from Cowes on 14 January 1930. Although G-AAOG to 'OJ arrived in the following month, N.F.S. did not survive long enough to take delivery of G-AAOK to 'OZ, which were never built. A considerable number were sold to private owners, but the main user was the N.S.Ae. & G.T. Co. Ltd. Reserve Flying School at Brough. The good name of the Bluebird IV was unfortunately sullied by the number of fatal crashes in which it was involved, including G-AAOA at Feltham on 6 April 1930 and G-AATP at East Heslerton, Yorks., both making unexplained dives into the ground from normal cruising flight, G-AATS, 'UG and 'UT operated for a short time from the Humber as twin-float seaplanes, the last being lost off Felixstowe when it alighted and sank during M.A.E.E. trials on 12 January 1931.

Flown by pioneering pilots, the Bluebird IVs were outstanding. G-AAJC the eighth Saro machine, went to Southern Rhodesia on survey work for Cobham-Blackburn Air Lines, becoming VP-YAI temporarily, before going on to South Africa. Another, G-AAOF, owned by H. R. Fields, found its way from Hull to Iceland by sea to become TF-ISL; a third, G-AAOC, went abroad with Mrs. Elizabeth Scott and ended its days in Madrid as EC-UUU. Two others, VH-UNS (Gipsy I) and 'OC (Genet Major I), were delivered to the Lasco School of Flying, Melbourne, in 1930 but the former was later sold to Ludwig Nudl who made the first-ever round-Australia commercial flight in it with R. W. McKenzie, 24 October–6 December 1931.

During 1931–32 VT-ACP was delivered to Coromandel Automobiles of Madras; VT-ADD and 'DK to Indo-American Automobiles of Bombay; and CF-ALN and 'UP were sent to Montreal for the Curtiss-Reid Aircraft Co.

Most famous Bluebird of all was undoubtedly the Gipsy II model G-ABDS in which, with only 40 hours solo in her log book, the Hon. Mrs. Victor Bruce made the first solo flight to encircle the globe. She left Croydon in July 1930 and flew 'DS to Rangoon by the usual route via Karachi, thence to Shanghai, and after a

The Hermes I engined Bluebird IV G-AACC, winner of the 1931 King's Cup.

213

The Gipsy III Bluebird IV floatplane G-ABGF used on the West African Survey flight in 1931.

magnificent 600 mile crossing of the Yellow Sea on 18 November 1930, to Seoul, Korea. After crossing from Tokyo to Vancouver by sea, the flight continued to New York, and following a second sea crossing to Le Havre, Croydon was reached on 20 February 1931. The next day's welcoming party at Heston was attended by almost every existing Bluebird, including the great G-ABDS itself and Robert Blackburn's private G-ABEU. So that the public might see it, 'DS was on show in the booking-hall of Charing Cross Underground Station during the first week in March. In November 1930, G-ABGF, the first to be fitted with a Gipsy III, was supplied to Miss Delphine Reynolds for a survey flight down the West African coast. Piloted by W. G. Pudney, they left Hanworth on 1 March 1931 and flew via Tangier to Bathurst, where Short floats were fitted. After two and a half months in the area, however, the acid in the water of the mangrove swamps of Sierra Leone corroded the metal airframe beyond repair.

Two Australian flights were also undertaken. H. F. Broadbent left Hanworth on 29 March 1931 in a Gipsy II model, G-ABJA 'City of Sydney', in an attempt to lower the record, but abandoned the flight at Constantinople on 1 April. A more leisurely trip of three weeks three days was accomplished by Lt. Cdr. G. A. Hall, who left Croydon in G-AAVG fitted with a Hermes II engine on 8 August 1932, and reached Wyndham from Koepang on 1 September, the machine later becoming VH-UQZ.

The last long-distance Bluebird flight was made by R. W. H. Knight who left Heston in G-AAIR on 8 October 1934 and flew 3,648 miles to Kano, Nigeria, in $54\frac{1}{2}$ hr. flying time.

The final Bluebird IVs were the Gipsy III powered G-ABPV, in which a Greek Air Force pilot was killed during a trial flight at Athens on 24 October 1931, and G-ABMI supplied to the Hon. Mrs. Victor Bruce. Two earlier machines had involved careers, one of which, sold in Germany as D-2536 in April 1932, was to have been first G-ABEX and then G-ABVZ, but received neither of these markings. The other was to have been G-ABEY, but was used on the Brough Reserve School as G-ABZX until withdrawn from use at the end of 1935. It was then converted as a flying testbed for the Blackburn Cirrus Minor 1 engine, becoming

G-ADXG in theory, but actually flying under B conditions as B-10. No Bluebird exists today, the last being G-AATE, sent by owner P. H. Ford from Hooton to Hamsey Green for overhaul in October 1938 and broken up there in 1947.

SPECIFICATION

Manufacturers: The Blackburn Aeroplane and Motor Co. Ltd., Brough, East Yorks., subcontracted to Saunders-Roe Ltd., East Cowes, Isle of Wight.

Power Plants: One 100 h.p. de Havilland Gipsy I.
One 120 h.p. de Havilland Gipsy II.
One 120 h.p. de Havilland Gipsy III.
One 90 h.p. A.D.C. Cirrus III.
One 100 h.p. A.D.C. Cirrus Hermes I or II.
One 135 h.p. Armstrong Siddeley Genet Major I.

Dimensions: Span, 30 ft. 0 in. Length, 23 ft. 2 in. Height, 9 ft. 0 in. Wing area, 246 sq. ft.

Weights: (Gipsy I) Tare weight, 1,070 lb. All-up weight, 1,750 lb.

Performance: (Gipsy I) Maximum speed, 120 m.p.h. Cruising speed, 85 m.p.h. Initial climb, 730 ft./min. Range, 320 miles.

Production:

Three aircraft G-AABV, 'CB and 'CC by Blackburn and 55 by Saunders-Roe Ltd., Cowes, including eight for export: (c/n SB.201) to Detroit, U.S.A. 10.29; (SB.242–244) untraced; (SB.247) VT-ACP; (SB.248) CF-AUP; (SB.250) VT-ADD; (SB.251) CF-ALN.

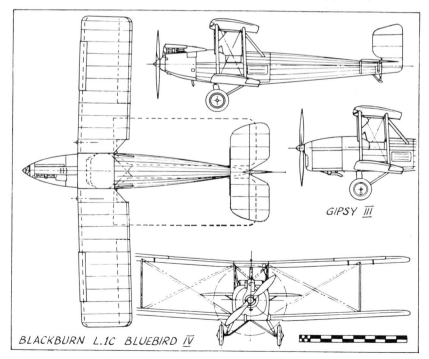

GIPSY III

BLACKBURN L.1C BLUEBIRD IV

The first production Blackburn Segrave G-ABFP.

Blackburn Segrave

As its name implies, this aeroplane was initially the brainchild of Sir Henry Segrave, a First World War fighter pilot, leading racing driver and holder of the world's land-speed record. When his interest in flying returned in the late 'twenties he drew up plans for what he considered to be the ideal aircraft for luxury air touring, a twin-engined four-seater with ability to fly on one engine and land slowly, but at the same time possessing an impressive cruising speed. None knew better than he the economies in power and the improvement in performance that result from careful streamlining. Thus in a biplane age with several of the longest lived and most widely used of our classic biplane types yet unbuilt, the machine was revolutionary with its streamlined fuselage and cantilever wing into which two 120 h.p. de Havilland Gipsy III inverted engines were faired. Only the crudity of its cabin glazing and the narrow track undercarriage would today reveal its true age.

The machine was known as the Segrave Meteor, detailed design and construction being entrusted to Saunders-Roe Ltd. by the Aircraft Development Corporation, of which Sir Henry was technical director. The all-white prototype, G-AAXP, made its first flight at Cowes on 28 May 1930, its mixed parentage leading to the official designation Saro-Segrave Meteor appearing on the Certificate of Registration. The Blackburn Aeroplane Co. Ltd. then took over production, translating the original wooden fuselage into an all-metal stressed skin version, the revised machine being known as the Blackburn-Segrave Meteor and later as the Blackburn Segrave. Further development and construction was seriously retarded by the tragic death of Sir Henry Segrave in the accident to the speedboat *Miss England II* on Lake Windermere on 13 June 1930 but two Blackburn Segraves, G-ABFP and 'FR, made their appearance in 1931, while a third, G-ABZJ, remained half completed.

The famous 1929 Schneider Trophy pilots Flt. Lt. R. L. R. (later Air Marshal Sir Richard) Atcherley and Flt. Lt. G. H. Stainforth formed the crew of the prototype G-AAXP in the 1930 King's Cup Race. Engine trouble prevented the 'dark horse', now red, from showing its paces, and it limped back to Hanworth, the starting point. Later the same year it was flown to Italy by T. Neville Stack for demonstration at the request of the Italian Air Force for whom it was flown by

Gen. Italo Balbo, its performance exciting enthusiastic comment. In 1932 it was acquired by J. G. D. Armour, a prominent Hanworth private owner, who used it for Continental and other touring, thus fulfilling the purpose of its design. The new owner also raced it for the 1932 King's Cup, but ill luck again dogged the machine, a forced landing at Filton with a broken petrol pipe putting it out of the race. Nevertheless the course was completed at an average speed of 131 m.p.h.

G-ABFP, first of the metal-fuselaged Segraves, also red, was delivered at Heston for the private use of Gordon Selfridge Jnr. in March 1931 and flown in the Easter tour of Spain, but on its return it went back to the makers to be fitted with an improved tail unit, with which it flew on test in Class B markings as B-1. After a sales tour to Athens in October 1931 it was sold to the British Air Navigation Co. Ltd., Heston, for cross-Channel charters but in 1933 went to Redhill under private ownership and was flown to Nairobi. It landed back at Croydon on 7 October piloted by a S.A.A.F. officer and was then used at Brough for the trial installation of two 120 h.p. Blackburn Cirrus Hermes IVA engines.

The sister aircraft, Segrave G-ABFR, was exhibited at the Hendon S.B.A.C. Show in July 1932, but was seen no more in the south for some years, being employed on the Brough–Waltham (Grimsby) ferry across the Humber. Like its comrade, it went to Redhill, becoming the property of the Redhill Flying Club Ltd. in May 1936, spares being obtained by cannibalisation of the prototype, pieces of which were still in evidence in 1947.

An interesting design exercise into the rigidity of single-spar cantilever wings was carried out with the third airframe. A unique all-metal structure, with a circular-section duralumin tubular spar, being designed by F. Duncanson of the Blackburn staff. This Duncanson wing was more tapered than the original, part of the hollow spar housing the fuel. The 260 lb. in weight thus saved permitted the installation of Gipsy Major engines and the provision of a fifth seat in the cabin without increasing the all-up weight. Markedly different from a standard Segrave, the machine was re-registered and flew in silver and black as G-ACMI early in 1934. No others were built, and 'MI was used for experimental flying at Brough. Data thus gained led to the construction of the Blackburn H.S.T.10 transport, which had the Duncanson wing, a retractable undercarriage and two Napier

The experimental metal Segrave G-ACMI flying near Brough with wool tufts over the rudder hinges.

217

Rapier engines. Military commitments forced the company to abandon its development, and after the prototype had appeared under B conditions as B-9, it was given to Loughborough College as an instructional airframe.

SPECIFICATION

Manufacturers: Saunders-Roe Ltd., East Cowes, Isle of Wight, and the Blackburn Aeroplane and Motor Co. Ltd., Brough, East Yorks.

Power Plants: Two 120 h.p. de Havilland Gipsy III.
Two 120 h.p. Cirrus Hermes IVA.
Two 130 h.p. de Havilland Gipsy Major.

Dimensions: Span, 39 ft. 6 in. Length, 28 ft. 6 in. Height, 7 ft. 9 in. Wing area, 230 sq. ft.

Weights: Tare weight, 2,240 lb. All-up weight, 3,300 lb.

Performance: Maximum speed, 138 m.p.h. Cruising speed, 112 m.p.h. Initial climb, 800 ft./min. Ceiling, 14,000 ft. Range, 450 miles.

Production:

One prototype Segrave Meteor G-AAXP built by Saunders-Roe Ltd. 1930 and three production Blackburn Segraves G-ABFP, G-ABFR and G-ABZJ/G-ACMI detailed in Appendix E.

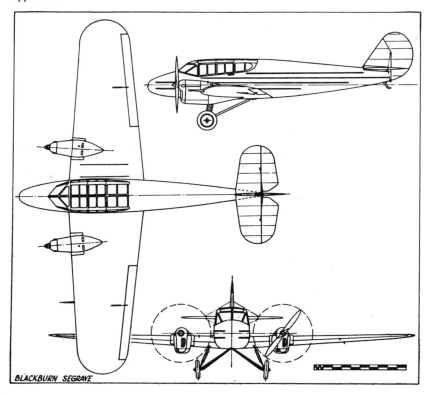

BLACKBURN SEGRAVE

The last airworthy Blackburn B-2, G-AEBJ, flying near Brough on 15 June 1960.

Blackburn B-2

The Blackburn B-2 was a side-by-side two-seat trainer developed from the Gipsy III version of the Bluebird IV. A normal fin-and-rudder assembly was fitted, but the fuselage was Alclad covered and made incredibly strong to withstand the hard knocks of intensive instructional flying. Like all the early models, the prototype G-ABUW, was fitted with a Gipsy III engine and made its first public appearance at the Hendon S.B.A.C. Show on 27 June 1932 and on 8 July was on the King's Cup Race starting line at Brooklands. Piloted by Flt. Lt. J. W. Gillan, it finished eighteenth, closely followed by Flg. Off. P. G. Sayer who came twenty-second in G-ABWI.

At the invitation of the Portuguese Government, 'UW was shipped from London Docks to Lisbon in the following September and demonstrated by W. E. P. Johnson, whose performance in getting in and out of a football pitch near the point of disembarkation drew very favourable comment. Competitive trials then took place against a Fleet trainer, a Caproni biplane, and Christopher Clarkson in a Tiger Moth, but the Portuguese preferred tandem seating and after a final flourish by Johnson and Clarkson, who flew an inverted formation over Lisbon, the contract was awarded to the Tiger Moth. On its return 'UW joined 'WI at the North Sea Aerial & General Transport Co. Ltd.'s Reserve Flying School at Brough, recently re-equipped with the remainder of the first production batch, G-ACAH and G-ACBH to 'BK. At the end of 1933 these were joined by G-ACLC and 'LD, the first two of a second production batch. In the King's Cup Race at Hatfield on 14 July 1934, 'AH, now fitted with a 120 h.p. Hermes IVA engine, was flown into fourth place by Flt. Lt. H. M. David at 114·18 m.p.h. Trial installations had also been made with a Gipsy Major engine in G-ACPZ and a Hermes IVA in G-ACRA, both of which went into service at Brough along with G-ACUE and 'ZH, the last two of the second six.

The fifth production B-2, G-ACBJ, in wartime training markings, flying near Brough in 1940.

With the formation of Flying Training Ltd. in 1935 and the opening of No. 5 Elementary and Reserve Flying Training School, 'PZ, 'RA and 'ZH were transferred to Hanworth to supplement a new batch, G-ADFN to 'FV, 'LF and 'LG. The Hermes IVA motor, also built by Blackburns, now became standard and was fitted in the new batches. On 12 November 1935 G-ACUE was wrecked at Little Weighton near Brough and was replaced by the first of a new batch, G-ADZM and 'ZN, both later transferred to Hanworth with G-ACLC. The year 1936 was an eventful one for the B-2s and saw the remaining production machines, G-AEBE to 'BO, go into service, 'BE and alternate aircraft belonging to the N.S.Ae. & G.T. Co. Ltd. and the rest to Flying Training Ltd. Several were lost in accidents during the year, G-ACER being so seriously damaged by fire at Brough on 8 May 1936 that it was at first considered a write-off, G-AEBH wrecked at Kingsbury, Middlesex, on 17 August, and G-ABWI burnt out in a fatal crash at Selby, Yorks., on 9 October. When the N.S.Ae. & G.T. Co. Ltd. was finally wound up at the end of the year, most of the B-2s were transferred to the ownership of Blackburn Aircraft Ltd., but G-ACEO and 'EP went to Hanworth, while 'ZH went north in exchange.

During the remaining pre-war period many thousands of hours of instructional flying were completed, during which two more were lost: G-AEBF destroyed at Sunbury on 9 September 1937 and G-AEBI demolished in a ground collision with a Hawker Hart at Hanworth on 31 January 1938. The last three of the 42 B-2 production aircraft bore the R.A.F. serials L6891, '2 and '3, and were added to the strength of No. 4 E.F.T.S. at Brough in June 1937. When war came, all the B-2s were hastily repainted with training yellow fuselages and camouflaged wings and continued normal instruction until they were given to the A.T.C. in February 1942, by which time four more had been lost, two in an air collision over the Humber on 24 June 1940. After the 1939–45 war several B-2s were still to be seen at schools and colleges and relics were visible more than 20 years later, notably the remains of the fuselage of G-ACBH at Dixon's Yard, Ramsden Heath, Essex.

Only two lived to fly again: G-ACLD, rebuilt with Cirrus Major III engine, was unsuccessfully raced for the Southend and Folkestone Trophies in 1947, but was an important exhibit at the annual vintage displays at Royal Aeronautical Society

Garden Parties until it crashed in time-honoured manner by stalling off a turn at low altitude during a display at York on 16 June 1951. The sole survivor was thus G-AEBJ, maintained in immaculate condition by its makers as a collector's piece to be flown at the more important events on the aviation calendar.

SPECIFICATION

Manufacturers: The Blackburn Aircraft Ltd., Brough, East Yorks.

Power Plants: One 120 h.p. de Havilland Gipsy III.
One 120 h.p. Cirrus Hermes IVA.
One 130 h.p. de Havilland Gipsy Major.
One 135 h.p. Blackburn Cirrus Major I.
One 150 h.p. Blackburn Cirrus Major III.

Dimensions: Span, 30 ft. 2 in. Length, 24 ft. 3 in. Height, 9 ft. 0 in. Wing area, 246 sq. ft.

Weights: Tare weight, 1,175 lb. All-up weight (normal), 1,850 lb.; (aerobatic), 1,770 lb.

Performance: Maximum speed, 112 m.p.h. Cruising speed, 95 m.p.h. Initial climb, 700 ft./min. Range, 320 miles.

Production: Forty-two British registered aircraft listed in Appendix E.

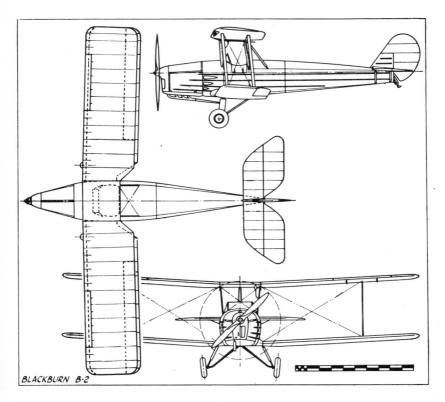

BLACKBURN B-2

The first production Boulton and Paul P.9 at Mousehold Aerodrome, Norwich, in April 1920. (*Boulton and Paul*)

Boulton and Paul P.6 and P.9

After the 1914–18 war J. D. North of Boulton and Paul Ltd. designed the small two-seat wood and fabric P.6 biplane, with R.A.F. 1A engine, which used Sopwith Camel parts in the fuselage and could be fitted with alternative sets of mainplanes for full-scale wing section research. It therefore flew with the experimental marking X25 but was registered to the makers on 20 May 1919 as K-120/G-EACJ for communications flying but is believed not to have carried this lettering.

The P.6 flew at the company's Mousehold aerodrome early in 1919, only a few weeks before the prototype P.9, a slightly larger version built at Norwich in six weeks to the order of Lt. A. L. Long who shipped it to Australia for patrolling sheep stations. On arrival Long flew it on newspaper and mail flights in Tasmania and made the first northbound crossing of the Bass Strait when he inaugurated the Hobart–Melbourne mail service on 15 December 1919.

Long's P.9 and the earlier P.6 used identical tail units and centre sections and neither boasted a constructor's number, but seven production P.9s which followed used a simplified, strutless tail incidence gear, had a different rudder horn balance shape and extra centre section struts, as well as a raised rear decking to accommodate suitcases behind the rear seat. The first of these, G-EAPD and 'SJ, flew at Mousehold in April 1920 and were used respectively by the makers and Brig. Gen. J. G. Weir. Due to the success of the prototype in Tasmania the next three were for Australia where they flew unregistered until they became G-AUBT, 'CP and 'CT in June 1921. One, inscribed 'Sun-Rayse' and believed later to have become G-AUCT, was bought by C. J. de Garis who flew as passenger when F. S. Briggs ferried it from Glenroy to a night landing at Sydney on 3 July 1920, and when the same pilot established the inter-city records: Mildura–Sydney on 6 July (550 miles in 6 hr. 10 min. flying time) and Sydney–Melbourne on 9 July (6 hr. 30 min.). After the P.9 crashed on the return flight on 11 July the remains were sold back to Aviation Ltd. and it is said to have been rebuilt as a monoplane in 1922.

G-AUCP, entrant H. O. Jolley and piloted by E. W. Percival, won the Herald Cup Race in high winds at Essendon, Melbourne, on 12 June 1923. It crashed at Willaura on 16 December 1927, its last owner being A. T. Tilt.

222

In April 1922 G-EASJ was acquired by F. T. Courtney who kept it at Croydon for flying to and from his various test flying assignments, and in September that year flew in the round-Britain King's Cup Race piloted by C. T. Holmes and competed against the sixth P.9, G-EAWS, flown by J. E. Tennant. In 1928 the Henderson School of Flying Ltd. took G-EASJ to the Cape for a joyriding tour which ended in its sale to the local pioneer airman John Wilkinson at Young's Field aerodrome, Cape Town.

The last P.9, built to an Australian order cancelled in 1921, was certificated in July 1923 as G-EBEQ for Boulton and Paul communications duties but was sold to Flg. Off. F. O. Soden in September 1926. Late in 1927 it went to Stag Lane where it was flown extensively by the new owner, Lt. H. Kennedy, who left Croydon for Paris on 7 October 1928 en route to Switzerland. It went through the ice in an attempted take-off from the frozen lake at St. Moritz on 9 February 1929 but was rebuilt locally and registered to Gerber and Greiner at Dübendorf as CH-259 in the following year.

The little Boulton and Paul P.6 painted up as the firm's communications machine in 1919. (*Boulton and Paul*)

The unregistered P.9 prototype which Lt. A. L. Long took to Tasmania in 1919. (*Boulton and Paul*)

SPECIFICATION

Manufacturers: Boulton and Paul Ltd., Riverside Works, Norwich.
Power Plant: One 90 h.p. R.A.F. 1A.

	P.6	P.9
Span	25 ft. 0 in.	27 ft. 6 in.
Length	19 ft. 0 in.	24 ft. 8 in.
Wing area	—	323 sq. ft.
Tare weight	1,100 lb.	1,244 lb.
All-up weight	1,725 lb.	1,770 lb.
Maximum speed	103 m.p.h.	104 m.p.h.
Cruising speed	—	85 m.p.h.
Initial climb	—	650 ft./min.
Range	—	300 miles

Production: (a) Boulton and Paul P.6
    One aircraft only: K-129/G-EACJ (c/n given as X25).

        (b) Boulton and Paul P.9
    One unregistered prototype and seven production aircraft: (c/n P.9-1) G-EAPD; (P.9-2) G-EASJ; (P.9-3, 4 and 5) G-AUBT, G-AUCP and G-AUCT, order not known; (P.9-6) G-EAWS; (P.9-7) G-AUDB ntu/G-EBEQ.

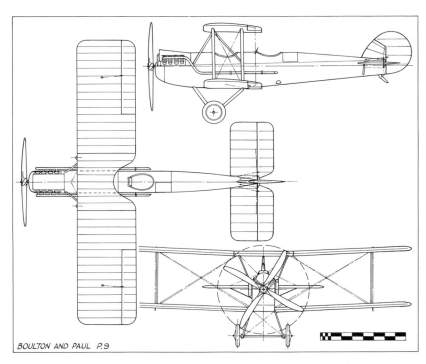

BOULTON AND PAUL P.9

The Hispano engined Fighter Type 17A built for the Belgian Government in 1924. (*Bristol Photo*)

Bristol Fighter

The Bristol F.2B Fighter biplane was designed by Capt. F. S. Barnwell in 1916, and built in the standard manner of the period with rectangular-section fabric-covered fuselage of wire braced spruce longerons and cross struts. The mainplanes were of conventional two-spar, two-bay design with the lower wing clear of the fuselage, which was thus in a mid-gap position. Although some Fighters were retained as standard equipment for the peace-time R.A.F., large numbers were taken over, dismantled and stored by the Aircraft Disposal Co. Ltd. in 1919–20. Following complete overhauls to airframe and engines, they emerged in a steady trickle from the Croydon factory as virtually new aeroplanes to be sold all over the world for civil and military purposes. They were fitted with either the Falcon III or 300 h.p. Hispano-Suiza engines, and by the end of 1923 twenty-two had been registered as British civil aircraft.

Handley Page Ltd. were the first to own 'Brisfits', G-EASH, 'SU and 'SV with Hispano engines being registered in April 1920, and a fourth, G-EAWA, in the following November. They were in fact the demonstration aircraft of the H.P. controlled Aircraft Disposal Co. Ltd. and were up for sale at £800 each. Although the initial outlay was low, running costs were excessive, and none were sold on the home market, the majority of the British machines carrying civil marks purely for test flying and delivery flights to the Belgian Air Force.

The Bristol Aeroplane Co. Ltd. supplied several foreign air forces with a modified version fitted with a 300 h.p. Hispano-Suiza engine, enlarged fin, Frise-type ailerons, and a redesigned oleo undercarriage replacing the old bungee type. Five (c/n 6140–6144), designated Type 17, were ferried to Spain in civil mark-ings M-MRAZ, 'AY, 'AX, 'AI and 'CO, and the first of these, M-MRAI, left Croydon on 13 September 1921 piloted by Larry Carter. A number of others, remanufactured with Hispano-Suiza engines by the Aircraft Disposal Co. Ltd., included M-MRAC, 'AE, 'AG, 'AH, 'AL to 'AR, 'AU and 'AV, which were flown away from Croydon by Hereward de Havilland, C. F. Wolley Dod, L. R. Tait-

Cox, L. Carter, F. T. Courtney, E. D. C. Herne, R. Stocken, F. C. Broome and others during the period August 1921–March 1922.

The first Type 17A, G-EBCN, was demonstrated in Norway before sale to the Belgian concern SABCA together with 15 certificated but unregistered machines (c/n 2324–2338). The only other Hispano-Suiza engined Bristol Fighter was G-EBIO, an A.D.C. demonstration aircraft first registered in 1923, and formerly H1254, which was a common sight at Croydon Airport and all over Europe for many years until sold to Flt. Lt. D. V. Ivins in August 1931. He used it for weekend trips from Jersey, arriving at Heston late on Friday afternoons, and in May 1932 flew it in the *Morning Post* Race from Heston round the Eastern Counties. The veteran averaged 85 m.p.h., but proved no match for the light aircraft, and came tenth. At the opening of Speke Airport on 1 July 1933, however, honour was satisfied when Ivins flew it to victory at 114·25 m.p.h. in the race to Blackpool and back.

A new era in the history of the type began in 1922, when 60 Army Co-operation Mk. IIs were built at Filton for the R.A.F., and all wartime Mk. Is returning to the works for reconditioning were modified up to the same standard. In 1926–27, 80 Mk. III, or Type 96, were also built, of which 30 were dual-control trainers, and after March 1927 all Mk. IIs coming up for reconditioning were also converted into Mk. IIIs. The modification programme reached its final stage in July 1928, when a number were strengthened and fitted with Handley Page auto-slots, long-travel undercarriages, cambered fins and horn balanced rudders for the R.A.F. overseas, while some were converted to dual control for the University Air Squadrons. These were designated Mk. IV, or Type 96A, and in 1931, when all marks were declared obsolete, they were offered for public sale, resulting in the appearance of a further 21 as British civil aircraft. The first of these, G-ABXA, was equipped as a tanker and refuelled the Saro Windhover in the air during Mrs. Victor Bruce's unsuccessful attempt on the world's endurance record in August 1932. A few were privately owned, notably G-ABXV by the Hon. John Grimston and G-ACAC by W. L. Handley, the others including G-ABYF, used for banner towing, and 'YT, in which Cinque Ports Club instructor K. K. Brown came second in the 1933 Folkestone Trophy Race. In 1933 Commercial Airways (Essex) Ltd. planned an all-Bristol Fighter flying school at

Walley Handley's civil Bristol Fighter (275 h.p. Rolls-Royce Falcon III) G-ACAC at Woodley in 1934. (*E. J. Riding*)

Nigel Tangye finishing in the Cinque Ports Wakefield Cup Race at Lympne, 25 August 1935, in London Film Productions' Bristol Fighter G-ADJR. (*Aeroplane*)

The Shuttleworth Trust's Fighter Mk. II D8096, which in 1936 was earmarked for civil conversion to G-AEPH. Photograph taken at Filton on 5 April 1957. (*Bristol Photo*)

Abridge, Essex, but although a quantity of major components was delivered by a local dealer, of the five registered, only the Hanworth-overhauled G-ABZG materialized.

C. P. B. Ogilvie, well-known collector of veteran aircraft, acquired two machines which were registered G-ADJR and G-AEPH. The former was made airworthy at Heston and sold in August 1935 to London Film Productions Ltd., for whom it was flown by Nigel Tangye as a camera ship. It was on this machine that he gave his memorable aerobatic display at the International Meeting at Lympne in 1935. With the machine in dark-green camouflage and numbered 4, he repeated his performance in the old crocks event at the 1936 Hendon R.A.F. Display. When the Ogilvie collection moved to Watford after the Second World War, the would-be G-AEPH went with it, and some years later was acquired by the Shuttleworth Trust, for which it was rebuilt and subsequently maintained by the makers. After restoration as nearly as possible to Mk. II standard, complete with Scarff ring and genuine R.A.F. serial D8096, it took the air again on 14 February 1951, flown by Bristol's chief test pilot, A. J. Pegg. It thereafter made annual flying appearances at Royal Aeronautical Society Garden Parties and other functions. The old crocks event at the 1937 R.A.F. Display also boasted a Bristol Fighter, this time an all-silver Mk. IV, F4587, flown by Sqn. Ldr. N. R. Buckle, who in 1938, with no more displays at which to fly it, registered it as a private machine G-AFHJ but unfortunately it was destroyed during the war.

SPECIFICATION

Manufacturers: The British and Colonial Aircraft Co. Ltd., Filton, Bristol; restyled The Bristol Aeroplane Co. Ltd. in August 1920.

Power Plant: (Types 14, 96 and 96A): One 275 h.p. Rolls-Royce Falcon III.
(Types 17 and 17A): One 300 h.p. Hispano-Suiza.

Dimensions: Span, 39 ft. 3 in. Length, 25 ft. 10 in. Height, 9 ft. 4 in. Wing area, 405·6 sq. ft.

Weights: Tare weight, 1,934 lb. All-up weight, 2,800 lb.

Performance: Maximum speed, 123 m.p.h. Initial climb, 1,200 ft./min. Ceiling, 21,500 ft.

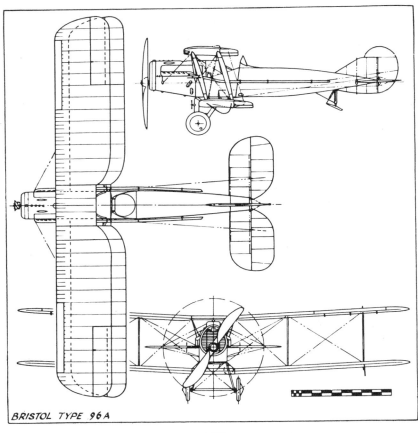

BRISTOL TYPE 96A

The Bristol Type 20 G-EAVO showing the main external features and the wing bracing system. (*Bristol Photo.*)

Bristol Types 20 and 77

The Bristol M.1C single-seat fighter designed by Capt. F. S. Barnwell in 1916 was a complete breakaway from contemporary practice, not only by virtue of its wire-braced, shoulder-mounted and crescent-shaped monoplane wing, but also because it represented a serious attempt to produce an aerodynamically clean airframe. The fuselage, although internally of standard wooden construction, was faired to a circular section in order to streamline the 110 h.p. Le Rhône rotary engine. In spite of the low power, the result was a fast and highly manoeuvrable aircraft, but prejudice against the monoplane in those days was such that only 125 were ordered, the majority being shipped to the Near East in 1917–18.

Six war surplus machines were acquired for civil purposes in 1919, four by the Bristol Aeroplane Co. Ltd. and a fifth by Maj. H. C. Chichester Smith, who flew it in the first post-war Aerial Derby at Hendon on 21 June 1919 and again in the Hendon Trophy Race on 12 July 1919. It was never fully converted as a civil aeroplane and was sold to the Grahame-White Aviation Co. Ltd. The sixth was C5001 bought from the Aircraft Disposals Board at Waddon in July 1919 by the Australian pilot Capt. Harry Butler who flew it from a field at Minlaton, near Adelaide, as G-AUCH and won the first Australian Aerial Derby on 8 September 1920. The veteran Horrie Miller bought it in 1930, replaced the Le Rhône by a 120 h.p. Gipsy II, and won the Adelaide Aerial Derby in 1931 and 1932. Registered VH-UQI and named 'Puck', it is now permanently exhibited at Minlaton as the Harry Butler Memorial.

Those repurchased by the manufacturers were reconditioned as c/n 5885–5888, the second being sold in the U.S.A. and the third, G-EAVO, left Croydon for Spain as M-AFAA in November 1921, on delivery to Señor Juan Pombo, piloted by Larry Carter. The other two, G-EASR and 'VP, had brief careers, that of 'VP (formerly one of the four M.1B prototypes) being the most eventful. In 1922 it was rebuilt with a 100 h.p. Bristol Lucifer three-cylinder radial and in this form, as the Bristol M.1D, came first in the Croydon Whitsun Handicap piloted by Bristol's chief test pilot, C. F. Uwins. On 7 August of the same year Larry Carter averaged 107·85 m.p.h. to bring it to victory in the Aerial Derby Handicap at Croydon, where a month later a Martlesham test pilot, Flt. Lt. Rollo

Major Chichester Smith's Bristol M.1C C4964/G-EAER at Hendon in June 1919 with the R.A.F. markings hardly obliterated. (*Flight Photo 293*)

The Lucifer engined Type 77 racing version G-EAVP. (*Bristol Photo*)

Larry Carter with M-AFAA (formerly G-EAVO) at Croydon in November 1921.

de Haga Haig, flew it in the first King's Cup Race. He got no farther than Aylesbury, where he made a forced landing. In the following year, when Bristol designs were retrospectively allotted type numbers, the M.1C machines became the Type 20 and the M.1D the Type 77.

G-EAVP made its final appearance in the Grosvenor Challenge Cup Race which started at Lympne on 23 June 1933, and in which it was flown by Major E. L. Foote. During the race he complained of petrol fumes, but carried on after a hurried repair to a leaking fuel tank. Later in the race, while flying low over the Fox Hills Estate near Chertsey, Surrey, the aircraft made an unexplained dive into the ground and was burnt out, Major Foote being killed.

SPECIFICATION

Manufacturers: The British and Colonial Aeroplane Co. Ltd., Filton, Bristol.

Power Plants: (Type 20) One 110 h.p. Le Rhône.

One 120 h.p. de Havilland Gipsy II.

(Type 77) One 100 h.p. Bristol Lucifer.

Dimensions: Span, 30 ft. 9 in. Length, 20 ft. 5½ in. Height, 7 ft. 9½ in. Wing area, 145 sq. ft.

Weights: (Type 20) Tare weight, 896 lb. All-up weight, 1,348 lb.

(Type 77) All-up weight, 1,300 lb.

Performance: (Type 20) Maximum speed, 130 m.p.h. Initial climb, 1,500 ft./min. Ceiling, 20,000 ft. Duration, 1¼ hours.

(Type 77) Maximum speed, 125 m.p.h.

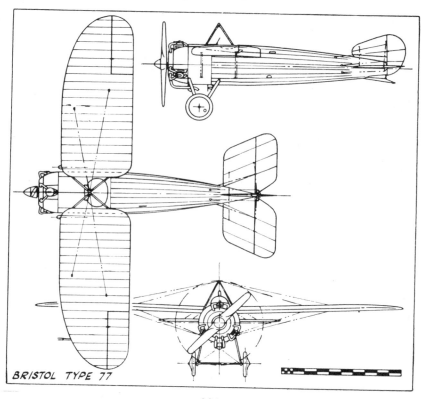

BRISTOL TYPE 77

The two-seat open cockpit Type 29 dual control Tourer G-EAXA, forerunner of the Type 81 Puma Trainer. (*Bristol Photo*)

Bristol Tourers, Seely and Puma Trainers

The Bristol Tourer was a brave attempt at producing a commercial aeroplane at low cost during the financially difficult period which followed the First World War. It was essentially a cheap, war surplus Fighter F.2B fitted with lower-powered engines in order to reduce running costs. Four distinct types were built, all flown from the front seat, but permitting a choice of enclosed cabin or open cockpit for one passenger, or in a widened rear fuselage, a similar choice for two passengers side by side. For convenience these will be referred to by the retrospective Bristol type numbers 27, 29, 28 and 47 subsequently allotted to them in 1923.

The solitary Type 27 was an unarmed Bristol Fighter, H1460, with tankage for 5 hours and a hinged coupé cover over the rear seat, which C. F. Uwins flew from Filton to Hounslow on 1 May 1919, the day civil flying recommenced after the 1914–18 war. He carried Herbert Thomas on an official engagement and the aircraft was later sold to the Air Board. The first real Tourer, G-EAIZ, a Type 29 created by fitting the Puma engine from Barnwell's crashed Badger X (see page 305) into a converted Fighter airframe, was followed by a similar machine, G-EANR, for exhibition at the Paris Salon in December 1919. Early in 1920 'NR was sold in the U.S.A. and is said to have been used for transporting silver bullion in Nicaragua. One more two-seat Type 29 and four three-seat Type 47s were also shipped to America, and one to the Newfoundland Air Survey Company who flew it on skis during the gold rush at Stag Bay, Labrador. Two three-seat seaplanes (c/n 5873 and 5874), the first of which was flown at Avonmouth by C. F. Uwins on 15 October 1920, remained unsold and were never registered.

Only two Tourers were delivered to users within the United Kingdom. First came the blue-and-silver Type 47 G-EART acquired by the pioneer Croydon airline operated by S. Instone and Co. Ltd. in March 1920. For a period of about a year it was used on charter work, probably its most notable assignment being on

232

3 May 1920, when Capt. F. L. Barnard flew it from Croydon to Cramlington, Newcastle, in four hours, carrying the Controller General of Civil Aviation, Maj. Gen. Sir Frederick Sykes, and his bride on their honeymoon. The first private owner to use an aeroplane for extensive touring was A. S. Butler, who bought the Type 29 G-EAWB in November 1920, one of his first trips being to the French Riviera via Le Bourget, Lyon and Aix on 2–3 April 1921. With fairings closing the gap between the fuselage and the lower mainplane, he raced it in the Aerial Derby at Hendon on 16 July 1922, coming second at 107·12 m.p.h. Thereafter it was based at Croydon, and became a familiar sight in the London area until its C. of A. expired in the following year.

Two three-seaters, G-EAWQ (closed) and 'WR (open), were ferried to Spain for a Senor Bayo as M-AAEA and M-AEAA by A. Forson and H. de Havilland respectively but Forson was killed when 'EA struck a mountainside after take-off from San Sebastian on 23 April 1921. It was replaced temporarily by G-EAVU until two-seater M-AFFA and three-seaters M-AAAF and M-AFFF were flown out a few months later.

The remaining eight three-seaters were all sold in Australia, G-AUCA in June 1921 for a 9,000 mile air route survey by Col. Brinsmead, Controller of Civil Aviation; six, G-AUDF to 'DK, to West Australian Airways (whose inaugural Geraldton–Derby service, flown on 5 December 1921, was marred by the fatal crash of G-AUDI); and a spare airframe (c/n 6113) believed used to restore G-AUCA as G-AUDX after it crashed at Bourke, N.S.W., on 16 March 1923. One of the W.A.A. fleet, G-AUDH, crashed in July 1924 but survived in rebuilt form until 1931 as G-AUDZ, while another, G-AUDK, achieved fame in retirement when it was flown 7,500 miles round Australia in 10 days 5 hours by Kingsford Smith and Ulm in June 1927. One other famous Tourer was G-AUEB, a locally converted Hispano-Suiza Fighter, H1248, used by Q.A.N.T.A.S., by the Flying Doctor Service, and in the goldfields in New Guinea until 1928.

Competing aircraft in the Air Ministry's development competition for small commercial aeroplanes which opened at Martlesham on 3 August 1920 were required to reach certain standards of design, performance and economy of operation. The Bristol entry, known as the Seely Puma, although resembling a Tourer superficially was, in fact, a different aeroplane known as the Type 36. It used many Fighter F.2B detail parts and retained the Puma engine, but the fuselage was deepened and a steel skid was fitted to the undercarriage to prevent nosing over when the multi-disc Ferodo brakes were applied. On 7 August 1920 it reached a

M-AEAA, formerly G-EAWR, the first Type 47 Tourer for Spain, showing the two-seat side-by-side rear cockpit and entrance ladder. (*Bristol Photo*)

speed of 108·3 m.p.h. and a week later achieved a slow-speed run of 49·07 m.p.h. but failed to carry off any of the prize money. It was used in later years for Bristol Jupiter radial engine development at Filton, and in 1928 was fitted with an experimental exhaust turbo-blown Jupiter III and handed over to the R.A.E. as J7004 with the new designation Type 85.

In 1922 a two-seat Tourer, G-EAXA, built as a Type 29 in May 1921, was fitted with dual controls and evaluated as a trainer. Experience with 'XA resulted in the construction of four more dual control Tourers in 1923—24 for advanced flying instruction at the newly formed Reserve Flying School at Filton. These were known as Type 81 and registered G-EBFR to 'FU, the third and fourth machines having the oleo undercarriage first fitted to export Fighters Type 17A. Six with enlarged rudders were supplied to the Greek Navy as Type 81As and five others fitted with 180 h.p. Wolseley Viper engines were delivered to the Bulgarian Department of Posts and Telegraphs at Sofia, two as Type 88 and the others, which had night flying equipment and enlarged rudders, as Type 88A.

A West Australian Airways Type 28 cabin Tourer, G-AUDG, with locally-made horn balanced rudder. (*John Hopton*)

C. F. Uwins in the pilot's seat of the Type 36 Seely Puma. The cabin was similar to that of the Type 27 and 28 Tourers and is shown in the open position. (*Bristol Photo*)

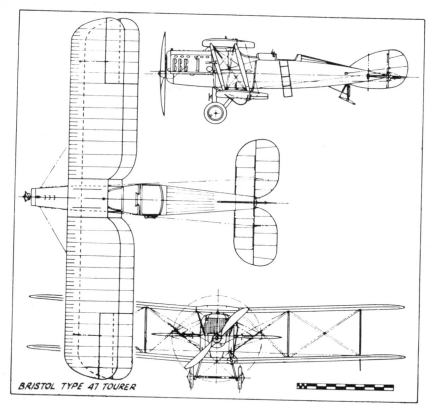

BRISTOL TYPE 47 TOURER

SPECIFICATION

Manufacturers: The Bristol Aeroplane Co. Ltd., Filton, Bristol.
Power Plants: One 180 h.p. Wolseley Viper.
              One 240 h.p. Siddeley Puma.
              One 300 h.p. Hispano-Suiza.

	Type 28	Type 29	Type 36	Type 47
Span	39 ft. 5 in.	39 ft. 5 in.	47 ft. 1 in.	39 ft. 5 in.
Length	26 ft. 1 in.	26 ft. 1 in.	29 ft. 6 in.	26 ft. 1 in.
Height	10 ft. 1 in.	10 ft. 1 in.	12 ft. 0 in.	10 ft. 1 in.
Wing area	407 sq. ft.	407 sq. ft.	560 sq. ft.	407 sq. ft.
Tare weight	1,900 lb.	1,700 lb.	—	1,900 lb.
All-up weight	3,000 lb.	2,800 lb.	3,000 lb.	3,000 lb.
Maximum speed	120 m.p.h.	120 m.p.h.	128 m.p.h.	120 m.p.h.
Ceiling	20,000 ft.	22,000 ft.	—	20,000 ft.
Range	400 miles	400 miles	—	400 miles

Production: (a) Type 27 Bristol Fighter F.2B Coupé
  One aircraft only: (c/n 5178) H1460.

(b) Type 28 Tourer three-seat coupé

Ten aircraft: (c/n 5891) U.S.A.; (6108) G-EAXK/G-AUDF; (6111) G-AUDG; (6113) spare airframe to Australia; (6114) G-EAWQ/M-AAEA; (6115) G-AUDH; (6116) G-AUDI; (6117) G-AUCA; (6118) G-AUDJ; (6119) G-AUDK. Also H1248 converted to G-AUEB in Australia.

(c) Type 29 Tourer two-seat open

Eight aircraft: (c/n 5867) G-EAIZ; (5868) G-EANR; (5881) U.S.A.; (5892) G-EAVU; (6120) G-EAXA; (6121) M-AFFA; (6122) G-EAWB; (6123) Newfoundland.

(d) Type 36 Seely Puma

One aircraft only: (c/n 5870) G-EAUE, later Type 85 as J7004.

(e) Type 47 Tourer three-seat open

Eight aircraft: (c/n 5876) G-EART; (5877–5880) U.S.A.; (6109) M-AAAF; (6110) M-AFFF; (6112) G-EAWR/M-AEAA.

(f) Type 48 Tourer three-seat open seaplane

Two aircraft only: (c/n 5873–5874) unregistered.

(g) Type 81 and 81A Puma Trainer

Ten aircraft: (c/n 6239–6242) G-EBFR to 'FU; (6712–6717) Greek Navy.

(h) Type 88 and 88A Viper Trainer

Five aircraft: (c/n 6383) B-BECA; (6384) B-BEHA; (6937) B-BEBA; (6938) B-BETO; (6939) B-BEKA.

The Type 81 Puma Trainer G-EBFU, together with 'FT, was fitted with the improved oleo undercarriage.

The Type 88A Tourer B-BEKA with enlarged, horn balanced rudder awaiting delivery to Bulgaria, Filton May 1926. (*Bristol Photo*)

The prototype three-seat Bristol Type 73 Taxiplane. (*Bristol Photo*)

Bristol Taxiplane, Lucifer and Type 83E

In 1922, following inquiries from South America, the Bristol Aeroplane Co. Ltd. made another attempt at marketing an economical three-seat general utility aeroplane, this time designed round their successful 100 h.p. Lucifer three-cylinder radial engine. The airframe was of orthodox wire-braced, fabric-covered, wooden construction, while for cheap and rapid production it had a square section fuselage with flat top, bottom and sides. A slight top decking was fitted only to the front fuselage, and rigging was simplified by using single bay wings with N-type interplane struts. Two passengers were carried behind the pilot in a large open cockpit entered by a door in the port side of the fuselage. A notable feature was that the Lucifer and its accessories were installed on a hinged mounting, quickly swung forward to give access to the rear of the engine.

The first Type 73 Taxiplane, G-EBEW, went to Martlesham in April 1923 but was found to be overweight with a second passenger in the rear cockpit and could only be certificated as a two-seater. Only two more were therefore completed.

The design effort was nevertheless turned to good account, and a two-seat trainer fuselage was built and fitted with all the major Taxiplane assemblies as the Type 83A Lucifer, and after successful demonstration at the Central Flying School the type was approved for primary instruction at Reserve Flying Schools. The narrow fuselage imparted an improved all-round performance, and six Lucifers, G-EBFZ to 'GE, went into service with the Bristol Reserve Flying School in June 1923. With the exception of G-EBGB, which was lost in an air collision with a Bristol 89 at Filton on 20 August 1929, the small fleet gave yeoman service until replaced by Tiger Moths in January 1932. The Lucifers were seldom seen far away from Filton, but at Lympne on 23 June 1923 G-EBGC competed for the

Grosvenor Trophy, during which test pilot C. F. Uwins landed at Tewkesbury with engine trouble. The 100 h.p. Lucifer was normally trouble free, and it is a truth that no engine failures were ever experienced at the Reserve School. By 1925 it had been developed into the 120 h.p. Lucifer IV with which the whole fleet was refitted. With this engine G-EBGD made another of their rare public appearances in the International Handicap at Lympne on 3 August 1925, when C. T. Holmes flew a magnificent race to come second at 93·69 m.p.h.

Five Bristol Type 83B Lucifers, with increased elevator and rudder area, were sold to Hungary, 12 to Chile and one to Bulgaria during 1926, the first two having the temporary British civil registrations G-EBNB and 'NC for demonstration flying at Filton before the purchasing commissions. All Type 83As were raised to this standard at overhaul, but early in 1928 G-EBGA was experimentally fitted with a large horn balanced rudder without fin to become the Bristol Type 83C. This proved to be the first of several modifications made to that machine, which finally flew as a single-seater with additional formers rounding out the fuselage to provide adequate streamlining for the radial engine. Cowlings were modified to

The first production two-seat Bristol Type 83A Lucifer. (*Bristol Photo*)

Bristol Lucifer B-BEPK built for Bulgaria in 1926, showing the wide-chord rudder fitted to Type 83B. (*Bristol Photo*)

The trial installation Lucifer G-EBGA in the first of its two Type 83C configurations had a horn-balanced rudder without fin. It afterwards received wide-chord strut fairings and other minor modifications. (*Bristol Photo*)

Capt. F. S. Barnwell taxying G-EBGA at the Whitchurch Meeting of September 1931, after the aircraft had been reconstructed as the Type 83D with wide chord fin and rudder. (*Aeroplane*)

incorporate cylinder head fairings, clean entry was ensured by fitting a large spinner, and a long-travel undercarriage was substituted. The machine was then subjected to flight trials which resulted in the reduction of G-EBGA to its original flat-sided, unfaired condition, but fitted with a large balanced rudder with fin. In this form it became the Bristol Type 83D Lucifer, and was followed in 1928 by the unnamed Bristol Type 83E advanced trainer G-EBYT. This was a two-seater of almost identical appearance to G-EBGA in its Type 83C condition, but powered by a 210 h.p. Titan five-cylinder radial and fitted with the wide-chord fin and rudder of the Type 83D. A further modification involved the positioning of the undercarriage radius rods behind, instead of in front, of the shock legs. The sole public appearance of the Bristol Type 83E was in the King's Cup Race held at

Brooklands on 20 July 1928, the pilot being Sqn. Ldr. A. G. Jones-Williams, who finished fourth after flying from Renfrew to Brooklands via Lympne on the second day at an average speed of 123·43 m.p.h. Later in 1928 the machine was used for flight testing the geared Titan, being equipped with the Type 83C rudder and a four-bladed airscrew. It was dismantled at the end of 1930.

With the exception of G-EBGA, all the black and silver Lucifers were scrapped in December 1931, the survivor undergoing a complete overhaul to emerge wearing the new orange-and-black livery of the School. In this condition it took part in the races at the Bristol and Wessex Aeroplane Club's meeting at Whitchurch on 26 September 1931 and in February 1933 was sold to the well known enthusiast L. G. Anderson at Hanworth. Here it was modified into a tandem three-seater with two passengers in the rear cockpit. After spending the rest of the year joyriding with C. W. A. Scott's British Hospitals Air Pageants, it was scrapped.

The Bristol Type 83E advanced trainer as tuned for the 1928 King's Cup Race.
(*Bristol Photo*)

After the installation of the geared Titan engine, the Type 83E was fitted with the Type 83C rudder. The actual fin removed from it was later fitted to the Type 83D G-EBGA.
(*Bristol Photo*)

SPECIFICATION

Manufacturers: The Bristol Aeroplane Co. Ltd., Filton, Bristol.
Power Plants: (Type 73 and 83) One 100 h.p. Bristol Lucifer.
 (Type 83E) One 210 h.p. Bristol Titan.

	Type 73	Type 83A	Type 83E ungeared Titan
Span	31 ft. 1 in.	31 ft. 1 in.	31 ft. 1 in.
Length	23 ft. 3 in.	24 ft. 0 in.	25 ft. 6 in.
Height	8 ft. 10 in.	8 ft. 10 in.	9 ft. $3\frac{1}{2}$ in.
Wing area	291 sq. ft.	291 sq. ft.	291 sq. ft.
Tare weight	1,210 lb.	1,340 lb.	—
All-up weight	2,000 lb.	1,840 lb.	2,000 lb.
Maximum speed	90 m.p.h.	96 m.p.h.	—

Production: (a) Type 73 Taxiplane
 Three aircraft only: (c/n 6153) G-EBEW; (6154) G-EBEY; (6155) G-EBFY.

 (b) Type 83A Lucifer
 Twenty-four aircraft: (c/n 6373–6378) G-EBFZ to G-EBGE; (6922) G-EBNB; (6923) G-EBNC; (6924–6935) 12 to Chile; (6936) B-BEPK; (6960–6962) 3 to Hungary.

 (c) Type 83E
 One aircraft only: (c/n 7266) G-EBYT.

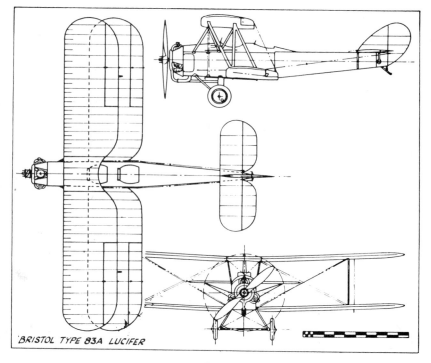

BRISTOL TYPE 83A LUCIFER

The original Bristol Type 76 Jupiter Fighter G-EBGF. (*Bristol Photo*)

Bristol Jupiter Fighter and
Type 89 and 89A Trainers

In August 1920 the Bristol Aeroplane Co. Ltd. acquired the assets of the Cosmos Engineering Co. Ltd. of Bristol, manufacturers of the nine cylinder Jupiter air-cooled radial engine. Development of this engine was continued until 1923, when it was fitted into one of the evergreen Fighter F.2B airframes. With this power unit and an oleo undercarriage of the type first fitted to the export Fighter Type 17A G-EBCN, it was known as the Bristol Type 76 Jupiter Fighter, and made its first public appearance in the New Types Park at the Hendon R.A.F. Display on 30 June 1923, registered G-EBGF.

In the following month it was flown 755 miles from Croydon to Gothenburg in one day by Capt. N. Macmillan to take part in a flying contest held at Torslanda in conjunction with the Gothenburg International Aero Exhibition at which a second Jupiter Fighter fitted with Frise-type ailerons was exhibited on the British stand. Impressed by Macmillan's victory in the aerobatic competition for two-seaters and his prize-winning climb to 26,000 ft., the Swedish government decided to purchase G-EBHG subject to satisfactory performance in Arctic conditions. It was therefore fitted with a ski undercarriage and carburettor heating and went north to Kiruna in Lapland where the extreme ease of starting the Jupiter engine in sub-zero temperatures, never before obtained with water-cooled or rotary engines, effectively clinched the deal and Lt. Gardin of the Swedish Army flew it back 800 miles from Kiruna to Malmslätt at an average speed of 124 m.p.h.

Thereafter G-EBHG was known as the Swedish Fighter and given the type number 76B. Type 76A was the third aircraft, G-EBHH, equipped with special alcohol tanks in addition to the normal fuel system, to feed the experimental bifuel Jupiter installed in it.

The previously mentioned Type 81A G-EBIH had not yet been completed, and when the first Jupiter Fighter had shown its paces the use of the water-cooled Puma was abandoned and G-EBIH was consequently flown with a derated Jupiter

III as the prototype Type 89 two-seat advanced trainer. The bifuel Fighter G-EBHH was also converted to Type 89, and accompanied 'IH to the Reserve School, where they were joined by G-EBJA and 'JB in 1924 and by G-EBML and 'MN in the following year. Two others were laid down, but were not completed, and in 1926 a further two, G-EBNZ and 'OA, were delivered to Renfrew for use by the Reserve School managed by William Beardmore and Co. Ltd.

Later in 1926 the final derivative of the famous old Bristol Fighter F.2B took off from Filton. This was the Bristol 89A prototype, G-EBOC, a Jupiter-engined trainer, outwardly identical to the Type 89, but with a plywood-covered monocoque fuselage of entirely new design. The black Cerric finish of the plywood fuselages earned the Filton School Bristol 89As the soubriquet of 'Black Maria'. The prototype was followed by four production models fitted with Jupiter VI motors for the Beardmore School, and by September 1931, when the last Type 89A, G-ABPM, left the works, the Filton Reserve School had taken delivery of

The tenth production Type 89A, G-AAGF, with plywood fuselage. The Frise type ailerons can also be seen in this view. (*Bristol Photo*)

another nine. Unlike the Renfrew machines, they were fitted with surplus Jupiter IVs. The faithful 89s and 89As continued in service at Renfrew until 1930, when the Beardmore School shut down, and at Filton until 1934, when they were superseded by Hawker Hart Trainers. G-EBYL was fitted with Handley Page auto-slots in 1930, another with a set of steel wings, and G-ABPM undertook taxying and landing tests with some of the earliest low pressure 'doughnut' tyres, all features likely to improve handling and serviceability in tropical conditions.

During their years of service the Bristol 89s and 89As seldom went far afield and earned little publicity apart from that gained when five were destroyed, together with a Type 83A Lucifer, by colliding in the air in pairs near Filton on three widely separated occasions.

SPECIFICATION

Manufacturers: The Bristol Aeroplane Co. Ltd., Filton, Bristol.
Power Plants: (Type 76) One 425 h.p. Bristol Jupiter IV.
  (Type 89) One 320 h.p. Bristol Jupiter IV (derated).

Dimensions: Span, 39 ft. 3 in. Length, 25 ft. 0 in. Height, 9 ft. 0 in. Wing area, 405 sq. ft.

Weights: (Type 76) Tare weight, 2,190 lb. All-up weight, 3,079 lb.

(Type 89) Tare weight, 2,326 lb. All-up weight, 3,250 lb.

Performance: (Type 76) Maximum speed, 134 m.p.h. Initial climb, 1,250 ft./min.

(Type 89) Maximum speed, 110 m.p.h. Cruising speed, 94 m.p.h.

Production: (a) Type 76 Jupiter Fighter

Three aircraft only: (c/n 6379) G-EBGF; (6380) G-EBHG; (6381) G-EBHH.

(b) Type 89

Nine aircraft: (c/n 6382) G-EBIH; (6522–6524) G-EBJA to 'JC; (6525) spare airframe; (6918) G-EBML; (6919) G-EBMN; (6963) G-EBNZ; (6964) G-EBOA.

(c) Type 89A

Fifteen aircraft: (c/n 6965) G-EBOC; (6966) G-EBOD; (6967) G-EBQS; (7124) G-EBQT; (7156) G-EBSB; (7157) G-EBSH; (7221) spare airframe; (7234) G-EBVR; (7265) G-EBYL; (7350) G-AAGF; (7351) G-AALO; (7352) G-AAWJ; (7711) G-ABPL; (7712) G-ABPM. One by Wm. Beardmore & Co. Ltd., Renfrew, from spares and salvaged components: (c/n R.58) G-EBWN.

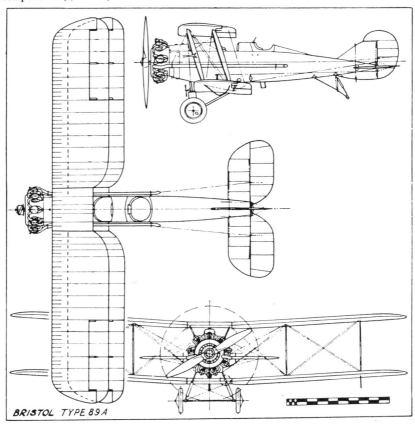

BRISTOL TYPE 89A

The prototype Type 91 Brownie two-seater in its original form. (*Bristol Photo*)

Bristol Type 91 Brownie

Although only three Brownies were built, their ingenious metal construction and progressive modification contributed an important chapter to the story of British light aeroplane development. They were designed by Capt. F. S. Barnwell specifically for the Air Ministry's two-seater light aeroplane trials for machines with engines of up to 1,100 c.c., held at Lympne from 27 September to 4 October 1924. The three fuselages, outwardly of the usual Bristol fabric-covered, square-section, flat-sided variety, struck a completely new note internally and were built of light gauge steel tubing braced with piano wire. All had the 32 h.p. Bristol Cherub flat-twin and were fitted with simple, wire braced, steel tube undercarriages. The first Type 91 Brownie, G-EBJK, was fitted with 17 ft. wooden wings and made its first flight at Filton on 6 August 1924, piloted by Bristol's chief test pilot C. F. Uwins. It flew well, and its tare weight was down to the stipulated 500 lb., and, following some rapid repairs after fouling telephone wires and crash landing at Filton on 5 September, C. F. Uwins took it to Lympne. Here it flew as competitor No. 1, and returned as winner of the second prize of £1,000 and the Duke of Sutherland's prize of £500 for the best take-off and pull up. Competitor No. 2 was the second Brownie, G-EBJL, which had made its maiden flight on 22 September, only five days before the trials. This machine was fitted with dural wings and was known as the Type 91A. Unfortunately it developed wing flutter during practice flying at Lympne, but landed without damage, the mishap being attributed to the unorthodox rubber tensioning in the aileron circuit. Although out of the competition, it went to Martlesham in the following month for Air Ministry evaluation. The small competition fuel tank fitted to G-EBJK prevented its participation in the Grosvenor Trophy Race held on the last day of the Lympne meeting, and its place was taken by the third Brownie, Type 91A G-EBJM. This had flown for the first time on 24 September and in it T. W. Campbell gained third place at 70·09 m.p.h., to complete a most successful week for the Bristol team.

Thereafter the Brownies did a considerable amount of test flying in the course of Cherub engine development, but C. F. Uwins took 'JM to Lympne for another race meeting over August Bank Holiday 1925. It bettered 70 m.p.h. to come third in the International Handicap and second in the Grosvenor Trophy Race. Though they were ultra-lights born of the ill-conceived rules for the 1924 Trials, the Brownies had proved themselves sturdy vehicles and ripe for further development. Thus in 1926 they were all considerably modified with improved Cherub III

The Type 91A Brownie G-EBJM after conversion to single-seater. (*Bristol Photo*)

The original Brownie G-EBJK after conversion to Type 91B with revised rudder and nose shape. (*Bristol Photo*)

engines, which still had single ignition but were fitted with duplicated plugs. G-EBJK appeared as the Type 91B with a revised nose shape to compensate for the lower thrust line of the engine, a sprung undercarriage, larger fuel tank, horn-balanced rudder and specially built 17 ft. 4½ in. steel wings. Again piloted by C. F. Uwins it won third prize in the *Daily Mail* Trials for two-seaters with engines weighing less than 170 lb., held at Lympne from 10–18 September 1926, also coming second in the Motor Manufacturers Race on the last day. The Type 91A G-EBJM was also at the meeting, this time as a single-seater with 14 ft. dural wings, the front seat covered by a curved decking. No change of designation was involved, and the remaining Brownie, G-EBJL, also underwent the same conversion. This was sold to the Bristol and Wessex Aeroplane Club Ltd. on 5 September 1927, and continued in service until the end of the following year. Its sister machine, G-EBJM, was leased to the London Aeroplane Club Ltd. at Stag Lane, but as a relief from club flying it was raced at the 1927 Bournemouth Easter and Whitsun meetings and at the Hampshire Air Pageant by famous pilots of those days—P. G. Lucas, L. J. C. Mitchell, F. G. M. Sparkes, G. H. Craig and M. L. Bramson. It was at the Hampshire Pageant at Hamble on 15 May 1927 that 'JM came face to face with its relative, the Type 91B G-EBJK, flown as usual by C. F. Uwins, but neither Brownie won a race. G-EBJM returned to club life for a time, while 'JK went home to Filton as F. S. Barnwell's private aircraft. On 21

March 1928 he struck a tree with the starboard wing during an early morning take-off from Farnborough, and although its designer was unhurt, 'JK had reached the end of its career.

SPECIFICATION

Manufacturers: The Bristol Aeroplane Co. Ltd., Filton, Bristol.
Power Plant: One 32 h.p. Bristol Cherub III.

	Type 91	Type 91A	Type 91B	Single Seater
Span	34 ft. 7 in.	36 ft. 7 in.	37 ft. 7 in.	30 ft. 7 in.
Length	26 ft. 3 in.	26 ft. 3 in.	25 ft. 11 in.	26 ft. 3 in.
Height	6 ft. 6 in.	6 ft. 6 in.	5 ft. 7 in.	6 ft. 6 in.
Wing area	204 sq. ft.	208 sq. ft.	210·5 sq. ft.	172 sq. ft.
Tare weight	500 lb.	500 lb.	690 lb.	500 lb.
All-up weight	870 lb.	870 lb.	1,010 lb.	720 lb.
Maximum speed	70 m.p.h.	70 m.p.h.	78 m.p.h.	70 m.p.h.
Range	100 miles	100 miles	125 miles	100 miles

Production: Three aircraft only: (c/n 6526–6528) G-EBJK to G-EBJM.

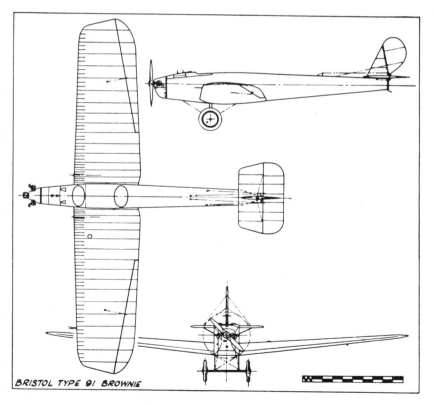

BRISTOL TYPE 91 BROWNIE

247

The silver and green Bulldog Mk. II demonstrator G-AAHH at Heston in July 1929.
(*Aeroplane*)

Bristol Type 105 Bulldog

The Bulldog Mk. I was a single-seat fighter designed by F. S. Barnwell and first flown at Filton by C. F. Uwins in May 1927. It was a small unequal span biplane of fabric-covered, high tensile steel construction, with a 440 h.p. Bristol Jupiter VII radial, which in developed form became one of the R.A.F.'s most famous fighters. Foreign air forces also bought it and inevitably several Bulldogs were completed as demonstrators or test vehicles flown in civil or Class B markings.

During the construction of the first R.A.F. Bulldog Mk. IIs, J9567–J9591, in 1928, an extra machine with 450 h.p. Jupiter VIA was built for company use as G-AAHH and flown by C. F. Uwins at Heston during the Olympia Aero Show of July 1929 prior to demonstrations in Sweden. J9591, last machine of the first R.A.F. batch, also completed in October 1929, was loaned to the Bristol company as testbed for the geared Mercury IVA and remained at Filton in civil marks as G-AATR until fitted with a Jupiter VIIF and handed back to the R.A.F. in September 1931.

The third testbed aircraft, completed in January 1930, flew under B conditions as R-1 to continue the Mercury III test programme interrupted by the crash of the Bristol Type 101 (q.v.), after which a 440 h.p. Gnome-Rhône Jupiter VI was substituted in readiness for a European sales tour. Registration G-ABAC was allotted on 30 May, but on 4 June the aircraft was damaged in the air while T. W. Campbell was practising flick rolls and crashed after he baled out. A replacement, G-ABBB, also fitted with 440 h.p. Gnome-Rhône 9ASB radial, was exhibited at the Paris Salon in November 1930.

This aircraft was a strengthened version with wide-track undercarriage and revised fin, designated Bulldog Mk. IIA, which temporarily became R-11 in 1935 for a 100-hour endurance flight test with the new Bristol Aquila I sleeve-valve radial. In 1939 G-ABBB was presented to the Science Museum and remained in store until the makers reconditioned it, and cannibalised four vintage engines to produce one serviceable Jupiter VIIFP with which it flew again at Filton, piloted by Geoffrey Auty, on 22 June 1961. It was then repainted in squadron colours as K2227, handed over to the Shuttleworth Trust in a ceremony at Filton on 12 September and thereafter lived at Henlow, but the career of this, the sole survivor of the 441 Filton-built Bulldogs, was regrettably short for it overturned when landing during a display at North Weald on 11 June 1962 and although it flew again at Filton on 7 August 1963 after repair, was completely wrecked in an accident during the Farnborough S.B.A.C. Show on 13 September 1964.

An unregistered, cleaned-up Bulldog Mk. IIIA prototype, c/n 7560, with spatted undercarriage, first flew as R-5 on 17 September 1931 but crashed at Martlesham on 30 March 1933. A second prototype, G-ABZW, did not carry the

Bulldog Mk. II G-ABAC with Gnome-Rhône Jupiter VI engine at Filton in June 1930.

Bulldog Mk. IIA G-ABBB/R-11 with Bristol Aquila I installed, Filton, September 1935.

Bulldog Mk. IVA G-ABZW after sale to the Air Ministry in July 1935 as K4292 with long-chord cowling and Hamilton variable-pitch airscrew.

Bulldog Mk. IVA G-ACJN/R-8 in pearl and black glossy cellulose finish for the Hendon S.B.A.C. Show, June 1934.

civil marks but was finished in R.A.F. colours as R-7 and shown at the Paris Salon in November 1932. Its first flight was made at Filton on 13 April 1933 and after Martlesham trials was reworked as the Bulldog Mk. IVA day-and-night fighter with 560 h.p. Bristol Mercury VIS.2. Although outclassed by the Gloster F.7/30, R-7 was purchased by the Air Ministry in July 1934 as K4292.

A second Bulldog Mk. IVA, built to demonstrate the Mercury VIS.2 and registered G-ACJN in August 1933, became testbed for the sleeve-valve Perseus IA in October 1933 and flew as R-8 until seriously damaged on 17 February 1934. It was then rebuilt with cockpit heating and distinctive exhibition finish for the 1934 Hendon R.A.F. and S.B.A.C. Displays but later that year reverted to the Mercury VIS.2 in short-chord cowlings and appeared thus with a three-bladed Hamilton v.p. metal airscrew at the 1935 Hendon S.B.A.C. Show.

SPECIFICATION

Manufacturers: The Bristol Aeroplane Co. Ltd., Filton, Bristol.

Power Plants: One 440 h.p. Bristol Jupiter VIIF or VIIFP.
One 440 h.p. Gnome-Rhône Jupiter VI or 9ASB.
One 450 h.p. Bristol Jupiter VIA.
One 450 h.p. Bristol Mercury III or IVA.
One 500 h.p. Bristol Aquila I.
One 600 h.p. Bristol Perseus IA.
One 640 h.p. Bristol Mercury VIS.Z

	Bulldog II	Bulldog IIA	Bulldog IIIA	Bulldog IVA
Span	33 ft. 10 in.	33 ft. 10 in.	33 ft. 8 in.	33 ft. 8 in.
Length	25 ft. 2 in.	25 ft. 2 in.	25 ft. 4 in.	25 ft. 4 in.
Height	8 ft. 9 in.	8 ft. 9 in.	9 ft. 1 in.	9 ft. 1 in.
Wing area	307 sq. ft.	307 sq. ft.	294 sq. ft.	294 sq. ft.
Tare weight	2,200 lb.	2,222 lb.	2,800 lb.	2,690 lb.
All-up weight	3,490 lb.	3,660 lb.	4,000 lb.	4,010 lb.
Maximum speed	178 m.p.h.	178 m.p.h.	208 m.p.h.	224 m.p.h.
Service ceiling	29,300 ft.	29,300 ft.	31,000 ft.	33,400 ft.

Civil production: Six aircraft detailed in Appendix E.

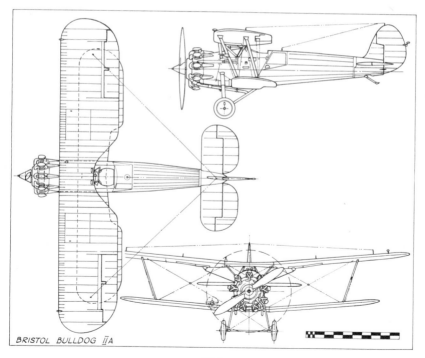

BRISTOL BULLDOG IIA

G-APAV, the last production Bristol Freighter, taking off from Southend in blue, white and gold SABENA livery in 1964. (*John Goring*)

Bristol Type 170 Freighter

At VJ-Day plans were in hand for a Bristol transport capable of operating from jungle airstrips, and two prototype serials, VK901 and VK903, had already been allotted. With the coming of peace it was just the type of rugged, heavy duty aircraft wanted by the newly revived air transport industry, so that chief designer, A. E. Russell, and his team quickly adapted the designs to produce the Bristol Type 170, first British civil transport built after the Second World War. It was an all-metal, twin-engined, high-wing monoplane built solely for low initial cost and cheapness of operation. Expensive alloys were dispensed with in favour of steel, a minimum of costly machined parts was used, and no special tools were required for its maintenance or repair. The 2,360 cu. ft. capacity, rectangular-section fuselage was clear of all obstructions, and the crew of three was accommodated high in the nose of a flight deck reached by an internal ladder. The wing was fitted with pneumatically operated split flaps and carried the quickly interchangeable Hercules power units in underslung nacelles. Considerable research into the economics of retractable undercarriages led to the adoption of a cheap, low drag, fixed type which required negligible maintenance.

Two versions were produced. The Series I, or Freighter, capable of carrying a load of $4\frac{1}{2}$ tons, was fitted with a strengthened floor and hydraulically operated nose doors to admit road vehicles or other heavy freight. The alternative Series II passenger version, known as the Wayfarer, was without nose doors but had additional windows and a small crew door in the front fuselage. The prototype, G-AGPV, was merely a flying shell, without nose doors, which made its first flight at Filton on 2 December 1945, piloted by C. F. Uwins. Early flight trials showed the need to lower the tailplane by 3 ft. and to increase its span by 4 ft. and after this modification it could be flown 'hands off'. The second machine was the prototype 34-seat Wayfarer 2A G-AGVB, which first flew on 30 April 1946. It was granted the Type 170's first unrestricted C. of A. on 7 May to become the first post-war British passenger aircraft to gain this distinction. In the colours of Channel Islands Airways it made a proving flight to Jersey two days later, piloted by A. J. Pegg, and in under six months had made 358 trips and carried its ten thousandth passenger. The next Type 170 built was G-AGVC, the first Freighter I with fully operable nose doors and its first flight on 23 June 1946 heralded a series of overseas sales tours.

G-AGPV was delivered to Boscombe Down as VR380 for trials on 24 September 1946 and nine days later the fourth Freighter, G-AGUT, now VR382, was handed over to the Telecommunications Research Establishment, Defford, where both aircraft served as flying laboratories until November 1958. G-AGUT was then cannibalised at Blackbushe to support 'PV which enjoyed a brief civil career until retired by Trans European Airways in 1963.

G-AGVC left Filton on 3 August 1946 and was away for two years, during which it crossed the Atlantic by the northern route, was demonstrated in Rio de Janeiro, saw service in Canada with Canadian Pacific Airways, and was chartered to Linea Aeropostale Venezolana to carry meat from the interior to Caracas. The first production Wayfarer 2A, G-AHJB, was less fortunate. When over the South Atlantic on 4 July 1946 outward bound from Bathurst, Gambia, en route to Natal and Buenos Aires, it was unable to make a landfall due to an error in the radio compass reading and was ditched 150 miles off shore. Wayfarer 2As G-AHJC and 'JF made demonstration flights in all parts of Europe and the Middle East, after which most of the early production aircraft were leased to Airwork Ltd., Skytravel Ltd., British American Air Services Ltd., British Aviation Services Ltd. and Air Contractors Ltd., for Forces' leave contracts and the carriage of fruit, freight, racehorses and cattle. The Bristol 170 then went into quantity production,

The prototype Bristol 170 in its original form with round windows and high set tailplane. (*Bristol Photo*)

VT-CHL and VT-CID, Wayfarer Mk. IIAs delivered to Dalmia Jain Airways, Delhi, late in 1946, showing the extra forward windows of the passenger version. (*Bristol Photo*)

253

Freighter 21 G-AIFV crossing the Channel on the Silver City Airways Ferryfield–Le Touquet car ferry.

and following a second series of sales tours in which G-AIMC 'Merchant Venturer' flew to Australia and New Zealand in 1947, G-AILZ 'African Enterprise' toured Africa in 1949 and G-AIFN 'Giovanni Caboto' went to Italy in 1949, the type was sold in 18 countries and to seven air forces. G-AIMC was damaged beyond repair on 23 October 1947 when the parking brake failed and it rolled off the sloping airstrip at Wau, New Guinea.

First sales were to the Argentine Air Force which ordered 15 Mk. IA aircraft, the first of which flew as G-AHJE before delivery by air from Filton on 24 October 1946 as LV-XII. There was little demand for the Wayfarer version, and only 16 were built, all but four of which eventually returned to Filton for conversion to Freighters. Variants were few, but on 2 December 1947 a special Freighter I G-AICM, fitted with optically clear panels in the underside of the nose doors for Hunting Aerosurveys Ltd., left Filton for photographic survey work in the Anglo-Iranian Oil Company's oilfields. Freighter Mk. II G-AILY never left Filton for after brief flight tests in 1948 it was retained for various ground trials under the Class B marking R37.

As flight experience mounted, however, progressive modification took place on most machines, first being the fitting of rounded wing tips to increase the span to

Freighter Mk. IA TC-330, formerly T.30 and G-AICH, in Argentine Air Force colours 1966. (*Aviation Photo News*)

108 ft. and create the Freighter XI, the prototype of which, G-AIFF, was exhibited at the 1947 Radlett S.B.A.C. Show. Local strengthening and the use of 14 ft. propellers permitted an increase in the all-up weight to 39,000 lb., and with more powerful Hercules 672/673 a further rise to 40,000 lb. was permitted and the Mk. 21 came into being, G-AIFF again being the prototype.

Only two aircraft were built as Mk. XIs, SE-BNG (initially G-AIMB) with de-icing and a heated cargo hold for A. B. Turist-Trafik-Transportflyg, delivered in August 1947 and lost on a mountainside near Salerno, Italy, on 18 November; and ZS-BVI, a mixed traffic version for Suidair International. This was restored as G-AIME in December 1947 but flew as R38 before modification to Mk. 21. G-AIFO was exhibited with Hercules 672s at the Farnborough S.B.A.C. Show in 1948 at which a dual purpose model known as the 21E was also offered with nose doors and freight floor but with a full complement of removable seats for airline work. Several early production aircraft were brought up to Mk. 21 and 21E standard and in 1948 an order for 30 specially equipped Mk. 21P with nose door windows as fitted to G-AICM was placed by the Pakistan Air Force. Deliveries of new aircraft were also made to Australia, France, Saudi Arabia, Spain, and the United Kingdom.

13 July 1948 proved to be an epoch making day in the annals of British air transport, a day when the Freighter began the life's work for which it will always be remembered. Using G-AGVC modified to carry two cars forward and their occupants in seats in the rear, Silver City Airways Ltd. inaugurated their now famous cross-Channel vehicle ferry between Lympne and Le Touquet. The sharp contrast between the pleasures of 25 minutes of flight and the discomforts of the sea brought almost instant popularity. A constantly changing fleet came into service to deal with the sheer immensity of the traffic, until on 13 July 1954, six years to the day after the first crossing, the company opened its modern air terminal at Ferryfield. In 1948–49 the Freighter also made a valuable contribution to the Berlin airlift, Silver City's G-AGVB, 'VC, G-AHJC and 'JP making 213 sorties and Airwork's G-AHJD and G-AICS an additional 74.

Two Freighter 21s, G-AIFF and G-AHJJ, were lost in crashes in the English Channel and at Llandow on 6 May 1949 and 2 March 1950 respectively, and investigations showed that they had suffered structural failure while demonstrating single engine climb, which caused unsuspected overstressing of the fin. As a consequence, not only were existing aircraft modified, but G-AGVC was rebuilt

Freighter Mk. 31 VH-TBB, the former Pakistani S4432, used on the Melbourne–Sydney–Brisbane scheduled services of Mayne Nickless Air Express in 1969. (*J. Guthrie*)

F-BKBI, Cie Air Transport Freighter Mk. 32 'Onze Novembre', formerly G-ANWI, at Le Touquet in 1966. (*Aviation Photo News*)

Freighter Mk. 32 G-ANVR 'Valiant' in British Air Ferries styling at Coventry/Baginton in 1971. (*Air Portraits*)

with a considerable dorsal fin as the prototype Freighter Mk. 31 and flown initially as G-18-2 with Hercules 734s and all-up weight of 44,000 lb. Production of the Mk. 21 ceased with the ninety-second machine, which was followed by the first two Mk. 31s, G-AINK and 'NL, which were evaluated by Boscombe Down as WH575 and WJ320 respectively. Ninety-three production 31s were then built, including the 31E G-AMLL operated by Jersey Airlines and G-AMLP 'Vanguard', G-AMSA 'Voyager' and G-ANMF 'Victory' used on the Southend–Calais and Ostend Air Bridge by Air Charter Ltd.

Military customers included Burma, Canada, Iraq, New Zealand and Pakistan which placed the largest single Freighter contract for 38 Mk. 31M variants. Two were equipped as V.I.P. transports and in 1961 five were fitted with spray booms for anti-locust operations. A number were sold later to Australia and New Zealand for civil use and one, G-ARSA, was flown to Southend in August 1961 to be broken up as spares for the British United Airways fleet. A special Mk. 31C went to the A. & A.E.E., Boscombe Down, in February 1955 as XJ470 and remained in service until 1968.

The last two Freighters to be delivered were both Mk. 31s, ZK-BVM for Straits Air Freight Express in February 1958 and G-APLH for Dan-Air in the following month. S.A.F.E. eventually operated one of the largest Freighter fleets including secondhand machines from Pakistan and Spain as well as several leased from the R.N.Z.A.F. Two were also built up locally, ZK-CVY using the fuselage of ZK-BMA and the wing of ZK-CVL; and ZK-CWF from the fuselage of ZK-AYG and the wing of ZK-CLU.

In 1951–1952 the Freighter Mk. 21 G-AICT flew in Class B markings as G-18-40 with 0·7 scale Britannia tail unit for flight testing the aerodynamic servo tab controls, and as production work on the Britannia expanded, it became necessary in 1953 to transfer the Freighter production line to Weston-super-Mare. In that year the Freighter 32, final version with elongated nose for the carriage of a third car, came into service. The first six, G-AMWA to 'WF, were delivered to Silver City Airways Ltd. and, following vast traffic increases, were joined by G-ANWG to 'WI in 1954. With a fleet of 17 Freighters, additional ferries were opened to Cherbourg, to the Channel Islands and to Northern Ireland, 50,000 trips being completed by May 1955. A final five Mk. 32s, G-ANWJ to 'WN, were delivered in 1956, traffic continued to increase and fares were annually reduced. For the Ferryfield to Le Touquet section of the London–Paris air-coach service, G-AMWA was fitted as a 60-seat Super Wayfarer in 1958. Thus, when Silver City Airways celebrated the tenth anniversary of the cross-Channel ferry, 215,000 cars, 70,000 motor cycles and cycles and 759,000 passengers had been carried on 125,000 flights. Two other Freighter 32s, G-ANVR 'Valiant' and G-ANVS 'Vigilant' joined the Air Charter fleet and were followed in 1957 by G-AOUU 'Venture', 'UV 'Valour', G-APAU 'Versatile' and 'AV 'Viceroy', two-hundred-and-fourteenth and last Freighter to be built. A joint service was then opened to Ostend, G-AOUV being painted in the blue livery of the Belgian airline SABENA. With the Freighter out of production, mounting traffic in the following year resulted in a unique modification whereby the company's Mk. 31 aircraft 'Vanguard' and 'Viceroy' were fitted with elongated noses and revised rudders to become Mk. 32s.

In later years first G-APAU and then 'AV replaced G-AOUV as the SABENA liveried aircraft. Also, in October 1962, Air Charter and Silver City merged to form British United Air Ferries (later British Air Ferries) but from 1967 the fleet was progressively run down and the aircraft scrapped, although some were transferred to the associated Compagnie Air Transport in France.

Freighter 21 G-AICT, used by Channel Airways 1957–65, as it was in 1951–52 when fitted with 0·7-scale Britannia tail surfaces. (*Bristol Photo*)

The former Dan-Air Freighter Mk. 31 G-AINL at Prestwick on 22 February 1970 during its delivery flight to Lamb Airways in Canada as CF-YDO. (*J. Guthrie*)

SPECIFICATION

Manufacturers: The Bristol Aeroplane Co. Ltd., Filton, Bristol and Old Mixon, Weston-super-Mare, Somerset.

Power Plants: (Mks. I, IIA and XI) Two 1,675 h.p. Bristol Hercules 632.
(Mk. 21) Two 1,690 h.p. Bristol Hercules 672.
(Mks. 31 and 32) Two 1,980 h.p. Bristol Hercules 734.

	Mk. I	Mk. IIA	Mk. XI
Span	98 ft. 0 in.	98 ft. 0 in.	108 ft. 0 in.
Length	68 ft. 4 in.	68 ft. 4 in.	68 ft. 4 in.
Height	21 ft. 8 in.	21 ft. 8 in.	21 ft. 8 in.
Wing area	1,405 sq. ft.	1,405 sq. ft.	1,487 sq. ft.
Tare weight	23,482 lb.	25,616 lb.	24,510 lb.
All-up weight	36,500 lb.	37,000 lb.	39,000 lb.
Maximum speed	240 m.p.h.	240 m.p.h.	195 m.p.h.
Cruising speed	163 m.p.h.	163 m.p.h.	165 m.p.h.
Initial climb	1,420 ft./min.	1,420 ft./min.	1,000 ft./min.
Ceiling	22,000 ft.	22,000 ft.	18,900 ft.
Range	300 miles	300 miles	490 miles

	Mk. 21	Mk. 31	Mk. 32
Span	108 ft. 0 in.	108 ft. 0 in.	108 ft. 0 in.
Length	68 ft. 4 in.	68 ft. 4 in.	73 ft. 4 in.
Height	21 ft. 8 in.	21 ft. 8 in.	21 ft. 8 in.
Wing area	1,487 sq. ft.	1,487 sq. ft.	1,487 sq. ft.
Tare weight	26,484 lb.	26,910 lb.	29,465 lb.
All-up weight	40,000 lb.	44,000 lb.	44,000 lb.
Maximum speed	195 m.p.h.	195 m.p.h.	195 m.p.h.
Cruising speed	165 m.p.h.	165 m.p.h.	165 m.p.h.
Initial climb	1,000 ft./min.	1,000 ft./min.	1,000 ft./min.
Ceiling	21,000 ft.	24,500 ft.	24,500 ft.
Range	490 miles	490 miles	490 miles

Production:

Two hundred and fourteen aircraft including British registered examples listed in Appendix E and the following for export:

Mk. IIA: (c/n 12802) F-BCJA (T.A.I. 'Commandant Dagnaux').

Mk. 21P: (12928–12936) Pakistan Air Force G801 to G809.

Mk. 31: (13255) ZK-BVM.

Mk. 31C: (13217) XJ470.

Mk. 31E: (13162) F-OAOT/F-BFOT; (13165) F-OAOU.

Mk.31M: (13058–13061) R.N.Z.A.F. NZ5905/ZK-BEO, NZ5906–NZ5908; (13134–13135) NZ5910, NZ5911/ZK-BJP; (13154–13161) R.P.A.F. S4401/ZK-CAL, S4402/ZK-CAM, S4403/ZK-CLU, S4404/ZK-CLT, S4405, S4406/ZK-CRK, S4407/ZK-CRL, S4408; (13163) S4410; (13164) S4413; (13166–13175) S4415, S4417, S4419, S4409/G-ARSA, S4421/ZK-CRM, S4411, S4422, S4424, S4426, S4412; (13176–13185) S4427/AP-AME/VH-TBA, S4414, S4429, S4416/AP-AMN/ VH-BFA/ZK-CVK, S4418, S4420, S4430, S4423, S4425, S4428; (13186–13193) S4431, S4432/VH-TBB, S4434, S4433, S4435, S4437, S4436/VH-BFB/ZK-CVL, S4438/VH-ADL; (13210) Burmese Air Force UB722/VH-TBD; (13214–13215) Iraqi Air Force 368, 369; (13218) NZ5912; (13219) R.C.A.F. 9699/CF-WAE; (13249) 9700/CF-WAG; (13253) 9850/CF-WAD.

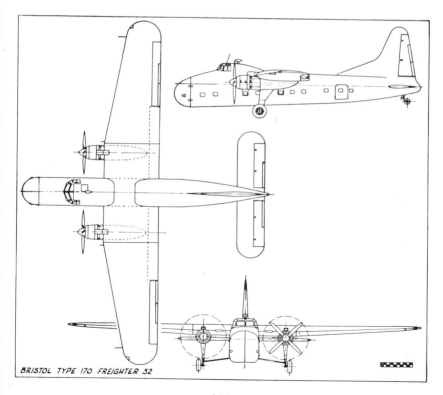

BRISTOL TYPE 170 FREIGHTER 32

The prototype Bristol Type 171 helicopter, G-ALOU, leaving Filton for the Paris Aero Show on 26 April 1949. (*Bristol Photo*)

Bristol Types 171 and 173

The Bristol 171 Mk. 1 was a four-seat helicopter designed by Raoul Hafner and powered by a 450 h.p. Pratt & Whitney Wasp Junior radial engine driving a three-bladed rotor. VL958, first of two prototypes, was first flown at Filton by H. A. Marsh on 27 July 1947, and the second, VL963, first flown in February 1948 was later registered G-ALOU and on 25 April 1949 received the first C. of A. ever issued to a British helicopter, enabling it to be flown to Le Bourget next day for exhibition at the Paris Salon.

The Mk. 2 version, VW905, with Alvis Leonides, shown statically at the Farnborough S.B.A.C. Show in September 1948, first flew at Filton on 3 September 1949 but the rotor disintegrated during the second take-off. When fitted with a strengthened rotor it flew for many years at Boscombe Down and the R.A.E., Bedford, until relegated to ground testing at Farnborough where it was scrapped in December 1962 without ever having carried its allotted civil registration G-AJGU.

The Bristol 171 Mk. 3 was a five-seater with shortened nose to improve downward view and 8 in. wider to accommodate three on the rear seat. All but two of the fifteen civil registered machines constructed in 1949 eventually bore R.A.F. markings for development flying to a Ministry of Supply contract, the exceptions being G-ALSR, evaluated by British European Airways as 'Sir Gareth' until handed over to the Empire Test Pilots' School, Farnborough, in October 1954 as XH682; and G-ALSX, company demonstrator from 1951 until delivered to Williamson Diamonds Ltd. at Mwadui, Tanganyika, in Bristol Freighter G-AILW in February 1958 as VR-TBS. It remained unused however until flown back in G-AINL in December 1959 for further company use as G-48-1 at their Old Mixon factory at Weston-super-Mare.

Bristol 171 Mk. 3 WT939, which carried civil marks G-ALTB solely for Arctic trials, was airfreighted to Canada for the purpose in R.C.A.F. Bristol Freighter 9696 in July 1951 and returned there for further tests in October 1953 prior to naval trials aboard the carrier *Perseus* in January 1954. Another, intended originally to be G-ALSZ, was used by the R.A.A.F. at the Woomera rocket range as A91-1 until 1965 when it was disposed of to J. Rose Motors Ltd. of Victoria as VH-GVR. After a crash during spraying operations at Falls Creek on 25 January 1967 the remains were acquired by a local preservation society for eventual exhibition at Moorabbin Airport.

Two machines with an additional freight hold aft of the engine bay, completed for B.E.A. as G-AMWG 'Sir Gawain' and G-AMWH 'Sir Geraint', inaugurated a 50/- return Eastleigh–Heathrow/Northolt experimental service on 15 June 1954 but G-AMWG was sold to Ansett-A.N.A. in 1956 for charter work as VH-INQ.

Large scale production of the Bristol 171 Mk. 4 Sycamore military version with 550 h.p. Leonides engines took place at Filton and Old Mixon, fourteen being allotted civil registrations G-AMWI to 'WU, G-AOBM and 'DL. These were mainly for the R.A.F., R.A.A.F. and the Belgian Air Force but G-AMWI was demonstrated all over Europe, took part in Pye airborne television experiments in 1956, and trained German pilots 1957–58. G-AOBM flew to Avonmouth Docks on 25 May 1955 to be shipped to Canada for demonstration flying as CF-HVX and in February 1956 made an outstanding flight from Winnipeg to Mexico City before returning to Old Mixon for overhaul and sale to the Royal Australian Navy. G-AODL was sold to Australian National Airways in May 1956 as VH-INO 'Yarrana' for flying crane work and crop spraying in Tasmania, ex-

Bristol Type 171 Mk. 2 VW905/G-AJGU. (*Bristol Photo*)

The five-seat Bristol Type 171 Mk. 3 G-ALSX at Weston-super-Mare in February 1958, ready for airfreighting to Tanganyika as VR-TBS. (*Bristol Photo*)

261

British European Airways' Bristol Type 171 Mk. 3A G-AMWG, showing the rear extension for carrying light freight. (*Bristol Photo*)

Bristol Type 173 Mk. 2 G-AMJI in B.E.A. colours as 'Sir Bors'. (*Bristol Photo*)

R.A.N. Sycamores XN448 and XR592, ex G-AOBM and G-AMWI, being similarly employed by J. Rose Motors Ltd. from 1966 as VH-SYC and VH-BAW respectively.

The Bristol 173 was a 13-passenger/2-crew transport helicopter driven by two sets of Sycamore Leonides Major power plants and rotors. The first prototype, G-ALBN, which made its first real flight at Filton piloted by C. T. D. Hosegood on 24 August 1952, was shown at the S.B.A.C. Show a month later before evaluation by the R.A.F. as XF785 and naval trials aboard the carrier *Eagle*. The second prototype, G-AMJI, designated Bristol 173 Mk. 2, had stub wings initially and became XH379 for naval trials in 1954 prior to lease to B.E.A. as 'Sir Bors'.

Three Bristol 173 Mk. 3 prototypes with four-bladed rotors and taller aft pylons were provisionally registered G-AMYF to 'YH but were completed for the Ministry of Supply as XE286–XE288, the first of which began hovering tests on 9 November 1956. XE288, which appeared at Old Mixon in B.E.A. livery in the same year, was allotted a second civil registration, G-AORB, but neither it nor XE287 progressed beyond the ground running stage.

SPECIFICATION

Manufacturers: The Bristol Aeroplane Co. Ltd., Filton, Bristol (style changed 1.56 to Bristol Aircraft Ltd.).

Westland Aircraft Ltd. (Bristol Helicopter Division), Old Mixon, Weston-super-Mare, Somerset.

Power Plants:
- (171 Mk. 1) One 450 h.p. P. & W. Wasp Junior R-985.
- (171 Mks. 2–4) One 550 h.p. Alvis Leonides LE.21HM or 524/1.
- (173 Mks. 1–2) Two 545 h.p. Alvis Leonides 73.
- (173 Mk. 3) Two 850 h.p. Alvis Leonides Major.

	171 Mks. 3 and 3A	171 Mk. 4	173 Mks. 1 and 2	173 Mk. 3
Rotor diameter	48 ft. 7 in.	48 ft. 7 in.	48 ft. 7 in.	48 ft. 9 in.
Length	42 ft. 0 in.	42 ft. 0 in.	55 ft. 2 in.	54 ft. 2 in.
Height	13 ft. 10 in.	14 ft. 7 in.	15 ft. 0 in.	17 ft. 0 in.
Tare weight	3,450 lb.	3,810 lb.	7,820 lb.	9,840 lb.
All-up weight	5,600 lb.	5,600 lb.	10,600 lb.	13,500 lb.
Cruising speed	132 m.p.h.	132 m.p.h.	115 m.p.h.	115 m.p.h.
Range	330 miles	330 miles	185 miles	300 miles

Production: (a) Bristol Type 171

Two Mk. 1; one Mk. 2; 17 British civil and six other Mks. 3 and 3A; 14 British civil and 140 other Mk. 4.

(b) Bristol Type 173

One Mk. 1; one Mk. 2; and three Mk. 3—all detailed in Appendix E.

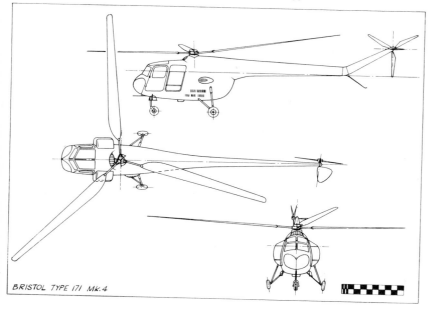

BRISTOL TYPE 171 Mk.4

The colourful Uganda-registered African Safari Airways Britannia 313 5X-UVH taking off from Southend on 11 May 1968. (*John Goring*)

Bristol Type 175 Britannia

On 5 July 1948, after some 12 months of discussion, three prototypes of the Bristol 175 were ordered by the Ministry of Supply and allotted serials VX442, VX447 and VX454. All were to be Centaurus powered, to have 130-ft. wing span and carry 42 passengers on B.O.A.C.'s Empire routes at an all-up weight of 104,650 lb. Two were to be suitable for conversion to Proteus propeller-turbines when sufficiently developed, but soon after the B.O.A.C. contract was placed on 28 July 1949 for a fleet of 25 the Centaurus engine was discarded and a Proteus powered transatlantic Type 175 with increased tankage and accommodating up to 83 passengers was accepted by B.O.A.C. as the production version.

Two prototype aircraft were then completed to the new specification as G-ALBO and G-ALRX, and the third airframe became the functional mock up. When therefore the Bristol chief test pilot A. J. Pegg took G-ALBO, Proteus 625 engines, on its maiden flight at Filton on 16 August 1952 it was the culmination of more than four years' work. By August 1953 its intended Proteus 705 engines were available, and with modified nacelles, turned up wing tips and additional power, its second S.B.A.C. Show appearance took place at Farnborough a month later. The second prototype, G-ALRX, also with Proteus 705s, was lost after only 51 hours' test flying. South of Ledbury at 10,000 ft. on 4 February 1954, fire in the starboard inner engine bay forced A. J. Pegg to put it gently down on the soft mud of the River Severn at Littleton Wharf where it was subsequently submerged by the rising tide and became a total loss. Development flying continued with G-ALBO, which was joined in the task in 1954 by the first production aircraft, G-ANBA, which was a more representative aeroplane. The very extensive development programme was further shared by G-ANBB and 'BC, G-ANBA going to Johannesburg and Khartoum in March 1955 to complete the tropical trials begun by G-ALBO in Tripoli in the previous year. At the same time the permissible all-up weight progressed from the 130,000 lb. of G-ALBO to the final figure of 155,000 lb. in 1956. G-ANBC and 'BD were granted full Cs. of A. at the end of 1955 and were delivered to B.O.A.C. at London Airport on 30 December 1955, later going to Hurn for crew training.

264

Over Southern Rhodesia on 4 April 1956 all four engines of the north-bound Britannia suffered flame-outs in the space of five minutes during flight in cu-nim at high altitude. This proved to be a recurring phenomenon, and only with difficulty was the resultant engine damage traced to dry ice accretion. B.O.A.C. proving flights were suspended until improved internal fairing of the engine intakes and the fitting of automatic relight glow-plugs remedied the trouble. The first two B.O.A.C. Britannias, G-ANBA and 'BB, had meanwhile gone to Short and Harland Ltd. at Belfast for modification up to full production standard while operational experience was being built up with G-ANBD to 'BI on trooping flights to Cyprus and on the Hungarian refugee air-lift between Vienna and London. Following successful trials in which G-ANBH went to Entebbe and Calcutta to be flown deliberately into the worst possible icing conditions, the Britannias were finally accepted for B.O.A.C. service. Thus with the departure of G-ANBI for Johannesburg on 1 February 1957 the Corporation had the distinction of putting the world's first long-range propeller-turbine powered transport into scheduled service.

G-ANBK, once part of the B.O.A.C. Britannia 102 fleet, in landing configuration at Heathrow in 1966. (*Richard Riding*)

In 1955, B.O.A.C. decided to order a small number of enlarged Britannias having two additional fuselage bays forward of the wing and one bay aft, increasing the fuselage length by 10 ft. 3 in. and permitting the carriage of up to 99 passengers in tourist seating. The fitting of integral fuel tanks in the outer wing panels to create B.O.A.C.'s long awaited non-stop transatlantic transport followed logically, and up-rated Proteus 755 engines for this version were flight tested in the outer nacelles of the Britannia prototype G-ALBO. Subsequently the Corporation took delivery of a fleet of 18 of the long-range, long-bodied version registered G-AOVB to 'VT.

By this time it had become necessary to differentiate between the several major variants then under construction for British and overseas purchasers, with the result that Bristol Aircraft Ltd. adopted a system combining Britannia series numbers with the customer type designations. The original basic type became the Series 100, the prototype G-ALBO was designated variant 101 and B.O.A.C. production aircraft were variant 102. Similarly the stretched version was referred to as the Series 300 and the prototype G-ANCA, now M.o.S. owned and first

XA-MEC, first Britannia 302 for Aeronaves de Mexico, landing at Filton in October 1957.

flown at Filton on 31 July 1956, was called the Britannia 301. Two similar aircraft, G-ANCB and 'CC, were sold in Mexico in 1957 as series 302s and five with extra tankage for Capital Airlines became Britannia 305s, all seven being built at Belfast by Short and Harland Ltd. The Capital sale eventually fell through but the 305s were disposed of to another U.S. operator, Northeast Airlines, in whose livery the first aircraft, G-ANCD, flew for a short period pending the issue of the C.A.A. type certificate on 10 April 1958 and their intended delivery as N6595C to N6599C inclusive. Long-range models with integral tanks were designated Series 310; the prototype G-AOVA (5,100 mile non-stop London–Vancouver polar flight in 14 hr. 40 min. on 29 June 1957) became the 311 and production models for B.O.A.C., commencing G-AOVB, Series 312.

G-AOVB was in fact the first of the B.O.A.C. fleet of 18 Series 312s to be delivered at London Airport, whither it was ferried from Filton by chief test pilot W. Gibb on 10 September 1957. It left on 28 September for proving flights in the U.S.A. and the Caribbean, making the crossing from London Airport to Idlewild, New York, non-stop in 11 hours 39 minutes. Two days later extreme meteorological conditions caused compressor blade rubbing in two engines, necessitating a landing at Miami, Florida. After further flight trials at Singapore in December 1957 with two suitably modified engines in G-AOVA, the long-haul Britannia was at last accepted. B.O.A.C. was then privileged to inaugurate the first turbine powered transatlantic service from London to New York direct on 19 December 1957, flown by G-AOVC, the same machine inaugurating the eastbound service two days later.

Other operators of this Series were El Al (Israel Airlines) which had four Britannia 313s 4X-AGA to 'GD; Canadian Pacific with six 314s CF-CZA to 'ZD, 'ZW and 'ZX (supplemented in 1959 by the last two Britannias to be built—Series 324s CF-CPD and 'PE); Hunting-Clan Air Transport Ltd. to which two Britannia 317s G-APNA and 'NB were delivered at the end of 1958; and Cubana de Aviacion, purchaser of four 318s CU-T668 to CU-T671. On 19 December 1957, the day B.O.A.C. began transatlantic Britannia services, El Al's 4X-AGA crossed in the opposite direction on a New York–Tel Aviv proving flight and established a distance record of 6,100 miles at an average speed of 401 m.p.h. Cubana's CU-T668 was leased to Eagle Airways in 1960 as G-APYY but in 1962 went to Ceskoslovenske Aerolinie as OK-MBA, becoming the first Britannia to operate behind the Iron Curtain. Later in 1962 it was joined by OK-MBB, formerly CU-T671.

Three long-fuselage, mixed traffic Britannias, built at Belfast with Short Bros. and Harland-designed freight doors and heavy duty flooring, were designated Series 252 and flown initially as G-APPE to 'PG but were then delivered to R.A.F. Transport Command as XN392, XN398 and XN404. They became Britannia C. Mk. 2s in Service use, joining 20 Britannia C. Mk. 1s (or Series 253). XL636, first of 15 built by Short Bros. and Harland. Ltd., was delivered on 4 June 1959, all 23 aircraft serving the world-wide route network of Nos. 99 and 511 Squadrons, Lyneham.

In June 1958, after Northeast Airlines had cancelled the order for the five Britannia 305s, G-ANCD was repainted in Cubana colours and left on an extensive sales tour to Spain, Portugal and Latin America. After covering some 27,400 miles in 23 days, it returned to Filton on 30 June and was leased to El Al as Series 306 4X-AGE. Returning to Filton in March 1959 it was refurbished for Air Charter Ltd. as a Series 307, joining G-ANCE, delivered on 12 September 1958. Both became part of the British United Airways fleet when that airline formed in 1960 and during 1966 freight doors and strengthened flooring were designed and installed at Stansted by Aviation Traders (Engineering) Ltd. They then emerged as Britannia 307Fs and operated the 'Africargo' services of B.U.A. The next two, G-ANCF and 'CG were delivered to the Argentine in December 1959, but the last, G-ANCH, remained at Bristol until it left for Ghana Airways as 9G-AAG on 17 July 1960. 9G-AAH, formerly G-AOVA and redesignated Series 319, followed on 8 November.

B.O.A.C.'s 14 surviving Britannia 102s were stored at Cambridge in 1962 to await sale and the 17 remaining 312s were progressively withdrawn from use from the end of 1963. During their eight years with B.O.A.C. they frequently carried stick-on titles of companies such as Nigeria Airways and British West Indian Airways, and the combined fleet of 33 aircraft flew 130,024,000 revenue

Britannia 307 G-ANCD at Filton on 24 March 1959 just before departure on its delivery flight to Air Charter Ltd. at Southend.

G-AOVB, first of the long-range Britannia 312s delivered to B.O.A.C. (*B.O.A.C.*)

miles without a single fatality among 2,163,171 fare-paying passengers. All Series 102 aircraft were leased eventually to the independents, the first, G-ANBK, to B.K.S. Air Transport Ltd. in April 1964.

The greater part of the Britannia 312 fleet was acquired by British Eagle International Airlines Ltd. which inaugurated a daily London–Glasgow Britannia service on 3 November 1963. These and others acquired from foreign operators, were employed extensively on inclusive tour and trooping work, and some were fitted with the Aviation Traders freight door before the airline went into liquidation in November 1968.

Only four foreign airlines operated secondhand Britannias, the first being Globe Air of Switzerland which bought two from El Al in 1964 but ceased operations after HB-ITB crashed on approach to Nicosia, Cyprus, on 20 April 1967. The survivor, HB-ITC, which passed to African Safari Airways as 5X-UVH in 1968, was joined by 5X-UVT, formerly G-ATGD, in 1969. During 1967 a third El Al machine went to the newly-formed Air Spain alongside three British Eagle Britannia 312s, the four being registered EC-BFJ to 'FL and 'SY.

Other British operators were Monarch Airlines Ltd., Luton, which began flying in 1968 with two ex-Caledonian 312s, G-AOVH and 'VI, and four former British Eagle aircraft; Lloyd International Airways Ltd. with two 312F freighters; and Donaldson International Airlines Ltd. which opened up in 1969 with the ex-B.U.A. Britannia 317s G-APNA and 'NB and the 312 G-AOVC.

Planned future development included the installation of the Orion supercharged propeller-turbine engine, the flight testing of which began in the port outer nacelle of the veteran Britannia 101 G-ALBO on 31 August 1956. The intention to equip the Series 301 G-ANCA with four of these engines for final proving was frustrated by its loss near Bristol during a test flight on 6 November 1957, with the loss of 15 lives, including that of the pilot, E. H. Statham. G-ALBO was then used for air testing the improved Proteus 765 which eventually powered most of the long-fuselage Britannias and first flew with this engine in the port inner position on 1 November 1957. When Government finance for the Orion ceased in 1958, G-ALBO became redundant and remained at Filton until 30 November 1960 when it was flown, still with its odd assortment of engines, to No. 4 School of Technical Training, St. Athan, where it was used as an instructional airframe until scrapped in June 1968.

Airline liveries: Transglobe G-ATGD taking-off from Southend, 8 December 1965; Donaldson G-APNB 'Carillon' landing there on 28 March 1969; Caledonian G-AOVJ 'County of Aberdeen' at Southend, November 1966: 5Y-ALT, African Air Safari's Britannia 313, formerly 5X-UVH and G-ASFU. (*John Goring photos except 'LT Aviation Photo News*)

SPECIFICATION

Manufacturers: Bristol Aircraft Ltd., Filton House, Bristol; sub-contracted to Short Bros. and Harland Ltd., Queen's Island, Belfast.

Power Plants: (Britannia 102)   Four 3,870 e.h.p. Bristol Proteus 705.
(Britannia 252, 312, 317)   Four 4,120 e.h.p. Bristol Proteus 755 or 761.

Dimensions: Span, 142 ft. 3 in. Height, 36 ft. 8 in. Wing area, 2,075 sq. ft. Length, (Britannia 102), 114 ft. 0 in.; (Britannia 252, 312 and 317), 124 ft. 3 in.

Weights: (Britannia 102) Tare weight, 86,400 lb. All-up weight, 155,000 lb.
(Britannia 252) Tare weight, 91,000 lb. All-up weight, 180,000 lb.
(Britannia 312) Tare weight, 88,000 lb. All-up weight, 180,000 lb.

Performance: (Britannia 102) 1. With maximum fuel a payload of 14,000 lb. could be carried 3,800 miles at a mean speed of 335 m.p.h.
2. With maximum payload of 25,000 lb., the range was 2,740 miles at a mean speed of 335 m.p.h.

(Britannia 312) 1. With maximum fuel a payload of 18,000 lb. could be carried 5,760 miles at a mean speed of 355 m.p.h.
2. With maximum payload of 28,000 lb. the range was 4,100 miles at a mean speed of 355 m.p.h.

Production:
Sixty-one British registered aircraft and the following for foreign operators and the Royal Air Force: Series 253 (c/n 13397–13400) XL635–XL638; (13434–13436) XM489–XM491; (13448–13449) XL639–XL640; (13453–13457) XL657–XL660; (13508–13514) XM496–XM498 and XM517–XM520. Series 314 (c/n 13394) CF-CZB. Series 318 (13433) CU-T669; (13437) CU-T670; (13515) CU-T671.

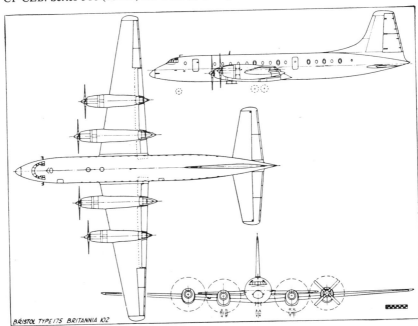

BRISTOL TYPE 175 BRITANNIA 102

BN-2A Islander G-AWNY flying over Southampton Water in January 1969 before delivery to SATAIR in Martinique, French West Indies.

Britten-Norman BN-2 Islander and Trislander

The Islander all-metal, 10-seat STOL monoplane was designed, built and certificated in 18 months for short-haul, third-level operation. Crewed by John Britten, Desmond Norman and flight observer A. J. Coombe, the prototype, G-ATCT, first flew at Bembridge on 13 June 1965 before exhibition at the Paris Aero Show a few days later. With fixed undercarriage and two 210 h.p. Rolls-Royce Continental engines, its empty weight was 1,000 lb. less than that of the Rapide of similar power, and its lines were as clean as American contemporaries yet at £17,500 it was only a fraction of the price.

Easily convertible to freighter, the private enterprise Islander created worldwide customer interest and large scale production of an improved version with 260 h.p. Lycoming engines further outboard in lengthened nacelles, 2 ft. wing tip extensions and redesigned tailplane, began in a specially built factory at Bembridge. The first, G-ATWU, flown on 20 August 1966, was used as a development aircraft and the next three, G-AVCN, 'KC and 'RA were delivered to Glosair/Aurigny Air Services and Loganair Ltd. in August 1967 for inter-island services based on Alderney and at Kirkwall respectively. The unique short-span prototype G-ATCT and its pilot Peter Hillwood were lost when it crashed into Ringwiel Lake near Leeuwarden, Holland, when returning from demonstration in Germany on 9 November 1966.

G-AVOS, which left for Shannon on 28 September 1967, was the first of a large number to make the Atlantic crossing with, in the cabin, four 45 gallon drums connected to the existing 112 gallon fuel system and thus equipped G-AWNS, (re-registered N676SA and first to be ferried in U.S. markings), flew 2,260 miles non-stop between Gander and Fort Lauderdale, Florida. It was one of several Islanders used by Suburban Airlines and Montauk-Caribbean Airways for commuter services in and out of the 1,000 ft. STOL strips at New York's John F. Kennedy and LaGuardia Airports. Others were sold to La Poseda Airways and Viking Airways

271

for local routes based on Laredo, Texas, and Rhode Island, N.Y. and to operators in the West Indian islands. N578JA forced landed on the Greenland icecap during delivery on 3 January 1969 and was abandoned; and N852JA was lost in the Caribbean later that year.

In August 1968 G-AVCN, G-AWBY and 'BZ (Aurigny Air Services) and G-AVKC and 'RA (Loganair) were modified to operate at an all-up weight of 6,000 lb. as the BN-2A and all aircraft from the 25th were built to this standard. World-wide sales continued, particularly in areas where there were only unprepared bush airstrips, e.g. TI-1063C to AVE Airlines serving banana plantations in Costa Rica, VH-AIA to Island Airways for Great Barrier Reef tourism and YV-T-MTM for airlifting construction materials in Venezuela. Some were ferried half round the world to Air Caledonie, Air Samoa and Air Tahiti for inter Pacific island services; to Malaysia-Singapore Airlines; and to Aerial Tours Pty. Ltd. for flying oil rig crews between Port Moresby and primitive jungle strips in Papua and New Guinea.

Flown by Capts. W. J. Bright and F. Buxton, G-AXUD won the London–Sydney Air Race in December 1969 in an elapsed time of 76 hr. 41 min. while on delivery to become Aerial Tours' seventh Islander, VH-ATZ. In the far north Lambair carried Canadian oil prospecting teams beyond the Arctic Circle in CF-XYK in an area where Regent Drilling Ltd. was bulldozing strips near the oil rigs for its own CF-RDI.

Later production aircraft flew initially under Class B markings before departure with foreign registrations and a number of allocated British marks were never used, e.g. the 16th machine G-51-4 was delivered to Transgabon on 6 March 1968 as TR-LNF, leaving G-AVXU unused.

By 1969 Islanders were already serving 56 companies in 27 countries, including Emden-based Ostfriesische Lufttaxi, Aerowest Dortmund and Stuttgarter Flugdienst for tourist traffic to the Frisian Islands and German Alps. On 25 June 1969 a new U.K. operator, Westward Airways Ltd., inaugurated a six-times daily Gatwick–Heathrow shuttle with G-AXFC and on 3 March 1970 Humber Airways Ltd. commenced scheduled services between Brough (later Leconfield) and Leavesden using Islanders G-AXRM and 'RN.

Special Islanders included G-AWID with four Micronair rotary atomisers for pest control in Thailand; G-AWNT with Wild RC.8 camera to replace Avro 19 Ser.2 G-APHV of Survey Flights Ltd.; and two with executive interiors for the

The short-span Islander prototype, G-ATCT. (*Aviation Photo News*)

The prototype Islander Mk. 3, G-ATWU, as it was at the end of September 1970 with small extra fin above the rear engine..(*via Air Pictorial*)

Sheikh of Abu Dhabi which also had UHF radio for use in their dual military transport role. G-AVUB, delivered initially to the Herts and Essex Aero Club, was landed on the aircraft carrier *Hermes* by test pilot Colin Newnes on 28 May 1968 and later handed over to Rolls-Royce Ltd. to be fitted with 285 h.p. turbo-supercharged Continental TSIO-520-Es with which it first flew as the BN-2S on 6 September 1968.

By 1970, in the face of very large orders, it was necessary to sub-contract component manufacture to Westlands, Weston-super-Mare, and assemblies for complete aircraft to British Hovercraft Ltd., East Cowes. The Bembridge factory was thereafter used solely for final assembly and for furnishing Islanders erected in Bucharest from British-made components and flown to Bembridge with British registrations. The seventh Rumanian, G-AXUT, was demonstrated en route at the Leipzig Trade Fair, arriving at Gatwick on 12 March 1970.

Earlier a 24 inch fuselage extension had been built into the second prototype G-ATWU, to produce the 14-seat BN-2E stretched version, first flown on 14 July 1968, but this configuration was abandoned in favour of a 90 inch extension combined with a third Lycoming engine mounted on top of a widened fin. It first flew at Bembridge in this form as the 17-seat Islander Mk. 3 (or Trislander) on

G-AYKR, second production BN-2A-3 Islander, showing the bulged cowlings and set-back air intake which identified the more powerful version. (*Tony Leigh*)

273

11 September 1970 and left for the S.B.A.C. Show at Farnborough the same afternoon.

The first BN-2A-3 Islanders with two 300 h.p. Lycoming IO-550K fuel-injection engines (which gave a significant boost to performance) also appeared in 1970 and the first two, G-AYKP and 'KR, left Bembridge for Australia on 4 and 5 November respectively, the first as the I.A.S. demonstrator VH-ISB and the other for Carpentaria Exploration Pty. Ltd. in Papua. The BN-2A-3 was identified by bulged engine cowlings and set-back air intakes and its designation should not be confused with that of the three engined Islander Mk. 3 (or Trislander), the first production model of which, G-AYWI, was delivered to Aurigny Air Services Ltd. at Staverton on 29 June 1971 and flew its first inter-island scheduled service on 1 October.

SPECIFICATION

Manufacturers: Britten-Norman Ltd., Bembridge, Isle of Wight.

Power Plants: (Prototype)   Two 210 h.p. Continental IO-360-A.
(BN-2 and BN-2A) Two 260 h.p. Lycoming O-540-E.
(BN-2A-3)   Two 300 h.p. Lycoming IO-540-K1B5.
(Trislander)   Three 260 h.p. Lycoming O-540-E4C5.

	Prototype	BN-2A Islander	Trislander
Span	45 ft. 0 in.	49 ft. 0 in.	53 ft. 0 in.
Length	35 ft. 3 in.	35 ft. 8 in.	43 ft. 9 in.
Height	13 ft. 8 in.	13 ft. 8 in.	13 ft. 4 in.
Wing area	298 sq. ft.	325 sq. ft.	337 sq. ft.
Tare weight	2,780 lb.	3,500 lb.	5,020 lb.
All-up weight	4,750 lb.	6,000 lb.*	9,350 lb.
Maximum speed	164 m.p.h.	168 m.p.h.	192 m.p.h.
Cruising speed	156 m.p.h.	150 m.p.h.*	185 m.p.h.
Initial climb	—	1,150 ft./min.	1,300 ft./min.
Range	950 miles	810 miles*	—

* BN-2A-3 Islander: A.U.W., 6,300 lb. Initial climb, 1,400 ft./min. Cruise, 170 m.p.h. Range, max. load, 400 miles.

Production: (a) Bembridge built

A large number of British registered aircraft and the following for export from Bembridge in foreign marks: (c/n 28) VH-ATI; (29) VH-ATK; (40) N587JA; (41) 9M-APD; (42) 9V-BBS; (43) F-OCMN; (44) LV-PLU n.t.u./N595JA; (45) N588JA; (46) I-TRAL; (49) N590JA/N88MA; (50) CF-XZS; (52) F-OCMO; (53) CS-AJP; (56) I-BATT; (57) N591JA; (58) N592JA; (59) VQ-GAB; (60) N593JA; (61) N594JA; (62) N290EA; (63) 9M-APE; (64) N596JA; (65) N291EX; (66) N598JA; (67) VH-ATW; (68) CS-AJQ; (69) N599JA; (71) N851JA; (72) N852JA; (74) N850JA; (77) N853JA; (78) CF-YZT; (80) N854JA; (82) CF-YZU; (83) TR-LOC; (84) D-IAWD; (87) N855JA; (88) D-IFDS; (89) VH-FLE; (90) N871JA; (92) N857JA; (93) YR-BNA; (94) VH-ATY; (98) CS-AJR; (99) A2-ZEV; (100) VH-ATV; (101) 4X-AYF; (102) TR-LOD; (103) N861JA; (104) F-OCFQ; (106) CF-AJL; (107) 4X-AYW; (108) N856JA; (109) 5W-FAF; (110) F-OCFR; (112) F-OCFS; (113) VH-EQE; (114) CF-AJM; (115) N858JA; (116) ST-ADJ; (118) 8R-GDN; (119) VH-ATU; (120) N869JA; (122) YR-BNC; (125) 8R-GDQ; (126) VH-ATX; (130) YR-BND; (131) F-OCOY; (133) VH-ATZ; (136)

F-OCOZ; (138) YR-BNF; (141) VH-FLF; (142) LN-RTO; (146) VH-EQK; (160) VP-LAE; (161) VP-LAF; (163) VP-LAG; (166) 4X-AYC; (175) N864JA; (176) N865JA; (177) VP-HBI; (178) N859JA; (180) EI-AUL; (181) OH-BNA; (184) N862JA; (185) N866JA; (186) N867JA/F-OGFA; (187) N870JA; (188) OY-DHS; (189) N44JA; (196) F-OCPY; (198) N31JA; (199) N32JA; (201) N33JA; (202) N34JA; (203) N35JA; (206) SE-FTA; (208) SE-FTB; (209) N36JA; (210) N37JA; (211) N38JA; (212) CF-GAQ; (213) N39JA; (214) 4X-AYB; (215) N111VA; (218) OH-BNB; (220) F-OCRG; (221) F-OCRH; (222) N40JA; (223) N41JA; (224) N132JL; (225) N131JL; (228) N42JA; (229) N43JA; (230) 8R-GDN; (231) 8R-GDQ; (232) N222TW; (234) N444TW; (236) OO-GVS; (237) I-BADE; (238) CF-ZVV; (239) N130JL; (240) CF-ZVY; (242) LV-PRE; (244) N45JA; (246) 9J-ACB; (248) HP-549; (249) N46JA; (250) N47JA; (251) 5Y-AMU; (252) N48JA; (254) 9J-ACC; (255) N49JA; (256) N50JA; (257) G-51-257; (258) PT-DVE; (259) PT-DVN; (260) 9J-ACE; (261) 9J-ACF; (263) CF-QPN; (264) G-51-264; (265) HP-551; (266) HP-570; (267) HP-569; (268) HP-568; (269) HP-571; (270) 9J-ACG; (274) HP-548; (275) G-51-275; (276) G-51-276; (280) G-51-280; (282) HP-550; (283) G-51-283; (284) 5Y-ANV; (286) N52JA; (287) 5Y-ANU; (290) G-51-290; (292) G-51-292; (293) N35JA/2; (294) N39JA/2; (295) G-51-295; (296) N56JA; (298) G-51-298; (300) G-51-300; (301) N53JA; (302) N57JA; (303) N58JA; (304) G-51-304; (306) N54JA.

(b) Rumanian built

The entire output British registered for ferrying to Bembridge, see Appendix E.

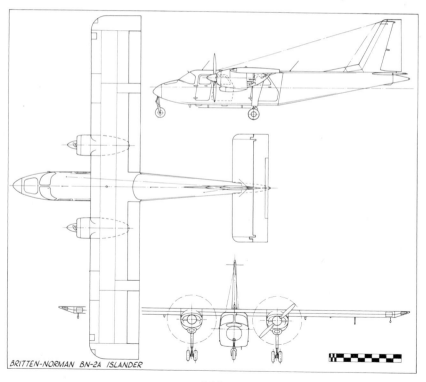

BRITTEN-NORMAN BN-2A ISLANDER

The eighth and final British registered Centaur IVA showing the enlarged rudder.

Central Centaur IV

The Centaur IV was a two-bay biplane of conventional wire-braced, fabric-covered, wooden construction, designed by A. A. Fletcher and built at Kilburn in 1919 by the Central Aircraft Company. This had been formed in 1916 as a subsidiary of the local woodworking firm of R. Cattle Ltd. The Centaur IV was originally to have been available in two distinct models, as a side-by-side two-seater or as a three-seater with the pilot in the front of an enlarged single cockpit. As no market existed for the private owner version, all eight aircraft were constructed as three-seaters. These formed the joyriding and instructional fleet of the ambitious flying school opened by the firm at Northolt with Herbert Sykes, O.B.E., as manager and Lt. F. B. Goodwin-Castleman as chief pilot. The prototype Centaur IV, K-108/G-EABI, was powered by a 70 h.p. Renault eight-cylinder V-type air-cooled engine, but all subsequent machines had the 100 h.p. Anzani nine-cylinder radial. This was uncowled and bolted direct to the original engine bulkhead with a supreme disregard for aesthetics. The extra power gave a much needed increase in performance, and their docility in the air was a legend, the average pupil going solo in three hours. Two of the first women to take up flying after the First World War were trained on Centaur IVs and on 24 June 1920 a third pupil, Miss Imelda Trafford, became the first woman to qualify for the Air Ministry's newly created 'A' Licence. Great enterprise was also shown in offering, and successfully selling, trips round London, over Welsh and Kentish beauty spots, cathedral cities and the Belgian battlefields at fares ranging from £2 3s. 6d. to £60. By June 1920 flights over London were averaging 100 a week and two aircraft were despatched to Bury St. Edmunds for a three-week joyriding 'season' at local request. In its passenger carrying form, with dual controls removed, it was referred to as the Centaur IVA.

The fifth and subsequent Centaur IVs were provided with increased rudder area by means of small additional triangular areas top and bottom. G-EAOR, the first aircraft so modified, was fitted with the conventional three-float undercarriage of the period to become the sole Centaur IVB. A week's joyriding was carried out at

The prototype Centaur IV (70 h.p. Renault) at Northolt in 1920. (*Royal Aeronautical Society*)

Southend with this floatplane after the Mayor had made the inaugural trip on 19 June 1920 and had made an enthusiastic second flight at his own expense immediately afterwards. It was eventually dismantled, and returned to London by rail for exhibition at the Olympia Aero Show in the July. Following its conversion to a landplane it crashed in October 1920, to become the type's sole casualty.

The post-war slump brought about a sharp decline in the company's activities, and in October 1921 the Centaur IVA G-EAOQ was sold in Belgium, making the delivery flight non-stop from Northolt. It was followed by G-EAQE and 'QF in December 1921, 'HS in July 1922 and 'OS in October 1922. At least five similar aircraft were also built to a Belgian order, some of which were active until 1938. The final British Centaur IVA, G-EAQF, was re-registered O-BOTI on arrival in Belgium, where it was used for instructional flying until withdrawn from use in November 1923. Two years later it was restored to flying condition, probably by the cannibalization of G-EAQE/O-BOTH, as it then took on a new lease of life with the markings properly belonging to its sister aircraft. Later, as OO-OTH, it fell victim to the tide of war in 1940.

When the Central Aircraft Company finally closed down in May 1926 the two surviving Centaur IVs, G-EABI and 'LL, were sold to the Gnat Aero and Motor Co. Ltd. who used them at Shoreham for instructing members of the

The Centaur IVB taxying off Southend on 19 June 1920 at the beginning of the Mayoral joyride. (*H. G. Martin*)

277

Southern Counties Aero Club and for joyriding along the South Coast until they were taken over by the reorganized Gnat Aero Company in March 1927 and finally scrapped in April 1930.

SPECIFICATION

Manufacturers: The Central Aircraft Company, Palmerston Works, 179 High Road, Kilburn, London, N.W.6.

	Centaur IVA		Centaur IVB
Engine	70 h.p. Renault	100 h.p. Anzani	100 h.p. Anzani
Span	34 ft. 2½ in.	34 ft. 2½ in.	39 ft. 1 in.
Length	27 ft. 6 in.	24 ft. 9 in.	27 ft. 1 in.
Height	—	—	9 ft. 6 in.
Tare weight	1,096 lb.	900 lb.	1,230 lb.
All-up weight	1,600 lb.	1,400 lb.	1,900 lb.
Maximum speed	70 m.p.h.	75 m.p.h.	75 m.p.h.
Duration	—	3 hours	3 hours

Production: Eight aircraft, c/n 201–208, listed in Appendix E.

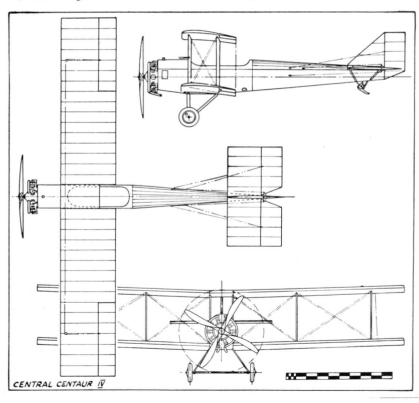

CENTRAL CENTAUR IV

Sqn. Ldr. H. R. Bilborough flying the Chilton D.W.1 G-AFGH near Denham in 1949.

Chilton D.W.1

The first Chilton D.W.1 was designed and built at Hungerford by two ex D.H. Technical School students, the Hon. Andrew Dalrymple and A. R. Ward, in 1937. It was intended to be cheap to manufacture and operate, yet have an exceptional performance on low power. This was handsomely achieved with an all-wood airframe with plywood skin, clean enough aerodynamically to require split flaps. Only the ailerons were fabric-covered. Power was supplied by a 32 h.p. Carden Ford, an automobile water-cooled unit, lightened and fitted with dual ignition for aircraft use.

Initial flight trials of the all-red prototype, G-AESZ, were made by Ranald Porteous at Witney in April 1937, but modifications to correct minor cooling and airscrew troubles postponed its public appearance until A. R. Ward flew it to the Southend Flying Club's 'At Home' on 4 September 1937. It was first sold to J. A. Talbot at Roborough, Plymouth, in 1938, and later to P. W. Bayliss at Wolverhampton, where it remained in storage throughout the war. Meanwhile two other Chilton D.W.1s, G-AFGH and 'GI, were completed, the first being exhibited in silver and blue at the Garden Party of the Royal Aeronautical Society at Heathrow on 8 May 1938. Only the front cowlings were different from the original and in April 1939 'GI went to Broxbourne as the property of F. D. Paul. On a mere 32 h.p., the Chilton's top speed of 112 m.p.h. was sensational, but when a suitable air-cooled engine, the French-built 44 h.p. Train 4T, became available, the heavy water-cooled unit was at once forsaken. The Train-engined Chilton G-AFSV, designated the D.W.1A, made its first flight in July 1939, and with it the Hon. A. Dalrymple won that year's Folkestone Trophy Race at an average speed of 126 m.p.h. Work also commenced on a third version, the D.W.2.

Surprisingly enough, all the Chiltons survived the war, all the jigs, spares and the half-completed D.W.2 being taken over by the College of Aeronautical Engineering Ltd. at Redhill. First to fly was G-AFSV, in which Ranald Porteous, who had done the flight trials of the prototype 10 years before, broke the 100 km. international closed circuit record at 124·5 m.p.h. during the Folkestone Trophy Meeting at Lympne on 31 August 1947. In September 1948 he bought G-AFGH, but sold it a few months later to Dr. Miles Bickerton, owner of Denham Aerodrome, but on 3 July 1949, just prior to the King's Cup Race, it was extensively damaged in a forced landing at South Chalfont. Rapid repairs involving

Sqn. Ldr. 'Manx' Kelly flying the Mikron-engined D.W.1A G-AFSV 'Barbara Ann III' near Booker in 1969. (*Air Portraits*)

the borrowing of the fuselage of G-AESZ were completed just in time for Sqn. Ldr. H. R. Bilborough to fly in the Grosvenor Cup Race and come thirteenth at 95·5 m.p.h. After the race the prototype was reconstructed, became the property of Dr. W. L. James at Southend and was groomed for the abortive 1951 King's Cup Race at Hatfield. The owner was subsequently seriously injured when the aircraft was forced to land at Felixstowe with engine trouble in 1953, and wrecked. Serviceable components of G-AFGH were sent to Redhill early in 1951, where the fuselage of the would-be D.W.2 was used to restore it to flying condition. In 1962 Messrs. J. T. Hayes and J. West took it to Branston, Lincoln, and commenced a painstaking rebuild with 55 h.p. Lycoming O-145-A2 flat four.

In a post-war Britain devoid of new high performance lightplanes the two remaining Chiltons could not fail to invite modification for racing purposes. In 1950 Lt. Cmdr. J. S. Sproule, R.N., added 5 m.p.h. to G-AFGI by fitting a bubble hood from an Olympia sailplane. After Hugh Kendall acquired it in 1951, the aircraft was stripped and re-covered, extensive modifications made to the engine

The third Chilton D.W.1, G-AFGI, after it had been rebuilt with the 55 h.p. Continental flat-four engine in 1966. (*P. R. March*)

bay and cowlings, and the heavy wheels replaced by lighter, braked Olympia units. Astonishing as its 112 m.p.h. had been in 1938, it now proceeded to win the *Daily Express* Race at Shoreham on 22 September 1951 at an average speed of 129 m.p.h. In 1966 a later owner, J. J. H. Dickson of Marlborough, also fitted a 55 h.p. Lycoming but loaned it to the Skyfame Museum, Staverton, in 1968.

The Train-engined D.W.1A G-AFSV eventually joined the prototype at Southend, where it was flown by J. R. Batt of Aviation Traders Ltd., and in the Goodyear Trophy Race at Wolverhampton on 17 May 1952 he averaged 122·5 m.p.h. This aircraft passed into the ownership of J. E. G. Appleyard at Yeadon in April 1955 to be fitted in the following year with a bubble canopy, and at the same time re-engined with a 62 h.p. Walter Mikron 2.

SPECIFICATION

Manufacturers: Chilton Aircraft Ltd., Chilton, Hungerford, Berks.
Power Plants: (D.W.1) One 30 h.p. Carden Ford.
                  One 55 h.p. Lycoming O-145-A2.
          (D.W.1A) One 45 h.p. Train 4T.
Dimensions: Span, 24 ft. 0 in. Length, 18 ft. 0 in. Height, 4 ft. 10 in. Wing area, 77 sq. ft.
Weights: (D.W.1) Tare weight, 398 lb. All-up weight, 640 lb.
Performance: (D.W.1) Maximum speed, 112 m.p.h. Cruising speed, 100 m.p.h. Initial climb, 650 ft./min. Range, 500 miles.

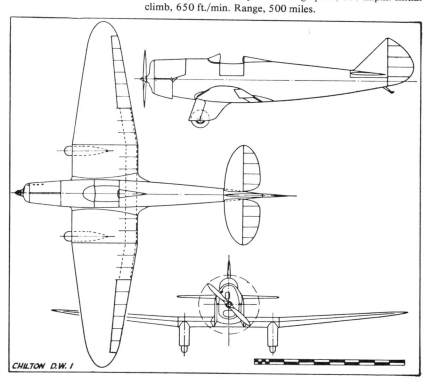

CHILTON D.W.1

Lesser Known British-built Civil Aircraft

This section of the book describes civil aircraft of British design which existed only in prototype form or in small numbers and includes designs intended for amateur construction which, although of foreign origin, have been built in Britain from British materials to British standards of airworthiness.

Whenever possible registration details are included in the text but when this is not possible through lack of space, they are listed in Appendix E. Omission of the date of issue of C. of A. indicates that none was issued. Dates are given in the British way, viz. day, month, year.

Abbreviations are confined to:

C.A.S	Chief of the Air Staff
d.b.r	Damaged beyond economical repair
M.A.E.E.	Marine Aircraft Experimental Establishment
N.S.Ae. & G.T.	North Sea Aerial & General Transport Co. Ltd.
ntu	Registration reserved but not taken up
R.Ae.S.	Royal Aeronautical Society
S.A.S	Scandinavian Airlines System
s.o.c.	Struck off charge

(Flight Photo 7358)

A.B.C. Robin

Single-seat cabin monoplane with plywood fuselage and folding wings designed by A. A. Fletcher and built at Walton-on-Thames 1929 by A.B.C. Motors Ltd. and fitted with their new 40 h.p. Scorpion engine. One aircraft only: G-AAID, c/n 1, first flown at Brooklands 6.29, exhibited at the Olympia Aero Show 7.29. Flown at Brooklands 11.29 with windscreen moved back to bring the fuel filler caps outside the cockpit, changed fuselage lines and enlarged fin and rudder. C. of A. issued 27.6.30, scrapped at Brooklands 1932. Span, 25 ft. 4 in. Length, 17 ft. 7 in. Tare wt., 415 lb. A.U.W., 680 lb. Cruise, 85 m.p.h.

Alliance P.1

Two-seat training biplane of wood and fabric construction built at Hendon 1918 as the Ruffy-Baumann R.A.B. 15, powered by one 80 h.p. Renault. Following absorption of the Ruffy, Arnell and Baumann Aviation Co. by the Alliance Aeroplane Co. Ltd., Acton, it was redesigned by J. A. Peters as the Alliance P.1 with horn balanced rudder and improved undercarriage. One aircraft only: K-159/G-EAGK, c/n P.1, registered 9.7.19, scrapped 11.20.

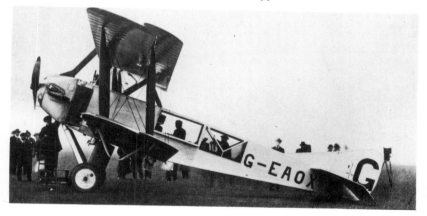

Alliance P.2 Seabird

Two-seater with 21-hour range, powered by one 450 h.p. Napier Lion, built 1919 by the Alliance Aeroplane Co. Ltd., Acton, for the Atlantic flight competition. Two aircraft only: K-160/G-EAGL (rear undercarriage radius rods), used instead by Capt. W. R. Curtis with designer J. A. Peters navigating for Acton–Madrid non-stop flight 31.7.19; G-EAOX (front radius rods), C. of A. 27.10.19, left Hounslow 13.11.19 to compete for the Australian Govt. £10,000 prize but crashed at Surbiton a few minutes later, Lt. R. Douglas and Lt. J. S. Ross killed. Span, 53 ft. 0 in. Length, 33 ft. 6 in. Tare wt., 2,600 lb. A.U.W., 7,400 lb. Max. speed, 140 m.p.h.

Alula D.H.6

D.H.6 fuselage and tail unit fitted with a 200 h.p. Bentley B.R.2 rotary and the Alula high-lift wing. Conversion by the Blackburn Aeroplane and Motor Co. Ltd. at Sherburn-in-Elmet 1920 to the designs of A. A. Holle of the Commercial Aeroplane Wing Syndicate Ltd. One aircraft only: G-EAWG, first flown 2.1.21 by Capt. Clinch, later modified with dihedral from the centre line and braced with a rigid structure below the wing. Flown by F. T. Courtney 4.21, dismantled and despatched to St. Cyr, near Paris for further tests.

(Royal Aeronautical Society)

Alula Semiquaver

The Martinsyde Semiquaver G-EAPX, 300 h.p. Hispano-Suiza, fitted with a wide track undercarriage and thick-section, mahogany planked Alula high-lift wing built by the Blackburn Aeroplane and Motor Co. Ltd and mounted directly on the fuselage. Scratched from the Aerial Derby as a result of taxying trials by F. T. Courtney 15.7.21, eve of the race. Flown at Northolt by R. W. Kenworthy 12.10.21, take-off speed 110 m.p.h., maximum speed close to the world speed record of 179 m.p.h. Believed taken to the Isle of Grain Experimental Establishment later in 1921 for testing and to have flown to Eastchurch. Scrapped after the R.A.E., Farnborough, found the factor of safety to be 1·75. Span, 28 ft. 6 in. Length, 19 ft. 3 in. Wing area $106\frac{1}{4}$ sq. ft.

Angus Aquila

Wooden single-seater with folding wings and aluminium-covered fuselage, designed and built 1930 by A. L. Angus (pictured) of Sutton Benger, Wilts. and powered by one 40 h.p. Salmson A.D.9 radial engine. One aircraft only: G-ABIK, c/n 1, taxying trials at Hanworth 1.31, destroyed in crash at Hanworth 21.3.31 and designer/pilot killed. Tare wt., 488 lb. A.U.W., 700 lb. Endurance 2 hr.

Armstrong Whitworth A.W.55 Apollo

Medium stage 26–31-passenger transport for the Ministry of Supply to civil specification 16/46 (Brabazon IIB), powered by four Armstrong Siddeley Mamba propeller-turbines. Two aircraft only: G-AIYN/VX220, c/n A.W.3137, with 1,135 e.h.p. Mamba A.S. Ma.1 engines (civil 503s), first flown 10.4.49, C. of A. 30.10.50 for trials at Boscombe Down; scrapped at Baginton 1955; G-AMCH/VX224, c/n A.W.3138, with 1,475 e.h.p. Mamba A.S. Ma.3s (504), first flown 12.12.52, to Empire Test Pilots' School, Farnborough, coded 15, dismantled at Farnborough 1957. Span, 92 ft. Length 71 ft $5\frac{1}{2}$ in. Tare wt., 31,000 lb. A.U.W., 47,000 lb. Range 1,130 miles at 280 m.p.h.

(A. J. Jackson)

Arpin A-1

Two-seat cabin monoplane designed and built by M. B. Arpin and Co. at West Drayton, Middlesex, 1937–38, powered by one 68 h.p. British Salmson A.D.9R pusher radial and fitted with MacLaren crosswind tricycle undercarriage. One aircraft only: G-AFGB, c/n 1, first flown at Hanworth by G. Wynne Eaton 7.5.38. Flown to R.Ae.S. Garden Party, Heathrow, next day. Re-engined 1939 as Mk. 2 with 90 h.p. Blackburn Cirrus Minor 1. To Old Sarum 11.12.39 for Army evaluation; stored until sold to T. L. McDonald, Balado, Fife, 12.45; scrapped 1946. Span 31 ft. 6 in. Length, 23 ft. 3 in. Tare wt., 740 lb. A.U.W. (Salmson), 1,261 lb. Cruise, 95 m.p.h. Endurance, 5 hours.

(Flight Photo 12150)

Arrow Active 1

Single-seat all-metal aerobatic biplane powered by one 115 h.p. Cirrus Hermes IIB, built 1931 by Arrow Aircraft Ltd., Leeds. One aircraft only: G-ABIX, c/n 1, C. of A. issued 21.5.31. Flown by Flt. Lt. E. C. T. Edwards in 1932 King's Cup Race at 132·2 m.p.h. Sold to Alex Henshaw 5·35, burnt out at Markschapel, Lincs. 30.12.35, owner landed by parachute. Span, 24 ft. 0 in. Length, 18 ft. 7 in. Tare wt., 853 lb. A.U.W., 1,210 lb. Max. speed, 140 m.p.h. Cruise, 125 m.p.h.

286

(*A. J. Jackson*)

Arrow Active 2

As Active 1, but with strutted centre section and 120 h.p. de Havilland Gipsy III. One aircraft only: G-ABVE, c/n 2, built 1932, C. of A. issued 29.6.32. Flown in 1932 and 1933 King's Cup Races by Flt. Lt. H. H. Leech at 137 m.p.h. Stored Yeadon until 1957, rebuilt with 145 h.p. Gipsy Major 1C for Norman Jones and the Tiger Club 1958. Span, 24 ft. 0 in. Length, 18 ft. 10 in. Tare wt., 925 lb. A.U.W., 1,325 lb. Max. speed, 144 m.p.h. Cruise, 128 m.p.h.

Auster J-1U Workmaster

Agricultural development of the Auster J-1N built for Crop Culture (Aerial) Ltd., Bembridge, for crop spraying in the Sudan, Central Africa and the U.K. Fitted with J-5R mainplane, J-5F ailerons, dorsal fin, 100 gallon insecticide tank, Micronair atomisers and powered by one 180 h.p Lycoming O-360-A1A. Prototype, G-APKP, first flown at Rearsby 22.2.58 followed by seven other British registered examples; (c/n 3501) F-OBHT/F-BJAS and (3507) F-OBRZ/TZ-ABX for export; and (3503) unfinished airframe. Span, 36 ft. 0 in. Length, 23 ft. 7 in. Tare wt., 1,800 lb. A.U.W., 2,650 lb. Cruise, 88 m.p.h.

Auster B.4

Four-seat pod and boom, rear loading, ambulance freighter, powered by one 180 h.p. Blackburn Cirrus Bombardier 702, built by Auster Aircraft Ltd., Rearsby. One aircraft only: G-AMKL, c/n 2983, first flown 7.9.51 as G-25-2; rebuilt with ventral fin 1952; evaluated by the Army and Boscombe Down as XA177; dismantled at Rearsby 1956. Span, 24 ft. 8 in. Length, 37 ft. 0 in. Tare wt., 1,730 lb. A.U.W., 2,700 lb. Max. speed, 121 m.p.h. Cruise, 103 m.p.h.

(*A. J. Jackson*)

Auster C.6 Atlantic

Four-seat executive tourer powered by one 185 h.p. Continental E-185-10 and equipped with tricycle undercarriage. One aircraft only: G-25-5/G-APHT, c/n 3447, statically exhibited fully furnished but without mainplanes at the S.B.A.C. Show, Farnborough, September 1957. Development of type abandoned, aircraft stored at Rearsby until 1959 when it was removed to long term storage at Burton-on-the-Wolds. Span, 36 ft. 0 in. Length, 23 ft. 10 in. A.U.W., 2,700 lb. Cruise, 127 m.p.h.

Austin Kestrel

Side-by-side two-seater powered by one 160 h.p. Beardmore, built for the 1920 Air Ministry Competition by the Austin Motor Co. Ltd., Northfield, Birmingham. One aircraft only: G-EATR, no c/n, reg'd. to the makers 10.6.20, C. of A. 7.8.20, awarded 3rd prize of £1,500 in small aeroplane class, pilot M. D. Nares. Put up for sale with spares 5.24, disposed of to Fraser's Flying School, Kingsbury, London, but never used. Span, 38 ft. 6 in. Length, 25 ft. 6 in. Tare wt., 1,966 lb. A.U.W., 2,740 lb. Max. speed, 110 m.p.h. Cruise, 83 m.p.h.

(Aeroplane)

Aviation Traders A.T.L. 90 Accountant 1

Medium range 28-passenger airliner powered by two 1,740 e.h.p. Rolls-Royce Dart 512 turboprops, built by Aviation Traders (Engineering) Ltd. at Southend. One aircraft only: G-ATEL, c/n A.T.L. 90, first flown as G-41-1 by L. P. Stuart-Smith 9.7.57, to Farnborough S.B.A.C. Show 9.57, last flight at Southend 10.1.58, development abandoned, cocooned until reduced to produce at Southend 2–3.2.60. Span, 82 ft 6 in. Length 62 ft. 1 in. Tare wt., 16,961 lb. A.U.W., 28,500 lb. Cruise 250 knots over max. stage length of 2,070 miles.

Avro 538

Single-seater powered by one 150 h.p. Bentley B.R.1, constructed from Avro 504K components by A. V. Roe and Co. Ltd., Manchester, 1919. One aircraft only: K-132/G-EACR, c/n 538/1. Used as communications aircraft by J. C. C. Taylor, ground engineer i/c the Avro Transport Company's nation-wide fleet of joyriding Avro 504Ks. Scrapped 9.20. Span, 28 ft. 0 in. Length, 20 ft. 6 in. Tare wt., 975 lb. A.U.W., 1,400 lb. Max. speed, 125 m.p.h. Cruise, 108 m.p.h.

Avro 539A

Single-seat floatplane powered by one 240 h.p. Siddeley Puma, built for 1919 Schneider Trophy by A. V. Roe and Co. Ltd., Hamble. One aircraft only: G-EALG, c/n 539/1, first flown 29.8.19. Modified with balanced rudder and elongated fin prior to contest 10.9.19, from which it was eliminated. Pilot H. A. Hamersley. Converted to landplane with smaller fin for Aerial Derby at Hendon 24.7.20. Pilot D. G. Westgarth-Heslam who force landed at Abridge, Essex. Span, 25 ft. 6 in. Length, 21 ft. 4 in. Tare wt., 1,670 lb. A.U.W., 2,119 lb.

Avro 539B

The Avro 539A rebuilt at Hamble for the 1921 Aerial Derby with 450 h.p. Napier Lion cooled by side-mounted radiators, plywood rear fuselage and revised undercarriage. One aircraft only: G-EAXM, c/n 539B/1, destroyed in landing accident at Hamble on 15 July 1921, eve of the race. D. G. Westgarth-Heslam seriously injured when the aircraft overshot into a railway cutting. Dimensions similar to Avro 539A landplane.

Avro 547

Five-seat commercial triplane using standard Avro 504K components, built 1920 by A. V. Roe and Co. Ltd. at Hamble and powered by one 160 h.p. Beardmore. One aircraft only: G-EAQX, c/n 547/1. Sold to H. E. Broadsmith, Sydney, N.S.W., 11.20 as G-AUCR and to Q.A.N.T.A.S. 6.21. Span, 37 ft. 3 in. Length, 29 ft. 10 in. Tare wt., 2,077 lb. A.U.W., 3,000 lb. Max. speed, 94 m.p.h. Cruise, 80 m.p.h.

Avro 547A

Modified version of Avro 547 powered by one 240 h.p. Siddeley Puma. One aircraft only: G-EAUJ, c/n 547A/1, C. of A. issued 25.8.20, built for the 1920 Air Ministry competition, in which it was piloted by H. A. Hamersley. Sold to F. G. Miles, Shoreham, as spares 1928. Span, 37 ft. 3 in. Length, 29 ft. 10 in. Tare wt, 2,077 lb. A.U.W., 3,200 lb. Max. speed, 95 m.p.h. Cruise, 80 m.p.h.

Avro 558

Single-seat ultra-light built for the 1923 light aeroplane trials by A. V. Roe and Co. Ltd. at Hamble. Two aircraft only, Nos. 5 and 11, powered by 500 cc. B. & H. and Douglas motor cycle engines respectively. No. 11, c/n 5089, was registered to G. E. Bush and H. A. Hamersley 19.9.23 as G-EBHW and established a class height record of 13,850 ft. over Lympne 13.10.23. Last heard of at Hendon 27.10.23. Span, 30 ft. 0 in. Length, 21 ft. 0 in. Tare wt., 294 lb. A.U.W., 480 lb.

Avro 562 Avis

Two-seater built for the 1924 Lympne Light Aeroplane Trials by A. V. Roe and Co. Ltd. at Hamble and powered by a 32 h.p. Bristol Cherub II. One aircraft only: No. 10, c/n 5105, first flown by H. J. Hinkler at Lympne 30.9.24. Won Grosvenor Trophy 1.10.24 at 65·87 m.p.h. Registered 19.12.24 as G-EBKP, C. of A. 1.2.26. Re-engined with three-cylinder 35 h.p. Blackburne Thrush for 1926 Lympne Trials, pilot W. Sholto Douglas. Fitted with Cherub I and sold to E. L. O. Baddeley 10.27 and to T. S. Baldwin, Totnes, 10.28, scrapped 1932. Span, 30 ft. Length, 24 ft. Tare wt., 565 lb. A.U.W., 943 lb. Max. speed, 75 m.p.h.

Avro 563 Andover

Twelve-passenger airliner powered by one 650 h.p. Rolls-Royce Condor IIIA, built 1925 by A. V. Roe and Co. Ltd., Hamble. One aircraft only: G-EBKW, c/n 5097, C. of A. issued 21.4.25, owned by the Air Council. Loaned to Imperial Airways Ltd. 1925 for cross-Channel proving flights, overhauled at Hamble 1926, to the R.A.F. 1.27 as J7264, erected at Halton. Span, 68 ft. 0 in. Length, 51 ft. 7 in. Tare wt., 6,800 lb. A.U.W., 10,685 lb. Max. speed, 110 m.p.h. Cruise, 90 m.p.h.

(Aeroplane)

Avro 627 Mailplane

Single-seat mailplane powered by one 525 h.p. Armstrong Siddeley Panther IIA, for trial flights by Canadian Airways Ltd. Built by A. V. Roe and Co. Ltd., Manchester, 1931. One aircraft only: G-ABJM, c/n 502, C. of A. issued 2.8.31, conversion of unfinished Avro 608 Hawk G-EBWM, c/n 5125. Toured Canada 1931, fastest time in 1932 King's Cup Race at 176 m.p.h., piloted by H. A. Brown. Converted to Armstrong Siddeley Tiger VI testbed 6.33, dismantled at Woodford 1934. Span, 36 ft. 0 in. Length, 30 ft. 10 in. Tare wt., 3,077 lb. A.U.W., 5,150 lb. Max. speed, 175 m.p.h.

(Flight Photo)

Avro 641 Commodore

Five-seat tourer powered by one 215 h.p. Armstrong Siddeley Lynx IVC and using the same metal construction and staggered N-strutted wings as the Avro Tutor. Prototype, G-ACNT, delivered Woodford-Heston 24.5.34, was followed by five production aircraft only. Two were sold in Egypt in 1936 and two were impressed during the 1939–45 war. The final machine, VT-AFN (c/n 759), supplied to the Maharajah of Vizianagram, was found unsuitable for Indian conditions and returned to Woodford to be scrapped in 1935. Span, 37 ft. 4 in. Length, 27 ft. 3 in. Tare wt., 2,225 lb. A.U.W., 3,500 lb. Cruise, 110 m.p.h.

(*Aeroplane*)

B.A.3 Cupid

Side-by-side two-seater powered by one 130 h.p. de Havilland Gipsy Major built at Hanworth 1935 by the British Aircraft Manufacturing Co. Ltd. One aircraft only: G-ADLR, c/n 701, C. of A. issued 29.8.35. Owner Charles Best, Hanworth; averaged 142 m.p.h. in King's Cup Race 7.9.35 piloted by J. G. Armour; sold in South Africa 1936 but not re-registered. Span, 35 ft. 0 in. Length, 23 ft. 4 in. Maximum speed, 135 m.p.h.

(*Aeroplane*)

B.A.IV Double Eagle

Six-seater with backward retracting undercarriage built by the British Aircraft Mfg. Co. Ltd. at Hanworth 1936–37. Three aircraft only (c/n 901–903): G-ADVV, two 130 h.p. D.H. Gipsy Majors, first flown as Y-1, C. of A. 3.7.36, C. Best, Hanworth; Sir Derwent Hall Caine, Hatfield 5.38; 5th in Isle of Man Race 1938 flown by T. W. Morton; impressed 7.41 as ES949, s.o.c. 4.44. G-AEIN, two 200 h.p. D.H. Gipsy VIs, C. of A. 2.7.36, Lord Willoughby de Broke, Hanworth; 3rd in King's Cup Race 11.7.36, pilot J. B. Wilson; flown in 1936 Johannesburg Race by Tommy Rose, retired at Almaza; North Western Air Transport Ltd., Speke 5.39; airframe impressed 7.41 for instructional use as ES950. ZS-AIY, C. of A. 18.6.37, aerial survey version for the Aircraft Operating Co. Ltd., flown to Johannesburg 7.37, re-registered ZS-AOC on arrival, impressed 1940 as S.A.A.F. 1415. Span, 41 ft. 0 in. Length, 29 ft. 10 in. Tare wt. (Gipsy Majors), 2,000 lb. A.U.W., 3,500 lb. Max. speed 165 m.p.h. Cruise, 145 m.p.h.

B.A.C.-Aérospatiale Concorde

Supersonic passenger transport built as a joint Anglo-French project by the British Aircraft Corporation Ltd. and Sud-Aviation. French prototype F-WTSS (c/n 001) first flown at Toulouse by André Turcat 2.3.69, British prototype G-BSST (Bristol c/n 13520) first flown Filton–Fairford by Brian Trubshaw 9.4.69. First Filton-built pre-production aircraft G-AXDN (13522) illustrated, registered 16.4.69, first flown 17.12.71. Production aircraft powered by four 35,080 lb. s.t. Rolls-Royce/SNECMA Olympus 593 turbojets. Span, 83 ft. 10 in. Length, 193 ft. 0 in. Tare wt., 166,200 lb. A.U.W., 385,000 lb. Cruise, 1,355 m.p.h. above 50,000 ft. Range, 4,530 miles.

(W. K. Kilsby)

Barnwell B.S.W. Mk. 1

Single-seat ultra-light, powered by one 28 h.p. Scott Squirrel, designed by F. S. Barnwell and built for his own use at Whitchurch 1938. One aircraft only: G-AFID, c/n 1, A. of F. issued 25.6.38, crashed at Whitchurch and F. S. Barnwell killed 2.8.38. The designation B.S.W. signified 'Barnwell Scott Whitchurch'. Span, 25 ft. 0 in. A.U.W., 750 lb.

Beagle B.218X

Experimental four-seat, low-wing monoplane of composite light alloy and fibre glass construction powered by two 145 h.p. Rolls-Royce Continental O-300-C flat-six engines. One aircraft only, c/n B.051, initially known as the Beagle-Miles M.218, first flown at Shoreham 19.8.62 by G. H. Miles as G-35-6, flown as G-ASCK at the Farnborough S.B.A.C Show 9.62, C. of A. 13.6.63, rebuilt as the Beagle B.242X in 1964. Span, 37 ft. 0 in. Length, 25 ft. 4 in. Tare wt., 2,164 lb. A.U.W., 3,200 lb. Max. speed, 185 m.p.h. Cruise 140 m.p.h.

Beagle B.242X

The Beagle B.218X reconstructed at Shoreham 1964 as an all-metal four-seat scaled-down version of the Beagle B.206 and powered by two 195 h.p. Rolls-Royce Continental IO-360-A flat-six engines. One aircraft only: G-ASTX, c/n B.053, first flown 27.8.64 by J. W. C. Judge, demonstrated at the Farnborough S.B.A.C. Show 9.64, C. of A. 18.6.65, tail surfaces modified and c/n changed 3.66 to B.242/001, production abandoned 1967. Span, 37 ft. 0 in. Length, 24 ft. 9 in. Tare wt., 2,510 lb. A.U.W., 3,600 lb. Max. speed, 212 m.p.h. Cruise, 162 m.p.h. Max. range 836 miles.

Beardmore W.B. IIB

Two-seater powered by one 160 h.p. Beardmore, built by William Beardmore and Co. Ltd. at Dalmuir, Dunbartonshire, 1920. Two aircraft only: G-EARX, c/n 5441/1, flown by Capt. Ward on Renfrew–Cricklewood proving flight 5.11.20, crashed at Huntingdon 12.12.20; G-EARY, c/n 5441/2, shown at Olympia Aero Show 7.20, flown by Capt. Ward on Renfrew–Croydon proving flight 17.9.20, C. of A. 21.2.22, w.f.u. 1922. Span, 34 ft. 10 in. Length, 27 ft. 7 in. Wing area, 354 sq. ft. Tare wt., 1,750 lb. A.U.W., 2,516 lb. Max. speed 107 m.p.h.

(*G. Clephane*)

Beardmore W.B.X

All-metal two-seater powered by one 185 h.p. Beardmore, built at Dalmuir 1920 for the Air Ministry commercial aeroplane competition at Martlesham. One aircraft only: G-EAQJ, c/n 5442, to Martlesham by road incomplete, weighed 7.8.20, flown only once by G. Powell 16.8.20, withdrawn from use at end of trials. Span, 46 ft. 0 in. Length, 26 ft. 0 in. Wing area, 540 sq. ft. Tare wt., 1,852 lb. A.U.W., 2,849 lb. Max. speed 91 m.p.h. Estimated endurance $4\frac{3}{4}$ hr.

(*W. K. Kilsby*)

Beardmore W.B.XXIV Wee Bee I

Two-seater powered by one 32 h.p. Bristol Cherub, built Dalmuir for the Air Ministry 1924 Lympne Light Aeroplane Trials. Won the principal money prize piloted by Maurice Pearcy. One aircraft only: G-EBJJ, c/n W.B. XXIV, C. of A. issued 4.3.30. Sold in Australia 1933 by Norman Edgar, Whitchurch; still flying in 1948 as VH-URJ. Span, 38 ft. 10 in. Length, 22 ft. 2 in. Tare wt., 462 lb. A.U.W., 840 lb. Max. speed, 87 m.p.h.

(*P. J. Bish*)

Bensen B-7M and B-8M Gyrocopters

Single-seat autogyro designed by Igor B. Bensen in the U.S.A. 1955. Six B-7M aircraft home-built in the U.K. 1959–62 fitted with 72 h.p. McCulloch target drone engines were followed by B-8M aircraft (90 h.p. McCulloch 4318E) built mainly from kits supplied by Campbell Aircraft Ltd., Hungerford. Three built at Luton by Napier 1961 flew as G-29-2 to 4. B-8M aircraft licence-built by Campbell appear separately in Appendix E. Rotor diameter, 20 ft. 0 in. Length, 11 ft. 4 in. Tare wt., 247 lb. A.U.W., 500 lb. Max. speed, 85 m.p.h. Cruise, 45 m.p.h.

(*Southern Newspapers*)

Bellamy Hilborne B.H.1 Halcyon

All-wood four-seater with retractable nosewheel undercarriage, powered by two 105 h.p. Walter Minor engines, designed by R. J. Hilborne and built at Eastleigh by the Hampshire Aero Club under the direction of V. H. Bellamy 1960–61. One aircraft only: G-ARIO, c/n HAC.5, registered to V. H. Bellamy 1.61. Construction reached the stage shown in the illustration 5.61 and engines were run 9.61 but the project was abandoned when the aircraft was damaged during taxying trials 2.62. Span, 30 ft. 5 in. Length, 23 ft. 7 in. A.U.W., 1,800 lb. Cruise, 150 m.p.h. Range, 300 miles.

Blackburn Sidecar

Side-by-side two-seat ultra-light powered by one 40 h.p. A.B.C. Gnat, built by the Blackburn Aeroplane and Motor Co. Ltd. at Brough 1919. One aircraft only: G-EALN, owner K. M. Smith, exhibited at Harrods 3.19 and afterwards sold to Haydon-White; re-engined with 100 h.p. Anzani 1921. Span, 27 ft. 3 in. Length, 20 ft. 6 in. Tare wt., 123 lb. Max. speed, 83 m.p.h.

300

(*Topical Press*)

Blackburn Pellet

Single-seat flying-boat powered by one 450 h.p. Napier Lion, built at Brough for the 1923 Schneider Trophy Race. One aircraft only, G-EBHF, launched at Brough 9.23, overturned and sank. Repaired and sent to Hamble by rail, launched from Fairey's slipway 26.9.23 and first flown by R. W. Kenworthy who was forced to alight on the sea off Calshot. Towed to Cowes where it sank in a take-off accident 27.9.23, Kenworthy rescued. Span, 34 ft. 0 in. Length, 28 ft. 7 in. A.U.W., 2,800 lb. Estimated max. speed, 160 m.p.h.

(*Flight Photo 12391*)

Blackburn Monoplane

Unnamed all-metal ten-seater powered by two 400 h.p. Armstrong Siddeley Jaguar IVC, built at Brough 1932. One aircraft only: G-ABKV, W/O 2780/1, constructed to Air Ministry order for comparative trials with near-identical biplane G-ABKW. First flown by A. M. Blake 4.10.32, shown at Hendon R.A.F. Display 14.6.33; to Farnborough 1.34 as K4241; to No. 2 A.S.U., Cardington 2.37, flew 232 hr. 10 min.; scrapped at Martlesham 12.37. Span, 86 ft. 0 in. Length, 55 ft. 3 in. Tare wt., 8,818 lb. A.U.W., 13,074 lb. Max. speed, 128 m.p.h. Cruise, 110 m.p.h.

Blackburn Biplane

Unnamed all-metal ten-seater powered by two 400 h.p. Armstrong Siddeley Jaguar IVC, built at Brough 1932. One aircraft only: G-ABKW, W/O 2781/1, constructed to Air Ministry order for comparative trials with near-identical monoplane G-ABKV. First flown by A. M. Blake 10.6.32, shown at Hendon R.A.F. Display 25.6.32; to Martlesham for test 27.1.33; registration cancelled 1.34. Both aircraft were designed by B. A. Duncan and nicknamed 'The Duncan Sisters'. Span, 64 ft. 0 in. Length, 55 ft. 0 in. Tare wt., 7,931 lb. A.U.W., 12,150 lb. Max. speed, 118 m.p.h. Cruise, 110 m.p.h.

(*Boulton and Paul*)

Boulton and Paul P.8

Long-range machine, powered by two 450 h.p. Napier Lion engines, designed by J. D. North and built at Norwich 1919 for the *Daily Mail* £10,000 transatlantic flight competition. Two aircraft only: Prototype (c/n P.8-1), unregistered, crashed on its maiden flight; G-EAPE (P.8-2), registered to Boulton and Paul Ltd. 6.11.19 and completed as a mailplane. First flown at Mousehold 10.5.20 but used only experimentally. Span, 61 ft. 0 in. Length, 40 ft. 0 in. Tare wt., 4,000 lb. A.U.W., 7,000 lb. Max. speed 149 m.p.h.

Boulton and Paul P.41 Phoenix I

Two-seat development prototype of an intended private owner's machine designed by J. D. North and built at Norwich 1929. It was a braced parasol monoplane of fabric-covered wooden construction powered by one 40 h.p. A.B.C. Scorpion, with the rudder identical to each half of the all-moving tailplane to reduce the number of spares. One aircraft only: G-AAIT (P.41-1), registered to Boulton and Paul Ltd. 11.6.29, shown at the Olympia Aero Show, London, 7.29 and flown at Mousehold by J. Dawson Paul later in the year. Dimensions and data were not released.

Boulton and Paul P.41 Phoenix II

The original Phoenix, G-AAIT, rebuilt in 1930 with redesigned fuselage and undercarriage, and re-engined with a 40 h.p. Salmson nine cylinder radial. Used for full-scale aerodynamic research at Mousehold. Withdrawn from use, registration cancelled 11.35. Span, 30 ft. 0 in. A.U.W., 1,000 lb.

303

Boulton and Paul P.64 Mailplane

Clean twin-engined, all-metal biplane designed by J. D. North to Spec. 21/28 to carry two crew and 175 cu. ft. of mail, powered by two 555 h.p. Bristol Pegasus I.M2 radials in nine-sided Townend-type cowlings. Prototype only, G-ABYK, first flown at Mousehold, Norwich, 3.33 by Sqn. Ldr. C. A. Rea. Wrecked when it struck the ground following an unexplained dive during the third test flight of the Martlesham trials 21.10.33. Flt. Lt. G. L. G. Richmond killed. Span, 54 ft. 0 in. Length, 42 ft. 6 in. Tare wt., 6,125 lb. A.U.W., 10,500 lb. Cruise 172 m.p.h. Range, 1,250 miles.

Boulton and Paul P.71A

Lightened version of the P.64 with slimmer and longer fuselage, three rudders and two 490 h.p. Armstrong Siddeley Jaguar VIA radials in circular cowlings. Two aircraft only: G-ACOX 'Boadicea' and G-ACOY 'Britomart' delivered to Imperial Airways Ltd. at Croydon 2.35 and there equipped with 7 removable seats as V.I.P. transports or light freighters. G-ACOX damaged beyond repair landing at Haren, Brussels, 25.10.35; G-ACOY lost in the English Channel 25.9.36. Span, 54 ft. 0 in. Length, 44 ft. 2 in. Tare wt., 6,100 lb. A.U.W., 9,500 lb. Cruise, 150 m.p.h. Range, 600 miles.

(Bristol Photo)

Bristol Badger X

The Badger X (X for Experimental), also known as 'Capt. Barnwell's Weekender' was built at Filton in 1919 by combining the wings and tail unit of the Badger Mk. I fighter F3497 and a new, flat sided plywood single-seat fuselage. This machine, K-110/G-EABU, c/n 5658, was powered by a 240 h.p. Siddeley Puma and first flew at Filton 13.5.19 piloted by C. F. Uwins. Withdrawn from use after Barnwell turned it over on the ground at Filton 22.5.19. Span, 34 ft. 2 in. Length, 24 ft.

(Bristol Photo)

Bristol Types 30 and 46 Babe

Single-seat lightplane built at Filton 1919–20. Three aircraft only: Mk. I (c/n 5866), Type 30, 35 h.p. Viale radial, first flown at Filton by C. F. Uwins 28.11.19, converted to Mk. III, Type 46A with 60 h.p. Le Rhône and flown as G-EAQD in 1920; Mk. III (5867), Type 46A, flown as G-EASQ, 1920, converted to low-wing monoplane Type 46B but not flown; (5875), unregistered Mk. II, Type 46, shown at the 1919 Paris Salon with incomplete 40 h.p. two-cylinder Siddeley Ounce. Span, 19 ft. 8 in. Length, 14 ft. 11 in. Tare wt., 460 lb. A.U.W., (Viale) 683 lb. (Le Rhône) 840 lb. Max. speed, 80 m.p.h.

Bristol Types 32 and 32A Bullet

Single-seater built at Filton 1919 as flying testbed for the 450 h.p. Cosmos (later Bristol) Jupiter radial. One aircraft only: G-EATS, c/n 5869, shown at the 1919 Paris Salon and averaged 129 m.p.h. in the Aerial Derby 24.7.20 piloted by C. F. Uwins. Rebuilt later in 1920 as Type 32A with new large-diameter fuselage which almost totally enclosed the Jupiter engine, metal-clad forward of the cockpit and streamlined by an outsize hemispherical spinner. Span, 31 ft. 2 in. Length, 24 ft. 1 in. Tare wt., 1,800 lb. A.U.W., 2,300 lb. Max. speed, 155 m.p.h.

Bristol Type 32B Bullet

Same aircraft further rebuilt in 1921 with short-span tapered mainplanes with the ailerons on the lower instead of the upper wing. Flown in the 1921 Aerial Derby by C. F. Uwins, coming fourth at an average speed of 141·38 m.p.h. With the spinner removed it was flown in the 1922 Aerial Derby by Rollo de Haga Haig, who came second at 145 m.p.h. Fitted with long-stroke oleo undercarriage 1.23, scrapped in 1924. Span, 22 ft. 4 in. Length, 24 ft. 1 in. Tare wt., 1,700 lb. A.U.W., 2,300 lb. Max. speed, 170 m.p.h.

(Bristol Photo)

Bristol Type 62

Transport for two crew and eight passengers built at Filton 1921. One aircraft only: G-EAWY, c/n 6124, initially fitted with a four-wheel undercarriage and powered by one 450 h.p. Napier Lion. Converted to two-wheel undercarriage 10.21, C. of A. issued 14.2.22. Used on the Croydon–Paris route of Handley Page Transport Ltd., making its fastest trip in 2 hours 15 minutes on 18.3.22. Span, 57 ft 3 in. Length, 42 ft. 0 in. Tare wt., 3,900 lb. A.U.W., 6,800 lb. Max. speed, 112 m.p.h.

(Bristol Photo)

Bristol Type 72

Single-seat racer designed by W. T. Reid with monocoque fuselage, enclosed 480 h.p. Bristol Jupiter IV with ducted cooling, and retractable undercarriage. One aircraft only: G-EBDR, c/n 6148, built at Filton 1922. Made only a few development flights, piloted by C. F. Uwins. Racing No. 10 allotted for the 1922 Aerial Derby, for which it was not ready, scrapped 1924. Span, 25 ft. 2 in. Length, 21 ft. 7 in. Estimated max. speed, 220 m.p.h.

Bristol Type 75

Jupiter IV engined development of the Type 62 for 2 crew and 8 passengers, first flown at Filton 7.22. Three aircraft only: (c/n 6145), G-EBEV, converted to Type 75A freighter, C. of A. 16.7.24, leased to Imperial Airways Ltd., first service to Cologne 22.7.24, withdrawn from use 1926; (6146) Type 79 Brandon ambulance version, first flown 19.3.24, to the R.A.F. 22.5.25 as J6997; (6147) unfinished airframe dismantled for spares 10.23. Span, 56 ft. 0 in. Length, 40 ft. 6 in. Tare wt., 4,000 lb. A.U.W., 6,755 lb. Max. speed, 110 m.p.h.

Bristol Type 99 Badminton

Single-seat equal-span racing biplane of fabric covered, wood and metal construction designed by F. S. Barnwell, powered initially by a 510 h.p. up-rated Bristol Jupiter VI and first flown at Filton by C. F. Uwins 5.5.26. One aircraft only: G-EBMK, c/n 6921, piloted by F. L. Barnard in the 1926 King's Cup Race but forced landed by the Thames at Oxford with fuel feed trouble. Span, 24 ft. 1 in. Length, 21 ft. $2\frac{3}{8}$ in. Tare wt., 1,840 lb. A.U.W., 2,460 lb. Max. speed, 160 m.p.h.

(*Bristol Photo*)

Bristol Type 99A Badminton

The Bristol Type 99 rebuilt in 1927 with wide-span, tapered wings, raised centre section, wide-chord interplane struts and uncowled 525 h.p. Bristol Jupiter VI. C. of A. issued 26.7.27 but crashed and F. L. Barnard killed 28.7.27 when it spun in after engine failure on take-off from Filton. Span, 33 ft. 0 in. Length, 21 ft. 5 in. Tare wt., 1,780 lb. A.U.W., 2,500 lb. Max. speed 160 m.p.h.

(*Bristol Photo*)

Bristol Type 109

Two-seater powered by one 480 h.p. Bristol Jupiter VIII, built at Filton 1928 for attempt on world long-distance record. One aircraft only: R-2/G-EBZK, c/n 7268, first flown 7.9.28. Attempt abandoned and machine modified for world flight by H. J. Hinkler; this also abandoned and aircraft used as Jupiter XIF testbed, completing its 250 hour sealed test in 1929. C. of A. issued 20.9.30, scrapped 1931. Span, 51 ft. 2 in. Length, 37 ft. 9 in. Tare wt., 4,600 lb. A.U.W., 9,800 lb.

(*Bristol Photo*)

Bristol Type 110A

Five-seater of fabric-covered metal construction designed by F. S. Barnwell. One aircraft only: G-AAFG, c/n 7348, exhibited at the Olympia Aero Show, London, 7.29. First flown at Filton with 220 h.p. Bristol Titan by C. F. Uwins 25.10.29. Later flown with 315 h.p. Bristol Neptune, damaged landing at Filton 2.31 and scrapped. Span, 40 ft. 6 in. Length, 33 ft. 6 in. Tare wt., 2,330 lb. A.U.W., 4,360 lb. Max. speed, 125 m.p.h.

(*Bristol Photo*)

Bristol Type 142

All-metal twin-engined low-wing executive transport for two crew and four passengers, powered by two 560 h.p. Bristol Mercury VIS. 2, built at Filton 1935 to the order of Lord Rothermere. One aircraft only: R-12/G-ADCZ, c/n 7838, first flight 12.4.35. Martlesham trials found it more than 50 m.p.h. faster than contemporary fighters. Presented to the nation 7.35 as K7557 'Britain First'. Shown at the Hendon R.A.F. Display 27.6.36. Forerunner of the Blenheim bomber. Span, 56 ft. 0 in. Length, 39 ft. 9 in. Tare wt., 6,822 lb. A.U.W., 9,357 lb. Max. speed, 307 m.p.h. Cruise, 250 m.p.h. Range, 1,000 miles.

(Bristol Photo)

Bristol Type 143

Ten-seat transport powered by two 600 h.p. Bristol Aquila I, built at Filton 1935. One aircraft only: R-14/G-ADEK, c/n 7839, first flown 20.1.36, demonstrated by C. F. Uwins at Bristol Aeroplane Club meeting, Whitchurch, 5.9.36, design not proceeded with due to pressure of Blenheim production, stored without engines and scrapped during 1939–45 war. Span, 56 ft. 6 in. Length, 42 ft. 0 in. Tare wt., 7,000 lb. A.U.W., 11,000 lb. Max. speed, 240 m.p.h. Cruise, 200 m.p.h.

(Bristol Photo)

Bristol Type 167 Brabazon

Transatlantic transport designed by L. G. Frise and A. E. Russell, built at Filton 1944–49, powered by eight 2,500 h.p. Bristol Centaurus 20 engines driving four pairs of contra-rotating airscrews. Two aircraft only: VX206/G-AGPW, c/n 12759, first flown 4.9.49 by A. J. Pegg, C. of A. issued 14.6.50, broken up at Filton 10.53; VX343/G-AIML, c/n 12870, intended as Brabazon 2 with Proteus turbo-props but broken up when half completed. Brabazon 1 G-AGPW was the largest landplane ever built in Britain and cost some £3 million. Span, 230 ft. 0 in. Length, 177 ft. 0 in. Tare wt., 159,310 lb. A.U.W., 290,000 lb. (or nearly 130 tons). Range, 5,500 miles at 250 m.p.h. cruising speed.

British Burnelli OA-1

British redesign of the American lifting-fuselage Burnelli U.B.14. Fifteen-seater powered by two 710 h.p. Bristol Perseus XIVC, built by Cunliffe Owen Aircraft Ltd., at Eastleigh 1938. One aircraft only: G-AFMB, c/n OA-1, based at Martlesham Heath in 1940, C. of A. 27.11.40; impressed 5.41 but ferried in camouflage and wartime civil marks to the Free French Air Force in West Africa by James Mollison 7.41, still there 12.43. Span, 73 ft. 6 in. Length, 44 ft. 0 in. Tare wt., 9,500 lb. A.U.W., 19,000 lb. Max. speed, 225 m.p.h. Range, 1,950 miles.

Britten-Norman BN-1F (J.A.P.)

Single-seat ultra-light powered by one 40 h.p. Aeronca J.A.P. J-99, designed and built at Bembridge 1950 by John Britten and Desmond Norman. One aircraft only: G-ALZE, c/n 1, internally sprung cantilever undercarriage. During early trials the engine failed on take-off and the aircraft was seriously damaged in the ensuing forced landing. Rebuilt as shown in the next illustration.

(A. W. J. G. Ord-Hume)

Britten-Norman BN-1F (Lycoming)

The original aircraft reconstructed in 1951 with 55 h.p. Lycoming flat-four engine, strut-braced undercarriage, increased rudder area and modified mainplane to take inset ailerons. First flown at Bembridge 26.5.51 by Geoffrey Alington; withdrawn from use 4.53, airframe stored for some years in a boathouse at Bembridge Harbour. Span, 23 ft. 0 in. Length, 16 ft. 7 in. Tare wt., 408 lb. A.U.W., 630 lb. Max. speed, 84 m.p.h. Cruise, 75 m.p.h.

(Flight Photo 70–7559)

Britten-Norman BN-3 Nymph

All-metal four-seater intended for purchaser-assembly from Bembridge-built kits with choice of engines. Prototype only: G-AXFB, c/n 5001, C. of A. 28.5.69, one 115 h.p. Lycoming O-235-C1B, initially, built in 53 days and first flown at Bembridge by Desmond Norman, with John Britten and A. J. Coombe, on 17 May 1969. Span, 39 ft. 4 in. Length, 23 ft. 6½ in. Tare wt., 1,140 lb. A.U.W., 1,825 lb. Cruise, 113 m.p.h. Range, 500 miles.

Brookland Mosquito

Single-seat gyrocopter with 1,500 cc. converted Volkswagen, designed by E. Brooks and built at Brookland Garage, Spennymoor, Co. Durham. Mk. 1, G-ATSW, first flown by designer at Tees-side 7.66; Mk. 2, G-AVYW, 1,600 cc. Volkswagen, flown 6.68. After the death of the designer in this aircraft at Tees-side 9.3.69, production continued as the Hornet (illustrated). Rotor diameter, 21 ft. 0 in. Length, 11 ft. 0 in. Tare wt., 290 lb. A.U.W., 510 lb. Cruise, 70 m.p.h. Range, 140 miles.

Broughton-Blayney Brawney

Single-seater with 30 h.p. Carden Ford designed by F. W. Broughton and built at Hanworth 1936 as a development of the Perman Parasol (see Vol. 3). Three aircraft only: G-AENM, 'RF and 'RG, whose brief careers will be found in Appendix E. Span, 25 ft. 6 in. Length, 15 ft. 6 in. Cruise, 70 m.p.h. Range, 200 miles.

Campbell Cricket

Single-seat gyrocopter powered by one 75 h.p. Volkswagen designed by Peter Lovegrove and assembled by Campbell Aircraft Ltd. at Membury Airfield near Newbury, Berks. Details of prototype G-AXNU, first flown by Geoff Whatley 11.69, and 33 production aircraft, are listed in Appendix E. Rotor diameter, 21 ft. 9 in. Length, 11 ft. 3 in. Tare wt., 295 lb. A.U.W., 650 lb. Cruise, 62 m.p.h.

Campbell Curlew

Two-seat cabin gyroplane designed by Campbell Aircraft Ltd for assembly at Membury. Mock-up of prototype, G-AXFJ, c/n CA.316, in its original form with 28 h.p. Mercury pusher engine, exhibited at the Paris Air Show 5.69. The production version with 160 h.p. Lycoming O-320-B was not built. Rotor diameter, 21 ft. 6 in. Length, 12 ft. 6 in. Tare wt., 550 lb. A.U.W., 900 lb. Cruise, 70 m.p.h.

Carden-Baynes Bee

Side-by-side two-seater powered by two 40 h.p. Carden Ford S.P.1 supercharged, water-cooled, converted car engines driving pusher airscrews. Built by Carden-Baynes Aircraft Ltd. at Heston 1936. One aircraft only: G-AEWC, c/n 1, first flown at Heston by Hubert Broad 3.4.37; scrapped 1939. Span, 29 ft. 10 in. Length, 23 ft. 0 in. Tare wt., 880 lb. A.U.W., 1,350 lb. Estimated max. speed, 110 m.p.h. Cruise, 100 m.p.h.

Carden-Baynes Scud III

Single-seat auxiliary sailplane powered by one retractable $2\frac{1}{2}$ h.p. Villiers two-stroke, built 1935 by Abbotts-Baynes Aircraft Ltd., Farnham, Surrey to the joint designs of Sir John Carden and L. E. Baynes. One aircraft only: BGA. 283, first flown at Woodley 8.8.35 by J. P. Dewsbery; registered to J. Clarke of Dunstable as G-ALJR 16.3.49; C. of A. issued 6.4.49; converted to glider as BGA. 684 at Kidlington 1953. Span, 45 ft. 6 in. Length, 20 ft. 0 in. A.U.W., 500 lb. Climb, 230 ft./min. Cruise (motor retracted), 35–40 m.p.h.

(*P. R. March*)

Cassutt 3M

Single-seat racer designed by T. W. A. captain, Tom Cassutt of Roslyn Heights, N.Y., in 1954. Three examples, G-AXDZ, 'EA and 'EB, powered by 90 h.p. Continental C-90-8F engines, built by Airmark Ltd. at Redhill 1969–72, the first of which made its racing debut at Halfpenny Green in the Goodyear Trophy Race 1.9.69 piloted by F. Gathercole at 171·5 m.p.h. G-AZHM, built by M. S. Crossley, first flown at Redhill 2.4.72. See Appendix E. Span, 15 ft. 0 in. Length, 16 ft. 0 in. Tare wt., 530 lb. A.U.W., 820 lb. Max. speed, 195 m.p.h.

(*Flight Photo*)

Central Centaur IIA (Open model)

Three bay biplane seating two pilots and six passengers in open cockpits, powered by two 160 h.p. Beardmore engines, designed by A. A. Fletcher and built by the Central Aircraft Company at Kilburn 1919. One aircraft only: K-170/G-EAHR, c/n 101, first flown 7.19 by F. T. Courtney. Destroyed in crash following take-off with crossed elevator cables, Northolt 7.20. Span, 63 ft. 8 in. Length, 39 ft. 3 in. Tare wt., 4,996 lb. A.U.W., 7,250 lb. Max. speed, 90 m.p.h.

(*Flight Photo*)

Central Centaur IIA (Cabin model)

Improved version with cabin for seven passengers, built at Kilburn 1920. One aircraft only: G-EAPC, c/n 102, first flown at Northolt by F. T. Courtney 5.20, C. of A. issued 30.6.20. Took part in Air Ministry commercial aeroplane competition, Martlesham 8.20, won no award, but achieved a speed range of 89–48 m.p.h. Spun in with the loss of six lives, including that of the pilot, Lt. F. P. Goodwin-Castleman, at Sharvel Lane, Hayes, Middlesex, 25.9.20. Specification similar to open model.

Military Types Used for Civil Purposes

Aircraft listed in this section were either demilitarised in small numbers for normal commercial or private usage or were military aircraft flown under civil markings for demonstration, test or overseas delivery. As it constitutes a breach of international law to fly an aircraft in military marks over foreign soil without special permission, British military aircraft being delivered by air usually receive temporary civil status.

The introductory notes to Appendix A apply equally to this section. British military types civilianised overseas are outside the scope of this book.

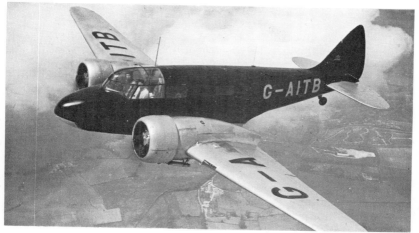

(*Hawker Siddeley Aviation Ltd.*)

Airspeed A.S.40 Oxford

Twin engined trainer of wooden construction built in quantity for the R.A.F. by Airspeed Ltd. and sub-contractors 1938–45, powered by two 370 h.p. Armstrong Siddeley Cheetah X radials. Two civil machines, G-AFFM and 'VS, prewar; civilianised in some numbers (over 30 in Britain) for early postwar transport and training with others in Denmark, Egypt, Finland, France, India, Kenya, Norway, Spain, Sweden and elsewhere. One Oxford, LX119/U-7/G-AJWJ, designated A.S.41 and first flown 3.6.46, was used by Miles Aircraft Ltd. as testbed for the Alvis Leonides radial. Span, 53 ft. 4 in. Length, 34 ft. 6 in. Tare wt., 5,380 lb. A.U.W., 7,600 lb. Cruise, 135 m.p.h. Range, 900 miles.

Armstrong Whitworth Wolf

Dual-control trainer powered by one 350 h.p. Armstrong Siddeley Jaguar III, built at Whitley 1923. Three civil aircraft only: G-EBHI, c/n A.W.18, first flew 16.2.23, C. of A. issued 4.9.23; G-EBHJ, c/n A.W. 28, first flew 16.8.23, C. of A. issued 10.12.23; G-AAIY, c/n A.W. 468, C. of A. issued 16.8.29. All used by the Armstrong Whitworth Reserve Flying School at Whitley and scrapped 1931, 'IY became instructional airframe at Air Service Training Ltd., Hamble. Span, 39 ft. 10 in. Length, 31 ft. 7 in. Tare wt., 3,350 lb. A.U.W., 4,100 lb. Max. speed, 112 m.p.h.

(*P. T. Capon*)

Armstrong Whitworth Atlas I

Two-seat Army Co-operation aircraft powered by one 385 h.p. Armstrong Siddeley Jaguar III, built at Whitley. Three civil aircraft only: G-EBLK, c/n A.W.139, C. of A. 29.8.25, shown at R.A.F. Display 3.7.26, w.f.u. 2.28; G-EBNI, c/n A.W.142, C. of A. 8.2.26, to R.A.F. 6.28 as J9129; G-EBYF, c/n A.W.346, C. of A. 2.10.28, flown Croydon–Constantinople 3.10.28 by J. L. N. Bennett-Baggs, w.f.u. 11.32. Span, 39 ft. 6½ in. Length 28 ft. 6½ in. Tare wt., 2,550 lb. A.U.W., 4,020 lb. Max. speed, 142 m.p.h. Cruise, 120 m.p.h.

Armstrong Whitworth Ajax

Trainer version of the Atlas I to Spec. 20/25, powered by one 385 h.p. Jaguar III.
One civil aircraft only: G-EBLM, c/n A.W.143, built at Whitley 1925, d/d to
Croydon 30.6.25, flown in the King's Cup Race by F. T. Courtney 3.7.25, ran
into ditch landing at Town Moor, Newcastle; Paris Aero Show 12.26; to R.A.F.
6.28, believed as J9128. Span, 39 ft. 4½ in. Length, 29 ft. 4 in. Tare wt., 2,640 lb.
A.U.W., 3,740 lb. Max. speed, 145 m.p.h.

Armstrong Whitworth Atlas Trainer

Improved dual-control trainer variant of the Atlas I, but with aerodynamically
balanced rudder without fin, powered by one 450 h.p. Jaguar IVC. Five civil
aircraft only: G-ABDY, c/n A.W. 536, C. of A. issued 25.9.30, demonstrator;
G-ABHV–'HX, c/n A.W. 563–5, Cs. of A. issued 13.4.31; G-ABOO, c/n A.W.
739, C. of A. issued 29.10.31. The last four used by Air Service Training Ltd.,
Hamble, for advanced and Reserve flying instruction, all scrapped in 1938.
Specification similar to Atlas I.

Armstrong Whitworth Atlas II

Two-seat fighter, general purpose and advanced training variant with cleaned-up airframe, built at Whitley 1931–33 and powered by one 525 h.p. Armstrong Siddeley Panther IIA in a double Townend ring. Eighteen known examples comprising three civil demonstrators registered to Sir W. G. Armstrong Whitworth Aircraft Ltd.: G-ABIV, c/n A.W.696, first shown publicly at Hanworth 6.31 by A.W. chief test pilot A. C. Campbell-Orde, C. of A. issued 10.12.31, shown at R.A.F. Display and S.B.A.C. Show, Hendon, 25–27.6.32, registration cancelled 12.34; G-ABKE; c/n A.W. 697, registered 24.3.31, to Martlesham Heath for evaluation, European tour 7.33, registration cancelled 5.36; G-ACAI, c/n A.W.830, registered 1.11.32, registration cancelled 12.35, see footnote.

Fifteen aircraft certificated in the name of the manufacturers prior to shipment to the Far East Aviation Co. Ltd., Hong Kong, for delivery to the Kwangsi Air Force at Luichow, South China: (a) G-ABRU to G-ABRZ, c/n A.W.768–773, Cs. of A. issued 8, 11, 12, 15, 18 and 19.1.32 respectively, sold abroad 1932. (b) VR-HAV, VR-HBA, VR-HBE, VR-HAX, VR-HBD and VR-HBG, c/n A.W.799–804, Cs. of A. issued 4, 5, 13, 20, 18 and 30.4.32 respectively: VR-HCQ and VR-HCR, c/n A.W.821 and 822, Cs. of A. issued 8 and 14.11.32. (c) One unregistered, c/n A.W.824, C. of A. issued 15.11.32.

Note: A British C. of A. issued 19.4.33 gave c/n A.W.799 (properly belonging to VR-HAV of a year earlier) for an Atlas II later registered in Hong Kong as VR-HCD. In view of the fact that an A.W.16, c/n 829, was certificated on that day, there are grounds for believing that the aircraft in question had, in fact, the c/n 830 and that VR-HCD was the subsequent identity of G-ACAI.

Span, (upper) 40 ft. 2 in. (lower) 30 ft. $10\frac{1}{4}$ in. Length, 29 ft. $6\frac{1}{2}$ in. Height 10 ft. 7 in. All-up weight, 4,600 lb. Maximum speed, 154 m.p.h. Service ceiling, 18,200 ft. With supercharged Panther: Maximum speed at 15,000 ft., 164 m.p.h. All-up weight, 5,300 lb. Service ceiling, 23,500 ft.

(*Flight Photo*)

Armstrong Whitworth A.W.14 Starling

Single-seat interceptor fighter built at Whitley 1928 with one 450 h.p. Armstrong Siddeley Jaguar IV supercharged radial. One civil aircraft only: J8027/G-AAHC, c/n A.W.277, demonstrator registered 10.5.29, shown at Olympia, London, in July 1929, cancelled 12.30. Span, (upper) 31 ft. 4 in. Length, 25 ft. 2 in. A.U.W., 3,095 lb. Max. speed, 177 m.p.h.

(*Flight Photo 10869*)

Armstrong Whitworth A.W.16

Single-seat fighter built at Whitley 1931–33 and powered by one 540 h.p. Armstrong Siddeley Panther IIIA radial. Eighteen known examples, comprising (a) three civil demonstrators: A-2, c/n A.W.460, C. of A. 7.12.31, converted to A.W.35 in 1935; G-ABKF, c/n A.W.722, C. of A. 31.12.31, cancelled 1.37; G-ABZL, c/n A.W.823, C. of A. 16.1.33, sold abroad 2.34 (b) three unregistered, c/n 698, 720 and 721, Cs. of A. 15.12.31 for Reid Massey (c) G-ABRH, 'RI and *continued on page 340*

(*Flight Photo 11994*)

Armstrong Whitworth A.W.23

Bomber transport to Spec. C.26/31 built at Whitley 1935 and powered by two 700 h.p. Armstrong Siddeley Tiger VI. One aircraft only, K3585, shown at R.A.F. Display and S.B.A.C. Show, Hendon, 29 June–1 July 1935, to Flight Refuelling Ltd., Ford, 4.39 with 840 h.p. Tiger VIIIs as G-AFRX, C. of A. 30.8.39. Flown to Boscombe Down by G. B. S. Errington and Geoffrey Tyson for world's first night refuelling experiments 24.2.40, destroyed in German air raid on Ford 6.40. Span, 88 ft. 0 in. Length, 80 ft. 9 in.

(*Flight Photo 11335SA*)

Armstrong Whitworth A.W.35 Scimitar

Major redesign of A.W.16 with lower front decking and 640 h.p. Panther VII. Two civil aircraft only: G-ACCD, c/n A.W.828, C. of A. 28.6.33, demonstrated at Copenhagen 8.34, scrapped 1936; G-ADBL, c/n 460, conversion of A.W.16 in 1935, preserved at Whitley, broken up in R. J. Coley's scrap yard, Hounslow, 10.58. Span, 33 ft. 0 in. Length, 25 ft. 0 in. Tare wt., 1,435 lb. A.U.W., 4,100 lb. Max. speed 217 m.p.h. Cruise 185 m.p.h.

Armstrong Whitworth A.W.38 Whitley 5

The conversion of 15 R.A.F. Whitley 5 heavy bombers into freighters for B.O.A.C. was a desperate gamble made in April 1942 for night supply flights from Gibraltar to beleaguered Malta. Powered by two 1,145 h.p. Rolls-Royce Merlin X engines they had no single-engined performance and took seven hours to reach the island, often landing during air attacks, and were unloaded at breakneck speed to enable them to be well clear before dawn. They proved uneconomical in the extreme, carried small loads, consumed vast quantities of fuel in the process, and were replaced by Lockheed Hudsons in August that year. Span, 84 ft. 0 in. Length, 70 ft. 6 in. Tare wt., 19,330 lb. A.U.W., 28,200 lb. Cruise, 185 m.p.h. Range, 2,000 miles.

Auster 9M

Auster Model B.5 three-seat A.O.P. type of fabric-covered metal construction powered by one 180 h.p. Blackburn Bombardier and supplied to the Army from 1955. G-AVHT, ex WZ711, reg'd. 3.67 to Capt. M. Somerton-Rayner, Middle Wallop; installation of 180 h.p. Lycoming O-360-A1D and Hartzell airscrew commenced 14.8.67, first flown 4.1.68 as Auster 9M, C. of A. 30.4.68. This and a number of standard Auster 9s are detailed in Appendix E. Span, 36 ft. 5 in. Length, 23 ft. 8½ in. Tare wt., 1,460 lb. A.U.W., 2,300 lb. Max. speed, 127 m.p.h. Cruise, 110 m.p.h.

(Flight Photo 3910)

Avro 566 Avenger I

Single-seat fighter powered by one 525 h.p. direct-drive Napier Lion VIII, built at
Hamble 1925. One aircraft only: G-EBND, c/n 5109, C. of A. issued 11.7.26.
Demonstrated by H. J. Hinkler. Exhibited in New Types Park at the 1926 R.A.F.
Display, Hendon. Span, 28 ft. 0 in. Length, 25 ft. 6 in. Tare wt., 2,368 lb. A.U.W.,
3,414 lb. Max. speed, 180 m.p.h. Cruise, 130 m.p.h.

(Aeroplane)

Avro 567 Avenger II

The Avro 566 rebuilt with 553 h.p. geared Napier Lion IX, reduced span and
single interplane struts for the King's Cup Race, Hendon, 20.7.28. Piloted by J.
Summers made fastest average time of 161·67 m.p.h. Left for Bucharest to be
demonstrated to the Rumanians 6.9.28. Handed over to Air Service Training Ltd.,
Hamble, as instructional airframe 5.31. Span, 28 ft. 0 in. Length, 25 ft. 6 in.
A.U.W. 3,414 lb.

Avro 571 Buffalo I

Two-seat, private venture torpedo-bomber of fabric covered wood and metal construction powered by one 450 h.p. Napier Lion VA, built at Manchester to Spec. 21/23 and first flown by H. J. Hinkler at Hamble in 1926. One aircraft only, G-EBNW, c/n R3/BTC/30021, rebuilt 1927 as the Avro 572 Buffalo II with 530 h.p. Napier Lion XIA, rectangular fabric-covered all-metal wings, Handley Page slots and four Frise-type ailerons. Converted to seaplane at Hamble 7.28 and transferred to the M.A.E.E., Felixstowe, as N239. Span, 46 ft. 0 in. Length, 37 ft. 3 in. Tare wt., 4,233 lb. A.U.W. 7,430 lb. Max. Speed 135 m.p.h. Cruise, 105 m.p.h. Range 650 miles.

(Flight Photo 39293S)

Avro 694 Lincoln B.Mk.2

Long distance bomber powered by four 1,635 h.p. Packard Merlin 68 engines built at Manchester 1945. Two civil aircraft only: G-APRJ and G-APRP (Appendix E) used by D. Napier and Son Ltd., Luton, for icing research 1948–62. Span, 120 ft 0 in. Length, 78 ft. 3½ in. Tare wt., 43,400 lb. A.U.W., 75,000 lb. Max. speed, 290 m.p.h. Cruise, 215 m.p.h.

(A. J. Jackson)

Avro 695 Lincolnian

Lincoln B.Mk.2 with Lancastrian nose and tail and ventral pannier. Five conversions only: One Lincoln Freighter G-ALPF by Airflight Ltd., Langley, C. of A. 22.6.49, used on the Berlin airlift by Surrey Flying Services Ltd., broken up at Southend 1952. Four similar Lincolnians (a) LV-ZEI 'Cruz del Sud' ex Argentine B-003 by A. V. Roe & Co. Ltd. at Langar, Notts., in 1948. (b) ZP-CBP-96, BR-97 and 'BS-98 ex RF417, RE376 and RF458 by Field Aircraft Services Ltd. at Tollerton for meat haulage in Paraguay (not delivered, scrapped). Span, 120 ft. 0 in. Length, 85 ft $7\frac{1}{2}$ in. Tare wt., 40,000 lb. A.U.W., 75,000 lb. Max. speed. 312 m.p.h. Cruise, 215 m.p.h.

Avro 701 Athena T. Mk. 2

Side-by-side two-seat advanced trainer powered by one 1,280 h.p. Rolls-Royce Merlin 35, built at Manchester 1949. One civil aircraft only: G-ALWA, c/n 1519, owned by Ministry of Supply, C. of A. issued 2.2.50 for demonstration tour of India, returned to Croydon 13.5.50, transferred to the R.A.F. as VR569 for the 1950 S.B.A.C. Show. Span, 40 ft. 0 in. Length, 38 ft. 0 in. Tare wt., 5,884 lb. A.U.W., 8,210 lb. Max. speed, 289 m.p.h. Cruise, 226 m.p.h.

(*Aviation Photo News*)

B.A.C. Lightning F.Mk.53

Single-seat, multi-role export fighter developed from the Lightning F.Mk.6 and powered by two 11,100 lb. s.t. (16,300 lb. with re-heat) Rolls-Royce Avon 302C. Armed with Firestreak missiles and gun, rocket, bomb or camera packs. Four British civil demonstrators are listed in Appendix E: G-AWON and 'OO shown at the Farnborough S.B.A.C. Show 9–15.9.68; G-AXEE at the Paris Aero Show 6.69; and also G-AXFW. Span, 34 ft. 10 in. Length, 53 ft. 3 in. A.U.W., 50,000 lb. Max. speed, Mach 2·27.

(*Richard Riding*)

B.A.C. 167 Strikemaster Mks.81–87

Export attack/trainer version of the B.A.C. 145 Jet Provost T.Mk.5 powered by one 3,410 lb. s.t. Bristol Siddeley Viper 535 and equipped with 3,000 lb. of underwing guns, SNEB rockets or long-range tanks. First flight of prototype, G-27-8, at Warton 26.10.67. Seven British civil demonstrators listed in Appendix E were shown at the Farnborough S.B.A.C. Shows of 1968 and 1970 and at the Paris Aero Show 1969. Span, 36 ft. 11 in. Length, 33 ft. $7\frac{1}{2}$ in. A.U.W., 11,500 lb. Max. speed, 480 m.p.h.

B.A.T. F.K.24 Baboon

Two-seat wooden trainer powered by one 170 h.p. A.B.C. Wasp I radial, built at Willesden in July 1918. One aircraft only: K-124/G-EACO, formerly R.A.F. D9731, registered to the British Aerial Transport Co. Ltd. 29.5.19. Raced at Hendon by Maj. Christopher Draper, winning the 20-mile cross-country event in July 1919. Span, 25 ft. Length, 22 ft. 8 in. Tare wt., 950 lb. A.U.W., 1,350 lb. Max. speed, 90 m.p.h.

(Northampton Evening Telegraph)

B.E.2c

Two-seat trainer designed by E. T. Busk in 1914 and built in large numbers with various engines by almost every major aircraft manufacturer of the day. One British civil conversion only: G-EAQR, ex-Admiralty 9468, engine not known, flown by G. Wigglesworth at Bekesbourne, Kent in 1920, crashed 24.8.21. One replica, G-AWYI, c/n 1 (illustrated), was built from Tiger Moth parts at Sywell by C. Boddington for film purposes in 1969, powered by an upright 130 h.p. Gipsy Major 1 and serialled 2984. Span, 37 ft. 0 in. Length, 27 ft. 3 in. Tare wt., 1,370 lb. A.U.W., 2,142 lb. Max. speed, 75 m.p.h. Duration, $3\frac{1}{4}$ hours.

(*Flight Photo 5778*)

B.E.2e

Two-seater built by the Royal Aircraft Factory, Farnborough, and numerous sub-contractors during the First World War. Eleven war-surplus aircraft converted for pleasure flights and private ownership 1919–20 (see Appendix E). All fitted with 90 h.p. R.A.F. IA engines except the 80 h.p. Renault powered G-EANW illustrated. Also C7198/G-AUBD, C6986/G-AUBF (Q.A.N.T.A.S.) and G-AUDV with 90 h.p. R.A.F. engines in Australia. Span, 40 ft. 9 in. Length, 27 ft. 3 in. A.U.W., 2,015 lb. Max. speed, 90 m.p.h.

Beagle E.3

Also known as the Beagle A.115 (or A.O.P. Mk.11), the E.3 was a three-seat STOL development of the Auster Mk.9 powered by one 260 h.p. Rolls-Royce Continental IO-470-D. One aircraft only: G-ASCC, c/n B.701, f/f at Rearsby 18.8.61 as G-25-12, flown at the Farnborough S.B.A.C. Show 9.61 by R. L. Porteous as XP254. Swiss Army trials on skis 10.63; stored at Burton-on-the-Wolds until restored 1.71 to A. D. Heath and M. D. N. Fisher and overhauled at Heathrow. Span, 36 ft. 5 in. Length, 23 ft. 8½ in. Tare wt., 2,119 lb. A.U.W., 2,550 lb. Max. speed, 148 m.p.h.

(*Air Ministry*)

Beardmore Inflexible

All-metal transport built on Rohrbach principles, powered by three 650 h.p. Rolls-Royce Condor II. One aircraft only, allotted civil marks G-EBNG during construction at Dalmuir 1925–27. No type number allotted, aircraft handed over to the R.A.F. as J7557 prior to completion, first flight at Martlesham 5.3.28, flown at 1928 Hendon R.A.F. Display, dismantled at Martlesham 1930 due to excessive structural weight and used to investigate exposure corrosion and methods of protective treatment. Span, 157 ft. 6 in. Length, 75 ft. 6 in. A.U.W., 37,000 lb. Max. speed, 109 m.p.h.

Blackburn Turcock

Single-seat fighter powered by one 490 h.p. Armstrong Siddeley Jaguar VI super-charged radial, built for the Turkish Government 1927. One aircraft only: G-EBVP to Works Order 9725, first flown at Brough by A. G. Loton 14.11.27, burned out after hitting a tree during speed trials at Martlesham 13.2.28. Span, 31 ft. 0 in. Length, 24 ft. 4 in. Tare wt., 2,282 lb. A.U.W., 2,726 lb. Max. speed, 176 m.p.h. Endurance $1\frac{3}{4}$ hours.

Blackburn Lincock I

Single-seat light fighter with plywood monocoque fuselage, powered by one 240 h.p. Armstrong Siddeley Lynx IV, built at Brough 1928. One aircraft only: G-EBVO, Works Order 9906, C. of A. 14.7.28, averaged 145·32 m.p.h. in the 1928 King's Cup Race piloted by Sqn. Ldr. J. Noakes; to Chicago for crazy flying displays by Flt. Lt. R. L. R. Atcherley 23.8.30 to 1.9.30; aerobatic displays in U.K. by A. M. Blake 1931; dismantled at Brough 8.31. Span, 22 ft. 6 in. Length, 18 ft. 1½ in. A.U.W., 2,000 lb. Max. speed 146 m.p.h.

Blackburn Lincock II and III

All-metal versions built at Brough 1929–30. Two civil aircraft only: (Mk.II) G-AALH, Works Order 2050/1, 255 h.p. Armstrong Siddeley geared Lynx IV, C. of A. 28.2.30, evaluated by the R.C.A.F. at Camp Borden 1930. (Mk.III) G-ABFK, Works Order 2920/2, 270 h.p. Lynx Major, C. of A. 11.10.30, European demonstrator. Both aircraft used by Cobham's Circus for aerobatics 1933–34; 'LH dismantled 3.35; 'FK fitted with Alfa Romeo radial at the College of Aeronautical Engineering, Brooklands 1935. Span, 22 ft. 6 in. Length, 19 ft. 6 in. Tare wt., 1,326 lb. A.U.W., 2,082 lb. Max. speed, 164 m.p.h. Range, 380 miles.

Blackburn Universal Freighter

Medium-range transport designed as the G.A.L. 60 by General Aircraft Ltd. prior to its merger with Blackburn Aircraft Ltd. Prototype WF320/G-AMUX, c/n 1000, powered by four 2,020 h.p. Bristol Hercules 730, built at Brough 1950. Major redesign as G.A.L. 65 with four 2,850 h.p. Bristol Centaurus 673, prototype WZ889/G-AMVW, c/n 1001, built at Brough as the Universal Freighter Mk. 2 in 1954. First production aircraft, XB259/G-AOAI, c/n 1002, built 1954 as Beverley C. Mk. 1 for the R.A.F. Fourth and last civil aircraft was XB260/G-AOEK, c/n 1003, C. of A. issued 22.9.55, for nine flights between Qatar on the Persian Gulf and Fahud in Oman, transporting a total of 129 tons of oil drilling gear. Span, 162 ft. 0 in. Length, 99 ft. 2 in. Tare wt., 79,100 lb. A.U.W., 135,000 lb. Cruise, 179 m.p.h. Range, 1,430 miles.

(Imperial War Museum Q.68925)

Boulton and Paul P. 7 Bourges IA

Highly manoeuvrable two-seat day bomber powered by two 320 h.p. A.B.C. Dragonfly engines, built at Norwich 1918. The first prototype became civil in its final form, as F2903/K-129/G-EACE. Looped, rolled and spun by F. T. Courtney at the first public demonstration of twin-engined aerobatics at Hendon, 6.19, scrapped 5.20. Span, 57 ft. 4 in. Length, 37 ft. 0 in. Tare wt., 3,820 lb. A.U.W., 6,326 lb. Max. speed, 123·5 m.p.h.

Boulton Paul P.108 Balliol T. Mk. 2

Side-by-side two-seat advanced trainer powered by one 1,280 h.p. Rolls-Royce Merlin 35, built at Wolverhampton 1950. One civil demonstrator: G-ANSF, c/n BP.6C, C. of A. issued 23.8.54: also seven others allotted civil marks for manufacturer's flight tests prior to delivery to the Ceylon Air Force, G-ANYL and 'YM 4.55; G-ANZV and 'ZW 5.55; G-APCN, 'CO and 'CP 8.57. Span, 39 ft 4 in. Length, 35 ft. 1½ in. Tare wt., 6,730 lb. A.U.W., 8,410 lb. Max. speed, 288 m.p.h. Cruise, 266 m.p.h.

Bristol Type 1 Scout C

Single-seat fighter built at Filton for the Royal Flying Corps during the First World War and retrospectively allotted Bristol type number 1 in 1923. One civil aircraft only: G-EAGR, c/n 1060, one 80 h.p. Le Rhône rotary; built with R.F.C. serial 5570 in March 1917; owned by Maj. J. A. McKelvie 7.19. Sqn. Ldr. H. V. Champion de Crespigny 3.26, Flt. Lt. A. M. Wray, Leuchars, 6.27, Smith at Hedon 9.30, and later to D. and J. Heaton and broken up in scrap yard at South Cave, East Yorks., 1933. Span, 24 ft. 7 in. Length, 20 ft. 8 in. Tare wt., 757 lb. A.U.W., 1,250 lb. Max. speed, 92·7 m.p.h. Endurance 2½ hours.

(*Bristol Photo*)

Bristol Type 26 Pullman Triplane

After the 1918 Armistice the unfinished airframe of the third Bristol Braemar four-engined heavy bomber was completed as the Pullman Triplane with cabin accommodation for two crew and 14 passengers. One aircraft only: C4298, c/n 3753, powered by four 400 h.p. Liberty engines, first flown 5.20, shown at Olympia Aero Show 7.20, sent to Martlesham 9.20 and there later dismantled. Allotted civil registration G-EASP for one month from 14.4.20. Span, 81 ft. 8 in. Length, 52 ft. 0 in. Wing area, 1,905 sq. ft. Tare wt., 11,000 lb. A.U.W., 17,750 lb. Max. speed, 135 m.p.h. Cruise, 100 m.p.h.

(*Bristol Photo*)

Bristol Type 84 Bloodhound

Two-seat fighter with metal fuselage and wooden wings, powered by one 425 h.p. Bristol Jupiter IV. Four aircraft only: (c/n 6222) G-EBGG, first flown 5.23 as Type 78 Fighter C; and three R.A.F. prototypes (6709–6711) J7248, J7236 and J7237 delivered 1925. Span, 40 ft. 2 in. Length, 26 ft. 6 in. Tare wt., 2,515 lb. A.U.W., 4,236 lb. Max speed, 130 m.p.h.

(*Bristol Photo*)

Bristol Type 84 Bloodhound (Modified)

G-EBGG fitted with Jupiter V for T. W. Campbell to fly in the 1925 King's Cup Race, C. of A. 30.6.25. Fitted with Jupiter VI and long-range tanks and on 8.3.26 Capts. F. Minchin and F. L. Barnard (illustrated) completed flights between Filton and Croydon totalling 25,074 miles in 225 hr. 54 min. with sealed engine. Left Croydon 30.6.26 and made a trouble-free 5,400 mile tropical proving flight to Cairo and back in a flying time of 56 hours. Jupiter VIII testbed until 1928, scrapped at Filton in 1931.

(*Bristol Photo*)

Bristol Type 93 Boarhound

Two-seat Army Co-operation biplane powered by one 425 h.p. Bristol Jupiter VI, built at Filton 1925 as a private venture for the Bristol Fighter replacement competition. One aircraft only: G-EBLG, c/n 6805, first flown by C. F. Uwins 8.6.25; C. of A. 8.6.26; crashed at Odiham 11.8.26 during trials at the School of Army Co-operation, Old Sarum, but rebuilt in one week. Withdrawn from use at Filton 4.27. Span, 44 ft. 9 in. Length, 31 ft. 6 in. Tare wt., 2,900 lb. A.U.W., 4,460 lb. Max. speed, 135 m.p.h. Endurance 3 hours.

Bristol Type 93A Beaver

General purpose variant of the Boarhound built at Filton 1927 as a private venture for the D.H.9A replacement competition. One aircraft only: G-EBQF, c/n 7123, first flown by C. F. Uwins 23.2.27, withdrawn from use at Filton after Martlesham trials 4.27. Two Type 93B Boarhound II reconnaissance fighters, c/n 7232 and 7233, sold to Mexico 1.28. Span, 44 ft. 9 in. Length, 31 ft. 6 in. Tare wt., 2,906 lb. A.U.W., 4,480 lb. Max. speed, 142 m.p.h. Endurance, 3 hours.

Bristol Type 101

Two-seat fighter with steel wings and plywood-covered fuselage, powered by one 450 h.p. Bristol Jupiter VI, built at Filton 1927. One aircraft only: G-EBOW, c/n 7019, first flown by C. F. Uwins 8.8.27 and exhibited at Copenhagen. Modified for 1928 King's Cup Race with ailerons on the top wing. Came second at 159·92 m.p.h. piloted by C. F. Uwins. C. of A. 18.7.28, became testbed for the 485 h.p. Bristol Mercury II. Broke up during a steep dive 29.11.29, pilot C. R. L. Shaw parachuted. Span, 33 ft. 7 in. Length, 27 ft. 4 in. Tare wt., 2,100 lb. A.U.W., 3,540 lb. Max. speed, 160 m.p.h.

(*Bristol Photo*)

Bristol Type 118

Two-seat general purpose biplane powered by one 595 h.p. Bristol Jupiter XF, built at Filton 1930. One aircraft only: R-3/G-ABEZ, c/n 7561, first flown by C. F. Uwins 22.1.31 as R-3, C. of A. 8.12.31; to the R.A.F. 2.32 as K2873 and fitted with 600 h.p. Bristol Mercury V for hot weather trials in Iraq. A similar, unregistered, aircraft, Type 120, c/n 7562, flown as R-6, later K3587. Span, 40 ft. 8 in. Length, 34 ft. 0 in. Tare wt., 3,632 lb. A.U.W., 5,200 lb. Max. speed, 165 m.p.h.

(*W. K. Kilsby*)

Bristol Type 142M Blenheim I

All-metal, mid-wing, three-seat day bomber evolved from the Bristol 142, powered by two 840 h.p. Bristol Mercury VIII, built in large numbers for use in the 1939–45 war. Thirty Blenheim Mk.1s allotted civil markings for delivery flights to foreign governments: G-AFCE and 'CF, c/n 8814–15, delivered via Heston and Paris to the Jugoslav Air Force 11.37; G-AFFP to 'FZ, c/n 8157–66 delivered by the same route to the Turkish Air Force 9.38; G-AFLA to 'LS, c/n 9222–39 to the Turkish Air Force 4.39; YU-BAA to 'AT diverted from the R.A.F. to Jugoslav Air Force via Aston Down 1940. Span, 56 ft. 10 in. Length, 39 ft. 9 in. Tare wt., 8,100 lb. A.U.W. 14,000 lb. Max. speed, 260 m.p.h.

Bristol Type 149 Blenheim IV

Three-seat day bomber powered by two 920 h.p. Bristol Mercury XV, fitted with long-range tanks and a lengthened nose to give improved accommodation for the navigator, superseding the Blenheim I in production in 1939. Twelve aircraft allotted British civil marks for delivery flights to the Greek Air Force: G-AFXD to 'XO, c/n 9392–93, 9397–98, 9403–04, 9416–17, 9422–23, 9428–29, Cs. of A. issued between 13.10.39 and 10.2.40. Span, 56 ft. 4 in. Length, 42 ft. 7 in. Tare wt., 9,790 lb. A.U.W., 14,500 lb. Max. speed, 266 m.p.h. Range, 1,950 miles.

continued from page 323
'RJ, c/n A.W.765–767, Cs. of A. 19.12.31; VR-HAZ and 'BK, c/n A.W.797 and 798, Cs. of A. 29.4.32; VR-HBH, 'BN and 'BQ, c/n 818–820, Cs. of A. 10, 12 and 19.5.32; four unregistered, c/n A.W.825–827 and 829, Cs. of A. 20, 21, 22.7.32 and 19.4.33 for the Far East Aviation Co. Ltd. and delivery to the Kwangsi and Canton Air Forces, the first three becoming Kwangsi 151–153. Span, 33 ft. 0 in. Length, 25 ft. 0 in. A.U.W., 3,600 lb. Max. speed, 185 m.p.h.

Foreign and Commonwealth Types

This section of the book describes all aircraft of foreign or Commonwealth design and construction flown in British civil markings since the inception of the registration system in 1919 and should be read in conjunction with Appendix E.

The introductory notes to Appendix A apply equally to this section.

(*H. J. Nobbs*)

Aero Commander 200D

Four-seat, all-metal tourer with retractable undercarriage evolved from the Meyers 200 and powered by one 285 h.p. Continental IO-520-A. Production commenced at the Albany, Georgia, factory of the Aero Commander division of the Rockwell Standard Corp. in July 1965. One British aircraft only: N2965T, c/n 338, imported 1966 by Atlantic Commander Ltd., Gatwick; registered 2.69 to Douglas Arnold Aviation Ltd., Fairoaks, as G-AWYH, C. of A. 4.6.69; to W. J. Roberts, Wadhurst, Sussex, 10.69. Span, 30 ft. 6 in. Length, 24 ft. 4 in. Tare wt., 1,940 lb. A.U.W., 3,000 lb. Max. speed, 235 m.p.h. Cruise, 215 m.p.h. Range, 1,000 miles.

Aero Commander 520 and 680E

All-metal executive/charter aircraft with two 260 h.p. Lycoming GO-435-C2B, the type number indicating total horsepower. Built at Culver City, California, U.S.A., by Aero Design and Engineering Inc. 1952–54. Three aircraft only imported 1960–63: G-ARJA, last of the type built; G-ARJJ and G-ASJU. Also two Model 680E (the E suffix denoting extended wing) with two 340 h.p. Lycoming GSO-480-B1A6: G-ASHI imported 1963 as HB-GOB; G-AWOE imported 1968 as N3844C. Span, 44 ft. 7 in. (680E) 49 ft. $6\frac{1}{2}$ in. Length, 34 ft. $4\frac{1}{2}$ in. Tare wt., 3,800 lb. A.U.W., 5,500 lb. Cruise, 197 m.p.h. Range, 1,150 miles.

Aero Commander 500A and 500B

Improved model with two 260 h.p. Continental IO-470-MS, swept tail surfaces and undercarriage retracting flat into elongated nacelles, introduced 3.60 by the Aero Commander division of the Rockwell Standard Corp., Oklahoma. G-ASIO and 'NJ imported for Scillonian Air Services Ltd. Gatwick–Scillies route 1963–64. Also G-ARGW, Model 500B with two 290 h.p. Lycoming IO-540-B1A, for Woods of Colchester Ltd. 12.60. Span, 49 ft. $6\frac{1}{2}$ in. Length, 35 ft. 1 in. Tare wt., 4,225 lb. A.U.W., 6,250 lb. (500B) 6,750 lb. Cruise, 190 m.p.h. Range, 1,420 miles.

Aero Commander 560F and 680F

Enlarged version of the 500B with two 350 h.p. Lycoming IGO-540-B1B and front fuselage lengthened by 10 in. Two British registered 560F: G-ARDK, transatlantic delivery by K. Burville 12.60; G-ASYA delivered as N1015 via Ringway 24.9.64. Also one Model 680F with two 380 h.p. Lycoming IGSO-540 and one Model 680FP pressurised: G-ATWN, 680F, delivered at Gatwick 25.9.64 as N390GA; G-AWCU, 680FP, delivered as HB-GBW. Data for 680F. Span, 49 ft. 6½ in. Length, 35 ft. 11 in. Tare wt., 4,800 lb. A.U.W., 8,000 lb. Cruise, 242 m.p.h. Range, 1,480 miles.

Aero Commander 680T

Nine-seat turbine development of the 680FLP Grand Commander with two 575 s.h.p. Garrett TPE-331s. Two aircraft registered 2.69 to Miles Aviation & Transport Ltd., Ford: G-AWXK (c/n 1540–6), d/d in the U.K. 3.67 as N6300, re-engined 1968 with two 730 e.h.p. Turboméca Astazou 12Ms as model 680TA, C. of A. 7.10.69, to France 10.70 as F-WSTM; G-AWXL (1532–2), d/d in U.K. 8.66 as N1186Z, C. of A. 22.1.69, to Switzerland 8.69 as HB-GEK. One 680V Turbo II Commander G-AYTX (1709–84) ex 9J-RGD, registered 3.71 to Shackleton Av. Ltd. Span, 49 ft. 2½ in. Length, 41 ft. 3¼ in. Tare wt., 5,100 lb. A.U.W., 8,500 lb. Cruise, 285 m.p.h. Range, 1,100 miles.

Aermacchi-Lockheed AL 60B-1

Six-seat utility aircraft powered by one 250 h.p. Continental IO-470-R, designed in the U.S.A. by Lockheed and manufactured by Aeronautica Macchi at Venegono, Italy. Three British aircraft only: G-ARZG, c/n 6219–39, d/d to Air Navigation & Trading Co. Ltd., Squires Gate 8.62; G-ATJS, 6227–47, ordered 1965 but not delivered; G-AXEZ, 6144-2, formerly OY-AFR, registered 5.69 to Junex of Sweden Ltd., Biggin Hill. See Appendix E. Span, 39 ft. 4 in. Length, 28 ft. 1 in. Tare wt., 2,024 lb. A.U.W., 3,850 lb. Cruise, 140 m.p.h. Range, 550 miles.

(*Aeroplane*)

Aeromere F.8L Falco III and IV

Wooden two-seater with 150 h.p. Lycoming O-320-A2A and retractable undercarriage, designed by Stelio Frati and built at Trento, Italy, by Aeromere S.p.A. The Falco IV with 160 h.p. Lycoming O-320-B3B manufactured by Laverda (formerly Aeromere). Five Falco IIIs G-APUO, G-APXD, G-AROT, G-ATAK and G-AZAY; and three Falco IVs G-ASYM, G-AVUJ and G-AWSU, imported 1959–71. Data for Falco IV: Span, 26 ft. 3 in. Length, 21 ft. 4 in. Tare wt., 1,212 lb. A.U.W., 1,808 lb. Max. speed, 202 m.p.h. Cruise, 180 m.p.h. Range, 850 miles.

(*R. P. Howard*)

Aeronca 50C Chief

Two-seater built 1938 by Aeronca Aircraft Corporation, Middletown, Ohio, and powered by one 50 h.p. Continental A-50-1. One British aircraft only: G-AFJC, c/n C-1028, C. of A. 29.8.38, Miss M. Butcher, Gatwick; to Aero Industries Ltd., Heston, 7.39, engine modified to Continental A-50-3. Stored in Burnley by T. Fletcher 1942–47; C. of A. at Walsall 28.3.47 for J. E. Steel; to K. C. Millican, Woolsington 5.48, scrapped 5.49. Span, 36 ft. 0 in. Length, 20 ft. 7 in. Tare wt., 650 lb. A.U.W., 1,130 lb. Max. speed, 100 m.p.h. Cruise, 90 m.p.h.

(*A. J. Jackson*)

Aeronca 7AC Champion

Two-seater powered by one 65 h.p. Continental A-65-8 and built by the Aeronca Aircraft Corporation at Middletown, Ohio, 1946–54. Five British registered examples only: G-AOEH, formerly the U.S. Embassy Flying Club's N79854, purchased in Belgium ex OO-TWF by the Brookwood Flying Group, Gatwick, 1956; G-ATHK, G-ATXC, G-AVDT and G-AWVN acquired from United States Air Force flying clubs at Alconbury and Chateauroux 1965–69, G-ATHK by F. Turner, Leicester East, G-AWVN by Farm Aviation Ltd., Rush Green, and the others by Horsted Aviation Ltd., Biggin Hill. Span, 35 ft. 0 in. Length, 21 ft. 6 in. Tare wt., 710 lb. A.U.W., 1,220 lb. Max. speed, 100 m.p.h. Cruise, 90 m.p.h.

Aeronca 15AC Sedan

Four-seater powered by one 145 h.p. Continental C-145-2, built at Middletown, Ohio. One British aircraft only: G-AREX, c/n 15AC-61, first registered in Vancouver 6.48 as CF-FNM, arrived Liverpool 25.6.59 for Dr. M. K. Moore, erected at Staverton; to R. C. Hayes, White Waltham, C. of A. 21.4.61; to Fich Institute of Data Processing, Denham 2.64; to A. McNamara, Tees-side, 4.66; to Maj. F. F. Chamberlain, Elgin, 3.69. Span, 37 ft. 6 in. Length, 25 ft. 3 in. Tare wt., 1,150 lb. A.U.W., 2,050 lb. Max. speed, 129 m.p.h. Cruise, 114 m.p.h.

Agusta-Bell 47J variants

Five-seat helicopters built under licence by Agusta at Gallerate, Italy, from 1957. One 47J-1 Ranger, G-APTH, with 240 h.p. Lycoming VO-435-A1D supplied to B.E.A. in 1959; six 47J-2 aircraft with metal rotor blades and 260 h.p. Lycoming VO-540-B1B3 engines; and one 47J-2A, G-ATFV, with boosted controls, were imported 1962–69 for taxi work, advertising and power line inspection work. Data for Agusta-Bell 47J-2A (illustrated): Rotor diameter, 37 ft. $1\frac{1}{2}$ in. Length, 32 ft. $4\frac{3}{4}$ in. Tare wt., 1,730 lb. A.U.W., 2,950 lb. Cruise, 93 m.p.h. Range, 260 miles.

Agusta-Bell 206A Jet Ranger

Fast five-seater powered by one 317 h.p. Allison 250-C18A free-turbine engine and introduced in 1966. Small fleet operated by Bristow Helicopters Ltd. and others used for executive charter in the U.K., including several Bell 206A aircraft (American-built) listed separately in Appendix E and operated by industry, e.g. B.S.R. Ltd. (G-AVTE); David Brown Tractors (G-AWOL and 'UC); or by airlines, e.g. Tradewinds (G-AXJC) and Court (G-AXMM). Rotor diameter, 33 ft. 4 in. Length, 28 ft. 8¼ in. Tare wt., 1,295 lb. A.U.W., 2,900 lb. Cruise, 130 m.p.h.

Air & Space 18A Gyroplane

Tandem two-seat autogyro, powered by one 180 h.p. Lycoming O-360-A1D driving a pusher airscrew, developed by the Umbaugh Aircraft Corp. 1957–62 and built in small numbers by Air & Space Mfg. Inc. at Muncie, Indiana, 1963–67. Two British registered aircraft only: G-ATZT, c/n 18–36, registered 30.9.66 to Short Bros. & Harland Ltd. but not imported; G-AYUE, c/n 18–61, N6150S, C. of A. 5.5.71, Campbell Aircraft Ltd., d.b.r. landing at Membury 21.5.71. Rotor diameter, 35 ft. 0 in. Length, 19 ft. 10 in. A.U.W., 1,800 lb. Cruise, 85 m.p.h. Range, 300 miles.

347

American Aviation AA-1 Yankee

Two-seat tourer, trainer or sport aeroplane with tricycle undercarriage and bonded honeycomb structure, powered by one 108 h.p. Lycoming O-235-C2C and built in Cleveland, Ohio, from 1967. Commencing March 1970, shipped to the U.K. in batches of four, erected at Leavesden and distributed by General Aviation Sales of Jersey, British registered examples being listed in Appendix E. Span, 24 ft. 5½ in. Length, 19 ft. 2¾ in. Max. speed, 144 m.p.h. Cruise, 134 m.p.h. Range, 466 miles.

Beech 17

Four-seat backward staggered biplane built at Wichita, Kansas, by the Beech Aircraft Corp. Four registered 1935–37: B-17L G-ADDH (225 h.p. Jacobs), B-17R floatplane G-ADLE (1935 World Flight by F. L. Farquhar), C-17Rs G-AENY and 'SJ (all with 420 h.p. Wright Whirlwinds). These and eight U.S.A.A.F./R.N. C-43 Travelers (450 h.p. Pratt & Whitney Wasp Juniors) civilianised 1947–51 as Model D-17S, see Appendix E. (Data for D-17S) Span, 32 ft. 0 in. Length, 26 ft. 0 in. Tare wt., 2,460 lb. A.U.W., 4,200 lb. Cruise, 202 m.p.h. Range, 500 miles.

Beech 18

All-metal eight-seater powered by two 450 h.p. Pratt & Whitney Wasp Juniors built at Wichita from 1937. Five Model C-18S Expediters registered 1948–57 included G-AIYI, an ex-U.S.A.A.F./R.N. AT-7; three war surplus UC-45Bs; and G-APBX converted from a pre-1939 Model 18A. For details of these, two Model D-18S, one E-18S and one tri-gear H-18 G-ASNX (10-seaters with 2 ft. greater span), see Appendix E. (Data for H-18) Span, 49 ft. 8 in. Length, 35 ft. 2½ in. Tare wt., 5,680 lb. A.U.W. 9,900 lb. Max. speed, 236 m.p.h. Cruise, 209 m.p.h.

Beech 23 Musketeer

Imports of this four-seater began in 1962, initially by Short Bros., Gatwick and later by Eagle Aircraft Services Ltd., Leavesden. Appendix E details five Model 23 (160 h.p. Lycoming O-320-D2B), two A.23 Musketeer II and two A.23A Custom III (165 h.p. Continental IO-346-A), nine two-seat A.23-19 Sport III (150 h.p. Lycoming O-320-E2C), and two A.23-24 Super III (200 h.p. Lycoming IO-360-A1B). (Data for Sport III) Span, 32 ft. 9 in. Length, 25 ft. 0 in. Tare wt., 1,325 lb. A.U.W., 2,200 lb. Max. speed, 140 m.p.h.

(Flight Photo 71–5599)

Beech A.24R Sierra

Four/five-seat stretched version of the Musketeer with retractable undercarriage and constant-speed airscrew, powered by one 200 h.p. Lycoming IO-360-A1B fuel injection engine, in production at the Beech plant at Liberal, Kansas, U.S.A., from 1969. One British registered aircraft imported 1971 by Eagle Aircraft Services Ltd., Leavesden: G-AYPA, c/n MC-91, C. of A. 20.5.71. Span, 32 ft. 9 in. Length, 25 ft. 0 in. Tare wt., 1,625 lb. A.U.W., 2,750 lb. Max. cruise, 162 m.p.h. Max. range, 650 miles.

Beech 35 Bonanza

All-metal low-wing monoplane with butterfly tail and retractable undercarriage for private, club or business use, produced at Wichita from 1947. Appendix E lists five British registered four-seat Model A.35s (185 h.p. Continental E-185-1) and one G.35 (225 h.p. Continental E-225-8) and seven larger five-seat H.35 (240 h.p. Continental O-470-G), M.35 (250 h.p. IO-470-C), N.35 and P.35 (illustrated) (260 h.p. IO-470-N) and S.35 (285 h.p. Continental IO-520-B) (Data for S.35) Span, 33 ft. $5\frac{1}{2}$ in. Length, 26 ft. $4\frac{1}{2}$ in. Tare wt., 1,855 lb. A.U.W., 3,300 lb. Max. speed, 212 m.p.h. Cruise, 200 m.p.h.

(*Air Portraits*)

Beech 35-33 Debonair

Four-seater similar to Model 35 Bonanza but with conventional tail surfaces, simplified interior and less equipment. Two British registered examples only: G-ASHR, a 1960 Model 33 (225 h.p. Continental IO-470-J) imported from Ireland for Metropolitan Developments Ltd., Renfrew, in 1965; and G-AVHG, Model C.33 (225 h.p. Continental IO-470-K) with enlarged rear window and internal modifications, new aircraft imported 1968. Span, 32 ft. 10 in. Length, 25 ft. 6 in. Tare wt., 1,780 lb. A.U.W., 3,050 lb. Max. speed, 195 m.p.h. Range, 1,070 miles.

(*W. H. Blunt*)

Beech 60 Duke

Fast pressurised six-seater of advanced design powered by two 340 h.p. Lycoming TIO-541-E1A4 turbosupercharged flat-six engines. One British registered aircraft only: G-AXEN (c/n P-94) delivered to Eagle Aircraft Services Ltd., Leavesden, from Germany via Luton 20.4.69 as N7204D, C. of A. 22.8.69, to Germany 9.70 as D-ICAV. Span, 39 ft. 3 in. Length, 33 ft. 10 in. Tare wt., 4,100 lb. A.U.W., 6,725 lb. Cruise, 210 m.p.h. Max. range, 1,195 miles.

(*Flight Photo 41655S*)

Beech 65 Queen Air

Six-seat executive transport powered by two 340 h.p. Lycoming IGSO-480-AIA6, in production at Wichita from 1958, imported initially by Short Bros. and later by Eagle Aircraft Services Ltd., Leavesden. Three aircraft listed in Appendix E include Model 65 G-ARFF of Davy-Ashmore Ltd. and two A.65As with swept fin and two Lycoming IGSO-480-A1E6 engines, viz. the Guinness Co.'s G-AVNA and Eagle Aviation's demonstrator G-AWKX. Span, 45 ft. 10½ in. Length, 33 ft. 4½ in. Tare wt., 4,740 lb. A.U.W., 7,700 lb. Max. speed, 239 m.p.h. Cruise, 205 m.p.h.

(*A. J. Jackson*)

Beech 65-80 Queen Air

Six/nine-seat version of the Queen Air with swept vertical tail surfaces and two 380 h.p. Lycoming IGSO-540-A1A engines introduced in 1961. Ten listed in Appendix E include Marshall of Cambridge's G-ASDA, the Pye Co.'s G-ASRX, Ind Coope's G-ASXV, Gulf Aviation's Bahrein-based G-AVDR and 'DS, and Rootes Motor's Model B.80 G-AWOI (two Lycoming IGSO-540-A1D and 50 ft. 4 in. span). (Data for 65–80) Span, 45 ft. 10½ in. Length, 35 ft. 3 in. Tare wt., 4,800 lb. A.U.W. 8,000 lb. Max. speed, 252 m.p.h. Cruise 189 m.p.h.

Beech 65-90 King Air

Improved Queen Air with pressurised fuselage and two 525 s.h.p. Pratt & Whitney PT6A-20 propeller-turbines introduced in 1964. Five British registered aircraft: G-ATGB (c/n LJ-80), N774K, not imported; G-AWPM (LJ-417), C. of A. 21.3.69, United Biscuits Ltd., Denham; G-AWWK (LJ-446), 8.6.69, Marchwiel Plant & Eng. Co. Ltd., Halfpenny Green; G-AXFE (LJ-481), 12.11.69, David Brown Gear Industries Ltd., Crosland Moor; G-AZBM (LJ-532) and G-AZGG (LJ-543), C90s, registered to Eagle Aircraft Services Ltd. 12.7.71 and 6.10.71 respectively. Span, 45 ft. 10½ in. Length, 35 ft. 6 in. Tare wt., 5,200 lb. A.U.W., 9,300 lb. Cruise, 270 m.p.h. Range, 1,160 miles.

Beech 65-100 King Air

Enlarged, pressurised version of the earlier model to carry two crew and up to 15 passengers, incorporating a 50 inch fuselage stretch, two extra windows, reduced span, enlarged tail surfaces and dual main landing gear. Power supplied by two 680 s.h.p. Pratt & Whitney PT6A-28 propeller-turbine engines. Two British registered aircraft to date: G-AYGY, c/n B-79, 5.12.70, The Distillers Co. Ltd., Turnhouse; G-AYLW, c/n B-80, 3.2.71, T.I. (Group Services) Ltd., Elmdon. Span, 45 ft. 10½ in. Length, 39 ft. 11¼ in. Tare wt., 6,405 lb. A.U.W., 10,600 lb. Cruise, 260 m.p.h. Max. range, 1,087 miles.

(*John Goring*)

Beech 95 Travel Air

Five-seater using Beech 35 Bonanza cabin married to the wings, tail unit and retractable undercarriage of the Beech 45 Mentor military trainer, powered by two 180 h.p. Lycoming IO-360-B1B. G-APUB, ferried Wichita–Azores–Southend by B. J. Snook 7.59, was the first of several variants from Beech 95 to E.95 registered in Britain. Span, 37 ft. 10 in. Length, 25 ft. 11 in. Tare wt., 2,555 lb. A.U.W., 4,200 lb. Cruise, 200 m.p.h. Range, 1,035 miles.

(*Flight Photo F647113*)

Beech 95-55 Baron

Twin-engined five/six-seat business aircraft introduced in 1960. Eleven British registered Model A.55 and B.55 (two 260 h.p. Continental IO-470-L) include the Iliffe *Flight* G-ASDO (illustrated), Ind Coope G-ASNO and General Engineering Co. G-ASOH. Thirteen improved C.55A and D.55s (two 285 h.p. Continental IO-520-C) include G-AWAD to 'AO acquired by the College of Air Training, Hamble, in 1968 for advanced training. (Data for D.55) Span, 37 ft. 10 in. Length, 28 ft. 3 in. Tare wt., 3,015 lb. A.U.W., 5,300 lb. Max. speed, 236 m.p.h. Cruise, 225 m.p.h.

(A. J. Jackson)

Bell 47B

Two-seat, two-bladed helicopter powered by one 178 h.p. Franklin 6V4-178-B3, built 1947 at Buffalo, N.Y., by the Bell Aircraft Corporation. One British aircraft only: G-AKCX, c/n 49, formerly NC1296, C. of A. issued 11.8.47, demonstration aircraft of Irvin-Bell Helicopter Sales Ltd., Prestwick. Damaged beyond repair at Heathfield, near Prestwick, 7.2.49. Rotor diameter, 31 ft. 1½ in. Length, 30 ft 10¾ in. Tare wt., 1,556 lb. A.U.W., 2,150 lb. Max. speed, 100 m.p.h. Cruise, 85 m.p.h.

(A. J. Jackson)

Bell 47B-3

Two-seat, two-bladed helicopter powered by one 178 h.p. Franklin 6V4-178-B32, built 1947 at Buffalo, N.Y. Two British aircraft only, both supplied to British European Airways Corporation for training purposes: G-AKFA 'Sir Balin', c/n 69, C. of A. issued 24.9.47, damaged beyond repair landing at Gatwick 4.1.55; G-AKFB 'Sir Balan', c/n 73, C. of A. issued 24.9.47. Both originally had open cockpits. Specification as Bell 47B.

(*Richard Riding*)

Bell 47D and 47G variants

Three-seat helicopters with 'goldfish bowl' cabin and 200 h.p. Franklin, 200 h.p. or 260 h.p. Lycoming engines produced at Buffalo from 1948 and under licence by Agusta at Gallerate, Italy, and Westland Aircraft Ltd., Yeovil. Some fifty British registered examples in six variants detailed in Appendix E were used for taxi, advertising, photography and crop spraying, as well as for Army pilot training at the Bristow civil school, Middle Wallop. Data for Bell 47G-4A (illustrated): Rotor diameter, 37 ft. 2 in. Length, 32 ft. 6 in. Tare wt., 1,778 lb. A.U.W., 2,950 lb. Cruise, 84 m.p.h.

(*E. J. Riding*)

Bellanca Pacemaker

Six-seater powered by one 300 h.p. Wright R-975 Whirlwind, built 1931 by the Bellanca Aircraft Corporation at New Castle, Delaware, U.S.A. One British aircraft, c/n 167, imported from Italy as I-AAPI by S. A. Courtauld, C. of A. issued 16.3.32. Flown to Iceland by F. S. Cotton en route to rescue the 1932 Courtauld Greenland Expedition. Later owned by the Hon. F. E. Guest at Hanworth and C. S. J. Collier at Doncaster. Impressed for naval communications as DZ209 in July 1941. Span, 46 ft. 4 in. Length, 27 ft. 9 in. Tare wt., 2,420 lb. A.U.W., 4,300 lb. Max. speed, 150 mp.h.

Bellanca 28-70

Two-seater powered by one 700 h.p. Pratt & Whitney Twin Wasp Junior SA-G. One aircraft only: EI-AAZ 'Irish Swoop', c/n 902, built for, but non-starter in, the 1934 Australia Race. Shipped to the U.S.A., where it became NR190M 'The Dorothy', in which James Mollison made a record crossing from New York to Croydon in 13 hours 17 minutes 30.10.36. Became British as G-AEPC on arrival, C. of A. validated from 21.10.36. Left on unsuccessful attempt on the Cape record 29.11.36, shipped back to Croydon and flown away by Mollison 1937.

Bellanca 14-13-2 Cruisair and 14-19-3

Four-seater with 150 h.p. Franklin 6A4-150-B3 built from 1955 by Downer Aircraft, Alexandria, Minnesota. The improved 14-19-3 (or '260') with 260 h.p. Continental IO-470-F and retractable tricycle undercarriage first flew in 1958. One British aircraft of each type: G-AREY (c/n 1564), 14-13-2, N9962F, 5.6.61, Chobham F/G, burned out at Blackbushe 8.8.69; G-ASRD, 14-19-3, (4125), EI-AKR, 25.3.64, Tasman Imports.Exports Ltd., Manningtree, crashed near Oswestry 12.8.66. (Data for 14-19-3) Span, 34 ft. 2 in. Length, 22 ft. 11 in. Tare wt., 1,690 lb. A.U.W., 2,700 lb. Max. speed, 208 m.p.h. Cruise, 185 m.p.h.

(*A. J. Jackson*)

Benes Mraz Be.550 Bibi

Two-seater powered by one 62 h.p. Walter Mikron II, built 1937 at Chocen, Czechoslovakia. One British aircraft only: G-AGSR, c/n 2, imported as OK-BET in 1938, stored during war, C. of A. issued 16.5.47, owner H. Clive Smith, Heston. Sold to N. C. Chorlton, 5.50, destroyed in fatal crash at White Waltham 25.10.51. Span, 37 ft. 8 in. Length, 23 ft. 11 in. Tare wt., 704 lb. A.U.W., 1,144 lb. Max. speed, 121 m.p.h. Cruise, 105·5 m.p.h.

(*E. J. Riding*)

Benes Mraz M.1C Sokol

Two/three-seater powered by one 105 h.p. Walter Minor 4-III, built 1947 by Automobilov Zavody at Chocen. One British aircraft only: G-AIXN, c/n 112, imported as OK-BHA by H. Clive Smith, C. of A. issued 15.5.47. to G. Shaw, Thornaby; A. R. Pilgrim, Elstree 1949; J. H. Southern, Barton 1959; E. N. Husbands, Swansea 1963; G. Priest, Horsham St. Faith 1968. Span, 32 ft. 9½ in. Length, 24 ft 0 in. Tare wt., 897 lb. A.U.W., 1,654 lb. Max. speed, 150 m.p.h. Cruise, 132 m.p.h.

(*Richard Riding*)

Björn Andreasson BA-4B

Single-seat aerobatic biplane designed by Björn Andreasson of Malmö Flygindustri and powered by one 100 h.p. Continental O-200-A. Design and production rights purchased by P. J. C. Phillips 1968 to whom the prototype, SE-XBS, c/n 1, was registered G-AWPZ, A. to F. 14.11.68. British production by Crosby Aviation Ltd. commenced at Barton 1970 with G-AYFU, 'FV and 'FW (c/n 001–003). Span, 17 ft. 6 in. Length, 15 ft. 4 in. Tare wt., 627 lb. A.U.W., 936 lb. (aerobatic) 880 lb. Max. speed, 143 m.p.h.

(*Miss D. E. Wright*)

Blériot XI

Single-seat monoplane with warping wings, powered by one 25 h.p. fan-type Anzani, designed by Louis Blériot and first flown at Issy near Paris, June 1909. A genuine original example, c/n 225, built 1910 for Jules Dupont, stored at Liége, Belgium, 1914–64, was registered to L. D. Goldsmith 2.11.67 as G-AVXV and restored to flying condition at Old Warden 1968. It thus became the oldest aircraft ever registered in Britain. Span, 28 ft. 0 in. Length, 25 ft. 0 in. Tare wt., 484 lb. A.U.W. 715 lb. Max. speed 40 m.p.h.

(*Richard Riding*)

Boeing-Stearman A75-N1

Two-seat Stearman trainer built in quantity by the Boeing Aircraft Co. at Wichita, Kansas, 1939–45. Over 4,000 postwar single-seat agricultural conversions with 450 h.p. Pratt & Whitney Wasp Junior R-985-AN-1 radials. Four British aircraft only: G-AROY (c/n 75-4775), N56418, imported for Aerial Farm Services Ltd., Stapleford, C. of A. 1.8.61; G-ATWK (75-1697), N55322, registered to M. J. L. Brook, Huddersfield 21.6.66, remained in U.S.A.; G-AWLO (75-8375), 5Y-KRR, M. T. Hynett, Farnborough; G-AZLE (75-8543), CF-XRD, Shoreham Av. Serv. Ltd. Span, 32 ft. 2 in. Length, 24 ft. 0¼ in. Tare wt., 2,300 lb. A.U.W., 3,200 lb. Max. speed, 125 m.p.h. Cruise, 80 m.p.h. Range, 300 miles.

(*Imperial War Museum CH.14069*)

Boeing 314A

Transport flying-boat carrying a maximum of 74 passengers (or 40 sleepers) and 10 crew, powered by four 1,600 h.p. Wright Cyclone 709-C14-AC1 radials and built at Seattle, Washington, for Pan American Airways 1938–39. Three purchased by B.O.A.C. 1941: G-AGBZ 'Bristol' (c/n 2081), NC18607, 10.7.41; G-AGCA 'Berwick' (2082), NC18608, 19.7.41; G-AGCB 'Bangor' (2084), NC18610, 27.7.41; all reverted to original U.S. marks when sold to General Phoenix Corp., Baltimore, 4.48. Span, 152 ft. 0 in. Length, 106 ft. 0 in. Tare wt., 48,000 lb. A.U.W., 84,000 lb. Max. speed, 210 m.p.h. Cruise 188 m.p.h. Range, 3,685 miles.

Boeing 377 Stratocruiser

Long-range transport accommodating 55–100 passengers and 5 flight crew, powered by four 3,500 h.p. Pratt & Whitney Wasp Major R-4360-TSB-6 radials. Fifty-five built at Seattle, Washington for B.O.A.C., S.A.S. and U.S. operators. G-AKGH to 'GM delivered to B.O.A.C. 1949–50 with G-ALSA to 'SD (originally ordered by S.A.S.), were supplemented in 1955 by G-ANTX to 'UC acquired from United Air Lines, and 'UM from Pan American. Ten were re-sold to Transocean Air Lines, Oakland, California, 1958–59. See Appendix E. Span, 141 ft. 3 in. Length, 110 ft. 4 in. Tare wt., 83,500 lb. A.U.W., 145,800 lb. Max. speed, 340 m.p.h. Cruise, 300 m.p.h. Range, 3,000 miles.

Boeing 707

Intercontinental jet transport for up to 180 passengers, produced at Renton from 1957 in variants designated by 'dash' numbers indicating capacity, size and power plants. First deliveries to Britain were 20 Series 436 and 465 for B.O.A.C. (four 17,500 lb. s.t. Rolls-Royce Conway 508) 1960–63; also Series 321, 323C, 336C, 349C, 355C, 365C, 373C, 379C, and 399C passenger/cargo versions (18,000 lb. s.t. Pratt & Whitney JT3D-3B turbofans) for B.O.A.C., British Caledonian and other operators. (Data for Series 436) Span, 145 ft. 9 in. Length, 152 ft. 11 in. Tare wt., 132,700 lb. A.U.W., 311,000 lb. Economical cruise, 522 m.p.h. Max. range, 6,955 miles. Also two Series 138B (Span, 130 ft. 10 in. Length, 134 ft. 6 in.), ex Qantas, to British Eagle 1968. See Appendix E.

Boeing 720-051B

Medium-range version of the Boeing 707 with four 17,000 lb. s.t. Pratt & Whitney JT3D-1 turbofans, new mainplane and shorter fuselage for operation from smaller airports at lower all-up weights. Three aircraft, all built 1961, acquired by Monarch Airlines Ltd., Luton: G-AZFB, c/n 18381, formerly N791TW and Northwest N730US, delivered at Luton 28.11.71; G-AZKM, c/n 18382, N792TW/N731US, delivered Luton 15.2.72; G-AZNX, c/n 18383, N793TW/N732US, registered 3.72. Span, 130 ft. 10 in. Length, 136 ft. 2 in. Tare wt., 109,590 lb. A.U.W., 233,000 lb. Cruise, 540 m.p.h. Max. range, 5,240 miles.

Boeing 737-204

Short haul transport carrying up to 119 passengers in 6 abreast seating, powered by two 14,000 lb. s.t. Pratt & Whitney JT8D-9 turbofan engines mounted below the mainplane. Deliveries from Seattle began in 1968, including G-AVRL to 'RN for Britannia Airways Ltd., Luton, who also acquired G-AVRO and G-AWSY in 1969 and G-AXNA to 'NC in 1970. Span, 93 ft. 0 in. Length, 100 ft. 0 in. Tare wt., 61,020 lb. A.U.W., 103,500 lb. Economical cruise, 506 m.p.h. Range, 1,200 miles at max. load.

Boeing 747-36

Long-range transport carrying up to 490 passengers in 10-abreast seating, powered by four 43,500 lb. s.t. Pratt & Whitney JT9D-3 two-spool turbofan engines. Largest commercial aircraft in the world when deliveries began from Boeing's new Everett, Washington, plant in December 1969. Twelve registered to B.O.A.C. 30.7.68 as G-AWNA to 'NL for delivery in 1970–71. See Appendix E. Span, 195 ft. 8 in. Length, 231 ft. 4 in. Tare wt., 353,398 lb. A.U.W., 710,000 lb. Economical cruise, 593 m.p.h. Max. range, 6,150 miles.

(*Aviation Photo News*)

Bölkow-Klemm Kl 107C

Three-seat trainer/tourer of semi-monococque wooden construction powered by one 150 h.p. Lycoming O-320-A1A, built at Nabern, Germany, by Bölkow Apparatebau GmbH as a development of the earlier Klemm Kl 107. Production ceased in 1960. One British registered aircraft only: G-ASAW (c/n 150), C. of A. 18.6.62, imported by Flair-Aviation Sales Co. Ltd., Biggin Hill; crashed in the sea off Littlehampton, Sussex 5.1.65. Span, 35 ft. 6¾ in. Length, 27 ft. 2¾ in. Tare wt., 1,377 lb. A.U.W., 2,138 lb. Max. speed, 146 m.p.h. Cruise, 127 m.p.h. Range, 510 miles.

(K. A. Palmer)

Bölkow Bö 207

A four-seat derivative of the Bölkow-Klemm K1107C with 180 h.p. Lycoming O-360-A1A, modified wing, clear-vision canopy and revised tail surfaces. Three British registered aircraft only, imported by Flair-Aviation Sales Co. Ltd., Biggin Hill: G-ARYN (c/n 212), 19.3.62, re-sold to Bölkow 7.63 as D-EHUK; G-ASAY (257), 7.6.62, damaged in forced landing at Libin, Belgium, 17.12.62, rebuilt 10.63 as D-EGLU; G-ASCW (256), remained in Germany, registered to Bölkow 7.64 as D-EGLO. Span, 35 ft. 6 in. Length, 27 ft. 3 in. Tare wt., 1,575 lb. A.U.W. 2,645 lb. Max. speed, 160 m.p.h. Cruise 124 m.p.h. Range, 775 miles.

(A. J. Jackson)

Bölkow Bö 208 Junior

The A.B. Malmö Flygindustri MFI-9 all-metal two-seat trainer built under licence by Bölkow from 1962 as the Bö 208A-1 Junior (100 h.p. Continental O-200A); Bö 208A-2 (Rolls-Royce version); and Bö 208C with larger cabin and 1 ft. 11 in. increase in wing span. One MFI-9, G-AVEA, registered 11.1.67; nine Bö 208A-1 or -2 imported 1963–65 by Flair-Aviation Sales Co. Ltd.; 18 Bö 208C imported 1965–67, some by K. N. Rudd (Engineers) Ltd., Shoreham. (Data for Bö 208C) Span, 26 ft. 3 in. Length, 19 ft. 0 in. Tare wt., 840 lb. A.U.W., 1,325 lb. Max. speed, 143 m.p.h. Cruise, 130 m.p.h. Range 620 miles.

Bölkow Bö 209 Monsun

Aerobatic two-seater with folding wings built by Messerschmitt-Bölkow-Blohm at Munich, Germany, from February 1970 as the Bö 209B (150 h.p. Lycoming O-360-E2C) and the Bö 209C (160 h.p. Lycoming IO-320-D1B, v.p. airscrew and retractable nose wheel). First British imports by Air Touring Services Ltd., Biggin Hill, were: G-AYNE, Bö 209B, (c/n 114), not delivered, became D-EBPC; G-AYPE, Bö 209C, (123), 8.4.71; G-AZBB, Bö 209C, (137), 23.7.71; G-AZDD, Bö 209B, (143), 31.8.71, (Bö 209C): Span, 27 ft. 7 in. Length, 21 ft. 0 in. Tare wt., 1,067 lb. A.U.W., 1,878 lb. Max. cruise, 158 m.p.h. Max. range, 650 miles.

(P. R. March)

Brantly B-2, B-2A and B-2B

Two-seat light helicopter powered by one 180 h.p. Lycoming VO-360-A1A, produced by the Brantly Helicopter Corporation, Frederick, Oklahoma, U.S.A., from 1959. Eight Model B-2, five Model B-2A with redesigned cabin, and twelve Model B-2B with 180 h.p. Lycoming IVO-360-A1A fuel injection engines imported 1959–68, all but the first two by British Executive Air Services Ltd., for training at Kidlington and executive use by other companies. Rotor diameter, 23 ft. 8¾ in. Length, 21 ft. 9¼ in. Tare wt., 1,040 lb. A.U.W., 1,600 lb. Max. speed, 100 m.p.h., Cruise, 90 m.p.h. Range, 260 miles.

(*P. R. March*)

Brantly 305

Five-seat version of the Brantly B-2B powered by one 305 h.p. Lycoming IVO-540-A1A, in production at Frederick, Oklahoma from 1964. Eight imported by British Executive Air Services Ltd. 1964–67, mainly as executive transports for large British industrial consortiums and including one re-exported to Ireland Rotor diameter, 28 ft. 8 in. Length, 25 ft. 10 in. Tare wt., 1,405 lb. A.U.W., 2,900 lb. Max. speed, 120 m.p.h. Cruise, 105 m.p.h. Range, 250 miles.

(*Flight Photo 8364*)

Breda 15

Two-seater powered by one 100 h.p. de Havilland Gipsy I, built at Milan 1930 by the Societa Italiana Ernesto Breda. Six British aircraft only: G-AAVL (c/n 1419), 15.4.30, H. E. Burgess, Heston; W. W. Adams, Heston, 11.30; Pan Aero Pictures Ltd., Brooklands, 3.35, dismantled 1937. G-AAVN (1414), 15.4.30, H. E. Burgess, Heston, dismantled 1932. G-ABBZ to 'CC (1638–1641), registered to International Aircraft Ltd. 17.7.30, cancelled 12.32. Span, 36 ft. 6 in. Length, 22 ft. 10 in. Tare wt., 926 lb. A.U.W., 1,543 lb. Maximum speed, 112 m.p.h.

(*Associated Press*)

Breda 15 (Ugo Antoni Wing)

Last British registered Breda 15, G-ABCC (c/n 1641), restored jointly to the Gloster Aircraft Co. Ltd. and Ugo Antoni Safety Aircraft Ltd., Brockworth, 26.6.33 and fitted with the Ugo Antoni variable-camber wing by Gloster Aircraft Ltd. First flown at Brockworth with standard rudder 10.33; flown with larger rudder by Rex Stocken 11.33; side slipped into trees and damaged beyond repair due to wing flutter in turbulence at Chosen Hill, Churchdown, Glos., 1.12.33. Pilot H. J. Saint uninjured.

Breda 33

Two-seater powered by one 130 h.p. de Havilland Gipsy III, built at Milan 1932. One British aircraft only: G-ABXK, c/n 3208, C. of A. issued 29.7.32. Flown by the late Miss Winifred Spooner in the 1932 Circuit of Europe, crated at Heston and returned to the manufacturers 10.32. Span, 32 ft. 2 in. Length, 24 ft. 6 in. Tare wt., 1,058 lb. A.U.W., 1,720 lb. Max. speed, 137 m.p.h. Cruise, 125 m.p.h.

(A. J. Jackson)

Brochet M.B.50 Pipistrelle

All-wood single-seater designed by Maurice Brochet in 1947 for amateur construction in France. F-PFAL, c/n 02, built 1948 and powered by one 45 h.p. Train 4A, registered to P. R. Holmes 17.4.67, shipped to England, overhauled and flown at Rochester as G-AVKB. Later based at Ramsgate by P. G. Horsting. Span 26 ft. 2¾ in. Length, 16 ft. 0 in. Tare wt., 529 lb. A.U.W., 772 lb. Max. speed, 87 m.p.h. Cruise, 72 m.p.h.

(W. L. Lewis)

Brochet M.B.84

Tandem, two-seat dual-control cabin monoplane, designed by Maurice Brochet in 1951 and featuring a spring steel undercarriage and 65 h.p. Continental A-65-8 engine. One British registered aircraft only; G-AYVT, c/n 9, F-BGLI, 'Le Vieux Paul' ferried Le Touquet to Purleigh strip, Essex, via Southend 25–26.2.71 by owner W. H. Cole. C. of A. 17.9.71. Span, 34 ft. 3 in. Length, 21 ft. 7½ in. Tare wt., 878 lb. A.U.W., 1,200 lb. Cruise, 96 m.p.h. Range, 310 miles.

Brunswick Zaunkoenig V-2

Single-seater powered by one 51 h.p. Zündapp Z9-92, built as an essay into slow-speed controlled flight by the students of Brunswick Technical High School, Germany. First flown by Prof. Winter 4.45 as D-YBAR, hidden at Hartzberg and survived the war to go to Farnborough as VX190. Registered to the Ultra Light Association as G-ALUA, A. to F. 1.7.49 and flown extensively by subsequent owners. Completely rebuilt by M. Loyal and flown again at Fairoaks 6.69. Span, 26 ft. 5 in. Length, 19 ft. 11 in. Tare wt., 553 lb. A.U.W., 776 lb. Max. speed, 87·3 m.p.h. Min. speed, 31 m.p.h.

Bücker Bü 131 Jungmann

Two-seat aerobatic biplane, one 105 h.p. Hirth HM 504A, first built 1934 by Bücker Flugzeugbau GmbH at Rangsdorf, Germany. Two British civil aircraft only: G-ASLI, c/n 957, ex HB-EVA, A. to F. 6.12.63, D. J. Reay; G-ATJX, c/n 36, ex D-EDMI, A. to F. 8.11.65, R. H. Fautley; both based at Navestock strip, Essex. Span, 24 ft. 3 in. Length, 21 ft. 8 in. Tare wt., 836 lb. A.U.W., 1,470 lb. Max. speed, 115 m.p.h.

(*Air Portraits*)

Bücker Bü 133C Jungmeister

Single-seat aerobatic trainer powered by one 160 h.p. Siemens Sh 14A-4 and first flown in 1935. Widely used by European air forces and licence-built outside Germany. Four British examples only, all originally built in Switzerland by Dornier-Werke A.G. for the Swiss Air Force and imported for competition flying 1969–1970: G-AXIH, G-AXMT, G-AXNI and G-AYFO. Span, 21 ft. $7\frac{1}{2}$ in. Length, 19 ft. 4 in. Tare wt., 925 lb. A.U.W., 1,140 lb. Max. speed, 134 m.p.h. Cruise, 102 m.p.h. Range, 310 miles.

(*A. J. Jackson*)

Bücker Bü 181 Bestmann

Two-seater powered by one 105 h.p. Hirth HM.504, first built 1939 by Bücker Flugzeugbau, GmbH at Rangsdorf. One British civil aircraft only: G-AKAX, c/n 120417, registered to O. F. McLaren Ltd. 10.7.47, never flown, parked in the open at Denham until broken up 1950. Span, 34 ft. 9 in. Length, 25 ft. 5 in. Tare wt., 1,056 lb. A.U.W., 1,650 lb. Max. speed, 133·5 m.p.h. Cruise, 120 m.p.h.

(H. C. Wilden)

Callair A-9 and B-1

Single-seat agricultural aircraft developed by Callair Inc. and built at Afton, Wyoming, U.S.A., by the Intermountain Mfg. Co. (IMCO) from 1963 and powered (A-9) by one 235 h.p. Lycoming O-540-B2B5 or (B-1) one 425 h.p. Lycoming IO-720-A1A. Two British civil aircraft only: G-AVZA (A-9), c/n 1200, ex SE-EUA, C. of A. 8.2.68, Farm Aviation Ltd., Rush Green; G-AWPT, (B-1), c/n 10002, ex SE-EWA, C. of A. 13.11.68, Shackleton Av. Ltd., Sywell, to Ethiopia 7.69 as ET-ADE. (Data for A-9) Span 35 ft. 0 in. Length 24 ft. 0 in. Tare wt., 1,400 lb. A.U.W., 3,000 lb. (B-1 4,500 lb). Max. speed 130 m.p.h. Cruise, 120 m.p.h.

(A. J. Jackson)

Canadair C-4

Pressurised transport based on the Douglas DC-4 but powered by four 1,760 h.p. Rolls-Royce Merlin 626 engines and built by Canadair Ltd. at Cartierville, Montreal, Canada, for Trans-Canada Air Lines and B.O.A.C. 1947–49. Twenty-two British registered aircraft flew on the B.O.A.C. world network until disposed of to other operators from 1958 as shown in Appendix E. Span, 117 ft. 6 in. Length, 93 ft. 7½ in. Tare wt., 46,832 lb. A.U.W., 82,000 lb. Cruise, 302 m.p.h. Range, 3,940 miles.

Canadair CL-44D-4

Long-range swing-tail commercial freighter based on the Bristol Britannia and powered by four 5,730 e.s.h.p. Rolls-Royce Tyne 515 propeller-turbines. First of 27 built flew at Cartierville 16.11.60 and a number initially delivered to The Flying Tiger Line and Seaboard World Airlines were later sold to British operators commencing with G-AWDK to Transglobe A/W Ltd., Gatwick, in February 1968. See Appendix E. Span, 142 ft. $3\frac{1}{2}$ in. Length, 136 ft. $10\frac{3}{4}$ in. Tare wt., 88,520 lb. A.U.W., 210,000 lb. Max. cruise, 402 m.p.h. Range (max. load) 3,250 miles.

(*Royal Aeronautical Society*)

Caudron G.3

Two-seat trainer powered by one 90 h.p. Anzani, designed in France 1912 and built under licence by the British Caudron Co. Ltd. at Cricklewood 1914–18. Nine British civil aircraft only, as shown in Appendix E. In use for a few months only in 1919 for instruction and passenger flights and by Brooklands private owners G. Eyston and L. C. G. M. Le Champion. French built OO-ELA, illustrated, 100 h.p. Anzani, bought from M. J. E. Leduc by K. H. F. Waller and ferried Brussels–Brooklands 20.5.36. Registration G-AETA not used; acquired by the Nash Collection; taken over by the R.Ae.S. and handed over to the R.A.F. on permanent loan 1964; rebuilt at Stradishall 1966; preserved at Henlow for the R.A.F. Museum. Span, 43 ft. 5 in. Length, 22 ft. 6 in. Tare wt., 981 lb. A.U.W., 1,619 lb. Max. speed, 71 m.p.h. Cruise, 56 m.p.h.

(*Flight Photo 10259*)

Caudron C.193

Two-seater powered by one 95 h.p. Renault built by Avions Caudron at Issy-les-Moulineaux 1930. One British aircraft only: G-ABFX, c/n 6479, formerly F-AJSI, C. of A. issued 8.11.30. Privately owned by Harold Swann, Heston. Sold abroad, 6.31. Span, 37 ft. 8 in. Length, 24 ft. 9 in. Tare wt., 1,012 lb. A.U.W., 1,650 lb. Max. speed, 108·6 m.p.h.

(*P. R. Duffy*)

Caudron C.276 Luciole

Tandem two-seat cabin biplane built as a C.275 by Avions Caudron at Issy during the 1930s, re-engined with one 105 h.p. Hirth HM 504A-2 as C.276. One British aircraft only: G-ATIO, c/n 7207/26, formerly F-PHQM, flown Dinard—Baldonnel 6.65 in Dakota 3 F-BAXR, registered to 20th Century Fox Productions Ltd. 9.9.65 for use in the film *Blue Max* during which it was destroyed. Registration cancelled 23.11.65. Span, 32 ft. 5½ in.

(P. R. Duffy)

Caudron C.277 Luciole

Caudron C.272 open cockpit Luciole, from which the C.275 was evolved, re-engined with one 120 h.p. Renault Bengali 4 Pdi as a C.277. One British aircraft only: G-ATIP, c/n 7546/135 built 1937 as F-AQFB, ferried Dinard–Biggin Hill–Baldonnel 6.65 by J. E. Hutchinson, registered to 20th Century Fox Productions Ltd. 9.9.65 for the film *Blue Max*; to Rousseau Aviation, Dinard, 2.66 as F-BNMB; to Ireland 5.67 as EI-ARF. Span, 32 ft. 5½ in. Length, 25 ft. 2 in. Tare wt., 1,173 lb. A.U.W., 1,852 lb. Max. speed, 107 m.p.h. Cruise, 93 m.p.h.

(E. J. Riding)

Cessna C-34 Airmaster

Four-seater powered by one 145 h.p. Warner Super Scarab 40, built by Cessna Aircraft Corporation at Wichita, Kansas, 1934–37. Two British aircraft only: G-AEAI, c/n 314, C. of A. issued 14.5.36, imported by Surrey Flying Services Ltd., Croydon, 1935, impressed 10.41 as HM502, restored by E. D. Wynne at Staverton 1946, burned out on the ground at Squires Gate 20.9.50; G-AFBY, c/n 319, Super Scarab 50, C. of A. issued 6.12.37, imported 1937 by Tecalemit Ltd., flown throughout the war, last owner W. Jaworski 12.49, scrapped at Cowes 11.51. Span, 33 ft. 10 in. Length, 24 ft. 7 in. Tare wt., 1,300 lb. A.U.W., 2,220 lb. Max. speed, 162 m.p.h. Cruise, 145 m.p.h.

Cessna 150

All-metal two-seater powered by one 100 h.p. Continental O-200-A, mass produced at Wichita from 1958. The 1964 Cessna 150D had slimmer rear fuselage with wrap-around rear canopy and the 1966 Cessna 150F introduced a swept fin and rudder. Mass produced in France by Reims Aviation with F prefix and Rolls-Royce engines from 1965 including the 1969 aerobatic Cessna FA.150. Imported in large numbers, see Appendix E. Span, 32 ft. 8½ in. Length, 23 ft. 9 in. Tare wt., 985 lb. A.U.W., 1,600 lb. Cruise, 120 m.p.h. Endurance, 6 hours.

Cessna 170

All-metal four-seater with 145 h.p. Continental O-300-A (170A) or C-145-2 (170B), mass produced at Wichita 1948–56. One British registered Model 170A and two 170B only: G-ABLE,* 170A, (19903), N1327D, VR-NAH, C. of A. 28.3.61, E. A. Scrimshire, Panshanger; G-APVS (26156), N2512C, 9.10.59, D. Scholes and partners, Yeadon; G-AWOU (25829), CR-ADU, VQ-ZJA, 29.5.69, Anglian Air Charter Ltd., North Denes. Span, 36 ft. 0 in. Length, 24 ft. 11½ in. Tare wt., 1,205 lb. A.U.W., 2,200 lb. Cruise, 121 m.p.h. Range, 590 miles.

* *Re-allocation* (see Appendix D, Volume 3—Vickers-Supermarine 179 of 1931).

(*Richard Riding*)

Cessna 172 Skyhawk and 175 Skylark

Nose-wheel version of the Cessna 170 introduced in 1955, marketed as the 172A with swept fin in 1960, through to the 172D with wrap-around rear canopy in 1963. Assembled by Reims Aviation with F prefix from the F.172D via later marks to the FR.172G Reims Rocket (210 h.p. Continental IO-360-D) in 1970. Cessna 175 Skylark luxury variant (175 h.p. Continental GO-300-E) introduced 1960. Production ceased with the 175C of 1962 with additional rear seat. Data for 175: Span, 36 ft. 2 in. Length, 26 ft. 6 in. Tare wt., 1,410 lb. A.U.W., 2,450 lb. Cruise, 142 m.p.h. Range, 720 miles.

(*Air Portraits*)

Cessna F.177 Cardinal RG

Four-seat cantilever touring monoplane powered by one 200 h.p. Lycoming IO-360-A1B6 with retractable gear (RG), introduced by Cessna 12.70, built by Reims Aviation and marketed in Britain by Brymon Aviation Ltd., Fairoaks, and Westair Flying Services Ltd., Squires Gate. G-AYPF to 'PI, first four of many British owned examples, were registered 1.71. Span, 35 ft. 6 in. Length, 27 ft. 3 in. Tare wt., 1,630 lb. A.U.W., 2,800 lb. Cruise, 165 m.p.h. Range, 765 miles.

(*A. J. Jackson*)

Cessna 180

All-metal four-seater with 225 h.p. Continental O-470-A six-cylinder engine introduced in 1953 using the same wing as the Cessna 170 with a redesigned fuselage and tail assembly. Details of ten aircraft of this type registered in Britain 1960–65 are listed in Appendix E. Span, 36 ft. 2 in. Length, 25 ft. 6 in. Tare wt., 1,525 lb. A.U.W., 2,800 lb. Max. speed, 170 m.p.h. Cruise, 164 m.p.h. Range, 1,215 miles.

(*John Goring*)

Cessna 182 Skylane

A nose-wheel version of the Cessna 180 with 230 h.p. Continental O-470-L in production at Wichita from 1956. The 182C of 1960 introduced a swept fin and rudder, the 182D of 1961 a shortened undercarriage and the 182E of 1962 a slim rear fuselage permitting all-round visibility from the cabin. Over 30 British registered examples up to the Cessna 182N of 1970 will be found in Appendix E. Span, 36 ft. 2 in. Length, 27 ft. 3 in. Tare wt., 1,550 lb. A.U.W., 2,800 lb. Max speed, 167 m.p.h. Cruise, 159 m.p.h. Range, 1,190 miles

Cessna 185 Skywagon

Utility six-seater with 260 h.p. Continental IO-470-F based on the Cessna 180 but with strengthened structure for freight work or agricultural flying. Four British civil examples only: G-ARMJ, 185, (c/n 185-0100), N9900X, C. of A. 24.7.61, Cowick Hall Av. Ltd., Snaith; G-ATAC, 185D with ventral cargo pack, (185-0807), to Mali 2.65 as TZ-ABW; G-AXVT (A.185F-01617), to Mali 3.70 as TZ-APR; G-AYNN (185-0518), 8R-GCC, 8.4.71, Britten-Norman Ltd., Bembridge. Span, 36 ft. 0 in. Length, 26 ft. 2 in. Tare wt., 1,506 lb. A.U.W., 3,200 lb. Max. speed, 176 m.p.h. Cruise, 168 m.p.h.

Cessna A.188 Agwagon

Single-seat agricultural aircraft, with 170 gallon hopper in front of the pilot, embodying some Cessna 180 components. Powered by one 300 h.p. Continental IO-520-D engine and first flown in 1965 as the Model 188 with 230 h.p. Continental O-470-R. Three British registered Cessna A.188s only, imported for crop spraying: G-AXFF (c/n 188-0366), N8116V, C. of A. 16.5.69; G-AXGF (188-0344), N8094V, C. of A. 10.6.69, crashed at Dyfynog, Breconshire 11.8.70; G-AYJM (188-0444), C. of A. 10.10.70. Span, 41 ft. $1\frac{1}{4}$ in. Length, 25 ft. $4\frac{3}{4}$ in. Tare wt., 1,800 lb. A.U.W., 3,300 lb. Cruise, 141 m.p.h.

(*Tony Leigh*)

Cessna 205, 206 and 207

The Cessna 205 six-seater (260 h.p. Continental IO-470-S) was introduced in 1962. The Cessna 206 Super Skywagon (285 h.p. Continental IO-520-A) with double freight doors was the 1964 version, subvariants being the utility U.206 and 'plush' P.206 Super Skylane. A stretched seven-seat version introduced in 1969 was designated Cessna 207. Ten aircraft British registered by 1971. Data for Cessna 206: Span, 36 ft. 7 in. Length, 28 ft. 0 in. Tare wt., 1,785 lb. A.U.W., 3,600 lb. Cruise, 163 m.p.h. Range, 1,075 miles.

(*Air Portraits*)

Cessna 210 Centurion

All-metal six-seater with 260 h.p. Continental IO-470-E in production from 1960 and the first single-engined Cessna aircraft with retractable undercarriage. The Cessna 210D of 1964 had the 285 h.p. Continental IO-520-A and the T.210H of 1969 was powered by the turbo-supercharged version. Fifteen British registered examples are listed in Appendix E. (Data for Cessna 210D) Span, 36 ft. 7 in. Length, 28 ft. 4 in. Tare wt., 1,830 lb. A.U.W., 3,100 lb. Max. speed, 199 m.p.h. Cruise, 191 m.p.h. Range, 1,035 miles.

379

(*Richard Riding*)

Cessna 310 and Cessna 320 Skyknight

Four/five-seater (two 240 h.p. Continental O-470-M) first marketed in 1953. The Cessna 310D of 1960 introduced swept tail surfaces and two extra windows, the Cessna 310L of 1966 being the first with 260 h.p. Continental IO-470-V fuel injection engines. The 1961 high-altitude version (two turbo-supercharged 260 h.p. Continental TSIO-470-D) was known as the Cessna 320 Skyknight. More than 30 British registered Cessna 310s and two 320s listed in Appendix E. Data for Cessna 310: Span, 36 ft. 11 in. Length, 28 ft. 10 in. Tare wt., 3,094 lb. A.U.W., 5,100 lb. Cruise, 223 m.p.h.

(*Richard Riding*)

Cessna 336 and 337 Skymaster

Twin-engined six-seater produced at Wichita from 1962, powered by two 195 h.p. Continental IO-360-A engines mounted in tandem and driving tractor and pusher airscrews respectively. Replaced in 1965 by a new version with 210 h.p. engines and retractable undercarriage known as the Cessna 337 Super Skymaster. British registered aircraft of both types, including the Reims-built Cessna F.377E, are listed in Appendix E. Data for 337: Span, 38 ft. 0 in. Length, 29 ft. 3 in. Tare wt., 4,056 lb. A.U.W., 6,570 lb. Cruise, 192 m.p.h. Range, 1,390 miles.

Cessna 411 and variants

Light transport for two crew and four passengers introduced in 1965 and powered by two 340 h.p. Continental GTSIO-520 turbo-supercharged engines. A lower powered economy Model 401 with 300 h.p. Continental TSIO-520-Es appeared in 1966, the pressurised Model 421 in 1967 and the Model 414 in 1970. Technical and registration details of British owned examples of all four types appear in Appendix E. (Data for 411): Span, 39 ft. 10 in. Length, 33 ft. 5½ in. Tare wt., 3,820 lb. A.U.W., 6,500 lb. Max. speed, 232 m.p.h. Range, 1,030 miles at 223 m.p.h.

Champion 7EC Traveller

Tandem two-seat, fabric-covered cabin monoplane with 90 h.p. Continental C-90-12F marketed 1950–51 as the Aeronca 7EC Champion. Production rights were later acquired by Champion Aircraft Inc. and the first Champion-built aircraft flew in February 1955. One British registered example only: G-AVDU, c/n 739, built at Osceola 1960, imported from France ex N9837Y by Horsted Aviation Ltd., Biggin Hill, C. of A. 25.4.67; F. M. Burdick, Sudbury, Suffolk. Span, 33 ft. 5 in. Length, 21 ft. 8 in. Tare wt., 929 lb. A.U.W., 1,500 lb. Max. speed, 135 m.p.h. Cruise, 112 m.p.h.

(*M. J. Hooks*)

Champion 7FC Tri-Traveller

De-luxe version of the Continental C-90-12F powered Champion 7EC with fixed tricycle undercarriage built in large numbers at Osceola by Champion Aircraft Inc. 1957–64. Seven imported by Maitland Drewery Ltd. 1960 (one written off unloading), for instructional use at Biggin Hill and an eighth, G-AVJY, by A. Indyk, Denham, 1967. Span, 33 ft. 5 in. Length, 21 ft. 8 in. Tare wt., 968 lb. A.U.W. 1,450 lb. Max. speed, 135 m.p.h. Cruise, 108 m.p.h.

(*George Pennick*)

Champion 7GCBA Challenger

Agricultural two-seater with increased span and spray booms evolved from the Champion 7EC and powered by one 180 h.p. Lycoming O-360-A2B. Built in considerable numbers from 1959. One British registered example only: G-ASSN, c/n 14, ex N9873Y, C. of A. 2.7.65, Airspray (Colchester) Ltd., Boxted; crashed at Boreham, Essex 27.7.65. Span, 34 ft. 5½ in. Length, 22 ft. 1 in. Tare wt., 1,050 lb. A.U.W., 2,400 lb. Max. speed, 125 m.p.h. Cruise, 115 m.p.h. Range, 630 miles.

382

(*M. D. N. Fisher*)

Champion 7KCAB Citabria

Fully aerobatic tandem two-seater of fabric-covered steel tube construction built by the Bellanca Aircraft Corporation and powered by one Rolls-Royce Continental IO-320-E2A with inverted fuel system. The name Citabria was a reversal of the word Airbatic. One British registered aircraft only: G-AYXU, c/n 232–70, formerly N7587F, registered 28.4.71 to Farm Aviation Ltd., Rush Green, Herts. Span, 33 ft. 5 in. Length, 22 ft. 8 in. Tare wt., 1,039 lb. A.U.W., 1,650 lb. Max. cruise, 125 m.p.h. Range, 530 miles.

APPENDIX D

This section of the book gives details of British registered civil aircraft for which illustrations have not been found despite many years of intensive search. It also describes those which were not completed and therefore not photographed and also those still under construction in 1972.

The introductory notes to Appendix A apply equally to this section.

Aircopta
Rotorcraft of undisclosed design registered 10.64 to Messrs. N. Dunmow and B. Coleman of Leytonstone, London, as G-ASXK, c/n 01.

Avro 636
Two-seat fighter trainer powered by one 460 h.p. Armstrong Siddeley Jaguar VIC, built at Woodford 1935. Reservation for one civil demonstrator, G-ADHP, c/n 821, not taken up and construction abandoned. Span, 33 ft. 0 in. Length, 27 ft. 6 in. Tare wt., 2,766 lb. A.U.W., 3,721 lb. Max. speed, 175 m.p.h.

Beardmore W.B.IX
Amphibian flying-boat for ten passengers and pilot laid down at Dalmuir, Dunbartonshire, for the 1920 Air Ministry Competition. Powered by four 200 h.p. Beardmore engines fitted inside the hull and driving two tractor airscrews through gears and shafting. The tail unit was carried on outriggers above a short hull. One aircraft only: G-EAQI, c/n 5404, construction abandoned. Span, 107 ft. Length, 61 ft. Tare wt., 9,520 lb. A.U.W., 14,000 lb. Estimated max. speed, 93 m.p.h. Range, 400 miles.

Bede BD-4
Two/four-seat, all-metal sporting and utility monoplane for amateur construction from plans and kits of parts marketed in the U.S.A. by Bede Homebuilts Inc. and powered by one 108 h.p. Lycoming O-235-C1 or one 180 h.p. Lycoming O-360. Two British registered aircraft only: G-AYKB, c/n 151, under construction by K. Bywater at Luton in 1971; G-AYYM, c/n 29, by K. Savidge at Pittsburgh, Penn., U.S.A., in 1971. Span, 25 ft. 6 in. Length, 21 ft. 10½ in. Tare wt., 840/880 lb. A.U.W., 1,400/1,800 lb. Max. speed, 156/180 m.p.h. Cruise, 145/175 m.p.h. Range (both), 1,200 miles.

Bird Gyrocopter
Single-seat autogyro registered 3.7.69 to Gerald Bird at Keighley, Yorks., as G-AXIY, c/n GB.001.

Bristol Type 130 Bombay

Late in 1939, at a time of grave wartime crisis, it was intended to convert three Bombay bomber transports for civil purposes. They were to have been registered G-AFYM, 'YN and 'YO but the scheme fell through and no other information is available. Standard R.A.F. Bombays were built by Short and Harland Ltd. at Belfast 1938–39 and powered by two 1,010 h.p. Bristol Pegasus XXII. Span, 95 ft. 9 in. Length, 69 ft. 0 in. Tare wt., 13,800 lb. A.U.W., 20,000 lb. Max. speed, 192 m.p.h. Cruise, 160 m.p.h. Range, 2,230 miles.

Bristol Type 156 Beaufighter X

Two-seat monoplane fighter powered by two 1,770 h.p. Bristol Hercules XVIII. Six unused war surplus aircraft RD135, RD448, RD427, ND929, NV306 and LZ185, were serviced at Ringway by the Fairey Aviation Co. Ltd. in April 1947 for private sale as G-AJMB to G-AJMG. All but 'MF were sold to R. Dickson and partners (a film company) and flown to Thame in July 1948. G-AJME crashed on approach to Thame 28.7.48, killing the pilot, and 'MF is believed to have been scrapped at Ringway. The remainder left for the Near East July–August 1948. Span, 57 ft. 10 in. Length, 41 ft. 8 in. Tare wt., 15,600 lb. A.U.W., 25,200 lb. Max. speed, 303 m.p.h. Range, 1,470 miles.

British Marine BM-1

The Sikorsky S-42A four-engined transoceanic flying-boat for 32 passengers and three crew, which was to have been built under licence by British Marine Aircraft Ltd., an associate of the British Aircraft Manufacturing Co. Ltd. A factory was built at Hamble in 1936 and all tools and jigs were manufactured for the prototype, G-AEGZ, c/n 1, but the works was turned over to sub-contract work under the Expansion Scheme and the BM-1 was not built. The American original was powered by 750 h.p. Pratt & Whitney Hornet S1EG radials. Span, 118 ft. 2 in. Length, 68 ft. 0 in. Tare wt., 20,924 lb. A.U.W., 40,000 lb. Max. speed, 190 m.p.h. Cruise, 160 m.p.h.

Bushby-Long Midget Mustang I

Single-seat, low-wing aerobatic monoplane of all-metal, stressed skin construction with 85 h.p. Continental C-85-8FJ (or 135 h.p. Lycoming O-290-D2), designed, built and first flown in 1948 by David Long, then chief engineer of the Piper company. Drawings and jigs were taken over by Robert W. Bushby of Glenwood, Illinois, U.S.A., who made plans and kits of parts available to amateur constructors. One British registered aircraft only: G-AWIR, c/n PFA.1315, under construction by A. Jarman at Oadby, Leics., in 1971. Span, 18 ft. 6 in. Length, 16 ft. 5 in. Tare wt., 575/590 lb. A.U.W., 875/900 lb. Max. speed, 190/210 m.p.h. Cruise, 148/165 m.p.h. Range, 400/375 miles.

Camco Mk. IIA V-Liner

An American designed, tandem-wing amphibious aircraft consisting of a V-section tubular structure acting as an airborne advertisement hoarding and supported at each end by a 69 ft. span monoplane wing with boat hull and wing tip floats. Power was supplied by two 750 h.p. Rolls-Royce Continental GTSIO-580D engines mounted above the front wing with a 100 h.p. O-200A engine over the rear wing to provide electrical power for the flashing illuminated signs. One aircraft only: G-AWPR, c/n 1657, partially built for the Central Aircraft Mfg.

Co. Inc. (Camco) by Slingsby Sailplanes Ltd. at Kirkbymoorside, Yorks., but scrapped after the half completed airframe was seriously damaged in the factory fire 18.11.68. Span, 69 ft. 0 in. Length, 378 ft. 0 in. A.U.W., 9,000 lb.

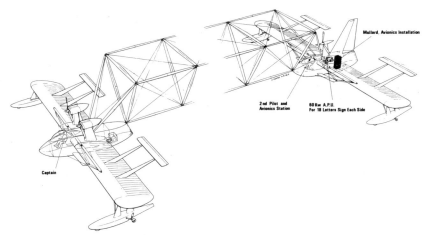

An artist's impression of the Camco Mk.IIA V-Liner which, had it been completed, would have weighed over four tons and incorporated over 2,000 ft. of aluminium tubing, 40 miles of wiring and 3,500 electric bulbs. (*Air Pictorial*)

Central Centaur V

Tourer of similar construction and appearance to the Centaur IV (see page 276), powered by one 110 h.p. Anzani. Normally flown as a side-by-side two seater but with removable decking for rapid conversion to four-seater. Reservation dated 15.9.19 for one aircraft only: G-EANA, c/n 301, construction abandoned. Span, 36 ft. 6 in. Length, 26 ft. 6 in. Tare wt., 1,200 lb. A.U.W., 1,800 lb. Max. speed, 80 m.p.h.

Central Centaur VIII

Reservation dated 26.4.20 for one aircraft only: G-EAST, c/n 400, which was not constructed. It would have been a triplane, but no further details were published.

Chasle YC-12 Tourbillon

Single-seat, low-wing aerobatic monoplane powered by one 65 h.p. Continental engine, designed and first flown in prototype form in France 1970. One British registered aircraft only: G-AYBV, c/n MA-001-W, under construction by B. A. Mills at Eversden, Cambs., in 1971. Span, 22 ft. 0 in. Length, 19 ft. 6 in. Tare wt., 630 lb. A.U.W., 950 lb. Max. cruise, 127 m.p.h. Max. range, 500 miles.

Register of British Civil Aircraft

Temporary civil registrations beginning at K-100 and reaching K-175, used for approximately one month from 30 April 1919, were supplanted by a lettered sequence commencing G-EAAA but by international agreement in 1928 a new system began at G-AAAA after G-EBZZ had been reached. The letter Q was discontinued in 1927, the last aircraft to carry it being G-EBTQ, a Fokker F.VIIA. Class B registrations comprising the national G, manufacturers' numbers and aircraft identity digits, are used when an aircraft is flown for test or certification, e.g. Islander G-51-2 where 51 indicated Britten-Norman Ltd. and 2 the particular aircraft. Before 1947 makers' letters were followed by a number.

This appendix is the first instalment of more than 16,500 individual aircraft registrations issued in Great Britain since 1919. They are grouped alphabetically by types and variants, following precisely the same order as that in which they are described in the chapters and appendixes. Registration data for aircraft which existed only in prototype form or very small numbers, is included with their descriptions in the appropriate appendix.

Abbreviations are limited to those included in the introductory notes to Appendix A, those common to aviation parlance, and the following:

A/B	Air Bridge	f/f	first flown
A/C	Aero Club	F/G	Flying Group
A.D.C.	Aircraft Disposal Co. Ltd.	F/S	Flying Services Ltd.
A/F	Air Force	G/C	Gliding Club
A/S	Air Services Ltd.	N.A.T.	Northern Air Transport Ltd.
A/T	Air Transport Ltd.	P.S.I.O.W.	Portsmouth, Southsea and
A.S.T.	Air Service Training Ltd.		Isle of Wight Aviation Ltd.
A.T. & T.	Aircraft Transport & Travel Ltd.	rest.	registration restored
B.A.F.	British Air Ferries Ltd.	S.A.F.E.	Straits Air Freight Express
B.A.S.	British Aviation Services Ltd.	S. of F.	School of Flying Ltd.
B.A.T.	British Air Transport Ltd.	t/a	trading as
B.U.A.F.	British United Air Ferries Ltd.	T.M.A.	Trans Mediterranean Airways
canc.	registration cancelled	u/c	undercarriage
d.b.f.	destroyed by fire	U.L.F.C	Ultra Light Flying Club
d/d	delivered	w.f.u.	withdrawn from use
F/C	Flying Club		

Details for each aircraft are given in the following order: constructor's number in parentheses; variant number (where necessary); previous identities; date of issue of Certificate of Airworthiness, Authorisation or Permit to Fly; representative ownership changes; fate or disposal. If no C. of A. was issued or the date of issue of an export C. of A. was not available for publication, the date of registration is substituted.

Where first flight dates are included, or where certification came late in the life of an aircraft, this is made clear. Airworthy aircraft and those on overhaul in January 1972 have no disposal details.

Space considerations compel a condensed form for all foreign types as well as for British machines built in very large numbers and if, in these cases, the last recorded fact is the date of issue of C. of A., the aircraft was still active in March 1972.

Aero Commander 500A and 500B

G-ARGW (981-22), 500B, 28.11.60; G-ASIO (1113-55), 500A, N4441, 27.5.63; G-ASNJ (1272-95), 500A, N78352, 11.2.64, to Austria 3.69 as OE-FPZ

Aero Commander 520 and 680E

G-ARJA (150), 520, N2638B, 4.5.61, to Sweden 11.63 as SE-EFY; G-ARJJ (16), 520, N4115B, 20.5.61, burned out on ground at Fairoaks 19.8.69; G-ASHI (658-255), 680E, HB-GOB, 14.11.63; G-ASJU (82), 520, N4176B, 9.12.66; G-AWOE (753-41), 680E, N3844C, 5.1.70

Aero Commander 560F and 680F

G-ARDK (992-6), 560F, 28.3.61, sold in Portugal 11.71; G-ASYA (1283-56), 560F, N1015, 13.11.64; G-ATWN (943-14), 680F, N390GA, 21.7.66; G-AWCU (1377-142), 680FP, HB-GBW, 29.3.68

Aermacchi-Lockheed AL60B-1

G-ARZG (6219-39), 3.9.62, destroyed in ground collision with Viking G-AGRW at Squires Gate 7.7.65; G-ATJS (6227-47), not delivered, registered in Italy 8.68 as I-VARH; G-AXEZ (6144-2), OY-AFR, 31.7.69, ditched off Yarmouth, I.O.W. 30.8.69

Aeromere F.8L Falco Series III

G-APUO (209), 4.9.59, crashed near Denham 31.1.60; G-APXD (216), 11.3.60; G-AROT (224), 10.5.62; G-ATAK (204), D-ENYB, 7.4.65; G-AZAY (230), D-EFAK, 30.9.71

Aeromere-Laverda F.8L Super Falco Series IV

G-ASYM (404), D-ECFA, 27.4.65; G-AVUJ (412), 30.11.67; G-AWSU (416), 8.3.69

Aeronca C-2 G-ABHE after conversion to glider in 1937.

Aeronca C-2
G-ABHE (A.100), 4.12.30, converted to glider in 1937; wrecked by gale at Maiden Newton, Dorset 11.38; G-ABKX (A.114), 7.4.31, sold abroad 5.31

Aeronca C-3
G-ADSO (A.579), CF-AYC, 4.12.30, scrapped circa 1941; G-ADSP (A.580), CF-AYB, scrapped during the war; G-ADYP (A.596), 21.1.36, scrapped during the war; G-ADYR (A.597), 21.1.36, w.f.u. 10.36; G-ADYS (A.600), 21.1.36, stored at Farnborough in 1971; G-ADYT (A.601), 21.1.36, sold abroad 12.37; G-ADZZ (A.599), 21.1.36, crashed at Hythe, Kent 15.8.36; G-AEAC (A.603), 21.1.36, to South Africa 3.36 as ZS-AGX; G-AEAE (A.604), 22.1.36, w.f.u. 12.36; G-AEAF (A.598), 21.1.36, to Holland 5.36 as PH-ALG; G-AEFT (A.610), 27.4.36, Lt. C. E. Humphreys, Yeovilton 1972; G-AEFU (A.609), 14.4.36, to Ireland 4.37 as EI-ABN; G-AELX (A.663), 1.10.36, lost in the Irish Sea 9.6.51; G-AELY (A.664), 19.12.36, scrapped during the war; G-AEOO (A.709) and G-AEOP (A.711), not certificated, scrapped at Denham 1949

Aeronca 100
G-AENW (AB.101), 10.11.36, Aircraft Exchange & Mart, Hanworth 7.37; scrapped during the 1939–45 war

G-AESP (AB.109), 15.4.37, Aircraft Exchange & Mart; J. Patston, Eyebury, 7.38; A. R. Pilgrim, Elstree 10.47; Speedbird F/C 11.48; to spares 1959

G-AESX (AB.106), 3.2.37, Aircraft Exchange & Mart 7.38; scrapped during 1939–45 war

G-AETG (AB.110), 23.2.37, London Air Park F/C 10.38; W. Cobbett, Fairoaks 8.56; R. W. Mills, Elstree 8.66; crashed at Booker 7.4.69

G-AETR (AB.112), 18.5.37, London Air Park Flying Club 10.38; W. S. Henry, Newtownards 7.46; crashed in Strangford Lough, Co. Down 2.3.47

G-AEUW (AB.108), 23.2.37, Aircraft Exchange & Mart 7.38; scrapped during 1939–45 war

G-AEVE* (AB.120), Aircraft Exchange & Mart 7.38; C. of A. 8.12.38; Peterborough Flying Club 3.39; dismantled at Warton, Lancs. 1947

G-AEVR (AB. 111), 31.3.37, Aircraft Exchange & Mart 7.38; Peterborough Flying Club 3.39; scrapped during the 1939–45 war

G-AEVS (AB.114), 18.5.37, Aircraft Exchange & Mart 7.38; Speedbird F/C 9.48; B. J. Snook 8.51; Mrs. E. Walters, Sherburn 3.57; Yorkshire Flying Club 10.58; H. Dodd, Newcastle 11.63; H.A.P.S., Biggin Hill 1968

G-AEVT (AB.115), 5.8.38, Aircraft Exchange & Mart; rebuilt by A. W. G. Ord Hume and P. Simpson at Pinner 1948–1949; crashed at Loughborough 11.7.50

G-AEWU (AB. 116), ferried to Hanworth 30.6.38; C. of A. 5.8.38; London Air Park F/C 10.38; P. Gooch, Fairoaks 11.48; P. J. Colbourne, Farnborough 6.51; crushed when portable hangar collapsed at Farnborough 2.55

G-AEWV (AB.117), 5.8.38, London Air Park F/C 10.38; Defford A/C 8.53; I. Trethewey, Fairoaks 12.56; A. Offen, Fairoaks 9.61; J. Chapman, Bedford 12.62

G-AEWW (AB.118) and G-AEWX (AB.119), not certificated, scrapped during 1939–45 war

G-AEXA (AB.113), 18.5.37, Aeronautical Corp. of Great Britain, Peterborough; Peterborough Flying Club 3.39; scrapped during 1939–45 war

G-AEXB (AB.134), 18.5.37, R. Grubb, Hamble; lost in the Irish Sea 8.7.37

G-AEXD (AB.124), 4.5.37, ferried to Hanworth 16.7.38; London Air Park Flying Club 10.38; Speedbird Flying Club 10.48; G. Bramhill, Skegness 8.60; M. Palmer, Fairoaks 12.62; D. S. Everall, Shrewsbury 2.67

389

G-AFLT† (AB.131), not certificated, registered to Aircraft Exchange and Mart Ltd., 31.10.38; Peterborough Flying Club 3.39; scrapped in 1941; registration re-allotted to Miles M.65 Gemini 1A in 1949

G-AFLU† (AB.130), 20.12.38, Peterborough Flying Club; Blackpool Flying Club 2.48; Speedbird Flying Club 1.49; cannibalised at Farnborough 11.52

G-AFXC ‡ (F.C.1), not certificated, registration not taken up

        * Aeronca 300   † Aeronca 700   ‡ Ely Type F.C.1

Aeronca 7AC Champion

G-AOEH (2144), N79854, OO-TWF, A. to F. 30.6.56; G-ATHK (791), N82339, A. to F. 24.3.66; G-ATXC (1304), N82661, A. to F. 3.10.66, crashed at Biggin Hill 24.1.67; G-AVDT (6932), N3594E, A. to F. 17.5.67; G-AWVN (6005), N2426E

Agusta-Bell 47G (see also Bell 47G)

G-ASTB (1535), 47G-3B-1, 14.12.64, lost in the English Channel 1.7.66; G-AXCD (220), 47G-2, Austrian Air Force 3B-XF, 20.5.69, to Iran 5.69 as EP-HBC; G-AXCE (234), 47G-2, 3B-XG, 20.5.69, to Iran 5.69 as EP-HBB; G-AXCF (244), 47G-2, 3B-XK, to Iran 5.69 as EP-HBA; G-AXHW (2517), 47G-4, 9L-LAK, 15.4.70; G-AYOF (122), 47G-2, F-OCGB, registered 21.12.70; G-AYOG (119), 47G-2, F-BIFO, registered 21.12.70; G-AZJK (001), 47G-2, I-SIAP, registered 3.12.71; G-AZJL (221), 47G-2, I-CIEB, registered 3.12.71

Agusta-Bell 47J-2

G-ARWA (2005), SE-HAZ, 19.1.62, to Italy 5.68 as I-CIEM; G-ASLR (2057), 27.9.63; G-ASNV (2061), 10.3.64; G-ASWR (2078), 20.10.64, w.f.u. 9.70; G-ATFV (2093), 13.7.65, sold in Zambia 8.71; G-ATTO (2012), HB-XAR, 7.5.66, ditched in the Gulf of Guinea 2.11.68; G-AWSI (2008), D-HEFA, 12.3.69, sold in Norway 10.70

Agusta-Bell 206A Jet Ranger (see also Bell 206A)

G-AVIG (8004), 15.8.67, to Trinidad 9.67 as 9Y-TCZ; G-AVIH (8007), 15.8.67, to Bermuda 8.67 as VR-BCM, to South Africa as ZS-HDI, rest. 7.71, to Nigeria 7.71 as 5N-AIW; G-AVSN (8008), 2.11.67; G-AVSV (8014), 24.11.67, to Bermuda 10.68 as VR-BCU, rest. 10.69; G-AVSW (8016), 15.12.67, to Nigeria 3.68 as 5N-AHM; G-AVSX (8027), 11.2.68, to Iran 3.68 as EP-HAO; G-AVSY (8031), 28.2.68, to Bermuda 3.68 as VR-BCQ; G-AVSZ (8032), 28.2.68, to Bermuda 3.68 as VR-BCR; G-AVVH (8026), 4.12.67; G-AVYX (8025), 7.3.68; G-AVZG (8017), 30.1.68; G-AVZH (8022), 13.3.68; G-AWFV (8042), 10.4.68, to Nigeria 4.68 as 5N-AHN; G-AWGU (8044), 26.4.68; G-AWIL (8049), 3.5.68, to Australia 8.68 as VH-BHV; G-AWIM (8050), 3.5.68, to Australia 8.68 as VH-BHW; G-AWJW (8052), 15.7.68; G-AWLL (8076), 5.8.68; G-AWLV (8072), 23.7.68; G-AWMK (8073), 1.8.68, to Bermuda 12.68 as VR-BCV; G-AWOY (8094), 5.9.68; G-AWRV (8095), 28.3.69; G-AWVO (8111), to Indonesia 4.69 as PK-HBG

G-AXAP (8116), to Indonesia 4.69 as PK-HBH; G-AXKE (8166), to Indonesia 8.69 as PK-HBJ; G-AXKF (8170), to Indonesia 8.69 as PK-HBK; G-AXNG (8173), to Angola 10.69 as CR-ALJ; G-AXOU (8179), 27.1.70; G-AXRY (8188), 1.6.70, to Nigeria 9.70 as 5N-AIO; G-AYBE (8192), 19.8.70; G-AYIY (8199), 22.1.71, to Bermuda 1.71 as VR-BDR; G-AZAG (8101), HB-XCY, 26.7.71

Airspeed A.S.4 Ferry

G-ABSI   (4), 21.4.32, Sir Alan Cobham; C. W. A. Scott 3.36; Air Publicity Ltd., Heston 11.36; P.S.I.O.W. 6.39; impressed 4.40 as AV968, later 2758M

Airspeed Courier X9437 awaiting sale at Kemble in December 1945 prior to restoration to the civil register as G-ACVF. (*Aeroplane*)

G-ABSJ (5), 10.6.32, Sir Alan Cobham; National Aviation Day Displays Ltd. 11.32; to Himalaya Air Transport & Survey Co. 9.34 as VT-AFO

G-ACBT (6), 7.2.33, J.C. Sword t/a Midland & Scottish Air Ferries Ltd., Renfrew; dismantled at Renfrew about 1941

G-ACFB (9), 2.6.33, J. C. Sword t/a Midland & Scottish Air Ferries Ltd.; Air Publicity Ltd., Heston 11.36; dismantled at Heston; impressed 2.41 at Meir, Stoke-on-Trent as DJ715

Airspeed A.S.5 Courier

G-ABXN (7), 4.8.33, Airspeed Ltd., Portsmouth; Sir Alan Cobham 1.34; North Eastern Airways Ltd., Croydon 3.37; Miss J. Parsons, Hanworth 8.39; scrapped at White Waltham 9.40

G-ACJL (10), 27.9.33, Aircraft Exchange & Mart Ltd., Hanworth; flown to Australia 10.34; re-registered 10.35 as VH-UUF; withdrawn from use 10.36

G-ACLF (12), 13.12.33, R. K. Dundas Ltd.; North Eastern Airways Ltd., Croydon 2.37; P.S.I.O.W. 4.39; impressed 3.40 as X9342; dismantled Kemble 1943

G-ACLR (11), 21.11.33, Airspeed Ltd.; P.S.I.O.W. 8.36; impressed 3.40 as X9344; crashed at Bolt Head Aerodrome, Devon 1.8.42

G-ACLS (13), 1.5.34, Airspeed Ltd.; Air Taxis Ltd., Croydon 7.34; crashed at Grenoble, France 17.10.34

G-ACLT (14), 22.2.34, Airspeed Ltd.; North Eastern Airways 2.37; Air Taxis Ltd., Croydon 5.39; impressed 3.40 as X9394; d.b.r. Hawarden 4.42

G-ACNZ (20), 22.6.34, AVM A. E. Borton; to P.S.I.O.W., Portsmouth with Lynx IVC 11.39; impressed 3.40 as X9346; scrapped at Kemble 4.44

G-ACSY (16), 26.2.34, Airspeed Ltd.; operated by London, Scottish & Provincial Airways Ltd., crashed near Sevenoaks, Kent 29.9.34

G-ACSZ (19), 30.5.34, Airspeed Ltd.; operated by London, Scottish & Provincial A/W; North Eastern A/W 2.37; crashed at Doncaster 29.5.37

G-ACVE (22), 15.8.36, Airspeed Ltd.; Union Founders Trust Ltd. 19.8.36; crashed on take-off at Portsmouth Airport 20.8.36

G-ACVF (23), 15.8.36, North Eastern A/W 3.37; impressed 4.40 as X9437; restored to R. J. Jones, Southend 1.2.46; w.f.u. at Southend 18.12.47

G-ACVG   (24), 2.1.35, R. K. Dundas Ltd., Hanworth; re-registered to the Maharajah of Jaipur as VT-AFY; reverted to Dundas 4.36 in India

G-ACZL   (25), 28.3.35, Airspeed Ltd.; P.S.I.O.W. 4.35; impressed 3.40 as X9345; d.b.r. taking off from field at Shenfield, Essex 15.10.40

G-ADAX (26), 15.4.35, P.S.I.O.W.; impressed 3.40 as X9347 for No. 3 Ferry Pilots' Pool, A.T.A., Hawarden; flown to Portsmouth 17.3.41 and scrapped

G-ADAY (27), 17.5.35, P.S.I.O.W.; impressed 3.40 as X9343 for No.3 Ferry Pilots' Pool, A.T.A., Hawarden; flown to Portsmouth 12.3.41 and scrapped

Airspeed A.S.6A Envoy Series I

G-ACMT (17), 9.10.34, Airspeed Ltd; converted to Series II 1936; sold in Spain 12.36, flew into mountainside and destroyed on active service

G-ACVH (28), 6.10.34, Airspeed Ltd., forced landed in Langstone Harbour, Hants. in 1934

G-ACVI   (29), 4.10.34, 'Miss Wolseley', Lord Nuffield, Castle Bromwich; to Ansett Airways 8.36 as VH-UXM, Whirlwind engines 1945, w.f.u. 3.51

G-ACVJ   (30), 29.12.34, R. K. Dundas Ltd.; to Commercial Air Hire Ltd., Heston 7.36; sold in Spain, arrived at Barcelona 22.8.36

G-ACYJ   (31), 9.11.34, C. T. P. Ulm; re-registered 11.34 as VH-UXY 'Star of Australia', lost in the Pacific Ocean 4.12.34

G-ADAZ (32), 28.3.35, North Eastern A/W 'Tynedale'; to A.S.T., Hamble 11.38; impressed 14.2.41 as DG663, Northolt Station Flight until 19.3.42

G-ADBA (33), 18.4.35, Cobham Air Routes (operated by Olley A/S); to Union Founders Trust 8.36; North Eastern A/W 2.37; to R.A.F. 1.39 as P5778

G-ADBB (34), 6.4.35, North Eastern Airways Ltd., 'Wharfedale'; sold in Spain 9.36

G-ADBZ (35), 13.4.35, North Eastern Airways Ltd., 'Swaledale'; leased to Air Dispatch Ltd., Croydon 1936, crashed at Titsey Hill, Surrey 22.1.37

G-ADCA (36), 2.5.35, Portsmouth, Southsea and Isle of Wight Aviation Ltd., sold in Spain 8.36

G-ADCB (37), 28.8.35, Airspeed Ltd.; to Mitsubishi Shoji Kaisha 7.35 as J-BDDO

G-ADCC (38), 10.5.35, Airspeed Ltd.; to Mitsubishi Shoji Kaisha 4.35 as J-BDAO

G-ADCE (40), 27.8.35, Airspeed Ltd.; to Mitsubishi Shoji Kaisha 7.35 as J-BDEO

Airspeed A.S.6D Envoy Series III

G-ADCD (39), 31.7.36, Airspeed Ltd.; to South African Airways Ltd. 8.36 as ZS-AGA; to South African Air Force 5.38

G-AEBV (52), 21.4.36, Brian Allen Aviation Ltd., Croydon; sold in Spain, arrived at Barcelona 22.8.36

Airspeed A.S.6J Envoy Series III

G-AEGF (55), British Scandinavian A/W; C. of A. 29.12.36, E. Hoffman, Vienna; to D. V. Reinders 1940 as PH-ARK, destroyed by E.A. at Ypenburg 10.5.40

G-AEGG (56), British Scandinavian A/W; C. of A. 30.12.36, E. Hoffman, Vienna; to D. V. Reinders 1940 as PH-ARL, destroyed by E.A. at Ypenburg 10.5.40

G-AENA (60), 17.9.36, Capt. M. H. Findlay and K. H. F. Waller 'Gabrielle', Brooklands; crashed at Abercorn, Northern Rhodesia 1.10.36

G-AERT (68), 22.1.37, Airspeed Ltd.; left Portsmouth 27.1.37 on delivery flight to Military Governor of Lui Chow, South China

G-AEXE　(67), 13.5.37, Airspeed Ltd.; left Portsmouth 26.6.37; d/d to Military
　　　　　Governor at Lui Chow 7.7.37; disappeared without trace 8.37

G-AEXX　(66), 7.5.37, Flt. Lt. E. H. Fielden (King's Flight), Hendon; flew as L7270 until
　　　　　rest. 4.46 to G. Farquharson; to Sweden 6.46 as SE-ASN

G-AFJD　(76), registered 2.8.38 to High Commissioner for India; to Delhi
　　　　　Communications Flight, Willingdon Airport 8.38 as N9107; scrapped 6.42

G-AFJE　(77), registered 2.8.38 to High Commissioner for India; to Delhi
　　　　　Communications Flight 8.38 as N9108; crashed at Mingaladon 24.4.42

G-AHAC　(79), P5626, 18.4.46, Brevet Flying Club, Hanworth; N. C. Alderson 9.46;
　　　　　Private Charter Ltd., Heston 3.48; scrapped at Tollerton 5.50

Airspeed A.S.6K Envoy Series III

G-AFWZ　(59), VT-AIC, 27.5.37, registerered 1.8.39 to R. K. Dundas Ltd.; impressed
　　　　　for No. 24 Sqn., Hendon 3.40 as X9370; destroyed in air raid 7.10.40

Airspeed A.S.8 Viceroy

G-ACMU　(18), 12.10.34, Airspeed Ltd.; T. Neville Stack 10.34; Australia Race 10.34;
　　　　　retired at Athens, returned; sold in Spain 12.36

Airspeed A.S.40 Oxford

G-AFFM　(75), 31.8.38, Secretary of State for Air (operated by British A/W), struck
　　　　　barrage balloon cable, Gosport 20.11.39, crashed and burned out

G-AFVS　(83), 30.6.39, Airspeed Ltd.; to Canada for winterisation trials 8.39, did not
　　　　　arrive, believed sunk in the 'Athenia'

G-AHDZ　ex ED190, 28.3.46, Scottish Aviation Ltd., Prestwick; Union Aéromaritime,
　　　　　Le Bourget 7.54 as F-BBIU

G-AHGU　(3277), V3815, 9.5.46, Bristol Aeroplane Co. Ltd., Filton; Air Couriers Ltd.,
　　　　　10.56; Overseas Av., Biggin Hill 7.60; d.b.r. Fairoaks 11.10.60

G-AHTW　(3083), V3388, 19.6.46, Boulton Paul Ltd., Wolverhampton; w.f.u. 12.60;
　　　　　repainted as V3388 at Elstree 2.64; to Skyfame Museum, Staverton 25.3.64

G-AHXA　ex V3870, 23.12.46, Payloads (Charter) Co., Croydon; to the Egyptian Air
　　　　　Transport Company 9.8.47 as SU-AER, w.f.u. by 1.54

G-AIAT　ex NM387, 10.5.48, B.O.A.C., Heathrow or Hurn; A.S.T. 4.51; Airwork
　　　　　Services Ltd., Perth 9.60; T. H. Marshall 11.60; w.f.u. at Christchurch

Oxford G-AHDZ at Le Bourget, Paris in 1954 after being sold to Union Aéromaritime as
F-BBIU.

393

G-AIAU   ex NM457, 24.4.48, B.O.A.C., Heathrow or Hurn; Cyprus Airways Ltd. 2.53; scrapped at Nicosia 6.54

G-AIAV   ex NM536, 9.3.48, B.O.A.C., Heathrow or Hurn; to Far East Flying School, Hong Kong 7.51 as VR-HFC

G-AIAW   ex NM649, 15.6.48, B.O.A.C.; Short & Harland Ltd., Rochester 9.50; stored at Thruxton as SE-CAM 11.54 to 11.55; to Iberia 9.56 as EC-APF

G-AIAX   ex DF356, 29.7.49, B.O.A.C., Heathrow or Hurn; A.S.T. 4.51; Airwork Services Ltd., Perth 9.60; T. H. Marshall 11.60; w.f.u. at Christchurch

G-AIAY   ex DF521, B.O.A.C., not converted for civil use, scrapped at Hurn 5.47

G-AIRZ   ex HN610, 22.2.47, B.O.A.C., Heathrow or Hurn; Hunting Aerosurveys Ltd., Luton 'The Odyssey' 3.51, crashed near Luxembourg 18.7.52

G-AITB   ex MP425, 29.5.47, Air Service Training Ltd., Hamble; Airwork Services Ltd., Perth 9.60, w.f.u. at Perth 5.61; to R.A.F. Museum, Hendon 1972

G-AITF   ex ED290, 27.3.47, Air Service Training Ltd., Hamble; Airwork Services Ltd., Perth 9.60, withdrawn from use at Perth 5.61

G-AIUH   (3507), NM277, 6.1.49, Reid & Sigrist Ltd., Desford; Hunting Aerosurveys Ltd. (with Consul nose); re-registered in Kenya 1959 as VP-KOX

G-AIVY   (828), 8.3.48, B.S.A.A. 'Star Mentor'; B.O.A.C. 'Star Mentor', Langley 1949; Cyprus Airways Ltd., 10.53, scrapped at Nicosia 9.56

G-AJGR   ex LX533, 4.7.47, Hunting Aerosurveys Ltd., Elstree; scrapped 2.52

G-AJNC   (5137), ED251, 26.6.47, Fairey Aviation Co. Ltd., White Waltham; to the Air Survey Co., Salisbury, Southern Rhodesia 11.51 as VP-YIY

G-ALTP   ex PH321, 26.1.50, Air Service Training Ltd., Hamble; T. H. Marshall 5.61, beyond repair after fire in port engine at Christchurch 1.1.62

G-ALTR   ex PH368, 9.1.50, Air Service Training Ltd., Hamble; T. H. Marshall, Christchurch 5.61, d.b.r. on take-off from Bordeaux 14.8.61

G-ALXV   to G-ALXY inclusive, ex X6811, NJ352, EB759 and AT660 respectively, registered to the Lancashire Aircraft Corp. Ltd. 1.50; not converted for civil use, scrapped at Squires Gate, Blackpool 6.50

G-AMCU, 'CV, 'CW, 'CY and 'CZ (5244–5246, 5248 and 5249) ex PH305, NM803, BG571, PH373 and HN786 respectively, registered 1.51 to Airspeed Ltd.; not converted for civil use, burned at Christchurch 1952–53

G-AMCX   (5247), ex PH517, Airspeed Ltd., later the de Havilland Aircraft Co. Ltd.; left Croydon 14.9.51 as EC-WGE on delivery to R. Bay, later EC-AGE

G-AMFJ   to G-AMFM inclusive and G-AMHE, ex DF276, NM413, HM831, LB417 and LX427 respectively, registered successively to Airspeed Ltd., Aerocontacts Ltd. and Britavia Ltd.; all sold in Israel 1951–1952

G-AOUT   ex MP301 and Belgian Air Force O-6, registered 8.56 to Eagle Aviation Ltd.; used for film purposes and burned at Ringway 8.56

Airspeed A.S.41 Oxford
G-AJWJ   (460), LX119, registered to Miles Aircraft Ltd., Woodley 6.47; flown as Leonides testbed in Class B marks as U-7; scrapped at Woodley 12.48

Airspeed A.S.57 Ambassador 1
G-AGUA   (61), RT665 ntu., 5.5.49, Ministry of Aircraft Production; dismantled at Christchurch 1951; to Filton 1952; scrapped at Stansted

G-AKRD   (62), RT668 ntu., 4.8.49, Ministry of Aircraft Production; B.E.A. 'Golden Lion' 1951; Proteus testbed 1953; to Rolls-Royce 12.55; f/f Hucknall 8.58 as Tyne testbed G-37-3; Dart testbed 1961; scrapped Hucknall 10.69

Ambassador 2 G-ALZS at Southend in 1960, temporarily in the colours of Norrønafly Oslo as LN-BWE. (*John Goring*)

Airspeed A.S.57 Ambassador 2

G-ALFR   (5210), 24.5.51, B.E.A. 'Golden Hind'; to Napier, Luton 1955 as Eland testbed; rebuilt for flying by Dan-Air 1961; w.f.u. at Lasham 3.67

G-ALZN   (5212), 20.8.51, f/f 12.1.51, B.E.A. 'Elizabethan' (fleet flagship); Overseas Av. (C.I.) 3.61, not used; Dan-Air 4.62; w.f.u. at Lasham 5.68

G-ALZO   (5226), 25.11.52, B.E.A. 'Christopher Marlowe'; delivered to R. Jordanian A/F 5.60, serial 108; restored 2.63 to Dan-Air

G-ALZP   (5213), 19.12.51, B.E.A. 'Sir Richard Grenville'; to R. Jordanian A/F 10.60, serial 109, not d/d; to Morocco as CN-MAK; Decca Navigator Co. Ltd., Gatwick 11.63; to South Seas A/W, Wellington 1971 as ZK-DFC

G-ALZR   (5214), 12.2.52, B.E.A. 'Sir Walter Raleigh'; Rolls-Royce 8.57; f/f Hucknall 26.2.59 as Tyne testbed G-37-4; freight door conversion at Southend; B.K.S. 11.64; Dan-Air 11.69; d.b.r. at Gatwick 26.7.69

G-ALZS   (5215), 24.1.52, B.E.A. 'William Shakespeare'; to Norrønafly 1960 as LN-BWE; to Globe Air 11.60 as HB-IEK 'Vogel Gryff'; rest. 11.63 to Autair Ltd., Luton; damaged beyond repair at Luton 14.9.67

G-ALZT   (5216), 26.1.52, B.E.A. 'Sir John Hawkins'; to B.K.S. Air Transport Ltd., Southend 5.5.58; withdrawn from use at Newcastle/Woolsington 1968

G-ALZU   (5217), 5.3.52, B.E.A. 'Lord Burghley', crashed on take-off from Munich 6.2.58 on Belgrade–Ringway charter with Manchester United team

G-ALZV   (5218), 5.4.52, B.E.A. 'Earl of Leicester'; to Globe Air 2.62 as HB-IEM 'Wilde Maa'; rest. to Autair International 12.63; scrapped at Luton 1968

G-ALZW   (5219), 28.4.52, B.E.A. 'Sir Francis Walsingham'; B.K.S. Air Transport Ltd., Southend 15.5.58, last flight 13.2.67; scrapped at Southend 4.68

G-ALZX   (5220), 29.5.52, B.E.A. 'Sir John Norris'; to Butler A/T 6.6.57 as VH-BUI; rest. to Dan-Air 11.59; d.b.r. landing at Beauvais 14.4.66

G-ALZY   (5221), 10.7.52, B.E.A. 'Sir Philip Sidney'; to R. Jordanian A/F 26.12.59 as 107; rest. 2.63 to Dan-Air; w.f.u. at Lasham 1967

G-ALZZ   (5222), 6.8.52, B.E.A. 'Edmund Spenser'; Norrønafly LN-BWF 1960; to Globe Air 5.61 as HB-IEL 'Lalle Keenig'; rest. 9.63 to Autair; scrapped at Luton 5.69

G-AMAA (5223), 2.9.52, B.E.A. 'Sir Francis Knollys'; d/d to Shell Aviation Ltd., Heathrow 26.1.60; to Dan-Air Ltd., Lasham as spares 2.67

G-AMAB (5224), 3.10.52, B.E.A. 'Sir Francis Bacon', d.b.r. in forced landing 4 miles south-west of Düsseldorf, Germany, due to engine failure 8.4.55

G-AMAC (5225), 1.11.52, B.E.A. 'Sir Robert Cecil'; to B.K.S. Air Transport Ltd., Southend 17.6.60; last flight 3.7.68, w.f.u. at Southend 12.68

G-AMAD (5211), 19.3.52, B.E.A. 'Sir Francis Drake'; B.K.S. A/T 23.7.57; f/f with freight door, Southend 10.6.68; crashed Heathrow 3.7.68

G-AMAE (5227), 19.12.52, B.E.A. 'Earl of Essex'; to Butler A/T 6.6.57 as VH-BUK; returned to Heathrow 13.9.58; rest 11.59 to Dan-Air; w.f.u. 6.71

G-AMAF (5228), 16.1.53, B.E.A. 'Lord Howard of Effingham'; Overseas Av. (C.I.), never used; dismantled at Wymeswold 1962; to spares at Luton 11.63

G-AMAG (5229), 4.2.53, B.E.A. 'Sir Thomas Gresham'; to Shell Aviation Ltd., Heathrow 8.2.59; Dan-Air 6.66; d.b.r. landing at Manston 30.9.68

G-AMAH (5230), 5.3.53, B.E.A. 'Sir Christopher Hatton'; to Butler A/T 6.6.57 as VH-BUJ; returned to Heathrow 14.8.58; rest. 11.59 to Dan-Air; w.f.u. 3.71

Airspeed A.S.65 Consul

G-AGVY (3204), V3679, 15.3.46, Bata Shoe Co. Ltd.; Airlinks Ltd., Gatwick 5.47; Air Enterprises Ltd., Gatwick 12.48; crashed in the Lebanon 11.2.49

G-AHEF (4044), 16.5.46, Airspeed Ltd., Portsmouth; de Havilland Aircraft Co. Ltd., Christchurch 8.51; scrapped at Christchurch 8.60

G-AHEG (1052), T1206, 26.4.46, Airwork Ltd., Heston; Metal Containers Ltd., Langley 4.48; Platts (Barton) Ltd. 12.54; Meridian Airmaps Ltd. 12.59 w.f.u. at Shoreham 5.61, taken away as scrap 7.63

G-AHEH (3362), LX641, 22.5.46, B.A.T., Redhill; W. A. Rollason, Croydon 8.50; to Air Jordan 9.50 as TJ-ABB; rest. 8.53; to Iberia 6.54 as EC-AJX

G-AHFS (2942), HN769, 15.6.46, B.A.T., Redhill; to Aero Propaganda A.B., Bromma, Sweden 5.8.51 as SE-BTU; crashed at Sundsvall 24.11.54

G-AHFT (2593), HN423, 24.5.46, Morton Air Services Ltd., Croydon; temp. to Israel 1948 as United Nations UN.99; lost in the English Channel 14.6.52

G-AHJX (541), LB529, 13.7.46, Morton Air Services Ltd., Croydon; crashed at Guernsey 12.5.50; fuselage converted for use as hen house

G-AHJY (2647), HN471, 21.6.46, Airwork Ltd., Heston; Atlas Aviation Ltd., Elstree 2.47; crashed at Deepcar 12.4.51 en route to Iceland as TF-RPM

G-AHJZ (2686), HN494, 26.6.46, de Havilland Aircraft Co. Ltd., Hatfield; to Group d'Études Aéronautiques, Toussus-le-Noble 4.57 as F-BFAT

G-AHMA (3428), LX732, 29.7.46, Atlas Aviation Ltd., Elstree; crashed at Villlemoireau, Isère, France while en route Gatwick–Geneva 23.12.46

G-AHMB (3112), LX281, 29.7.46, Southern Aircraft (Gatwick) Ltd. 'Southernaire'; Dennis Aviation Ltd., Elstree 10.46; to Israel 26.8.49 as 4X-ACO

G-AHMC (2778), HN583, 4.7.46, Westminster Airways Ltd., Blackbushe; H. L. White 12.47; to Israel ex Gatwick via Dublin 2.3.49, Haifa 13.3.49

G-AHMD (3545), NM329, 2.8.46, Lancashire Aircraft Corp. Ltd., to long term storage at Yeadon 1952; burned at Squires Gate 20.4.56

G-AHRK (3096), LX265, 18.7.46, B.A.S., Thame; to N. Rhodesia 2.49 as VP-RBM; rest. 9.49 to Silver City A/W; to Iberia 4.52 as EC-AGI

G-AHXP (2996), HN840, 21.8.46, International Airways Ltd., Croydon 'Blanche Fury'; sold in Israel 23.10.49

G-AHYW (3923), PG936, 3.9.46, Portsmouth Av.; d.b.r. in forced landing N.E. of Salisbury, S. Rhodesia, while en route to Capetown 16.10.46

G-AHZV (4397), RR356, 19.9.46, Lancashire Aircraft Corp. Ltd., Squires Gate; long term storage until 3.54; scrapped at Stansted 3.56

G-AHZW (3091)), LX260, 13.9.46, Lancashire Aircraft Corp. Ltd., Yeadon; to Italy
11.53; rest. 3.54 to Lancashire Aircraft Corp. Ltd.; w.f.u. 3.58

G-AIAH (4316), PK252, 27.9.46, Morton Air Services Ltd., Croydon; used by the
A.A. 1956; Mrs. M. Treacy 10.59; burned at Portsmouth 2.11.61

G-AIBC (4399), RR358, 24.9.46, Westminster Airways Ltd., Blackbushe; Kenbank
Enterprises Ltd. 6.48; R. A. Short 1.51; scrapped at Southend 6.52

G-AIBF (3422), LX726, 17.8.46, Silver City Airways Ltd. (operated in Malta for Malta
Airways Ltd.); scrapped at Blackbushe 4.54

G-AICZ (4317), PK253, 9.9.46, Westminster Airways Ltd., Blackbushe; H. L. White
12.47; sold in Israel 4.48

Consul G-AHJZ at Hatfield in April 1957, ready for delivery to the Groupe d'Études
Aéronautiques (Airnautic) as F-BFAT.

G-AIDW (2956), HN783, 22.8.46, Guernsey Air Charter Ltd., Elstree; Dexford Motors
Ltd., Southend 12.48; scrapped at Southend 11.9.51

G-AIDX (4318), PK254, 7.11.46, Intava Ltd., Luton; Anglo American Oil Co., 2.49;
Esso Ltd., Croydon 6.51; to Farner-Werke, Grenchen 10.56 as HB-LAT

G-AIDY (3094), LX263, 3.10.46, British Air Transport Ltd., Redhill; damaged beyond
repair in emergency night landing, Berck, France 14.6.48

G-AIDZ (4404), RR363, 8.10.46, British Air Transport Ltd., Redhill; to Escadrille
Mercure, Le Bourget, Paris, 7.51 as F-BFVS

G-AIEA (4320), PK256, 3.10.46, B.A.T., Redhill; conv. to Oxford at Croydon 10.50;
to Sté. Afrique de Travaux et E.P.A., Libreville as F-OAHJ

G-AIHC (4312), PK248, registered 4.9.46 to Airspeed Ltd.; to Air Transport Brussels
9.46 as OO-GVP; crashed at Tambur in the Sudan 6.1.47

G-AIIM (4342), PK290, registered 17.9.46 to Airspeed Ltd., to Turkish A/F 9.46

G-AIIN (4344), PK292, 28.10.46, Westminster A/W, Kenley; Airwork Ltd.,
Blackbushe 3.49; to C. Myers, Bulawayo 11.49 as VP-YIC; re-reg'd ZS-DDM
2.50

G-AIIO (4349), PK297, 21.10.46, Airspeed Ltd.; Extractors (Hull) Ltd., White
Waltham; crashed in the Alps 17.7.48

G-AIIS (4398), RR357, 8.10.46, Thomas Barclay Ltd., t/a as International Airways
Ltd.; d.b.r. at Normanton, Yorks. 1.11.49; scrapped Croydon 2.51

G-AIKO (4339), PK287, 5.12.46, Chartair Ltd., Malta; to Air Jordan 12.50 as
TJ-ABE; restored 8.53; to Aerotechnica S.A., Madrid 5.54 as EC-AJV

G-AIKP (4323), PK259, 22.11.46, O. H. Simpson, Portsmouth; to Silver Flight Ltd.,
Durban 10.47 as ZS-BJX; scrapped at Durban 1.50

G-AIKR (4338), PK286, 5.12.46, Chartair Ltd., Thame; Airwork Ltd., Perth, 1.47; Rapid F/G, Baginton 2.62; to Canadian Air Museum, Rockcliffe 10.65

G-AIKS (4340), PK288, 22.11.46, Skytravel Ltd., Speke; Bowmaker Ltd. 6.51 (operated in Malta by Air Malta Ltd.); burned at Squires Gate 20.4.56

G-AIKT (4356), PK304, 27.11.46, Lord Londonderry, Newtownards; Air Enterprises Ltd., Croydon 6.51; Derby Aviation Ltd. 7.58; w.f.u. at Burnaston 3.59

G-AIKU (4348), PK296, 5.11.40, Butlins Ltd., Elstree; S. E. Norman, Southend 7.50; to Air Jordan, Amman 5.51 as TJ-AAX

G-AIKX (4354), PK302, 16.12.46, Chartair Ltd.; Samuel Hodge & Sons Ltd., Broxbourne 3.50; All Power Transformers, Blackbushe 9.55; scrapped Croydon 9.56

G-AIKY (4324), PK260, 5.12.46, British Aviation Services Ltd.; to Malayan A/W Singapore 4.47 as VR-SCD 'Raja Udang'; rest. 1.53; to El Al 5.53 as 4X-AEK

Consul MC-ABA on test near Portsmouth, October 1946, in short-lived Monégasque markings before becoming G-AJAX. (*Flight Photo 19731S*)

G-AIKZ (4325), PK261, 5.12.46, Skytravel Ltd., Speke; Bowmaker/Air Malta Ltd. 6.51; to Soc. Transportes Aerei Mediterranei, Rome 5.56 as I-VALH

G-AILA (4322), PK258, Airspeed Ltd., to the Turkish Air Force 9.46

G-AIOL (4321), PK257, 5.12.46, D. L. Steiner, Speke 'Liverpool Hawk'; Thomas Barclay Ltd. t/a International A/W, Croydon; to Israel 11.49 as 4X-ACR

G-AIOM (4347), PK295; 19.12.46, Chartair Ltd.; forced landed in field 6 miles north of Lyons, France 24.1.48 and destroyed by flood water

G-AION (4352), PK300, 20.12.46, Airspeed Ltd.; to Sté. Algérienne de Transports Aériens, Algiers 12.46 as F-BCJD; to Aigle Azur Indochine, Hanoi 1.49

G-AIOO (4357), PK305, 19.12.46, Payloads (Charter) Co., Gatwick; to South Africa as ZS-BNT (ntu); rest. 7.47 to Payloads; crashed at Perpignan 27.11.47

G-AIOP (671), HN642, allotted OO-MAB (ntu), 19.2.47, Hornton A/W, Gatwick; Transair Ltd., Croydon 5.50; to Nordisk Air Transport 4.51 as SE-BTB

G-AIOR (4341), PK289, 23.12.46, Airspeed Ltd.; Dennis Aviation Ltd., Gatwick 12.46; to Israel 1.9.49 as 4X-ACP

G-AIOS (4329), PK265, 20.12.46, Morton Air Services Ltd., Croydon; Mrs. M. Treacy, Portsmouth 10.59; to Hanwell, Mx. as a film property 13.4.61

G-AIOT (4330), PK266, 2.1.47, Patrick Duval Av., Elmdon 'County of Warwick'; Israel 1948 as UN.97; Air Enterprises 12.48; w.f.u. Thruxton 8.55

G-AIOU (4355), PK303, 10.1.47, Morton Air Services Ltd., Croydon; crashed in the Egyptian desert near Cairo 24.5.48

398

G-AIOV   (4361), PK309, 3.2.47, Patrick Duval Av. 'County of Worcester'; Air Enterprises 12.48; to Soc. Transportes Aerei Med. 5.56 as I-VALZ

G-AIOW   (4353), PK301, 17.1.47, Morton Air Services Ltd., Croydon; withdrawn from use and dismantled at Croydon 12.54

G-AIOX   (2188), EB748, 19.2.47, Transcontinental A/S, Gatwick; Airspan Travel Ltd., Redhill 'Gorgeous Gussie' 7.49; to Air Jordán 12.50 as TJ-ABD

G-AIOY   (4334), PK282, 10.1.47, S. Yager, White Waltham 'Carlos Amigos'; Solar A/S, White Waltham 2.49; to Aero Propaganda A.B. 8.50 as SE-BTD

G-AIOZ   (4335), PK283, 23.1.47, Grayson A/S, Denham; I. R. K. Maclaren (operator Milburnair Ltd., Croydon) 2.47; crashed Tatsfield, Surrey 15.8.47

G-AIRP   (4400), RR359, 2.11.46, Payloads (Charter) Co., Croydon; Brevet Flying Club Ltd., Croydon 2.50; dismantled at Langley 5.51

G-AIUR   (967), HN174, 4.2.47, Chartair Ltd., Malta; temporarily in United Nations service in Israel 1948 as UN.95; withdrawn from use 2.49

G-AIUS   (750), HM757, 14.2.47, Air Kruise (Kent) Ltd., Lympne; Silver City A/W; 3.54; V. H. Bellamy 9.58; accident Tangier 17.6.59; sold as CN-TEJ

G-AIUT   (3375), LX666, 10.2.47, Congo Air Charter, Langley; to C. Myers, Bulawayo 11.49 as VP-YID; to Commercial A/S, Cape Town 2.50 as ZS-DDN

G-AIUU   (5104), W6562, 11.4.47, International A/W, Croydon; temporarily United Nations UN.102 in Israel 1948; dismantled at Croydon 10.50

G-AIUV   (5098), HN191, 11.4.47, Hornton Airways Ltd., Gatwick; sold in Israel 4.4.50

G-AIUW   (5100), PH503, 11.4.47, Hornton Airways Ltd., Gatwick; Transair Ltd., Croydon 5.50; to Elsham Ltd., Israel 22.5.50 as 4X-ACQ

G-AIUX   (5106), LB257, 15.4.47, Chartair Ltd., Thame; B.S.A.A. 'Star Master' 11.48; B.O.A.C., Hurn 1949; to E.A.A.C., Nairobi 5.54 as VP-KMI

G-AIUY   (5116), HN323, 17.4.47, Olley A/S, Croydon; Cambrian A/S, Cardiff 2.53; Morton A/S, 10.53; to Soc. Transp. Aerei Med. 5.56 as I-VALC

G-AIUZ   (5105), V4125, 11.4.47, Transair Ltd., Croydon; crashed near Berne, Switzerland 2.9.48 while en route Croydon–Geneva; scrapped at Croydon

G-AIVA   (5102), BG152, 5.5.47, Transair Ltd., Croydon; S. J. Cooke, Croydon 12.51; to Real Aero Club de Gran Canaria, Las Palmas 2.53 as EC-AHU

G-AJAX   (3331), LX599, MC-ABA (ntu), 15.10.46, Atlas Av., Elstree; Proctor Springwood Ltd., 6.48; J. Taubman, Langley 4.49; to Israel 4.49

G-AJFZ   (5097), T1013, 20.2.47, P. H. Meadway, Portsmouth 'Monica'; dismantled at Portsmouth 7.49

G-AJGA   (5117), X6740, 8.5.47, Northern Air Charter Ltd., Woolsington; Astral Av. 6.48; Skyways Ltd., Squires Gate 4.55; scrapped at Stansted 3.56

G-AJGB   (5110), LX156, 30.5.47, D. L. Steiner, Speke; Thomas Barclay Ltd., Croydon 6.48; International Airways Ltd., Croydon 2.49; w.f.u. 2.51

G-AJGC   (5119), LW833, 22.4.47, D. L. Steiner, Speke; destroyed in forced landing near La Rochelle after radio failure while returning from Madrid 13.11.47

G-AJGD   (5120), HN633, 16.5.47, D. L. Steiner, Speke; Olley A/S, Croydon 6.48; d.b.r. in forced landing at Dukes Meadows, Chiswick 15.7.49

G-AJGE   (5121), R5973, 30.5.47, Pullman Airways Ltd., Elstree; lost in the Mediterranean between Benina and Castel Benito 27.2.48

G-AJGF   (5122), HN199, 22.5.47, Patrick Laing Air Services Ltd.; leased to Transair Ltd., Croydon 1949; sold in Israel 25.8.49

G-AJGG   (5123), HN733, 10.6.47, Chartair Ltd., Croydon; to Air Jordan 12.50 as TJ-ABG; rest. 9.52 to Adie Av.; to A. Raimondi, Nice 8.56 as F-BGOP

G-AJGH	(5124), AT676, 22.5.47, British Aviation Services Ltd., Thame; sold abroad 9.47; rest. 4.48 to Air Charter Ltd.; sold in Belgium 6.50
G-AJGI	(5125), LW832, 9.5.47, D. L. Steiner, Speke; B. R. W. Betts and Co. 12.47; d.b.r. in forced landing near Châlons, France 14.11.47
G-AJLH	(5126), NJ376, 17.6.47, Northern Air Charter Ltd., Woolsington; Astral Av. 6.48; Lancashire Aircraft Corp. Ltd.; scrapped at Bovingdon 5.51
G-AJLI	(5127), LX760, 4.6.47, Westminster Airways Ltd., Blackbushe; Fairflight Ltd., 10.50; S. J. Cooke, Croydon 9.51; to Iberia 2.52 as EC-AGK
G-AJLJ	(5128), HM627, 22.5.47, Air Enterprises Ltd., Croydon; with United Nations Israel Commission, Beirut 1948 as U.96; scrapped Croydon 1950
G-AJLK	(5129), HN780, 10.6.47, Westminster A/W, Blackbushe; to Air Jordan 1.51 as TJ-ABF; rest. to W. A. Rollason; to Air Jordan 5.51 as TJ-AAY
G-AJLL	(5130), HN479, 6.6.47, Chartair Ltd.; to Sté. Algérienne de Transp. Aériens 1.49 as F-BCJE; to Aigle Azur Indochine 1950; dest. Gia Lam 4.3.54
G-AJLM	(5131), LW899, 17.6.47, J. T. Donaldson, Perth 'Eaglesway'; West Indies Trading Co., Jersey 8.50; to Gök-Tur Sirketi Co., Turkey 8.52 as TC-GÖK
G-AJLN	(5132), V4159, 10.7.47, Transair Ltd., Croydon; English Electric Co., Samlesbury 3.49; to Dept. of Civil Aviation, Lydda 5.53 as 4X-AEN
G-AJLO	(5133), X6859, 8.3.49, Airspeed Ltd.; to Congo Belge Force Publique, Leopoldville 3.49 as C-34; to Natal Aviation Ltd., Durban 9.55 as ZS-DNL
G-AJLP	(5135), DF402, 22.5.47, Prince Aly Khan, Croydon; Flyaway Ltd., Croydon 8.49; to Air Jordan 9.50 as TJ-ABC, reduced to spares at Amman 12.51
G-AJLR	(5136), R6029, 10.6.47, Olley A/S, Croydon; Cambrian A/S, Cardiff 2.53; Morton A/S 10.53; All Power Transformers Ltd. 9.56; w.f.u. Fairoaks 4.63
G-AJND	(5138), EB718, D. L. Steiner, Speke; C. of A. 28.11.47, delivered direct to Union of Burma Airways Ltd., Rangoon 11.47 as XY-ABJ
G-AJNE	(5139), LW900, 25.6.47, D. L. Steiner, Speke; Air Enterprises, Croydon 10.53; J. Crewdson, Burnaston 6.56; Airwork 11.56; w.f.u. Blackbushe 5.61
G-AJNF	(5145), HN847, 23.6.47, Milburnair Ltd., Gatwick; R. K. Dundas Ltd., Portsmouth 11.47; to the Maharajah of Bikaner 1.48 as VT-CRG
G-AJNG	(5146), DF522, 27.6.47, Westminster A/W, Blackbushe; B.A.S., Blackbushe 11.48; Chartair Ltd., Thame 9.49; to Aero Nord A.B. 3.52 as SE-BUP
G-AJNH	(5150), HM915, 29.7.47, Airspeed Ltd.; to Société Indochinoise de Transports Aériens 7.47 as F-BDPY; d.b.r. at Tonkin 18.5.49
G-AJNI	(5157), DF515, 29.7.47, Airspeed Ltd., to Société Indochinoise de Transports Aériens 7.47 as F-BDPV; d.b.r. at Haiphong 28.6.49
G-AJNJ	(5158), EB908, registered 16.6.47 to Airspeed Ltd.; to Burma 11.47
G-AJNK	(5159), MP347, 13.1.48, Airspeed Ltd.; R. K. Dundas Ltd., Portsmouth 1.48; to the Maharajah of Bundi 1.48 as VT-CZQ
G-AJNL	(5160), HN831, 10.12.47, Airspeed Ltd.; to Union of Burma Airways Ltd., Rangoon 11.47 as XY-ABK
G-AJWO	(5148), AT760, 2.7.47, Airspeed Ltd.; E. R. van den Burgh, Croydon 8.47; to J. Charmoz, Tangier 6.48 as F-OAFD
G-AJWP	(5161), NM642, 30.9.47, Airspeed Ltd.; to Société Indochinoise de Transports Aériens 9.47 as F-BDPX, d.b.r. at Namdinh 16.3.49
G-AJWR	(5162), HN829, 16.10.47, Airspeed Ltd.; to Société Indochinoise de Transports Aériens 10.47 as F-BEDP, destroyed by fire, Saigon 26.10.50
G-AJWS	(5170), HN756, 14.11.47, E. R. van den Burgh, Croydon; to R. Bouchier, Tangier 9.48 as F-OAGD 'Hyper Bichon'; rest. 10.53 to de Havillands; Hants & Sussex Av. 8.61; to Aerofotographica, Rome 27.6.63 as I-SAFI

Consul G-AJWO after sale in Tangier, June 1948, as F-OAFD.

G-AJWT   (5169), HN713, 4.9.47, Airwork Ltd.; to United Air Services Ltd., Dar-es-Salaam 3.48 as VR-TAR, d.b.r. at Mombasa 4.3.48, scrapped in 1952

G-AJWU   (5180), HM917, 28.11.47, Airspeed Ltd.; to Union of Burma Airways Ltd., Rangoon 11.47 as XY-ABI

G-AJWV   (5172), HM636, registered 14.8.47 to Airspeed Ltd.; military version for Burmese Air Force; order cancelled; dismantled at Portsmouth 7.49

G-AJWW   (5173), HN717, 29.12.47, Airspeed Ltd.; to Société Indochinoise de Transports Aériens 12.47 as F-BEDT

G-AJWX   (5174), NJ302, 10.12.47, Airspeed Ltd., to United Air Services Ltd., Dar-es-Salaam, Tanganyika, 12.47 as VR-TAS, scrapped 1952

G-AJWY   (5175), EB974, 25.3.48, Airspeed Ltd.; to United A/S 3.48 as VR-TAU; to Air Jordan, Amman 9.50 as TJ-ABA, crashed at Jerusalem 31.10.50

G-AJWZ   (5176), AT657, 14.6.48, Airspeed Ltd.; to the Government of French Indo-China 6.48 as F-OABU, French registration cancelled 3.52

G-AJXE   (5164), HN734, 23.9.47, M.C.A. Flying Unit, Gatwick; B.K.S. A/T, Southend 11.55; T. D. Keegan, Keevil 11.57; d.b.r. at Elstree 21.11.59

G-AJXF   (5165), NM314, 9.10.47, M.C.A. Flying Unit, Gatwick; Skyways Ltd., Stansted 9.55; Skyways Coach-Air Ltd., Lympne 6.59; scrapped 8.60

G-AJXG   (5166), NM334, 6.11.47, M.C.A. Flying Unit, Gatwick; B.K.S. Air Transport Ltd., Southend 11.55; burned at Southend 19.6.60

G-AJXH   (5167), HN719, 4.11.47, M.C.A. Flying Unit, Gatwick; Eagle Aircraft Services Ltd., Blackbushe 3.56; to Iberia, Madrid 4.57 as EC-ANL

G-AJXI   (5168), V4283, 6.11.47, M.C.A. Flying Unit, Gatwick; W. S. Shackleton Ltd., Whitchurch 9.56; to G.E.C.A., Toussus-le-Noble 2.57 as F-BHVY

G-AKCK   (5177), HN827, 10.6.48, Airspeed Ltd.; to the Government of French Indo-China 6.48 as F-OABT, French registration cancelled 3.52

G-AKCV   (5178), NM593, 2.12.48, Airspeed Ltd.; to Congo Belge Force Publique, Leopoldville 12.48 as C-32; to Natal Aviation Ltd., Durban 9.55 as ZS-DNM

G-AKCW   (5179), NJ318, registered 14.8.47 to Airspeed Ltd.; to M.o.S. as VX587; to Alvis Ltd. as Leonides testbed; scrapped at Baginton in 1956

G-AKSA   (5188), registered 26.1.48 to Airspeed Ltd., Portsmouth; delivered to the Burmese Air Force 8.49

G-ALTZ   (5134), HN844, Aer Lingus EI-ADB, 30.6.47; to B.S.A.A.C. 6.49 as 'Star Monitor'; B.O.A.C., Hurn 10.49; L. M. Berner & Co. Ltd., Elmdon 6.56; abandoned unserviceable at Leopoldville, Belgian Congo 13.11.57

G-AMBT (5202), 6.6.50, Airspeed Ltd., Portsmouth; to the Government of French Indo-China 7.50 as F-OAHG

G-AMBU (5243), 6.6.50, Airspeed Ltd., Portsmouth; to the Government of French Indo-China 7.50 as F-OAHH

G-AMID (5250), 16.4.51, Airspeed Ltd., Portsmouth; de Havilland Aircraft Co. Ltd. 9.51; to Aigle Azur Indochine, Hanoi 3.52 as F-BGPF

G-AVIL, the Ulster Flying Club's Alon A-2. (*Richard Riding*)

Alon A-2 Aircoupe (*see also Ercoupe 415-CD and Forney F-1A*)
G-ATRY (A-140), 16.6.66; G-ATWP (A-188), 23.9.66; G-AVIL (A-5), N5471E, 4.5.67

American Aviation AA-1 Yankee
G-AYFX (0318), N6118L, 16.4.70; G-AYHA (0369), 17.8.70; G-AYHB (0397), 17.8.70, crashed near Fleetwood, Lancs. 1.1.71; G-AYHC (0398), 17.8.70, d.b.r. at Perpignan, France 12.5.71; G-AYHD (0399), 25.8.70; G-AYLM (0442), 24.2.71; G-AYLN (0443), 11.3.71; G-AYLO (0444), 17.2.71; G-AYLP (0445), 22.2.71; G-AZIX (302), registered 25.11.71; G-AZKS (0334), N6134L, registered 23.12.71

ANEC I
G-EBHR Lympne No. 18, reg'd. 29.8.23 to Hubert Blundell; to A. G. Simpson, Perth, W.A. 19.8.24, first flown as G-AUEQ 10.24, reg'n. cancelled 9.32

G-EBIL (1), Lympne No. 17, completed 28.9.23, reg'd. 21.11.23 to Surrey Light A/C, Brooklands; R.A.F. 8.24 as J7506; to ANEC IA 7.25; sold abroad 1.26

ANEC II
G-EBJO (2), Lympne No. 7, reg'd. 17.7.24 to A.N.E.C. Ltd.; N. H. Jones 9.26, C. of A. 12.4.27; A. H. Wheeler, Henlow 2.29; A. J. Edmunds, Heston 3.33; F. C. H. Allen, Selsey Bill 1.35; E. J. Guild, W. Malling 5.36; Shuttleworth 1.37

ANEC IV
G-EBPI (1), 8.9.26, Air Navigation and Engineering Co. Ltd.; converted to Genet II; G. N. Warwick 4.27, crashed near Peebles, Scotland 20.7.28

Armstrong Whitworth F.K.3

G-EABY   B9629, 14.5.19, E. D. C. Herne, Aerodrome Hotel, Hendon, N.W.9, named 'Porthcawl', registration cancelled 5.20

G-EABZ   B9518, 14.5.19, E. D. C. Herne, registration cancelled 5.20

G-EAEU   B9612, 10.7.19, Kingsbury Aviation Co., Stag Lane Aerodrome, Edgware, Middlesex, crashed 12.19

G-EALK   B9603, L. G. Lowe, 1 Hamilton Place, Piccadilly, London; believed not converted for civil use, scrapped 1920

Armstrong Whitworth F.K.8

G-EAET   D5150, London and Provincial Aviation Co. Ltd., Stag Lane Aerodrome, Edgware, Middlesex; crashed 8.19, believed at Great Yarmouth

G-EAIC   H4473, 7.8.19, T. Neville Stack, crashed 6.20

G-EAJS   H4612, 10.9.19, G. L. P. Henderson; left Hounslow 11.11.19 on delivery to P. O. Flygkompani, Barkaby, Sweden

G-EALW   F7484, 13.7.20, By Air Ltd., Coventry; fatal crash near Bedford 16.8.20

G-EATO   F7384, 15.7.20, R. E. Duke, scrapped in 1922

G-EATP   H4600, registered 9.6.20 to Maj. Tryggve Gran, R.A.F. Andover; flown to Oslo 24–25.6.20, crashed during subsequent European tour

G-EAVQ   H4585, 20.10.20, Handley Page Ltd., Cricklewood, believed sold in the Argentine, registration cancelled at census 10.1.23

G-EAVT   H4573, 3.11.20, Handley Page Ltd., Cricklewood, believed sold in the Argentine, registration cancelled at census 10.1.23

Armstrong Whitworth Siskin

G-EBEU   Mk.II (A.W.10), reg'd. 21.8.22 to Sir W. G. Armstrong Whitworth Aircraft Ltd., f/f as single seater, C. of A. 11.7.23 as two seater, w.f.u. 11.24

G-EBHY   Mk.II (A.W.11), single seater reg'd. as above 1.10.23, C. of A. 25.6.24, sold to the Royal Swedish Air Force 2.9.25

G-EBIK   Mk.IV, reg'd. 10.11.23 to Sir W. G. Armstrong Whitworth Aircraft Ltd.; reported as still under construction 31.1.24, registration lapsed

G-EBJQ   Mk.III (A.W.66), registered 29.7.24 to Sir W. G. Armstrong Whitworth Aircraft Ltd. for King's Cup Race, withdrawn from use by 20.11.24

G-EBJS   Mk.III (A.W.67), reg'd. as above, withdrawn from use by 20.11.24

G-EBLL   Mk.IV (A.W.143), reg'd. 4.6.25 to Sir W. G. Armstrong Whitworth Aircraft Ltd. for King's Cup Race, withdrawn from use by 3.2.28

G-EBLN   Mk.V (A.W.97), reg'd. as above, C. of A. 30.7.25, w.f.u. by 1.1.27

G-EBLQ   Mk.V (A.W.102), registered as above 25.6.25, C. of A. 30.7.25, destroyed in fatal crash at Whitley 19.7.26

G-ABHT   Mk.III two seater (A.W.651), reg'd. 24.12.30 to Sir W. G. Armstrong Whitworth Aircraft Ltd.; to A.S.T. 5.31, crashed Sarisbury, Hants. 8.6.31

G-ABHU   Mk.III two seater (A.W.652), registered as above; to Air Service Training Ltd. 6.31, crashed 1.38

Armstrong Whitworth Argosy I

G-EBLF   (A.W.154), 29.9.26, Imperial Airways Ltd. 'City of Glasgow'; Jaguar IVA radials fitted in 1931, withdrawn from use 9.34

G-EBLO   (A.W.155), 30.6.26, Imperial Airways Ltd. 'City of Birmingham'; Jaguar IVA radials fitted in 1931, crashed at Aswan, Egypt 16.6.31

G-EBOZ   (A.W.156), 23.4.27, Imperial Airways Ltd. 'City of Wellington', later 'City of Arundel', Jaguar IVA radials in 1931, written off 10.34

Armstrong Whitworth Argosy II

G-AACH   (A.W.362), 19.5.29, Imperial Airways Ltd. 'City of Edinburgh', crashed and burned out at Croydon Airport 22.4.31

G-AACI   (A.W.363), 3.6.29, Imperial Airways Ltd. 'City of Liverpool', crashed and burned out near Dixmude, Belgium 28.3.33

G-AACJ   (A.W.364), 6.7.29, Imperial Airways Ltd. 'City of Manchester'; United Airways Ltd., Blackpool 7.35; British Airways Ltd. 1.36; registration cancelled 12.36

G-AAEJ   (A.W.400), 21.8.29, Imperial Airways Ltd. 'City of Coventry', dismantled at Croydon 1935

Armstrong Whitworth Argosy II G-AACJ at Stanley Park Aerodrome, Blackpool, in British Airways titling 1936. (*E. J. Riding*)

Armstrong Whitworth A.W.15 Atalanta

G-ABPI   (A.W.740), 15.8.32, Imperial Airways Ltd. 'Atalanta', damaged near Whitley 20.10.32, rebuilt as 'Arethusa'; to Indian Trans-Continental Airways 8.33 as VT-AEF; impressed by Indian Air Force 3.41 as DG-453

G-ABTG   (A.W.785), 12.9.32, Imperial Airways Ltd. 'Amalthea', crashed at Kisumu, Kenya 27.7.38

G-ABTH   (A.W.741), 27.9.32, Imperial Airways Ltd. 'Andromeda', w.f.u. 6.39

G-ABTI   (A.W.742), 2.1.33, Imperial Airways Ltd. 'Atalanta'; impressed by the Indian Air Force 3.41 as DG451, d.b.r. at St. Thomas' Mount, Madras, 22.8.42

G-ABTJ   (A.W.743), 18.1.33, Imperial Airways Ltd. 'Artemis'; impressed by the Indian Air Force 3.41 as DG452, scrapped 6.44

G-ABTK   (A.W.744), 18.3.33, Imperial Airways Ltd. 'Athena', burned out in hangar fire at Willingdon Airport, Delhi, India 29.9.36

G-ABTL   (A.W.784), 4.4.33, Imperial Airways Ltd. 'Astraea'; impressed by the Indian Air Force 3.41 as DG450, withdrawn from use 9.42

G-ABTM   (A.W.786), 20.4.33, Imperial Airways Ltd. 'Aurora'; to Indian Trans-Continental Airways Ltd. 8.33 as VT-AEG; impressed 3.41 as DG454

Armstrong Whitworth A.W.27 Ensign 1

G-ADSR (A.W.1156), f/f 24.1.38, C. of A. 29.6.38, Imperial A/W* 'Ensign'; to Mk. 2; flew 2,099 hr., w.f.u. at Almaza, Cairo 9.44, scrapped 3.1.45

G-ADSS (A.W.1157), f/f 25.6.38, C. of A. 18.11.38, (VT-AJE 'Ellora'†), Imperial A/WW 'Egeria'; to Mk. 2; flew 2,686 hr., scrapped at Hamble 26.3.47

G-ADST (A.W.1158), f/f 7.11.38, C. of A. 14.11.38, Imperial A/W* 'Elsinore'; to Mk. 2; flew 3,495 hr., flown to Hamble 19.2.46, scrapped 28.3.47

G-ADSU (A.W.1159), f/f 12.11.38, C. of A. 2.12.38, (VT-AJF 'Everest'†), Imperial A/W* 'Euterpe'; to Mk. 2; w.f.u. 2.45, scrapped at Almaza, Cairo 3.46

G-ADSV (A.W.1160), f/f 24.11.38, C. of A. 2.12.38, Imperial A/W* 'Explorer'; to Mk. 2; flew 3,720 hr., flown to Hamble 25.2.46, scrapped 23.3.47

G-ADSW (A.W.1161), f/f 11.12.38, C. of A. 8.5.39, Imperial A/W* 'Eddystone'; to Mk. 2; flew 3,595 hr., flown to Hamble 5.6.46, scrapped 21.4.47

G-ADSX (A.W.1162), f/f 27.2.39, C. of A. 12.6.39, Imperial A/W 'Ettrick'; abandoned at Le Bourget 1.6.40, fitted with Daimler-Benz engines by Germans

G-ADSY (A.W.1163), f/f 19.6.39, C. of A. 23.6.39, Imperial A/W* 'Empyrean'; to Mk. 2; flew 3,478 hr., flown to Hamble 7.1.46, scrapped 26.3.47

G-ADSZ (A.W.1164), f/f 25.6.39, C. of A. 30.6.39, Imperial A/W 'Elysian'; shot up by Me 109s and burned out on ground at Merville, France 23.5.40

G-ADTA (A.W.1165), f/f 19.8.39, C. of A. 23.8.39, (VT-AJG 'Ernakulam'†), Imperial A/W 'Euryalus', damaged landing Lympne 23.5.40, to spares at Hamble

G-ADTB (A.W.1166), f/f 30.8,39, C. of A. 19.9.39, Imperial A/W* 'Echo'; to Mk. 2; flew 3,534 hr., flown to Hamble 19.2.46, scrapped 20.3.47

G-ADTC (A.W.1167), f/f 5.10.39, C. of A. 7.10.39, (VT-AJH 'Etah'†), Imperial A/W 'Endymion'; destroyed by incendiary bombs, Whitchurch 24.11.40

* Transferred to B.O.A.C. 4.40   † Registration and name not used

Armstrong Whitworth A.W.27 Ensign 2

G-AFZU (A.W.1821), f/f 20.6.41, C. of A. 26.6.41, B.O.A.C. 'Everest'; shot up by He 111 over Biscay 9.11.41; flew 2,406 hr., scrapped Hamble 16.4.47

G-AFZV (A.W.1822), f/f 28.10.41, C. of A. 1.11.41, B.O.A.C. 'Enterprise'; abandoned in W. Africa 3.2.42; became F-AFZV, later F-BAHO; seized by the Germans, transferred to the Luftwaffe and fitted with Daimler-Benz engines

Armstrong Whitworth A.W.38 Whitley 5

G-AGCF (A.W.2694), BD360, 5.5.42, B.O.A.C.; returned to R.A.F. 7.43 as BD360

G-AGCG (A.W.2695), BD361, 5.5.42, B.O.A.C.; returned to R.A.F. 7.43 as BD361

G-AGCH (A.W.2696), BD362, 5.5.42, B.O.A.C.; returned to R.A.F. 3.43 as BD362

G-AGCI (A.W.2716), BD382, 8.6.42, B.O.A.C.; ditched off Gibraltar 26.9.42

G-AGCJ (A.W.2717), BD383, 21.5.42, B.O.A.C.; returned to R.A.F. 10.43 as BD383

G-AGCK (A.W.2718), BD384, 21.5.42, B.O.A.C.; returned to R.A.F. 10.43 as BD384

G-AGDU (A.W.1126), Z9208 ex No. 58 Sqn., Linton-on-Ouse, C. of A. 18.7.42, B.O.A.C.; returned to R.A.F. damaged 8.42

G-AGDV (A.W.1134), Z9216, reg'd. 17.3.42 to B.O.A.C.; returned to R.A.F. 4.42 as Z9216; missing on training flight from No. 19 O.T.U., Kinloss 5.43

G-AGDW Z6660 ex No. 58 Sqn., Linton-on-Ouse, registered 17.3.42 to B.O.A.C.; returned to R.A.F. 4.42 as Z6660

G-AGDX (A.W.2719), BD385, 22.5.42, B.O.A.C.; returned to R.A.F. 7.43 as BD385

G-AGDY (A.W.2720), BD386, 22.5.42, B.O.A.C.; returned to R.A.F. 7.43 as BD386

G-AGDZ (A.W.2721), BD387, 22.5.42, B.O.A.C.; returned to R.A.F. 1.43 as BD387
G-AGEA (A.W.2722), BD388, 26.5.42, B.O.A.C.; returned to R.A.F. 1.43 as BD388
G-AGEB (A.W.2723), BD389, 8.5.42, B.O.A.C.; returned to R.A.F. 1.43 as BD389
G-AGEC (A.W.2724), BD390, 8.5.42, B.O.A.C.; returned to R.A.F. 7.43 as BD390

Auster 3

G-AHLI (540), NJ911, 17.9.46, Vickers-Armstrongs Ltd., South Marston; Seven Flying Group, Booker 2.67; A. V. Orchard, Valley 6.71
G-AHLK (700), NJ889, 17.9.46, Vickers-Armstrongs Ltd., South Marston; J. W. C. Judge, Shoreham 4.58; H. W. Bonner, Shoreham 6.69; F. W. Shaw and Sons (Worthing) Ltd., Shoreham 1.72
G-AREI (518), MT438, VR-SCJ, VR-RBM, 9M-ALB, 29.3.61, M. Somerton-Rayner, Middle Wallop; Laarbruch Flying Club, Germany 8.67; N. C. Milne, White Waltham 5.70; P. J. Pearce, Thruxton 4.71
G-ATAX (546), NJ916, PH-UFP, 23.1.64, Geilenkirchen Flying Club, Germany; to Holland 7.65 as PH-UFP; rest. 7.68 to Laarbruch Flying Club, Germany

Auster 4

G-AJXX (875), MT104, 26.7.48, T. Leadbetter, Elmdon; T. W. Hayhow, Thornaby 9.49; Darlington & District Aero Club 2.52; to French Morocco 3.52 as F-DAAK
G-AJXY (792), MT243, 2.9.48, T. Leadbetter, Elmdon; S. Bicham, Orkney 9.50; Alconbury A/C 4.58; C. King, Biggin Hill 11.63; H. M. Alliott, Fairoaks 1.66
G-AJYB (847), MS974, 24.3.49, J. G. Crampton, Spalding; accident at Costessey, Norwich 30.10.51; E. H. Gould, Bournemouth 1.61; conv. to Auster J-1N
G-AKYT (891), MT165, 18.6.48, York F/C 7.48; R. S. Field, Macmerry 2.51; Darlington & District A/C, Croft 6.51 as Mk. 4A; to France 8.51 as F-BECV
G-ALJE (918), MT186, 18.7.50, Darlington & District A/C, Croft; sold to the Moroccan Aero Club 12.50 as F-DAAY
G-ALNU (819), MS952, 13.7.50, R. A. Short, Croydon; to France 9.51 as F-BFXZ; later to Morocco as CN-TEI
G-ALVV (865), MT143, 14.9.50, G. C. S. Whyham, Squires Gate; J. D. Barber, Denham 6.53; Aerocontacts Ltd., Gatwick 12.54; to Spain 3.55 as EC-AKU
G-ALYH (849), MT107, 28.4.50, South Hants U.L.A.C., Christchurch; Elstree F/C 7.51; B.K.S. Aerocharter Ltd., Düsseldorf 8.53; reduced to spares 1959
G-AMJV (976), MT340, 30.12.52, Darlington & District A/C, Croft; sold to Sté. Commerciale d'Aviation Marocaine, Casablanca 1.53 as F-DABR
G-AMLU (756), MT193, registered 24.8.51 to Boardsides Aircraft Servicing Ltd., Wyberton, Boston, Lincs; burned out in hangar fire, Wyberton 6.4.52
G-ANGX (881), MT108, registered to R. K. Dundas Ltd., Elstree 12.53; sold in Australia 11.54 as VH-AZJ, later VH-TLS, VH-DDW and VH-BHA
G-ANHL (902), MT133, 13.8.54, R. K. Dundas Ltd.; E. E. Chick, Elstree 9.54; D. J. Porter, Biggin Hill 4.60; R. E. Webb, Eastleigh 9.63, w.f.u. 10.65
G-ANHM (846), MT137, registered 12.53 to R. K. Dundas Ltd., Elstree; to Australia 11.54 as VH-AZO, later VH-ILS and VH-SNG
G-ANHN (900), MT163, 9.7.54, Aerocontacts Ltd., Gatwick 8.54; Vendair (London) Ltd., Croydon 7.57; to Bölkow Apparatebau GmbH, Nabern 5.58 as D-EGUK
G-ANHP (906), MT170, 8.9.54, R. K. Dundas Ltd., Elstree; to K. Murmann, Bochum, Germany 11.55 as D-ELIT

G-ANHS (737), MT197, 2.9.54, L. M. Henry, Elstree; N. Rivett & T. G. Crane, Foulsham 3.61; J. Rushton, Wolverhampton 12.65; J. N. West, Elmdon 9.69

G-ANHU (799), MT255, 22.10.54, R. K. Dundas, Elstree; J. F. Harris, Elstree 11.54; F. A. Webber, Elstree 5.61; to Spain 10.64 as EC-AXR

Auster 5

G-AGLK (1137), RT475, 14.9.44, converted 8.57 to Auster 5D; G-AGLL (1138), 14.9.44, d.b.r. 10.49; G-AHGV (757), MT191, 8.1.47, crashed at Humberstone, Leics. 14.5.49; G-AIKA (889), MT188, 4.11.46, to New Zealand 11.50 as ZK-AVU; G-AIKB (1408), TJ341, 4.12.46, crashed at Wrexham 26.3.48; G-AIKC (1078), NJ699, 6.12.46, to Paraguay 5.47 as ZP-TDK; G-AIKE (1097), NJ728, 11.12.46, d.b.r. at Luton 1.9.65; G-AIPE (1416), TJ347, to Holland 6.52 as PH-NET; G-AIPF (1039), NJ638, 10.1.47, to Turkey 4.52 as TC-ALIS; G-AIPN (1151), RT488, 16.4.47, to France 2.52 as F-BGPD; G-AIPO (1544), TJ543, 26.3.47, to Dakar 8.51 as F-DAAI

G-AJAK (1021), NJ625, 16.4.47, to France 2.57 as F-BIAU, to Ireland 12.58 as EI-AKN, rest. as G-AJAK 5.61, crashed at Ramsgate 16.2.67; G-AJAN (1248), RT618, 28.4.47, to France 9.50 as F-BEEI; G-AJCH (2054), TW510, 5.10.48, to the Falkland Islands 9.49 as VP-FAA; G-AJCI (817) MS951, 5.10.48, to the Falkland Islands 9.49 as VP-FAB; G-AJFI (1557), TJ531, 4.4.47, to Finland 3.50 as OH-AUA; G-AJGJ (1147), RT486, 20.9.47; G-AJHJ (1067), NJ676, 8.5.47, w.f.u. at Haldon 6.49; G-AJHV (806), MS941, 12.7.50, crashed at Hanover, Germany 30.12.53; G-AJII (1588), TJ537, 16.6.47, to France 11.50 as F-BFXG; G-AJIK (1161), RT498, 24.6.47, sold in the Lebanon 2.52; G-AJIL (1086), NJ702, 24.6.47, to France 12.47 as F-BECZ; G-AJJA (1211), RT576, 15.5.47, crashed at Elmdon 18.1.48; G-AJJB (1563), TJ520, 11.4.47, to Kenya 12.52 as VP-KKL; G-AJJG (1107), NJ732, 11.9.47, to Tunis 8.50 as F-OAHS; G-AJJH (1014), NJ617, 23.7.47, to France 12.52 as F-BGOX; G-AJJR (1050), NJ667, 28.7.47, to Australia 8.51 as VH-ABA

G-AJLE (1550), TJ541, 13.8.47, to Sweden 11.53 as SE-BZC; G-AJLF (844), MT110, scrapped at Squires Gate 2.49; G-AJLG (742), MT175, 19.7.48, to Sweden 10.53 as SE-BZA; G-AJTM (1445), TJ402, 7.10.47, to Kenya 3.55 as VP-KNE; G-AJTN (1052),

Auster 5 G-AKWK being serviced at Elstree in April 1952 before delivery to Turkey as TC-AYLA. This, TC-ALIS (G-AIPF) and TC-URER (G-AJTV) are among the few known examples of six letter registrations. (*Planet News*)

NJ668, 9.1.48, to Switzerland 6.50 as HB-EUA; G-AJTV (1433), TJ367, 3.7.47, to Turkey 4.52 as TC-URER; G-AJVK (1537), TJ514, 27.1.48, to Tunis 9.49 as F-OAEF; G-AJVN (1435), TJ372, 12.9.47, to New Zealand 9.50 as ZK-AVX; G-AJVT (1495), TJ478, 13.3.48; G-AJVU (1834), TW502, 16.7.47, to New Zealand 8.50 as ZK-AUH; G-AJVV (1817), TW478, crashed at Denham 18.9.52; G-AJVW (1833), TW503, 17.9.47, to New Zealand 7.48 as spares; G-AJXC (1409), TJ343, 3.10.47; G-AJXV (1065), NJ695, to France 12.47 as F-BEEJ; G-AJYC (1193), RT553, 26.8.48, to Kenya 8.49 as VP-KGD; G-AJYD (1105), NJ731, 13.10.48, to New Zealand 11.50 as ZK-AWD; G-AJYH (1400), TJ352, 2.9.49, to Holland 10.49 as PH-NAD; G-AJYI (977), MT343, 16.3.49, to France 1951 as F-BFXF; G-AJYP (804), MS939, 18.5.50, to Singapore 7.52 as VR-SDQ

G-AKJT (1583), TJ530, 19.7.48, to India 4.52 as VT-DGB; G-AKJU (2058), TW513, 13.1.58, converted to J-1N, crashed at Whatfield, Suffolk 15.8.71; G-AKLH (791), MT269, used as spares 7.48; G-AKMB (1529), TJ480, 5.4.48, to Sweden 4.52 as SE-BUR; G-AKMC (1516), TJ458, 31.5.48, to New Zealand 7.50 as ZK-AVF; G-AKMI (1530), TJ471, 28.7.48, to France 2.52 as F-BGPB; G-AKOT (1469), TJ433, 13.5.48, crashed at Gorleston 9.9.62; G-AKOU (1412), TJ342, 13.10.48, to New Zealand 7.50 as ZK-AVH; G-AKOW (1579), TJ569, 24.3.48, to Holland 11.50 as PH-NEG, to Germany 6.61 as D-EJON, rest. 1.63 as G-AKOW; G-AKOX (1264), RT637, 6.9.48, to Holland 4.52 as PH-NEP; G-AKPH (1099), NJ719, 10.4.48, dismantled at Rutherglen 1.61; G-AKPI (1088), NJ703, 15.6.48; G-AKPJ (1586), TJ567, 24.9.48, to New Zealand 9.50 as ZK-AXP; G-AKRC (856), MT100, 9.4.48, to Finland 5.52 as OH-AUF; G-AKSI (1159), RT497, 14.5.48, to Switzerland 5.48 as HB-EON; G-AKSJ not taken up, aircraft re-registered G-AKSP; G-AKSP (1448), TJ401, 13.4.48, to France 7.49 as F-BDAY; G-AKSY (1567), TJ534, 9.4.48, to France 2.52 as F-BGOO; G-AKSZ (1503), TJ457, 13.5.48, to France 3.52 as F-BGPQ; G-AKTA (1319), TJ227, 11.6.48, to France 6.51 as F-BFXX; G-AKTF (1443), TJ399, 27.5.48, crashed off Beachy Head 7.2.60; G-AKWG (1134), RT471, 27.10.48, crashed off Gosport 19.4.50; G-AKWH (2051), TW507, 29.6.48, to Kenya 11.49 as VP-KID; G-AKWI (984), MT346, sold abroad 5.48; G-AKWK (1375), TJ299, 27.8.48, to Turkey 4.52 as TC-AYLA; G-AKWS (1237), RT610, 1.6.48; G-AKWT (998), MT360, 23.7.48, crashed at Tollerton 7.8.48; G-AKXP (1017), NJ633, 14.6.48; G-AKXR (1289), TJ200, 2.6.49, to Sweden 8.58 as SE-CGL; G-AKYU (2057), TW512, 8.12.48, to Dakar 11.54 as F-DADS

The Dorset Gliding Club's unique, Compton Abbas-based Auster 5/150, once D-EGOF, was fitted with the 150 h.p. Lycoming and dorsal fin at Rearsby in 1966. (*P. J. Bish*)

G-ALBJ (1831), TW501, 5.1.50; G-ALBK (1273), RT644, 13.10.48; G-ALBW (1470), TJ410, 7.7.48, crashed at Booker 24.7.52; G-ALCT (1532), TJ513, 11.5.49, to Sweden 10.53 as SE-BZB; G-ALEY (895), MT124, 3.12.48, to New Zealand 11.50 as ZK-AYB; G-ALFA (826), MS958, 10.3.49; G-ALJB (1557), TJ545, 2.8.49, crashed at Harraton Hall, Co. Durham 13.5.51; G-ALJC (1829), TW500, 1.7.49, to Morocco 4.51; G-ALJD (1079), NJ691, 25.5.51, to Dakar 8.51 as F-DAAG; G-ALKJ (2052), TW508, 19.1.50, to Australia 3.50 as VH-AJD; G-ALKK (1652), TJ638, 15.9.50, to New Zealand 11.50 as ZK-AXQ; G-ALNV (1216), RT578, 5.7.49, dismantled at Leicester East 10.59; G-ALNW (1606), TJ585, 12.7.52, to Belgium 8.52 as OO-VAV; G-ALXZ (1082), NJ689, 22.3.50, to Holland 4.52 as PH-NER, to Germany 1.61 as D-EGOF, rest. 1.66 as G-ALXZ, flown 5.67 as Auster 5/150; G-ALYB (1173), RT520, 21.4.50, w.f.u. at Rearsby 5.63; G-ALYD (824), MS957, 26.9.50

G-AMAO (1095), NJ721, dismantled at Croydon 4.53; G-AMAP (1417), TJ351, 11.5.50, to France 7.51 as spares; G-AMBZ (1036), NJ636, 28.6.50, to New Zealand 7.50 as ZK-AVG; G-AMDS (1115), NJ738, 24.11.50, to Australia 5.51 as VH-ASP; G-AMFR (1828), TW499, 7.12.50, to New Zealand 12.50 as ZK-AWU; G-AMFS (1802), TW464, 15.1.52, to Holland 4.52 as PH-NEO; G-AMFT (1827), TW498, to Australia 4.51 as VH-ARX; G-AMJM (1792), TW452, 22.6.51, to France 9.51 as F-BBSO; G-AMNI (1030), NJ637, 15.3.52, to France 4.52 as F-BGPC; G-AMNU (1603), TJ587, 29.8.52, to Germany 10.56 as D-EFIR; G-AMOR (1781), TW451, 19.3.52, to Finland 5.52 as OH-AUE; G-AMSZ (838), MS971, 27.6.52; G-AMVD (1565), TJ565, to France 4.52 as F-BGTF; G-AMZP (1312), TJ219, 28.5.53, to Madagascar 8.53 as F-OANT

G-ANDU (1510), TJ459, converted to Auster 5M, C. of A. 9.12.53, to Sweden 6.55 as SE-CAO; G-ANEP (1384), TJ309, 5.11.53, d.b.f. at Düsseldorf 12.3.54; G-ANFU (1748), TW385, 18.12.53; G-ANGA (1807), TW468, 30.12.53, to Australia 2.56 as VH-BGN; G-ANGW (845), MS980, to Austria 11.55 as OE-AAT; G-ANHO (899), MT169, 13.10.54, crashed at Biggin Hill 9.5.64; G-ANHR (759), MT192, 20.8.54 G-ANHT (764), MT218, to Belgium 11.54 as OO-DBA; G-ANHV (922), MT277, to Sweden 2.55 as SE-CAP; G-ANHW (1396), TJ320, 21.5.54, converted to Auster 5D q.v.; G-ANHX (2064), TW519, converted to Auster 5D q.v.; G-ANHZ (1753), TW384, 29.6.54

G-ANIA (2050), TW506, 12.7.54, to Switzerland 7.54 as HB-EUB; G-ANIB (1818), TW475, to France 7.54 as F-BHCO; G-ANIC (1816), TW474, to spares at Caen, France 7.54; G-ANID (1811), TW471, 1.10.54, crashed near Oxford 13.2.58; G-ANIE (1809), TW467, 3.3.54; G-ANIF (1709), TW460, 13.5.54, to Sweden 1.58 as SE-CGO; G-ANIG (1795), TW457, 11.6.54, to Spain 7.54 as EC-AJJ; G-ANIH (1779), TW449, 12.5.55; G-ANII (1739), TW374, 9.7.54, to the French Colonies 11.55 as F-OARN; G-ANIJ (1680), TJ672, 27.9.55, converted to Auster 5D q.v.; G-ANIK (1674), TJ657, crashed near Leeds 4.3.62; G-ANIL (1575), TJ527, 6.4.55, to Germany 6.57 as D-ECIL; G-ANIM (1542), TJ515, 15.4.54, to Norway 6.54 as LN-BDK; G-ANIN (1494), TJ506, 15.7.54, d.b.r. at Barrow 19.11.59; G-ANIO (1425), TJ422, 6.5.55, to Norway 2.60 as LN-BNB; G-ANIP (1453), TJ394, to Greece 9.56 as SX-ADA; G-ANIR (1438), TJ380, 27.2.56, to Malawi 7.67 as 7Q-YDG; G-ANIS (1429), TJ375, 28.1.55; G-ANIT (1407), TJ339, 9.3.54, crashed off Hastings 2.7.54; G-ANIU (841), MS977, to Norway 2.55 as LN-BDU; G-ANKI (1790), TW446, 21.1.54 to Germany 11.56 as D-ELYD; G-ANLU (1780), 7.5.54; G-ANPG (1000), MT363, 1.4.54, w.f.u. 3.55; G-ANRP (1789), TW439, 25.6.54

G-AOCP (1800), TW462, 19.6.56, d.b.r. 5.70; G-AOCU (986), MT349, 20.7.56; G-AOHA (1796), TW456, 16.3.56, to Paraguay 1957 as ZP-TDL; G-AOJL (1791), TW455, 1.6.56, to Sweden 5.59 as SE-CMB; G-AORI (1154), RT489, 18.5.56, crashed at Stagsend, Beds. 7.12.56; G-AOSL (1815), TW477, 26.9.56, converted to Auster 5M;

G-AOTJ (1760), TW388, 2.8.56, crashed near Dumfries 7.10.63; G-AOVW (894), MT119, 20.6.69; G-AOXT (1756), TW386, 23.11.56, to Trinidad 5.57 as VP-TBZ; G-AOYA (2055), TW515, 26.4.57, to the Gold Coast 8.57 as VP-AAG

G-APIC (1668), TJ651, 30.11.57, to Singapore 12.58 as VR-SED; G-APJX (1439), TJ373, 6.3.59, wrecked by gale at Inverness 28.9.69

Auster 5C

G-ALKI   (1272), TJ187, 17.4.50, Grp. Capt. A. H. Wheeler, Farnborough; to E. G. McNutt, Waipukurau, New Zealand 10.51 as ZK-AZF

Auster 5D

G-AGLK   (1137), RT475, 13.8.57, E. H. Gould, Christchurch; Royal Artillery Aero Club, Middle Wallop 11.58; W. C. E. Tazewell, Shoreham 6.67

G-AJYU   (2666), prototype converted from TW453 (c/n 1793), 6.9.50, Auster Aircraft Ltd., Reasby; to Denmark 8.51 as OY-ACI; to Sweden as SE-CMG

G-ALYG   (835), MS968, 9.8.57, W. Sturrock, Grantham; N. Lockwood, Irby-on-Humber private strip 7.58

G-ALZM   (1035), NJ635, 4.8.55, D. E. Bianchi, White Waltham; to New Zealand 8.55 to Aerial Work (Marlborough) Ltd. as ZK-BMD

G-AMII   (1013), NJ626, 12.9.51, Warden Aviation Ltd., Old Warden; to Australia 11.51 as VH-AZI

G-ANHW (1396), TJ320, 14.5.55, Airways Aero Ass'n., Croydon; Cotswold A/C, Staverton 7.57; Industrial Publicity 6.66; G. J. Arnold, Swanton Morley 12.67

G-ANHX   (2064), TW519, 11.5.57, Glamorgan Aviation Ltd., Rhoose; The Rochford Hundred Flying Group, Southend 9.64; G. B. Pearce, Lympne 8.69; C. B. Lloyd and R. S. Kelly, Lympne 6.71

G-ANHY   (1757), TW387, 3.2.55, R. K. Dundas Ltd., Elstree; to New Zealand to A. M. Bisley and Co. 2.55 as ZK-BGU

G-ANIJ   (1680), TJ672, 22.11.56, Channel Islands A/C, Jersey; Airlines (Jersey) Ltd. 2.58; G. Donaldson and M. Melly, Woodvale 3.66

G-AOCR   (1060), NJ673, 5.10.56, D. E. Bianchi, White Waltham; to Ireland 3.57 as EI-AJS; rest. 11.57; Channel Islands A/C, Jersey 6.59; B. O. Shepherd, Christchurch 3.68; G. W. Johnson, Stapleford 11.69

G-AOUL   (1755), TW389, 1.12.56, Luton Flying Club, crashed at Baldock 16.5.61

Auster Alpha 5 (*New construction 1957–59*)

G-AOFJ   (3401), 9.1.57, W. T. Clarke, Speke; Chester F/C, Calveley 7.60; G. H. Clement, Wolverhampton 9.61; Miss P. Innocent, Lulsgate 3.69

G-APAF   (3404), 14.5.57, Travelair Ltd.; Process Units (Halifax) Ltd., Yeadon 6.59; Yorkshire Territorial F/G, Yeadon 6.62; A. Brier, Sherburn 5.69

G-APAH   (3402), 1.5.57, C. W. Morley, Stapleford; w.f.u. Stapleford 9.60; in store at Southend 1972

G-APBE   (3403), 9.5.57, Associated Newspapers Ltd.; E. A. Holt, Croydon 9.57; Experimental F/G, Biggin Hill 8.59; Thurleigh F/G, Bedford 5.68

G-APBW   (3405), 13.6.57, J. E. Allcard, Croydon; Angel Court F/G, Biggin Hill 5.66; P. J. Rae, Panshanger 10.68; G. C. Starling, Cambridge 11.69

G-APHU   (3407), 13.9.57, F. Hewitt, Croydon; Mrs. Y. M. Kaiser, Fairoaks 11.59; re-registered in Austria under the same ownership 2.60 as OE-DBZ

G-APNM (3409), 17.7.58, Auster Aircraft Ltd., to Sweden 1.59 as SE-CFN

G-APNN   (3410), 17.7.58, Auster Aircraft Ltd., to Sweden 10.59 as SE-CME

G-APRE   (3411), 23.12.58, Auster Aircraft Ltd., to Sweden 2.59 as SE-CGK

G-APRF   (3412), 8.1.59, J. D. C. White, Woolsington; to Sierra Leone 8.59 as VR-LAF; rest. 11.60 to J. D. C. White; Experimental F/G, Biggin Hill 9.61; E. Drake, Biggin Hill 3.70

G-APTU   (3413), 23.7.59, Grantchester Garage Ltd., Cambridge; Anglian Air Charter Ltd., North Denes 2.61; W. E. Taylor Ltd., Thorn's Cross 5.69; B. G. F. King, Melksham 1.71

G-APUL   (3414), 8.10.59, Auster Aircraft Ltd.; to Germany 10.59 as D-ECUZ

The unique Auster J-1S G-AMVN (*M. D. N. Fisher*)

Auster J-1 Autocrat

G-AERO, see G-AHHE; G-AFWN (124), 20.11.45, to Germany 9.56 as D-EKOM; G-AGOH (1442), 8.10.45; G-AGTO (1822), 19.12.45; G-AGTP (1823), 19.12.45, converted to J-1N; G-AGTR (1824), 29.12.45, to Germany 12.58 as D-ENUM; G-AGTS (1825), 29.12.45, crashed at Denham 25.11.47; G-AGTT (1826), 28.12.45; G-AGTU (1837), 29.12.45, to Southern Rhodesian Air Force 8.47 as SR-28; G-AGTV (1838), 29.12.45, to Ireland 7.62 as EI-AMK; G-AGTW (1839), 28.12.45, to Gabon 8.51 as F-OAJK; G-AGTX (1840), 28.12.45, w.f.u. 1.65; G-AGTY (1841), 6.12.45, crashed at Denham 19.7.54; G-AGVF (1857), 18.1.46, converted to J-1N; G-AGVG (1858), 25.1.46; G-AGVH (1859), 21.1.46, to Malaya 11.50 as VR-RBO; G-AGVI (1860), 23.1.46; G-AGVJ (1861), 23.1.46, converted to J-1N, w.f.u. 8.64; G-AGVK (1844), 31.12.45, to France 12.48 as F-BFYS; G-AGVL (1871), 31.1.46, crashed at Panshanger 22.1.67; G-AGVM (1872), 8.2.46, converted to J-1N, crashed at Lulsgate 19.5.59; G-AGVN (1873), 6.2.46; G-AGVO (1874), 13.2.46, to Australia 2.52 as VH-AJE; G-AGVP (1875), 9.2.46, to Trinidad 6.57 as VP-TBV; G-AGVR (1876), 12.2.46, to Australia 2.51 as VH-WRB; G-AGVS (1877), 12.2.46, to Nyasaland 2.48 as VP-NAJ; G-AGVT (1878), 13.2.46, d.b.r. at Heston 16.3.47; G-AGVU (1879), 7.3.46, to France 2.52 as F-BBRU

G-AGWY (1880), 7.3.46, to Germany 3.56 as D-ELYM; G-AGWZ (1881), 13.2.46, crashed at Haddington, East Lothian 20.5.47; G-AGXB (1892), 19.3.46, d.b.r. at Tollerton 16.12.62; G-AGXC (1893), 22.3.46, crashed at Denham 16.1.52; G-AGXD (1894), 25.3.46, to Australia 4.55 as VH-DDY; G-AGXE (1895), 30.3.46, to South Africa 4.47 as ZS-BPM; G-AGXF (1896), 30.3.46, crashed at Bridport 5.4.52; G-AGXG (1897), 30.3.46, d.b.r. at Denham 6.3.55; G-AGXH (1898), 2.4.46, converted to J-1N, derelict at Lympne 12.71; G-AGXI (1899), 1.4.46, to South Africa 11.48 as ZS-DBM; G-AGXJ (1900), 2.4.46, to France 8.53 as F-BGRX; G-AGXK (1951), 8.4.46, crashed at Staverton 20.8.53; G-AGXL (1961), 13.4.46, crashed in France 26.6.47; G-AGXM (1962), crashed at Loch Leven 12.7.53; G-AGXN (1963), 13.4.46, converted to J-1N; G-AGXO (1964), 13.4.46, to Spain 12.53 as EC-AJS; G-AGXP (1965), 17.4.46; G-AGXR (1966), 15.4.46, to Uganda 8.46 as VP-UAL; G-AGXS (1967), 15.4.46, to Spain 6.55 as EC-ALD; G-AGXT (1968), 25.4.46, converted to J-1N, crashed at Bickmarsh 7.6.69; G-AGXU (1969), 27.4.46, converted to J-1N; G-AGXV (1970), 27.4.46; G-AGXW (1971), 27.4.46, to New Zealand 2.50 as ZK-AUB; G-AGXX (1982), 10.5.46, crashed at Cambridge 16.12.51; G-AGXY (1983), 10.5.46, to Iraq 9.46 as YI-ABM, rest. 7.50 as G-AGXY, dismantled at Perth 9.54; G-AGXZ (1984), 10.5.46, to South Africa 7.48 as ZS-DAE

G-AGYD (1985), 10.5.46, converted to J-1N; G-AGYE (1986), 16.5.46, crashed at La Baule, France 28.7.48; G-AGYF (1987), 16.5.46, crashed at Southend 29.8.54; G-AGYG (1988), 16.5.46, to France 6.49 as F-BDAX; G-AGYH (1989), 16.5.46, converted to J-1N; G-AGYI (1990), 16.5.46, converted to J-1N, crashed at Brighton 3.9.58; G-AGYJ (1991), 16.5.46, to Australia 1.52 ass VH-BGB; G-AGYK (2002), 7.6.46, w.f.u. 11.71; G-AGYL (2003), 7.6.46, crashed near Brecon 6.7.64; G-AGYM (2004), 7.6.46, converted to J-1N; G-AGYN (2005), 7.6.46, to Norway 4.56 as LLN-BFV; G-AGYO (2006), 30.5.46, crashed at Kemsing 24.8.51; G-AGYP (2007), 17.6.46, converted to J-1N, crashed at East Didsbury 14.4.61; G-AGYR (2008), 19.6.46, crashed at Kirkburton 11.12.50; G-AGYS (1866), 31.1.46, to France 1950 as F-BGXX; G-AGYT (1862), 25.1.46, converted to J-1N

G-AHAL (1870), 31.1.46, converted to J-1N; G-AHAM (1885), 8.3.46; G-AHAO (1886), 4.3.46, to Sweden 12.53 as SE-BYU; G-AHAP (1887), 28.2.46; G-AHAR (1888), 28.2.46, to France 12.50 as F-BGRZ; G-AHAS (1889), 28.2.46, to Sweden 3.46 as SE-ART; G-AHAT (1849), 8.1.46, converted to J-1N; G-AHAU (1850), 9.1.46; G-AHAV (1836), 21.1.46; G-AHAW (1865), 21.1.46, to New Zealand 9.50 as ZK-AWH; G-AHAX (1955), 2.4.46, to New Zealand 5.50 as ZK-AUO; G-AHAY (1956), 15.4.46; G-AHCF (1960), 9.4.46, to Spain 1.51 as EC-DAZ; G-AHCJ (1972), 2.5.46, crashed at Speeton 5.9.48; G-AHCK (1973), 2.5.46, converted to J-1N; G-AHCL (1977), 20.5.46, converted to J-1N; G-AHCM (1979), 10.5.46, converted to J-1N, to Holland 1.63 as PH-AAF; G-AHCN (1980), 10.5.46, converted to J-1N; G-AHCO (1992), 30.5.46, to Germany 5.58 as D-EGEH; G-AHCP (1993), 30.5.46, crashed at Sywell 28.6.47

G-AHHD (1976), 30.5.46, to Holland 1.48 as PH-FCB; G-AHHE (1994), re-registered G-AERO, 31.5.46, to New Zealand 7.50 as ZK-AUX; G-AHHF (2009), 21.6.46, to Denmmark 6.46 as OY-DGO; G-AHHG (2010), 21.6.46, to Denmark 6.46 as OY-DGI; G-AHHH (2011), 21.6.46, to France 11.50 as F-BAVR, rest. 11.70 as G-AHHH; G-AHHI (2012), 19.6.46, to Belgium 5.46 as OO-ANL, re-registered 9.51 as OO-PIT, rest. 2.57 as G-AHHI, crashed at Squires Gate 4.1.59; G-AHHJ (2013), 19.6.46, to Egypt 12.49 as SU-AGR; G-AHHK (2014), 19.6.46; G-AHHL (2015), 19.6.46, crashed near Avranchès, France 27.9.61; G-AHHM (2016), 19.6.46, crashed off Cromer 31.12.59; G-AHHN (2017), 21.6.46; GG-AHHO (2018), 21.6.46, to Germany 10.56 as D-EGUT; G-AHHP (2019), 21.6.46, converted to J-1N; G-AHHR (2020), 21.6.46, crashed at Rochester 12.3.55, rebuilt as J-1N registered G-AOXR, to the Cape Verde Islands 7.62 as CR-CAJ; G-AHHS (2021), 24.6.46, ditched off Berck, France 15.4.63; G-AHHT (2022), 24.6.46, converted to J-1N; G-AHHU (2023), 2.7.46, converted to J-1N, w.f.u. 6.63; G-AHHV (2024), 2.7.46, to Palestine 7.46 as VQ-PAS; G-AHHW (1995), 23.5.46, converted to J-1N, to France 8.62 as F-BKGX

G-AHSH (2028), 15.6.46, to Dakar 9.52 as F-DAAV; G-AHSI (2029), 4.7.46, to Spain 2.55 as EC-AMB; G-AHSM (2107), 10.7.46, to Port Gentil 3.51 as F-OAJG; G-AHSN (2105), 10.7.46, crashed at Denham 11.7.55; G-AHSO (2123), 14.9.46, converted to J-1N; G-AHSP (2134), 26.9.46, to France 11.52 as F-BGRO; G-AHSR (2135), 23.9.46, to Australia 8.50 as VH-AIH; G-AHSS (2136), 26.9.46, converted to J-1N; G-AHST (2137), 23.9.46, converted to J-1N; G-AHSU (2138), 1.10.46, to Egypt 11.49 as SU-AGS; G-AHSV (2139), 26.9.46, to France 12.47 as F-BENL; G-AHSW (2140), 26.9.46; G-AHSX (2141), 30.9.46, to Liberia 9.52 as EL-AAD; G-AHSZ (2112), 10.7.46, to Port Gentil 3·50 as F-OAGT

G-AIBH (2113), 10.7.46, converted to J-1N; G-AIBI (2122), 14.9.46, crashed in Graham Land, Antarctica 15.9.47; G-AIBJ (2145), 1.8.50, to Brazil 1.48 as PT-ADI; G-AIBK (2146), 1.10.46, to Ireland 4.47 as EI-ACY; G-AIBL (2147), 1.10.46, to Australia 1.53 as VH-BDQ; G-AIBM (2148), 4.10.46; G-AIBO (2149), 7.10.46, to Iraq 3.48 as YI-ABO; G-AIBP (2150), 10.10.46, to Australia 5.52 as VH-ASI; G-AIBR (2151), 10.10.46, d.b.r. at Gamston 5.9.70; G-AIBS (2154), 11.10.46, crashed at Peterborough 22.5.51; G-AIBT (2155), 10.10.46, to Australia 9.51 as VH-AYO; G-AIBU (2156), 11.10.46, to India 1.47 as VT-CIR; G-AIBV (2157), 15.10.46, to New Zealand 8.49 as ZK-ATS; G-AIBW (2158), 10.10.46, converted to J-1N; G-AIBX (2159), 14.10.46; G-AIBY (2160), 11.10.46; G-AIBZ (2161), 16.10.46, converted to J-1N

G-AICB (2133), 25.9.46, crashed at Tollerton 21.3.48; G-AICC (2163), 15.10.46, to Egypt 10.46 as SU-AEX; G-AIFZ (2182), 6.11.46, converted to J-1N; G-AIGA (2183), 12.11.46, crashed at Brixham 6.8.47; G-AIGB (2184), 8.11.46, to Switzerland 12.46 as HB-EOZ; G-AIGC (2185), 8.11.46, to Germany 12.58 as D-EBOT; G-AIGD (2186), 8.11.46; G-AIGE (2187), 13.11.46, w.f.u. at Southend 4.55; G-AIGF (2188), 20.11.46, converted to J-1N; G-AIGG (2189), 4.12.46, to Australia 7.53 as VH-AVW; G-AIGH (2190), 6.12.46, to Spain 12.53 as EC-AIS; G-AIGI (2191), 16.12.46, to Dakar 1.54 as F-DADG; G-AIGJ (2153), 15.10.46, crashed at Antwerp 27.11.48; G-AIGK (2173), 23.10.46, d.b.r. at Lowick, Northants. 10.10.68; G-AIGL (2174), 23.10.46, to Australia 10.52 as VH-AIK; G-AIGM (2177), 30.10.46, converted to J-1N; G-AIGO (2164), 21.10.46, to Australia 7.51 as VH-ALO; G-AIGP (2165), 21.10.46; G-AIGR (2172), 20.10.46, converted to J-1N; G-AIGS (2175), 8.11.46, to New Zealand 8.51 as ZK-AUI; G-AIGT (2176), 28.10.46, converted to J-1N; G-AIGU (2180), 5.11.46, converted to J-1N; G-AIGV (2207), 25.1.47, to Iceland 9.55 as TF-ACC; G-AIGX (2167), 10.10.46 crashed at Beziers, France 9.8.48; G-AIGY (2168), 10.10.46, crashed at Pwllheli 1.8.50

G-AIJF (2304), 18.4.47, crashed at West Hartlepool 29.8.49; G-AIJG (2305), 18.4.47, destroyed in air collison with D.H.87B G-AFDT over Dinas Powis 20.12.51; G-AIJH

After 24 years in Holland as a camera ship, PH-OTO returned to Sywell in 1970 to be overhauled for a British owner as G-AXUJ. (*Air Portraits*)

(2306), 18.4.47, to Finland 11.51 as OH-AUC; G-AIJI (2307), 18.4.47, converted to J-1N; G-AIJJ (2217), 20.1.47, to Burma 9.47, as XY-ABE; G-AIJW (2192), 16.12.46, to Dolosie 7.51 as F-OAJI; G-AIJX (2193), 10.1.47, ditched off the Pembroke coast 15.8.47; G-AIJY (2194), 10.1.47, crashed at Speeton 5.9.48; G-AIJZ (2195), 10.1.47, crashed near Hereford 25.10.70

G-AIKD (2120), 12.9.46, to France 1.50 as F-BEXT; G-AIPT (2200), 21.1.47, to South Africa 11.47 as ZS-DBN; G-AIPU (2202), 21.1.47, to France 7.51 as F-BFXO; G-AIPV (2203), 21.1.47, w.f.u. 11.71; G-AIPW (2204), 22.1.47; G-AIPX (2205), 23.1.47, crashed at Somerford 18.9.49; G-AIPY (2206), 23.1.47, to Australia 11.50 as VH-AJQ; G-AIPZ (2208), 28.1.47, to Ireland 11.53 as EI-AGJ; G-AIRA (2209), 31.1.47, to Barbados 4.52 as VQ-BAA; G-AIRB (2214), 13.2.47, crashed at Coleford, Hereford 11.4.71; G-AIRC (2215), 27.2.47; G-AIZU (2228), 24.3.47, w.f.u. 8.65; G-AIZV (2229), 24.3.47, converted to J-1N, to Sudan 4.62 as ST-ABP; G-AIZW (2230), 20.3.47, to Sweden 8.58 as SE-CGR; G-AIZX (2231), 24.3.47, to France 6.50 as F-BFPQ; G-AIZY (2233), 24.3.47; G-AIZZ (2234), 24.3.47

G-AJAB (2235), 24.3.47, converted to J-1N; G-AJAC (2236), 26.3.47, converted to J-1N; G-AJAE (2237), 26.3.47, converted to J-1N; G-AJAF (2238), 26.3.47, to New Zealand 3.50 as ZK-AUF; G-AJAG (2239), 26.3.47, to Australia 4.52 as VH-ABB; G-AJAH (2240), 26.3.47, w.f.u. at Ipswich 11.69; G-AJAI (2241), 24.3.47, to Austria 10.55 as OE-AAH; G-AJAJ (2243), 26.3.47, converted to J-1N; G-AJAL (2216), 27.2.47, to Spain 6.48 as EC-ADG; G-AJAR (2232), 26.3.47, d.b.r. in 1963; G-AJAS (2319), 24.4.47, converted to J-1N; G-AJDV (2244), 31.3.47, crashed at Bisley 13.4.63; G-AJDW (2320), 28.4.47; G-AJDX (2321), 24.4.47, to Burma 6.49 as XY-ABU; G-AJDY (2322), 28.4.47; G-AJDZ (2323), 30.4.47, to Trinidad 11.52 as VP-TBG

G-AJEA (2324), 30.4.47, ditched off the Devon coast 20.8.55; G-AJEB (2325), 7.5.47, converted to J-1N; G-AJEC (2327), 30.4.47, to New Zealand 11.54 as ZK-BJL; G-AJED (2308), 28.4.47, crashed near Uckfield 19.7.51; G-AJEE (2309), 17.4.47; G-AJEF (2310), 17.4.47, to New Zealand 5.50 as ZK-AUL; G-AJEG (2311), 17.4.47, crashed at Merville, France 11.12.48; G-AJEH (2312), 17.4.47, converted to J-1N; G-AJEI (2313), 17.4.47; G-AJEJ (2314), 22.4.47, crashed at Luton 18.2.49; G-AJEK (2315), 22.4.47, to France 3.52 as F-BCUZ; G-AJEL (2316), 22.4.47, crashed in Ireland 10.8.48; G-AJEM (2317), 20.1.48, to France 8.49 as F-BFPB, rest. 1.65; G-AJEN (2328), 7.5.47, crashed at Puncknowle, Dorset 31.8.52; G-AJEO (2329), 23.5.47, d.b.r. at Southend 22.4.60; G-AJEP (2330), 19.5.47, converted to J-1N, crashed at Christchurch 22.11.59; G-AJET (2242), 31.3.47, to South Africa 6.48 as ZS-DAD; G-AJEU (2301), 16.4.47, to Spain 8.52 as EC-AHF; G-AJEV (2247), 17.4.47, to South Africa 1.49 as ZS-DCP; G-AJEW (2302), 17.4.47, to Germany 5.57 as D-EDIG

G-AJID (2218), 20.1.47; G-AJIE (2219), 20.1.47, ditched off Jersey 10.5.59; G-AJIF (2248), 3.4.47, to South Africa 12.47 as ZS-BWK; G-AJIG (2249), 3.4.47, to Germany 7.56 as D-EGAD; G-AJIH (2318), 28.4.47; G-AJIM (2331), 9.5.47, to Denmark 4.48 as OY-AAK, rest. 7.61; G-AJIN (2332), 13.5.47, to Germany 6.57 as D-EJYN; G-AJIO (2333), 22.5.47, crashed in the North Sea 9.3.55; G-AJIP (2334), 22.5.47, converted to J-1N; G-AJIR (2335), 22.5.47, to Haute-Volta 5.51 as F-OAKY; G-AJIS (2336), 22.5.47, converted to J-1N; G-AJIT (2337), 22.5.47, w.f.u. at Shobden 7.66; G-AJIU (2338), 22.5.47; G-AJIV (2339), 22.5.47, d.b.r. at Portreith 8.7.51; G-AJIW (2340), 22.5.47, converted to J-1N; G-AJIX (2341), 21.5.47, to Australia 10.51 as VH-AQN; G-AJIY (2342), 21.5.47; G-AJIZ (2343), 21.5.47, to Gabon 6.52 as F-OAKL

G-AJPW (2345), 22.5.47, to the Sudan 6.52 as SN-ABA; G-AJPX (2346), 2.6.47, to Australia 8.51 as VH-AYJ; G-AJPY (2347), 2.6.47, to Australia 6.51 as VH-PAB; G-AJPZ (2348), 2.6.47, to France 7.49 as F-BFPE; G-AJRA (2349), 23.5.47, to Portugal

9.48 as CS-ACI; G-AJRB (2350), 23.5.57; G-AJRC (2601), 9.6.47; G-AJRD (2602), 9.6.47, ditched off Shanklin 29.8.47; G-AJRE (2603), 9.6.47; G-AJRF (2604), 9.6.47, to Holland 8.55 as PH-NFC; G-AJRG (2605), 9.6.47, to France 5.50 as F-BDRP; G-AJRH (2606), 9.6.47, converted to J-1N; G-AJRI (2607), 9.6.47, crashed in the Congo 1.10.48; G-AJRJ (2608), 9.6.47, to India 10.48 as VT-CYR; G-AJRK (2609), 9.6.47; G-AJRM (2611), 9.6.47, to France 7.47 as F-BDPR; G-AJRN (2612), 9.6.47, to Ireland 9.70 as EI-AUM; G-AJRO (2613), 24.10.50, crashed at Colyton, Devon 20.11.51; G-AJRP (2615), 9.6.47, to Australia 4.52 as VH-AMK

G-AJUC (2303), 25.6.47, to Uganda 8.47 as VP-UBA; G-AJUD (2614), 25.6.47; G-AJUE (2616), 25.6.47; G-AJUF (2617), 25.6.47, to Norway 3.52 as LN-ORF; G-AJUG (2619), 18.7.47, to Malaya 1.50 as VR-RBL; G-AJUH (2620), 2.1.48, to New Zealand 11.50 as ZK-AWI; G-AJUI (2621), 17.6.48, to Holland 6.48 as PH-NDM; G-AJUJ (2622), 18.6.47, crashed at Liskeard 12.4.52; G-AJUK (2623), 14.8.47, crashed at Spalding 6.5.51; G-AJUL (2624), 15.7.47, converted to J-1N; G-AJUM (2625), 25.6.47, crashed at Kingsbury Episcopi 6.10.58; G-AJUN (2626), 17.9.47, to Australia 1.52 as VH-ALM; G-AJUO (2627), 25.6.47, converted to J-1N; G-AJUP (2628), 10.9.47, crashed at Harwich 5.4.53; G-AJUR (2629), 10.9.47, crashed in France 15.10.53; G-AJUS (2630), used as spares at Rearsby in 1951; G-AJUT (2631), 1.12.48, to Ireland 1.49 as EI-AFG, rest. 2.54, to Kenya 8.54 as VP-KMN; G-AJUU and 'UV (2632 and 2633), used as spares at Rearsby in 1951; G-AJUX (2635), 31.8.49, to New Zealand 2.50 as ZK-AUG; G-AJUY (2636), 5.9.47, to New Zealand 3.50 as ZK-AWT; G-AJUZ (2637), 5.9.49, to New Zealand 2.51 as ZK-AXO

G-AJXO (2642), 27.5.48, to French Congo 7.46 as F-OAIA; G-AJXS (2645), 27.10.48, d.b.f. at Shoreham 5.9.51; G-AJXU (2618), 25.6.47, to Portugal 7.47 as CS-ACN

G-ALUE (2104), 10.7.46, registered 7.49 ex EI-ACO, crashed at Buxton 20.9.52; G-AMTM (3101), 17.9.52; G-AMVN (3102), 24.10.52, to Kenya 12.52 as VP-KKG, converted to J-1S, rest. 8.63, destroyed in air collision with Forney F-1A G-AROP over Fyfield, Essex 24.4.69; G-AOXR see G-AHHR; G-APUK (1843), 31.12.45, registered 6.59 ex SE-ARA and D-EGEG, to Nigeria 12.60 as VR-NDJ/5N-ADW, rest. 8.64; G-ARGT (2199), 21.1.47, registered 12.60 ex VP-YLT, converted to J-1N; G-ARRL (2115), 10.7.46, registered 6.61 ex VP-KFK, converted to J-1N, w.f.u. 11.71; G-AXUJ (1957), PH-OTO, 29.9.70

Note: G-AJXK and 'XL (2638 and 2639) believed not built. Registrations were re-allotted to a Miles Aerovan and Douglas Dakota 3 respectively.

Auster J-1N Alpha (*New Rearsby construction 1957–62*)

G-AORN (3352), 14.2.57, F. Mann t/a Crop Culture (Aerial) Ltd., Bembridge; crashed while crop spraying near Boston, Lincs. 6.7.58

G-APAE (3372), 20.5.57, Auster Aircraft Ltd., Rearsby; to Anders Ekman, Multra, Sweden 9.57 as SE-CGN

G-APAR (3370), 16.4.57, Crop Culture (Aerial) Ltd., West Africa; Portsmouth Aero Club 8.60; crashed near Storrington, Sussex 16.4.63

G-APCY (3377), 4.7.57, Britten-Norman Ltd.; to Nigeria 8.59 as VR-NDQ/5N-ACX; rest. 11.62, Farnborough F/G, Blackbushe 6.63; R. Leigh, Grimsby 4.68

G-APIK (3375), 12.11.57, Crop Culture (Aerial) Ltd., Bembridge; W. London A/C 11.60; J. P. Webster, Baginton 8.67; J. S. Buckland, Biggin Hill 12.68

G-APIL (3386), 6.12.57, Crop Culture (Aerial) Ltd., Bembridge; crashed at Tombel, South Cameroons 30.9.59

G-APJY	(3380), 13.1.58, Crop Culture Ltd., Bembridge; Cumberland A/S, Silloth 5.59; Lakes G/C Ltd., Tebay 1.64; crashed at Walney Island 10.10.65
G-APJZ	(3382), 3.2.58, Crop Culture (Aerial) Ltd., Bembridge; to Nigeria 2.61 as VR-NDR/5N-ACY; rest. 1.63 to Bees Flight Ltd., Sandown
G-APKD	(3384), 25.3.58, Auster Aircraft Ltd.; Crop Culture (Aerial) Ltd., Bembridge 6.59; Portsmouth Aero Club 8.61; F. Hefford, Boscombe Down 2.69
G-APKL	(3383), 11.7.58, Crop Culture; Portsmouth Aero Club 9.59; H. Birkett, White Waltham 6.62; crashed on beach near Le Touquet 8.7.63
G-APKM	(3385), 25.3.58, J. W. Chater Ltd., Doncaster; R. Woods, Woolsington 7.60; L. Wood, Woolsington 7.65; K. C. Bachmann, Tolleshunt d'Arcy strip 10.70
G-APKN	(3387), 17.2.59, Auster Aircraft Ltd.; Skegness Air Taxis Ltd., Wyberton 3.59
G-APOA	(3381), 14.7.58, Fison-Airwork Ltd., Bourn; Airwork (Helicopters) Ltd., Redhill 10.60; Bristow Helicopters Ltd., Redhill 6.62
G-APPV	(3389), 28.11.58, Auster Aircraft Ltd.; to A. B. Motorfirman A. Lindberg, Lyckaele, Sweden 5.59 as SE-CMA
G-APSM	(3388), 4.3.59, Auster Aircraft Ltd.; to the Tunisian Government 3.59 as TS-AAA
G-APSN	(3390), 4.3.59, Auster Aircraft Ltd.; to the Tunisian Government via Croydon 7.3.59 as TS-AAB
G-APTO	(3391), 28.4.59, Auster Aircraft Ltd.; to Hans W. Pfeiffer, Plettenberg Ohle, Germany, via Southend–Ostend 28.4.59 as D-EGIV
G-APTR	(3392), 2.12.59, G. S. Salariya, Blakeney, Glos.; D. W. Wilson, Wolverhampton 9.61; Halfpenny Green Flying Club 4.62; J. P. Webster, Baginton 9.65
G-APUA	(3393), 12.5.59, Auster Aircraft Ltd.; to A. B. Stockholms Aero, Bromma 8.59 as SE-CMD
G-ARUY	(3394), 13.2.62, Beagle Flying Group, Shoreham; Miss T. R. Stevens, Roborough 6.63; G. Godfrey, Jersey 10.67
G-ASEE	(3359), I-AGRI, 19.12.63, Air Navigation & Trading Co. Ltd., Squires Gate; J. C. Hardy, Hurn 12.68; H. J. Williams, Hemswell 11.70
G-AZIH	(3395), completion of stored airframe, registered 11.71 to I. R. F. Hammond and L. A. Groves, Portsmouth

Auster J-1B Aiglet

G-AJUW	(2634), 8.5.50, Aerial Spraying Contractors Ltd., Boston; Skegness Air Taxis Ltd. 7.56; Crop Culture Ltd. 3.57; to J-1N; to Ireland 3.63 as EI-AMY
G-AJYR	(2646), 10.8.50, Aerial Spraying Contractors Ltd., Boston; Skegness Air Taxis Ltd., 7.56; crashed at Boston, Lincs. while crop spraying 6.7.64
G-AJYT	(2660), 10.8.50, Aerial Spraying Contractors Ltd., Boston; Skegness Air Taxis Ltd., 7.56; crashed near Skegness while crop spraying 4.7.63
G-AJYW	(2663), 1.9.50, Auster Aircraft Ltd.; W. S. Shackleton Ltd., Fairoaks 8.51; to the Waikato Aero Club 1.52 as ZK-BAQ
G-ALAB	(2708), 3.8.51, Aerial Spraying Contractors Ltd., Boston; lost in the Mediterranean between Tunis and Ajaccio, Corsica 10.11.53
G-AMIH	(2706), 30.4.51, T. W. Hayhow, Fairoaks 'Lady Lady'; W. S. Shackleton Ltd., Fairoaks 1.53; to the Aéro Club de Bangui 2.53 as F-OAMZ
G-AMJE	(2707), 3.8.51, Aerial Spraying Contractors Ltd., Boston; crashed at Fahl in the Sudan while crop dusting 11.10.52

The prototype Aiglet at Boston Aerodrome, Lincs., 20 March 1951, on the occasion of its first public crop spraying demonstration. (*Shell*)

G-AMKU (2721), 17.9.51, Pest Control Ltd.; to the Sudan 6.53 as SN-ABD/ST-ABD; rest. 7.58 to Fison-Airwork Ltd., Bourn; G. A. Barlow, Redhill 3.62; Southdown Flying Group, Slinfold strip, Sussex 10.64
G-AMMM (2719), 4.10.51, Auster Aircraft Ltd.; to W. Africa 11.51 as F-OAJV
G-AMMR (2744), 10.1.52, Aerial Spraying Contractors Ltd., Boston; Skegness Air Taxis Ltd. 7.52; R. F. Saywell, Gatwick 4.57; withdrawn from use 4.60
G-ANGV (3122), 3.3.54, W. S. Shackleton Ltd.; to New Zealand 3.54 as ZK-BDX
G-ANNZ (3128), 13.3.54, Aerial Spraying Contractors Ltd., Boston; Skegness Air Taxis Ltd., 8.56; R. F. Saywell, Gatwick 4.57; to Italy 5.61 as I-UEST
G-APMU (2793), ex VP-KKS, reg'd. 5.58 to R. H. Buxton; C. of A. 26.5.58; lost in Mediterranean on delivery flight from Nairobi to Fairoaks 12.7.58
G-ARBM (2792), ex VP-SZZ, reg'd. 7.60 to J. M. Tussaud; C. of A. 17.8.60; E. C. & Mrs. Winter, Elstree 9.60; to Aero-Views Ltd., Dublin 9.62 as EI-AMO

Auster J-1U Workmaster
G-APKP (3497), 5.5.58, Crop Culture (Aerial) Ltd., Bembridge; crashed while crop spraying at Mongonu, Nigeria 10.10.63
G-APMH (3502), 24.4.59, Crop Culture (Aerial) Ltd.; to SINCMA 8.59 as F-OBOA; rest. 1.66 to S. Donghi, Italy; Air Tows Ltd., Lasham 7.68; Cornish Gliding and Flying Club, Perranporth 5.70
G-APMI (3506), 24.4.59, Crop Culture (Aerial) Ltd., Bembridge; to SINCMA 8.59 as F-OBOB
G-APMJ (3504), 13.3.60, Cumberland Aviation Services Ltd., Silloth; crashed near Loch Enoch, Kirkcudbrightshire 18.10.63
G-APMK (3505), 2.6.61, Crop Culture (Aerial) Ltd., Bembridge; destroyed in accident 9.69
G-APSP (3498), ex F-OBHQ, 24.4.59, Crop Culture (Aerial) Ltd.; Crop Culture (Overseas) Ltd. 8.59; destroyed 17.12.68
G-APSR (3499), ex F-OBHR, 24.4.59, Crop Culture (Aerial) Ltd.; to Jamaica 10.61 as VP-JCD; rest. 3.63 to Crop Culture (Overseas) Ltd.; Ripper Robots Ltd., Sudan 1.66
G-APXE (3500), ex F-OBHS, 18.12.59, Crop Culture (Overseas) Ltd.; Ripper Robots Ltd., Sudan 1.66; withdrawn from use in the Sudan 12.66

Auster J-2 Arrow

G-AGPS (1660), registered 10.7.45 to Taylorcraft Aeroplanes (England) Ltd. for experimental work and communications; dest. by gale at Rearsby 16.3.47

G-AICA (1878/1), ex Z-1, 20.9.46, Auster Aircraft Ltd.; to France 10.50 as F-BAVS

G-AIGN (2351), 21.11.46, R. Burton, Tollerton; to Royal Queensland Aero Club, Archerfield 11.49 as VH-BNP, re-engined with 108 h.p. Lycoming O-235-C1

G-AIGW (2352), 21.11.46, Auster Aircraft Ltd., Rearsby; to Australia 2.47 as VH-BDE 'The Privateer'; converted to Auster J-4 as VH-KFB

G-AIJU (2361), 31.12.46, Kenning Aviation Ltd., Burnaston; Wolverhampton F/S 6.48; to Australia 11.49 as VH-BNQ; converted to Auster J-4 as VH-KFF

G-AIJV (2362), 31.12.46, Auster Aircraft Ltd., Rearsby; sold 8.49 as VP-JAR; destroyed by storm at Palisadoes Airport, Kingston, Jamaica 9.11.61

G-AJAM (2371), 7.3.47, Wheels & Wings Ltd., Elmdon; B. Hynes, Denham 8.49; A. C. T. Carey, Denham 4.51; B. Woodcock & partner, Caistor 5.65

G-AJPS (2389), 5.6.47, Somerton Airways Ltd., Cowes; to Australia 7.51 as VH-ABF; later re-registered VH-BYL and converted to Auster J-4

G-AJPT (2390), 5.6.47, Auster Aircraft Ltd., Rearsby; to Australia 5.50 as VH-ACD; later re-engined with 125 h.p. Continental C-125-2

G-AJPU (2392), 5.6.47, J. M. Rollo, Perth; Air Navigation & Trading Co. Ltd., Squires Gate 9.55; C. W. Morley, Southend 8.56; w.f.u. at Rearsby 1.58

G-AJPV (2393), 5.6.47, Auster Aircraft Ltd.; to Australia 5.50 as VH-KAE

G-AJRL (2365), 2.1.47, Auster Aircraft Ltd.; to Royal Queensland Aero Club, Archerfield as VH-BYZ; re-engined with 108 h.p. Lycoming O-235-C1

G-AJRR (2372), 27.1.47, Auster Aircraft Ltd., Rearsby; to Australia 5.50 as VH-KBR; crashed in Tasmania 25.9.54

G-AJXZ (2386), OO-AXE, 23.5.48, Auster Aircraft Ltd.; A. S. Mackenzie-Lowe, Hastings 8.49; R. Allerton-Austin 2.51; to Australia 8.51 as VH-AFD

G-AWLX (2378), OO-ABZ and F-BGJQ, A. to F. 24.4.69, D. P. Golding, Thruxton

Auster J-3 Atom

G-AHSY (2250), registered 10.9.46 to Auster Aircraft Ltd., Rearsby; dismantled at Rearsby 1950; rebuilt as Auster J-4 (2941) G-AJYX later in 1950

G-AJIJ (2401), registered 10.4.47 to Auster Aircraft Ltd.; construction abandoned; registration cancelled 11.1.49

Auster J-4

G-AIGZ (2066), 20.12.46, H. F. Fulford, Sheffield; to Australia 5.51 as VH-AAL; dest. in air collision with Tiger Moth VH-APF, Bankstown 12.8.55

G-AIJK (2067), 20.12.46, Birmingham A/C, Elmdon; F. L. Clark, Croft 2.51; Leicestershire A/C, 5.53; M. Beckett, Sheffield 8.67; w.f.u. 8.68

G-AIJL (2068), 21.1.47, Yorkshire Aeroplane Club, Sherburn; to Australia 5.51 as VH-AAG; crashed at Lansvale, N.S.W. 17.1.58

G-AIJM (2069), 20.12.46, R. H. Thorne, Farnborough; H. Best-Devereux, Elstree 8.54; Blyborough Contracting Co. 9.60; L. A. Clark, Doncaster 11.68; Rotherham F/G, Sheffield 5.70; E. R. Stevens, Rearsby 9.71

G-AIJN	(2070), 20.12.46, Kenning Aviation Ltd., Burnaston; H. Gadsby, Leicester 6.48; to Australia 6.51 as VH-AAO, later VH-KFC and VH-CDQ
G-AIJO	(2071), 20.12.46, R. Gunton, Cowes; Morgan Aviation Ltd., Cowes 2.49; Miss G. Pendleton, Lympne 9.49; to Luxembourg 5.50 as LX-REX
G-AIJP	(2072), 27.2.47, Rearsby Flying School; Skyfreight Ltd., Speke 3.49; to Australia 11.51 as VH-AET; shot down at sea off Sydney 30.8.55
G-AIJR	(2073), 2.1.47, Loxham's Flying Services Ltd., Squires Gate; Blackpool A/C 4.53; Dr. S. Parker, Halfpenny Green 8.64; B. Moss, Sheffield 6.67; B. A. Harris, Halfpenny Green 11.71
G-AIJS	(2074), 2.1.47, Dr. L. Hyder, Ipswich; Luton F/C 6.57; Kagan Textiles Ltd., Yeadon 5.58; Links Air Touring Group, Lincoln 10.64; A. R. Weston, Sibson 1.71
G-AIJT	(2075), 2.1.47, Spa & Warwick Timber Co., Wellesbourne Mountford; North Luffenham F/C 7.54; J. C. Quantrell, Norwich 12.60; Merlin F/C 8.67
G-AIPG	(2076), 28.2.47, Cecil Kay Aircraft Ltd., Elmdon; B. F. Francis, Elstree 5.48; R. E. Harrington, Elstree 4.53; to Kenya 7.55 as VP-KNB
G-AIPH	(2077), 27.2.47, Wright Aviation Ltd., Speke; Dragon Airways Ltd., Speke 3.54; W. Westoby, Squires Gate 11.59; Merlin F/C, Hucknall 7.63
G-AIPI	(2078), 21.1.47, Auster Aircraft Ltd., Rearsby; T. W. Shipside Ltd., Tollerton 9.48; to French West Africa 1.51 as F-OAMY; w.f.u. 6.64
G-AIPJ	(2079), 21.1.47, Southend Municipal Flying School; T. Shipside Ltd., Tollerton 5.49; to Australia 5.51 as VH-AAK, later VH-PJN
G-AIPK	(2080), 10.2.47, Birmingham Aero Club, Elmdon; Warwickshire A/C, Elmdon 4.48; to W. G. Bradshaw, Christchurch, New Zealand 10.50 as ZK-AXC
G-AIPL	(2081), 13.2.47, Aircraft (Hereford) Ltd.; Inter-City A/S Ltd., Hereford 4.49; to Australia 5.51 as VH-AEA and fitted with crosswind undercarriage
G-AIPM	(2082), 17.3.47, R. Knight, Tollerton; C. W. Blankley, Grantham 7.49; F. Briggs, Portsmouth 7.50; to Australia 10.51 as VH-AEC
G-AIPP	(2083), 3.7.47, Auster Aircraft Ltd., Rearsby; to Switzerland 7.47 as HB-EOX; later to the Congo as F-OAHD and thence to Portugal
G-AIPR	(2084), 7.5.47, H. C. N. Goodhart, Thruxton; Heron F/G, Yeovilton 6.58; Yorkshire Flying Club, Yeadon 8.59; G. S. Claybourn, Doncaster 8.66; M.P.M. F/G, Elstree 11.71
G-AIPS	(2085), 30.7.47, Capt. P. A. W. B. Everard, Ratcliffe; Miss E. I. Kidner, 12.48 (used by Airways Aero Assoc'n.); crashed at Denham 15.6.51
G-AIRD	(2086), 3.4.47, T. Shipside Ltd., Tollerton; Boston Air Transport Ltd. 10.49; B. G. Sellars, Wyberton 11.57; crashed Stainfield, Lincs. 5.1.58
G-AIZP	(2087), 18.6.48, Auster Aircraft Ltd., Rearsby; crashed at Shardlow, Derby 19.11.49 while in use by the Rearsby Flying School
G-AIZR	(2088), 10.2.51, Auster Aircraft Ltd., Rearsby; to Brazzaville, Congo 2.51 as F-OAKI
G-AIZS	(2089), 12.9.51, Auster Aircraft Ltd., Rearsby; to Senegal 9.51 as F-OALT
G-AIZT	(2090), 11.5.51, Auster Aircraft Ltd., Rearsby; crashed and burned at Gaddesby, Leicestershire 2.12.56
G-AJYX	(2941), 13.10.50, Auster Aircraft Ltd.; crashed near Melton Mowbray after pilotless take-off from Rearsby 22.4.51
G-APJM	(2091), 30.6.58, E. E. Chick, Elstree; North Middlesex F/G, Elstree 6.59; crashed in the English Channel near the Varne Lightship 27.5.61

Auster J-5 and *J-5A

*G-AJER   (2093), registered 17.2.47 to Auster Aircraft Ltd., Rearsby; to Kingsford
                Smith Aviation Pty. Ltd. 3.49 as VH-KSB

*G-AJYA (2226), built 2.47 as J-1 VP-YGP; registered 10.8.48 to Auster Aircraft Ltd.,
                Rearsby; to Egypt 3.49 as SU-AGA; withdrawn from use 8.59

G-AJYE   (2874), 8.11.48, D. S. Hind, Hurn; R. T. Briscoe, Gold Coast 11.49 and re-
                registered VP-AAB; to the Niger Colony 1952 as F-OAMQ

G-AJYG   (2876), 26.1.49, Auster Aircraft Ltd., Rearsby; to the Director of Civil
                Aviation, Lisbon 2.49 as CS-ADZ; w.f.u. at Alverca 7.62

*G-AJYL   (2889), 28.10.49, Auster Aircraft Ltd., Rearsby; R. K. Dundas Ltd., Croydon
                9.51; to Govt. of W. Pakistan, Lahore 10.51 as AP-AFI/AP-AJV

G-AMMI (2901), 20.12.51, R. K. Dundas Ltd., Croydon; to Australia 1.52 as
                VH-KAG; crashed near Ungarie, New South Wales 30.8.61

G-AMMU (2902), 31.12.51, d/d to R. K. Dundas Ltd., Croydon 3.2.52; to Govt. of W.
                Pakistan, Lahore 2.52 as AP-AFP; crashed at Mohamed Goth 19.12.58

*G-AMPJ (2905), 8.4.52, Aerial Spraying Contractors Ltd., Wyberton; Skegness Air
                Taxis Ltd. 5.56; crashed while spraying at Langworth, Lincoln 26.6.56

*G-AMPK (2906), 8.4.52, Aerial Spraying Contractors Ltd., Wyberton; to the Aero Club
                Dolisie, French Equatorial Africa 4.52 as F-OAKN

G-AMPU (2903), 25.4.52, Cyprus Airways Ltd., Nicosia; re-reg'd. 6.52 as VQ-CAA;
                rest. to Airspray Ltd., Boxted 6.58; burned out at Kosti, Sudan 3.1.61

G-AMPV (2904), 22.4.52, Cyprus Airways Ltd., Nicosia; re-reg'd. 6.52 as VQ-CAB;
                rest. 9.60 to Grantair Ltd., Sywell; d.b.r. landing at Ringway 10.6.61

*G-AMPX (3000), 7.4.52, T. A. Stephenson Ltd., Blackbushe; W. S. Shackleton Ltd.,
                Fairoaks 9.53; to H. Allen Mills, New Zealand 1.54 as ZK-BDW

Auster J-5B Autocar

G-AJYK   (2908), 4.1.50, Auster Aircraft Ltd.; Airviews Ltd., Barton 4.50; crashed four
                miles north of Leicester 18.9.50

G-AJYM (2909), 4.1.50, Mitchell Engineering Co. Ltd., Peterborough; crashed at
                Boston, Lincolnshire 7.4.50

G-AJYN   (2910), 9.3.50, J. V. Heriz-Smith, Elstree; W. S. Shackleton Ltd., Old Warden
                2.57; converted to J-5P; to Spain 6.3.57 as EC-ANK

G-AJYO   (2913), 26.6.50, T. F. Ringer, Docking strip, Norfolk; P. J. Riseborough,
                Hillington strip, Kings Lynn 9.60

G-AJYV   (2927), 4.9.50, A. S. Mackenzie-Lowe, Hastings; I. M. Erskine, White
                Waltham 7.52 'Bluesky'; left Croydon 19.9.53 en route to Bilbao to become
                EC-AIR

G-AJYY   (2928), 20.4.51, L. R. Snook, Portsmouth; Longford Engineering Co. Ltd.,
                Bognor 11.51; H. Mitchell, Portsmouth 2.55; to Australia 4.55 as VH-DYY

G-AMFO (2923), 12.3.51, Sissleys Cycles Ltd., Southend; Hunting Aerosurveys Ltd.,
                Elstree 2.53; crashed at Kirkaldy, Fife 8.7.55

G-AMFP   (2933), 11.1.51, Aviation Traders Ltd.; Southend Flying School 12.55;
                F. H. Greenwell, Tees-side 8.67; Rochford Hundred Flying Group, Southend
                7.69

G-AMLI   (2954), 16.10.51, J. W. Cox, Elstree; W. S. Shackleton Ltd., Elstree 12.51; to
                W. L. Pascoe, New Zealand 2.52 as ZK-BAE

G-AMMZ (2948), 18.2.52, Hunting Aerosurveys Ltd., Luton; L. S. Dawson, Yeadon
                8.57; A. Barker, Yeadon 6.59; crashed at Brough-under-Stainmore 28.10.60

The 18th production J-5B Autocar, G-AJYV 'Bluesky', flying near White Waltham in 1952.

G-AMNB (2950), 14.12.51, Royal Artillery Flying Club, Thruxton; to W. J. Polson, New Zealand 12.53 as ZK-BET; crashed at Oruanui 22.12.57
G-AMNC (2953), 18.1.52, Bristol Aeroplane Co. Ltd., Filton; Bristol Aircraft Ltd. 3.56; converted to J-5P; to New Zealand 9.57 as ZK-BVL
G-AMPW (2961), 30.4.52, Bees Flight Ltd., Sandown; R. J. Rimmer, White Waltham 3.63; Miss J. V. Inglis, Turnhouse 10.64
G-ANNX (3075), 15.2.54, Kuwait F/C, Kuwait; re-registered 8.60 as 9K-AAF
G-ANNY (3076), 15.2.54, Kuwait F/C; crashed in low water, Kuwait 25.10.54
G-AXMN (2962), F-BGPN, 29.8.69, Robinson Aircraft Ltd., Blackbushe

Auster J-5E
G-AJYS (2917), Auster Aircraft Ltd., Rearsby; dismantled 1951, fuselage stored until 1961, then modified to J-5B standard and sold as spare airframe

Auster J-5F Aiglet Trainer
G-AMKF (2709), G-25-1, 8.9.51, Auster Aircraft Ltd., Rearsby; to Australia 1.52 as VH-AFS, later re-reg'd. to W. C. de Courcey, Townsville as VH-WDC
G-AMMS (2720), 18.3.52, Auster Aircraft Ltd.; conv. to J-5K (c/n 2745) q.v.
G-AMNM (2731), 8.4.52, R. K. Dundas Ltd., Croydon; to Assam, India 4.52 as VT-DGD, registration cancelled 2.53
G-AMOS (2718), single seater with Gipsy Major 1G, 10.4.52, T. W. Hayhow, Fairoaks, 'Liege Lady'; crashed in Austrian Alps 20 miles from Salzburg 10.4.53
G-AMOV (2768), 8.10.52, D. Martyn, Cardiff, 'Titus Andronicus'; to the North West Whaling Co., Perth, W.A. 5.54 as VH-BTQ; withdrawn from use 6.61
G-AMRF (2716), 8.4.52, R. Chisholm, Ipswich; temporarily VT-DHA 1953–54; Girls Venture Corps 8.55; Rolls-Royce F/C 7.68; D. Shorrock, Squires Gate 3.69; J. M. Hosey, Stansted 7.71
G-AMRL (2779), 17.11.52, H. B. Showell, Fleggburgh; Scottish Aero Club, Perth 6.58; Rolls-Royce Coventry F/C, Baginton 7.68; P. White, Booker 5.70; to Ireland 11.70 as EI-AUS

The prototype Auster J-5F Aiglet Trainer, G-AMKF, at Bankstown, Sydney, in 1952, after sale to Kingsford Smith Aviation Services Pty. as VH-AFS.

G-AMTA (2780), 29.9.52, Airways Aero Assoc., Croydon; Lord Trefgarne, Fairoaks 8.62; Avon F/G, Hurn 5.67; Strabor Aircraft Ltd., Rochester 4.70

G-AMTB (2781), 11.11.52, Airways Aero Assoc., Croydon; Glamorgan F/C, Rhoose 9.63; Mell-Air Ltd., Goxhill 4.65; w.f.u. 9.65; sold as spares 9.68

G-AMTC (2782), 26.11.52, Airways Aero Assoc., Croydon; temporarily D-EFEP 1958–60; Coventry (Civil) Av. Ltd., Baginton 1.63; d.b.r. Manaccan 11.6.65

G-AMTD (2783), 1.10.52, Airways Aero Assoc., Croydon; Biggin Hill F/C 12.62; G. E. Paterson, Cambridge 2.67; Aiglet Flying Group, Newtownards 5.70; to Ireland 2.72 as EI-AVL

G-AMTE (2784), 1.10.52, Airways Aero Association, Croydon; J. W. Hainge, Kidlington 10.57; Cumberland Aviation Services Ltd., Carlisle 11.66; Astra Flying Group, Fairoaks 4.70

G-AMTR (2789), 22.9.52, Club Aviation Ltd., Staverton; Steels (Aviation) Ltd., Staverton 12.61; D. Smart, Wick 9.62; crashed at Lybster, Caith. 29.1.64

G-AMUI (2790), 17.12.52, A.S.T., Hamble; Newcastle A/C 6.60; Bristol & Wessex Aeroplane Club, Lulsgate 5.61; Mell-Air Ltd., Goxhill 8.65; w.f.u. 2.66

G-AMUJ (2791), 22.12.52, A.S.T., Hamble; Hants & Sussex Aviation Ltd., Portsmouth 5.60; crashed at South Rauceby, Sleaford, Lincs. 8.6.60

G-AMVM (2758), 22.1.53, W. S. Shackleton Ltd., Blackbushe; to the Belgian Congo 2.53 as OO-CHT; later based at Luluaburg as 9O-CHT

G-AMYD (2773), 16.4.53, College of Aeronautics, Cranfield; G. H. Maskell, Wilstead, Beds. 1.72

G-AMYE (2775), 22.4.53, Airwork Ltd., Blackbushe; to New Zealand 8.53 to the Otago Aero Club as ZK-BDO; crashed near Dunedin 18.5.54

G-AMZI (3104), 22.5.53, D. R. Carnegie, Panshanger; J. D. Power, White Waltham 11.62; A. J. Camp, Radlett 8.65; Handley Page Power F/G 9.68

G-AMZT (3107), 21.8.53, College of Aeronautics; A. H. Roscoe, Wilstead, Beds. 9.69

G-AMZU (3108), 21.8.53, College of Aeronautics; D. J. Deacon, Wilstead, Beds. 10.69

G-ANAO (3109), 6.10.53, W. S. Shackleton Ltd., Rearsby; to New Zealand 11.53 as ZK-BDY for Southland Aero Club; crashed in Tuapeka River 26.5.61

G-ANAU (3110), 31.7.53, Parker's Stores Ltd., Macmerry; to the Otago Aero Club, New Zealand 7.56 as ZK-BRA; later to Southern Districts Aero Club

G-ANNV (3113), 15.2.54, Kuwait Flying Club; re-registered 8.60 as 9K-AAD

G-ANNW (3120), 15.2.54, Kuwait Flying Club; re-registered 8.60 as 9K-AAE

G-ANSV   (3124), 26.7.54, Barrow, Hepburn & Gale Ltd.; Luton F/C 3.59; Coventry (Civil) Aviation, Baginton 6.59; crashed Hockley Heath, Warks. 11.8.65

G-ASLS   (2767), Arab Legion Air Force A-408, OD-APA, 24.3.64, Marquis of Headfort, Biggin Hill; withdrawn from use at Kells, Ireland 3.67

G-ASLT   (2771), Arab Legion Air Force A-409, OD-APB, 2.1.64, Marquis of Headfort, Biggin Hill; A. J. Nathan, Elstree, later Cairo 6.67

Auster J-5G Cirrus Autocar

G-AMKG (2982), 25.3.52, Auster Aircraft Ltd.; to Australia 7.52 as VH-ADX

G-AMOY (2985), 20.6.52, Pest Control Ltd., Bourn; crashed at Khartoum 12.10.54

G-AMOZ (2986), 10.9.52, Pest Control Ltd., Bourn; to Pest Control (Sudan) Ltd. 1.56 as SN-ABI; crashed at Aba Island, Sudan 18.10.56

G-AMPA   (2987), 3.7.52, Pest Control Ltd., Bourn; to Pest Control (Sudan) Ltd. 1.56 as SN-ABE; later to Fisons Pest Control (Sudan) Ltd. as ST-ABE

G-AMPB   (2988), 25.6.52, Pest Control Ltd., Bourn; to Pest Control (Sudan) Ltd. 1.56 as SN-ABF; later to Fisons Pest Control (Sudan) Ltd. as ST-ABF

G-AMPC   (2989), 3.7.52, Pest Control Ltd., Bourn; to Pest Control (Sudan) Ltd. 1.56 as SN-ABG; later to Fisons Pest Control (Sudan) Ltd. as ST-ABG

G-AMYR   (3052), 11.5.53, N. A. Rogers, Renhold strip, Beds.; R. K. Dundas Ltd., Croydon 3.56; to Yemen 11.56 as YE-AAM

G-AMZV   (3065), 27.7.53, Saunders-Roe Ltd., Bembridge; leased to Giro Aviation Ltd., Southport 5.60; Mell-Air Ltd., Weston-super-Mare 7.62; crashed 28.8.66

G-ANBS   (3068), 24.9.53, Pest Control Ltd., Bourn; to Pest Control (Sudan) Ltd. 1.56 as SN-ABH; later to Fisons Pest Control (Sudan) Ltd. as ST-ABH

G-ANSW (3091), 10.9.54, A. B. T. Thompson; to Australia 9.54 as VH-BYT

G-ANVG   (3095), 15.11.54, W. S. Shackleton Ltd.; to Australia 1.55 as VH-AZK

G-ANVM (3158), 17.1.55, W. S. Shackleton Ltd.; to Australia 9.55 as VH-KCA

G-ANVN   (3153), 14.1.54, Secretary of State for the Colonies; to Malaya as XJ941; rest. to original owner 1.57; to Tanganyika 10.57 as VR-TBR

G-ANVT   (3159), 26.1.55, W. S. Shackleton Ltd.; G. W. Asher, Burnaston 5.55; to Kingsford Smith Aviation Pty Ltd., Sydney 9.55 as VH-KCE

G-AOIY   (3199), 29.3.56, Parker's Stores Ltd., Turnhouse; J. O. Hodgson, Sleaford 7.60; Sherwood F/C, Tollerton 7.62; L. N. Garner, Sutton Bridge 4.65

G-ARDA   (3157), VR-NBB, 16.1.64, S. Blakemore, Lympne; Air Navigation & Trading Co. Ltd., Squires Gate 11.64; crashed at Squires Gate 6.2.66

G-ARKG   (3061), AP-AHJ, 25.5.61. J. M. Tussaud, Elstree; Norfolk & Norwich Aero Club 8.61; H. A. Styles, North Denes 6.65; C. Thompson, Hemswell 1.71

G-ARNB   (3169), AP-AHL, 8.8.61, J. M. Tussaud, Elstree; P. G. Beck, Swanton Morley 11.61; Anglian Air Charter Ltd., North Denes 5.64

G-ARUG   (3272), G-25-9, 6.7.62, Beagle-Auster Aircraft Ltd., Rearsby; Portsmouth A/C 7.62; M. Cockburn, Compton Abbas 3.69

G-ARUT   (2974), AP-AJW, 7.5.62, J. M. Tussaud, Elstree; H. E. Smead, Elstree 7.62; written off in forced landing near Barnet, Herts 13.8.65

G-ASFK   (3276), 21.5.63, Anglian Air Charter Ltd., North Denes

Auster J-5K Aiglet Trainer

G-AMMS (2745), 18.3.52, Auster Aircraft Ltd., J. K. Edwards, Zürich 9.54; M. D. Ewart & Co. Ltd., Elstree 10.56; L. W. Brown, White Waltham 6.64; w.f.u. 11.71

G-AMYI (3151), 18.6.54, Auster Aircraft Ltd.; converted to J-8L; Yorkshire Aero Club, Sherburn 2.55; Denham Auster Group 9.62; D. S. Vernon, Goodwood 10.71

Auster J-5L Aiglet Trainer

G-ANSS (3123), 1.10.54, Miss B. P. Rowell, left Shoreham for Nairobi 2.11.54; to S. Rhodesia 11.55 as VP-YNK; later to Belgian Congo as OO-CFM

G-ANWX (3131), 1.3.55, E. Rylands, Samlesbury; Skyways Ltd., Lympne 6.57; J. W. Benson, Bicester 9.65; Mrs. E. Walker, Tees-side 3.70

G-ANXC (3135), 6.5.55, Auster Aircraft Ltd.; converted to J-5R Alpine; Crop Culture (Aerial) Ltd., Bembridge 10.57; to Uganda 10.59 as VP-UBD

G-ANXW (3132), 16.3.55, Kuwait Flying Club; re-registered 8.60 as 9K-AAG

G-ANXX (3133), 17.3.55, Kuwait Flying Club; re-registered 8.60 as 9K-AAH

G-ANXY (3134), 17.3.55, Kuwait Flying Club; re-registered 8.60 as 9K-AAI

G-AOEZ (3141), 19.12.55, Eric Bemrose Ltd., Elstree; T. R. Davey, Lulsgate 9.61; Biggin Hill Flying Club 8.64; crashed near Sandown, I.O.W. 30.7.66

G-AOFS (3143), 5.1.56, H. B. Showell, Fleggburgh; to Dublin 1.60 as EI-ALN; rest. 3.61; Metnor Ltd., Woolsington 9.61; G. Howard, Panshanger 6.69

G-APLG (3148), 21.5.58, Glamorgan Aviation Ltd., Rhoose; Shropshire F/G, Sleap 4.60; Blackpool A/C 8.63; G. Shufflebottom, Lulsgate 6.67; w.f.u. 6.68

G-APVG (3306), 3.9.59, Auster Aircraft Ltd.; D. W. Wilson, Wolverhampton 9.60; College of Aeronautics, Cranfield 6.61

Auster J-5P Autocar

G-ANXZ (3161), 22.3.55, Kuwait F/C, Kuwait; re-registered 8.60 as 9K-AAJ

G-ANYE (3165), 22.3.55, Kuwait F/C, Kuwait; re-registered 8.60 as 9K-AAK

G-AOBV (3171), 26.5.55, B. de Ferranti, Ringway; Meridian Air Maps Ltd., Shoreham 4.59; British Oxygen Co. Ltd. 7.61; J. B. Martin, Ringway 2.66; G. Lee, Stapleford 1.71

G-AOCY (3258), 31.8.56, Bristol Aero Engines Ltd., Filton; Bristol and Wessex Aeroplane Club, Lulsgate 2.60; crashed at Bampton, Devon 30.6.62

Auster J-5P Autocar G-ARLY in the colours of Bournemouth Air Taxis, Hurn, 1962.
(*P. R. March*)

G-AODC (3187), 11.7.55, S. J. J. Blackburn; to the East Austrian Flying School, Vienna 7.55 as OE-DAC

G-AOFM (3178), 29.6.55, Hunting Aerosurveys Ltd., Elstree; Hunting Surveys Ltd. Elstree 2.59; J. E. Stevens, Ringway 11.69; withdrawn from use 11.71

G-AOFT (3193), 7.11.55, W. S. Shackleton Ltd.; to New Zealand 12.55 as ZK-BLZ

G-AOGM (3197), 17.1.56, Hunting Clan A/T, Luton; J. D. Coleman, Panshanger 7.57; Hunting Surveys Ltd., Elstree 3.64; J. E. Stevens, Ringway 11.69

G-AOHF (3191), 18.5.56, Auster Aircraft Ltd.; to Ireland 11.56 as EI-AJH; rest. 3.57 to Gloster Aircraft Ltd.; B.P. Irish, White Waltham 3.62; F. B. Fairchild 11.67; R. E. Rudd, Thruxton 11.69; to Australia 4.70 as VH-EDF

G-AOHZ (3252), 29.3.56, North Perrott Estate Co. Ltd., Crewkerne; Luton F/C 7.59; Hunting Surveys Ltd. 2.63; R. Willing, Ringway; d.b.f. at Manton, Yorks. 5.5.71

G-APKI (3274), 2.5.58, Dunlop Rubber Co. Ltd., Baginton; G. Hayman, Perranporth 11.67; L. Phillips. Perranporth 4.70; crashed at Perranporth 16.5.71

G-ARLY (3271), 18.7.61, Auster Aircraft Ltd.; Bournemouth Air Taxi Co., Hurn 10.61; E. J. Morton, Elmdon 8.66; J. W. Benson, Bicester 3.69

Auster J-5Q Alpine

G-AOZL (3202), 2.3.57, J. V. Heriz-Smith, Elstree; Dr. W. Zehden, Elstree 10.64

G-APCB (3204), 28.6.57, Jack Heywood Ltd., Yeadon; Allison & Thelwell Ltd., Yeadon 8.58; F. H. Bird, Sheffield 2.62; J. Wilson, Speke 2.67

Auster J-5R Alpine

G-AOGN (3301), 19.6.56, W. S. Shackleton Ltd.; to Australia 11.56 as VH-BTI

G-AOGV (3302), 21.6.56, N. A. Rogers, Renhold, Beds.; Tyne Tees Air Charter Ltd., 7.61; S. T. Burdett, Skegness 4.67; A.B.H. Aviation Ltd., Sibson 5.66

G-APAA (3303), 27.7.56, Automobile Association; J. McLachan, Turnhouse 6.58; Willie Jig F/G, Lulsgate 6.63; D. G. Ellis, Sandown 6.70; A. J. Morrey 8.71

G-APCX (3304), 26.7.57, R. B. Haigh, Stansted; College of Aeronautics, Cranfield 4.60; Girls Venture Corps 6.61; H. Winch, Rhoose 7.68; J. M. Joyce, Elstree 11.70

G-APFW (3307), 24.9.57, P. Cox, Leicester East; Grantchester Garages Ltd., Cambridge 7.60; ditched in the English Channel off Le Touquet 7.2.61

Auster J-5V Autocar

G-APUW (3273), 21.4.60, W. T. Clarke, Speke; E. S. Collins Ltd., Weeley Heath, Essex 4.63; N. J. White, Halfpenny Green 5.65; J. P. Webster, Baginton 1.69

Auster J-8F Aiglet Trainer

G-ANVJ (3152), construction abandoned, marks reallotted to Percival Proctor 4

Auster B.8 Agricola

G-ANYG (B.101), Auster Aircraft Ltd. 1.55, first flown 8.12.55 as G-25-3; re-registered 6.56 as ZK-BMI, C. of A. 29.6.56, dismantled at Rearsby 1959

G-APFZ (B.118), 14.2.58, Auster Aircraft Ltd.; Aerial Agriculture Ltd. 5.59; to Air Contracts Ltd., Masterton 9.62 as ZK-CCV; crashed Pongroa 19.2.63

Auster 6
G-ALGW (1928), TW562, K. J. Nalson, Croydon; sold to Austers unconverted 1950
G-APRO WJ370, 16.5.61, Air Comm. A. H. Wheeler, Old Warden; converted to Auster 6A, 8.64

Auster 6A Tugmaster
G-ARCY (2482), TW624 and 7433M, test flown as G-25-9; C. of A. 10.8.60, F. Horridge, Lasham; crashed at Lasham 9.9.60
G-ARDX (1905), TW524, 25.8.60, F. Horridge, Lasham; crashed at Lasham 1.1.64
G-ARGB (2593), VF635, 14.3.61, F. Horridge, Lasham; Three Counties A/C, Blackbushe 3.64; Air Tows Ltd., Lasham 11.67; J. S. Thorne, Compton Abbas 4.71
G-ARGI (2299), VF530, 22.6.61, Coventry G/C, Edge Hill; Jackaroo Syndicate, Edge Hill 12.61; Doncaster Gliding Club 10.67
G-ARHM (2515), VF557, 3.3.61, Midland Gliding Club, Sleap; Cambridge University Gliding Club 12.64; P. E. Brown, Husbands Bosworth 2.67; University of Aston in Birmingham Gliding Club 1.72
G-ARIH (2463), TW591, 9.2.61, H. Britten, Sywell; West Wales F/G, Haverford-west 5.62; West Wales G/C 9.64; Air Tows Ltd., Lasham 5.67; Ulster G/C 4.70
G-ARKC (2261), VF492, 22.5.61, F. Horridge, Lasham; Three Counties Aero Club, Blackbushe 3.64; Lands End Gliding Club 5.65; J. S. Thorne, Compton Abbas 12.68; crashed at Bidford-on-Avon 12.6.71
G-ARRX (2281), VF512, 28.7.61, F. Gaze, Hereford; F. B. Miles, Staverton 11.67; C. Rowe-Jones, Worcester 7.68
G-ARXU (2295), VF526, 7.4.62, F. Horridge, Lasham; Air Tows Ltd., Lasham 5.64
G-ARYD WJ358, registered 4.63 to Airwork Services Ltd., Perth; conversion abandoned at Perth 9.63
G-ASEF VW985, 22.5.63, Airgineers Ltd., Staverton; R.A.F. Gliding & Soaring Assoc., Bicester 8.63; dismantled at Bicester 1966 after accident
G-ASEG (2506), VF548, 18.12.64, Airgineers Ltd., Staverton; Halfpenny Green Flying Club 7.66; Worcestershire Gliding Club, Bickmarsh 11.70
G-ASHY (3724), VX110, 25.10.63, Beagle-Auster Aircraft Ltd., Rearsby; to B. Svens-son and T. Rosenberg, Stockholm, Sweden 1.64 as SE-ELA
G-ASIF (2556), VF615, 21.5.63, F. Horridge, Lasham; Air Tows Ltd., Lasham 5.64; C. F. Hobley, Kidlington 4.67; R.A.F. G/S Assoc., Bicester 5.68
G-ASIP (2549), VF608, delivered to Heathrow 10.4.63, converted for B.E.A. G/C, Booker, C. of A. 28.2.64; Bristol Gliding Club, Nympsfield 3.67
G-ASNB (3725), VX118, 21.2.64, F. Horridge, Lasham; Air Tows Ltd., Lasham 7.64; West Wales Gliding Club, Haverfordwest 10.65
G-ASOC (2544), VF603, 20.5.64, J. W. Benson, Bicester; R.A.F. G/S Assoc., Bicester 12.66
G-ASTI (3745), WJ359, 22.7.64, F. Horridge, Lasham; Air Tows Ltd., Lasham 7.64

Auster Model P Avis
G-AJXW Mk. 1 (2838), Z-2, 22.3.48, Auster Aircraft Ltd., Rearsby; dismantled at Rearsby, registration cancelled 4.2.49
G-AJYF Mk. 2 (2907), Auster Aircraft Ltd., Rearsby; damaged beyond repair in forced landing at Queniborough, Leics. 2.8.50

Auster 9 and 9M

G-AVHT WZ711, converted to Auster 9M, C. of A. 30.4.68, Capt. M. Somerton-Rayner, Middle Wallop

G-AVXY XK417, registered 7.11.67 to E. B. Pearce, Thruxton; R. J. Moody, Shaftesbury 2.68; in the yard of A. R. Else Ltd., Wisbech in 1971

G-AXRR XR241, registered 7.11.69 to Capt. M. Somerton-Rayner, Middle Wallop for London–Sydney Air Race, December 1969; presented to the Shuttleworth Trust, Old Warden, and reverted to military marks 1.70 as XR241

G-AXWA XN437, registered 13.1.70 to T. Platt, Oldham

G-AYUA XK416, 7855M, registered 12.3.71 to G. B. E. Pearce, Lympne

G-AZBU 7826M, registered 15.7.71 to L. C. Mansfield, Hassocks

The prototype Austin Whippet in original paint scheme and temporary civil marking K-158.

Austin Whippet

G-EAGS (AU.1), K-158, reg'd. 7.19 to Austin Motor Co., C. of A. 4.12.19; C. P. B. Ogilvie, Hendon 1920; not flown after C. of A. expiry 19.11.21

G-EAPF (AU.2), reg'd. to Austin Motor Co. 11.19; C. P. B. Ogilvie 7.23; F. O. Soden 3.24, C. of A. 7.10.24; Midland A/C 7.26; E. R. King 5.28; H. M. Pearson, Hamble 4.29; to F. G. Miles, Shoreham; out of commission in 1931

G-EAUZ (AU.3), registered to A. J. Greenshields, La Emilia Ballesteros F.C.C.A., Argentine 30.7.20, withdrawn from use circa 1929

Aviation Traders A.T.L.98 Carvair (*see page 95 for previous identities and date of first flight*)

G-ANYB (1), 30.1.62, Channel A/B, Southend 'Golden Gate Bridge'; B.U.A.F., Southend 12.62; B.A.F., Lydd 12.67; scrapped at Lydd 8.70

G-AOFW (12), 1.4.64, B.U.A.F., Southend; to Aviaco 4.64 to 11.64 as EC-AVD; restored 11.64 to B.U.A.F.; B.A.F., Southend 12.67

G-APNH (11), 10.1.65, B.U.A.F., Southend 'Menai Bridge'; B.A.F., Southend 12.67, beyond repair in nose wheel collapse at Le Touquet 18.3.71

G-ARSD (2), 2.4.62, Channel A/B, Southend 'Chelsea Bridge'; B.U.A.F., Southend 12.62; B.A.F., Lydd 12.67; scrapped at Lydd 8.70

G-ARSF (3), 6.7.62, Channel A/B, Southend 'Pont de l'Europe'; crashed landing at Rotterdam 28.12.62; wreck to Southend 23.2.63; to Stansted 3.63

G-ARSH (4), G-41-2, 14.9.62, Channel A/B; to Intercontinental 9.62 as N9758F; re-reg'd. 1.63 as LX-IOG; to Cie Air Transport, Le Touquet 5.65 as F-BMHU; crashed on take-off from Karachi 8.3.67

G-ARZV (6), Channel A/B, f/f Stansted–Southend 21.12.62; C. of A. 8.3.63; to Aer Lingus 3.63 as EI-AMP; to Eastern Provincial Airways 7.68 as CF-EPX; crashed at Twin Falls, Idaho 28.9.68

G-ASDC (7), 25.3.68, B.U.A.F., Southend 'Pont du Rhin'; B.A.F., Southend 12.67

G-ASHZ (9), 14.6.63, B.U.A.F., Southend 'Maasbrug'; B.A.F., Southend 12.67

G-ASKD (14), D-ANEK, Aviation Traders Ltd., Stansted; C. of A. 23.4.64; to Aer Lingus 4.64 as EI-ANJ; to Eastern Provincial A/W 6.68 as CF-EPW

G-ASKG (10), 1.8.63, B.U.A.F., Southend 'Channel Bridge'; B.A.F., Southend 12.67; to Cie Air Transport, Le Touquet 3.69 as F-BRPT; withdrawn from use 1970

G-ASKN (13), 23.3.64, B.U.A.F., Southend 'Pont d'Avignon'; B.A.F., Southend 12.67

G-ATRV (15), 31.3.66, B.U.A.F., Southend; to Cie Air Transport, Le Touquet 5.67 as F-BOSU; withdrawn from use 1970

G-AXAI (17), 3.4.69, B.A.F., Southend

Avro 504K

G-EAAK, E4222, 9.5.19, Avro/Hounslow, w.f.u. 5.20; G-EAAL, E4154, 29.5.19, Avro/Southsea, Vickers Ltd., Brooklands 2.23, converted to Avro 548 in 1925; G-EAAM, E3289, 9.5.19, Avro/Hounslow, w.f.u. 5.20; G-EAAN, E4225, 5.5.19, Avro/Weston-super-Mare, w.f.u. 5.20; G-EAAX, D6205, 12.5.19, Grahame-White, Hendon, w.f.u. 5.21; G-EAAY, C724, 7.5.19, Grahame-White, Hendon, Lady Ulica Beecham, Hendon 9.24, Liverpool Av. Co. 5.25, Southern Counties Av. Co., Brooklands 'Jake' 4.26, F. G. Miles, Shoreham 10.26, L.J. Skytrips Ltd., 4.27, L. R. G. Errington, Bekesbourne 7.30, crashed 1931

Shown with registration on a white panel in 1919 style, G-EAAY had eight owners and was one of the longest-lived of the early civil 504Ks. (*P. T. Capon*)

G-EABA, E3480, 27.5.19, Grahame-White, Hendon, w.f.u. 5.21; G-EABE, E4137, 18.5.19, Grahame-White, Hendon, E. F. Edwards, Whitley Bay 9.23, crashed 12.5.24; G-EABF, C748, 11.7.19, Grahame-White, Hendon, w.f.u. 7.21; G-EABG, C749, 30.5.19, Grahame-White, Hendon, w.f.u. 5.21; G-EABH, B8758, 7.8.19, Grahame-White, Hendon, w.f.u. 8.21; G-EABJ, E4359, 19.5.19, Avro/Blackpool No. 3, w.f.u. 5.20; G-EABK, D8287, 18.5.19, Avro/Southport, w.f.u. 5.20; G-EABL, E4324, 19.5.19, Avro/Alexandra Park, w.f.u. 5.20; G-EABM, E4360, 19.5.19, Avro/Southport No. 2, w.f.u. 5.20; G-EABN, C723, 9.5.19, Grahame-White, Hendon, w.f.u. 5.21; G-EABO, D6202, 27.5.19, Grahame-White, Hendon, to Canada 5.20 as G-CAAE; G-EABP, F9802, 18.5.19, Grahame-White, Hendon, to Belgium 7.21; G-EABT, D6201, 20.5.19, London & Provincial Av. Co., Stag Lane, w.f.u. 8.19; G-EABV, D6229, 18.5.19, Avro, crashed 12.19; G-EABW, C747, 25.5.19, Grahame-White, Hendon, w.f.u. 7.22; G-EABX, E4230, 20.5.19, Grahame-White, Hendon, Manchester Av. Co. 8.22, cancelled 8.23

G-EACA, E6765, 18.6.19, G. J. Lusted, Shoreham, H. Sykes, Kingsbury 2.21 'Psyche', crashed near Stag Lane 1.10.21; G-EACB, E1671, registered 9.5.19, to Avro, cancelled 9.20; G-EACD, E4224, 16.5.19, Avro, crashed 12.19; G-EACL, D9298, 10.6.19, J. D. V. Holmes, East Hanney, crashed near Northampton 5.8.19; G-EACS, D9341, 20.5.19, Avro, w.f.u. 5.20; G-EACV, E4233, 24.6.19, Vickers Ltd., Joyce Green, crashed 4.20; G-EACW, E1663, 2.6.19, Avro/Southsea, landed in the sea 11.19

G-EADA, E4221, 19.5.19, Avro, converted to Avro 504N in 1923; G-EADD, E1665, 25.5.19, Avro, w.f.u. 5.20; G-EADH, E3502, 31.5.22, West of Scotland Av. Co., Kingwill and Jones Flying Co. 5.22, w.f.u. 6.26; G-EADI, E3292, 25.5.19, Avro/Morecambe, w.f.u. 5.20; G-EADM, E4336, 10.6.19, Avro/Southsea, sold in Belgium 8.21; G-EADN, E3293, 5.6.19, Avro, sold in Belgium 7.21; G-EADO, F8706, 16.6.19, Central Aircraft Co., Northolt, crashed 12.19; G-EADP, E3481, 11.8.19, Central Aircraft Co., Northolt 'White Wings', Midland Av. Co. 10.21, Manchester Av. Co. 3.23, Northern Av. Co. 3.24, crashed 3.5.24; G-EADQ, D7588, 6.6.19, Central Aircraft Co., Northolt, to the Irish Air Corps 6.22; G-EADR, D6245, 10.7.19, Bournemouth Av. Co., crashed 8.20; G-EADS, H2507, 24.6.19, Vickers Ltd., Joyce Green, crashed 4.20; G-EADU, D9329, 1.7.19, Central Aircraft Co., Northolt, J. M. Drysdale, Caversham 9.20, D. M. Matthews 8.23, J. E. A. Binnie, Renfrew 9.23, N. S. McConnell, Renfrew 7.24, w.f.u. 10.24; G-EADW, E4343, 24.6.19, Avro, wrecked by gale at Rhyl 8.19; G-EADX, D6230, 24.5.19, Avro, w.f.u. 5.20; G-EADY, E3408, 7.8.19, Navarro Av. Co., Astra Engine Works, Hendon 5.20, sold in South Africa 1.21

G-EAEA, D9304, 3.7.19, Navarro Av. Co., Astra Engine Works, Hendon 5.20, sold in South Africa 1.21; G-EAEB, B8774, 3.7.19, Navarro Av. Co., S. Summerfield and Co. 7.20, crashed 3.10.21; G-EAEC, E3501, 1.9.19, Cambridge S. of F., Hardwicke, to Australia 8.19, became G-AUDQ in 1921; G-EAEN, D9018, 13.6.19, Avro/Southport No. 11, crashed 1.20; G-EAEO, E4362, 13.6.19, Avro/Morecambe No. 10, w.f.u. 6.20; G-EAEV, H2586, 24.6.19, Avro, w.f.u. 6.20; G-EAEY, H2560, 1.7.19, Vickers Ltd., Joyce Green, crashed 4.20; G-EAEZ, H2561, 30.6.19, Vickers Ltd., Joyce Green, crashed 4.20

G-EAFC, E1660, 10.7.19, Avro/Southport No. 16, wrecked by gale at Rhyl 8.19; G-EAFD, E4329, 25.6.19, Avro/Southport No. 12 (flew as D4329), J. Blake and Co., Liverpool 3.20, w.f.u. 6.20; G-EAFE, D7648, 10.7.19, Avro, crashed 8.9.21; G-EAFP, E3363, 1.7.19, Central Aircraft Co., Northolt, to Australia 12.21 as G-AUFP; G-EAFQ, E4180, 7.8.19, T. J. Rogers, Stallard Airways, Herne Bay 9.21, crashed at Hildenborough, Kent 11.21; G-EAFS, D9340, 10.7.19, Avro/Southport No. 15, w.f.u. 7.20; G-EAFU, H2583, 10.7.19, South African Aerial Transport Co., sold in South Africa 7.19; G-EAFV,

H2584, as 'FU; G-EAFW, H2591, as 'FU; G-EAFX, H6543, registered to Golden Eagle Av. Co., Squires Gate 1.7.19, wrecked by gale 8.19, rebuilt as G-EASG

G-EAGB, H5173, 15.12.19, Aerial Photos Ltd., Edinburgh, Midland Av. Co. 8.22, crashed 22.10.23; G-EAGC, H5172, 12.8.19, London & Provincial Av. Co., Stag Lane, Aerial Photos Ltd. 12.19, Manchester Av. Co. 3.23, cancelled 3.24; G-EAGD, D5499, registered 4.7.19 to London & Provincial Av. Co., damaged and rebuilt as G-EALE; G-EAGI, E4234, 14.8.19, Central Aircraft Co., Northolt, crashed 7.20; G-EAGJ, C746, 2.8.19, Central Aircraft Co., Northolt, crashed at Twickenham 12.19; G-EAGO, D9343, 2.8.19, Avro, crashed at Southport 8.19; G-EAGT, D6217, 2.8.19, Kingsbury Av. Co., Astra Engine Works, Hendon 5.20, Oxfordshire Av. Co. 8.20, crashed 3.21; G-EAGV, H6598, 2.8,19, North Sea Aerial Nav. Co., Leeds, crashed 9.20; G-EAGW, H6599, 2.8.19, North Sea Aerial Nav. Co., Leeds, crashed at Scarborough 7.20; G-EAGZ, D8984, 7.8.19, C. A. Crichton, t/a Northern Aircraft Transport & Travel Co. Ltd., w.f.u. 7.20

G-EAHK, E4340, 12.8.19, Bournemouth Av. Co., J. W. Gibson 2.20, J. Barnes 2.21, w.f.u. 8.21; G-EAHL, E4118, 12.8.19, Cambridge S. of F., Hardwicke, Leatherhead Av. Co., Croydon 10.20, Manchester Av. Co. 3.23, crashed 7.7.23; G-EAHM, E1707, 2.8.19, T. D. Lewis, crashed 12.19; G-EAHO, H1959, 7.8.19, H. V. David, crashed at Aberystwyth 28.8.19; G-EAHU, E1611, 7.8.19, Aerial Photos Ltd., Edinburgh, W. L. Woodward, Castle Bromwich 5.22, crashed at Castle Bromwich 10.6.22; G-EAHV, H2297, 7.8.19, Aerial Photos Ltd., Edinburgh, w.f.u. 8.21; G-EAHW, E3364, 6.9.19, Handley Page Ltd., Cricklewood, crashed in Southwark Park, London 31.3.20; G-EAHX, E3366, 6.9.19, Handley Page Ltd., Cricklewood, w.f.u. 9.20; G-EAHY, H7513, 26.8.19, West of Scotland Av. Co., William Beardmore Ltd., Renfrew 9.23, w.f.u. 8.28; G-EAHZ, H2411, 26.8.19, West of Scotland Av. Co., F. J. V. Holmes 8.21, crashed 1.3.23

G-EAIA, F8717, 26.8.19, West of Scotland Av. Co., Border Av. Co. 8.20, R. Atkinson 3.23, cancelled 3.24; G-EAIB, D9303, 12.8.19, J. D. V. Holmes, East Hanney, Anderson and Pool Av. Co., Ipswich 6.20, w.f.u. 8.20; G-EAIG, E1675, registered 3.9.19 to Aerial Photos Ltd., Edinburgh, cancelled 10.19; G-EAIH, H2595, 8.8.19, Avro/Amsterdam, sold in Belgium 7.21; G-EAII, H2596, 7.8.19, Avro/Amsterdam, crashed 8.21; G-EAIJ, H2597, 7.8.19, Avro/Amsterdam, w.f.u. 7.20; G-EAIO, E3359, 22.9.19, Aircraft Transport & Travel Ltd., Hendon, w.f.u. 8.20; G-EAIP, E4143, registered to A.T. & T. 7.8.19, cancelled 8.19; G-EAIQ, E4144, 28.8.19, A.T. & T., scrapped 11.20; G-EAIR, E4164, 28.11.19, A.T. & T., Croydon, Surrey Flying Services Ltd., Croydon 9.21, crashed at Hayling Island 21.8.23; G-EAIS, E4170, registered to A.T. & T. 7.8.19, sold abroad 4.20; G-EAIV to 'IY (AAEC.1 to 4), Australian Aircraft and Engineering Co. Ltd., Sydney ('IV and 'IY registered G-AUCB and 'BE respectively 6.21)

G-EAJE, H2549, 1.8.19, J. D. Atkinson, to D.D.L., Copenhagen 1921 as T-DOLM; G-EAJF, H2556, 1.8.19, J. D. Atkinson, to Danish Army 11.21 as 'Avro 1'; G-EAJG, H1956, 14.7.19, Eastbourne Av. Co., T. Baden Powell 3.22, crashed at Penshurst 20.8,22; G-EAJK, D7619, 29.8.19, Central Aircraft Co., Northolt, Vulcan Av. Co. 5.21, crashed 8.21; G-EAJP, E1728, 14.8.19, Navarro-Wellesley Av. Co., Astra Engineering Works, Hendon 5.20, sold abroad 1.21; G-EAJQ, H2587, 20.8.19, Avro/Amsterdam, H. W. B. Hansford, Lyme Regis 8.20, crashed 10.20; G-EAJU, H2592, 20.8,19, Avro/Amsterdam, Gnat Aero Co., Shoreham 5.22, J. C. Don, Shoreham 8.28, d.b.r. Brighton 21.7.29; G-EAJZ, H2594, 27.8.19, Avro/Brighton, W. G. Pudney, Canvey, Essex 11.22, D. M. Matthews, Renfrew 7.23, crashed 11.8.23

G-EAKB, H2588, 26.8.19, Avro, w.f.u. 8.20; G-EAKR, E4246, 19.9.19, Avro, crashed in France 20.9.19; G-EAKV, J803, 17.9.19, Avro, to Switzerland 9.19 as CH-10;

Although flown without markings, the single Avro 546 was actually a converted Avro 536, G-EAOM. The widened fuselage imparted a 9 in. increase in the span.

G-EAKW, H2593, 26.8.19, Avro/Hamble, w.f.u. 8.20; G-EAKX, H2600, 18.9.19, Avro/Brighton, Berkshire Aviation Tours, East Hanney 12.20, Northern Air Lines, Barton 6.29, L. J. Rimmer 8.33, dismantled at Hooton 9.34; G-EAKY, H2599, 9.9.19, Avro, w.f.u. 8.20; G-EAKZ, E3297, 9.9.19, Avro/Brighton, w.f.u. 9.20

G-EALA, E1640, 7.10.19, Avro, R. Taylor 7.22, crashed 21.8.22; G-EALD, H1925, 10.6.19, Eastbourne Av. Co., R. H. Leavey t/a Provincial Flying Services 5.22, crashed 27.8.22; G-EALE, D5499, 26.8.19, Aerial Photos Ltd., Edinburgh, Midland Av. Co. 8.22, crashed 24.4.23

G-EAMI, E3399, 19.9.19, W. G. Pudney, Canvey, written off 7.12.21; G-EAMN, J747, 26.9.19, Avro, w.f.u. 9.20; G-EAMO, J746, 26.9.19, Avro/Brighton, sold in Chile 9.21; G-EAMP, J745, 11.10.19, Avro, w.f.u. 10.20; G-EAMQ, J748, 7.10.19, Avro, w.f.u. 10.20; G-EAMZ, E3724, 26.9.19, Avro, F. P. Raynham 5.23, M. W. Piercey 7.24, Earl of Kinnoul 6.25, crashed at Le Bourget 9.6.25

G-EANC, H2318, registered 16.9.19 to Avro, cancelled 10.20; G-EAND, J749, 26.9.19, Avro, sold in Belgium 6.21; G-EANE, J751, 25.10.19, Avro, sold in Chile 9.21; G-EANF, J752, 3.10.19, Avro, w.f.u. 10.20; G-EANG, J753, 7.10.19, Avro, sold in Belgium 6.21; G-EANN, H2514, 13.4.20, Sir P. Sassoon, Lympne, H. Sykes, Kingsbury 'Psyche' 3.20, Adastral Air Lines 9.20, crashed in France; G-EANO, J756, 11.10.19, Avro, w.f.u. 10.20; G-EANP, J754, registered 22.9.19 to Avro, to the Japanese Navy 9.21; G-EANQ, J755, 11.10.19, Avro, Border Av. Co. 4.20, crashed at Carlisle 5.12.21; G-EANT, E3358, 4.10.19, G.N. Ltd., Brooklands, w.f.u. 10.20; G-EANX, G-EANY and G-EANZ, J757–J759, Cs. of A. 25.10.19, 7.11.19 and 3.10.19, Avro, to the Japanese Navy 9.21

G-EAOA to 'OD, J760–J763, registered 3.10.19 to Avro, to the Japanese Navy 9.21; G-EAOE, E3505, registered 6.10.19 to Lt. Col. R. B. Bourdillon, Farnborough, B. Martin, Cleethorpes 5.22, crashed 13.6.22; G-EAQU, E3021 and G-EAQV, E9443, 18.2.20, A. A. Mitchell, one crashed at Kelso, Roxburgh 24.5.20; G-EARP, 6.4.20, Pudney-Brettel-Owen Co., w.f.u. 3.21; G-EARZ, H6551, 12.4.20, Bournemouth Av. Co., crashed 9.20

G-EASA, F9809, 12.4.20, Bournemouth Av. Co., S. Summerfield 11.21, crashed 8.5.22; G-EASB, F9810, 12.4.20, Bournemouth Av. Co., C. P. B. Ogilvie, Hendon 5.25, crashed near Ripley, Yorks. 12.26; G-EASF, D5858, 9.4.20, Cobham and Holmes Av.

Co., O. P. Jones 7.20, F. J. V. Holmes 3.22, Northern Air Lines, Barton 6.29, L. J. Rimmer, dismantled at Hooton 1937; G-EASG, H6543, 22.4.22, Golden Eagle Av. Co., Squires Gate, J. S. Boumphrey 7.21, Liverpool Av. Co. 7.22, Southern Counties Av. Co., Brooklands 5.25, crashed 2.9.26; G-EATB, F8902, 22.6.20, A. R. van den Bergh, w.f.u. 6.21; G-EATU, E3045, 28.2.21, C. L. Pashley, Shoreham, Gnat Aero Co., Shoreham 9.27, crashed on the Downs in 1928; G-EATV, D6387, 26.6.20, International Av. Co., crashed 11.20; G-EATZ, E3022, registered 24.6.20 to J. M. Drysdale, re-registered G-EAVC

G-EAVC, E3022, registered 17.8.20 to W. R. Bailey, not converted; G-EAVD, E6757, registered 18.8.20 to Handley Page Ltd., flown to Brussels 16.8.20; G-EAVI, E1644, 25.7.21, W. A. Hadden, w.f.u. 8.24; G-EAWI, E3672, 1.4.21, Surrey Flying Services Ltd., crashed near Croydon 9.21; G-EAWJ, D2035, 22.3.21, Surrey Flying Services Ltd., w.f.u. 2.22; G-EAWK, E3671, 22.6.21, Welsh Av. Co., Swansea, Evan Williams 4.22, crashed in Swansea Bay 2.10.22; G-EAWL, E9341, 20.4.21, Welsh Av. Co., Evan Williams 4.22, dismantled 4.23; G-EAWM, E9245, 29.3.21, Welsh Av. Co., Evan Williams 4.22, dismantled 4.23; G-EAXY, D9058, 9.7.21, Royal Aero Club, Croydon, w.f.u. 7.23; G-EAYB, H6608, 22.7.21, Royal Aero Club, Croydon, crashed 7.23; G-EAYC, H6609, 22.7.21, Royal Aero Club, Hendon, crashed 22.5.22; G-EAZF/H7426, G-EAZG/H6605, G-EAZK/H6611 and G-EAZL/H6601, Aircraft Disposal Co. Ltd., Croydon, sold in Belgium 11.21; G-EAZQ/H2516, G-EAZR/H2553, G-EAZS/H2558, G-EAZU/H2509 and G-EAZV/H2565, Aircraft Disposal Co. Ltd., sold in Belgium 1.22 (G-EAZF and 'ZL crashed on test at Croydon); G-EAZW, H2295, 22.8.22, Manchester Av. Co., Northern Av. Co. 3.24, crashed at Brighouse, Yorks. 3.5.24; G-EAZX, E1860, 24.7.22, Manchester Av. Co., Northern Av. Co. 3.24, crashed 2.8.24

G-EBAF, H7467, Aircraft Disposal Co. Ltd., Croydon, sold in Belgium 1.22; G-EBAV, F9783, 20.4.22, Leatherhead Av. Co., crashed at Slough 20.8.22; G-EBAY, registered to H. Sykes 9.1.22, named 'Psyche'; A. Fraser, Kingsbury 7.22, cancelled 7.23; G-EBBF, E1843, 16.7.23, A. Fraser, Kingsbury, w.f.u. 7.24; G-EBBP, H6653, Aircraft Disposal Co. Ltd., sold in Belgium 4.22; G-EBCB, H221, 2.5.22, Kingwill and Jones Flying Co., Clacton, written off 2.29; G-EBCC/H6656, G-EACD/H7487 and G-EBCF/H2065, Aircraft Disposal Co. Ltd., sold in Belgium 5.22; G-EBCK, E3379, 29.4.22, F. J. V. Holmes, East Hanney, F. Neale, Epping 1.23, B. Roberts 2.25, H. Sykes, Ramsey 'Psyche'

Surrey Flying Services' blue and silver Avro 504K G-EBDP at Croydon in 1925.

5.26, w.f.u. 1.28; G-EBCL, E9227, 20.4.22, W. R. Bailey, crashed 5.22; G-EBCO, H7482, Aircraft Disposal Co. Ltd., sold in Belgium 5.22; G-EBCQ, H6547, 22.5.22, Leatherhead Av. Co., Manchester Av. Co. 12.22, crashed 24.8.23; G-EBCR/H7474, G-EBCS/H2062 and G-EBCT/H2071, Aircraft Disposal Co. Ltd., sold in Belgium 7.22; G-EBDC/H2060 and G-EBDJ/H2052, Aircraft Disposal Co. Ltd., sold in Belgium 5.22; G-EBDP, F2284, 22.6.22, Surrey Flying Services Ltd., Croydon, w.f.u. 7.25; G-EBEL, E3291, 15.8.22, London Av. Co. Ltd., sold abroad 1.23; G-EBEO, C691, registered to A. S. J. Chapman 2.8.22, cancelled 8.24

G-EBFV, 14.5.23, F. J. V. Holmes, East Hanney, William Beardmore Ltd., Renfrew 10.23, crashed 6.10.24; G-EBFW, E1850, 28.5.23, Surrey Flying Services Ltd., Croydon, crashed at Yeovil 17.9.27; G-EBGH, H6602, registered to Manchester Av. Co. 8.5.23, crashed 5.6.23; G-EBGI, H2416, 12.6.23, Manchester Airways, w.f.u. 5.24; G-EBGV, E9358, 26.6.24, Aircraft Disposal Co. Ltd., Croydon, sold abroad 6.24; G-EBGY (R/LE/10390), 25.7.23, Wm. Beardmore Ltd., Renfrew, crashed 12.6.24; G-EBGZ (R/LE/10407), 25.7.23, Wm. Beardmore Ltd., Renfrew, L. J. Rimmer, Hooton 10.29, dismantled at Hooton 1934; G-EBHB, registered 17.7.23 to Manchester Airways, cancelled 8.24; G-EBHE (R3/CL/10365), 11.4.23, Avro 504N converted to 504K in 1932, W. Mackay, crashed 1.37; G-EBHM, E3794, 21.8.23, Surrey Flying Services Ltd., Croydon

G-EBII, E1826, 12.11.23, Surrey Flying Services Ltd., Croydon, w.f.u. 11.24; G-EBIN, 4.1.24, F. J. V. Holmes, crashed 25.7.24; G-EBIS (R/LE/12663), 9.2.24, Wm. Beardmore Ltd., Renfrew, North British Av. Co., Hooton 2.29, crashed 22.4.35; G-EBIZ, 19.5.24, Cornwall Av. Co., St. Austell, w.f.u. 3.33; G-EBJE, 21.1.26, Southern Counties Av. Co., J. R. Cobb, Brooklands 1.26, F. G. Miles 8.26, Southern Aircraft Ltd., Shoreham 7.28, w.f.u. 9.34, rebuilt 1963 for R.A.F. Museum as E449; G-EBKB, E2969, 13.9.24, F. J. V. Holmes, Northern Air Lines, Barton 4.29, in the sea off Scarborough 13.9.31; G-EBKR, E3382, 24.3.25, F. J. V. Holmes, C. L. Kent 8.27, Wolverhampton Aircraft Co. Ltd., 5.30, crashed at Church Lawton, Cheshire 22.7.32; G-EBKS, 1.6.25, Southern Counties Av. Co., Brooklands, w.f.u. 6.27; G-EBKX, E3386, 9.5.25, F. J. V. Holmes, Northern Air Lines, Barton 7.29, L. J. Rimmer, Hooton 8.33, crashed at Crosby, Lancs. 21.7.34; G-EBLA (R/LE/18615), 1.7.25, North Sea Aerial and General Transport Co. Ltd., Brough, A. G. Cooper 4.28, in the sea off Weymouth 19.6.28

G-EBNH, 6.4.26, T. J. Carslake, Hooton, South Wales Airways, crashed at Bridgend, Glam. 7.5.28; G-EBNR, F8864, 16.3.26, Cornwall Av. Co., St. Austell, w.f.u. 2.30; G-EBNU, E448, 23.4.26, Aircraft Disposal Co. Ltd., Croydon, to Finnish Air Force 9.26 as AV-57; G-EBOB, F8865, 2.6.26, F. J. V. Holmes, w.f.u. 3.29; G-EBQR, 14.4.27, Western Aviation Ltd., Cheltenham, Aviation Tours Ltd. 4.33, cancelled 4.37; G-EBSE, H2234, 29.7.27, Cornwall Av. Co., St. Austell, w.f.u. 4.32; G-EBSG, H257, 29.7.27, South Wales Airways, Western Aviation Ltd., Cheltenham 5.28, cancelled 11.34; G-EBSJ, H2365, 16.4.28, A. H. Matthews, Maylands, North British Av. Co. 7.34, cancelled 5.35; G-EBSL, D6330, 27.8.27, F. J. V. Holmes, Northern Air Transport Ltd., Barton, crashed 9.5.32; G-EBSM, H9859, 10.8.27, F. J. V. Holmes, J. Bunning Ltd., Pontypool 5.28, w.f.u. 5.29; G-EBVL, 9.1.28, L. E. R. Bellairs, Shoreham, Southern Aircraft Ltd., Shoreham 7.28, F. C. Fisher, Christchurch 8.31, scrapped 1939; G-EBVW, 18.5.28, F. J. V. Holmes, Shrewsbury, N.A.L. 7.29, dismantled at Hooton 12.31; G-EBWF, 21.3.28, L.J. Skytrips Ltd., Alliston Av. Co. 5.29, scrapped at Hornchurch 12.32; G-EBWO, 26.7.28, Dr. M. C. Wall, Woodley, Phillips and Powis Ltd., Woodley 11.28, crashed 4.29

G-EBXA, 4.4.28, W.B., North British Av. Co. 7.29, w.f.u. 12.33; G-EBXV, 26.5.28, Western Av. Ltd., Aviation Tours Ltd. 4.33, w.f.u. 4.37; G-EBYB, 26.5.28, Gnat Aero

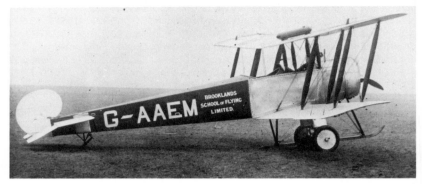

Avro 504K G-AAEM in the red and silver livery of the Brooklands School of Flying Ltd., 1929.

Co., Southern Aero Club, Shoreham 3.30, dismantled 2.33; G-EBYE, 30.6.28, Henderson S. of F., Brooklands, Midland Aero Flights Ltd. 8.28, R. H. Jackson 11.28, Brooklands S. of F. 1.30, crashed at Brixton, London 2.2.31; G-EBYW, 3.9.28, Surrey F/S, Aviation Tours Ltd. 5.30, Kinmel Bay F/S, Rhyl 5.34, w.f.u. 3.38; G-EBZA, 13.7.28, L.J. Skytrips Ltd., L. R. G. Errington 8.30, w.f.u. 12.31; G-EBZB, H2262, 2.10.26, Surrey Flying Services Ltd., M. W. Allenby, Wilmington 11.32, w.f.u. 10.33

G-AAAF, 7.9.28, Cornwall Av. Co., Surrey Flying Services Ltd. 8.33, H. V. K. Atkinson, Witney 6.35, Flying Hire Ltd., Chilworth 8.35, burned at Gatwick 1939; G-AACA, 3.11.28, L. J. May, Brooklands S. of F. 2.29, F. J. V. Holmes 6.32, w.f.u. 12.33; G-AACG, F8811, 12.11.28, L. J. Anderson, w.f.u. 1.32; G-AACW, 27.7.29, Southern Aircraft Ltd., Home Counties A/S 11.30, crashed at Gatwick 25.1.31; G-AACX, 20.11.28, Dominion Aircraft Ltd., Gatwick, crashed 4.29; G-AADY, J8373, 23.2.29, Henderson S. of F., W. Cornell 10.29, D. A. N. Watt, Ford 11.30, w.f.u. 12.31; G-AAED, 12.3.29, J. Sale and A. Barnett, Shoreham, crashed at Stag Lane 4.7.29; G-AAEM, 28.3.29, Brooklands S. of F., Popular Flights Ltd. 7.29, w.f.u. 12.31; G-AAES, 29.3.29, T. J. Carslake, burned at Hooton 1935; G-AAEZ, 27.3.29, Aeroplane Services Ltd., Castle Bromwich, H. C. Howard 5.30, N.A.L. 8.31, W. Mackay 8.33, w.f.u. 12.34

G-AAFE, 31.5.29, Inland F/S, Maylands, w.f.u. 12.30; G-AAFJ, J8375, 3.4.29, Henderson S. of F., H. C. Howard 5.30, Mrs E. M. Watt, Ford 11.30, w.f.u. 12.31; G-AAFT, J8379, 26.3.29, A. B. Forsyth, Inland F/S 5.29, w.f.u. 3.31; G-AAGB, 17.4.29, Surrey F/S, crashed 12.34; G-AAGG, 6.5.29, Phillips and Powis Ltd., Woodley, Rollason Av. Co., Croydon 3.31, w.f.u. 12.35; G-AARV (SP/1312), 7.11.30, S. Payne Jnr., crashed at Bekesbourne 2.1.31; G-AASS, F2540, 16.5.30, L. G. Anderson, Hanworth, South Wales Airways 11.30, submerged by tide at Swansea Sands 1.8.31; G-AAST, F9819, 11.1.30, E. Brown, w.f.u. 12.32; G-AASX, 7.5.30, Alliston Av. Co., R. M. Stobie, Brough 7.30, w.f.u. 12.32; G-AATY, 17.3.30, Wolverhampton Aero Club, scrapped at Driffield 1937

G-AAUJ (K.A.S.1), 28.3.30, Kent Aircraft Services, Kingsdown, crashed at Harrogate 5.10.32; G-AAUK (K.A.S.2), 28.3.30, Kent Aircraft Services, crashed on Epsom Downs 4.6.31; G-AAUL (K.A.S.3), 21.5.30, Kent Aircraft Services, crashed at Dovercourt, Essex 2.8.31; G-AAVW, F9720, 18.9.30, L. G. Anderson, L. D. Trappitt 1.31, w.f.u. 12.35; G-AAWB, Kent A/S, not converted; G-AAWC (K.A.S.5), 21.5.30, Kent Aircraft Services, P. H. Meadway 9.30, w.f.u. 12.32; G-AAWD (K.A.S.4), 16.6.30, Kent Aircraft

Services, dismantled 10.36; G-AAYH, H9833, 6.6.30, N.A.T., to Ireland 3.32 as EI-AAM; G-AAYI, H9861, 29.5.30, Cornwall Av. Co., w.f.u. 12.31; G-AAYM, 9.6.30, Surrey Flying Services Ltd., Aviation Tours Ltd. 4.33, L. J. Rimmer 8.33, w.f.u. 12.34

G-ABAA, 11.9.30, G. & H. Aviations Ltd., Stag Lane, Luff's Aviation Tours Ltd. 3.33, Williams and Co., Squires Gate 5.36, dismantled at Brooklands 1939; G-ABAB, 4.7.30, G. & H. Av. Ltd., R. O. Roch 6.31, last flight 16.10.32; G-ABAU, J8353, 19.6.30, H. Sinclair, burned in hangar fire at Broomfield, Chelmsford 18.9.32; G-ABAV, J8348, 9.7.30, N.A.T., crashed at Holyhead 9.30; G-ABAW, J8347, 21.6.30, N.A.T., w.f.u. 12.33; G-ABAY, 7.8.30, Surrey Flying Services Ltd., wrecked at Croydon 13.1.35; G-ABBF, H202, 2.7.31, Rollason Av. Co., Mrs. E. M. Watt, Ford 11.30, R. E. Pancoast-Bliss, Croydon 7.31, Southend Flying Club 10.31, dismantled at Bekesbourne 7.32

G-ABGI, 12.6.31, Mrs. V. Brailey, L. J. Rimmer 8.33, w.f.u. 1.36; G-ABGJ, no C. of A., Mrs. V. Brailey, w.f.u. 12.34; G-ABHI, J8342, 7.3.31, N.A.T., Cornwall Av. Co. 4.32, w.f.u. 1.34; G-ABHJ, J8343, 7.3.31, N.A.T., L. J. Rimmer 8.33, crashed at Hooton 1933; G-ABHK, J8351, 24.3.31, N.A.T., L. J. Rimmer 8.33, crashed at Hooton 1933; G-ABHP, J8371, 14.3.31, N.A.T., to Ireland 3.32 as EI-AAN; G-ABJF (K.A.S.6), 30.3.31, P. Turner, Thanet Av. Ltd. 3.32, w.f.u. 5.34

G-ABLL, J8333, 3.6.31, N.A.T., L. J. Rimmer 8.33, crashed at Lowton Moor 8.34; G-ABLV, H3086, 16.5.31, R. H. Thomas, Wenvoe, S. Wales, scrapped 1936; G-ABLW, H3087, 16.5.31, R. H. Thomas, South Wales Airways 8.33, w.f.u. 1.34; G-ABML, E438, Calder Valley Aero Club, Burnley, not converted; G-ABOL (K.A.S.7), no C. of A., Kent Aircraft Services, crashed 12.32; G-ABSL, 5.5.32, C. B. Field, Kingswood Knoll, Surrey, Modern Airways Ltd. 8.32, L. J. Rimmer 4.33, w.f.u. 8.36; G-ABSM, H1986, 15.6.32, C. B. Field, E. L. Gandar Dower, Shoreham 10.32, w.f.u. 12.37; G-ABSN, H2965, 7.7.32, London & Provincial Av. Co., Herne Bay, L. J. Rimmer 8.33, F. B. Chapman, Gosport 12.34, w.f.u. 4.38

G-ABTX, J. Mackay, not converted; G-ABUK, J8365, 7.4.32, N.A.T., crashed at Hedon, Hull 3.9.32; G-ABWK, E9353, 27.6.32, Essex Flying Club, Abridge, Kinmel Bay A/S 8.33, sold abroad 12.35; G-ABYB, 7.9.32, Essex Aero Club, Orsett, H. M. Talbot-Lehmann, Chelmsford 10.32, w.f.u. 6.33; G-ABZC, 5.4.33, Devonshire Aviation Tours Ltd., crashed at Chard, Som. 30.4.33; G-ACAU, 26.4.33, C. B. Field, crashed at Epping 22.5.33; G-ACAV, 27.5.33, C. B. Field, w.f.u. 3.37.

G-ATXL, replica (H.A.C.1), 17.9.66, V. H. Bellamy, Kings Somborne, Hants., to Cole Palen collection, Old Rheinbeck, N.Y. 12.70

Avro 504K Mk.II

G-ADGB   J8758, 19.6.35, L. J. Braddock and partners, Croydon; Zenith Airways Ltd., Camber Sands, Sussex 6.35; registration cancelled 6.36
G-ADGC   J9689, registered 23.4.35 to L. J. Braddock and partners, Croydon; Zenith Airways Ltd., Camber Sands, Sussex; registration cancelled 1.36
G-ADGM   K1962, 11.7.35, Aviation Commerce Ltd., Croydon; Aircraft and Autos Ltd., Croydon 7.35; Brooklands Aviation Ltd. 6.36; registration cancelled 12.36
G-ADGN   H2962, 10.8.35, Aviation Commerce Ltd., Croydon; reg'n cancelled 3.38

Avro 504L

G-EADJ   H2581, 26.6.19, A. V. Roe and Co. Ltd., Windermere; registration lapsed at C. of A. expiry 25.6.20
G-EADK   H2582, 2.8.19, A. V. Roe and Co. Ltd., Windermere and Folkestone; registration lapsed at C. of A. expiry 1.8.20

K-144/G-EAFB, first of the Eastbourne Aviation Co. Ltd.'s joyriding Avro 504Ls (three individual cockpits), taxying out at Hove, Sussex, in August 1920. (*Royal Aero Club*)

G-EAFB   (E.1), K-144, 22.7.19, Eastbourne Aviation Co. Ltd.; registration lapsed at C. of A. expiry 21.7.20

G-EAFF   (A.T.C.12), K-145, 12.8.19, A. V. Roe and Co. Ltd., Hayling Island and Isle of Wight, Hants.; sold in Belgium 7.21

G-EAFG   (A.T.C.13), K-146, 7.8.19, A. V. Roe and Co. Ltd., Paignton, Devon; wrecked off Alderney, Channel Islands, in fog 5.10.19

G-EAGU   H2585, 16.8.19, A. V. Roe and Co. Ltd.; registration lapsed 15.8.20

G-EAJH   (E.2), 22.8.19, Eastbourne Aviation Co. Ltd.; sank off Hove, Sussex 19.8.20

G-EAJX   (A.T.C.16), 20.8.19, A. V. Roe and Co. Ltd.; reg'n. cancelled 10.20

G-EAKA   H2590, 27.8.19, A. V. Roe and Co. Ltd., sold abroad 8.21

G-EALB   H2589, 17.9.19, A. V. Roe and Co. Ltd.; registration cancelled 10.20

G-EALH   (A.T.C.15), 26.8.19, A. V. Roe and Co. Ltd.; reg'n. cancelled 10.20

G-EALI   (A.T.C.17), 3.9.19, A. V. Roe and Co. Ltd.; reg'n. cancelled 10.20

G-EALO   (E.3), 19.9.19, Eastbourne Aviation Co. Ltd.; crashed 2.21

G-EANB   (A.T.C.18), 6.11.19, A. V. Roe and Co. Ltd.; to Sweden 7.21 as S-IAA 'Masen'; re-registered 1923 as S-ABAA; struck off register 16.10.26

G-EANS   (E.4), 20.10.19, Eastbourne Aviation Co. Ltd.; crashed 9.20

G-EASD   (E.5), 1.6.20, Eastbourne Aviation Co. Ltd.; to Sweden 3.21 as S-AAP; re-registered 1923 as S-AHAA and in 1928 as SE-HAA

G-EASE   (E.6), 10.9.20, Eastbourne Aviation Co. Ltd., reg'n. cancelled 3.21

Avro 504M

G-EACX   (A.T.C.10), K-134, 25.6.19, A. V. Roe and Co. Ltd., Hounslow Heath, Middlesex; registration lapsed 24.6.20

Avro 504N (*including radial engined 504Ks**) Lynx engine unless otherwise stated.

G-EADA   E4221, Lucifer, registered 29.5.19 to A. V. Roe and Co. Ltd. as 504K, converted to 504N in 1923, registration cancelled 1924

G-EADL*   E4348, Lucifer, registered 5.6.19 to A. V. Roe and Co. Ltd.; Cosmos Engineering Co. Ltd., Filton 10.19; crashed at Kingswood, Bristol 1.20

G-EAFH*   (A.T.C.14), K-147, Wasp I, registered 19.6.19 to A. V. Roe and Co. Ltd.; converted to Avro 548 in 1920

G-EAJB*   H2598, Lucifer, 20.8.19, A. V. Roe and Co. Ltd., converted to Avro 548 in 1927

G-EBFB* H2518, Lucifer, registered 24.1.23 to the Aircraft Disposal Co. Ltd., Croydon; registration cancelled 1.25

G-EBHC* (R3/LY/10331), registered 20.7.23 to Sir W. G. Armstrong Whitworth Aircraft Ltd., Whitley; crashed 3.8.23

G-EBHD* (R3/LY/10348), 1.8.24, Sir W. G. Armstrong Whitworth Aircraft Ltd., Whitley; R. O. Roch, Hanworth 1.31; Modern Airways 3.32; canc. 9.36

G-EBHE* (R3/LY/10365), 12.12.23, Sir W. G. Armstrong Whitworth Aircraft Ltd., Whitley; converted to Avro 504K (Clerget) in 1932

G-EBHT* (R3/LY/10382), 14.2.24, Sir W. G. Armstrong Whitworth Aircraft Ltd.; Modern Airways Ltd. 3.32; registration cancelled 12.32

G-EBKQ (5104), K-8, 2.7.25, A. V. Roe and Co. Ltd., Hamble; conv. to Avro 582 in 1927; Titan testbed 1928; A.S.T., Hamble 6.30 as 504O; canc. 11.35

G-EBVY (R3/CN/126), 1.2.28, A. V. Roe and Co. Ltd., Hamble; L. G. Anderson, Hanworth 11.32; crashed at Tooting, London 30.1.35

G-ABVC* F8834, Lucifer, 9.6.33, H. C. Chater, Lympne; reg'n. cancelled 11.45

G-ABVH* J8372, Mongoose IIIA, 8.4.32, F. J. V. Holmes, Penshurst; Air Travel Ltd., Penshurst 1.34; registration cancelled 12.46

G-ABVY* H2524, Mongoose IIIA, 21.5.32, F. J. V. Holmes, Penshurst; Air Travel Ltd., Penshurst 1.34; registration cancelled 10.36

G-ACCX* Mongoose IIIA, 8.4.33, F. J. V. Holmes, Penshurst; wrecked at Leighton Buzzard 19.6.34

G-ACLV J8573, 9.3.34, Air Travel Ltd., Penshurst; Aerial Sites Ltd., Hanworth 7.34; registration cancelled 12.46

G-ACNV K1808, 11.4.34, E. B. Fielden; Air Pageants Ltd., Witney 7.34; registration cancelled 3.37

G-ACOD F8713, 11.4.34, Air Travel Ltd., Penshurst; fatal air collision with Westland Wessex G-ADFZ over Blackpool 7.9.35

G-ACOK F2588, Mongoose IIIA, 24.4.34, National Aviation Day Displays Ltd.; L. J. Rimmer, Hooton 3.36; crashed at Rhyl 14.8.38

G-ACOM E430, Mongoose IIIA, Air Travel Ltd., Penshurst; Plane Advertising Ltd., West Malling 10.38; Herts and Essex Aero Club 4.39; scrapped in 1940

G-ACPV K1250, 10.8.34, L. G. Anderson, Hanworth; Aerial Sites Ltd., Hanworth 8.34; Publicity Planes Ltd., Heston 3.38; impressed 1.41 as BV209

G-ACRE E9408, 7.5.34, H. B. G. Micklemore, Hedon; Air Publicity Ltd., Heston 6.34; crashed at Gamlingay, Cambs. 13.2.38

G-ACRS K1802, 15.5.34, National Aviation Day Displays Ltd.; crashed at Cove, Hants 30.6.34

G-ACZC 8.1.35, Earl of Cardigan, Marlborough; Campbell Black's Air Display Ltd. 1936; R. A. C. Holme, Doncaster 1938; impressed 6.40 as AX854/2453M

G-ADBD K1245, Mongoose IIIA, 17.5.35, Air Travel Ltd., Penshurst; National Av. Day Displays 7.35; Canute Air Park Co., crashed at Southend 22.7.36

G-ADBM K1055, 1.3.35, Air Travel Ltd., Penshurst; H. C. Wardle, Shoreham 3.35; Air Publicity Ltd., Heston 9.35; impressed 6.40 as AX871

G-ADBO K2354, 4.3.35, L. G. Anderson, Hanworth; Air Publicity Ltd., Heston 7.36; registration cancelled 12.46

G-ADBP K2353, 19.3.35, L. G. Anderson, Hanworth; Air Publicity Ltd., Heston 7.36; impressed 6.40 as AX874; instructional airframe 1942

G-ADBR K1819, 22.3.35, L. G. Anderson, Hanworth; Air Publicity Ltd., Heston 10.36; registration cancelled 12.46

L. J. Rimmer's Avro 504N G-AEGW (Mongoose IIIA) at Hooton in 1939. (*E. J. Riding*)

G-ADBS   K1251, Mongoose IIIA, 1.4.35, L. G. Anderson, Hanworth; crashed at Bodmin, Cornwall 16.8.35

G-ADDA   K1810, 26.3.35, Air Services Ltd., Croydon; Air Publicity Ltd., Heston 8.35; registration cancelled 12.46

G-ADEI   E3460, 8.6.35, H. B. G. Micklemore, Hedon; crashed at Hanworth 16.5.39

G-ADET   J8533, 11.6.35, Air Publicity Ltd., Heston; impressed 6.40 as AX875

G-ADEV   H5199, 24.8.35, Air Publicity Ltd., impressed 9.40 as BK892

G-ADFW   K1061, 4.5.35, Lincolnshire Flying Services Ltd., Louth; canc. 11.45

G-AEAA   (14), 3.6.36, F. C. J. Allen, Ford; registration cancelled 9.38

G-AECR   K2396, Mongoose IIIA, L. J. Anderson, Hanworth; sold abroad 3.38

G-AECS   J8548, 4.4.36, L. J. Anderson, Hanworth; Bournemouth Flying School Ltd. 5.38; dismantled at Christchurch 1940

G-AEDD   K1823, 11.4.36, Air Travel Ltd., Penshurst; Plane Advertising Ltd., Abridge 5.36; Publicity Planes Ltd., Hanworth 5.38; crashed at Walsall, Staffs. 13.3.39

G-AEGW   J9702, Mongoose IIIA, 2.9.36, Air Travel Ltd., Penshurst; L. J. Rimmer and W. F. Davidson, Hooton 3.37; burned in hangar fire, Hooton 8.7.40

G-AEIJ   J8507, 27.6.36, Air Travel Ltd., Penshurst; Plane Advertising Ltd., Abridge; lost in the Irish Sea 21.1.37

G-AEMP   J9017, 16.9.36, Air Travel Ltd.; Plane Advertising Ltd., Abridge 9.36; Publicity Planes Ltd., Heston 1939; impressed 1.41 as BV208

G-AFRM   K1964, registered 15.3.39 to Martin Hearn Ltd., Hooton; destroyed in hangar fire at Hooton 8.7.40

Avro 504Q

G-EBJD   (5103), registered 12.6.24 to the Oxford University Arctic Expedition; abandoned at Liefde Bay, Spitzbergen 9.24; registration cancelled 6.25

Avro 504R Gosport

G-EBNE   (5110), Gnome Mono, 15.6.24, A.V. Roe and Co. Ltd.; flown with Genet Major 1928; later K-6; to A.S.T., Hamble 1930 as instructional airframe

438

G-EBNF   (5111), Gnome Mono, 6.7.26, Light Planes (Lancs.) Ltd., Woodford; A. V. Roe and Co. Ltd. 9.27; crashed at Cheadle Hulme, Cheshire 21.10.28.

G-EBOX   (R3/G/80086), Gnome Mono, registered 20.7.26 to A. V. Roe and Co. Ltd., Woodford; sold abroad 8.26

G-EBPH   (R3/R/70000), Avro Alpha, 9.12.26, A. V. Roe and Co. Ltd., Woodford; converted to Avro 585; crashed 1.30

G-EBUY   (R3/CN/100), Mongoose, 26.11.27, A. V. Roe and Co. Ltd., Woodford and Hamble; to R.A.F. Martlesham 1.29 as J9175

G-AACT   (R3/CN/238), Mongoose, A. V. Roe and Co. Ltd., crashed 1.30

Avro 534 Baby and variants

G-EACQ   Avro 534, (534/1), K-131, registered 29.5.19 to A. V. Roe and Co. Ltd., Hamble; H. J. Hinkler, Hamble 4.20; to Australia 4.21 as G-AUCQ

G-EAPS   Avro 534A, (534/2), registered 21.11.19 to A. V. Roe and Co. Ltd., Hamble; crashed 7.9.21

G-EAUG   Avro 534B, (534B/1), registered 9.7.20 to A. V. Roe and Co. Ltd., Hamble; crashed near Ipswich about 3.8.20

G-EAUM   Avro 543, (543/1), registered 12.7.20 to A. V. Roe and Co. Ltd.., Hamble; C. of A. 3.8.23; c/n amended to 5062 at engine change 1926; L. E. R. Bellairs and F. G. Miles 11.27; R. A. Whitehead 7.28; H. H. Leech, Farnborough 9.28; H. R. A. Edwards 9.29; Roper Brown, Southend 8.32; cancelled 12.34

G-EAXL   Avro 534C, (534C/1), registered 27.6.21 to A. V. Roe and Co. Ltd., Hamble; crashed in Southampton Water 6.9.22

G-EAYM   Avro 534D, (5049), registered 17.9.21 to E. Villiers, Calcutta; withdrawn from use at Calcutta in 1929

G-EBDA   Avro 534, (5064), registered 28.4.22 to A. V. Roe and Co. Ltd., Hamble; flown to Russia 6.22

G-EBFE   Avro 554, (5040), registered 1.2.23 to the Aerial Survey Company, Newfoundland; scrapped in Newfoundland 1927

Avro 536

G-EAAO   (A.T.C.4), K-106, 16.5.19, A. V. Roe and Co. Ltd., Hounslow Heath; crashed at Sandhurst, Berks. 6.8.19

G-EAAP   (A.T.C.3), K-105, 14.5.19, A. V. Roe and Co. Ltd., Hounslow Heath; crashed 12.19

G-EAAQ   (A.T.C.2), K-104, 14.5.19, A. V. Roe and Co. Ltd., Hounslow Heath; crashed in Southwark Park, London 9..9.19 with registration K-104

G-EACC   (A.T.C.1), K-114, 3.7.19, A. V. Roe and Co. Ltd., flown at Hamble 5.19 as landplane and from 7.19 as seaplane; reg'n. cancelled 7.21

G-EACG   (A.T.C.9), K-116, 17.6.19, A. V. Roe and Co. Ltd., Southsea; crashed 12.19

G-EADC   (A.T.C.5), K-137, 3.6.19, A. V. Roe and Co. Ltd., Southsea; dismantled at Hamble 12.19

G-EADV   (A.T.C.11), K-139, experimental long-range two seater registered 6.6.19 to A. V. Roe and Co. Ltd., Hamble; scrapped 12.19

G-EAGM   (A.T.C.6), K-161, 12.7.19, A. V. Roe and Co. Ltd., Weston-super-Mare; crashed at Weston-super-Mare 1.9.19

G-EAHA   (A.T.C.7), K-165, 12.8.19, A. V. Roe and Co. Ltd., believed sold in Holland, registration cancelled 9.20

G-EAHB   (A.T.C.8), K-166, 17.7.19, A. V. Roe and Co. Ltd., Margate; dismantled at Hamble 12.19

The Curtiss engined Avro 545 G-EAPR at Hamble, October 1919, awaiting the fitting of the rudder.

G-EAID   (B.1), K-173, 7.8.19, A. V. Roe and Co. Ltd.; stored at Alexandra Park Aerodrome, Manchester 8.21

G-EAIE   (B.2), K-174, 7.8.19, A. V. Roe and Co. Ltd., Blackpool (Fleet No. 19); stored at Alexandra Park Aerodrome, Manchester 8.21

G-EAIF   (B.4), K-175, 5.8.19, A. V. Roe and Co. Ltd.; stored at Alexandra Park Aerodrome, Manchester 8.21

G-EAJR   (B.5), 20.8.19, A. V. Roe and Co. Ltd.; stored at Alexandra Park 8.21

G-EAKD   (B.3), 22.8.19, A. V. Roe and Co. Ltd.; stored at Alexandra Park 8.21

G-EAKJ   (B.6), 9.9.19, A. V. Roe and Co. Ltd., Brighton; Surrey Flying Services Ltd., Croydon 4.24; registration cancelled 1.29

G-EAKK   (B.7), 9.9.19, A. V. Roe and Co. Ltd.; stored at Alexandra Park 8.21

G-EAKL   (B.8), 19.11.19, A. V. Roe and Co. Ltd., stored at Alexandra Park 8.21; believed rebuilt as G-EBOY in 1926

G-EAKM   (B.9), registered 18.8.19 to A. V. Roe and Co. Ltd.; Surrey Flying Services Ltd., Croydon 7.25; C. of A. 18.8.25; crashed at Taplow 6.7.28

G-EAKN   (B.10), registered 18.8.19 to A. V. Roe and Co. Ltd.; F. J. V. Holmes, Monkmoor Aerodrome, Shrewsbury 9.23; C. of A. 17.4.24; crashed 1.9.24

G-EAKO   (B.11), registered 18.8.19 to A. V. Roe and Co. Ltd.; stored at Alexandra Park Aerodrome, Manchester 8.21

G-EAKP   (B.12), registered 18.8.19 to A. V. Roe and Co. Ltd.; Surrey Flying Services Ltd., Croydon 7.25; C. of A. 15.7.25; registration cancelled 1.29

G-EBOF   26.6.26, Surrey Flying Services Ltd., Croydon; withdrawn from use 12.30

G-EBOY   (P.8), 28.8.26, Surrey Flying Services Ltd., Croydon; w.f.u. 12.30

G-EBRB   13.5.27, Surrey Flying Services Ltd., Croydon; crashed 12.6.28

G-EBTF   1.9.27, Surrey Flying Services Ltd., Croydon; withdrawn from use 12.30

Avro 546

G-EAOM   (A.T.C.23), 22.12.19, A. V. Roe and Co., Ltd., Hamble and Brighton; registration cancelled 12.20

Avro 548

G-EAAL*   E4154, 4.12.25, de Havilland Aircraft Co. Ltd., Stag Lane, Edgware; T. H. Richardson, Stag Lane 'Vida' 11.26; crashed near Stag Lane, 4.6.28

G-EAFH (A.T.C.14), K-147, 22.6.20, Avro, Hamble; Welsh Av. Co., Swansea 5.21; Dr. E. D. Whitehead Reid, Bekesbourne 3.22; Capt. J. S. Lord, Squires Gate 2.28; Giro Av. Co. Ltd., Southport 3.31; crashed at Southport 31.5.35

G-EAJB* H2598, 12.4.27, Henderson School of Flying Ltd., Brooklands; cancelled 1.29

G-EALF J743, 8.12.20, A. V. Roe and Co. Ltd., Hamble; written off 7.21

G-EAPQ H2322, 16.3.20, A. V. Roe and Co. Ltd., Hamble; W. G. Pudney, Croydon 3.22; written off 19.10.22

G-EAVH (548/4), 15.10.20, A. V. Roe and Co. Ltd., crashed at Montevideo, Uruguay 21.8.21

G-EAYD H7428, Aircraft Disposal Co. Ltd., Croydon; crashed 13.10.21

G-EBAG H2025, Aircraft Disposal Co. Ltd.; C. of A. 4.9.23; de Havilland Aircraft Co. Ltd.; Southern Counties Av. Co. 6.25; Northern A/W 6.27; canc. 1.29

G-EBAJ E3043, 26.1.22, Marconi's Wireless Telegraph Co. Ltd., Croydon; G. L. P. Henderson, Brooklands 7.26; registration cancelled 5.28

G-EBBC H2212, 9.3.22, Derwent Hall Caine; Surrey Flying Services Ltd., Croydon 8.22; withdrawn from use 25.11.25

G-EBFL H2053, 6.6.23, de Havilland Aircraft Co. Ltd.; crashed 24.7.23

G-EBFM H2070, 6.6.23, de Havilland Aircraft Co. Ltd., Stag Lane; G. L. P. Henderson, Brooklands 5.26; crashed at Brooklands 20.9.28

G-EBHK H7488, 12.8.25, Aircraft Disposal Co. Ltd.; withdrawn from use 1.1.26

G-EBHL H2067, 4.9.23, de Havilland Aircraft Co. Ltd., Stag Lane; written off after accident 6.11.25

G-EBOK (R/R3/Re/70022), 24.7.26, Light Planes (Lancashire) Ltd., Woodford; Lancashire School of Flying Ltd., Squires Gate 8.28; cancelled 1.37

G-EBPJ E9337, 4.12.26, Nigel Norman; Norfolk & Norwich A/C, Mousehold 11.27; British Flying & Motor Services Ltd., Maylands 10.28; cancelled 12.30

G-EBPO E3387, 14.12.20, Newcastle A/C, Cramlington; J. J. Robertson 11.27; Pleasure F/S 2.29; Cramlington Aircraft Ltd. 11.29; canc. 9.31

G-EBRD 3.6.27, Henderson School of Flying Ltd.; scrapped in South Africa 1928

The Avro 548 was fitted with the V-8 Renault driving a four bladed airscrew. G-EBVE illustrated here was used by the Henderson School of Flying Ltd. at Brooklands in 1928.

G-EBSC	21.7.27, Henderson School of Flying Ltd.; crashed in South Africa 5.28
G-EBVE	8.3.28, Henderson School of Flying Ltd.; d.b.r. at Brooklands 11.28
G-EBWH	18.4.28, Henderson School of Flying Ltd., Brooklands; damaged beyond repair at Canvey Island, Essex 22.7.28
G-EBWJ	24.5.28, Henderson School of Flying Ltd.; Brooklands School of Flying Ltd. 11.28; C. B. Crawshaw, Hooton 5.31, sold as scrap circa 1932
G-AABW	(G516), 23.3.29, Surrey Flying Services Ltd., Croydon; crashed at Welling, Kent 19.9.29
G-AADT	13.4.29, Brooklands School of Flying Ltd.; E. Willox, Dyce 11.30; registration cancelled 12.31
G-ABMB	H2232, 9.7.31, Giro Aviation Co. Ltd., Southport; scrapped circa 1940
G-ABSV	7.4.32, Giro Aviation Co. Ltd., Southport; scrapped circa 1940

* Conversion of civil Avro 504K listed previously.

Avro 548A

G-EBIT	(5100), 9.5.24, North Sea Aerial & General Transport Co. Ltd., Brough; Lancashire S. of Aviation, Squires Gate 2.28; cancelled 3.38
G-EBIU	(5101), 9.5.24, North Sea Aerial & General Transport Co. Ltd., Brough; Lancashire S. of Av., Squires Gate 2.28; d.b.r. at Rhyl 17.5.37
G-EBIV	(5102), 9.5.24, North Sea Aerial & General Transport Co. Ltd.; Golds & Leeding 5.28; Maj. E. G. Clerk, Squires Gate 3.30; cancelled 3.38
G-EBKN	E449, 17.4.25, Aircraft Disposal Co. Ltd., Croydon; A. G. Head, Shoreham 2.30; parts used to rebuild Avro 504K G-EBJE in 1969 as E449 for R.A.F. Museum

Avro 552

G-EAPR	H2323, 11.7.23, A. V. Roe and Co. Ltd., Hamble; converted 1927 to Cierva C.8V as G-EBTX; reconverted to Avro 552 in 1931 as G-ABGO, see below
G-ABGO	22.4.31, L. G. Anderson, Hanworth; Inca Aviation Ltd., Hanworth 8.33; crashed at Coal Aston, Sheffield 25.10.33
G-ACAW	20.6.33, C. B. Field, Kingswood, Surrey; Plane Advertising Ltd., Abridge, Essex 4.34; registration cancelled 9.37

H. J. Hinkler at Croydon in the prototype Avian after its conversion to Avro 581E with Cirrus I engine.

G-ACAX (12), 22.12.34, C. B. Field, Kingswood, Surrey; Plane Advertising Ltd., Abridge, Essex 12.35; crashed at Sandridge, Herts 27.3.36

G-ACRP (9), 3.7.34, C. B. Field, Kingswood, Surrey; Plane Advertising Ltd., Abridge, Essex 10.34; registration cancelled 3.36

Avro 581 Avian prototype
G-EBOV (5116), 8.9.26, A. V. Roe and Co. Ltd., Hamble; converted to Avro 581A; H. J. Hinkler 4.27; conv. to Avro 581E; preserved at Brisbane

Avro 594 Avian I
G-EBQL (R3/AV/117), 12.4.27, A. V. Roe and Co. Ltd., Woodford; Light Planes (Lancs) Ltd. 11.27; converted to Mk.IV; crashed at Barton 18.11.33

G-EBQN (R3/AV/100), 12.4.27, Royal Aircraft Establishment Aero Club, Farnborough; impressed 1.40 as 2081M for use at Eastchurch

Avro 594 Avian II
G-EBRC (R3/AV/118), 13.5.27, A. V. Roe and Co. Ltd., Woodford; demonstration aircraft; lost at sea off Ventnor, Isle of Wight 6.9.27

G-EBRR (R3/AV/119), 14.7.27, A. V. Roe and Co. Ltd., Woodford; Light Planes (Lancs) Ltd., Woodford 7.27; crashed 1.29

G-EBRS (R3/AV/120), 18.7.27, A. V. Roe and Co. Ltd.; Mrs. S. C. Elliott-Lynn 7.27; to Basle Air Transport 8.27, believed as CH-202

G-EBSD (R3/AV/121), 28.7.27, Alpha engine; Avro 594C 10.27; Taxiplanes Ltd. 6.28; F. S. Lee 1.29; L. M. J. Balfour 1.30; crashed 1932

G-EBTP (R3/AV/124), 1.9.27, H. Hollingdrake, Woodford; to South Africa 2.29 as ZS-AAN

Avro 594 Avian III
G-EBTU (R3/AV/125), 23.9.27, W. N. Lancaster 'Red Rose'; to Australia 5.28 as VH-UTU; burned out at Singleton N.S.W. 6.6.36

G-EBTY (R3/AV/128), 23.9.27, J. P. Drew; D. K. Fairweather, Renfrew 1.29; to Mk. IV; H. V. Armstrong, Woodford 8.39; impressed 12.39 as 2077M

G-EBUG (R3/CN/101), 17.11.27, Lady Heath; sold to Amelia Earhart, U.S.A. 6.28, believed as NC7083

G-EBVA (R3/CN/104), 27.1.28, L. E. R. Bellairs, Shoreham; Surrey F/S, Croydon 10.29; R. Pick, Leeming 1.35; dest. by fire, Brooklands 24.10.36

G-EBVI (R3/CN/107), 18.1.28, Hampshire Aeroplane Club, Hamble; crashed 7.34

G-EBVU (R3/CN/111), 27.1.28, A. V. Roe and Co. Ltd.; Capt. H. D. Wolff (Cape Argus, Cape Town) 5.28; flown out by Lt. Murdoch; canc. 12.28

G-EBVZ (R3/CN/112), 26.1.28, Winifred Brown, Woodford; Sir Ralph Hare 2.34; crashed at Scarcliffe, Derby 19.5.34

G-EBWK (R3/CN/114), 1.3.28, Merseyside Aero & Sports, Hooton; S. D. Scott, Cowes 10.32; Bedford S. of F., Barton 10.38; sold as spares 12.40

G-EBWP (R3/CN/113), 5.3.28, A. V. Roe and Co. Ltd., Woodford; to South Africa 7.28 as G-UAAR, crashed 18.2.30 as ZS-AAR

G-EBWR (R3/CN/116), 12.3.28, A. V. Roe and Co. Ltd., Woodford; J. G. Crammond 9.28; E. K. Rayson, Buenos Aires 10.28; sold in Argentina 12.30

G-EBWU (R3/CN/117), 10.3.28, Lancs. S. of F., Squires Gate; Lt. Caspar John 6.30; Gravesend Av. 2.33; Cinque Ports F/C, Lympne 12.36; K. Lingford, Lympne 11.37; to National Studios, Elstree as stage property 8.44

G-EBWW (R3/CN/118), 15.3.28, F. P. Raynham, Woodford; sold abroad 20.3.29
G-EBXD (R3/CN/121), 5.4.28, A. V. Roe and Co. Ltd., Woodford; Light Planes
        (Lancs.) Ltd., Woodford 10.28; R. G. Davies, Woodford 4.36; canc. 12.37
G-EBXE (R3/CN/123), 3.4.28, Norfolk & Norwich A/C; Phillips & Powis Ltd.,
        Woodley 3.33; F. R. Wilson, Sywell 7.34; d.b.f. at Brooklands 24.10.36
G-EBXJ (R3/CN/133), 19.6.28, H. J. V. Ashworth, Tollerton; H. H. Selvey 10.31;
        D. S. Hunt, Tollerton 11.32; sold abroad 10.35
G-EBXO (R3/CN/124), 27.4.28, Agra Engineering Co. Ltd., Haldon; W. A. Dawson,
        Derby 10.30; S. H. Holland, Gatwick 2.33; registration cancelled 12.35

Avro 594 Avian IIIA

G-EBXX (R3/CN/233), 26.5.28, Liverpool and District Aero Club Ltd., Hooton;
        Blackpool & West Coast Air Services Ltd., Squires Gate 1.32; canc. 12.34
G-EBXY (R3/CN/234), 26.5.28, first two owners as 'XX above; J. Proctor, Squires
        Gate 1.36; Avian Syndicate, Heysham 11.38; impressed 12.39 as 2078M
G-EBXZ (R3/CN/235), 7.6.28, A. V. Roe and Co. Ltd., Woodford; to Australia 6.28 as
        VH-UHX
G-EBYA (134), 5.7.28, Liverpool & District A/C, Hooton; A. V. Roe and Co. Ltd.,
        Woodford 6.28; E. Hayes, Shrewsbury 7.28; registration cancelled 4.31
G-EBYM (151), 4.7.28, A. V. Roe and Co. Ltd., Woodford; sold in Spain to the Marques
        di Cordoba 7.28 as M-CAAE, later EC-AAE
G-EBYN (152), 5.7.28, A. V. Roe and Co. Ltd., Woodford; sold in Spain to the Marques
        di Cordoba 7.28 as M-CDDD
G-EBYO (153), 5.7.28, A. V. Roe and Co. Ltd., Woodford; Miss E. Scott 6.29; Mrs. V.
        Brailey 5.31 (Cardiff A/C); crashed at St. Lythans, Cardiff 13.12.31
G-EBYP (154), 4.7.28, A. V. Roe and Co. Ltd., Woodford; J. G. Crammond 9.30; W. F.
        Jennings, Croydon 1.32; registration cancelled 1.37
G-EBYR (155), 5.7.28, E. W. Percival; to Australia 12.30 as G-AUJY
G-EBZD (161), 17.7.28, Airways Publications Ltd., Croydon; C. M. Browne, Croydon
        12.29; crashed at Carshalton, Surrey 2.4.31
G-EBZM (160), 3.2.28, A. V. Roe and Co. Ltd.; Merseyside Aero and Sports Ltd.,
        Hooton 2.29; Giro Av. Co. Ltd., Southport 12.32; preserved at Stockport
G-AAAP (169), 5.9.28, A. V. Roe and Co. Ltd., Hamble; sold to American owner G. H.
        Storck 9.28 as floatplane NX6663; to U.S.A. as landplane NC6663
G-AAAU (177), A. V. Roe and Co. Ltd., Woodford; registration not used
G-AABU (181), A. V. Roe and Co. Ltd., Woodford; registration not used
G-AABZ (173), 29.9.28, Director of Surveys, Tanganyika; to Tanganyika 6.32 as
        VR-TAG
G-ABPU (170), EI-AAA, 5.10.28, British registered 10.9.31 to J. F. Legard; to India
        12.34 as VT-AGC
G-ACGT (171), EI-AAB, 24.10.28, U.K. registered 8.5.33; Coventry Av. Group,
        Whitley 3.35; C. S. Burney, Brooklands 6.36; preserved at Linthwaite, Yorks.

Avro 594 Avian IV

G-AAAT (172), 7.9.28, A.D.C. Aircraft Ltd., Croydon; W. P. Cubitt, Mousehold 2.31;
        Malcolm & Farquharson Ltd., Heston 6.35; scrapped at Heston 9.36
G-AABX (183), 3.10.28, P. T. Eckersley, Woodford; Light Planes (Lancs) Ltd., Barton
        11.37; H. V. Armstrong 12.38; impressed 2.40 as 2080M
G-AACE (236), 22.10.28, A. V. Roe and Co. Ltd., Woodford; R.A.E. Aero Club,
        Farnborough 9.30; impressed 1.40 as instructional airframe 2082M

G-AACF   (237), 22.10.28, Northern Air Lines, Wythenshawe; National Flying Services 4.30; Guernsey A/C 1.35; damaged by gale, Guernsey 16.11.35; stored until seized during the German occupation and shipped to Germany 3.41

G-AADF   (204), 14.12.28, Southern A/C, Shoreham; S. G. Stephens, Shoreham 1.30; F. W. Green, Cambridge 5.35; impressed 2.40 as 2074M

G-AADL   (182), 3.1.29, J. D. Siddeley; Northern Air Lines, Wythenshawe 5.29; London Air Park F/C, Hanworth 1.35; Aylesbury Airport Ltd., Chilworth 8.36; W. L. Lewis, Hanworth 6.37; Premier Aircraft Constr. Ltd. Maylands 11.37

G-AAEC   (223), 12.2.29, Light Planes (Lancs) Ltd.; W. Greenhalgh, Speke 12.36; impressed 12.39 as instructional airframe 2076M

G-AAGP   (304), 26.4.29, A. V. Roe and Co. Ltd., Woodford; sold to J. Ortiz, Madrid 1.30 as EC-FAF

G-AAGR   (232), 6.5.29, E. Cohen, Woodford; Air Travel Ltd., Penshurst 1.36; Airports Ltd., Gatwick 11.37; Earl of Cardigan, Marlborough 4.38; impressed 1.40 as instructional airframe 2071M

G-AAHD   (318), 17.5.29, A. V. Roe and Co. Ltd., Woodford; A. W. Brett, Mousehold 11.29; H. B. Chantrey, Heston 7.32; to Sweden 8.33 as SE-ADT

G-AAHE   (319), 18.5.29, W. P. Cubitt, Mousehold; A. C. P. Johnstone, Gravesend 1.31; D. I. M. Kennard 6.32; L. E. Clark, Ford 7.36; reg'n. cancelled 12.46

G-AAHK   (317), 24.6.29, Pinchin Johnson & Co. Ltd., Woodford; E. Hart 7.32; Strathtay A/C 8.36; Bedford S. of F., Barton 9.38; canc. 12.46

G-AAHN   (320), 29.5.29, A. P. Turner, Le Bourget; Chilworth F/C 6.36; Aylesbury Airport Ltd. 8.36; H. V. Armstrong 12.38; impressed 12.39 as 2079M

G-AAIJ   (325), 13.6.29, A. V. Roe and Co. Ltd., Woodford; to Spain 6.29 as M-CIAA

G-AAIK   (326), 13.6.29, A. V. Roe and Co. Ltd., Woodford; to Spain 6.29 as M-CAIA

G-AAIX   (330), 22.6.29, A. V. Roe and Co. Ltd., Woodford; G. Surtees 1.30; F. E. Buckland, Hawkwell, Essex 3.35; scrapped at Southend 1940

G-ACBV   (R3/AV/423), origin not known, 5.8.33, Phillips & Powis Aircraft Ltd.; R. Somerset, Hanworth 4.35; H. Hughes, Elstree 6.36; canc. 12.46

G-ADEO   (A25/1), 18.7.36, The Alpha Club, Hamble; impressed 1.40 as 2075M

The Cirrus Engine Company's Avian IV, G-AAAT, with prototype Cirrus Hermes I engine.

Avian IVM, G-AABR, used by A. V. Roe & Co. for trial installations 1928–30. It is shown here with a closely cowled Genet Major engine.

Avro 616 Avian IVM

G-AABR (178), 24.9.29, A. V. Roe and Co. Ltd., Woodford; cancelled 9.30

G-AABS (179), 25.6.30, A. V. Roe and Co. Ltd., Woodford; cancelled 5.31

G-AABT (180), 21.11.29, A. V. Roe and Co. Ltd., Woodford; cancelled 10.30

G-AACV (239), 9.5.29, A. V. Roe and Co. Ltd.; Airwork Ltd., Heston 3.31; J. K. Matthew, Heston 2.33; P. Randolph, Sherbourne 3.33; sold abroad 12.34

G-AAHJ (316), 25.6.29, A. V. Roe and Co. Ltd., Woodford; A.D.C. Aircraft Ltd., Croydon 2.30; crashed at Fen Ditton, Cambridge 13.6.31

G-AAKA (324), 26.9.29, Malayan Motors Ltd., Singapore; Singapore Flying Club 7.32; registration cancelled 12.32

G-AATL (415), 3.2.30, Henlys Ltd., Heston; Lt. Col. T. W. Hay 8.30; J. R. Chaplin 8.32; Phillips & Powis Ltd., Woodley 1.33; crashed 6.37

G-AATV (435), 31.1.30, Shell Co. of Egypt Ltd., Almaza; re-registered 3.33 as SU-AAG; rest. 12.34; to New Zealand 3.35 as ZK-ADQ; crashed 13.6.48

G-AAUN (438), 13.5.30, Director of Surveys, Tanganyika; reg'd. 9.31 as VR-TAA

G-AAVM (416), 24.4.30, Henlys Ltd., Heston; crashed 12.34; rest. to South Staffs Aero Club, Walsall 5.36; registration cancelled 12.46

G-AAVP (417), 29.3.30, Airwork Ltd., Heston; Henlys Ltd., Heston 2.31; P. H. Johnson, Hedon 2.33; V. H. Buchan, Shoreham 7.32; cancelled 8.45

G-AAWF (354), 2.4.30, Ferrand and Rayson Ltd., Buenos Aires; H. C. Paul, Hanworth 2.35; registration cancelled 2.36

G-AAWH (418), 18.4.30, Henlys Ltd.; C. Hunter, Heston 1.32; G. H. Miles, Shoreham 11.35; R. H. Henderson, Hanworth 9.36; impressed 2.40 as 2083M

G-ABCD (420), 14.7.30, L. M. J. Balfour; Hon. B. Lewis, Heston 2.35; S. N. Jones, Walsall 8.35; S. Staffs A/C, Walsall 8.38; dest. 12.38

G-ABCO (422), 25.7.30, Henlys Ltd., Heston; C. H. Wilson, Woodford 7.31; R. N. Birley, Woodford 7.36; crashed 12.37

G-ABDP (472), 9.9.30, Airwork Ltd., Heston; J. E. D. Shaw, Kirkbymoorside 4.32; Herts & Essex A/C, Broxbourne 9.38; Grimsby Av., 10.38; cancelled 12.46

G-ABHL (489), 15.1.31, A. V. Roe and Co. Ltd., Woodford; cancelled 9.31

G-ABIC (486), 16.2.31, Director of Surveys, Tanganyika; named 'Tanganyika'; re-registered 6.32 as VR-TAD

G-ABIE (491), 30.1.31, Anglo American Oil Co. Ltd., 'High Test'; R. A. Carder, Heston 4.32; S. Jackson, Heston 7.32; crashed in Italy 23.10.34

G-ABIW (500), 3.3.31, K. Greenacre, Gatwick; R. Somerset, Hanworth 7.37; Isle of Wight Flying Club, Sandown 2.39; registration cancelled 12.46

G-ABKA (503), 21.5.31, Air Service Training Ltd., Hamble; burned out at Heston 18.7.32 when flare set fire to grass during night flying

G-ABKB (504), 20.6.31, Air Service Training Ltd., Hamble; impressed as instructional airframe 2.40 as 2073M

G-ABME (529), 23.5.31, A. J. A. Wallace Barr, Heston; A. H. Tweddle, Hanworth 7.35; to Australia 11.36 as VH-UVR; registration cancelled 2.59

G-ABMO (532), 27.8.331, Merseyside Aero & Sports Ltd., Hooton; F. A. Montague, Heston 8.36; A. T. Lawson-Tancred 4.37; impressed 1.40 as 2070M

G-ABSC (562), 8.2.32, Air Service Training Ltd., Hamble; L. Lipton, Southend 8.38; scrapped at Gravesend during 1939–45 war

G-ABUN (587), 29.3.32, Air Service Training Ltd., Hamble; L. Lipton, Southend 9.38; registration cancelled 12.46

G-ABVL (588), 6.4.32, A. M. D. Grenfell; Merseyside Aero & Sports Ltd., Hooton 3.33; to Sweden 7.36 as SE-AEZ; crashed in Lake Vättern 1939

G-ACIF (656), 29.7.33, Merseyside Aero & Sports Ltd., Hooton; J. Allen, Woodley 9.36; C. B. Wilkington, Doncaster 10.37; reg'n. cancelled 12.46

G-ACKE (414), VH-UOB, 6.2.30, British reg'd, 13.9.33; Merseyside Aero & Sports Ltd., Hooton 12.34; H. M. Woodhams, Baginton 1.49; d.b.r. 26.7.50

G-ACNK (479), 11.11.30, ex South African, registered 6.2.34 to Flt. Lt. E. H. Wheelwright, Shaibah; P.O. W. N. Stubbs, Shaibah 1.36; J. H. Van, Hanworth 6.39; impressed 2.40 as instructional airframe 2072M

Avro 616 Sports Avian

G-AAWI (454), 24.5.30, Light Planes (Lancs.) Ltd., Woodford; H. R. Starkey-Howe, Heston 12.35; to South Africa 2.37 as ZS-ANP; to SAAF 1940 as '2028'

G-AAXH (456), 20.6.30, Henlys Ltd., Heston; A. Wynn Eaton, Heston 4.35; British Landing Gears Ltd., Hanworth 7.36; scrapped 1.49

G-AAYU (419), 29.5.30, A. V. Roe and Co. Ltd., Woodford; S. Gleave, Woodford 2.36; crashed at Cheltenham 21.9.36

G-ABCE (421), 25.7.30, H. H. Youngman, Heston; H. G. Selfridge, Heston 7.30; to Holland 6.35 as PH-OVG; to France 11.36 as F-APFL

G-ABDN (423), 25.8.30, A. V. Roe and Co. Ltd., Woodford; R. A. Carder, Heston 8.30; H. B. Chantrey, York 5.32; crashed at Skegness 6.6.33

G-ABEA (424), 6.9.30, N. Holden, Selsey Bill; to Kenya 10.31 as VP-KAN

G-ABED (474), 17.12.30, Winifred Brown, Woodford, 'Jerry'; Raquan Asphalt, Broxbourne 10.36; Herts & Essex A/C 8.38; d.b.f. Hooton 8.7.40

G-ABEE (473), 12.12.30, A. V. Roe & Co. Ltd.; R. H. Dobson 5.31; A. Voor-sanger, Woodford 10.32; H. R. A. Edwards 6.34; in storage at Stockport in 1972

G-ABIB (490), 24.1.31, British Petroleum Co. Ltd., Heston; J. G. Ormston, Broxbourne 2.32; to India 11.33 as VT-AEV

G-ABIM (501), 11.3.31, Shell Mex & B.P. Ltd.; R. Frogley, Broxbourne 1.35; V. A. Ercolani, Broxbourne 6.36; Grimsby Av. Ltd. 10.38; cancelled 12.46

Avro Five G-ABBY, the Air Service Training navigational trainer, flying near Hamble in 1934. (*Aeroplane*)

G-ABKI   (505), 9.4.31, Henlys Ltd., Heston; L. E. R. Bellairs, Shoreham 4.31; Malcolm & Farquharson Ltd., Heston 5.35; to Sweden 10.35 as SE-AEN

G-ABLF   (522), 1.5.31, Henlys Ltd., Heston; Brooklands Aviation Ltd. 8.35; A. Bilbe-Robinson, Brooklands 12.35; to Australia 8.36 as VH-UVX

G-ABSS   (576), 24.12.31, W. Cunningham, Ronaldsway, I.O.M.; H. Mason, Speke 8.35; crashed in the River Mersey 1.2.36

G-ACGV (649), 8.6.33, Merseyside Aero & Sports Ltd., Hooton; Dr. J. W. A. Hunter, Barton 6.36; presented to the R.A.F. 8.40 as 2235M

Avro 616 Avian IVA and Avian V
G-ABCF   (467), 26.9.30, Avian IVA, Sir Charles Kingsford Smith, Sydney; G. Menzies, New Zealand 12.30; crashed at Sydney, Australia 12.4.31

G-ABLK   (523), 21.7.31, Avian V, Sir Charles Kingsford Smith, Sydney; W. N. Lancaster, Heston 4.33; lost in the Sahara 12.4.33; wreck found 3.62

Avro 618 Ten
G-AADM (241), 26.8.29, A. V. Roe and Co. Ltd.; to Australian National Airways Ltd. 8.29 as VH-UMF 'Southern Cloud'; lost in the Strathbozie Mts. 21.3.31

G-AASP   (384), 23.4.31, A. V. Roe and Co. Ltd.; Iraq Petroleum Transport Co. Ltd., 4.31; Imperial Airways Ltd. 'Achilles' 6.33; destroyed 3.4.40

G-ABLU   (528), 18.6.31, Imperial Airways Ltd. 'Apollo'; Iraq Petroleum Transport Co. Ltd. 10.32; Imperial Airways Ltd. 6.33; crashed in Belgium 30.12.33

G-ABSP   (525), 22.12.31, Airwork Ltd., Heston; to Egyptian Army Air Force, Cairo 1.32 as F200; crashed at Assiut, Egypt 10.12.33

G-ABSR   (526), 29.12.31, Airwork Ltd., Heston; to Egyptian Army Air Force, Cairo 1.32 as F201; to Indian National A/W, Delhi 9.34 as VT-AFX

G-ACGF   (527), 3.5.33, Midland and Scottish Air Ferries Ltd., Renfrew; registration cancelled 12.46

Avro 619 Five
G-AASO   (383), 10.3.30, A. V. Roe and Co. Ltd.; Wilson Airways Ltd., Nairobi 9.30; damaged beyond repair near Broken Hill, N. Rhodesia 18.1.32

G-ABBY (458), 8.4.31, A. V. Roe and Co. Ltd; Air Service Training Ltd., Hamble 5.33; scrapped at Hamble after C. of A. expiry 7.3.41

Avro 621 Tutor

G-AAKT (321), 7.1.30, A. V. Roe and Co. Ltd., Woodford; to the R.A.F. 1930
G-AARZ (322), 17.6.30, A. V. Roe and Co. Ltd., Woodford; test flown as K-4; used by National Aviation Day Displays Ltd. 1932–34; crashed 10.6.34
G-AATU (437), 12.12.30, A. V. Roe and Co. Ltd., Woodford; w.f.u. 10.31
G-ABAP (461), 18.7.30, Director of Surveys, Tanganyika; re-registered 2.32 as VR-TAB; impressed locally during 1939–45 war.
G-ABAR (462), 30.9.30, Director of Surveys, Tanganyika; re-registered 2.32 as VR-TAC; impressed locally during 1939–45 war.
G-ABFL (477), 20.10.30, A. V. Roe and Co. Ltd., Woodford; demonstration machine tested to destruction 1.31
G-ABGH (485), 17.11.30, A. V. Roe and Co. Ltd., Hamble; floatplane trials; transferred to the R.A.F. at Felixstowe 12.32
G-ABHA (487), 4.3.31, Director of Surveys, Tanganyika; re-registered 6.32 as VR-TAE; impressed locally during 1939–45 war
G-ABIR (497), 12.3.31, Air Service Training Ltd., Hamble; impressed 10.41 as HM504; d/d to No. 1403 A.T.C. Sqn., Radford, Notts. 4.42 as 3065M
G-ABIS (498), 27.3.31, Air Service Training Ltd., Hamble; impressed 10.41 as HM505; d/d to No. 1493 A.T.C. Sqn., Leeds 12.41 as 3064M
G-ABZP (624), 3.11.32, National Aviation Day Displays Ltd.; North Eastern Airways Ltd., Doncaster 6.37; Doncaster Aero Club 7.38; scrapped 1940
G-ABZR (625), 3.11.32, National Aviation Day Displays Ltd.; crashed during air display at Cape Town 17.2.33
G-ACOV K1791, 29.5.34, Air Pageants Ltd.; crashed 12.34
G-ADMG (795), A. V. Roe and Co. Ltd., Woodford; to the Greek Air Force 12.35 as E-69
G-ADYW K1231, 23.6.36, T. C. L. Westbrook, Eastleigh; reg'n. cancelled 12.46
G-AFZW K3237, 3.4.40, Portsmouth, Southsea and I.O.W. Aviation Ltd., Portsmouth; impressed 4.40 as AV980; to instructional airframe as 2427M
G-AHSA K3215, 20.7.47, J. Neasham, Croft; F. C. Bettison, Stansted 4.51; G. S. Haywood, Burnaston 8.51; Shuttleworth Trust 1959; restored as K3215
G-AIYM K3363, A. P. Fraser, Redhill 7.47; scrapped at Croydon in 1949
G-AKFJ K6105, 17.12.47, W. Sturrock, Bracebridge Heath, Lincs.; Doncaster Ultra Light Aircraft Group 9.48; crashed on take-off, Doncaster 30.7.49

Avro 624 Six

G-AAYR (457), 25.6.30, A. V. Roe and Co. Ltd., Woodford; to the Far East Aviation Co. Ltd., Hong Kong 12.31 as VR-HAQ

Avro 625 Avian Monoplane

G-AAYV (459), 27.6.30, A. V. Roe & Co. Ltd.; conv. to biplane; S. H. Beech, Meir 11.34; London Transport F/C, Broxbourne 9.36; written off in 1939
G-AAYW (460), 27.6.30, Flt. Lt. R. L. R. Atcherley, Market Drayton; W. L. Handley, Elmdon 6.40; scrapped during 1939–45 war

Avro 626

G-ABFM (478), 30.12.30, A. V. Roe and Co. Ltd.; sold in the Argentine 9.31

G-ABGG (476), K-7, 6.8.31, A. V. Roe and Co. Ltd., Woodford; sold abroad 1.37

G-ABJG (496), 3.6.31, A. V. Roe and Co. Ltd., Woodford; modification test machine flown as K-10; converted to Avro 637 prototype; cancelled 12.46

G-ABRK (553), 15.3.32, A. V. Roe and Co. Ltd., Earl of Amherst, Heston 7.32; W. R. Westhead, Heston 2.35; C. Lewis, Hanworth 12.36; sold abroad 9.37

G-ABYM (622), 24.8.32, Air Service Training Ltd., Hamble; scrapped 1939

G-ACFW (648), 12.10.33, A. V. Roe and Co. Ltd., Woodford; scrapped in 1950

G-ACFZ (643), 12.6.33, A. V. Roe and Co. Ltd., Hamble; floatplane trials aircraft; sold in Brazil 9.36

G-ADKZ (862), 2.8.35, A. V. Roe and Co. Ltd.; flown to Czechoslovakia 12.35

G-ADUJ (868), 15.11.35, A. V. Roe and Co. Ltd.; sold in Australia 12.35

G-AEGA (923), 14.5.36, A. V. Roe and Co. Ltd.; flown to Austria 1.37

G-AEGB (924), 22.5.36, A. V. Roe and Co. Ltd.; flown to Austria 1.37

G-AEGC (925), 2.6.36, A. V. Roe and Co. Ltd.; flown to Austria 1.37

G-AEVI (982), 15.4.37, A. V. Roe and Co. Ltd.; flown to Austria 6.37

G-AEVJ (983), 23.4.37, A. V. Roe and Co. Ltd.; flown to Austria 6.37

G-AEVK (984), 30.4.37, A. V. Roe and Co. Ltd.; flown to Austria 6.37

G-AHRZ K5069, 27.7.46, Southern Aircraft (Gatwick) Ltd., Gatwick; scrapped at Gatwick in 1948

G-AHVO K5066, 9.7.46, Southern Aircraft (Gatwick) Ltd.; L. E. Gisborne, Denham 10.46; A. G. Harding, Hastings 9.48; scrapped at Hastings in 1950

Avro 631 Cadet

G-ABRS (558), 15.3.32, A. V. Roe and Co. Ltd., Woodford; to the Far East Aviation School, Hong Kong 10.34 as VR-HCS; reg'n. cancelled 2.36

G-ABVU (592), 8.6.32, A. V. Roe and Co. Ltd., Woodford; Light Planes (Lancs) Ltd., Barton 3.36; scrapped at Barton 5.51

G-ABVV (589), 28.5.32, Maj. J. E. Durrant Shaw, Kirkbymoorside; crashed at Welburn, Yorks. 30.5.39 while glider towing out of Sutton Bank

G-ABWJ (597), 18.6.32, A. V. Roe and Co. Ltd., Woodford; to Brazil 1.37 as PP-TJC

G-ABWS (606), 9.6.32, Air Service Training Ltd., Hamble; impressed 9.41 as 2957M and delivered to the Air Training Corps at Stroud, Glos.

G-ABXU (607), 25.6.32, Air Service Training Ltd., Hamble; impressed 1.42 as 2958M and delivered to No. 1821 A.T.C. Sqn. at Oakdale, Wales

G-ABYC (621), 27.7.32, Yardley and Co. Ltd., Hamsey Green; Light Planes (Lancs) Ltd., Barton 11.34; scrapped at Barton 5.51

G-ABZF (623), 4.10.32, A. V. Roe and Co. Ltd., Hooton 6.33; F. G. Miles, Woodley 1935; scrapped in 1936

G-ACCH (627), 27.3.33, Air Service Training Ltd., Hamble; to spares 12.41

G-ACCI (628), 27.3.33, Air Service Training Ltd., Hamble; impressed 7.41 as 2945M and delivered to No. 1431 A.T.C. Sqn., Newbiggin-by-the-Sea

G-ACCJ (629), 3.4.33, Air Service Training Ltd., Hamble; impressed 7.41 as 2946M and delivered to No. 1084 A.T.C. Sqn., Market Harborough

G-ACCK (630), 3.4.33, Air Service Training Ltd., Hamble; impressed 8.41 as 2952M and delivered to No. 473 A.T.C. Sqn., Hartlepool

G-ACCL (631), 6.4.33, Air Service Training Ltd., Hamble; scrapped 3.42

450

G-ACCM (632), 22.4.33, Air Service Training Ltd., Hamble; night crash in the River Thames, Purfleet, Essex 17.4.36

G-ACCN (633), 25.4.33, Air Service Training Ltd., Hamble; impressed 7.41 as 2939M and delivered to No. 392 A.T.C. Sqn., Newmarket

G-ACMG (682), 3.1.34, Light Planes (Lancs.) Ltd., Barton; damaged beyond repair at Adlington, Cheshire 3.12.34

G-ACNE (692), 9.3.34, Air Service Training Ltd., Hamble; damaged beyond repair in take-off accident, Hamble 10.7.40

G-ACNF (693), 12.3.34, Air Service Training Ltd., Hamble; impressed 8.41 as 2953M and delivered to No. 273 A.T.C. Sqn., Wallasey, Cheshire

G-ACRY (701), 22.5.34, Air Service Training Ltd., Hamble; crashed in the Solent off Hillhead, Hants., 4.6.34

G-ACRZ (702), 22.5.34, Air Service Training Ltd., Hamble; impressed 2.42 as 2962M and delivered to No. 696 A.T.C. Sqn., Stroud, Glos.

G-ACUH (724), 10.7.34, Air Service Training Ltd., Hamble; crashed near Southampton 10.9.34

G-ADAU (806), 18.2.35, Air Service Training Ltd., Hamble; impressed 2.42 as 2970M and delivered to No. 36F A.T.C. Sqn., Enfield, Middlesex

G-ADAV (805), 18.2.35, Air Service Training Ltd., Hamble; impressed 8.41 as 2954M and delivered to No. 1178 A.T.C. Sqn., Wigan, Lancs.

G-ADCX (813), 17.4.35, Air Service Training Ltd., Hamble; impressed 9.41 as 2956M and delivered to the A.T.C. at Seaford, Sussex

Avro 638 Club Cadet

G-ACAY (626), 2.6.33, A. V. Roe and Co. Ltd.; H. Constant, Heston 6.33; Southend Flying Services Ltd. 22.1.37; scrapped at Southend in 1940

G-ACGY (650), 6.6.33, Light Planes (Lancs.) Ltd., Barton; to the Aero Club de Mocambique 2.39 as CR-AAS

G-ACHN (651), 22.6.33, Airwork Ltd., Heston; Airwork Flying Club Ltd., Heston 11.38; crashed during 1939–45 war

G-ACHO (652), 26.6.33, Airwork Ltd., Heston; Airwork Flying Club Ltd., Heston 11.38; shipped abroad 6.41

Douglas Fairweather's Hermes IVA Club Cadet at Southend in 1935 after being sold to the local flying club. (*A. J. Jackson*)

G-ACHP (653), 26.6.33, Airwork Ltd., Heston; Airwork Flying Club Ltd., Heston 11.38; impressed to Saunders-Roe Ltd., Cowes 7.42 as HM570; Vintage Aeroplane Club, White Waltham 1952; crashed at Denham 1.1.56

G-ACHW (654), 3.8.33, F. Tyzack, Sywell; S. P. Tyzack, Sywell 9.33; Southend Flying Services Ltd. 12.38; scrapped at Southend in 1940

G-ACHY (655), registered 12.6.33 to A. V. Roe and Co. Ltd.; construction abandoned

G-ACIL (661), K-11, 18.7.33, D. K. Fairweather, Renfrew; Southend Flying Services Ltd. 9.35; crashed at Thundersley, Essex 22.12.35

G-ACJZ (667), 16.9.33, S. L. Turner, Heston; Southend Flying Services Ltd. 7.35; scrapped at Southend in 1940

G-ACNY (686), 24.3.34, Lord Londonderry, Newtownards; Airwork Flying Club Ltd., Heston 11.38; shipped abroad 6.41

G-ACTB (704), 1.6.34, Henlys Ltd., Heston; Southend Flying Services Ltd. 9.35; scrapped at Southend in 1940

G-ACTX (718), 27.6.34, Airwork Ltd., Heston; Lord Londonderry, Newtownards 7.36; Southend Flying Services Ltd. 1938; scrapped at Southend in 1940

G-ACTY (719), registered 11.6.34 to Airwork Ltd., construction abandoned

G-ACTZ (720), 14.7.34, Airwork Ltd., Heston; shipped abroad 2.41

G-ACZS (797), 8.2.35, Henlys Ltd., Heston; Airwork Ltd., Heston 3.37; H. S. Ford, Heston 5.38; Airwork Ltd., Heston 8.38; shipped abroad 6.41

G-ADBC (807), 7.2.35, Earl of Essex, Manorbier; Brian Allen Aviation Ltd., Croydon 6.36; to France 4.37 as F-AQCJ

G-ADEH (816), 10.4.35, York County Aviation Club, Sherburn; Tollerton Aero Club Ltd. 11.37; scrapped at Tollerton in 1950

Avro 639 Cabin Cadet

G-ACGA (639), K-14, registered 12.4.33 to A. V. Roe and Co. Ltd., Woodford; scrapped at Woodford in 1936

G-ACMD (686), registered 22.11.33 to A. V. Roe and Co. Ltd., Woodford; not flown with cabin; completed as Avro 638 Club Cadet G-ACNY

Avro 640 Cadet three seater

G-ACFH (640), 28.4.33, Scottish Motor Traction Co. Ltd., Renfrew; Utility Airways Ltd., Hooton 7.35; burned in hangar fire, Hooton 8.7.40

G-ACFS (644), 18.5.33, Scottish Motor Traction Co. Ltd., Renfrew; Utility Airways Ltd., Hooton 7.35; burned in hangar fire, Hooton 8.7.40

G-ACFT (645), 18.5.33, Scottish Motor Traction Co. Ltd., Renfrew; Aircraft Facilities Ltd., Hooton 7.35; burned in hangar fire, Hooton 8.7.40

G-ACFU (646), 18.5.33, Scottish Motor Traction Co. Ltd., Renfrew; T. Campbell Black; crashed at Leigh, Lancs. 2.8.37

G-ACFX (647), 23.6.33, Midland and Scottish Air Ferries Ltd., Renfrew; to Perak Flying Club 11.36 as VR-RAJ

G-ACJX (666), 14.10.33, Henlys Ltd., Heston; dismantled 11.34

G-ACLU (679), 11.4.33, Sir Alan Cobham; C. W. A. Scott's Flying Display Ltd., Croydon 3.36; A. Harris, Broxbourne 12.36; sold abroad 4.39

G-ACOZ (697), 11.4.33, Sir Alan Cobham; C. W. A. Scott's Flying Display Ltd., Croydon 3.36; scrapped in 1941

G-ACPB (696), 11.4.34, Sir Alan Cobham; C. W. A. Scott's Flying Display Ltd., Croydon 3.36; J. L. Bebb, Croydon 2.37; burned at Hooton 8.7.40

Avro 641 Commodore

G-ACNT   (691), 18.5.34, W. R. Westhead, Heston; A. V. Roe and Co. Ltd., Woodford 4.35; dismantled at Woodford 13.10.39; believed scrapped in 1950

G-ACRX   (700), 3.7.34, Earl of Amherst, Heston;; Airwork Ltd. 5.35; V. H. Tait, Almaza 9.35; sold in 1936 as SU-AAS; later to Egyptian Army Air Force

G-ACUA   (721), 11.8.34, Airwork Ltd., Heston; to Egypt 1936 as SU-AAU; later sold to the Egyptian Army Air Force

G-ACUG   (722), 28.9.34, Maj. J. E. Durrant Shaw, Kirkbymoorside; impressed 2.41 as DJ710; to H.Q. Training F.P. Pool; crashed at White Waltham 10.8.41

G-ACZB   (729), 24.4.35, Henlys Ltd., Heston; Sir W. G. Armstrong Whitworth Aircraft Ltd., Whitley 3.36; impressed 8.41 as HH979; scrapped 8.42

The fourth production Commodore in the white and blue colours of Major J. E. Durrant Shaw.

Avro 642/2m

G-ACFV   (642), 29.1.34, Midland and Scottish Air Ferries Ltd. Renfrew 'Marchioness of Londonderry'; Commercial Air Hire Ltd., Croydon 5.35; to W. R. Carpenter Ltd., New Guinea 9.36 as VH-UXD; dest. by enemy action 3.42

Avro 643 Cadet

G-ACIH   (657), 9.3.34, Midland and Scottish Air Ferries Ltd., Renfrew; North of Ireland A/C, Newtownards 11.38; to M. P. Cahill, Dublin 4.61 as EI-ALU

G-ACXJ   (758), 12.9.34, V. H. Tait, Almaza; Airwork Ltd., Heston 10.35; York County Aviation Club, Sherburn 11.36; scrapped during 1939–45 war

G-ACZA   (794), 23.1.35, Henlys Ltd., Heston; Earl of Amherst, Shoreham 7.36; to the Perak Flying Club 1.38

G-ADEG   (817), 8.4.35, York County Aviation Club, Sherburn; Tollerton Aero Club Ltd. 11.37; scrapped at Tollerton in 1950

G-ADEX   (820), 29.5.35, Hon. R. F. Watson, Heston; L. C. Lewis, Hanworth 1.37; sold abroad 9.37

G-ADFD   (819), 24.5.35, Bristol & Wessex Aeroplane Club, Whitchurch; to the A.T.C., Wimborne, Dorset 1951; scrapped in 1961

G-ADIE   (848), 5.6.35, Sir W. Firth, Brooklands; North of Ireland A/C, Newtownards 9.38; to Ireland 9.60 as EI-ALP

Avro 643 Mk. II Cadet

G-ADJT (849), 14.9.35, A. V. Roe and Co. Ltd., Woodford; to France 3.38 as F-AQMX

G-ADTF (870), 13.11.35, Air Service Training Ltd., Hamble; impressed 8.41 as 2950M and delivered to No. 1102 A.T.C. Sqn., Melksham

G-ADTG (871), 13.11.35, Air Service Training Ltd., Hamble; impressed 7.41 as 2943M and delivered to No. 1478 A.T.C. Sqn., Golders Green, Middlesex

G-ADTH (872), 9.12.35, Air Service Training Ltd., Hamble; canc. 4.3.42

G-ADTI (873), 9.12.35, Air Service Training Ltd., Ansty; crashed at Filton 17.2.37

G-ADTJ (874), 19.12.35, Air Service Training Ltd., Ansty; impressed 12.41 as 2960M and delivered to No. 303 A.T.C. Sqn., Worksop

G-ADTK (875), 20.12.35, Air Service Training Ltd., Ansty; impressed 2.42 as 2971M and delivered to No. 227 A.T.C. Sqn., Dagenham, Essex

G-ADTL (876), 4.1.36, Air Service Training Ltd., Ansty; impressed 2.42 as 2961M and delivered to No. 1131 A.T.C. Sqn., Olney

G-ADTM (877), 9.1.36, Air Service Training Ltd., Ansty; crashed at Westend, Southampton 6.2.36

G-ADTN (878), 4.1.36, Air Service Training Ltd., Ansty; impressed 12.41 as 2972M, and delivered to the A.T.C. in Shropshire

G-ADTO (879), 9.1.36, Air Service Training Ltd., Ansty; struck off register as scrapped 1.11.45

G-ADTP (880), 9.1.36, Air Service Training Ltd., Ansty; impressed 8.41 as 2949M and delivered to No. 68 A.T.C. Sqn., Holywell

G-ADTR (881), 9.1.36, Air Service Training Ltd., Ansty; destroyed by fire in crash at Radcot Bridge, Bampton, Oxon. 16.8.40

G-ADTS (882), 11.1.36, Air Service Training Ltd., Ansty; impressed 8.41 as 2948M and delivered to No. 522 A.T.C. Sqn. at Lays School, Dundee

G-ADTT (883), 17.1.36, Air Service Training Ltd., Ansty; impressed 7.41 as 2944M and delivered to No. 973 A.T.C. Sqn., Southgate, Middlesex

G-ADTU (884), 17.1.36, Air Service Training Ltd., Ansty; impressed 7.41 as 2947M and delivered to No. 1417 A.T.C. Sqn., Leeds

G-ADTV (885), 23.1.36, Air Service Training Ltd., Ansty; impressed 7.41 as 2942M and delivered to No. 444 A.T.C. Sqn., Shoreditch, London

G-ADTW (886), 24.1.36, Air Service Training Ltd., Ansty; impressed 9.41 as 2955M and delivered to No. 499 A.T.C. Sqn., Port Talbot

G-ADTX (887), 30.1.36, Air Service Training Ltd., Ansty; impressed 7.41 as 2940M and delivered to No. 291 A.T.C. Sqn., Chelsea, London

G-ADTY (888), 31.1.36, Air Service Training Ltd., Ansty; impressed 7.41 as 2941M and delivered to No. 437 A.T.C. Sqn., Poplar, London

G-ADTZ (889), 4.2.36, Air Service Training Ltd., Ansty; cancelled 11.45

G-AEAR (922), 8.5.36, Air Service Training Ltd., Hamble; impressed 12.41 as 2959M and delivered to No. 1203 A.T.C. Sqn., Bridgnorth

G-AEIR (926), 6.7.36, Air Service Training Ltd., Hamble; crashed in the sea after take-off from Hamble 8.6.40

G-AENL (949), 13.10.36, Air Service Training Ltd., Hamble; impressed 8.41 as 2951M and delivered to No. 580 A.T.C. Sqn., Dauntsey's School, Wilts.

Avro 652

G-ACRM (698), 1.3.35, Imperial Airways Ltd., Croydon 'Avalon'; Air Service Training Ltd., Hamble 7.38; impressed for No. 811 Sqn. 2.41 as DG655

G-ACRN (699), 8.3.35, Imperial Airways Ltd., 'Ava'; Air Service Training Ltd. 7.38; impressed 2.41 as DG656; d.b.r. at Lee-on-Solent 1.10.41

Avro 652A Anson Mk. 1 and Mk. 10

G-AHBN, NK271, 23.4.46, to Italy 7.48 as I-AHBN; G-AHFV, AW996, 17.10.46, ditched off Isle of Wight 3.7.47; G-AHKF, NK602, 14.8.46, to Kenya 4.47 as VP-KDW; G-AHKG, EG449, 25.6.46, to Kenya 10.47 as VP-KEO; G-AHKH, EG526, 30.9.46, to Singapore 4.52 as VR-SDL; G-AHKI, EG771, 2.7.46, to Kenya 8.47 as VP-KEM; G-AHKJ, EG413, 20.11.46, crashed at Croydon 12.3.47; G-AHMZ, EG637, 12.9.46, to Kenya 2.50 as VP-KHP; G-AHNS, MG634, 22.11.46, to French Morocco 6.55 as F-DAEJ; G-AHNT, MG866, 22.7.46, repainted 3.56 as EI-AHO, scrapped at Portsmouth 3.58; G-AHRD, EG633, 16.7.46, to Kenya 10.47 as VP-KDX; G-AHUD (RY/LW/11943), 15.6.46, w.f.u. 2.49; G-AHXS, N9531, 20.3.47, w.f.u. 12.55; G-AHXT (RY/LW/4394), 28.2.47, w.f.u. 9.52

G-AHXS, a former R.A.F. Anson 1, N9531, civilianised at Ringway in 1947 by the Fairey Aviation Co. Ltd. It was used for aerial survey.

G--AIEZ (RY/LW/23942), 24.10.46, to Israel 5.49; G-AIFA (RY/LW/5183), 19.9.46, to Tanganyika 3.48 as VR-TAT; G-AIFB (RY/LW/8315), 13.9.46, to Israel 5.49; G-AIFC (RY/LW/7274), 25.9.46, to Israel 5.49; G-AIFD (RY/LW/2356), 11.10.46, to Aden 8.52 as VR-AAH; G-AIIC, EG492, 26.9.46, d.b.r. in Tanganyika 4.47; G-AINZ, MG218, 18.12.46, scrapped 1948; G-AIOA, NK601, 17.2.47, scrapped 1948; G-AIOB, NK843, 9.1.47, to Sweden 5.50 as SE-BRW; G-AIPA, EF866, 24.3.47, w.f.u. 4.60; G-AIPB, LT288, not converted, cancelled 4.48; G-AIPC, MG588, 9.5.47, w.f.u. 8.55; G-AIPD, NK616, 17.6.47, to Denmark 11.53 as OY-DYY; G-AIRL, MG970, not converted; G-AIRM, MG585, 21.5.48, to Southern Rhodesia 3.54 as VP-YLC; G-AIRN, NK667, 10.5.48, crashed in Italy 22.2.52; G-AIRO, N9895, not converted; G-AIRW, MH167, 5.10.48, to Kenya 7.50 as VP-KHS; G-AIRX, AX232, to Kenya 4.52 as VP-KJK; G-AITJ, MG874, 27.3.47, scrapped 1950; G-AITK, W2628, to Sweden 1950 as SE-BRT; G-AITL, EG324, 11.7.47, w.f.u. 11.51; G-AIWH, NK787, 27.4.47, to Aden 8.52 as VR-AAG; G-AIWV, NK668, 26.8.47, to Singapore 8.52 as VR-SDM; G-AIWW, MG569, 15.11.47, destroyed 16.12.47; G-AIWX, AX360, 8.5.48, scrapped 1950; G-AIXO (RY/LW/248), 28.4.47, to Israel 10.52; G-AIXT, MH236, 23.5.47, crashed at Croydon 18.7.47; G-AIXU, NK823, to spares in 1950; G-AIXV, MG241, 3.7.47, to Denmark 5.54 as OY-FAD; G-AIXW, NK648, 23.9.48, crashed at Mons, France

26.4.50; G-AIXX, R9695, 27.4.48, to France 6.48 as F-BEDZ; G-AIXY, MG966, 3.7.47, w.f.u. 1.50; G-AIXZ, EG646, 8.3.48, d.b.r. at Jersey 5.2.51; G-AIZH, MG472, not converted

G-AJBA, AX409, 28.3.47, crashed near Paris 10.2.50; G-AJCO, NK370, not converted; G-AJCP, MG829, not converted; G-AJCR, NK878, not converted; G-AJCS, NK947, not converted; G-AJCT, NK957, not converted; G-AJFX, NK826, 14.5.47, d.b.r. at Gizeh, Egypt 10.7.51; G-AJHK, NK842, 6.5.47, w.f.u. 1948; G-AJSC, AX261, VH-ALX, 25.2.48, w.f.u. 7.50; G-AJSD, DJ165, VH-AKI, 9.5.47, w.f.u. 1949; G-AJSE, DG696, VH-ALY, 25.2.48, w.f.u. 7.50; G-AJSI, EG135, VP-KDH, 20.2.47, w.f.u. 1952

G-AKEW, DJ168, 20.8.48, to Kenya 1.50 as VP-KHL; G-AKFK, NK770, 19.3.48, w.f.u. 12.52; G-AKFL, NK674, 11.6.48, crashed at Beirut, Lebanon 18.12.49; G-AKFM, MG495, 23.4.48, to Kenya 1951 as VP-KME; G-AKMV, EG239, 17.6.48, to Kenya 1.51 as VP-KHT; G-AKVW, L7909, 25.6.48, to Aden 1.53 as VR-AAI; G-AKXX, AX256, scrapped 2.49; G-AKXY, LV201, scrapped 2.49

G-ALEK, NK242, to Belgium 2.49 as OO-SRA; G-ALEL, MG247, scrapped 1.49; G-ALEM, MG756, scrapped 1.49; G-ALEN, EG435, scrapped 1.49; G-ALFD, EG689, 11.11.50, w.f.u. 11.51; G-ALFJ, NL116, crashed at Croydon 8.3.49; G-ALFP, NK971, 7.5.53, to Israel 10.52; G-ALHZ, NK451, not converted; G-ALIA, NK862, not converted; G-ALIB, NK489, not converted; G-ALIC, NK933, not converted; G-ALUM, MG901, 14.10.49, to Denmark 3.54 as OY-DYC; G-ALUR, MG471, 22.6.51, to Finland 7.52 as OH-ANA; G-ALUS, NK737, scrapped 10.50; G-ALVN, LT452, 9.11.49, to Israel 4.50; G-ALVO, LV320, 17.1.50, to Israel 4.50; G-ALWX, EG674, 16.3.51, scrapped 6.53; G-ALXB, LV273, 9.3.50, to French Morocco 10.55 as F-DAEK; G-ALXC, MH182, 31.5.50, to Ireland 3.54 as EI-AGQ, rest. 8.56, w.f.u. at Southend 1961; G-ALXD, LT959, to spares 7.50; G-ALXE, R9785, to Israel 5.50; G-ALXF, EG436, to Singapore 3.52 as VR-SDK; G-ALXG, N9904, not converted; G-ALXH, W1731, re-allotted 9.56 to Anson 11 q.v.; G-ALYE, LV280, to Israel 6.50

G-AMBE, EG228, not converted, w.f.u. 12.61; G-AMBF, DJ669, not converted; G-AMBG, MH124, not converted; G-AMBV, EG316, not converted; G-AMDA, N4877, 14.10.53, to Skyfame Museum, Staverton 1963 as N4877

Avro 652A Anson Mk. 11

G-AGLM (1204), NL246, 24.11.44, Secretary of State for Air, Croydon; M.C.A., Croydon 7.45; returned to R.A.F. 2.46 as NL246

G-ALID NK873 ⎫
G-ALIE NL186 ⎬ registered 16.2.49 to R. L. Whyham; not converted; scrapped at
G-ALIF NL132 ⎱ Kingstown Aerodrome, Carlisle in 1953
G-ALIG NL182 ⎭

G-ALIH NL229, 7.6.51, R. L. Whyham, Squires Gate; B.K.S. Ltd., Düsseldorf 4.54; E. K. Cole Ltd., Southend 8.54; w.f.u. 9.67; to Newark Air Museum 11.70

G-ALII NK996, details as G-ALID, scrapped at Squires Gate, Blackpool in 1954

G-AMBC NL231 ⎱ details as for G-ALID, scrapped at Kingstown, Carlisle in 1953
G-AMCI NK987 ⎰

Avro 652A Anson Mk. 12

G-AGLB (1205), NL152, 15.12.44, Secretary of State for Air, Madrid; returned to R.A.F. 11.48 as NL152

456

G-AGUI, one of two Avro 19 Series 1 aircraft supplied to the Ethiopian Government in 1945.

Avro 19 Series 1

G-AGNI (1214), MG159, 23.1.45, Ministry of Aircraft Production; Universal F/S Ltd., Hanworth 10.47; crashed in the Irish Sea 11.6.48

G-AGPB (1271), 3.1.46, Minister of Civil Aviation; damaged beyond repair in accident at Bovingdon 27.9.50

G-AGPG (1212), 6.8.45, A. V. Roe and Co. Ltd., Woodford; conv. to Ser.2 in 1952; Ekco Electronics Ltd., Southend 10.67; Pye Telecom. Ltd., Southend 11.69

G-AGPU (1241), 15.10.45, Secretary of State for Air, Lisbon; to the R.A.F. 2.48

G-AGUD (1275), 23.11.45, Railway A/S, Croydon; B.E.A.C. 2.47; Minister of Civil Aviation 7.48; Wiltshire S. of F. 8.54; to Germany 1.55 as N9951F

G-AGUE (1276), 23.11.45, Railway Air Services Ltd., Croydon; crashed at Speke 16.8.46

G-AGUH (1273), 2.1.46, Min. of Aircraft Prod'n.; to Ethiopia 2.47 as IEAF.120; rest. 8.49 to Hawker Aircraft Ltd.; Armstrong Siddeley Motors Ltd. 8.50; Bristol Siddeley Engines Ltd. 5.59; scrapped at Filton 10.60

G-AGUI (1274), 2.1.46, Min. of Aircraft Prod'n.; to Ethiopia 2.47 as IEAF.121; rest. to D. Sangster, Croydon 1.49; burned at Croydon 21.2.54

G-AGUX (1277), 23.11.45, Railway Air Services, Croydon; B.E.A.C. 2.47; Fairey Aviation Co. Ltd. 4.48; crashed at Villa Cisneros, Rio de Oro 15.12.51

G-AGVA (1278), 28.11.45, Railway A/S, Croydon; B.E.A.C. 2.47; Wiltshire S. of F., Thruxton 8.54; A.V.I. Enterprises Ltd. 5.55; to Germany 6.56 as D-IGOR

G-AGWA (1332), 24.6.46, Minister of Civil Aviation, Gatwick; Wiltshire School of Flying Ltd., Thruxton 8.54; to Germany 1.55 as N9923F

G-AGWD PH860, 10.1.46, Minister of Civil Aviation; registration cancelled 2.46 on sale to Misrair, Cairo as SU-ADN 'Tanta'

G-AGWE (1286), TX201, 12.6.46, Minister of Civil Aviation, Gatwick; Decca Navigator Co. Ltd. 2.53; conv. to Ser. 2; Kemp's Aerial Surveys Ltd., Thruxton 1.67

G-AGWF TX202, (1287), 12.6.46, Minister of Civil Aviation, Gatwick; Sperry Gyroscope Co. Ltd. 11.51; Fairways (Jersey) Ltd. 10.55; derelict at Croydon in 1960

G-AGZS (1330), 1.10.46, Minister of Civil Aviation, Gatwick; crashed at Petersfield, Hants. 4.1.52

G-AGZT (1331), 1.10.46, Minister of Civil Aviation, Gatwick; Channel A/S, Jersey 4.53; Fairways (Jersey) Ltd. 5.55; derelict at Croydon in 1960

G-AHIB (1317), 14.5.46, Railway A/S; B.E.A.C. 2.47; R. L. Whyham, Squires Gate 4.50; LEC Refrigeration Ltd., Bognor 6.57; w.f.u. at Wymeswold 2.60

G-AHIC (1318), 17.6.46, Railway A/S; B.E.A.C. 2.47; College of Aeronautics, Cranfield 10.51; conv. 11.61 to Ser. 2; Kemp's Aerial Surveys Ltd., Thruxton 2.65

G-AHID (1319), 17.6.46, Railway Air Services, Croydon; B.E.A.C. 2.47; Minister of Civil Aviation 5.48; conv. to Ser. 2; to Kenya 5.50 as VP-KKK

G-AHIE (1320), 24.6.46, Railway Air Services, Croydon; B.E.A.C. 2.47; Minister of Civil Aviation 5.48; R. L. Whyham, Squires Gate 4.50; burned 3.59

G-AHIF (1321), 28.6.46, Railway A/S, Croydon; B.E.A.C. 2.47; F. A. Laker, Southend 4.50; to A. B. Svenska Aero 9.50 as SE-BRS; crashed Karlstad 20.9.50

G-AHIG (1322), 2.7.46, Railway A/S, Croydon; B.E.A.C. 8.46; R. L. Whyham, Squires Gate 8.50; Fairways (Jersey) Ltd. 4.55; ditched off Calshot 6.8.55

G-AHIH (1323), 24.6.46, Railway A/S, Croydon; B.E.A.C. 2.47; Minister of Civil Aviation 5.48; Wiltshire S. of F. 7.54; to Germany 9.54 as N9924F

G-AHII (1324), 28.6.46, Railway A/S; B.E.A.C. 2.47; Starways Ltd., Speke 'Starlight' 3.50; Airtech Ltd., Thame 2.51; to Sweden 3.51 as SE-BTM

G-AHIJ (1325), 5.7.46, Railway A/S, Croydon; B.E.A.C. 8.46; Sperry Gyroscope Co. Ltd., Cranfield 11.51; to Pakistan 12.52 as AP-AGA

G-AHIK (1326), 11.7.46, Railway A/S, Croydon; B.E.A.C 8.46; Starways Ltd., Speke 'Starflight' 3.50; to Sweden 1.52 as SE-BUI

G-AHKC (1327), TX246, 2.5.46, Ministry of Supply; to Misrair, Cairo 5.46 as SU-ADQ 'Mona'

G-AHKD (1328), TX248, 2.5.46, Ministry of Supply; to Misrair, Cairo 5.46 as SU-ADP 'Radwa'

G-AHKE (1329), TX249, 2.5.46, Ministry of Supply; to Misrair, Cairo 5.46 as SU-ADO 'Arafat'

G-AHXK (1351), 8.10.46, Hunting Air Travel Ltd., Croydon; Sivewright A/W Ltd., Ringway 'Mancunia' 4.48; Hawker Aircraft Ltd., Langley 8.52; conv. to Ser. 2 in 1954; to Nicholas Air Charter Pty. Ltd. 8.62 as VH-RCC

G-AHXL (1352), 1.8.46, Hunting Air Transport Ltd., Croydon; Airways Training Ltd., Aldermaston 10.47; B.E.A.C. 11.48; to Sweden 7.50 as SE-BRP

G-AHXM (1353), 8.8.46, Hunting Air Transport Ltd., Croydon; Sperry Gyroscope Co. Ltd., Cranfield 11.49; written off landing at Blackbushe 5.11.51

G-AHYN (1359), 13.8.46, Sivewright A/W Ltd., Ringway 'Salfordia'; Sir W. G. Armstrong Whitworth Aircraft Ltd., Bitteswell 1.52; Tippers Air Transport Ltd., Baginton 10.64; W. Stevens, Elmdon 8.66; w.f.u. 4.68

G-AHYO (1360), 16.8.46, Westminster Airways Ltd., Blackbushe; crashed in Northern Rhodesia 31.10.46

G-AIIA PH858, registered 7.10.46 to the Secretary of State for Air; returned to the R.A.F. 1.3.48, stationed at Bovingdon in 1960

G-AIRV PH830, registered to the Secretary of State for Air, Heliopolis, Egypt 22.10.46; returned to the R.A.F. 21.3.49

Avro 19 Series 2

G-AHKX (1333), 17.12.46, Smiths Aircraft Instruments Ltd., Luton; later Staverton; Meridian Air Maps Ltd., Shoreham 4.61; Treffield Aviation Ltd., Rhoose 6.65; Kemp's Aerial Surveys Ltd., Thruxton 1.67

G-AIKM (1364), 31.10.46, Short & Harland Ltd., Rochester; British South American A/W, Heathrow 'Star Visitant' 10.48; crashed at Luton 21.4.49

G-AIXE (1376), 17.3.47, Sivewright Airways Ltd., Ringway 'Mancunia'; wrecked in forced landing at Chelford, Cheshire 7.1.48

G-AIYK (1375), 24.1.47, Hunting Air Travel Ltd., Luton; to Republic Air Charters, Dublin 4.55 as EI-AGW; to Algiers 4.57 as F-OBAG

G-AJDH VL336, 31.5.50, Secretary of State for Air, Aldergrove; to Malta Communications Flight 1954 as VL336; scrapped in Malta 11.54

G-AKDU (1423), 25.9.47, Secretary of State for the Colonies, Bulawayo, Southern Rhodesia; crashed at Heany, Bulawayo 30.7.50

G-AKDV (1424), 25.9.47, Secretary of State for the Colonies, Thornhill, Southern Rhodesia; crashed at Sombula, Southern Rhodesia 2.3.50

G-AKFE VP512, 12.9.47, Secretary of State for Air, Vienna (later Belgrade); returned to the R.A.F. 4.56; stationed at Bovingdon 1960

G-AKUD (1449), VM373, 20.4.48, Minister of Supply, Paris/Buc, later Boscombe Down; to R.A.F. 4.49 as VM373; rest. 5.54; to Liberia 8.55 as EL-ABC

G-ALFN (1508), VM336, 8.2.49, Secretary of State for Air, Teheran; to the R.A.F. after return to the United Kingdom 5.50

G-AMNA VL298, 4.1.52, Secretary of State for Air, Fayid, Egypt; returned to the R.A.F. 4.53

G-ANWW VS512, 14.5.55, Air Survey Co. Ltd., White Waltham; to Air Survey Co. of Rhodesia Ltd. 6.56 as VP-YOF; crashed at Maidenhead 8.7.58

G-APCF VS514, 18.7.58, Air Couriers (Transport) Ltd., Croydon; to Cie de Travaux et Services Aériens, Algiers 7.58 as F-OBIJ

G-APCG VS519, 3.12.57, Air Couriers (Transport) Ltd., Croydon; to Société Algérienne de Constructions Aéronautiques (SACA) 11.57 as F-OBAI

G-APCH VS558, 19.6.58, Air Couriers (Transport) Ltd., Croydon; to SACA, Algiers 6.58 as F-OBHB

G-APCI VS559, 14.5.59, Air Couriers (Transport) Ltd., Croydon; to Cie Generale de Transports en Algérie 5.59 as F-OBMP

G-APCJ VS561, 16.10.57, Air Couriers (Transport) Ltd., Croydon; to SACA, Algiers 10.57 as F-OBAH

G-APCK VV866, 28.1.58, Air Couriers (Transport) Ltd., Croydon; to SACA, Algiers 12.57 as F-OBGO

G-APHV VM360, 5.9.58, Hants & Sussex Aviation Ltd., Lasham; B.K.S. Air Survey Ltd., Southend 8.60; Survey Flights Ltd., Newtownards 6.64; Kemp's Aerial Surveys Ltd., Thruxton 3.69

G-APTL VM305, 18.3.60, Air Couriers (Transport) Ltd., Biggin Hill; W. S. Shackleton Ltd. 4.60; to Persia 5.60 as EP-CAA

G-AVCK TX157, registered to T.A.T. Ltd. 30.11.66; d/d Shawbury–Baginton 1.4.67; to Condor Aviation, Halfpenny Green 9.67; scrapped 1969

G-AVEV VV297, registered to T.A.T. Ltd. 27.1.67; delivered Shawbury–Baginton 9.2.67 and dismantled for spares on arrival

G-AVGR TX176, registered to W. Stevens 7.2.67; delivered to Staverton 14.3.67; scrapped at Staverton 3.69

G-AVHU TX211, registered to Mrs. L. A. Osborne 3.3.67; delivered Shawbury–Southend 14.3.67 and repainted as TX211 for Southend Air Museum

G-AVIJ TX182, registered to T.A.T. Ltd. 10.3.67; delivered Baginton–Halfpenny Green for Condor Aviation 9.67; scrapped 1969

Avro 19 Series 2 G-AWML, formerly R.A.F. Transport Command TX166, painted up for Biafra relief flights, Southend July, 1968. (*John Goring*)

G-AVPP   VM330, registered to T.A.T. Ltd. 22.6.67; delivered Shawbury–Halfpenny Green for Condor Aviation 8.7.67; dismantled for spares 1.68

G-AVTA   PH845, registered to T.A.T. Ltd. 8.8.67; delivered Shawbury–Halfpenny Green for Condor Aviation 2.9.67; scrapped 1969

G-AVVO   VL348, registered to T.A.T. Ltd. 6.10.67; d/d Shawbury–Halfpenny Green 10.11.67; further d/d to Southend 3.9.68; to Southend Air Museum 11.70

G-AVVP   VP509, registered to T.A.T Ltd. 6.10.67; delivered Shawbury–Halfpenny Green for Condor Aviation; scrapped 1969

G-AVVR   VP519, registered to T.A.T. Ltd. 6.10.67; delivered Shawbury–Halfpenny Green for Condor Aviation 15.2.68; scrapped 1969

G-AWMG VV958, 2.8.68, J. M. Smith trading as Mercy Missions, Fernando Po; crashed in Biafra while on famine relief flight 6.9.68

G-AWMH TX227, 2.8.68, J. M. Smith trading as Mercy Missions, Fernando Po; ditched off the Liberian coast near mouth of River Cess 20.6.69

G-AWML TX166, registered to Mrs. L. A. Osborne 25.7.68; d/d Shawbury–Southend 24.7.68; to Baginton 1.9.68; scrapped at Weston-super-Mare 5.70

G-AWRS   TX213, registered to Hewitt's Investments Ltd., Shoreham 14.10.68; Junex of Sweden Ltd., Biggin Hill 3.70

G-AWSA   VL349, registered to J. R. Hawke 21.10.68; stored at Norwich Airport 11.68; to the United States 8.69 as N5054

G-AWSB   VM351, registered 21.10.68 to J. R. Hawke; to the United States as N7522 and delivered via Prestwick and Stornoway 28.11.68

G-AYWA   (1361), OO-CFA, OO-DFA, OO-VIT, registered 14.4.71 to Kemp's Aerial Surveys Ltd., Thruxton

Avro 683 Lancaster

G-AGJI   DV379, 12.1.44, B.O.A.C., Hurn; scrapped at Colerne 12.47

G-AGUJ   PP689, 12.3.46, British South American Airways 'Star Pilot'; B.O.A.C. 9.49; dismantled at Langley 12.49

G-AGUK PP688, 30.1.46, British South American Airways 'Star Gold'; scrapped at Langley 1.47

G-AGUL   PP690, 1.4.46, British South American Airways 'Star Watch'; crashed at London Airport, Heathrow 23.10.47

G-AGUM PP751, 6.5.46, British South American Airways 'Star Ward'; B.O.A.C. 9.49; dismantled at Dunsfold 12.49

G-AGUN   PP744, civilianised 7.46 as G-AHVN (see below)
G-AGUO   PP746, returned to the R.A.F., not converted for civil use
G-AHJT   LL809, 13.5.46, Ministry of Supply; Flight Refuelling Ltd., Ford 8.46;
         scrapped at Tarrant Rushton 1.50
G-AHJU   LM681, 13.5.46, Ministry of Supply; Flight Refuelling Ltd., Ford 8.46;
         scrapped at Tarrant Rushton 9.51
G-AHJV   LM639, 13.5.46, Ministry of Supply; Flight Refuelling Ltd., Ford 8.46;
         scrapped at Tarrant Rushton 1.50
G-AHJW   ED866, 13.5.46, Ministry of Supply; Flight Refuelling Ltd., Ford 8.46;
         crashed near Andover 22.11.48
G-AHVN   PP744, 10.9.46, B.O.A.C, Hurn; Flight Refuelling Ltd., Tarrant Rushton 3.49;
         scrapped at Tarrant Rushton 1.50
G-AJWM   PP741, 19.7.48, British European Airways Corporation, White Waltham;
         flown to Rome and handed over to Alitalia 11.48
G-AKAB   PP739, 10.10.47, Skyways Ltd., Dunsfold 'Sky Trainer'; dismantled at
         Dunsfold as Lancastrian spares 11.48
G-AKAJ   HK557, registered 30.6.47 to Flight Refuelling Ltd. for one ferry flight to
         Tarrant Rushton to be dismantled for spares
G-AKAK   PP743 ⎤
G-AKAL   PP742 ⎬ details as G-AKAJ above
G-AKAM   PP734 ⎦
G-ALVC   NX726, registered 24.8.49 to Eagle Aviation Ltd. for one ferry flight to Luton
         to be dismantled for York spares
G-ASXX   NX611, WU-15, registered 10.64 to M. D. N. Fisher and W. R. Snadden,
         Biggin Hill; d/d to Biggin Hill 13.5.65; restored as NX611; flown away
         19.5.67; for sale at Squires Gate 3.72

Avro 685 York

G-AGFT   Registration reserved 5.11.42 but not taken up
G-AGJA   (1207), MW103, 21.2.44, B.O.A.C. 'Mildenhall'; B.S.A.A.C. 'Star Fortune'
         5.49; B.O.A.C. 'Kingston'; Lancashire Aircraft Corp. 6.51; trooping 1951–52
         as WW541 and 1952–54 as WW508; Skyways Ltd. 2.55; w.f.u. 1.59
G-AGJB   (1208), MW108, 14.4.44, B.O.A.C. 'Marathon'; trooping 1951 as WW503;
         Aviation Traders Ltd. 11.53; dismantled for spares at Stansted 1955
G-AGJC   (1209), MW113, 22.7.44, B.O.A.C. 'Malmesbury'; trooping 1951 as WW504;
         Skyways Ltd. 12.57; withdrawn from use at Stansted 1.58
G-AGJD   (1210), MW121, 28.7.44, B.O.A.C. 'Mansfield'; crashed on take-off at Castel
         Benito, Tripoli, 1.2.49
G-AGJE   (1211), MW129, 26.9.44, B.O.A.C. 'Middlesex'; B.S.A.A.C. 'Star Way' 5.49;
         B.O.A.C. 'Panama' 9.49; Lancashire Aircraft Corp. Ltd. 7.51; trooping 1951–
         54 as WW580; Skyways Ltd. 2.55; w.f.u. at Stansted 10.56
G-AGNL   (1213), TS789, 30.1.46, B.O.A.C. 'Mersey'; Lancashire Aircraft Corp. Ltd.
         7.51; trooping 1951–54 as WW581; scrapped at Stansted 3.54
G-AGNM   (1215), TS790, 28.12.45, B.O.A.C. 'Murchison'; Eagle Aviation Ltd. 10.49;
         trooping 1950–51 as XA192; Skyways Ltd. 12.52; trooping 1952 as
         WW511; scrapped at Stansted 12.58
G-AGNN   (1216), TS791, 10.10.45, B.O.A.C. 'Madras'; to South African Airways 5.47
         as ZS-BGU; rest. 9.47 to B.O.A.C.; B.S.A.A.C. 'Star Crest' 7.48; B.O.A.C.
         'Atlantic Trader' 9.49; trooping 1951 as WW465; Skyways Ltd. 5.57; with-
         drawn from use at Stansted 7.57

South African Airways' York ZS-BTT, formerly B.O.A.C. G-AGNS 'Melville', being made ready for service at Hurn, 17 August 1947. (*E. J. Riding*)

G-AGNO (1217), TS792, 31.8.45, B.O.A.C. 'Manton'; Lancashire Aircraft Corp. 6.51; trooping 1951–54 as WW577, later WW576; Skyways Ltd. 3.55; withdrawn from use at Stansted and scrapped 12.56

G-AGNP (1218), TS793, 14.9.45, B.O.A.C.; 'Manchester'; South African Airways 5.47 as ZS-BRA; rest. 9.47 to B.O.A.C.; Lancashire Aircraft Corp. 7.53; trooping 1954 as WW509; to Air Liban 9.53 as OD-ABT; to OD-ACZ 6.57

G-AGNR (1219), TS794, 22.9.45, B.O.A.C.; South African A/W 4.47 as ZS-ATP 'Springbok'; rest. 5.47 B.O.A.C. 'Moira'; crashed at Az-Zubair 16.7.47

G-AGNS (1220), TS795, 20.10.45, B.O.A.C. 'Melville'; South African A/W 4.47 as ZS-BTT; rest. 9.47 to B.O.A.C.; B.S.A.A.C. 'Star Glory' 5.49; B.O.A.C. 'Pacific Trader' 9.49; trooping 1951 as WW466; damaged beyond repair on take-off at Idris, Libya 22.4.56

G-AGNT (1221), TS796, 31.10.45, B.O.A.C. 'Mandalay'; South African Airways 6.47 as ZS-ATU; rest. 10.47 to B.O.A.C.; Lancashire Aircraft Corp. 7.53; trooping 1953–54 as WW514; Skyways Ltd. 3.55; w.f.u. at Stansted 12.56

G-AGNU (1222), TS797, 14.12.45, B.O.A.C. 'Montgomery'; South African Airways 1.46 as ZS-ATR 'Impala'; rest. 9.47 to B.O.A.C.; B.S.A.A.C. 'Star Dawn' 7.49; B.O.A.C. 'Nassau' 9.49; Air Charter Ltd. 'New Endeavour' 9.52; trooping 1954 as XD670; to Trans Mediterranean A/W 12.56 as OD-ACO

G-AGNV (1223), TS798, 9.12.45, B.O.A.C. 'Morville', later 'Middlesex'; Skyways Ltd. 4.55; d/d to Skyfame Museum, Staverton 9.10.65; repainted as LV633

G-AGNW (1224), TS799, 24.1.46, B.O.A.C. 'Morecambe'; South African A/W 3.46 as ZS-ATS 'Sable'; B.O.A.C. 'Caribbean Trader' 9.47; Lancashire Aircraft Corp. 6.51; trooping 1952 as WW581; to Persian A/S 2.55 as EP-ADB

G-AGNX (1225), TS800, 6.2.46; B.O.A.C. 'Moray'; B.S.A.A.C. 'Lima' 7.49; B.O.A.C. 9.49; Lancashire Aircraft Corp. 5.51; trooping 1952 as WW582; dismantled at Stansted 6.53

G-AGNY (1226), TS801, 23.2.46, B.O.A.C. 'Melrose'; Eagle Aviation Ltd. 10.49; Skyways Ltd. 1.53; trooping 1953 as WW510; crashed at Kyritz, East Germany 26.6.54

G-AGNZ (1227), TS802, 7.6.46, B.O.A.C. 'Monmouth'; South African Airways 5.47 as ZS-BRB; rest. 6.47 to B.O.A.C.; Eagle Aviation Ltd. 10.49; crashed near Gatow, Berlin after engine fire on take-off 24.8.52

G-AGOA (1228), TS803, 28.8.46, B.O.A.C. 'Montrose'; Lancashire Aircraft Corp. 6.51; trooping 1952 as WW542; scrapped at Squires Gate 1.54

462

G-AGOB   (1229), TS804, 22.6.46, B.O.A.C. 'Milford'; Lancashire Aircraft Corp. 6.51; trooping 1952 as WW501; Skyways Ltd. 3.55; w.f.u. Stansted 2.62

G-AGOC   (1230), TS805, 19.4.46, B.O.A.C. 'Malta'; B.S.A.A.C. 'Star Path' 5.49; B.O.A.C. 9.49; dismantled at Hurn 11.49

G-AGOD   (1231), TS806, 2.7.46, B.O.A.C. 'Midlothian'; Lancashire Aircraft Corp. 6.51; trooping 1952–54 as WW576, later WW577; Skyways Ltd. 3.55; to Persian Air Services 12.55 as EP-ADC; later to T.M.A. as OD-ACP

G-AGOE   (1232), TS807, 17.7.46, B.O.A.C. 'Medway'; Lancashire Aircraft Corp. Ltd. 8.52; scrapped at Stansted 1.55

G-AGOF   (1233), TS808, 16.9.46, B.O.A.C. 'Macduff'; South African A/W 4.47 as ZS-ATT; rest. 9.47 to B.O.A.C.; Lancashire Aircraft Corp. 3.52; trooping 1952–53 as WW579; scrapped at Squires Gate 2.55

G-AGSL   (1236), TS809, 25.10.46, B.O.A.C. 'Morley'; Lancashire Aircraft Corp. 6.51; trooping 1952 as WW579; scrapped at Squires Gate 6.54

G-AGSM   (1237), TS810, 8.10.46, B.O.A.C. 'Malvern'; Lancashire Aircraft Corp. 6.51; trooping 1952 as WW540; scrapped at Stansted 3.50

G-AGSN   (1238), TS811, 8.11.46, B.O.A.C. 'Marlow'; Lancashire Aircraft Corp. 8.51; trooping 1952 as WW578; withdrawn from use at Stansted 1952

G-AGSO   (1239), TS812, 2.5.46, B.O.A.C. 'Marston'; trooping 1951 as WW476; Skyways Ltd., Stansted 12.57; withdrawn from use 4.58

G-AGSP   (1240), TS813, 11.5.46, B.O.A.C. 'Marlborough', later 'Santiago'; scrapped at London/Heathrow 5.55

G-AHEW   (1300), 27.5.46, British South American Airways Corporation 'Star Leader'; crashed at Bathurst, Gambia 7.9.46

G-AHEX   (1301), 20.6.46, British South American Airways Corporation 'Star Venture'; crashed at Caravellas, Brazil 5.1.49

G-AHEY   (1302), 5.7.46, B.S.A.A.C. 'Star Quest'; B.O.A.C. 9.49; Lancashire Aircraft Corp. 4.52; trooping 1952 as WW506; Skyways Ltd. 3.55; to Arab Airways 6.56 as JY-ABZ; rest. 10.56; scrapped at Stansted 8.62

G-AHEZ   (1303), 24.7.46, B.S.A.A.C. 'Star Speed'; crashed at Dakar 13.4.47

G-AHFA   (1304), 18.8.46, B.S.A.A.C. 'Star Dale'; B.O.A.C. 9.49; Lancashire Aircraft Corp. 12.51; trooping 1952 as WW504; lost in Atlantic 2.2.53.

G-AHFB   (1305), 28.8.46, B.S.A.A.C. 'Star Stream'; B.O.A.C. 9.49; Lancashire Aircraft Corp. 9.51; trooping 1952 as WW499, later WW586; Airspan Travel Ltd. 8.54; Skyways Ltd. 1.55; to Arab Airways 6.57 as JY-AAC; rest. 5.58 to Skyways Ltd., Luton; scrapped at Luton 4.63

G-AHFC   (1306), 12.9.46, B.S.A.A.C. 'Star Dew'; B.O.A.C. 9.49; Lancashire Aircraft Corp. 4.52; trooping 1953 as WW507; Skyways Ltd. 3.55; to Air Liban 10.55 as OD-ACJ; to Saudi Arabia as HZ-CAA and Persia as EP-ADD

G-AHFD   (1307), 21.9.46, B.S.A.A.C. 'Star Mist'; B.O.A.C. 9.49; Lancashire Aircraft Corp. 11.51; trooping 1952 as WW500; Skyways Ltd. 3.53; to Middle East Airlines, Beirut, Lebanon 6.57 as OD-ADB

G-AHFE   (1308), 30.9.46, B.S.A.A.C. 'Star Vista'; B.O.A.C. 9.49; Lancashire Aircraft Corp. 8.51; trooping 1952 as WW468, later WW578; Skyways Ltd., Stansted 3.55; withdrawn from use at Stansted 2.60

G-AHFF   (1309), 18.10.46, B.S.A.A.C. 'Star Gleam'; B.O.A.C. 9.49; Lancs. Aircraft Corp. 1.52; trooping 1953 as WW503; Skyways Ltd. 3.55; w.f.u. 9.59

G-AHFG   (1310), 25.10.46, B.S.A.A.C. 'Star Haze'; B.O.A.C. 9.49; Lancashire Aircraft Corp. 9.51; trooping 1952 as WW468; Skyways Ltd. 3.55; withdrawn from use at Stansted 10.56

G-AHFH (1311), 31.10.46, B.S.A.A.C. 'Star Glitter'; B.O.A.C. 9.49; Lancashire Aircraft Corp. 11.51; trooping 1952 as WW502; Skyways Ltd., Stansted 3.55; to Middle East Airlines, Beirut, Lebanon 6.57 as OD-ADA

G-AHFI (1316), 13.5.46, Skyways Ltd., Dunsfold 'Skyway'; crashed at Gatow Airport, Berlin 16.3.49

G-AHLV (1340), 3.6.46, Skyways Ltd., Dunsfold 'Sky Courier'; withdrawn from use at Stansted 2.52

G-AIUP (1374), 14.2.47, Skyways Ltd., Dunsfold 'Sky Consul'; crashed on landing at London/Heathrow 25.7.47

G-ALBX (PC4494), FM400, 17.10.48, Skyways Ltd., Dunsfold 'Sky Dominion'; crashed at Neustadt, near Wunsdorf, Germany 19.6.49

G-AMGK (1356), LV-AFZ, 22.3.51, Eagle Aviation Ltd., Luton; trooping 1952–53 as XA191, later WW512; Skyways Ltd., Stansted 12.52; to Air Liban 11.54 as OD-ABV; rest. 11.55 to Skyways Ltd.; w.f.u. at Stansted 7.61

G-AMGL (1354), LV-AFV, 21.9.51, Eagle Aviation Ltd., Luton; Air Charter Ltd., Stansted 'New Era' 8.51; trooping 1952 as XA192; crashed near Hamburg, Germany 11.3.52

G-AMGM (1355), LV-AFY, 10.2.52, Eagle Aviation Ltd., Luton; Air Charter Ltd., Stansted 'New Venture' 2.52; crashed at Lyneham 27.11.52

G-AMRI MW138, 23.8.52, Air Charter Ltd., Stansted 'New Enterprise'; to Air Liban, Beirut, Lebanon 6.55 as OD-ACD

G-AMRJ MW326, 24.5.52, Air Charter Ltd., Stansted 'New Era II'; trooping 1953–55 as XG897; to Air Liban, Beirut, Lebanon 6.55 as OD-ACE

G-AMUL MW308, 7.2.53, Scottish Aviation Ltd., Prestwick; trooping 1953–55 as XF284; destroyed in take-off crash at Stansted 30.4.56

G-AMUM MW332, 20.5.53, Scottish Aviation Ltd., Prestwick; trooping 1953–54 as XF285; damaged beyond repair landing at Luqa, Malta 13.4.54

G-AMUN MW321, 30.1.53, Scottish Aviation Ltd., Prestwick; trooping 1953–55 as XD667; crashed on night approach to Stansted 23.12.57

G-AMUS MW110, 24.12.53, Air Charter Ltd., Stansted 'New Britain'; trooping 1955 as XF919; Hunting Clan A/T Ltd., Heathrow 2.56; to spares 5.58

G-AMUT MW185, 29.11.52, Air Charter Ltd., Stansted; to Maritime Central Airways 3.55 as CF-HTM; rest. 3.58 to Dan-Air Services Ltd., Lasham; damaged beyond repair at Luqa, Malta 20.5.58

G-AMUU MW183, 25.2.53, Air Charter Ltd., Stansted 'Nouvelle Calédonie'; trooping 1953–55 as XD668; Hunting Clan Air Transport Ltd., Heathrow 2.56; w.f.u. 2.59

G-AMUV MW226, 7.11.52, Air Charter Ltd., Stansted 'New Venture II'; trooping 1953–55 as XD623, later XD669; Dan-Air Services Ltd., Lasham 3.56; crashed in forced landing with engine fire, Gurgaon, India 25.5.58

G-AMVY MW292, Hunting A/T Ltd.; not converted; to spares at Bovingdon 4.54

G-AMVZ MW302, Hunting A/T Ltd.; not converted; to spares at Bovingdon 8.54

G-AMXM MW323, 3.5.54, Hunting A/T Ltd., Bovingdon; Hunting Clan A/T Ltd., Heathrow 2.58; to Trans Mediterranean Airways 7.59 as OD-ADM

G-ANAA MW100, Surrey F/S Ltd., Stansted; not conv.; dismantled Stansted 9.55

G-ANAB MW104, Surrey Flying Services Ltd.; details as G-ANAA above

G-ANAC MW236, Surrey Flying Services Ltd.; details as G-ANAA above

G-ANAW MW139, Surrey F/S Ltd., Stansted; Skyways Ltd. 5.55; scrapped 9.55

G-ANGF MW254, 22.4.54, Hunting Air Transport Ltd., Bovingdon; Hunting Clan A/T Ltd., Heathrow 2.56; to Trans Mediterranean Airways 7.59 as OD-ADL

York G-AHFD in Skyways' colours at Stansted in 1956. (*Flight Photo 27227S*)

G-ANGL   MW231, 1.7.54, Skyways Ltd., Stansted; leased to Aden Airways Ltd. in 1954; to Persian Air Services 2.55 as EP-ADA

G-ANRC   MW327, 23.7.54, Scottish Aviation Ltd., Prestwick; trooping 1954 as XG898; burned out in take-off accident at Stansted 22.9.54

G-ANSY   MW193, 30.9.54, Scottish Aviation Ltd., Prestwick; trooping 1954–55 as XG929; total loss in take-off accident at Luqa, Malta 25.2.56

G-ANTH   MW177, Lancashire Aircraft Corp. Ltd.; Skyways Ltd., Stansted 5.55; scrapped at Stansted 11.55

G-ANTI   MW143, 18.1.55, Dan-Air Services Ltd., Lasham; w.f.u. Lasham 5.63

G-ANTJ   MW149, 23.12.58, Dan-Air Services Ltd., Lasham; w.f.u. Lasham 12.62

G-ANTK   MW232, 30.10.56, Dan-Air Services Ltd., Lasham; withdrawn from use at Lasham 10.64; presented to local Air Scouts for airfield bunkhouse

G-ANUN   MW253, Scottish Aviation Ltd.; re-registered G-ANVO (below) to avoid radio telephonic confusion with the company's York G-AMUN

G-ANVO   MW253, G-ANUN, 31.12.54, Scottish Aviation Ltd., Prestwick; trooping 1955 as XJ264; Skyways Ltd., Luton 8.58; w.f.u. at Luton 6.63

G-ANXJ   MW141, delivered to Aviation Traders Ltd., Southend 26.1.55; scrapped

G-ANXK   MW178, delivered to Aviation Traders Ltd. at Thame 1955 and scrapped

G-ANXL   MW196, as G-ANXK above

G-ANXM   MW227, delivered to Aviation Traders Ltd., Southend 24.1.55; scrapped

G-ANXN   MW258, 26.3.56, Air Charter Ltd., Stansted 'New Charter'; Dan-Air Services Ltd., Lasham 11.56; withdrawn from use at Lasham 6.63

G-ANXO   MW318, Aviation Traders Ltd.; not converted; scrapped at Thame

G-ANYA   MW210, 25.7.56, Scottish Airlines (Prestwick) Ltd.; Skyways Ltd., Stansted 8.58; withdrawn from use at Stansted 8.59

G-AOAN   MW199, d/d to Scottish Airlines (Prestwick) Ltd. 4.4.55; Field Aircraft Services Ltd., Tollerton 12.55; scrapped at Tollerton 3.57

G-APCA   MW295 'Ascalon II', Field Aircraft Services Ltd., Heathrow; to Trans Mediterranean Airways 8.57 as OD-ACQ, later to Persia as EP-ADE

Avro 688 Tudor 1

G-AGPF   (1234), TT176, 18.11.47, Ministry of Supply and Aircraft Production; to Ministry of Supply 1949 as VX192; scrapped at Woodford 12.50

G-AGRC (1251), Ministry of Supply and Aircraft Production; first flown 12.1.46; scrapped at Woodford 12.48

G-AGRD (1252), 22.11.46, Ministry of Supply and Aircraft Production; scrapped at Woodford 3.49

G-AGRE (1253), 25.9.46, B.O.A.C.; Ministry of Civil Aviation 11.46; flown to Woodford for prototype Tudor 4B conversion

G-AGRF (1254), 6.12.46, B.O.A.C. 'Elizabeth of England'; converted to Tudor 4B in 1948

G-AGRG (1255), 10.1.47, Ministry of Civil Aviation; used by B.S.A.A. as Tudor Freighter 1 'Star Cressida'; converted to Super Trader 4 in 1956

G-AGRH (1256), 10.12.46, Ministry of Civil Aviation; used by B.S.A.A. as Tudor Freighter 1; converted to Super Trader 4B in 1956

G-AGRI (1257), 3.2.48, Ministry of Civil Aviation; Aviation Traders Ltd. 9.53; used by Air Charter Ltd. as XF739; dismantled at Southend 10.54

G-AGRJ (1258), 24.2.47, Ministry of Civil Aviation; Aviation Traders Ltd., Southend 9.53; Air Charter Ltd. 8.54; scrapped at Stansted 8.56

G-AGRK (1259), Ministry of Supply and Aircraft Production; transferred to the Ministry of Supply as TS874; dismantled at Woodford 12.50

G-AGRL (1260), Ministry of Supply and Aircraft Production; transferred to the Ministry of Supply as TS875; dismantled at Woodford 12.50

G-AGST (1249), TT181, Ministry of Supply; rebuilt as Tudor 4 and later as Tudor 8 VX195; scrapped at Farnborough 1951

Avro 689 Tudor 2

G-AGRY (1262), VX202, 1.9.48, Ministry of Supply and Aircraft Production; Airflight Ltd. 9.48; Fairflight Ltd. 4.50; Air Charter Ltd., Stansted 1953; trooping 1953–54 as XF537; scrapped at Stansted 7.59

G-AGRZ (1263), Ministry of Supply and Aircraft Production; to Ministry of Supply 1.51 as VZ366; rest. 11.53 to Flight Refuelling Ltd., Tarrant Rushton; Aviation Traders Ltd., Southend 3.54; scrapped 7.59

G-AGSA (1264), Ministry of Supply and Aircraft Production; on loan to Rolls-Royce Ltd., Hucknall 1.49 as VZ720; scrapped at Farnborough 10.53

G-AGSU (1235), prototype, Ministry of Supply; crashed at Woodford 23.8.47

G-AGSV (1250), Ministry of Supply; construction abandoned

Avro 688 Tudor 3

G-AIYA (1367), VP301, 14.2.50, Ministry of Civil Aviation; Aviation Traders Ltd., Southend 9.53; converted 5.54 to Tudor 1; Air Charter Ltd., Stansted 9.54; withdrawn from use at Stansted 5.55

G-AJKC (1368), VP312, 14.2.50, Ministry of Civil Aviation; Aviation Traders Ltd., Southend 9.53; Air Charter Ltd. 9.54; scrapped at Southend 8.56

Avro 688 Tudor 4 and 4B

G-AGRE (1253), 12.11.48, British South American Airways 'Star Ariel'; lost over the Western Atlantic between Bermuda and Jamaica 17.1.49

G-AGRF (1254), 8.12.48, British South American Airways; dismantled at Hurn and sold to Aviation Traders Ltd.; to Southend as spares 9.53

G-AGRG (1255), 31.1.54, Aviation Traders Ltd.; conv. to Super Trader 4 'El Alamein' for Air Charter Ltd. 7.56; burned out at Brindisi 27.1.59

Super Trader 4B 'Trade Wind' G-AHNI of Air Charter Ltd. The hinges of the freight door are visible forward of the ladder.

G-AGRH (1256), 25.10.55, Aviation Traders Ltd.; conv. to Super Trader 4B 'Zephyr' for Air Charter Ltd. 7.56; crashed in Turkey 23.4.59

G-AHNH (1341), construction abandoned

G-AHNI (1342), 24.2.50, British South American Airways 'Star Olivia'; Aviation Traders Ltd. 9.53; converted to Super Trader 4B 'Trade Wind' for Air Charter Ltd. 1956; scrapped at Stansted 6.59

G-AHNJ (1343), 18.7.47, B.S.A.A. 'Star Panther'; to spares at Ringway 1953

G-AHNK (1344), 30.9.47, B.S.A.A. 'Star Lion'; to spares at Ringway 1953

G-AHNL (1345), 14.2.50, Ministry of Civil Aviation; Aviation Traders Ltd., Southend 9.53; converted to Super Trader 4B for Air Charter Ltd. 1956; scrapped at Southend 2.60

G-AHNM (1346), 6.3.50, Ministry of Civil Aviation; Aviation Traders Ltd. 9.53; converted to Super Trader 4B 'Cirrus' for Air Charter Ltd. 1956; scrapped at Stansted 6.59

G-AHNN (1347), 23.3.48, B.S.A.A. 'Star Leopard'; Ministry of Civil Aviation 11.51, Hurn (later Ringway); to spares at Ringway 1953; to Southend

G-AHNO (1348), 24.2.50, Ministry of Civil Aviation, Ringway; Aviation Traders Ltd. 9.53; converted to Super Trader 4B 'Conqueror' for Air Charter Ltd. 1956; scrapped at Stansted 8.59

G-AHNP (1349), 5.11.47, British South American Airways 'Star Tiger'; lost in the Western Atlantic, north-east of Bermuda 30.1.48

G-AHNR (1350), construction abandoned

Avro 689 Tudor 5

G-AKBY (1417), 24.9.48, Airflight Ltd.; crashed at Llandow, South Wales 12.3.50

G-AKBZ (1418), 3.11.48, B.S.A.A. 'Star Falcon'; scrapped at Stansted 7.59

G-AKCA (1419), 7.12.48, British South American Airways 'Star Hawk'; Surrey Flying Services Ltd., Stansted 9.51; loaned to Lome Airways, Canada 1953 as CF-FCY; scrapped at Stansted 7.59

G-AKCB (1420), 31.12.48, B.S.A.A. 'Star Kestrel'; scrapped at Stansted 7.59

G-AKCC (1421), 26.1.49, B.S.A.A. 'Star Swift'; William Dempster Ltd., Stansted 4.50 'President Kruger'; damaged beyond repair at Bovingdon 26.10.51

G-AKCD (1422), 11.2.49, British South American Airways 'Star Eagle'; William Dempster Ltd., Stansted 4.50; scrapped at Stansted in 1956

Avro 689 Tudor 7

G-AGRX (1261), Ministry of Supply and Aircraft Production; first flown 17.4.46; to Ministry of Supply 3.49 as VX199; rest. 11.53 to Flight Refuelling Ltd., Tarrant Rushton; to Aviation Traders Ltd. as spares 3.54

Avro 691 Lancastrian 1

G-AGLF (1172), VB873, 7.2.45, B.O.A.C.; Skyways Ltd., Dunsfold 'Sky Diplomat' 5.46; crashed at Landing Ground H.3 in the Syrian Desert 11.5.47

G-AGLS (1173), VD238, 9.3.45, B.O.A.C. 'Nelson'; scrapped at Hurn 1.51

G-AGLT (1174), VD241, 20.3.45, B.O.A.C. 'Newcastle'; scrapped at Hurn 1.50

G-AGLU (1175), VD253, 29.3.45, B.O.A.C.; damaged beyond repair, Hurn 15.8.46

G-AGLV (1176), VF163, 13.4.45, B.O.A.C.; Skyways Ltd., Dunsfold 'Sky Lane' 5.46; to Skyways (E.A.) Ltd. 1.49 as VP-KGT; scrapped at Dunsfold 3.52

G-AGLW (1177), VF164, 26.4.45, B.O.A.C. 'Northampton'; scrapped at Hurn 1.51

G-AGLX (1178), VF165, 14.5.45, B.O.A.C.; lost in the Indian Ocean, north of the Cocos Islands 24.3.46

G-AGLY (1179), VF166, 29.5.45, B.O.A.C. 'Norfolk'; scrapped at Hurn 1.51

G-AGLZ (1180), VF167, 2.6.45, B.O.A.C. 'Nottingham'; to Qantas 11.47 as VH-EAU; scrapped at Mascot, Sydney 9.52

G-AGMA (1181), VF152, 11.6.45, B.O.A.C. 'Newport'; scrapped at Hurn 2.51

G-AGMB (1182), VF153, 15.6.45, B.O.A.C. 'Norwich'; crashed at Singapore 27.8.48

G-AGMC (1183), VF154, 21.6.45, B.O.A.C.; crashed at Sydney, Australia 2.5.46

G-AGMD (1184), VF155, 29.6.45, B.O.A.C. 'Nairn'; to Qantas 7.47 as VH-EAS; destroyed by fire at Dubbo, N.S.W. 7.4.49

G-AGME (1185), VF156, 3.7.45, B.O.A.C. 'Newhaven'; scrapped at Hurn 1.50

G-AGMF (1186), VF160, 25.7.45, B.O.A.C.; crashed at Broglie, France 20.8.46

G-AGMG (1187), VF161, 21.8.45, B.O.A.C. 'Nicocia'; scrapped at Hurn 1.51

G-AGMH (1188), VF162, 28.8.45, B.O.A.C.; crashed at Karachi 17.5.46

G-AGMJ (1189), VF145, 11.9.45, B.O.A.C. 'Naseby'; scrapped at Hurn 1.51

G-AGMK (1190), VF146, 20.9.45, B.O.A.C. 'Newbury'; scrapped at Hurn 1.51

G-AGML (1191), VF147, 26.9.45, B.O.A.C. 'Nicobar'; to Qantas 9.47 as VH-EAT; broken up at Mascot, Sydney 9.52

G-AGMM (1192), VF148, 3.10.45, B.O.A.C. 'Nepal'; wrecked at Castel Benito, Tripoli, Libya 7.11.49

G-AGMN to G-AGMY (1193–1204), VF149–VF151 and VF137–VF144, were intended for B.O.A.C. but not completed.

Avro 691 Lancastrian 2

G-AJPP See G-AKFI below

G-AKFH 23.10.47, Skyways Ltd., Dunsfold 'Sky Scout'; to Skyways (E.A.) Ltd. 3.48 to 4.49 as VP-KFD; burned out landing at Gatow, Berlin 26.6.49

G-AKFI VL979, 1.12.47, Skyways Ltd., Dunsfold 'Sky Consort'; re-registered 5.48 as G-AJPP to avoid radio confusion with Skyways York G-AHFI; Aeronautical and Industrial Research Corp., Dunsfold 6.48; sold in Pakistan 7.48

G-AKMW VL977, 23.12.47, British South American Airways 'Star Bright'; Skyways Ltd., Dunsfold 'Sky Empire' 12.48; withdrawn from use at Dunsfold 5.51

G-AKPY VL971, 16.3.48, B.O.A.C. 'Natal'; scrapped at Hurn 1.50

G-AKPZ VL972, 9.3.48, B.O.A.C. 'Nile'; scrapped at Hurn 4.49

G-AKRB VM737, 1.3.48, B.O.A.C. 'Nyanza'; scrapped at Hurn 1.50

Skyways' Lancastrian 2 'Sky Consort' G-AKFI bearing re-registration G-AJPP with which it flew for a few weeks before sale to Pakistan in 1948. (*E. J. Riding*)

G-AKSN   VL973, 9.5.49, Skyways Ltd., Dunsfold 'Sky Consort'; withdrawn from use at Dunsfold 5.51

G-AKSO   VL974, 6.4.49, Skyways Ltd., Dunsfold 'Sky Kingdom'; withdrawn from use at Dunsfold 5.51

G-AKTB   VM378, 28.4.48, British South American Airways 'Star Glory'; Flight Refuelling Ltd., Tarrant Rushton 4.49; withdrawn from use 5.51

G-AKTC   VL978, British South American Airways; used for spares at Langley 6.48

G-AKTG   (R3/LB/485398), British South American Airways; spares, Langley 8.48

Avro 691 Lancastrian 3

G-AGWG   (1279), 5.12.45, British South American Airways 'Star Light'; crashed in Bermuda 13.11.47

G-AGWH   (1280), 9.1.46, B.S.A.A. 'Star Dust'; lost over the Andes Mts. 2.8.47

G-AGWI   (1281), 24.1.46, B.S.A.A. 'Star Land'; Flight Refuelling Ltd., Tarrant Rushton 1.49; scrapped at Tarrant Rushton 9.51

G-AGWJ   (1282), 28.1.46, B.S.A.A. 'Star Glow'; crashed at Bathurst, Gambia 30.8.46

G-AGWK   (1283), 15.2.46, B.S.A.A. 'Star Trail'; crashed in Bermuda 5.9.47

G-AGWL   (1284), 13.2.46, B.S.A.A. 'Star Guide'; Flight Refuelling Ltd., Tarrant Rushton 1.49; scrapped at Tarrant Rushton 9.51

G-AHBT   (1288), 23.8.46, Silver City Airways Ltd., Dunsfold 'City of New York'; Skyways Ltd., Dunsfold 'Sky Ranger' 7.47; w.f.u. at Dunsfold 3.52

G-AHBU   (1289), 16.9.46, Skyways Ltd., Dunsfold 'Sky Path'; crashed at Nutts Corner Aerodrome, Belfast 3.10.47

G-AHBV   (1290), 18.9.46, Silver City Airways Ltd., Dunsfold 'City of Canberra'; Skyways Ltd., Dunsfold 3.49; withdrawn from use at Dunsfold 3.52

G-AHBW   (1291), 15.10.46, Silver City Airways Ltd., Dunsfold 'City of London'; to QANTAS 1.48 as VH-EAV; damaged beyond repair at Sydney 17.11.51

G-AHBX   (1292), 2.4.47, British European Airways Corpn., White Waltham; to Alitalia, Rome, 2.48 as I-AHBX 'Maestrale'; d.b.f. at Dakar 23.12.49

G-AHBY   (1293), 2.4.47, British European Airways Corp., White Waltham; to Alitalia, Rome 11.47 as I-AHBY 'Libeccio'

G-AHBZ   (1294), 6.11.46, Skyways Ltd., Dunsfold 'Sky Ambassador'; Aeronautical and Industrial Research Corp., 7.48; to Pakistan 3.49 as AP-ACQ

G-AHCA (1295), 6.11.46, Skyways Ltd., Dunsfold; burned out in hangar fire at Dunsfold 8.12.46

G-AHCB (1296), 8.1.47, British European Airways Corp., White Waltham; to Alitalia, Rome 7.47 as I-AHCB 'Grocale'

G-AHCC (1297), 12.12.46, Skyways Ltd., Dunsfold 'Sky Chieftain'; scrapped at Dunsfold 3.52

G-AHCD (1298), 10.1.47, B.S.A.A. 'Star Valley'; British European Airways Corp., White Waltham 4.47; to Alitalia, Rome 12.47 as I-AHCD 'Sirocco'

G-AHCE (1299), 2.4.47, British European Airways Corp., White Waltham; to Alitalia, Rome 8.47 as I-DALR 'Borea'

Avro 691 Lancastrian 4

G-AKFF TX284, 10.9.47, Skyways Ltd., Dunsfold 'Sky Ruler'; B.S.A.A. 'Star Flight' 1948; Flight Refuelling Ltd., Tarrant Rushton 1949; scrapped 9.51

G-AKFG TX286, 29.9.47, Skyways Ltd., Dunsfold 'Sky Minister'; B.S.A.A. 'Star Traveller' 1948; Flight Refuelling Ltd., Tarrant Rushton 1949; scrapped at Tarrant Rushton 9.51

G-AKJO 25.10.47, Skyways Ltd., Dunsfold 'Sky Envoy'; Onzeair Ltd. 7.48; sold in Pakistan 7.48

G-AKLE TX285, Skyways Ltd.; used for spares at Dunsfold 9.48

Trans-Canada Air Lines' Lancaster XPP CF-CNA carrying wartime nationality stripes in 1945. It was sold to Flight Refuelling Ltd. as G-AKDS in 1947. (*J. F. McNulty*)

Avro Lancaster XPP (*Canadian conversions to Lancastrian 1*)

G-AKDO KB729, CF-CMV, 3.9.47, Flight Refuelling Ltd., Tarrant Rushton; withdrawn from use at Tarrant Rushton 5.51

G-AKDP FM185, CF-CMY, 26.1.48, Flight Refuelling Ltd., Tarrant Rushton; damaged beyond repair in forced landing in Russian Zone of Germany 10.5.49

G-AKDR FM186, CF-CMZ, 15.3.48, Flight Refuelling Ltd., Tarrant Rushton; withdrawn from use at Tarrant Rushton 5.51

G-AKDS FM187, CF-CNA, 11.12.47, Flight Refuelling Ltd., Tarrant Rushton; withdrawn from use at Tarrant Rushton 5.51

Avro 694 Lincoln B.Mk.2

G-APRJ   RF342, registered to D. Napier & Son Ltd., Luton 1.59; to Class B 1960 as G-29-1; to College of Aeronautics, Cranfield 11.62 as G-36-3; flown to Southend 9.5.67 as G-APRJ for preservation by Historic Aircraft Museum as G-29-1

G-APRP   RF402, used by D. Napier & Son Ltd., Luton for icing research from 1948 until dismantled as spares for G-APRJ in 1960. Temporarily civil in 1959.

British Klemm L.25C 1A Swallow

G-ACMK   (1), 19.1.34, British Klemm Aeroplane Co. Ltd., Hanworth; C. E. Berens, Hanworth 6.34; to Weston Air Services., Leixlip 6.47 as EI-ADS

G-ACMZ   (2), 10.2.34, Lord Willoughby de Broke, Kineton; derelict at Old Warden Aerodrome, Biggleswade in 1958

G-ACNU   (5), 10.3.34, Major H. Musker, Hanworth; used by the Civil Air Guard at Chigwell, Essex in 1938-39; sold abroad 19.4.40

G-ACOE   (6), 20.6.34, British Klemm Aeroplane Co. Ltd., Hanworth; to Germany 5.36 as D-ECOE

G-ACON   (7), 8.6.34, British Klemm Aeroplane Co. Ltd., Hanworth; Capt. A. D. Crabbe, Hanworth 6.34; crashed near Retford, Notts., 6.9.34

G-ACOW   (8), 21.4.34, British Klemm Aeroplane Co. Ltd., Hanworth; Hon. L. Lambart, Eastleigh 2.35; impressed 4.40 as X5010; d.b.r. at Cove, Hants. 10.4.40

G-ACPJ   (10), 25.4.34, The Earl of Essex; Duke of Richmond and Gordon, Heston 10.35; F. G. Smith, Cowes 7.47; dismantled in 1948

G-ACRD   (11), 3.5.34, Rt. Hon. F. E. Guest, Hanworth; Weston Acro Club, Weston-super-Mare 12.38; impressed for ground instruction 4.40 as X5011

G-ACSN   (9), 23.5.34, British Klemm Aeroplane Co. Ltd., Hanworth; to Spain 1.35 as EC-XXA, later military as 30-22, restored as EC-CAP in 1941

G-ACSO   (12), 29.5.34, Wrightson Aircraft Sales Ltd., Heston; Royal Artillery Flying Club, High Post 8.38; destroyed in hangar collapse at Bourn 1952

G-ACTP   (22), 6.7.34, Major H. Musker, Hanworth; Mrs. F. Grierson, Brooklands 7.36; Romford Flying Club, Maylands 8.38; scrapped in 1940

G-ACUB   (15), 6.7.34, Aberdeen Flying Club, Dyce; crashed 22.2.38

G-ACUF   (16), 18.7.34, J. L. MacAlpine; Airwork Ltd., Heston 1.36; Lt. F. L. Gates, Whitchurch 10.38; scrapped in 1940

G-ACUM   (17), 20.7.34, A. Sebag Montefiore, Heston; crashed and burned out at Beenham, Berks. 23.7.34

G-ACVV   (14), 25.7.34, E. C. Paget, Gravesend; L. J. Blow, Maylands 1939; derelict at Old Warden Aerodrome, Biggleswade in 1958

G-ACVW   (3), 5.3.34, Sir John Carberry, Nairobi; P. J. Urlwin-Smith, Brooklands 10.36; B. M. Groves, Heston 10.38; seized by the Russians 13.11.38

G-ACWA   (18), 1.8.34, E. Parry, Castle Bromwich; H. L. Johnson, Castle Bromwich 5.39; impressed 4.40 as X5008, believed as instructional airframe

G-ACXD   (20), 27.8.34, Albert Batchelor, Ramsgate; to Denmark 5.37 as OY-DOL

G-ACXE   (21), 12.10.34, Aberdeen Flying School Ltd., Dyce; stored at Knowle, Birmingham by D. C. Burgoyne until 1949; stored at Sandown in 1972

G-ACXS   (23), 15.9.34, Aberdeen Flying School Ltd., Dyce; derelict at Walsall, Staffs. in 1947

G-ACYY   (26), 6.11.34, British Klemm Aeroplane Co. Ltd., Hanworth; Ilford Aviation Co. Ltd., Abridge 7.36; Coventry (Civil) Aviation Ltd., Whitley 11.38; Civil Air Guard at Chigwell 1939; derelict at Maylands 1940

G-ACZK (28), 16.1.35, British Klemm Aeroplane Co. Ltd., Hanworth; to Miss Lily
Dillon, Dublin 1.35 as EI-ABD; impressed 1940, flown as EI-ABD

B.A. Swallow 2 (Pobjoy)

G-ADDB (32), 18.5.35, British Aircraft Mfg. Co. Ltd., Hanworth; R. G. Kingsmill,
Hanworth 10.36; Southern Motors & Aircraft Ltd., Hamsey Gn. 8.38; w.f.u.

G-ADJL (400), 29.5.35, G. R. D. Shaw, Sywell; A. J. Linnell, Sywell 4.38; flown at
Wittering during the war; dismantled at Elstree in 1953

G-ADJM (401), 17.7.35, R. Branston, Cambridge; E. S. Baker, Redhill 8.36; crashed in
the sea south of Dover 14.5.38, later salvaged and scrapped

G-ADJN (402), 26.8.35, J. H. Musker, Hanworth; R. A. Farquharson, Whitchurch,
Bristol 4.39; destroyed during German bombing raid on Lympne 9.40

G-ADLD (404), 31.7.35, M. G. Christie, Hanworth; A. Montieth, York 7.36; destroyed
during German bombing raid on Lympne 9.40

G-ADMB (405), 3.8.35, Col. H. L. Cooper, High Post; reg'n. cancelled 12.36

G-ADMF (406), 27.7.35, H. E. Hudson, Castle Bromwich; J. K. N. Evans, Castle
Bromwich 12.38; P. Blamire, Baginton 6.46; to Ireland 5.49 as EI-AFF

G-ADMX (408), 30.8.35, I. C. Maxwell, Rochester; W. R. Silcock, Hanworth 2.37;
Peterborough Flying Club, Horsey Toll 2.39; scrapped in 1940

G-ADPS (410), 5.9.35, Cotswold Aero Club, Churchdown; Cardiff A/C, Splott 11.38;
Walker & Thompson Ltd., Lympne 6.46; J. W. Benson, Bicester 4.70

G-ADPT (411), 4.10.35, British Aircraft Mfg. Co. Ltd., Hanworth; Edinburgh F/C,
Macmerry 10.36; Doncaster Aero Club 12.38; registration cancelled 12.46

G-ADSF (413), 24.9.35, Rt. Hon. F. E. Guest, Hanworth; Eastbourne Flying Club,
Wilmington 10.36; conv. Cirrus Minor; Cinque Ports Flying Club, Lympne
8.38; destroyed in German bombing raid on Lympne 9.40

G-ADXH (415), 22.11.35, Leicestershire Aero Club, Braunstone; G. H. Curtis,
Maylands, Romford 9.38; burned out in hangar fire, Maylands 6.2.40

G-AEAH (433), 20.1.36, British Aircraft Mfg. Co. Ltd.; re-registered to the manufacturers in India 10.36 as VT-AIK; Indian reg'n. cancelled 4.37

G-AEAU (416), 30.1.36, Bristol & Wessex Aeroplane Club, Whitchurch; C. D. Godfrey,
Cardiff 6.39; derelict at Exeter in 1949

G-AEAV (418), 30.1.36, Bristol & Wessex Aeroplane Club, Whitchurch; T. C. Sparrow,
Christchurch 7.47; scrapped at Christchurch 9.50

B.A. Swallow 2 VH-UUM, Pobjoy Cataract III engine, built to Australian order in 1935
and still flown by owner E. R. Burnett-Reid at Adelaide in 1970. (*John Hopton*)

G-AECA   (417), 21.2.36, G. R. Armstrong and J. Shand, Leeming; Doncaster A/C 2.39; T. L. McDonald, Balado 6.46; to South Africa 6.47 as ZS-DAV

G-AECY   (419), 28.2.36; J. R. Grice, Grimsby; W. J. Martin, Tollerton 1.37; registration cancelled 12.46

G-AEDX   (421), 17.3.36, P. R. Burton and V. M. Desmond, Castle Bromwich; C. E. Mercer, West Malling 5.39; impressed 7.41 as ES952, later 2786M

G-AEFM   (437), 7.5.36, D. R. Pobjoy, Rochester; C. M. McClure, Hanworth 6.39; registration cancelled as beyond economical repair 6.46

G-AEGM   (436), 8.5.36, Liverpool & District Aero Club, Hooton; destroyed by fire in crash following pilotless take-off at Hooton 27.6.36

G-AEGN   (438), 8.5.36, Liverpool & District A/C, Hooton; Bristol & Wessex Aero Club, Whitchurch 4.39; T. C. Sparrow, Christchurch 5.46; scrapped 9.50

G-AEHB   (425), 8.5.36, British Aircraft Mfg. Co. Ltd., Hanworth; P. G. Aldrich-Blake, Heston 6.36; forced down in the sea off Boulogne 3.7.36

G-AEHI   (424), 15.5.36, G. L. Prendergast, Lympne; stored at Weston-super-Mare during war; C. J. Packer, Weston 5.46; scrapped at Burton, Wilts. 6.48

G-AEHK   (426), 19.5.36, Viscount Gort, Woodley; impressed 4.40 as X5007

G-AEHL   (427), 15.5.36, R. M. Wilson, Heston; N. Holden, Selsey 9.36; Mrs. B. Macdonald, Witney 6.39; used as a glider at Thame 1941 as BK895

G-AEIC   (428), 19.5.36, H. Blount, Whitchurch; H. L. Griffiths, Walsall 5.38; M. Bryant, Wolverhampton 8.38; T. Shipside, Tollerton 11.46; scrapped 1948

G-AEIG   (429), 23.5.36, G. Dawson, Tollerton; M. Forte and J. Hood, Waddington 12.36; G. Dawson, Skegness 8.38; destroyed in air collision with Swallow 2 G-AFER over Cotgrave, Notts. 16.2.39

G-AEIH   (430), 19.6.36, W. A. Phillips, Hanworth; Cinque Ports Flying Club, Lympne 6.36; Cardiff Aeroplane Club 1.39; impressed 3.40 as X5006

G-AEIW   (431), 3.6.36, P. G. Aldrich-Blake, Heston; British Aircraft Mfg. Co. Ltd. 7.36; W. A. Fox, Roborough 11.36; to Ireland 3.39 as EI-ABY

G-AEKG   (442), 14.7.36, Eastbourne Flying Club, Wilmington; W. S. Aston, Roborough 10.38; E. L. Blow, Chigwell 1.39; derelict at Maylands in 1940

G-AELG   (449), 28.7.36, Newcastle Aero Club; E. Boulter, Sywell 4.46; C. D. Godfrey, Shoreham 7.46; Swansea F/S 3.50; Parachute Flying Group, Panshanger 9.56; R. E. Clear, Christchurch 9.57; to Ireland 8.62 as EI-AMU

G-AELH   (446), 24.7.36, P. G. Aldrich-Blake, Heston; Mrs. B. Macdonald, Witney 8.38; impressed 8.40 as a glider, became BK896 at Farnborough 11.40

G-AELJ   (448), 19.8.36, British Aircraft Mfg. Co. Ltd.; J. S. Owen, Hucknall 8.38; E. B. Taylor, West Molesey, Surrey 12.42; at garage in Wandsworth 4.46

G-AEMD   (452), 21.8.36, Mrs. F. Morris-Davis, Lympne; cancelled 12.46

G-AEMS   (453), 18.9.36, Merseyside Aero & Sports Ltd., Speke; crashed at Bromborough, Cheshire 1.5.38

G-AENC   (455), 18.9.36, A. J. Cormack, Macmerry; crashed 3.37

G-AEOW   (457), 28.11.36, British Aircraft Mfg. Co. Ltd.; London Air Park F/C, Hanworth 6.38; A. R. Pilgrim, Broxbourne 9.39; stored during war; restored 4.46 to same owner at Elstree; wrecked in gale at Heston 16.3.47

G-AEZM   (434), 12.3.36, ex VT-AHJ, Bombay Flying Club; O. R. Guard, Portsmouth 9.37; G. B. S. Errington, Portsmouth 'Puddlejumper II' 7.38; D. Kirk, Weston-super-Mare 9.44; L. W. Usherwood, Rochester 6.52; burned in shed 15.3.54

G-AFCL   (462), 2.11.37, W. L. Hope, Croydon; C. McCarthy, Croydon 1.38; G. H. Forsaith, Thruxton 10.48; A. Ethridge, Old Warden 5.65; A. M. Dowson 11.71

G-AFES   (464), 7.2.38, P. W. Kennedy, Croydon; to Ireland 3.38 as EI-ABX

G-AFGC   (467), 31.4.38, T. H. Clayton and Sir D. Hall Caine, Hanworth; R. M. Dryden 1.39; impressed 8.40 as BK 893; rest. 2.46 to B. Arden, Exeter; H. Plain, Exeter 2.50; put into storage at farm near Exeter 9.56

G-AFGD   (469), 31.4.38, T. H. Clayton and Sir D. Hall Caine, Hanworth; Cardiff A/C 1.39; impressed 8.40 as BK 897; sold to B. Arden, Exeter 9.43 and stored

G-AFGE   (470), 31.4.38, as 'GD; E. B. Taylor, Witney 10.38; impressed 8.40 as BK 894; sold to B. Arden, Exeter 9.43; L. W. Usherwood, Rochester 6.54; D. G. Ellis, Sandown 9.62; Shuttleworth Trust 7.69; Torbay Museum 5.70

B.A. Swallow 2 (Cirrus Minor)

G-AEIB   (441), 29.5.36, British Aircraft Mfg. Co. Ltd.; to Doncaster Aero Club, Ledsham, less engine 2.43; not flown again

G-AEKB   (444), 4.7.36, J. J. Lister, Doncaster; Leicestershire Aero Club, Braunstone 8.38; Hull Aero Club, Hedon 7.39; impressed 11.42 as 3568M

G-AEKC   (443), 30.6.36, York Aviation Services Ltd., Leeming; cancelled 12.46

G-AELI   (445), 12.8.36, W. Courtenay, Gatwick; Cinque Ports Flying Club, Lympne 8.37; destroyed in fatal crash near Lympne 21.9.38

G-AELV   (447), 28.8.36, Blackburn Aircraft Ltd., Grimsby; London Air Park Flying Club 3.39; crashed at Hanworth after pilotless take-off 24.5.39

G-AEMV   (454), 10.9.36, G. Western, Broxbourne; registration cancelled 10.47

G-AEMW   (456), 19.9.36, Eastbourne F/C, Wilmington; M. C. Scarlett, Perth 9.36; Strathtay A/C 9.38; G. McLean, Perth 7.46; L. F. Walters, Broxbourne 8.49; A. Thelwall, Elstree 11.63; crashed at Baldock 29.12.63

G-AEOZ   (458), 3.11.36, C. D. Godfrey, Cardiff; British Aircraft Mfg. Co. Ltd. 9.37; Coventry (Civil) Av. Ltd., Whitley 9.38; reg'n. cancelled 12.46

G-AERI   (465), 16.12.36, Blackburn Aircraft Ltd., Grimsby; London Air Park Flying Club, Hanworth 3.39; registration cancelled 7.46

G-AERK   (466), 21.12.36, A. Batchelor, Ramsgate; Weston Aero Club, Weston-super-Mare 1.39; dismantled for spares at Weston 3.40

G-AERR   (468), 13.1.37, H. N. Peake, Sulgrave, Oxon; Horton Kirby Flying Club 1.39; T. L. McDonald, Balado 6.46; to Ireland 6.48 as EI-AFD

G-AESI   (473), 25.1.37, Leicestershire Aero Club, Braunstone; crashed 6.38

G-AESL   (471), 20.1.37, Bristol & Wessex Aeroplane Club, Whitchurch; impressed 10.42 as 3412M and handed over to No. 1834 A.T.C. Sqn., Hayle, Cornwall

G-AEVC   (474), 3.3.37, Cinque Ports Flying Club, Lympne; registration cancelled 6.41; to No. 304 A.T.C. Sqn., Hastings 1943

G-AEVD   (460), 19.3.37, A. J. Cormack, Macmerry; British Aircraft Mfg. Co. Ltd. 1.38; G. H. Curtis, Maylands 9.38; burned in hangar fire, Maylands 6.2.40

G-AEVZ   (475), 24.3.37, Hull Aero Club, Hedon; stored Gainsborough during war; E. Clark, Doncaster 7.54; D. Pullen, Yeadon 10.58; dismantled at Crosby-on-Eden 3.64; preserved at Stockport 1972 by N. Aircraft Pres. Society

G-AEWB   (476), 15.4.37, Airwork Ltd., Heston; N. E. Goddard, Cheltenham 7.38; reg'n. cancelled 12.46; with No. 252 A.T.C. Sqn., Driffield in 1949

G-AEWH   (477), 23.3.37, Midland Bank Flying Club, Hanworth; crashed in Shepperton Reservoir, Middlesex 23.8.37

G-AEWI   (478), 23.3.37, Midland Bank F/C, Hanworth; Grimsby Aviation Ltd., Waltham 11.35; T. L. McDonald, Balado 2.46; D. A. Doughty, Croydon 8.48; Central F/G, Croydon 5.51; W. Smyth, Cambridge 12.56; scrapped 10.59

G-AEXH   (479), 24.4.37, E. E. Hughes-Williams, Castle Bromwich; Hull Aero Club, Hedon 3.39; D. Cook, Hedon 12.41; to No. 1423 Sqn. A.T.C. as 3636M

B.A. Swallow 2 G-AFGV, Cirrus Minor 1 engine, was delivered Perth–Dublin on 28 August 1950, became EI-AFN and was still extant at Kilkenny in 1970. (*G. J. R. Skillen*)

G-AEYV (480), 4.6.37, Cinque Ports Flying Club, Lympne; C. A. Wilson, Wilmington 4.38; registration cancelled 11.45

G-AEYW (481), 9.6.37, Cinque Ports Flying Club, Lympne; destroyed in German bombing raid on Lympne 9.40

G-AFBB (461), 6.11.36, Malcolm & Farquharson Ltd., Heston; to India 10.37 as VT-AIG; further sold in Australia 11.37 as VH-AAB; w.f.u. 3.69

G-AFCB (482), 14.10.37, Midland Bank Flying Club, Hanworth; Grimsby Aviation Ltd., Waltham 11.38; impressed 9.40 and flown at Ringway as BJ575

G-AFER (484), 20.5.38, S. Lawrence, Derby; destroyed in air collision with Swallow 2 G-AEIG over Cotgrave, Notts. 16.2.39

G-AFGS (483), 20.5.38, W. S. Shackleton Ltd., Hanworth; H. R. B. Waters, Hatfield 6.38; crashed in the sea off Folkestone 6.7.38

G-AFGV (485), 16.5.38, Doncaster Aero Club; McDonald Aircraft Ltd., Balado 11.45; I. H. Cameron, Perth 6.49; to Ireland 8.50 as EI-AFN

G-AFHC (486), 23.5.38, P. Mursell, Hamsey Gn.; B. Arden, Exeter 11.45, stored

G-AFHD (487), 23.5.38, R. H. Graham, Odiham; Tollerton Aero Club 4.39; R. Hollins, Tollerton 11.43; scrapped at Tollerton 12.46

G-AFHH (488), 4.6.38, A. W. Whittet, Brooklands; J. Lister, Doncaster 8.47; F. Haigh, Doncaster 8.49; T. Adair, Newtownards 7.52; to Ireland 10.53 as EI-AGH

G-AFHK (491), 17.6.38, Blackburn Aircraft Ltd., Brough; London Air Park Flying Club, Hanworth 2.39; scrapped at Hanworth 12.46

G-AFHL (492), 17.6.38, as G-AFHK above

G-AFHM (493), 17.6.38, Blackburn Aircraft Ltd., Brough; London Air Park Flying Club 2.39; T. L. McDonald, Balado 3.46; to Ireland 7.48 as EI-AEC

G-AFHN (494), 21.6.38, as G-AFHK above; crashed at Feltham, Mx. 15.7.39

G-AFHO (495), 21.6.38, as G-AFHK above

G-AFHP (496), 21.6.38, as G-AFHK above

G-AFHR (489), 29.6.38, W. S. Shackleton; to the Otago A/C, N.Z. 6.38 as ZK-AGO; impressed as NZ583; later to Queenstown & Mt. Cook A/W as ZK-AGR

G-AFHS (490), 24.6.38, J. Heath, Shoreham; R. L. Windus, Shoreham 6.56; crashed at Merstham, Surrey 24.7.60

G-AFHU (497), 25.6.38, Blackburn Aircraft Ltd., Brough; London Air Park Flying Club, Hanworth 2.39; scrapped at Hanworth 12.46

G-AFHV (498), 25.6.38, as G-AFHU above

G-AFHW (499), 25.6.38, as G-AFHU above

G-AFIG   (472), 12.8.38, Blackburn Aircraft Ltd., Brough; crashed at Sleaford, Lincs. 19.9.38

G-AFIH   (500), 5.7.38, Blackburn Aircraft Ltd., Brough; Doncaster Ultra Light F/G 9.49; W. S. Shackleton Ltd. 5.52; to Ireland 6.52 as EI-AGA

G-AFII   (501), 5.7.38, as G-AFHU above

G-AFIJ   (502), 5.7.38, Blackburn Aircraft Ltd., Brough; to P. Schärer, Grenchen, Switzerland 6.39 as HB-AKI; crashed in the French Alps 1.11.45

G-AFIK   (503), 11.7.38, Blackburn Aircraft Ltd., Brough; Peterborough Flying Club 8.39; London Air Park Flying Club, Hanworth 9.39; scrapped 12.46

G-AFIL   (504), 11.7.38, as G-AFIK above

British Klemm B.K.1 Eagle 1

G-ACPU   (2), 6.7.34, British Klemm Aeroplane Co. Ltd., E. L. Gandar Dower, Dyce 7.34; Miss M. Glass, Heston 2.39; impressed 9.41 as 2679M

G-ACRG   (1), 6.7.34, British Klemm Aeroplane Co. Ltd.; J. Fox, Hanworth 7.35; W. A. Phillips, Hanworth 5.36; C. McCarthy, Hanworth 2.37; crashed 6.38

G-ACTR   (25), 21.10.34; British Klemm Aeroplane Co. Ltd., Hanworth; to Adastra Airways Ltd., Sydney 9.34 as VH-USI; crashed at Mascot 24.1.37

G-ACVU   (30), 25.9.34, G. Shaw, Thornaby-on-Tees 'Spirit of Wm. Shaw & Co. Ltd.'; crashed in the Mediterranean off Corsica 13.4.36

B.A. Eagle 2

G-ACZT   (107), 18.12.34, Border Flying Club, Carlisle; Hon. Brian Lewis, Elstree 7.36; J. Carr, Newtownards 7.38; destroyed by enemy action at Ards 1941

G-ADEJ   (110), 28.3.35, British Klemm Aeroplane Co. Ltd., Hanworth; demonstration aircraft, crashed 12.35

G-ADES   (111), 16.5.35, Lord Willoughby de Broke, Sywell; to Switzerland 1.36 as HB-DES; owned by E. Muller, Basle in 1939

G-ADFB   (112), 29.4.35, British Klemm Aeroplane Co. Ltd., Hanworth; registered in Japan 12.35 after solo flight to Tokyo by Katsutaro Ano

G-ADGJ   (121), 16.6.35, British Aircraft Mfg. Co. Ltd.; flown to India by R. Vaughan-Fowler ex Hanworth 1.12.35; sold in India 7.36 as VT-AHT

G-ADID   (118), 24.3.36, British Aircraft Mfg. Co. Ltd., Hanworth; R. E. Gardner, Hamsey Green 5.38; W. Humble, Firbeck 5.39; impressed 10.41 as HM500

G-ADJO   (122), 1.8.35, British Aircraft Mfg. Co. Ltd.; J. C. Hargreaves, Alexandria, Egypt 11.36; H. C. Paul, Hanworth 5.38; sold abroad 9.38

G-ADJS   (119), 25.5.36, Villiers Hay Development Co. Ltd., Heston; R. L. Hunter, Heston 5.36; A. J. Cormack, Macmerry 12.37; impressed 4.41, DR610 ntu

G-ADPN   (124), 4.9.35, J. D. Armour, Hanworth; M. E. King, Mousehold, Norwich 5.36; crashed at Cardiff 20.9.36

G-ADPO   (125), 19.10.35, Air Hire Ltd., Heston; D. H. Tollemache, Heston 11.37; Nash Aircraft Sales & Hire Ltd., Croydon 2.39; scrapped at Hanworth 1940

G-ADVT   (130), 31.10.35, Air Commerce Ltd., Heston; Marquess of Donegal, Heston 4.36; impressed 3.41 as DP847; u/c collapsed at Linton-on-Ouse 19.10.43

G-ADYY   (116), 13.12.35, H. Holliday, Hanworth; S. Leigh, Heston 7.37; J. H. Crook, Heston 11.38; to Barbados 7.45 as VP-TAM; derelict in 1949

G-AEER   (126), 2.4.36, J. P. Wakefield, Brooklands; crashed at Breedon 2.10.37

G-AEFZ   (133), 5.5.36, Sir Alasdair MacRobert, Brooklands; J. H. Rabone, Hendon 8.38; impressed 6.41 as ES944; u/c collapsed at Turnhouse 29.5.43

The fixed undercarriage B.A. Eagle 2 G-AFAX (see page 170) at Parkes, N.S.W., as VH-ACN in 1969. (*Leslie Hunt*)

G-AEGO (127), 13.5.36, R. Branston, Cambridge; J. Ramsey, Hanworth 7.38; Aeronautical Research & Sales Corp., Hanworth 6.41; impressed 8.41 as HM506

G-AEKI (131), 3.7.36, J. W. Adamson, Leeming; Yorkshire Aviation Services Ltd., York 9.38; impressed 7.41 as ES948; u/c collapsed at Colerne 29.6.43

G-AENE (132), 23.9.36, L. T. Lillington, Braunstone; to France 5.37 as F-AQNE and based at Roubaix

G-AERB (137), 8.1.37, British Aircraft Mfg. Co. Ltd., Hanworth; Sir Derwent Hall Caine and T. H. Clayton, Hanworth 4.38; to France 5.38 as F-ARRB

G-AFAX (138), 6.8.37, H. O. Hamilton, Shoreham; J. D. Hodder, Rangoon 6.39; registered in Australia 3.40 as VH-ACN, still flying in 1970

G-AFIC (141), 30.6.38, Flg. Off. A. E. Clouston, Farnborough; to Rai Bajrang Singh, Partab Garh, Oudh 10.38 as VT-AKO; impressed 11.42 as MA945

G-AFIS (143), 22.9.38, Spikins (Twickenham) Ltd., Hanworth; to the Nawab of Sachur 1.39 as VT-AKP; impressed 12.40 as AW183

G-AFKH (142), 10.10.38, Luis Fontes, Woodley; sold to Ernst Spahni, Switzerland in 1939 as HB-EBE; crashed at Fribourg 28.7.49

B.A.C. Drone (*with date of Authorisation to Fly*)

G-ADMU (5), 3.8.35, A. E. Coltman, Braunstone; crashed at Braunstone 15.1.39

G-ADPJ (7), 23.8.35, Cdr. J. S. Dove R.N., Hanworth; F. Lawton, Huddersfield 8.36; A. C. Waterhouse, Desford 10.50; crashed at Leicester E. 3.4.55

G-ADSA (6), 23.10.35, Anglian Air Services, Maylands; Ely Aero Club 12.36; Ray Bullock, Fraddon 11.37; burned as scrap at St. Colomb, Cornwall

G-ADSB (3), 7.9.35, G. A. Carpmael, Hanworth; A. Carpmael, Denham 10.36; B. F. Collins, Hanworth 1937; conv. to glider by London Gliding Club 1938

G-ADUA (8), registered 26.9.35 to B.A.C. Ltd., Hanworth; used by the Ely Aero Club; crashed at Caxton Gibbet, Cambs. 20.12.36

G-AEAN (9), 31.1.36, B.A.C. Ltd., Hanworth; flown by C. W. A. Scott's Air Display; crashed on bungalow adjacent to Southend Airport 22.7.36

G-AEBC (10), 8.2.36, Thomas (Worcester) Ltd., Pershore; reg'n. cancelled 12.36

G-AECP (11), 5.3.36, Tenbury Baths Co. Ltd., Kidderminster; E. D. Ward, Speke 8.38; G. Briggs, Middleton, Lancs. 11.38; registration cancelled 12.46

G-AEDA (12), 2.4.36, R. E. Sharples, Yeadon; registration cancelled 12.46

G-AEDB   (13), 19.3.36, G. Scott-Pearce, Perth; Ely Aero Club 10.36; Cambridge F/S 6.37; D. C. Burgoyne, Birmingham 1.57; R. E. Ogden, Woodley 1.69

G-AEDC   (14), 25.3.36, F. E. Tasker, Maylands; A. J. Tricker, t/a A. J. T. Development Co. Ltd., Watchfield 5.37; registration cancelled 12.46

G-AEEN   (16), 18.5.36, A. Batchelor, Ramsgate; W. M. Peatfield, Ramsgate 2.37; destroyed in fatal crash at Ramsgate 24.8.37

G-AEEO   (15), 3.4.36, C. W. A. Scott's Air Display Ltd.; L. J. Rimmer, Hooton 10.36; J. S. Boumphrey, Hooton 11.36; burned in hangar fire at Hooton 8.7.40

G-AEEP   (17), 1.4.36, B.A.C. Ltd., Hanworth; Ely Aero Club 2.37; Cambridge Flying Services, Ely 8.38; registration cancelled 12.46

G-AEJH   (18), 29.5.36, East Midlands Aviation Co. Ltd., Sywell; A. J. Spiller and partner, Sywell 6.38; dismantled at Knowle, Birmingham 9.48

G-AEJK   (19), 29.5.36, Scottish Flying Club, Renfrew; J. B. Patston, Eyebury 9.37; E. J. Pope, Ealing 2.49; scrapped by Otley Motors Ltd., W.11

G-AEJL   (20), 11.6.36, V. Greenhouse, Shrewsbury; registration cancelled 3.37

G-AEJP   (21), 1.8.36, Aberdeen Flying Club, Dyce; lapsed at Perth 5.39

G-AEJR   (22), 15.7.36, L. A. Clark, Doncaster; Thorne's (Worcester) Ltd., 9.37; complete at Honiley in 1952; stored at Chadwick Manor near Elmdon 1953

G-AEJS   (23), 8.7.36, Coventry Air Training Club, Burton Green; A. E. Green, Leamington 4.39; Drone Syndicate, Hamsey Green 2.46; crashed at Gerrards Cross, 1½ miles S.W. of Denham Aerodrome 27.4.47

G-AEKM   (24), 8.7.36, E. Thomas, Barton; given to Robert Kronfeld for research 1939; registration cancelled 1.41

G-AEKN   (25), 14.1.37, Scottish Flying Club, Renfrew; scrapped in 1945

G-AEKO   (26), 5.8.36, H. B. Showell, Fleggburgh; A. A. Rice, Norwich 10.38; sold to Dr. Bruce, Attleborough; destroyed and cancelled 11.45

G-AEKT   (28), 6.11.36, Kronfeld Ltd., Hanworth; registration cancelled 12.46

G-AEKU   (29), 19.11.36, Kronfeld Ltd., Hanworth; R. J. Wynne, Shoreham 5.38; Lord Apsley, Hanworth 10.39; to storage at Tattersall's Garages, Preston

G-AEKV   (30), 29.10.36, Kronfeld Ltd., Hanworth; H. H. Cairns, Upper Heyford 1950; J. Fricker, Southend 1.52; E. H. Gould, Christchurch 3.56; R. T. Vigors, Kidlington 8.57; J. R. Garood, Booker 5.60; based at Colerne 1972

G-AENZ   (4), 9.11.36, L. E. Fallow, Middleton, Lancs.; T. J. Thomason, Dyce 4.46; registration lapsed

With the 35 h.p. Ava flat-four, two-stroke engine, Lord Sempill's G-AFBZ had a maximum speed of 78 m.p.h. (*Flight Photo 14963S*)

G-AESF (31), 5.1.37, U. Williams, Eastleigh; H. J. Curtis, Cumnor, Oxford 5.39;
        disposed of in Bristol 11.45
G-AFBZ (35), 6.9.37, Lord Sempill, Hanworth; registration cancelled 12.46

B.A.C. Lightning F.Mk.53

G-AWON G-27-56, registered 9.8.68 to the British Aircraft Corp. Ltd., Warton; shown at
        Farnborough 9.68; to Royal Saudi Arabian A/F 9.68 as 53-686
G-AWOO G-27-57, registered and exhibited as above but civil lettering not carried; to
        Royal Saudi Arabian Air Force 9.68 as 53-687
G-AXEE G-27-86, registered 24.4.69 to the British Aircraft Corp. Ltd., Warton; shown
        at Paris Aero Show 6.69; to Kuwait Air Force 7.69 as K418
G-AXFW G-27-87, registered 21.5.69 to the British Aircraft Corporation Ltd., Warton;
        to the Kuwait Air Force 7.69 as K419

B.A.C. 167 Strikemaster Mks. 81–87

G-AWOR (102), G-27-9, Mk. 81, registered to B.A.C. Ltd. 9.8.68 for the Farnborough
        S.B.A.C. Show 9.68; to the Royal Saudi Arabian A/F as 902
G-AWOS (106), G-27-13, Mk. 81, registered to B.A.C. Ltd. 9.8.68 for Farnborough as
        above; to the Royal Saudi Arabian Air Force 9.68 as 906
G-AXEF G-27-35, Mk. 81, registered to B.A.C. Ltd., Warton 24.4.69; shown at the
        Paris Air Show 6.69; to the South Yemen Air Force 7.69 as 503
G-AXFX G-27-36, Mk. 81, registered 21.5.69 to B.A.C. Ltd., Warton; to the South
        Yemen Air Force 7.69 as 504
G-AYHR Mk. 87, registered 22.7.70 to B.A.C. Ltd., Warton; to Class B markings 10.70;
        to the Kenya Air Force as 601
G-AYHS G-27-143, Mk. 84, registered 22.7.70 to B.A.C. Ltd., Warton; to Class B
        markings 10.70 as G-27-143; to the Singapore Air Force as 314
G-AYHT G-27-144, Mk. 84, registered 22.7.70 to B.A.C. Ltd., Warton; to Class B
        markings 10.70 as G-27-144; to the Singapore Air Force as 315
G-AYVK G-27-189, Mk. 83, registered 5.4.71 to B.A.C. Ltd., Warton; shown at Paris
        Air Show 6.71; left Warton for Kuwait 2.7.71 as 120
G-AYVL G-27-190, Mk. 83, registered 5.4.71 to B.A.C. Ltd., Warton; left Warton
        2.7.71 on delivery to the Kuwait Air Force as 121

B.A.C. One-Eleven Series 200

G-ASHG (004), first flown 20.8.63, British Aircraft Corp. Ltd., Wisley; crashed and
        burned during test flight, Cricklade, Wilts. 22.10.63
G-ASJA (005), first flown 19.12.63, C. of A. 29.2.64, British United Airways Ltd.,
        Gatwick; flown at Cambridge 3.70 as G-52-1; to E. T. Barwick Industries Inc.,
        U.S.A., 4.70 as N734EB
G-ASJB (006), first flown 14.2.64, British United Airways Ltd., Gatwick; damaged
        beyond repair landing at Wisley from test flight 18.3.64
G-ASJC (007), first flown 1.4.64, C. of A. 18.5.64, British United Airways Ltd.,
        Gatwick; British Caledonian Airways Ltd., Gatwick 9.71
G-ASJD (008), first flown 6.7.64, C. of A. 4.8.65, British United Airways Ltd.,
        Gatwick; Caledonian/B.U.A. 'City of Edinburgh' 3.71; to R.A.E., Bedford
        10.71 as XX105
G-ASJE (009), first flown 5.5.64, C. of A. 22.5.64, British United Airways Ltd.,
        Gatwick; British Caledonian Airways Ltd., Gatwick 9.71

G-ASJF	(010), first flown 28.7.64, C. of A. 21.5.65, British United Airways Ltd., Gatwick; British Caledonian Airways Ltd., Gatwick 9.71
G-ASJG	(011), first flown 31.10.64, C. of A. 4.12.64, British United Airways Ltd., Gatwick; British Caledonian Airways Ltd., Gatwick 9.71
G-ASJH	(012), first flown 17.9.64, C. of A. 16.4.65, British United Airways Ltd., Gatwick; British Caledonian Airways Ltd., Gatwick 9.71
G-ASJI	(013), first flown 22.12.64, C. of A. 21.1.65, British United Airways Ltd., Gatwick; British Caledonian Airways Ltd., Gatwick 9.71
G-ASJJ	(014), first flown 24.2.65, C. of A. 6.4.65, British United Airways Ltd., Gatwick; crashed after take-off from Milan/Linate 14.1.69
G-ASTJ	(085), first flown 25.10.65, C. of A. 29.10.65, British United Airways Ltd., Gatwick; British Caledonian Airways Ltd., Gatwick 9.71
G-ASUF	(015), first flown 9.6.64 as Braniff N1541; registered 7.64 to British Aircraft Corp. Ltd. as G-ASUF; delivered to Braniff 8.65 as N1541
G-ASVT	(095), registered 9.64 to British Aircraft Corporation Ltd. for rebuild of G-ASJB; project abandoned
G-ATTP	(039), first flown 19.2.66 as VP-YXA, C. of A. 30.4.66, British Eagle International Airways Ltd., Heathrow 'Swift'; to Zambia 12.67 as 9J-RCH
G-ATVH	(040), first flown 16.4.66 as VP-YXB, C. of A. 27.5.66, British Eagle International Airways Ltd., Heathrow 'Serene'; to Zambia 12.67 as 9J-RCI
G-AWDF	(134), first flown 4.3.68 as N1124J, registered 3.68 to B.A.C. for trials in Spain; delivered to Mohawk Airlines 25.3.68 as N1124J

B.A.C. One-Eleven Series 300

G-ATPH	(110), first flown 19.4.67, C. of A. 28.4.67, British Eagle International Airways Ltd., Heathrow; to Quebecair 4.69 as CF-QBN
G-ATPI	(112), first flown 12.5.67, C. of A. 22.5.67, British Eagle International Airways Ltd., Heathrow; to Quebecair 4.69 as CF-QBO
G-ATPJ	(033), first flown 20.5.66, C. of A. 7.6.67, British Eagle International Airways Ltd. 'Stalwart'; Dan-Air Services Ltd., Gatwick 3.70
G-ATPK	(034), first flown 14.6.66, C. of A. 22.6.67, British Eagle International Airways Ltd. 'Spur'; to Bahamas Airways 4.70 as VP-BCP; rest. 3.71 to Laker Airways Ltd., Gatwick
G-ATPL	(035), first flown 13.7.66, C. of A. 22.7.67, British Eagle International Airways Ltd. 'Superb'; Dan-Air Services Ltd., Gatwick 9.69
G-AVBW	(107), first flown 17.2.67, C. of A. 25.2.67, Laker Airways Ltd., Gatwick
G-AVBX	(109), first flown 28.3.67, C. of A. 7.4.67, Laker Airways Ltd., Gatwick
G-AVBY	(113), first flown 1.5.67, C. of A. 9.5.67, Laker Airways Ltd., Gatwick; leased to Air Congo 1967–68
G-AVYZ	(133), first flown 8.4.68, C. of A. 11.4.68, Laker Airways Ltd., Gatwick

B.A.C. One-Eleven Series 400

G-ASYD	(053), first flown 13.7.65, C. of A. 14.8.65, British Aircraft Corp. Ltd.; first flown as Series 500 prototype 30.6.67; first flown as Series 475 prototype 27.8.70
G-ASYE	(054), second prototype, first flown 16.9.65, C. of A. 23.9.65, British Aircraft Corp. Ltd.; to Victor Comptometers Inc. 9.66 as N3939V
G-ATVU	(074), first flown 6.6.66 as N5032; registered 2.6.66 to British Aircraft Corp. Ltd. for demonstration in Sweden; delivered to American Airlines 21.6.66 as N5032; leased to Merpati Nusantara, Indonesia 8.71 to 11.71

One-Eleven 432 G-AXMU, second for Gulf Aviation delivered on 2 November 1971, joined G-AXOX on scheduled operations in the Gulf area.

G-AVEJ (094), first flown 3.1.67 as G-16-1, C. of A. 15.2.677, B.A.C.; leased to Bavaria Flug 2.67 to 10.67; to Philippine A/L 11.67 as PI-C1141

G-AVGP (114), first flown 9.6.67, C. of A. 14.6.67, Channel Airways Ltd., Stansted; B.A.C. Ltd. 5.68; leased to Dominicana 8.68; to Autair 3.69 as 'Halcyon Cloud'; Cambrian Airways Ltd., Rhoose 4.70

G-AVOE (129), first flown 8.3.68, C. of A. 19.3.68, Autair International Airways Ltd., Luton 'Halcyon Day'; Cambrian Airways Ltd., Rhoose 1.70

G-AVOF (131), first flown 18.1.68, C. of A. 29.1.68, Autair International Airways Ltd., Luton 'Halcyon Breeze'; Cambrian Airways Ltd., Rhoose 12.69

G-AVTF (122), first flown 21.7.67 as LV-IZR; registered 11.8.67 to B.A.C. Ltd. for demonstration to TAROM, Bucharest; to Austral 10.67 as LV-PID

G-AWBL (132), first flown 22.4.68, C. of A. 30.4.68, Court Line Aviation Ltd., Luton 'Halcyon Dawn'; Cambrian Airways Ltd., Rhoose 2.71

G-AWEJ (115), first flown 30.4.68, C. of A. 7.5.68, Channel Airways Ltd., Stansted and Southend

G-AWGG (116), first flown 20.6.68, C. of A. 24.6.68, British Aircraft Corp. Ltd.; to Bavaria Flug, Munich 4.69 as D-ALLI

G-AWKJ (128), first flown 29.1.69, C. of A. 5.2.69, Channel Airways Ltd., Stansted and Southend; leased to British United Airways Ltd., Gatwick 1969–70

G-AWXJ (166), first flown 27.2.69, C. of A. 16.3.69, B.A.C. Ltd.; earmarked for Tell-Air 5.70 as HB-ITK ntu; to Robin Loh, Hong Kong 11.71 as 9V-BEF

G-AXBB (162), first flown 14.2.69 as G-16-6, C. of A. 10.3.69, B.A.C. Ltd.; leased to Quebecair 3.69; leased TAROM 5.69 to 8.69 as YR-BCP; to L.A.C.S.A., Costa Rica 11.69 as TI-1055C

G-AXCK (090), first flown 6.12.66 as N5044, C. of A. 24.4.69 for Dan-Air Services Ltd., Gatwick

G-AXCP (087), first flown 29.10.66 as N5041, C. of A. 4.4.69 for Dan-Air Services Ltd., Gatwick

G-AXMU (157), first flown 20.11.68 as VP-BCZ, C. of A. 21.8.69. Laker Airways Ltd., Gatwick; leased Philippine A/L 10.69 as PI-C1151; to Hurn 2.71 as G-16-14; delivered to Gulf Aviation Ltd., Bahrein 11.71

G-AXOX (121), first flown 28.8.68 as G-16-5, VP-BCY, C. of A. 13.11.69, Gulf Aviation Ltd., Bahrein

G-AYHM (161), first flown 20.9.68 as PI-C1151 but leased to T.A.E. 3.69 as EC-BQF; C. of A. 1.8.70 for B.A.C. Ltd.; leased to Bavaria Flug 8.70

G-AZED (127), first flown 6.12.67 as G-16-3, D-ANDY, registered 19.8.71 to Dan-Air Services Ltd., Gatwick

G-AZMI (066), first flown 8.4.66 as N5026, registered 20.1.72 to Orientair Ltd., Berlin

B.A.C. One-Eleven Series 475
G-AYUW (239), first flown 5.4.71 as G-16-17, C. of A. 2.6.71, British Aircraft Corp. Ltd.; arrived Lima, Peru for Faucett 26.7.71 as OB-R-953

B.A.C. One-Eleven Series 500 (*British European Airways aircraft*)
First flight date is followed by date of issue of C. of A.

G-AVMH (136), 7.2.68, 11.6.69; G-AVMI (137), 13.5.68, 7.6.68; G-AVMJ (138) 15.7.68, 13.8.68; G-AVMK (139), 8.8.68, 12.9.68; G-AVML (140), 30.8.68, 30.9.68; G-AVMM (141), 28.9.68, 4.10.68; G-AVMN (142), 14.10.68, 12.11.68; G-AVMO (143), 29.10.68, 19.11.68; G-AVMP (144), 15.11.68, 3.12.68; G-AVMR (145), 28.11.68, 10.2.69; G-AVMS (146), 14.12.68, 20.12.68; G-AVMT (147), 10.1.69, 17.3.69; G-AVMU (148), 29.1.69, 17.3.69; G-AVMV (149), 21.3.69, 2.4.69; G-AVMW (150), 27.4.69, 2.5.69; G-AVMX (151), 2.6.69, 9.6.69; G-AVMY (152), 9.7.69, 16.7.69; G-AVMZ (153), 5.8.69, 14.8.69

Caledonian Airways' One-Eleven 509 G-AWWZ 'Isle of Eriskay' at Gatwick, August 1969. (*Richard Riding*)

B.A.C One-Eleven Series 500 (*other operators*)
G-AWWX (184), first flown 11.2.69, C. of A. 12.3.69, Caledonian Airways Ltd., Gatwick 'Isle of Skye'; British Caledonian Airways Ltd. 9.71

G-AWWY (185), first flown 11.3.69, C. of A. 31.3.69, Caledonian Airways Ltd., Gatwick 'Isle of Iona'; British Caledonian Airways Ltd. 9.71

G-AWWZ (186), first flown 18.4.69, C. of A. 28.4.69, Caledonian Airways Ltd., Gatwick 'Isle of Eriskay'; British Caledonian Airways Ltd. 9.71

G-AWYR (174), first flown 25.3.69, C. of A. 10.4.69, British United Airways Ltd., Gatwick; Caledonian/BUA 'Isle of Tiree' 3.71; British Caledonian Airways Ltd.,.Gatwick 9.71

G-AWYS (175), first flown 16.4.69, C. of A. 23.4.69, B.U.A. Ltd.; Caledonian/BUA 'Isle of Bute' 3.71; British Caledonian Airways Ltd., Gatwick 9.71

G-AWYT (176), first flown 6.5.69, C. of A. 13.5.69, British United Airways Ltd., Gatwick; British Caledonian Airways Ltd., Gatwick 9.71

G-AWYU (177), first flown 10.6.69, C. of A. 17.6.69, British United Airways Ltd., Gatwick; British Caledonian Airways Ltd., Gatwick 9.71

G-AWYV (178), first flown 20.6.69, C. of A. 25.6.69, B.U.A. Ltd.; Caledonian/BUA 'Isle of Harris' 3.71; British Caledonian Airways Ltd. 9.71

G-AXJK (191), first flown 14.8.69, C. of A. 4.3.70, British United Airways Ltd., Gatwick; British Caledonian Airways Ltd., Gatwick 9.71

G-AXJL (209), first flown 20.2.70, C. of A. 2.3.70, B.U.A. Ltd.; Caledonian/BUA 'Isle of Mingulay' 12.70; British Caledonian Airways Ltd. 9.71

G-AXJM (214), first flown 17.3.70, C. of A. 24.3.70, British United Airways Ltd., Gatwick; British Caledonian Airways Ltd., Gatwick 9.71

G-AXLL (193), first flown 25.9.69 as G-16-8, C. of A. 10.12.69, British Midland Airways Ltd., East Midlands/Castle Donington

G-AXLM (199), first flown 22.12.69, C. of A. 6.2.70, British Midland Airways Ltd., East Midlands/Castle Donington

G-AXLN (211), first flown 4.2.70, C. of A. 12.3.70, British Midland Airways Ltd., East Midlands/Castle Donington

G-AXMF (200), first flown 25.11.69, C. of A. 5.12.69, Court Line Aviation Ltd., Luton 'Halcyon Breeze'

G-AXMG (201), first flown 8.12.69, C. of A. 16.12.69, Court Line Aviation Ltd., Luton 'Halcyon Sky'

G-AXMH (202), first flown 12.1.70, C. of A. 6.2.70, Court Line Aviation Ltd., Luton 'Halcyon Sun'

G-AXMI (203), first flown 27.1.70, C. of A. 19.2.70, Court Line Aviation Ltd., Luton 'Halcyon Day'

G-AXMJ (204), first flown 17.2.70, C. of A. 10.3.70, Court Line Aviation Ltd., Luton 'Halcyon Night'

G-AXMK (205), first flown 7.4.70, C. of A. 11.4.70, Court Line Aviation Ltd., Luton 'Halcyon Star'; leased to Aviateca 12.70 to 4.71 as TG-ARA; to Leeward Islands Air Transport 11.71 as VP-LAK

G-AXML (206), first flown 22.4.70, C. of A. 29.4.70, Court Line Aviation Ltd., Luton 'Halcyon Cloud'; leased to LANICA 1.72–3.72 as AN-BHJ

G-AXPH (194), first flown 8.10.69 as G-16-9, C. of A. 21.10.69, British Aircraft Corp. Ltd., Hurn; to Austral 11.69 as LV-JNS

G-AXSY (195), first flown 20.10.69, C. of A. 28.11.69, British Aircraft Corp. Ltd., Wisley; to Germanair, Frankfurt 12.69 as D-AMUR

G-AXVO (197), first flown 9.12.69 as G-16-11, C. of A. 9.1.70, British Aircraft Corp. Ltd., Wisley; to Germanair, Frankfurt 3.70 as D-AMOR

G-AXYD (210), first flown 6.3.70, C. of A. 16.3.70, Caledonian Airways Ltd., Gatwick 'Isle of Arran'; British Caledonian Airways Ltd., Gatwick 9.71

G-AYKN (215), first flown 9.10.70 as PI-C1171, registered 7.10.70 to B.A.C. Ltd. for Rumanian demonstrations 20–22.10.70; C. of A. 4.6.71; delivered to Philippine Air Lines 29.10.71 as PI-C1171

G-AYOP (233), first flown 3.3.71, C. of A. 26.3.71, Court Line Aviation Ltd., Luton 'Halcyon Beach'

G-AYOR (232), first flown 29.1.71, C. of A. 5.2.71, Court Line Aviation Ltd., Luton 'Halcyon Dawn'

G-AYOS (213), first flown 15.9.70 as PI-C1161, registered 4.1.71 to B.A.C. Ltd. for ferrying to Philippine Air Lines, Manila; stored at Hurn 12.71

G-AYSC (235), registered 4.2.71 to Court Line Aviation Ltd., Luton; first flown as D-AMAT 17.4.71 and delivered to Germanair, Frankfurt 21.4.71

G-AYWB (237), registered 14.4.71 to Court Line Aviation Ltd., Luton; first flown as TI-1084C 13.5.71 and delivered to L.A.C.S.A., Costa Rica 25.5.71

G-AYXB (192), first flown 15.9.69 as G-16-7, LV-JNR, C. of A. 30.4.71 for Court Line Aviation Ltd., Luton; returned to Austral via Casablanca 14.10.71 as LV-JNR at termination of lease

G-AZEB (188), first flown 17.7.69 as VP-BCN, registered 26.8.71 to Court Line Aviation Ltd., Luton 'Halcyon Bay'

G-AZEC (189), first flown 21.7.69 as VP-BCO, registered 26.8.71 to Court Line Aviation

G-AZMF (240), registered 14.1.72 to Lloyds Associated Aircraft Leasing Ltd. for operation by British Caledonian Airways Ltd.

B.A.T. F.K.23 Bantam

G-EACN (15), F1654, K-123, registered 29.5.19 to the British Aerial Transport Co. Ltd., Hendon; remains preserved by the Shuttleworth Trust, Old Warden

G-EACP (17), F1656, K-125, clipped-wing racer registered 29.5.19 to the British Aerial Transport Co. Ltd.; scrapped at Hendon in 1920

G-EAFM (16), F1655, K-154, registered 24.6.19 to the British Aerial Transport Co. Ltd., Hendon; shown at ELTA 7.19; crashed at Hendon 3.20

G-EAFN (18), F1657, K-155, registered 24.6.19 to the British Aerial Transport Co. Ltd., Hendon; raced at Hendon in 1919; registration lapsed 6.20

G-EAJW Registered 12.8.19 to the British Aerial Transport Co. Ltd., Hendon; sold in Holland 20.8.20

G-EAMM Registered 8.9.19 to the British Aerial Transport Co. Ltd., Hendon; registration lapsed 9.20

G-EAYA (22), F1661, registered 7.7.21 to the British Aerial Transport Co. Ltd., Hendon; sold to Frederick Koolhoven in 1924 and re-registered H-NACH

B.A.T. F.K.26

G-EAAI (29), K-102, 2.8.19, the British Aerial Transport Co. Ltd., Hendon; to C. P. B. Ogilvie, Hendon 1921; taken to Holland by F. Koolhoven 1937

G-EAHN (30), K-167, 8.8.19, the British Aerial Transport Co. Ltd., Hendon; crashed 7.20

G-EANI (31), 11.10.19, the British Aerial Transport Co. Ltd., Hendon; to C. P. B. Ogilvie, Hendon 1921; C. of A. renewed 8.21; d.b.r. Watford 1942

G-EAPK (32), 4.3.20, the British Aerial Transport Co. Ltd., Hendon; S. Instone and Co. Ltd., Croydon 'City of Newcastle' 17.8.20; crashed 31.7.22

B.E.2e

G-EACY C7175, 7.6.19, T. T. Laker (By Air Ltd.), Coventry; crashed 12.19

G-EAGH C7101, 30.9.19, Aircraft Manufacturing Co. Ltd., Hendon; registration lapsed 9.20

G-EAJA A1298, 22.8.19, Kingsford Smith-Maddocks Aeros Co.; Capt. A. H. Curtis, Hendon 10.19; written off 7.20

G-EAJN A1404, 19.8.19, Kingsford Smith-Maddocks Aeros Co.; D. Shepperson, Hendon 11.20; seaside passenger flights until 10.21; scrapped

G-EAJV   A1410, 19.8.19, Kingsford Smith-Maddocks Aeros Co.; A. J. Greenshields, Hendon; 7.20; C. R. Catesby, Hendon 9.20; crashed 10.21

G-EANW   C7185, L. Zborowski, Brooklands; J. R. King, Brooklands 7.25; R. L. Preston 9.25; C. of A. 13.2.26; P.O. T. H. Carr 7.26; written off 2.29

G-EARW   C6953, 13.4.20, A. A. Mitchell trading as the Scottish Aerial Transportation Co.; removed from register at census 10.1.23

G-EATT   C6968, 23.6.20, J. A. Dempsey; flown in Aerial Derby 1920; dismantled

G-EATW   C6964, 20.7.20, S. L. Pettit; crashed 1.21

G-EAVA   C7178, registered 3.8.20 to L. Zborowski, Brooklands; L. C. G. M. Le Champion, Brooklands 8.22; crashed 21.9.22

G-EAVS   C7179, 3.11.20, Handley Page Ltd., Cricklewood; Royal Aero Club, Croydon 10.21; crashed 10.5.22

Beagle-Auster D.4/108

G-ARLG   (3606), 27.4.61, Auster Aircraft Ltd., Rearsby; Beagle Aircraft Ltd., Rearsby 7.62; Wickenby Flying Club, Wickenby, Lincs. 1.71

Beagle-Auster D.6/180

G-ARCS   (3703), 2.11.60, A. Haggis, Speke; Geo. Matthews & Co. Ltd., Halfpenny Green, 9.62; H. E. Smead, Biggin Hill 2.66

G-ARDJ   (3704), 1.9.60, Auster Aircraft Ltd., Rearsby; Hon. E. G. Greenall, Jersey 4.63; F. G. Blain, Elstree 6.65; J. D. Radford, Tollerton 2.71

Beagle D.5/180 Husky

G-ASBV   (3677), 13.8.62, Beagle Aircraft Ltd., Rearsby; crashed at Ecuvillens, near Fribourg, Switzerland 20.10.63

G-ASNC   (3678), 23.4.64, Beagle Aircraft Ltd., Rearsby; M. Arnison-Newgass, Eastleigh 9.68; Airviews (M/c) Ltd., Ringway 10.70

G-ATCD   (3683), 28.5.65, Shackleton Aviation Ltd., Sywell; D. Ancill Ltd., Middleton Stoney; Oxford F & G Group 5.70

Beagle Husky 'Spirit of Butlin's', formerly G-AWSW, which Sir Billy Butlin presented to the Air Training Corps in 1969. (*Richard Riding*)

G-ATKB   (3682), 5.11.66, Beagle Aircraft Ltd., Rearsby; shipped to the Tanzanian Government, Dar-es-Salaam 7.66 as 5H-MMU

G-ATMH   (3684), 3.3.66, N. H. Jones (Tiger Club), Redhill; Devon and Somerset Gliding Club, North Hill 7.71

G-AVOD   (3688), 2.8.67, Turriff Construction Corp., Ltd., Baginton

G-AVSR   (3689), 26.10.67, J. Milne, Teheran, Persia; A. L. Young, Lulsgate 1.72

G-AWSW   (3690), 3.3.69, Beagle Aircraft Ltd., Rearsby; to No. 5 Air Experience Flt., Cambridge 7.69 as XW635 'Spirit of Butlin's'

Terrier 1 G-ASZX was originally intended for Sweden as SE-ELO and carried Beagle's export style blue and white livery. (*A. J. Jackson*)

Beagle A.61 Terrier 1

G-ARLH   (3720), VX109, 10.7.61, Beagle-Auster Aircraft Ltd.; to Leinster Aero Club 10.61 as EI-AMB; rest. 8.68 to Beagle Aircraft Ltd.

G-ARLM   (2573), 17.5.62, Airways Aero Association Ltd., White Waltham; registration cancelled 10.62; converted to Beagle A.61 Terrier 2 G-ASDK

G-ARLN   (3727), WE558, 4.5.62, Airways Aero Association Ltd., White Waltham; registration cancelled 10.62; converted to Beagle A.61 Terrier 2 G-ASDL

G-ARLO   (2500), TW462, 19.10.61, Beagle-Auster Aircraft Ltd.; Southern A/C, Shoreham 11.61; J. B. Campbell, Dyce 8.64

G-ARLP   (3724), VX123, 30.10.61, S. I. Phillips, White Waltham; Freemans' of Bewdley Ltd., Halfpenny Green 3.65

G-ARNO   (3722), VX113, 22.9.61, Sprague & Price Ltd., Speke; A. F. Butcher, South Marston 3.62; S. Boon, Chiseldon 12.68

G-ARRN   (2296), VF527, 22.6.61, Beagle-Auster Aircraft Ltd., Rearsby; Beagle Aircraft Ltd., Shoreham 5.62; withdrawn from use 6.62

G-ARSL   (2539), VF581, 21.7.61, L. N. Hocking, White Waltham; H. Brooks, Shoreham 12.64; S. Brod, Elstree 6.65; M. Costin, Tollerton 4.69

G-ARTM   (3723), WE536, 13.10.61, B. V. Wynne-Jones, White Waltham; E. van Mechelen, White Waltham 9.65; S. N. Cole, Sywell 11.70

G-ARUI   (2529), VF571, 18.4.62, J. A. Wilson, Luton; Dom (Air Services) Ltd., Cambridge 6.64; Cisavia Ltd., White Waltham 5.65

G-ARUX   (3729), WE611, 16.2.62, West London Aero Services Ltd., White Waltham; damaged beyond repair in crash landing at Luton 18.8.63

G-ARXL (3726), WE555, 15.3.62, West London Aero Services; Three Counties A/C, Blackbushe 3.65; M. Wren, Stapleford 10.67; crashed at Chatteris 16.5.70

G-ASKJ (3730), VX926, 27.9.63, Lincoln Aero Club, Kirton Lindsey; D. R. Wilcox, Sywell 7.67; F. H. Feneley, Little Staughton 6.69

G-ASZX (3742), WJ368, 15.4.65, D. C. Smith, Derby; B. Chapman, Spalding 6.66

G-ATHU WE539/7453M, 18.3.66, Air Tows Ltd., Lasham; L. Redshaw, Walney Island 6.66

G-AVCR WE572, registered 12.12.66 to J. C. Benson, Bicester; F. D. Spencer, Banbury 5.69; R.A.F. Gliding & Soaring Association, Bicester 1.72

G-AVCS WJ363, 18.5.67, R.A.F. Gliding & Soaring Association, Bicester; Maj. R. M. Rose, Coningby 7.69; J. N. Nicoll, Lincoln 9.71

G-AVYU (3746), WJ401, 20.5.68, R.A.F. Gliding & Soaring Association, Bicester

Beagle A.61 Terrier 2

G-ARLR (3721/B.601), VW996, 26.4.62, Beagle-Auster Aircraft Ltd.; A. R. Lightfoot, Carlisle 1.64; H. A. Worrall, Carlisle 11.70

G-ARZT (B.602), WE604, 4.7.62, Airways Aero Association, White Waltham; D. W. Head, Blackbushe 6.70

G-ARZU (B.603), WE535, 4.7.62, Airways Aero Association, White Waltham; A. R. Turton, Biggin Hill 1.69; M. S. Bayliss, Baginton 10.70

G-ASAC (B.606), 6.7.62, Airways Aero Association, White Waltham; crashed landing at Roborough Aerodrome, Plymouth 4.9.64

G-ASAD (B.610), 24.7.62, Airways Aero Assoc., White Waltham; Lapwing F/G, Denham 5.69; fell in the English Channel 9 miles SE Lympne 30.8.70

G-ASAE (B.611)), WE606, 25.7.62, Airways Aero Assoc., W. Waltham; destroyed in air collision with Chipmunk WP906 over Sobney, near Reading 4.11.62

G-ASAG (B.607), VF550, 13.7.62, A. F. Butcher, South Marston; Halfpenny Green Flying Club 7.64; crashed near Kidderminster 11.9.66

G-ASAJ (B.605), 4.7.62, Newcastle Aero Club, Woolsington; Casair Ltd., Carlisle 2.63; J. C. Riddell, Yeadon 4.65

G-ASAK (B.604), 4.7.62, Newcastle A/C, Woolsington; Casair Ltd., Carlisle 2.63; W. F. Barnes, Stapleford 10.65; Roding Valley F/G, Stapleford 11.66

G-ASAN (B.608), VX928, 13.7.62, British Executive Air Services Ltd., Kidlington; C.S.E. Ltd., Kidlington 5.64; R. G. Cooper, Blackbushe 10.64

G-ASAX (B.609), TW533, 25.7.62, Southern A/C, Shoreham; H. Smith, Yeadon 5.70

G-ASBT (B.612), WE603, 20.8.62, Beagle Aircraft Ltd., Rearsby; to the Hanseatischer Fliegerclub, Cologne 25.8.62 as D-EBMU

G-ASBU (B.613), 30.8.62, Beagle Aircraft Ltd., Rearsby; D. O'Rourke, Middleton St. George 8.66; Mrs. P. J. Wilcox, Sywell 7.69

G-ASCD (B.615), VW993, 26.7.62, Beagle Aircraft Ltd.; to Holland 12.62 as PH-SFT; rest. 7.68 to Shackleton Av. Ltd., Sywell; D. B. Hayles, Yeadon 1.71

G-ASCE (B.616), WE571, 4.9.62, Beagle Aircraft Ltd.; to Dr. M. Remy, Bex, Switzerland 9.62 as HB-EUD

G-ASCF (B.617), WE548, 1.10.62, Casair Ltd., Carlisle; Gregory Air Taxis Ltd., Woolsington 10.65; to Sweden 7.67 as SE-ELO

G-ASCG (B.618), VF633, 27.3.63, B. Smith, Carlisle; M. Avais, Usworth 9.65; W. G. Wright, Turnhouse 5.68; to Australia 6.69 as VH-UPS

G-ASCH (B.619), VF565, 3.10.63, Andrews Car Sales Ltd., Shoreham; Casair Ltd., Carlisle 2.64; Enstone Eagles Flying Group 6.69

G-ASCI   (B.620), VF629, 6.4.62, Beagle Aircraft Ltd., Rearsby; to Luftsportverein Oberberg, Gummersbach 11.62 as D-ENZO

G-ASDK   (B.702), 12.11.62, West London Aero Services Ltd., W. Waltham; Pensnett Autos Ltd., Halfpenny Gn. 4.65; W. C. Smeaton, Blackbushe 7.69; T. T. Parr, Lulsgate 1.71

G-ASDL   (B.703), 15.11.62, West London A/S Ltd., W. Waltham; P. F. Eycken, Elstree 7.66; Airways Aero Assoc., Booker 10.67; C. P. Lockyer, Booker 3.70

G-ASEY   (B.632), 28.2.63, A.E. Bolwell, Halfpenny Gn.; Halfpenny Green F/C 7.65; J. M. Pashley, Halfpenny Gn. 8.68; J. Woodward, Kidlington 7.70

G-ASFM   (B.623), VX942, 26.4.63, Beagle-Auster Aircraft Ltd.; fatal take-off crash while glider towing at Rearsby 23.5.64

G-ASIE   (B.626), VX924, G-35-11, 30.5.63, Beagle-Auster Aircraft Ltd.; to A.B. Nyge-Aero, Nyköping, Sweden 8.64 as SE-ELR

G-ASMZ   (B.629), VF516, 29.1.64, Casair Ltd., Carlisle; J. P. Taylor, Shobden 10.67; Shobden Aviation Co. Ltd. 1.70; Heron Flying Club, Yeovil 2.71

G-ASNT   (B.624), VF618, PH-SFR, 13.1.64, Wallace & Jones Aviation Ltd., Netherthorpe; crashed at Goring-on-Sea, Sussex 10.4.65

G-ASOI   (B.627), WJ404, 28.2.64, J. Dalgleish, Turnhouse; H. M. Robertson, Turnhouse 9.68; H. Gill, Portsmouth 11.69

G-ASOM   (B.622), VF505, 17.4.64, J. Lyons & Co. Ltd., White Waltham; G. Cluley, Halfpenny Green 2.67; D. F. Redman, Leavesden 3.69; J. Moore, Wickenby 8.71

G-ASOY   (B.621), WE551, 20.3.64, Beagle Aircraft Ltd.; Leicestershire Aero Club, Leicester East 4.65; crashed at Traben-Trarbach, Germany 20.7.65

G-ASPD   (B.640), VF544, 20.5.64, J. Twiname Ltd., Carlisle; Plant Holdings Ltd., Carlisle 2.68; crashed near Leuchars, Fife 1.4.68

G-ASRG   (B.633), WE599, 24.3.64, G. D. Craig & Son Ltd., Middleton St. George; N. Bolsover, M. St. G. 8.67; to Ireland 2.68 as EI-ASU

G-ASRL   (B.631), WE609, 24.4.64, Sir E. Holden, Middleton St. George; Shackleton Av. Ltd., Sywell 11.67; crashed at Kota Kota, Malawi 18.4.69

G-ASUI   (B.641), VF628, 14.8.64, St. Austell By-Pass Garage Ltd., Roborough

G-ASWM   (B.628), VF634, 6.10.64, W. M. Moore, Sywell; Stamford Aviation Ltd., Luton 1.70

G-ASYG   (B.637), VX927, 13.11.64, Don Everall Av. Ltd., Wolverhampton; B. J. Guest, Wolverhampton 5.70

G-ASYN   (B.634), VF519, 21.12.64, L. Brown, Horncastle; H. Wood, Yeadon 9.70

G-ASZE   (B.636), VF552, 28.1.65, Don Everall Av. Ltd., Wolverhampton; G. A. Solkow, Meir 5.68

G-ATBU   (B.635), VF611, 15.4.65, Leicestershire Aero Club, Leicester East; C. W. Shelton Ltd., Sibson 11.67; J. E. Lane, Skegness 10.71

G-ATDN   (B.638), TW641, 14.6.65, T. W. Corbett, Sleap; B. Walker & Co. Ltd., Staverton 11.68; T. A. Hampton, Roborough 6.69; W. E. Taylor and Son Ltd., Exeter 10.70

G-ATKJ   (B.639), VF575, 4.11.65, Beagle Aircraft Ltd.; damaged beyond repair following loss of airscrew when taking off with glider, Rearsby 27.12.65

G-ATMS   (B.643), VF620, 14.1.66, Beagle Aircraft Ltd.; Corby Aero Club 3.69

G-AYDW   (B.646), 2.7.70, Pensnett Autos Ltd., Baginton; R. Bosworth and R. White-house, Baginton 10.70

G-AYDX   (B.647), 13.7.70, Pensnett Autos Ltd., Baginton

Beagle A.61 Terrier 3

G-AVYK (B.642), WJ357, Beagle Aircraft Ltd.; K. G. Wilkinson, Booker 3.69; C. of A. 2.7.69

Beagle A.109 Airedale

G-ARKE (B.501), G-25-11, 25.5.61, Beagle-Auster Aircraft Ltd.; converted to A.111 at Cambridge 8.61; withdrawn from use at Rearsby 4.63

G-ARKF (B.502), first flown 15.6.61, Beagle-Auster Aircraft Ltd.; Beagle Aircraft Ltd. 5.62; dismantled at Rearsby 6.62

G-ARNP (B.503), 27.10.61, Beagle-Auster Aircraft Ltd.; Andrews Car Sales Ltd., Shoreham 12.63; J. D. Perkins, Norwich 11.69

Airedale prototype, G-ARKE, with enlarged spinner after modification to Beagle A.111 with Rolls-Royce Continental engine. (*Frank Hudson*)

G-ARNR (B.504), 13.7.62, Beagle-Auster Aircraft Ltd.; Beagle Aircraft Ltd. 5.62; withdrawn from use and stored at Burton-on-the-Wolds 7.63

G-ARNS (B.505), 4.9.62, Beagle-Auster Aircraft Ltd.; to the Cercle Aérophile de Monthey, Montreux 9.62 as HB-EUE

G-ARNT (B.506), 15.10.63, G. H. Westle, Yeadon; moved to Jersey 1965; A. M. Biddle, Lympne 10.69

G-AROJ (B.508), stored at Leicester East as HB-EUC; registered 3.64 to Lord Trefgarne & partner, Fairoaks; C. of A. 29.4.64; Vaughan Associates Ltd., Elstree 10.67; Capt. H. H. Winch, Minffordd, Merionethshire 9.70

G-ARRO (B.507), 19.11.63, Holmsund Flooring Ltd.; Montague Travel Ltd., Fairoaks 10.67

G-ARXB (B.509), 9.4.62, Beagle Aircraft Ltd., Rearsby; Five Star Flying Group, Elmdon 5.70

G-ARXC (B.510), 20.9.62, Pressed Steel Co. Ltd., Kidlington; to Shannon 11.68 as EI-ATD; rest. 3.70 to W. J. Lambert, Doncaster

G-ARXD (B.511), 26.4.62, Assoc. Iliffe Press Ltd., Fairoaks; Searchlight Films Ltd., Elstree 4.65; A. Bayes, Elstree 11.69

G-ARYZ (B.512), 17.5.62, Beagle Aircraft Ltd., Kidlington; B. Laird, Baginton 8.63; Executive Air Engineering Ltd., Baginton 7.68; A. S. Collard 12.70

G-ARZP (B.513), 25.5.62, Scott (Toomebridge) Ltd., Belfast; J. M. Waddington, Swansea 7.68; T. H. Coward, Eastleigh 5.69

489

G-ARZR (B.514), 28.5.62, Beagle Aircraft Ltd.; British Executive Air Services Ltd., Kidlington 6.63; L. N. Hocking, W. Waltham 6.64; destroyed in air collision with Condor G-AVRV off Folkestone, Kent 6.7.68

G-ARZS (B.515), 8.6.62, Beagle Aircraft Ltd.; Maidenhead Organ Studio Ltd., 11.63; R. C. Hayes, White Walthaam 10.65; G. H. Reeve, Newark 4.70

G-ASAF (B.517), 10.8.62, British Executive Air Services Ltd., Kidlington; to K. Jensen, Aalborg, Denmark 8.62 as OY-AOM

G-ASAH (B.518), 7.5.64, Ewart & Co. (Studio) Ltd., Elstree; Northair Av. Ltd., Yeadon 9.68; Kennair Ltd., Elstree 3.70; T. G. Davis, Elmdon 3.71

G-ASAI (B.516), 26.7.62, British Executive Air Services Ltd., Kidlington; C. A. Ramsey, Carlisle 1.64; A. Robinson, Elstree 11.69; H.B.R.D. F/G, Rotherham

G-ASBH (B.519), 31.7.63, D. H. Crump, Biggin Hill; M. H. Snelling, Valley 8.66; R. C. Magrath, White Waltham 1.70; L. Hocking, White Waltham 6.70

G-ASBI (B.520), 7.5.63, Lord Trefgarne; flown to Australia ex Gatwick 15.5.63, arrived Port Darwin 28.6.63; to Aviation Services Pty. 7.63 as VH-UEM

G-ASBJ (B.521), 20.6.63, Machaine, Watson & Co. Ltd.; flown to Malaya ex Shoreham 27.9.63; registered to the Perak Flying Club 11.63 as 9M-AMT

G-ASBK (B.522), Beagle Aircraft Ltd.; to Sanderson Acfield Services Ltd., Malton, Ontario 6.63 as CF-PDL

G-ASBX (B.524), 30.7.62, Beagle Aircraft Ltd., Rearsby; to Société Dumez, Lahore, Pakistan by air 2.63 to become AP-ANP

G-ASBY (B.523), 30.8.62, Beagle Aircraft Ltd.; W. D. Anderson, Turnhouse 12.63; W. H. Thorburn, Turnhouse 11.68; M. R. Millbourn, White Waltham 11.70

G-ASBZ (B.525), Beagle Aircraft Ltd.; shipped to Australia 8.62 as VH-UEP

G-ASCA (B.526), Beagle Aircraft Ltd.; shipped to Australia 8.62 as VH-UEH

G-ASCB (B.527), 19.10.62, Cumberland Aviation Services Ltd., Carlisle; crashed into river at Barqueiros do Douro, Portugal 26.7.64

G-ASEL (B.534), 22.2.63, Beagle Aircraft Ltd., Rearsby; to S.p.A. Aviaco, Milan/Linate 5.63 as I-CINA for the Milan Aero Club

G-ASEM (B.536), 22.2.63, Beagle Aircraft Ltd., Rearsby; to S.p.A. Aviaco, Milan 5.63 as I-COSO for Sig. G. Torrisi, Catania

G-ASRK (B.538), 13.5.64, Engineering Appliances Ltd., White Waltham

G-ASWB (B.543), 28.8.64, Kebbell Development Ltd., Elstree; W. C. Smeaton, Blackbushe 6.68; Tompa Metals Ltd., Speke 7.69

G-ASWF (B.537), 28.8.64, Shackleton Av. Ltd., Sywell; West Essex Flying Group, Stapleford 8.65; E. A. Pitcher, Stapleford 7.68; Farm Veterinary Supplies (Diss) Ltd. 1.71

G-ATAW (B.541), 8.4.65, A. C. Stewart, Middleton St. George; Northair Aviation Ltd., Yeadon 4.68; M. Beckett and partners, Yeadon 12.70

G-ATCC (B.542), 5.5.65, Shackleton Av. Ltd., Sywell; Northair Av. Ltd., Yeadon 4.68; M. Beckett, Doncaster 2.69; A. E. Lalley, Biggin Hill 3.70

G-AVKP (B.540), SE-EGA, 6.12.67, M. Armstrong, Perranporth

G-AWGA (B.535), D-ENRU, 3.6.65, registered 3.4.68 to W. S. Shackleton Ltd., Sywell; to Shannon 6.68 as EI-ATA; rest 10.69; W. J. Cassidy, Tees-side 3.70

Beagle B.121 Pup Series 1

G-AVDF (01), 23.5.67, Beagle Aircraft Ltd., Shoreham; withdrawn from use and stored at Shoreham 1969; registration cancelled 7.71

(02), unregistered static test airframe tested to destruction at Shoreham in 1967

Pup Series 1 N556MA over Shoreham before its transatlantic delivery flight to Miami Aviation. It first flew as G-AWEB on 24 August 1968.

G-AVZM   (05), 3.4.68, Beagle Aircraft Ltd., Shoreham; Domestic Wholesale Appliances (Shiftrealm) Ltd., Elstree 1.72

G-AVZN   (06), 17.4.68, Shoreham S. of F.; Rogers Aviation Ltd., Cranfield 9.69; Brooklands Flying Club, Sywell 6.71

G-AVZO   (07), 20.5.68, Flairavia Flying Group, Biggin Hill

G-AVZP   (08), 1.6.68, Shoreham S. of F.; J. E. Dixon, Norwich 10.69; Brooklands Flying Club, Sywell 9.70

G-AWDX   (09), 4.7.68, Flairavia Flying Club, Biggin Hill

G-AWDZ   (011), 21.8.68, Shoreham S. of F.; Rogers Aviation Ltd., Cranfield 9.69; Brooklands Flying Club, Sywell 6.71

G-AWEA   (012), 30.8.68, Peter Clifford Av. Ltd., Kidlington; Skywork Ltd., Stansted 1.69; to Belgium 5.69 as OO-WEA

G-AWEB   (013), 30.8.68, Beagle Aircraft Ltd., Shoreham; delivered to Miami Aviation Corporation via Gatwick and Shannon 11.9.68 as N556MA

G-AWEC   (014), 20.9.68, Shoreham S. of F.; Rogers Aviation Ltd., Cranfield 9.69; T. Dyson, Yeadon 6.71

G-AWKM   (017), 30.9.68, Cumberland Aviation Services Ltd., Carlisle; C.S.E. Aviation (Carlisle) Ltd. 1.71

G-AWKO   (019), 22.10.68, Cumberland Aviation Services Ltd., Carlisle; C.S.E. Aviation (Carlisle) Ltd. 1.71

G-AWRB   (021), 15.11.68, Truman Aviation Ltd., Tollerton; Nipper Aircraft Ltd., Castle Donington 2.69

G-AWVC   (026), 19.12.68, Wickenby Flying Club, Wickenby

G-AWWF   (033), 25.2.69, Three Counties Aero Club, Blackbushe

G-AWWH (035), 25.3.69, College of Aeronautics, Cranfield; blown over by gale and wrecked on ground at Dyce Airport, Aberdeen 21.9.69

G-AWYO   (041), 31.3.69, E.F.G. Flying Services Ltd., Biggin Hill

G-AXBE   (039), 12.6.69, Three Counties Aero Club, Blackbushe; damaged beyond repair in forced landing near Basingstoke, Hants. 15.3.70

G-AXDV   (049), 30.4.69, R. W. Husband, Netherthorpe

G-AXDW   (053), 16.5.69, College of Aeronautics, Cranfield

G-AXEW   (061), 6.6. 69, Medminster Ltd., t/a Surrey and Kent Flying Club, Biggin Hill

G-AXEX   (063), 16.6.69, Dr. W. P. Stevens, Tollerton

G-AXEY   (065), 16.6.69, Danish African Co. Ltd., Goodwood

G-AXHK   (071), 27.6.69, F. R. Blennerhassett t/a Middleton St. George Aero Club, Tees-side; overshot and damaged beyond repair at Tees-side 10.1.70
G-AXIA   (078), 14.7.69, College of Aeronautics, Cranfield
G-AXIB   (080), 22.7.69, W. S. Bateson, Squires Gate; destroyed in fatal crash at Squires Gate 16.5.70
G-AXIC   (082), 24.7.69, Dismore Aviation Ltd., Cambridge; Three Counties Aero Club, Blackbushe 4.70
G-AXMV   (099), 11.9.69, Medminster Ltd., t/a Surrey and Kent Flying Club, Biggin Hill
G-AXMW   (101), 11.9.69, Medminster Ltd., t/a Surrey and Kent Flying Club, Biggin Hill
G-AXNL   (113), 30.9.69, I. Booker-Milburn, Abbotsinch; P. A. Crawford, Roborough 11.71
G-AXNM   (114), 30.9.69, M. H. Gill, Carlisle; Brooklands Flying Club, Sywell 2.71
G-AXOZ   (115), 14.10.69, G. A. Gardner, Weston-super-Mare
G-AXPA   (116), 14.10.69, Medminster Ltd., t/a Surrey and Kent Flying Club, Biggin Hill
G-AXPB   (117), 16.10.69, A. A. Wild, Yeadon; A. A. Welch, Yeadon 12.69
G-AXPC   (119), registered 7.10.69 to Beagle Aircraft Ltd.; to the Vliegclub Rotterdam 10.69 as PH-VRS
G-AXPD   (121), 23.10.69, Beagle Aircraft Ltd.; Medminster Ltd., t/a Surrey and Kent Flying Club, Biggin Hill 1.70
G-AXPM   (122), 30.10.69, Beagle Aircraft Ltd.; R. W. Willoughby, Tollerton 4.71
G-AXSC   (138), 1.12.69, Beagle Aircraft Ltd.; Medminster Ltd., t/a Surrey and Kent Flying Club, Biggin Hill 1.70
G-AXSD   (139), 1.12.69, Beagle Aircraft Ltd.; College of Aeronautics, Cranfield 1.70
G-AXSE   (142), registered 13.11.69 to Beagle Aircraft Ltd.; to Konair Flying School, Constance 2.70 as D-EBBZ
G-AXTZ   (148), 19.12.69, L. Brown, Skegness
G-AXUA   (150), 10.3.70, F. R. Blennerhassett, t/a Middleton St. George Aero Club, Tees-side

The following Pup Series 1 aircraft, partly constructed when Beagle ceased production early in 1970, were registered 30.7.71 to Beagle Aircraft Ltd. and completed at Shoreham: (c/n 152) G-AZCJ; (158–162) G-AZCP to 'CU; (168) G-AZDA; (169) G-AZDB

Beagle B.121 Pup Series 2

G-AVLM (03), 30.4.68; G-AVLN (04), 5.3.68; G-AWDY (010), 9.8.68, to Switzerland 8.68 as HB-NAA; G-AWKK (015), 17.9.68, to U.S.A. 10.68 as N557MA; G-AWKL (016), 3.10.68, to Australia 10.68 as VH-EPA; G-AWKN (018), 19.10.68, to Switzerland 11.68 as HB-NAD; G-AWRA (020), 28.10.68, to New Zealand 2.69 as ZK-CYP; G-AWRC (022), 8.11.68, to Ireland 12.68 as EI-ATF, to Finland 3.69 as OH-BGD; G-AWRD (023), 9.12.68, to Switzerland 1.69 as HB-NAH; G-AWRE (024), 24.1.69, to Iraq 6.69; G-AWRF (025), 4.12.68, to Luxembourg 12.68 as LX-NIT; G-AWRW (027), 15.1.69; G-AWRX (028), 30.1.69, d.b.r. 8.70; G-AWWE (032), 26.2.69, d.b.r. at Fairoaks 12.9.70; G-AWWG (034), 20.2.69, to Iraq 3.69 as YI-AEK; G-AWYJ (038), 31.3.69

G-AXCV (044), 28.3.69, to New Zealand 4.69 as ZK-CYP(2); G-AXCW (045), 21.4.69; G-AXCX (046), 28.4.69; G-AXDU (048), 7.5.69; G-AXES (056), 29.5.69, to Kenya 10.69 as 5Y-AKG; G-AXET (057), 29.5.69; G-AXEU (062), 26.6.69; G-AXEV (070), 26.6.69; G-AXFZ (050), 23.5.69, to Iraq 6.69 as YI-AEL; G-AXHL (072), 2.7.69, to Iraq 7.69 as YI-AEM; G-AXHM (074), 2.7.69, to Iraq 7.69 as YI-AEN; G-AXHN

The first production Pup Series 2, G-AWDY/HB-NAA, over Shoreham before its ferry
flight to the Swiss Aero Club, August 1968

(075), 2.7.69, to Iraq 7.69 as YI-AEO; G-AXHO (077), 10.7.69; G-AXIE (087), 5.8.69;
G-AXIF (088), 5.8.69; G-AXJH (089), 14.8.69; G-AXJI (090), 14.8.69; G-AXJJ (091),
14.8.69; G-AXJN (092), 19.8.69; G-AXJO (094), 28.8.69; G-AXJP (095), 28.8.69, to
Austria 8.70 as OE-DUP; G-AXMX (103), 30.9.69, to Australia 12.69; G-AXNN (104),
30.9.69; G-AXNO (105), 23.9.69; G-AXNP (106), 23.9.69; G-AXNR (108), 26.9.69;
G-AXNS (110), 14.10.69; G-AXOJ (109), 16.10.69; G-AXPN (123), 10.9.71;
G-AXPO (124), to Australia 11.69 as VH-EPG; G-AXPP (125) to Australia 11.69 as
VH-EPH; G-AXPR (127), to Australia 11.69 as VH-EPJ; G-AXSA (133), to Switzerland
1.71 as HB-NAG; G-AXSB (135), to Germany 7.71 as D-EKAK; G-AZGF (076),
PH-KUF, registered 6.10.71 to Shackleton Aviation Ltd., Baginton

The following Pup Series 2 aircraft, partly constructed when Beagle ceased production
early in 1970, were registered 30.7.71 to Beagle Aircraft Ltd. and completed at Shoreham:
(c/n 153–157) G-AZCK to 'CO; (163–167) G-AZCV to 'CZ

A number of frustrated exports, crated in Australian marks at Rearsby during the same
period, were registered 15.9.71 to Domestic Wholesale Appliances (Shiftrealm) Ltd. and
overhauled at Elstree: (c/n 130) VH-EPL/G-AZEU; (131) VH-EPM/G-AZEV; (132)
VH-EPN/G-AZEW; (134) VH-EPO/G-AZEX; (136) VH-EPP/G-AZEY, to Switzerland
11.71 as HB-NAK; (137) VH-EPQ/G-AZEZ, C. of A. 19.10.71; (143) VH-EPR/
G-AZFA, C. of A. 19.10.71

Beagle B.125 Bulldog Series 1 (*see also Volume 3, Scottish Aviation Bulldog*)
G-AXEH   (001), 27.5.69, Beagle Aircraft Ltd., Shoreham; Scottish Aviation (Bulldog)
          Ltd., Prestwick 8.70
G-AXIG   (002), construction commenced 7.69, completed at Prestwick 1970; first flown
          14.2.71; C. of A. 16.2.71, Scottish Aviation (Bulldog) Ltd., Prestwick

Beagle B.206 prototypes
G-ARRM   (001), 206X, 9.10.62, British Executive & General Aviation Ltd., Shoreham;
          withdrawn from use at Shoreham after C. of A. expiry 23.12.64
G-ARXM   (002), 206Y, 5.6.63, British Executive & General Aviation Ltd., Shoreham;
          crashed at Wisborough Green, Sussex 25.5.64

Beagle B.206 Series 1

G-ASMK (005), 10.8.64, Beagle Aircraft Ltd., Shoreham; converted to Series 2 prototype 5.65; redesignated 1.66 as Series 2X; picketed at Shoreham 12.71

G-ASOF (007), 23.10.64, Beagle Aircraft Ltd.; Cumberland Aviation Services Ltd., Carlisle 11.68 'Helvellyn'; D. G. Walker, Biggin Hill 12.69; Lombank Ltd., Biggin Hill 1.71

G-ASWJ (009), 12.5.65, Rolls-Royce Ltd., Hucknall

G-ATDD (013), 21.7.65, Beagle Aircraft Ltd.; Cumberland Aviation Services. Ltd., Carlisle 'Blencathra' 11.68; James Spence Ltd., Biggin Hill 10.69; J. P. Air Services Ltd., Tollerton 1.71

G-ATEU (015), 29.9.65, Beagle Aircraft Ltd.; crashed on take-off at Mushingashi, N'dola, Zambia 17.1.66

G-ATHO (019), 28.10.65, Maidenhead Organ Studios Ltd., Booker; Shoreham Flying School 8.68; Chas. Spreckley & Co. Ltd., Booker 1.70

G-ATKO (022), 28.3.66, Imperial Tobacco Co. Ltd., Lulsgate; Beagle Aircraft Ltd., Rearsby 6.68; conv. to Ser. 2; picketed at Shoreham 12.71

G-ATKP (026), 8.3.66, Beagle Aircraft Ltd.; E. R. M. Adams and partners, Halfpenny Green 10.71

G-ATYC (039), 16.3.67, Beagle Aircraft Ltd.; Airways Training Ltd., Gatwick 5.68; Clerkenwell Trust & Finance Ltd., Biggin Hill 2.71; Northair Aviation Ltd., Yeadon 10.71

G-ATYW (038), registered 26.8.66 to Beagle Aircraft Ltd.; Northern Air Taxis Ltd., Yeadon 11.71

G-ATZO (044), 2.1.67, Beagle Aircraft Ltd.; to Irish Aviation Services, Dublin 3.67 as EI-APO; rest. 5.68 to Airways Training Ltd., Gatwick; R. J. Everett, Whatfield 2.72

Beagle 206 Series 1 G-ATHO and Series 2 G-ATLF at Gatwick in April 1966 showing the improved large loading door of the later mark.

Beagle B.206 Series 2

G-ATLF (023), 7.4.66, Beagle Aircraft Ltd.; left Gatwick for Australia 1.5.66; reg'd. 6.66 to Beagle Aircraft Sales (Australasia) Ltd. as VH-UNC

G-ATSD (027), 28.4.66, Beagle Aircraft Ltd., Shoreham; delivered to Aero Res S.A., Madrid ex Gatwick 1.5.66 as EC-BES

G-ATTL (028), 18.5.66, Beagle Aircraft Ltd.; ferried to Buenos Aires and re-registered to Cia Argentina de Aero Taxi as LV-DMR, later LV-IYB

G-ATUJ (029), 7.7.66, Beagle Aircraft Ltd., Shoreham; sold to National Airways Corporation, Johannesburg 4.67 as ZS-EMI; to Zambia 11.69 as 9J-ABB

G-ATUK (032), 23.6.66, Beagle Aircraft Ltd.; to the Sudan 1.67 as ST-ADA

G-ATVT (035), 25.8.66, Beagle Aircraft Ltd.; to Aero Res S.A., Madrid 12.66 as EC-BFR

G-ATYD (040), 2.9.66, Beagle Aircraft Ltd.; picketed at Shoreham 12.71

G-ATYE (041), 2.9.66, Beagle Aircraft Ltd.; Maidenhead Organ Studios Ltd., Booker 10.67

G-ATYX (043), 31.1.67, Beagle Aircraft Ltd.; delivered to Aero Res S.A., Madrid ex Gatwick 6.2.67 as EC-BJF

G-ATZP (046), 24.1.68, Beagle Aircraft Ltd.; to Zambian Flying Doctor Service 7.70 as 9J-AAM; to the U.S.A. 2.71 as N8010

G-ATZR (047), 20.7.67, Beagle Aircraft Ltd.; re-registered in Australia to Beagle Aircraft Sales (Australasia) Ltd. 1.68 as VH-UNL

G-AVAL (048), 26.7.67, G.K.N. Group Services Ltd., Baginton; Sterling Armament Co. Ltd., Luton 2.71; crashed near Tours, France 6.3.71

G-AVAM (049), 7.4.67, Boulay Investments Ltd., Jersey; fatal crash after take-off from Jersey airport 6.8.70

G-AVAN (050), 12.6.67, Beagle Aircraft Ltd.; flown to Australia ex Gatwick 16.6.67; to the Royal Flying Doctor Service, Sydney 10.67 as VH-FDA

G-AVCG (051), 5.12.67, Beagle Aircraft Ltd.; picketed at Shoreham 12.71

G-AVCH (052), 22.6.67, Beagle Aircraft Ltd.; flown to Australia ex Gatwick 12.7.67; to the Royal Flying Doctor Service, Sydney 8.67 as VH-FDB

G-AVCI (053), 25.5.67, British Ropes Ltd., Gamston

G-AVCJ (054), 23.5.67, Imperial Tobacco Co. Ltd., Lulsgate

G-AVHO (058), 6.9.67, British Aircraft Corporation Ltd., Wisley

G-AVHP (057), 26.5.67, Beagle Aircraft Ltd.; to the U.S.A. 10.67 as N996B

G-AVHR (056), registered 24.2.67 to Beagle Aircraft Ltd., Rearsby; on overhaul at Shoreham 11.71

G-AVHS (055), 31.8.67, Beagle Aircraft Ltd., Shoreham; delivered to the U.S.A. ex Gatwick 4.9.67; re-registered N1008B on arrival

G-AVLK (059), 22.3.68, Beagle Aircraft Ltd.; on overhaul at Shoreham 11.71

G-AVLL (060), 18.1.68, Beagle Aircraft Ltd.; to the Federal Military Government of Nigeria, Lagos 1.68 as 5N-AGW

G-AWRM (070), G-35-24, to Aero Comahue, Argentina 10.68 as LV-PLE 'Calfucura'; rest. to Beagle 5.69; C. of A. 27.5.69; Executive Flights Ltd., Guernsey 6.69; Jersey Fisheries Ltd., Jersey 2.71

G-AWRN (071), G-35-25, to Aero Comahue, Argentina 10.68 as LV-PLF 'Numuncura'; rest. 5.69 to Beagle; to Brazil 1.72 as PT-DYW

G-AWRO (072), G-35-26, to Aero Comahue, Argentina 10.68 as LV-PLG 'Caupolican'; rest. to Beagle 5.69; Northair Aviation Ltd., Yeadon 2.70; C. of A. 20.3.70

G-AXCB (061), 10.4.69, Beagle Aircraft Ltd.; to the Royal Flying Doctor Service, Sydney 4.69 as VH-FDF

G-AXPV (074), Mk.3 prototype G-35-28 reconverted to Mk.2, registered 28.10.69 to Beagle Aircraft Ltd.; picketed at Shoreham 12.71

G-AXZL (062), G-35-16, PT-DIP, 24.3.70, Northair Aviation Ltd., Yeadon

Beagle B.206 Series 3
G-AWLN (080), registered 8.7.68 to Beagle Aircraft Ltd., Rearsby; picketed at Shoreham 12.71

Beech 17
G-ADDH (23), B-17L, 4.6.35, damaged in forced landing at Orpington, Kent 21.10.36, sold abroad as spares 7.37; G-ADLE (50), B-17R, 16.8.35, crashed on Island of Laaland, Denmark 20.1.39; G-AENY (114), C-17R, 17.12.36, sold abroad 12.37; G-AESJ (118), C-17R, 22.4.37, impressed 5.41 as DS180

Beech D-17S
G-AHXJ (6686), U.S. Navy 23674, Royal Navy FT465, 17.2.47, destroyed in ground collision at Ypenburg 24.6.47; G-AIHZ (6905), U.S.A.A.F. 44-67799, FT535, sold in South Africa 6.48; G-AJJE (4925), 43-10877, FZ435, 8.5.47, to Southern Rhodesia 5.51 as VP-YIT; G-AJJJ (4922), 43-10874, FZ432, 11.4.47, to Australia 12.52 as VH-MJE; G-AJLA (4935), 43-10887, FZ439, registered 27.3.47, not converted, registration cancelled 31.12.48; G-AJLD (4921), 43-10873, FZ431, registered 2.4.47, not converted, to U.S.A. 10.48; G-ALNN (6699), 44-67722, FT473, LN-HAK, 14.4.49, sold abroad 4.49 as F-OACT; G-AMBY (295), U.S.A.A.F. 39-139, impressed 5.41 as DR628, sold as NC91397 in 1947, British C. of A. 27.7.51, to Southern Rhodesia 8.51 as VP-YIV

Beech C-18S Expediter
G-AIYI, U.S.A.A.F. 42-43477, Royal Navy FE883, 22.6.48, crashed at Sherburn-in-Elmet, Yorks. 24.8.49; G-AKCZ (6116), 43-35616, 11.1.49, to Northern Rhodesia 9.50 as VP-RCA; G-ALJJ (8468), PI-C843, VR-HED, 18.3.50, to Australia 11.50 as VH-KFD; G-ANVL (6395), N714A, sold in France 12.54 as F-BHCJ; G-APBX (269), VT-ANJ, 30.5.57, damaged beyond repair by fire on ground, Hurn 5.8.59

Beech 18 (*postwar models*)
G-ASNX (BA-663), H-18 tri-gear, 6.2.64, sold in the Congo 12.69 as 9Q-CSP; G-ASUG (BA-111), E-18S, 31.3.65, Loganair Ltd., Abbotsinch; G-ATUM (A-850), D-18S, N20S, D-IANA, to U.S.A. 11.68 as N15750; G-AXWL (CA-167), D-18S, N6685, 19.6.70, Sagittair Ltd., Heathrow; G-AYAH (CA-159), D-18S, N6123, 1.1.71, Sagittair Ltd., Heathrow

Beech 23 Musketeer I
G-ASBB (M-15), N3057G, 17.12.62; G-ASCL (M-107), 15.1.63, crashed at Kirkbymoorside, Yorks. 24.6.66; G-ASFB (M-231), 5.4.63; G-ASJO (M-518), 9.8.63; G-AWIK (M-534), PH-MUS, 14.8.68

Beech A23 Musketeer II
G-ASWP (M-587), 22.12.64; G-ATBI (M-696), 23.6.65

Beech A23A Musketeer Custom III
G-AVVU (M-1092), 20.5.68; G-AXSX (M-1287), 29.5.70

The first British registered Expediter, G-AIYI (luxury conversion for Prince Aly Khan), awaiting Customs clearance at Croydon in May 1949. (*E. J. Riding*)

Beech A23-19 (or 19A*) Musketeer Sport III

G-AVDP (MB-229), 29.6.67, crashed near Le Bourget 5.10.68; G-AVHF (MB-236), 18.8.67; G-AWFZ (MB-323), N2811B, 28.5.68; G-AWKU* (MB-352), 30.8.68, crashed at Lympne 16.4.69; G-AWTR* (MB-411), N2758B, 9.5.69; G-AWTS* (MB-412), N2763B, 14.5.69; G-AWTT* (MB-418), N2766B, 24.3.70, crashed at Northiam, Sussex 7.5.70; G-AWTU* (MB-423), N2769B, 5.6.70, sold in the Trucial States 3.71; G-AWTV* (MB-424), N2770B, 21.8.70

Beech A23-24 Musketeer Super III

G-AVYF (MA-316), 13.6.68; G-AXCJ (MA-352), 1.8.69

Beech C23 Musketeer

G-AYPB (M-1319), 2.4.71; G-AYWS (M-1351), 29.7.71; G-AYYU (M-1353), 12.10.71

Beech 35 and A35 Bonanza

G-AJVG (D-1098), 21.1.48, to Israeli Air Force 1949, to 4X-AER in 1956, to F-BCAQ in 1958; G-AKYV (D-446), ZS-BPX, 22.3.48, to Southern Rhodesia 4.48 as VP-YGS; G-ANZH (D-2108), N8698A, to French Morocco 2.56 as F-DABZ; G-AOAM (D-1990), VR-ABA, 19.4.55, to Belgium 5.56 as OO-ALU; G-APVW (D-11168), ZS-BTE, 4X-ACI, N9866F, 4.3.60; G-ASIZ (D-161), N2769V, 11.10.63, w.f.u. 11.71

Beech 35 Bonanza (*other Models*)

G-APTY (D-4789), G35, EI-AJG, 4.6.59; G-ARKJ (D-6736), N35, 5.5.61; G-ARZN (D-6795), N35, N215DM, 5.6.62; G-ASFJ (D-7171), P35, 25.4.63; G-ASJL (D-5132), H35, N5582D, 16.8.63; G-ATII (D-7693), S35, VR-BCD, 21.9.65; G-ATSR (D-6236), M35, EI-ALL, 1.7.66

Beech 35-33 Debonair

G-ASHR (CD-214), EI-ALI, 10.5.65; G-AVHG (CD-1090), model C33, 4.3.68

Beech 65 and A65* Queen Air

G-ARFF (LC-50), 16.10.60; G-ARII (LC-85), 29.3.61, to Australia 5.68 as VH-CTE; G-AROU (LC-114), 5.1.62, to the U.S.A. 2.69 as N1277C; G-AVNA* (LC-267), 20.10.67

Beech 65-70 Queen Air (*1968 model with engines of A65 and increased span of B80*)
G-AYPC (LB-35), 23.3.71

Beech 65-80, A80 and B80* Queen Air
G-ASDA (LD-64), 16.11.62; G-ASIU (LD-102), 24.7.63; G-ASKM (LD-116), 1.10.63; G-ASRX (LD-159), 15.7.64; G-ASVE (LD-185), A80, 2.10.64; G-ASXV (LD-205), 1.10.64; G-AVDR* (LD-339), 21.3.67; G-AVDS* (LD-337), 9.3.67; G-AVNG (LD-176), A80, D-ILBO, 25.5.67; G-AWKY* (LD-393), re-registered G-AWOI; G-AWOI* (LD-393), 17.9.68; G-AYIK* (LD-370), VQ-BAR, 8P-BAR, to the U.S.A. 11.70; G-AZFS* (LD-322), N900KQ, registered 29.9.71; G-AZOH* (LD-410), N789IR, registered 3.72

Beech 95 Travel Air
G-APUB (TD-240), 95, 7.6.59; G-AREJ (TD-423), B95, 27.9.60; G-ASIR (TD-543), D95A, 25.7.63; G-ASMF (TD-565), D95A, 29.1.64; G-ASYJ (TD-595), D95A, N8675Q, 24.11.64; G-ASZC (TD-532), B95A, OY-AOP, 6.1.65, to Finland 12.69 as OH-BTB; G-ATLX (TD-538), D95A, N7714N, 17.1.66, crashed at Zürich 8.11.69; G-ATRC (TD-504), B95A, EI-AMC, 24.3.66; G-AWCW (TD-717), E95, 21.6.68; G-AXUX (TD-417), B95A, OE-FAD, 6.2.70; G-AYNM (TD-629), N5887J, 10.2.71

The Guinness company acquired the swept fin Beech A.65 Queen Air G-AVNA in 1967 for business flights out of Leavesden. (*Richard Riding*)

Beech 95-A55* and B55 Baron
G-ASDO* (TC-401), 23.1.63; G-ASLG* (TC-495), 12.9.63, to the U.S.A. 12.70 as N18JH; G-ASNO (TC-574), 21.2.64; G-ASOH (TC-565), 10.6.64; G-ASRV (TC-677), 25.6.64; G-ATGR (TC-841), N6146V, 21.7.65; G-AWTW (TC-1200), 5.3.69; G-AXOV (TC-1307), 28.1.70; G-AXXR (TC-1347), 16.5.70; G-AYID (TC-1283), SE-EXK, 18.8.70; G-AYKA (TC-523), D-IKUN, 24.11.70, to Switzerland 2.71; G-AYPD (TC-1389), 22.3.71; G-AZDK (TC-1406), 6.12.71

Beech 95-C55A* and D55 Baron

G-AVET* (TE-362), 17.5.67; G-AWAD (TE-548), 26.3.68; G-AWAE (TE-546), 26.3.68; G-AWAF (TE-544), 17.4.68; G-AWAG (TE-542), 22.3.68; G-AWAH (TE-540), 13.3.68; G-AWAI (TE-538), 13.3.68; G-AWAJ (TE-536), 13.3.68; G-AWAK (TE-534), 13.3.68; G-AWAL (TE-532), 8.3.68; G-AWAM (TE-530), 12.3.68; G-AWAN (TE-528), 8.3.68; G-AWAO (TE-524), 5.3.68

Beech 95-58 Baron

G-AYGZ (TH-112), 24.11.70, Baron Air Charters, Southend; G-AZLG (TH-195), registered 30.12.71 to Eagle Aircraft Services Ltd., Leavesden

Bell 47D-1

G-APYL (Lfs 1-1953), SE-HAG rebuilt, 19.7.62, crashed near Perth 18.7.63; G-ASJW (12), N158B, 5.7.63, crashed at Saxilby, Lincs. 19.7.71; G-ASOL (4), N164B, 14.5.64; G-ATSF (31), N6064C, 26.4.66, crashed at Brigg, Lincs. 31.5.66; G-ATSH (183), N237B, 7.6.66, crashed near Cranbrook, Kent 11.6.71; G-AZJJ (147), I-MAGR, registered 3.12.71

Bell 47G-1

G-ANZX (17), 18.3.55, crashed at Conington, Hunts. 25.7.62; G-AODI (42), 10.8.55, crashed at Luton 25.2.59; G-AODJ (44), 6.11.55, crashed near Perth 12.7.60; G-AODK (45), 12.12.55, crashed at Kennoway, Fife 9.8.65; G-ARIA (6), N4929V, 8.3.61; G-ARXH (40), N120B, SE-HAE, CF-HDO, 4.4.62; G-ASDM (16), 5.12.62, d.b.r. 5.70; G-ATYV (177), F-BDRU, 9L-LAJ, 3.11.67

Bell 47G-2

G-ASYW (2219), VP-TCF, CP-671, VR-BBA, 22.12.64; G-ATZX (1469), HB-XAT, 2.11.66; G-AVDO (804), N62K, 14.4.67; G-AVKS (689), 9J-RDE, 18.7.67; G-AVZF (2225), LN-ORO, 28.3.68, to Sierra Leone 2.69 as 9L-LAM; G-AWSJ (218), Austrian A/F, 23.12.69; G-AWSK (211), Austrian A/F, 27.4.70; G-AXCC (1413), Austrian A/F code 3B-XA, 20.5.69, to Iran 7.69 as EP-HBD; G-AYOE (1515), F-OCBF, 5.5.71; G-AYOH (1637), Gabon Army, registered 21.12.70

Bell 47G-4A

G-AVSK (7576), N7178S, 19.9.67; G-AXRV (7690), to Sierra Leone 12.69 as 9L-LAO; G-AYAE (7682), 13.4.70; G-AZBR (7756), 23.7.71

Bell 47G-4A (*Westland-built, first flown as G-17-1 to G-17-16*)

G-AXKK (WA.716), 7.8.69; G-AXKL (WA.717), 7.8.69; G-AXKM (WA.718), 29.8.69; G-AXKN (WA.719), 29.8.69; G-AXKO (WA.720), 4.9.69; G-AXKP (WA.721), 4.9.69; G-AXKR (WA.722), 21.9.69; G-AXKS (WA.723), 21.9.69; G-AXKT (WA.724), 29.9.69; G-AXKU (WA.725), 10.10.69; G-AXKV (WA.726), 31.10.69; G-AXKW (WA.727), 29.10.69; G-AXKX (WA.728), 31.10.69; G-AXKY (WA.729), 5.11.69; G-AXKZ (WA.730), 3.12.69; G-AXLA (WA.731), 3.12.69

Note: The above formed the training fleet of Bristow Helicopters Ltd., Middle Wallop

Bell 47G-5

G-AWRZ (7832), HB-XCK, 29.10.68; G-AYEL (25007), 29.6.70; G-AYMY (25023), 29.4.71; G-AZBS (25045), registered 15.7.71

Bell 206A Jet Ranger
G-AVTE (66), 12.2.68; G-AWJL (181), 27.6.68, crashed at Broughton, Northants.
22.7.69; G-AWOL (239), 26.8.68; G-AWOM (280), 15.10.68; G-AWRI (306), 31.3.69;
G-AWUC (323), 31.3.69; G-AXAY (332), 14.5.69; G-AXGO (416), 27.6.69; G-AXJC
(417), 14.8.69; G-AXMM (405), N1469W, 21.8.69; G-AXXO (420), 18.3.70; G-AYCM
(529), 26.6.70; G-AYDK (337), 28.5.70, sold in Zambia 7.71; G-AYHN (225), N4702R,
7.8.70; G-AYMH (586), 2.12.70; G-AYMW (587), 13.1.71; G-AYMX (605), 18.8.71;
G-AYTF (385), N1453W, 17.3.71

Bensen B-7M Gyroplane (*with unified system of constructors' numbers*)
G-APSY   (2), McCulloch, built by J. Howell at Queens Gate, London; damaged in heavy
        landing at Biggin Hill 19.9.59; for sale 1968
G-APUD   (1), McCulloch, built by Wg. Cdr. K. H. Wallis at Southwick, Sussex, f/f at
        Shoreham, A. to F. 16.6.59; F. G. Purvis, Biggin Hill 12.66; w.f.u. 2.70
G-APUV   (3), McCulloch, built by Sqn. Ldr. R. A. Harvey; A. to F. 30.8.60; damaged at
        Manby 2.9.60; rebuilt at Leconfield 1961; I. Wallis, Sheffield 10.65; w.f.u.
        10.70
G-ARBF   (4), McCulloch, built by J. S. Sproule at Shoreham; A. to F. 31.10.60;
        damaged in heavy landing at Tangmere 29.4.61
G-ARBK   (5), McCulloch, built by P. E. Blyth at Maltby, Rotherham, Yorks; withdrawn
        from use 1962
G-ARFE   (6), 55 h.p. Lycoming, built by J. S. Rymill at Brookmans Park; f/f at
        Panshanger 1962; P. Pozerkis, Polebrook 3.64; withdrawn from use 5.65

Bensen B-8M Gyrocopter (*unified constructors' numbers*)
G-ARTJ   (7), built by W. G. Hosie; arrived Renfrew by road 28.8.62; at Bonnyrigg,
        Midlothian 5.65 awaiting Volkswagen engine
G-ARTN   (8), built by D. Campbell at Hungerford; A. to F. 22.2.62; G. Whatley,
        Membury 3.62; withdrawn from use and rebuilt as G-AVXB
G-ARUN   (9), registered to N. A. F. Edwards, Gillingham, Kent; not completed and
        constructor's number re-allotted as under:
G-ARZL   (9), registered to C. H. Force, Perranporth, Cornwall
G-ASLF   (10), built by G. D. Talby-Bates at Blaby, Leicester 1962; S. R. Hughes,
        Wolverhampton 12.64
G-ASLP   (11), built by R. Caygill, Mackworth, Derby
G-ASME   (12), built by A. D. Marks at Liverpool 1963 and exhibited there 2.68
G-ASNZ   (13), built by Yorkshire Gyrocopter Group at Barwick-in-Elmet; flown as
        glider 1964; shown at Church Fenton 5.66
G-ASWN   (14), built by D. R. Shepherd, Edinburgh
G-ASXH   (15), built by C. E. Rose, Blackbushe where first flown 22.11.64; to Kidlington
        2.67; to Membury 9.68
G-ATIB   (16), built by A. Atkinson at Huddersfield 1965; shown at Church Fenton 5.66
G-ATLP   (17), registered 9.12.65 to M. W. J. Whittaker, Dorchester
G-ATOZ   (18), registered 7.2.66 to J. D. M. Wilson, Pwllheli; initially flown from beach
        as a glider; withdrawn from use at Pwllheli 11.69
G-AWBO   (19), built by N. D. Hamilton-Meikle at Douglas, I.O.M.; A. to F. 10.6.68;
        fatal crash at Druidale near Ronaldsway, Isle of Man 15.9.69

Bensen B-8M Gyrocopter (*builders' initials as constructors' numbers*)
G-ARWW (SJB.1), S. J. Bartlam, Flamstead, Herts; A. to F. 23.2.62; T. A. Hampton,
        Warfleet Creek, Dartmouth 6.64; R. L. Toms, Hurn 10.69

G-29-3, second of three Bensen B-8MEJ Agricopters built at Luton by D. Napier and Son Ltd. for crop spraying, 1961, and believed later to have been registered G-ATWT.

G-ASCT (D.C.3), D. Campbell, Hungerford; A. to F. 11.10.62; L. D. Goldsmith and N. R. Cole, Blackbushe 1964; E. Barlow, Padstow 3.68; w.f.u. 9.70

G-ASFN (B.1/1), E. Brooks, Spennymoor; flown at Middleton St. George; withdrawn from use at Spennymoor 11.69

G-ASLU (DPR.1), D. P. Reason, Coventry; A. to F. 1.10.63; P. Pozerkis, Sywell 7.64; damaged beyond repair on take-off at Burtonwood 11.4.66

G-ATFA (WHE.111), W. H. Ekin, Belfast; A. to F. 11.8.65; C. L. Dalgleish, Raven Rock Farm strip, Colne, Lancs. 1.69

G-AVXB (PCL.1), P. C. Lovegrove, Didcot; A. to F. 21.6.68; M. E. Williams, Warrington 11.69

G-AWDW (DS.1330), D. C. J. Summerfield, Devonport; A. to F. 22.5.68; conv. to Campbell-Bensen CB-8S; A. M. Curzon-Howe-Herrick, Le Chastenet, France 1969 (see page 542)

G-AWGL (RGG.1), registered 9.4.68 to R. G. Goodman, Sutton Coldfield; withdrawn from use 12.70

G-AWPL (NFH.1), registered 11.9.68 to N. F. Higgins, Durrington

G-AXBG (RC.1), registered 12.3.69 to R. C. Curtis, Beckenham

G-AXCI (CEW.1), registered 20.3.69 to C. E. Winter, Leicester

G-AXDE (TJH.001), registered 9.4.69 to T. J. Hartwell, Bromham, Beds.

G-AXII (PCL.4), registered 25.6.69 to P. C. Lovegrove, Didcot, C. of A. 17.9.71

G-AYTY (J.H.W.1), registered 11.3.71 to J. H. Wood, Hempstead, Gloucester

G-AZAZ (RNEC.1), registered 2.7.71 to Royal Naval Engineering College, Davidstow Moor, Cornwall

Bensen Gyrocopter (*other production*)

G-ATWT (21102), built at Luton 1961 by D. Napier & Son Ltd.; believed ex G-29-3; A. J. Howlet, Swanton Morley 'Miss Celaneous'; A. to F. 8.12.66; D. Hutchinson, Hythe 11.67; B. G. Baker, Romford 4.70; withdrawn from use 10.70

G-AVIK (00/61/009), B-7MC, built by D. Campbell 1962; shipped to P. G. Nicholas, Mombasa, Kenya as VP-KRI; registered 14.3.67 to Lt. M. S. Kennard, Gillingham; A. to F. 20.9.68

G-AVST (B.7), B-7M seaplane, registered to E. R. Wilson, Pwllheli 8.8.67

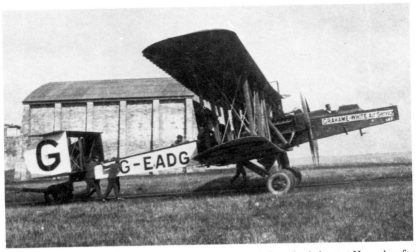

Kangaroo G-EADG of the Grahame-White Air Service being wheeled out at Hounslow for a mail flight to Newcastle in October 1919. (*B. A. Hewitt*)

Blackburn Kangaroo

G-EADE B9981, 21.6.19, The Grahame-White Aviation Co. Ltd., delivered Seaton Carew–Hendon 11.5.19; damaged beyond repair 7.19

G-EADF B9982, delivered Seaton Carew–Hendon 11.5.19 for The Grahame-White Aviation Co. Ltd., no C. of A., crashed on take-off at Hendon 31.5.19

G-EADG B9985, 6.6.19, delivered Seaton Carew–Hendon 11.5.19 for The Grahame-White Aviation Co. Ltd.; withdrawn from use at C. of A. expiry 7.6.21

G-EAIT B9978, 11.8.19, North Sea Aerial & General Transport Co. Ltd., Brough; cabin type converted to dual trainer 3.25; crashed at Brough 5.5.25

G-EAIU B9973, 1.9.19, North Sea Aerial & General Transport Co. Ltd., Brough; converted to prototype dual trainer 'Bonzo' 5.24; scrapped 1929

G-EAKQ B9972, 9.9.19, North Sea Aerial & General Transport Co. Ltd., Brough; sold to the Peruvian Army Flying Service, Las Palmas, Lima 7.21

G-EAMJ B9977, cabin type for Australia Race, registered to North Sea Aerial & General Transport Co. Ltd. 8.9.19; to dual trainer 'Felix the Cat' 1924; C. of A. 20.6.24; scrapped at Sherburn-in-Elmet 1929

G-EAOW B9970, 17.11.19, Blackburn Aeroplane & Motor Co. Ltd.; Australia Race machine abandoned in Crete 8.12.19

G-EBMD Origin not known, 21.1.26, North Sea Aerial & General Transport Co. Ltd., Brough; converted to dual trainer 'Wilfred' to Works Order 8837; scrapped at Sherburn-in-Elmet 1929

G-EBOM Origin not known, 13.7.26, North Sea Aerial & General Transport Co. Ltd., Brough; converted to dual trainer 'Pip' to Works Order 8839; crashed landing at Brough 25.9.28

G-EBPK Origin not known, 3.2.27, North Sea Aerial & General Transport Co. Ltd., Brough; converted to dual trainer 'Squeak' to Works Order 8840; scrapped at Sherburn-in-Elmet in 1929

Blackburn Swift

G-EAVN (6368), registered to the Blackburn Aeroplane & Motor Co. Ltd. 22.9.20; flown to Martlesham and handed over to the R.A.F. 23.12.20 as N139

Blackburn Dart

G-EBKF (8312/1), 21.4.25, North Sea Aerial & General Transport Co. Ltd., Brough; beyond repair in accident near Digby, Lincs. 7.1.32

G-EBKG (8312/2), 13.6.25, North Sea Aerial & General Transport Co. Ltd., Brough; withdrawn from use at Brough 25.1.28

G-EBKH (8312/3), 26.10.25, North Sea Aerial & General Transport Co. Ltd., Brough; withdrawn from use 9.5.33; scrapped at Hatfield, Yorks. 1952

Blackburn Velos

G-EBWB (9593/1), 28.3.28, North Sea Aerial & General Transport Co. Ltd., Brough; to scrap yard in York Road, Leeds 12.33; still there in 1939

G-AAAW (1440/1), 23.4.29, North Sea Aerial & General Transport Co. Ltd.; to I. R. Parker, Hooton 4.33; scrapped at Old Warden, Beds. in 1935

G-AAAX (1440/2), 9.5.29, North Sea Aerial & General Transport Co. Ltd., Brough; to scrap yard in York Road, Leeds 5.33; still there in 1939

G-AAAY (1440/3), 22.5.29, North Sea Aerial & General Transport Co. Ltd., Brough; withdrawn from use 3.33 and scrapped at Bentley, Yorks.

G-AAAZ (1440/4), 9.10.29, North Sea Aerial & General Transport Co. Ltd., Brough; withdrawn from use and scrapped 3.32

G-AAUM (9762/1), 2.1.31, North Sea Aerial & General Transport Co. Ltd., Brough; withdrawn from use and scrapped 1.34

Blackburn Bluebird I

G-EBKD (9803/1), 4.9.26, Robert Blackburn, crashed and burned out following air collision with Westland Widgeon G-EBPW at Bournemouth 6.6.27

Blackburn Bluebird II

G-EBRE (9803/2), 25.8.27, Suffolk and Eastern Counties Aero Club; damaged beyond repair at Hadleigh, Suffolk 6.1.30

G-EBRF (9803/3), 27.7.27, Yorkshire Aeroplane Club, Sherburn; L. C. Mitchell, Chard 6.30; Hon. A. B. Mildmay, Gravesend 7.36; burned at Gravesend 7.37

G-EBRG (9803/4), 13.9.27, Yorkshire Aeroplane Club; crashed at Sherburn-in-Elmet, Yorks. 5.2.28

G-EBSV (9803/5), 18.9.27, Yorkshire Aeroplane Club; F. R. G. Spikins, Hanworth 12.30; dismantled at Spikins' Garage, Twickenham, Middlesex 1932

G-EBSW (9803/6), 19.9.27, seaplane for Blackburn Aeroplane & Motor Co. Ltd.; to landplane for Flt. Lt. G. E. Lywood 6.30; w.f.u. at Whitchurch 12.33

G-EBSX and G-EBSY (9803/7 and 9803/8), 31.9.27 and 8.10.27, Blackburn Aeroplane and Motor Co. Ltd.; shipped to Brazil 17.10.27

G-EBSZ (9803/9), 20.9.27, Suffolk and Eastern Counties Aero Club, Hadleigh; C. N. Prentice, Colchester 3.31; R. D. Gerrans, Broxbourne 1.32; dismantled 1936

G-EBTA (9803/10), 13.10.27, Blackburn Aeroplane & Motor Co. Ltd., Brough; North Sea Aerial & General Transport Co. Ltd. 4.28; crashed 12.30

G-EBTB   (9803/11), 27.3.28, Blackburn Aeroplane & Motor Co. Ltd., Brough; Yorkshire Aeroplane Club, Sherburn-in-Elmet 5.28; crashed 3.29

G-EBTC   (9803/12), 8.7.28, North Sea Aerial & General Transport Co. Ltd., Brough; crashed 3.30

G-EBUH   (9803/13), 17.5.28, Blackburn Aeroplane & Motor Co. Ltd., Brough; Suffolk and Eastern Counties Aero Club 1928; withdrawn from use 1932

G-EBUI   (9803/14), 5.10.28, Blackburn Aeroplane & Motor Co. Ltd., Brough; crashed 3.29

Blackburn Bluebird III

G-EBWE   (629/1), 17.3.28, T. A. Gladstone, Brough; North Sea Aerial & General Transport Co. Ltd. 5.29; K. V. Wright, Farnborough 5.30; crashed at Nivelles, Belgium 8.9.31

G-AABB   (1450/1), 4.12.28, H. T. Merritt, Auckland; to S. J. Blackmore, Hamilton as ZK-AAQ; to Waikato Aero Club; crashed Te Rapa, Hamilton 2.4.33

G-AABC   (1450/2), 8.11.28, sold in Spain to Señor Fernando Pedioza 8.29

G-AABD   (1450/3), 27.3.29, Armstrong Siddeley Motors Ltd.; Yorkshire Aeroplane Club 4.29; C. E. Dooks, Bridlington 3.31; dismantled 1931

G-AABE   (1450/4), 27.3.29, Suffolk and Eastern Counties Aero Club; Southend Flying Services Ltd. 2.33; G. H. Charlton, Chilworth 3.36; crashed near Lichfield 22.3.36

G-AABF   (1450/5), 31.5.29, Suffolk and Eastern Counties Aero Club; H. R. Law 5.30; Mrs. G. Gallien and Miss S. O'Brien 6.31; crashed Hatfield 18.6.31

G-AABG   (1450/6), laid down as seaplane for the Suffolk and Eastern Counties Aero Club, order cancelled and aircraft not completed

Blackburn Bluebird IV

G-AABV   (1430/1), 6.2.30, Sqn. Ldr. L. H. Slatter; Dr. C. S. Glass, Meir 2.31; T. E. Richardson, Hedon 11.33; crashed at Hedon, Hull 6.3.34

G-AACB   (1730/1), registered 11.10.28 to Blackburns; registered in Norway 10.29 as floatplane N-40; registration not taken up

G-AACC   (1730/2), 28.6.29, Auto Auctions Ltd., Heston; R. McAlpine 5.31; R. A. Kent and P. H. Forth, Hooton 7.37; burned in hangar fire at Hooton 8.7.40

G-AAIR   (SB.202), 20.1.30, Auto Auctions Ltd.; Master of Sempill 5.31; Lord Douglas Hamilton 12.31; C. Berens, High Post 2.33; R. W. H. Knight, Christchurch 7.34; destroyed in fatal crash at Agades, Nigeria 17.4.35

G-AAJC   (SB.207), 8.1.30, Cobham-Blackburn Air Lines, Bulawayo; to Rhodesia and Nyasaland Airways 6.32 as VP-YAI; to Hon. J. Grimston, Cape Town 8.35

G-AAJD   (SB.202), registered to Blackburn Aeroplane & Motor Co. Ltd. in error 18.6.29, duplicating G-AAIR above; registration cancelled 1.30

G-AAJE   (SB.203), registered 18.6.29 to Blackburns; re-registered to National Flying Services Ltd., Hanworth 10.10.29 as G-AAOB q.v.

G-AAOA   (SB.200), 7.1.30, National Flying Services Ltd., Hanworth; delivered Cowes– Hanworth 14.1.30; crashed at Feltham, Middlesex 6.4.30

G-AAOB   (SB.203), 7.1.30, National Flying Services Ltd., Hanworth; delivered Cowes– Hanworth 14.1.30; dismantled at Hanworth 12.30

G-AAOC   (SB.204), 7.1.30, National Flying Services Ltd., Hanworth; A. V. M. Longmore 3.31; Mrs. E. Scott, Madrid 11.33; to Spain 12.33 as EC-UUU

G-AAOD (SB.205), 10.1.30, National Flying Services Ltd., Hanworth; dismantled at Hanworth 12.30

G-AAOE (SB.206), 11.1.30, National Flying Services Ltd.; R. E. H. Allen, Hanworth 9.31; sold abroad 12.34

G-AAOF (SB.209), 14.1.30, National Flying Services Ltd., Hanworth; H. R. Fields, Hedon 8.31; to Reykjavik F/C 1937 as TF-LOA; registration not used

G-AAOG (SB.213), 24.1.30, National Flying Services Ltd., Hanworth; damaged beyond repair in accident at Oulton, Leeds 13.4.30

G-AAOH (SB.214), 10.2.30, National Flying Services Ltd., Hanworth; S. Hargreaves, Hanworth 1.31; crashed at Bushey Park, Middlesex 27.1.31

G-AAOI (SB.221), 10.3.30, National Flying Services Ltd.; J. W. Gillan 4.31; York County Aviation Club 5.32; crashed at Sherburn-in-Elmet 20.1.34

G-AAOJ (SB.222), 14.3.30, National Flying Services Ltd., Hanworth; Miss W. Slack, Renfrew 5.31; dismantled at Gatwick 3.37

Registrations G-AAOK to 'OZ, reserved by National Flying Services Ltd. for additional Bluebird IVs, were not taken up.

G-AASU (SB.208), 10.1.30, Airwork Ltd., Heston; crashed at Hendon 7.6.30

G-AASV (SB.211), 4.4.30, E. L. Gandar Dower, Dyce; registration cancelled 12.37

G-AATE (SB.210), 10.1.30, J. Ellis, Sherburn; P. H. Ford, Heston 10.38; S. Bicham, Orkney 5.45 (not delivered); scrapped at Hamsey Green 1.47

G-AATM (SB.217), 4.2.30, North Sea Aerial & General Transport Co. Ltd., Brough; crashed at Coal Aston, Sheffield 27.8.32

G-AATN (SB.218), 27.2.30, Auto Auctions Ltd.; Sir R. McAlpine 4.30; to A. S. Gallimore, Karachi 13.9.32 as VT-ACR; crashed at Lingeh, Persian Gulf 5.33 while en route Karachi–England

G-AATO (SB.219), 27.2.30, Auto Auctions Ltd.; N. Holden, Selsey 6.30; Blackburn Aeroplane & Motor Co. Ltd. 1.32; crashed near Brough 4.8.32

The second pre-production Bluebird IV on Blackburn floats at Cowes in 1929.
(*Beken & Sons, Cowes*)

H. F. Broadbent's Australia flight Bluebird G-ABJA 'City of Sydney', Gipsy II engine, at Brough in February 1931.

G-AATP   (SB.220), 24.2.30, Auto Auctions Ltd.; P. Dujardin, Sherburn 4.30; York County Aviation Club, Sherburn 5.34; crashed at E. Heslerton 24.6.34

G-AATS   (SB.215), 5.2.30, H. J. Andrews, Brough; Maj. H. P. L. Higman, Hooton 6.33; crashed 12.36

G-AAUF   (SB.223), 25.3.30, Auto Auctions Ltd.; North Sea Aerial & General Transport Co. Ltd.; damaged beyond repair at Brough 16.7.32

G-AAUG   (SB.224), 28.3.30, Auto Auctions Ltd.; North Sea Aerial & General Transport Co. Ltd. 8.32; R. Giddings 7.37; crashed at High Post 20.3.38

G-AAUT   (SB.225), 16.5.30, North Sea Aerial & General Transport Co. Ltd., Brough; floatplane trials; sank off Felixstowe 12.1.31

G-AAUU   (SB.226), 4.4.30, Harald Peake M.P.; Henlys Ltd., Heston 5.34; sold abroad 6.35

G-AAUV   (SB.227), 5.5.30, Hon. L. Guinness; D. Ripley, Heston 2.31; Brooklands Aviation Ltd. 11.31; registration cancelled at census 12.32

G-AAUW   (SB.228), 21.5.30, Auto Auctions Ltd.; Maj. A. Holt 6.30; North Sea Aerial & General Transport Co. Ltd. 2.31; registration cancelled 12.32

G-AAUX   (SB.229), 27.5.30, Auto Auctions Ltd.; North Sea Aerial & General Transport Co. Ltd. 4.35; crashed at Waltham airfield, Grimsby 29.4.37

G-AAUY   (SB.230), 19.6.30 Auto Auctions Ltd., Heston; sold abroad 7.30

G-AAVF   (SB.231), 26.6.30, Earl of Amherst, Heston; F. A. I. Muntz, Heston 12.31; North Sea Aerial & General Transport Co. Ltd. 11.32; crashed 9.36

G-AAVG   (SB.232), 25.6.30, Auto Auctions Ltd.; H. R. Fields, Hedon 5.31; Lt. Cdr. G. A. Hall, R.A.N. 7.32; registered in Australia 7.33 as VH-UQZ

G-AAVH   (S.B.233), 5.8.30, Kennings Ltd.; loaned to Sheffield Aero Club, Coal Aston 8.30; S. Laurence, Alfreton 4.31; registration cancelled 12.34

G-AAVI   (SB.234), registered 29.8.30 to A. F. Horsman; re-registered to Delhi Flying Club 4.32 as VT-ADI, withdrawn from use 8.41

G-AAVJ   (SB.235), registration not taken up, believed crated for Japan

G-AAVK   (SB.236), registration not taken up, believed crated for Japan

506

G-ABDS (SB.245), 23.9.30, Hon. Mrs. Victor Bruce 'Bluebird'; world flight machine, withdrawn from use 12.31

G-ABEU (SB.246), 8.10.30, Robert Blackburn; North Sea Aerial & General Transport Co. Ltd. 1.32; to Switzerland 7.32 as CH-345, later HB-ULU

G-ABEV (SB.238), not taken up; aircraft re-registered G-ABPN q.v.

G-ABEW (SB.239), 3.5.32, not taken up; to the Indo-American Automobile Co., Bombay 6.32 as VT-ADK

G-ABEX (SB.240), 20.9.30, registration not taken up; re-registered G-ABVZ q.v.

G-ABEY (SB.241), registration not taken up; re-registered G-ABZX q.v.

G-ABGF (SB.252), 17.2.31, Miss Delphine Reynolds; to floatplane 3.31; totally unserviceable in Sierra Leone through acid corrosion 5.31

G-ABJA (SB.249), 19.3.31, H. F. Broadbent 'City of Sydney'; G. N. Wilson, Heston 1.32; to Irish Air Lines, Waterford 12.32 as EI-AAO

G-ABMI (SB.254), 1.7.31, Hon. Mrs. Victor Bruce 'Bluebird II'; crashed 2.33

G-ABOT (SB.237), 14.11.31, Norman Holden, Selsey; J. B. Taylor, Heston 9.35; S. G. Cummings, Brooklands 10.38; sank off Kirkmichael, I.O.M. 29.5.39

G-ABPN (SB.238), 20.11.31, Kennings Ltd.; Blackburn Aeroplane & Motor Co. Ltd. 9.33; loaned to Grimsby Aero Club; crashed at Waltham 16.10.35

G-ABPV (SB.253), 1.10.31, Blackburn Aeroplane & Motor Co. Ltd., Brough; crashed at Tatoi Aerodrome, Athens, Greece 24.10.31

G-ABVZ (SB.240), 22.4.32, Blackburn Aeroplane & Motor Co. Ltd., Brough; to Karl Winkler 12.32 as D-2536

G-ABZX (SB.241), registered 22.9.32 to the North Sea Aerial & General Transport Co. Ltd., Brough but cancelled and re-registered G-ADXG q.v.

G-ADXG (SB.241), registered 15.11.35 to the North Sea Aerial & General Transport Co. Ltd., Brough as Blackburn Cirrus Minor I test bed; transferred to Class B markings 1.36 as B-10

Blackburn Segrave

G-AAXP (1), prototype built as the Saro Segrave Meteor at Cowes 1930, C. of A. 27.6.30, Aircraft Investment Corporation; J. G. D. Armour 10.31; G. E. de Lengerke 6.32; withdrawn from use at Brough 9.32

G-ABFP (3169/1), 18.3.31, G. Selfridge, Heston; British Air Nav. Co. Ltd., Heston 2.32; Mrs. F. S. Burnside, Redhill 3.33; scrapped Brough 3.34

The Saro-built Segrave Meteor G-AAXP at Brough in 1931.

G-ABFR (3169/2), 26.5.32, North Sea Aerial & General Transport Co. Ltd., Brough;
F. R. Evans, Brough 10.35; British Air Transport Ltd., Redhill 5.36; withdrawn from use at Redhill 2.38

G-ABZJ (3854/1), registered 17.9.32 to J. G. D. Armour; registration cancelled 12.32;
same aircraft re-registered 22.11.33 to Blackburn Aeroplane & Motor Co.
Ltd., Brough as G-ACMI with Duncanson wing; first flown 2.2.34; dismantled
at Brough 10.35

Blackburn B-2

G-ABUW (3580/1), 23.6.32, R. Blackburn; North Sea Aerial & General Transport Co.
Ltd., 3.33; impressed 2.42, believed as 2887M to Leeds ATC

G-ABWI (4700/1), 30.6.32, Blackburn Aeroplane & Motor Co. Ltd.; North Sea Ae. &
G.T. Co. Ltd. 3.33; crashed at Ellerton, Selby, Yorks. 9.10.36

G-ACAH (4700/2), 15.3.33, N.S.Ae. & G.T. Co. Ltd., Blackburn Aircraft Co. Ltd.
12.36; to Hemel Hempstead A.T.C. 2.42 as 2907M

G-ACBH (4700/3), 22.3.33, N.S.Ae. & G.T. Co. Ltd.; Blackburn Aircraft Ltd. 12.36;
written off near Brough 16.3.40; impressed 2.42 as 2895M but only the
fuselage survived for handing over to Brentwood, Essex A.T.C.

G-ACBI (4700/4), 22.3.33, N.S.Ae. & G.T. Co. Ltd.; Blackburn Aircraft Ltd. 12.36;
fatal crash at Brough Haven, East Yorks. 30.7.37

G-ACBJ (4700/5), 22.3.33, N.S.Ae. & G.T. Co. Ltd.; Blackburn Aircraft Ltd. 12.36; to
Wimborne Minster, Dorset A.T.C. 2.42 as 2900M

G-ACBK (4700/6), 22.3.33, N.S.Ae. & G.T. Co. Ltd.; Blackburn Aircraft Ltd. 12.36; to
Rotherham, Yorks. A.T.C. 2.42 as 2906M

G-ACEM (5093/1), 3.4.33, N.S.Ae. & G.T. Co. Ltd.; Blackburn Aircraft Ltd. 12.36; to
Thanet, Kent A.T.C. 2.42 as 2890M; to Manston 7.46

G-ACEN (5093/2), 3.4.33, N.S.Ae. & G.T. Co. Ltd.; Blackburn Aircraft Ltd. 12.36;
fatal crash at Osgodby, Selby, Yorks. 26.12.40

G-ACEO (5093/3), 5.4.33, N.S.Ae. & G.T. Co. Ltd.; Flying Training Ltd., Hanworth
12.36; fitted Cirrus Major 11.39; impressed 2.42 as 2899M and handed over
to Eden Valley, Cumberland A.T.C.

G-ACEP (5093/4), 10.4.33, N.S.Ae. & G.T. Co. Ltd.; Blackburn Aircraft Ltd. 12.36;
registration cancelled 2.43

G-ACER (5093/5), 12.4.33, N.S.Ae. & G.T. Co. Ltd.; Blackburn Aircraft Ltd. 12.36;
crashed at Brough 11.9.40

G-ACES (5093/6), 11.5.33, N.S.Ae. & G.T. Co. Ltd.; Blackburn Aircraft Ltd. 12.36; to
Gelligaer, Wales A.T.C. 2.42 as 2904M

G-ACLC (5290/1), 2.2.34, N.S.Ae. & G.T. Co. Ltd.; Flying Training Ltd., Hanworth
2.36; Blackburn Aircraft Ltd. 12.36; destroyed in fatal air collision over the
River Humber with Blackburn B-2 G-ADFS 24.6.40

G-ACLD (5290/2), 12.4.34, N.S.Ae. & G.T. Co. Ltd.; Blackburn Aircraft Ltd. 12.36;
allotted 2885M in 1942 but remained with Blackburns; C. of A. renewed
2.7.46 with Gipsy III; renewed 6.8.47 with Cirrus Major III; crashed at
Rawcliffe, York 16.6.51; cannibalised to service G-AEBJ

G-ACPZ (5290/3), 18.5.34, Aircraft Exchange & Mart Ltd., Hanworth; Flying Training
Ltd. 5.35; to Gosport, Hants A.T.C. 2.42 as 2902M

G-ACRA (5290/4), 24.5.34, Blackburns; Flying Training Ltd. 5.35; to Malden and
Coombe, Surrey A.T.C. 2.42 as 2905M; scrapped at Witney 1946

G-ACUE (5290/5), 28.6.34, Blackburns; N.S.Ae. & G.T. Co. Ltd. 10.34; struck H.T.
cables and crashed at Little Weighton, East Yorks. 12.11.35

G-ACZH (5290/6), 12.1.34, Blackburns; Flying Training Ltd. 10.34; Blackburn Aircraft Ltd. 12.36; to East Ham, London A.T.C. 2.42 as 2886M

G-ADFN (5920/1), 30.5.34, Flying Training Ltd., Hanworth; No. 4 E.F.T.S., Brough 10.39; to Durham A.T.C. 2.42 as 2897M

G-ADFO (5920/2), 3.6.35, Flying Training Ltd., Hanworth; No. 4 E.F.T.S., Brough 10.39; d.b.r. in forced landing at Newport, Yorks. 3.9.40

G-ADFP (5920/3), 5.6.35, Flying Training Ltd., Hanworth; No. 4 E.F.T.S., Brough 10.39; to Pontefract, Yorks. A.T.C. 2.42 as 2892M

G-ADFR (5920/4), 7.6.35, Flying Training Ltd., Hanworth; No. 4 E.F.T.S., Brough 10.39; to Pinner, Middlesex A.T.C. 2.42 as 2894M

G-ADFS (5920/5), 9.6.35, Flying Training Ltd., Hanworth; No. 4 E.F.T.S., Brough 10.39; fell into Humber after air collision with G-ACLC q.v.

G-ADFT (5920/6), 17.6.35, Flying Training Ltd., Hanworth; No. 4 E.F.T.S., Brough 10.39; to Bexhill, Sussex A.T.C. 2.42 as 2908M

G-ADFU (5920/7), 20.6.35, Flying Training Ltd., Hanworth; No. 4 E.F.T.S., Brough 10.39; to Birmingham A.T.C. 2.42 as 2903M

L6891, first of three B-2 aircraft for the R.A.F., was originally to have been G-AEBM.

G-ADFV (5920/8), 25.6.35, Flying Training Ltd., Hanworth; No. 4 E.F.T.S., Brough 10.1.39; to Caterham, Surrey A.T.C. 2.42 as 2893M

G-ADLF (5920/9), 16.7.35, Flying Training Ltd., Hanworth; No. 4 E.F.T.S., Brough 10.39; to Port Talbot, Wales A.T.C. 2.42 as 2891M

G-ADLG (5920/10), 28.11.35, Flying Training Ltd., Hanworth; No. 4 E.F.T.S., Brough 10.39; to Welling, Kent A.T.C. 2.42 as 2888M

G-ADZM (6300/1), 12.2.36, N.S.Ae. & G.T. Co. Ltd.; Blackburn Aircraft Ltd. 12.36; to West Harrow, Middlesex A.T.C. 2.42 as 2896M

G-ADZN (6300/2), 27.2.36, Flying Training Ltd., Hanworth; No. 4 E.F.T.S. 10.39; fitted Cirrus Major; to Airedale, Yorks. A.T.C 2.42 as 2889M

G-AEBE (6300/3), 6.3.36, N.S.Ae. & G.T. Co. Ltd.; Blackburn Aircraft Ltd. 12.36; to Chipping Sodbury, Glos. A.T.C. 2.42 as 2898M

G-AEBF (6300/4), 20.3.36, Flying Training Ltd., Hanworth; crashed at Sunbury, Middlesex 9.9.37

G-AEBG (6300/5), 16.4.36, N.S.Ae. & G.T. Co. Ltd.; Blackburn Aircraft Ltd. 12.36; to Caerphilly, Wales A.T.C. 2.42 as 2938M

G-AEBH (6300/6), 6.5.36, Flying Training Ltd., Hanworth; crashed at Kingsbury, Middlesex 17.8.36

G-AEBI (6300/7), 29.5.36, N.S.Ae. & G.T. Co. Ltd.; Flying Training Ltd. 9.36; destroyed in ground collision with Hawker Hart, Hanworth 31.1.38

G-AEBJ (6300/8), 5.6.36, Flying Training Ltd., Hanworth; No. 4 E.F.T.S., Brough 10.39; retained by Blackburn Aircraft Ltd.; still airworthy in 1972

G-AEBK (6300/9), 20.7.36, N.S.Ae. & G.T. Co. Ltd.; Flying Training Ltd. 12.36; No. 4 E.F.T.S. 10.39; to Cheshunt, Herts. A.T.C. 2.42 as 2901M

G-AEBL (6300/10), 29.4.36, Flying Training Ltd., Hanworth; No. 4 E.F.T.S., Brough 10.39; to Hawick, Roxburghshire A.T.C. 2.42 as 2973M

G-AEBM (6795/1), registered 1.37 to Blackburn Aircraft Ltd.; sold to Air Ministry 6.37; No. 4 E.F.T.S. 6.37 as L6891; to Cosford 9.41 as 3158M

G-AEBN (6795/2), registered 1.37 to Blackburn Aircraft Ltd.; sold to Air Ministry 6.37; No. 4 E.F.T.S. 6.37 as L6892; to Cosford 9.41 as 3159M

G-AEBO (6795/3), registered 1.37 to Blackburns; sold to Air Ministry 6.37; No. 4 E.F.T.S. 6.37 as L6893; to No. 9 S. of T.T., Morecambe 10.41 as 3877M

Boeing 377 Stratocruiser (*all B.O.A.C. aircraft*)

G-AKGH (15974), 15.11.49, 'Caledonia', to Transocean 8.58 as N137A, later N402Q; G-AKGI (15975), 9.1.50, 'Caribou', to Transocean 1.59 as N100Q/N405Q; G-AKGJ (15976), 6.2.50, 'Cambria', to Transocean 1.59 as N102Q/N407Q; G-AKGK (15977), 16.2.50, 'Canopus', to Transocean 3.59 as N104Q/N409Q; G-AKGL (15978), 5.4.50, 'Cabot', to Transocean 8.58 as N86Q/N404Q, later N9600H; G-AKGM (15979), 24.3.50, 'Castor', to Transocean 3.59 as N105Q/N410Q; G-ALSA (14943), SE-BDP ntu, 'Cathay', crashed at Prestwick 25.12.54; G-ALSB (14944), OY-DFY ntu, 25.10.49, 'Champion', to Transocean 2.59 as N103Q/N408Q; G-ALSC (14945), LN-LAF ntu, 1.12.49, 'Centaurus', to Transocean 1.59 as N101Q/N406Q; G-ALSD (14946), SE-BDR ntu, 15.12.49, 'Cassiopeia', to Transocean 9.58 as N85Q/N403Q; G-ANTX (15965), N31225, 13.6.55, 'Cleopatra', to Transocean 8.59 as N107Q/N412Q; G-ANTY (15966), N31226, 28.4.55, 'Coriolanus', to Transocean 8.59 as N108Q/N413Q; G-ANTZ (15967), N31227, 21.5.55, 'Cordelia', to Transocean 8.59 as N106Q/N411Q; G-ANUA (15968), N31228, 2.6.55, 'Cameronian', to Transocean 8.59 as N109Q/N414Q; G-ANUB (15969), N31229, 6.4.55, 'Calypso', scrapped at Stansted 1959; G-ANUC (15971), N31231, 12.5.55, 'Clio', scrapped at Stansted 1959; G-ANUM (15927), N1027V, 2.9.55, 'Clyde', to Transocean 7.58 as N1027V/N401Q

Boeing 707-138B

G-AVZZ (17699), VH-EBD, 6.1.68, British Eagle International Airways Ltd. 'Enterprise', to Laker Airways Ltd., Gatwick 1.69; G-AWDG (17702), VH-EBG, 10.3.68, British Eagle 'Phoenix', to Laker Airways Ltd., Gatwick 1.69

Boeing 707-321

G-AYAG (18085), N759PA, 22.4.70, Lloyd International Airways Ltd., Stansted; G-AYBJ (17597), N719PA, 5.5.70, British Midland Airways Ltd., Castle Donington; G-AYRZ (18084), N758PA, 25.2.71, Lloyd International Airways Ltd., Stansted; G-AYSL (17599), N721PA, 6.4.71, Dan-Air Services Ltd., Gatwick; G-AYVE (18083), N757PA, 3.4.71, British Midland Airways Ltd., Stansted; G-AYVG (17598), N720PA, 29.4.71, Donaldson International Airways Ltd., Stansted; G-AYXR (17608), N730PA, Donaldson International Airways Ltd., Stansted

Boeing 707-323C

G-AYZZ (20089), N8417, 8.6.71, Caledonian/B.U.A., returned to American Airlines 10.71 as N8417

Boeing 707-324C

G-AZJM (18886), N17323, 30.12.71, Lloyd International Airways Ltd., Stansted

Boeing 707-336C (*B.O.A.C. aircraft*)

G-ASZF (18924), N2978G, 19.12.65; G-ASZG (18925), 20.12.65; G-ATWV (19498), 1.12.67; G-AVPB (19843), 13.8.68; G-AXGW (20374), 24.3.70; G-AXGX (20375), 8.4.70; G-AXXY (20456), 3.2.71; G-AXXZ (20457), 17.5.71; G-AYLT (20517), 29.6.71

Boeing 707-349C and 707-355C* (*British Caledonian Airways aircraft*)

G-AWTK (18975), N322F, 6.12.68, 'County of Angus'; G-AWWD (19355), N325F, 8.1.69, 'County of Argyll'; G-AXRS* (19664), N526EJ, PH-TRF, 7.11.69, 'County of Caithness'; G-AYEX* (19417), N525EJ, 27.6.70, 'County of Perth', to Britannia Airways Ltd., Luton 10.71

Boeing 707-365C

G-ATZC (19416), registered to British Eagle 14.9.66, not imported, sold to Airlift International Inc., Miami 2.67 as N737AL, to Transavia 1969 as PH-TRW, rest. 7.70 to Caledonian Airways Ltd. as 'City of Stirling', C. of A. 8.7.70; G-ATZD (19590), 23.12.67, British Eagle International Airways Ltd., Heathrow, leased in the Lebanon 2.68 with Bermudan marks VR-BCP, rest. to B.O.A.C. 12.68

Boeing 707-373C

G-AYSI (18707), N375WA, 2.4.71, Britannia Airways Ltd., Luton

Boeing 707-379C

G-AWHU (19821), N762U, 28.6.68, B.O.A.C. (replacing 707-465 G-ARWE)

Boeing 707-399C (*British Caledonian Airways aircraft*)

G-AVKA (19415), N319F, 2.6.68, 'Flagship Bonny Scotland'; G-AVTW (19767), 5.1.68, 'County of Ayr'

Caledonian Airways Boeing 707-399C G-AVKA 'Flagship Bonny Scotland' at Gatwick in 1968. (*Aviation Photo News*)

Boeing 707-436 (*B.O.A.C. aircraft*)
G-APFB (17703), N31241, 9.5.60; G-APFC (17704), N5088K, 17.5.60; G-APFD
N5091K, 28.4.60; G-APFE (17706), N5092K, 29.4.60, crashed on Mt. Fuji, Japan
5.3.66; G-APFF (17707), 13.5.60; G-APFG (17708), N5094K, 22.6.60; G-APFH
(17709), 13.7.60; G-APFI (17710), 23.7.60; G-APFJ (17711), 24.9.60; G-APFK
(17712), 29.9.60; G-APFL (17713), 21.10.60; G-APFM (17714), 4.11.60; G-APFN
(17715), 17.11.60; G-APFO (17716), 9.12.60; G-APFP (17717), 22.12.60; G-ARRA
(18411), 16.2.62; G-ARRB (18412), 12.2.63; G-ARRC (18413), 15.3.63

Boeing 707-465 (*B.O.A.C. aircraft*)
G-ARWD (18372), VR-BBW, 11.10.62; G-ARWE (18373), VR-BBZ ntu, 9.7.62,
burned out after emergency landing at Heathrow 8.4.68

Boeing 737-204 (*Britannia Airways aircraft*)
G-AVRL (19709), 6.7.68; G-AVRM (19710), 9.8.68; G-AVRN (19711), 8.5.69;
G-AVRO (19712), 30.4.69 'City of Birmingham'; G-AWSY (20236), 15.5.69;
G-AXNA (20285), 20.3.70; G-AXNB (20389), 21.4.70; G-AXNC (20417), 15.5.70

Boeing 747-36 (*B.O.A.C. aircraft*)
G-AWNA (19761), N17998, 25.8.70; G-AWNB (19762), 17.8.70; G-AWNC
(19763), 31.7.70; G-AWND (19764), 15.3.71; G-AWNE (19765), 8.3.71; G-AWNF
(19766), 17.3.71; G-AWNG (20269), 8.9.71
Later deliveries were: (c/n 20270–20273) G-AWNH to 'NK; (20284) G-AWNL
Registrations G-AWNM, G-AWNN, G-AWNO and G-AWNP not used

Bölkow Bö 208A-1 Junior
G-ASAS (514), 25.4.63, to Germany 2.64 as D-EKMY; G-ASFO (517), D-ENDI,
10.6.63; G-ASFP (523), remained in Germany as D-EGMU; G-ASFR (522), 19.4.64;
G-ASFS (516), D-ENDE, 25.4.63, crashed at Biggin Hill 29.1.66; G-ASFT (521),
27.7.63; G-AVEA* (04), SE-EBO, 8.3.67, to Denmark 7.69 as OY-DZL

* MFI-9 Junior

Bölkow Bö 208A-2 Junior
G-ASUO (537), D-EGQU, 17.7.64; G-ASWE (561), 27.9.64; G-ASZD (563), 14.1.65

Bölkow Bö 208C Junior
G-ATDO (576), 10.5.65; G-ATOC (600), 7.2.66, to Ireland 12.70 as EI-AUR;
G-ATRI (602), 3.3.66, d.b.r. in forced landing, Balloch, Loch Lomond 1.8.70; G-ATSI
(605), 24.3.66; G-ATSX (608), 7.4.66; G-ATTR (612), 2.5.66; G-ATUI (611), 5.5.66;
G-ATVB (614) 30.6.66; G-ATVX (615), 9.6.66; G-ATXZ (624), 2.10.64; G-ATYP
(617), 23.8.66; G-ATZA (629), 10.4.67; G-AVGX (630), 20.3.67; G-AVKR (648),
2.5.67; G-AVLO (650), 9.5.67; G-AVNH (655), 15.6.67, crash landed at Steyning,
Sussex 10.3.68; G-AVZI (673), 27.12.67

Boulton and Paul P.9
G-EAPD (P.9-1), 21.4.20, Boulton and Paul Ltd., Mousehold; cancelled 11.20
G-EASJ (P.9-2), 15.7.20, J. G. Weir, Renfrew; F. T. Courtney, Croydon 4.22;
   Henderson S. of F. Ltd., Brooklands 1.28; to South Africa 3.29 as G-UAAM
G-EAWS (P.9-6), 28.4.21, Boulton and Paul Ltd., Mousehold; damaged beyond repair
   after running away on the ground, Cramlington 12.6.29

G-EBEQ (P.9-7), first flown 4.9.22, C. of A. 31.7.23, Boulton and Paul Ltd., F. O. Soden 9.26; Lt. H. Kennedy, Stag Lane 12.27; seriously damaged at St. Moritz 9.2.29; sold in Switzerland 9.30 as CH-259; cancelled 1.32

Boulton and Paul P.64 Mailplane and P.71A

G-ABYK (P.64), Mailplane prototype registered 14.7.32 to the Air Council; crashed on test at Martlesham Heath, Suffolk 21.10.33

G-ACOX (P.71A-1), 19.9.34, Imperial Airways Ltd., Croydon 'Boadicea'; lost in the English Channel 25.9.36

G-ACOY (P.71A-2), 14.10.34, Imperial Airways Ltd., Croydon 'Britomart'; crashed while landing at Haren Aerodrome, Brussels 25.10.35

Boulton Paul P.108 Balliol T. Mk.2

G-ANSF (BP.6C), 23.8.54, Boulton Paul Ltd., Wolverhampton; shown and flown at Farnborough S.B.A.C. Show 6–13.9.54; withdrawn from use 9.56

G-ANYL (BP.7C), WN164, registered 1.55 to Boulton Paul Ltd.; delivered to the Ceylon Air Force 4.55 as CA306; crashed at Kandy later in 1955

G-ANYM (BP.8C), WN166, registered 1.55 to Boulton Paul Ltd.; delivered to the Ceylon Air Force 4.55 as CA307

G-ANZV (BP.9C), WN147, registered 3.55 to Boulton Paul Ltd.; delivered to the Ceylon Air Force 5.55 as CA308

G-ANZW (BP.10C), WN148, registered 3.55 to Boulton Paul Ltd.; delivered to the Ceylon Air Force 5.55 as CA309

G-APCN (BPA.10C), WG224, registered 6.57 to Boulton Paul Ltd.; delivered to the Ceylon Air Force 8.57 as CA310

G-APCO (BPA.11C), WG230, registered 6.57 to Boulton Paul Ltd.; delivered to the Ceylon Air Force 8.57 as CA311

G-APCP (BPA.12C), WN132, G-3-2, registered 6.57 to Boulton Paul Ltd.; delivered to the Ceylon Air Force 8.57 as CA312

Brantly B-2

G-APSE (14), registered 1.59 to Brantly Helicopter (Sales) Ltd., Swansea, returned to U.S.A. 11.60; G-APSF (15), 31.3.60, to U.S.A. 11.60 as N511Z; G-ARVY (145), N5998X, 13.3.62, d.b.r. at Kidlington 28.8.64; G-ARXO (175), 13.4.62, crashed at Kidlington 14.7.62; G-ARYX (182), 8.6.62, crashed on East Berkshire golf course 15.6.64; G-ARZI (165), 2.11.62; G-ARZJ (170), 20.7.62, crashed at Llanfairfechan 12.4.64; G-ARZK (171), 28.1.63, crashed at Kidlington 24.4.67

Brantly B-2A

G-ASEH (303), 18.2.63, w.f.u. at Kidlington 2.71; G-ASEI (304), 30.2.63, crashed near Bladon, Oxon. 19.10.65; G-ASEW (308), 5.4.63; G-ASHD (314), 30.4.63, crashed in River Colne off Brightlingsea 15.2.67; G-ASHK (315), 24.6.63, evaluated as XS681 in 1963

Brantly B-2B

G-ASHJ (319), 21.10.63, evaluated as XS683 in 1963; G-ASJX (325), 16.8.63, crashed in Perth 4.7.68; G-ASLO (330), N2168U, 24.9.63, to Ireland 11.71 as EI-AVK; G-ASXD (435), 10.3.65; G-ASXE (436), 11.6.65; G-ATFG (448), 24.9.65; G-ATFH (449), 28.9.65; G-ATGH (451), 17.1.66; G-ATJY (455), 18.1.66; G-AVCA (466), 16.3.67; G-AVIP (471), 26.5.67; G-AVJN (473), 6.10.67; G-AWDU (481), 9.5.68; G-AWIO (483), 25.7.68; G-AXSR (474), N2237U, 2.1.70

Brantly 305

G-ASUM (1005), N2236U, 25.1.66, to U.S.A. 1.67 as N16616; G-ASUN (1004), 16.10.64, d.b.r. 5.70; G-ASXF (1014), 9.3.66; G-ATLO (1021), 4.8.66; G-ATSJ (1024), 19.5.66; G-ATUR (1029), N12H, 12.10.66; G-ATUS (1030), 17.8.66, crashed at Barton 14.3.70; G-ATYB (1035), to Ireland 8.67 as EI-ARU

Bristol Fighter Types 14, 17 and 17A

G-EASH (5093), H1376, 29.11.20, Hispano-Suiza engine; Handley Page Ltd., used as demonstrator by the Aircraft Disposal Co. Ltd., w.f.u. 4.21

G-EASU (5356), H1639, Handley Page Ltd./A.D.C. Ltd.; sold abroad 9.20

G-EASV (5355), H1638, Handley Page Ltd./A.D.C. Ltd.; sold abroad 11.20

G-EAWA H951, Gloster-built, Handley Page Transport Ltd., Cricklewood; handed over to the Aircraft Disposal Co. Ltd.; registration lapsed

G-EAWZ (4999), H1282, Aircraft Disposal Co. Ltd., Croydon; crashed 9.21

G-EAYQ (5106), H1389, Aircraft Disposal Co. Ltd., ferried Croydon–Brussels 13.10.21 by M. Piercey and handed over to the Belgian Air Force

G-EBAK (5008), H1291, Aircraft Disposal Co. Ltd.; ferried Croydon–Brussels 29.12.21 by A. F. Muir and handed over to the Belgian Air Force

G-EBAL (5009), H1292, Aircraft Disposal Co. Ltd.; ferried from Croydon to Brussels 2.3.22 and handed over to the Belgian Air Force

G-EBAM (4957), H1240, Aircraft Disposal Co. Ltd.; ferried from Croydon to Brussels 25.2.22 by M. Piercey and handed over to the Belgian Air Force

G-EBAT (4959), H1242, Aircraft Disposal Co. Ltd.; believed crashed at Croydon 28.1.22 when taking-off for Brussels piloted by D. L. Forestier-Walker

G-EBAU (4961), H1244, Aircraft Disposal Co. Ltd.; ferried from Croydon to Brussels 15.2.22 by E. D. C. Herne and handed over to the Belgian Air Force

G-EBBD (3492), D7842, Aircraft Disposal Co. Ltd.; presented to the Queen of the Belgians and ferried to Brussels 28.1.22 by A. F. Muir

G-EBBO (4975), H1258, Aircraft Disposal Co. Ltd.; ferried Croydon–Brussels 11.3.22 by E. D. C. Herne and handed over to the Belgian Air Force

G-EBCN (6223), Type 17A, 31.1.23, Bristol Aeroplane Co. Ltd., Filton; sold to SABCA as pattern aircraft; registration cancelled 24.7.23

G-EBCU E2058, Armstrong Whitworth-built, Aircraft Disposal Co. Ltd.; ferried to Brussels 6.5.22 by E. L. Foote and handed over to the Belgian Air Force

G-EBCV (4998), H1281, Aircraft Disposal Co. Ltd.; ferried from Croydon to Brussels 12.7.22 and handed over to the Belgian Air Force

G-EBCW (4962), H1245, Aircraft Disposal Co. Ltd.; ferried from Croydon to Brussels 18.7.22 and handed over to the Belgian Air Force

G-EBDB E5219, Standard-built, Aircraft Disposal Co. Ltd.; ferried from Croydon to Brussels 12.7.22 and handed over to the Belgian Air Force

G-EBDN H927, Gloster-built, Aircraft Disposal Co. Ltd.; ferried from Croydon to Brussels 12.7.22 and handed over to the Belgian Air Force

G-EBEE H926, Gloster-built, Aircraft Disposal Co. Ltd.; ferried from Croydon to Brussels 18.7.22 and handed over to the Belgian Air Force

G-EBFD (3957), E2354, 10.2.23, Bristol Aeroplane Co. Ltd., Filton; sold to the Serbian Army 3.23

G-EBIO (4971), H1254, Hispano-Suiza engine, 24.12.24, Aircraft Disposal Co. Ltd.; D. V. Ivins, Jersey 8.31; R. C. Parker, Redhill 11.34; scrapped 1935

G-ACFP, a Fighter Mk. IV conversion owned by Empire Air Services, after the day's passenger flights at Southend, August 1933. (*A. J. Jackson*)

Bristol Fighter Types 96 and 96A

G-ABXA (7056), J8258, 1.7.32, Hon. Mrs. V. Bruce, Hanworth; Inca Aviation Ltd., Hanworth 11.33; withdrawn from use 11.34

G-ABXV (6464), F4711, 2.11.32, P. H. Thomas and Hon. J. Grimston; crashed and broke its back at Capenoch, Dumfriesshire, pilot Grimston, 18.9.33

G-ABYD (7574), J8446, 14.10.32, M. Cresswell, scrapped after accident 3.33

G-ABYE (7559), F4721, 14.12.32, M. Emmett, Woodley; Universal Aircraft Services Ltd., Witney 3.35; registration cancelled 4.38

G-ABYF (7573), J8429, 17.12.32, D. V. Ivins, Jersey; Airmedia Ltd., Hanworth (later Redhill) 4.35; dismantled at Redhill in 1939; cancelled 8.45

G-ABYL (7579), J8444, 14.10.32, E. B. H. Wright; scrapped in 1933

G-ABYT (7568), J8434, 28.7.33, A. T. Wilson; J. P. W. Topham, Lympne 4.34; scrapped at Lympne after collision with barbed wire fence in 1936

G-ABZG (7043), J8245, 9.8.33, Commercial Airways (Essex) Ltd., Abridge; scrapped at Abridge 5.38

G-ACAA (7434), F4516, 20.1.33, C. R. A. Oakley, Woodley; H. A. Carson 5.34; A. E. Green and A. P. Fraser, Elstree 2.36; registration cancelled 12.46

G-ACAC (7571), J8437, 12.4.33, W. L. Handley, Castle Bromwich; scrapped at Hooton 1.36

G-ACCG (7576), J6790, 24.3.33, Universal Aircraft Services Ltd., Witney; M. N. Mavrogordato, Witney 10.33; scrapped 7.39

G-ACFK (7431), J8285, Commercial Airways (Essex) Ltd., fully converted at Abridge but not issued with C. of A., sold for scrap 5.36

G-ACFL (7570), C4897, registered to Commercial Airways (Essex) Ltd. 22.3.33 but not converted at Abridge, sold for scrap 5.36 with G-ACFN (7144) ex F4542 and G-ACFO (7137) ex C4750.

G-ACFP (7581), F4434, 13.4.33, Empire Air Services Ltd., Hanworth; Hon. Mrs. Victor Bruce 11.33; sold for scrap 1.38

G-ACHR (7578), F4342, 24.7.33, R. C. Simpson; crashed at Guigmes, Seine-et-Marne, France 19.9.33

G-ACPE (7577), J8448, 9.10.34, A. F. Cawthorn, Hanworth; Josephine Dudley, Hanworth 7.35; R. G. Kingsmill, Hanworth 8.36; scrapped 1.39

515

G-ADJR   (7580), J8455, 22.6.35, C. P. B. Ogilvie, Heston; London Film Productions Ltd., Heston 8.35; scrapped 1.38

G-AEPH   (7575), D8096, C. P. B. Ogilvie, Hanworth; found at Elstree 1949 unconverted, bought by the Shuttleworth Trust and airworthy at Old Warden 1972

G-AFHJ   (7146), F4587, 1.9.38, Sqn. Ldr. N. R. Buckle, Hendon; destroyed by enemy action during the 1939–45 war

Bristol Type 20 M.1C and Type 77 M.1D

G-EAER   (2782), C4964, registered 13.6.19 to Maj. C. H. Chichester Smith, Hendon; sold to The Grahame-White Aviation Co. Ltd. in 1920

G-EASR   (5885), 20.12.20, Bristol Aeroplane Co. Ltd., Filton, withdrawn from use and registration cancelled 7.4.25

G-EAVO   (5887), registered 28.9.20 to the Bristol Aeroplane Co. Ltd.; sold in Spain as M-AFAA and delivered by L. Carter ex Croydon 11.21

G-EAVP   (5888), Type 77, Lucifer engine, registered 28.9.20 to the Bristol Aeroplane Co. Ltd.; crashed at Chertsey, Surrey 23.6.23

Bristol Type 30 and Type 46 Babe

G-EAQD   (5866), Mk.I, Type 30, 35 h.p. Viale, first flown at Filton 28.11.19; converted to Mk.III, Type 46A, with 60 h.p. Le Rhône; w.f.u. 12.20

G-EASQ   (5865), Mk.III, Type 46A, 60 h.p. Le Rhône, flown 1920; converted to low-wing monoplane Type 46B, not flown, w.f.u. at Filton 2.21

The Instone Air Line Type 47 Tourer showing the two-seat side-by-side rear cockpit. (*Bristol Photo.*)

Bristol Tourer

G-EAIZ   (5867), Type 29, 16.9.19, British and Colonial Aeroplane Co. Ltd., Filton; demonstration aircraft; withdrawn from use 9.20

G-EANR   (5868), Type 29, registered 23.9.19 to the British and Colonial Aeroplane Co. Ltd.; shipped to New York in May 1920, flown in Nicaragua

G-EART (5876), Type 47, 21.4.20, S. Instone and Co. Ltd., Croydon; withdrawn from use 2.21

G-EAUE (5870), Type 36, 10.12.20, Bristol Aeroplane Co. Ltd., Filton; sold to Air Ministry 22.12.23 in modified form as Type 85, serial J7004

G-EAVU (5892), Type 47, 25.10.20, Bristol Aeroplane Co. Ltd., Filton; dual control demonstrator; scrapped after its return from Spain 9.21

G-EAWB (6122), Type 29, 31.12.20, A. S. Butler, Croydon; withdrawn from use at C. of A. expiry 30.12.21

G-EAWQ (6114), Type 28, 5.1.21, Bristol Aeroplane Co. Ltd., Filton; to Spain as M-AAEA; crashed near Lasarte, San Sebastian 23.4.21

G-EAWR (6112), Type 47, 19.4.21, Bristol Aeroplane Co. Ltd., Filton; to Spain as M-AEAA; delivered to Madrid by Hereward de Havilland 24.4.21

G-EAXA (6120), Type 29, 17.6.21, Bristol Aeroplane Co. Ltd., Filton; modified to Type 81 Puma Trainer: crashed 10.5.24

G-EAXK (6108), Type 28, 21.6.21, Bristol Aeroplane Co. Ltd.; to West Australian Airways 7.22 as G-AUDF; crashed at Onslow W.A. 27.1.25

Bristol Type 73 Taxiplane

G-EBEW (6153), 21.6.23, Bristol Aeroplane Co. Ltd. Filton; scrapped 7.25

G-EBEY (6154), 21.6.23, Bristol Aeroplane Co. Ltd., tested at Martlesham 1.24; dismantled at Filton 5.25

G-EBFX (6154), G-EBEY re-registered in error; marks cancelled 12.6.23

G-EBFY (6155), 21.6.23, Bristol Aeroplane Co. Ltd.; dismantled at Filton 5.24 and used as spares for the Reserve School Type 83A Lucifers

Bristol Type 81 Puma Trainer

G-EBFR (6239), Bristol Aeroplane Co. Ltd., Filton; crashed at Filton 6.23 prior to issue of C. of A.

G-EBFS (6240), 21.6.23, Bristol Aeroplane Co. Ltd., Filton; scrapped 5.24

G-EBFT (6241), 21.6.23, Bristol Aeroplane Co. Ltd., Filton; crashed at Filton 10.3.25

G-EBFU (6242), 21.6.23, Bristol Aeroplane Co. Ltd., Filton; crashed at Filton in 1928, registration cancelled 1.29

Bristol Type 83A Lucifer and Type 83E

G-EBFZ (6373), 21.6.23, Bristol Aeroplane Co. Ltd., Filton; scrapped 12.31

G-EBGA (6374), 21.6.23, Bristol Aeroplane Co. Ltd., Filton; converted to Type 83B in 1926; to Type 83C in 1928; to L. G. Anderson, Hanworth 2.33; used by C. W. A. Scott's British Hospitals Air Pageants; scrapped 12.33

G-EBGB (6375), 21.6.23, Bristol Aeroplane Co. Ltd., Filton; destroyed in air collision with Bristol Type 89 G-EBIH over Filton 20.8.29

G-EBGC (6376), 23.10.23, Bristol Aeroplane Co. Ltd., Filton; scrapped 12.31

G-EBGD (6377), 3.10.23, Bristol Aeroplane Co. Ltd., Filton; scrapped 12.31

G-EBGE (6378), 3.10.23, Bristol Aeroplane Co. Ltd., Filton; scrapped 12.31

G-EBNB (6922), Bristol Aeroplane Co. Ltd., Filton; registered 14.12.25 for demonstrations to Chilean and Hungarian purchasing commissions; sold in Hungary 2.26 with C. of A. dated 28.4.26

G-EBNC (6923), details as for G-EBNB above.

G-EBYT (7266), Type 83E, Bristol Aeroplane Co. Ltd., Filton; scrapped 12.30

Bristol Type 76 Jupiter Fighter

G-EBGF   (6379), Type 76, 2.8.23, Bristol Aeroplane Co. Ltd., Filton; crashed 23.11.23 after engine seizure at 20,000 ft.; pilot T. W. Campbell escaped

G-EBHG   (6380), Type 76B, 26.5.24, Bristol Aeroplane Co. Ltd., Filton; to the Swedish Army 5.24 as 4300 (became 1300 in 1926 and 3667 in 1932); H. Fredrikson 2.35 as SE-AEE; crashed at Gothenburg 19.9.37

G-EBHH   (6381), Type 76A, registered 25.7.23 to the Bristol Aeroplane Co. Ltd., Filton; converted to Type 89, C. of A. 27.2.25; destroyed in air collision with Type 89 G-EBJA over Filton 23.9.25

Bristol Type 89

G-EBIH   (6382), 5.7.24, Bristol Aeroplane Co. Ltd., Filton; destroyed in air collision with Type 83A Lucifer G-EBGB over Filton 20.8.29

G-EBJA   (6522), 23.7.24, Bristol Aeroplane Co. Ltd., Filton; destroyed in air collision with Type 89 G-EBHH over Filton 23.9.25

G-EBJB   (6523), 9.4.25, Bristol Aeroplane Co. Ltd., Filton; crashed and burned out near Filton 15.12.25

G-EBJC   (6524), aircraft not completed; registration cancelled 11.5.25

G-EBML   (6918), 17.12.25, Bristol Aeroplane Co. Ltd., Filton; written off 14.5.27

G-EBMN   (6919), 17.12.25, Bristol Aeroplane Co. Ltd., Filton; written off 17.3.27

G-EBNZ   (6963), 9.6.25, Wm. Beardmore & Co. Ltd., Renfrew; withdrawn from use 10.29; written off 14.1.30

G-EBOA   (6964), 5.6.25, Wm. Beardmore and Co. Ltd., Renfrew; crashed 15.3.27

Bristol Type 89A

G-EBOC   (6965), 28.10.26, Bristol Aeroplane Co. Ltd., Filton; destroyed in air collision with Type 89A G-AAWJ over Filton 7.7.31

G-EBOD   (6966), 4.4.27, Bristol Aeroplane Co. Ltd., Filton; Wm. Beardmore & Co. Ltd., Renfrew 4.27; crashed on railway embankment near Pollockshaws Station, Glasgow 26.5.27; written off 14.1.30

G-EBQS   (6967), 27.6.27, Bristol Aeroplane Co. Ltd.; Wm. Beardmore & Co. Ltd., Renfrew 6.27; withdrawn from use 6.29; written off 14.1.30

G-EBQT   (7124), 11.6.27, Bristol Aeroplane Co. Ltd.; registered to Beardmore, Renfrew in error 6.27; crashed at Tewkesbury, Glos. 23.8.28

G-EBSB   (7156), 5.7.27, Wm. Beardmore & Co. Ltd., Renfrew; written off 14.1.30

G-EBSH   (7157), 1.9.27, Bristol Aeroplane Co. Ltd., Filton; withdrawn from use 11.33

G-EBVR   (7234), 10.3.28, Wm. Beardmore & Co. Ltd., Renfrew; written off 14.1.30

G-EBWN   (R.58), 31.7.28, Wm. Beardmore & Co. Ltd., Renfrew; withdrawn from use 7.29

G-EBYL   (7265), 14.9.28, Bristol Aeroplane Co. Ltd., Filton; withdrawn from use 10.33

G-AAGF   (7350), Jupiter VI engine, 16.5.29, Bristol Aeroplane Co. Ltd., Filton; written off 8.35

G-AALO   (7351), 24.10.29, Bristol Aeroplane Co. Ltd., Filton; written off 8.35

G-AAWJ   (7352), 22.8.30, Bristol Aeroplane Co. Ltd., Filton; destroyed in air collision with Type 89A G-EBOC over Filton 7.7.31

G-ABPL   (7711), Jupiter VIFM engine, 23.10.31, Bristol Aeroplane Co. Ltd., Filton; written off 12.34

G-ABPM   (7712), Jupiter VIFM engine, 7.11.31, Bristol Aeroplane Co. Ltd., Filton; written off 8.35

Bristol Type 91 Brownie

G-EBJK   (6526), Type 91, Bristol Aeroplane Co. Ltd., Filton; first flown 6.8.24; modified to Type 91B, C. of A. 4.9.26; crashed at Farnborough 21.3.28

G-EBJL   (6527), Type 91A two-seater, Bristol Aeroplane Co. Ltd., Filton; first flown 22.9.24; converted to Type 91A single-seater, C. of A. 8.9.27; Bristol & Wessex Aeroplane Club, Filton 9.27; withdrawn from use 11.32

G-EBJM   (6528), Type 91A, Bristol Aeroplane Co. Ltd., Filton; first flown 24.9.24; leased to the London Aeroplane Club, Stag Lane, Edgware 7.26; C. of A. 17.7.26; withdrawn from use 7.28

Bristol Type 105 Bulldog Mk.II (*registered to the manufacturers*)

G-AAHH   (7331), Jupiter VIA, 15.6.29, demonstrator; scrapped at Filton 1935

G-AATR   (7397), J9591, Mercury IVA, 13.1.30, on loan from the Air Ministry; returned to the R.A.F. 9.31 with Jupiter VIIF as J9591

G-ABAC   (7399), R-1, first flown 1.30 with Mercury III; re-engined with Gnome-Rhône Jupiter VI as G-ABAC, C. of A. 30.5.30, crashed after T. W. Campbell baled out over Filton 4.6.30

Bristol Type 105 Bulldog (*other Marks*)

G-ABBB   (7446), Mk.IIA, Gnome-Rhône 9ASB, 17.4.31; fitted 9.35 with Aquila I as R-11, stored 1939–57; flown 22.6.61; crashed at Farnborough 13.9.64 as K2227

G-ABZW   (7745), Mk.IIIA, Mercury VIS.2; converted 3.34 to Mk.IVA, sold to the Air Ministry 7.35 as K4292 with long-chord cowlings

G-ACJN   (7808), Mk.IVA, Perseus IA, flown as R-8; scrapped at Filton in 1938

Bristol Type 170 Freighter

G-AGPV   (12730), Mk.I, VK900, 29.8.46, Bristol Co.; to R.A.F. 9.46 as VR380; conv. to Mk.II at Blackbushe 1958; Air Condor Ltd., Southend 3.60; Trans European Aviation Ltd. 11.60; withdrawn from use at Baginton 7.63

G-AGUT   (12733), Mk.IIA, 23.9.46, Bristol Co.; to T. R. E. Defford 9.46 as VR382; by road to Shortcut Aviation Ltd., Blackbushe 7.3.58 as spares

G-AGVB   (12731), Mk.IIB, VK903, 7.5.46, leased Channel Islands A/W; conv. to Mk.21; Silver City 4.54; trooping 1955–56 as XF656; to Cie Air Transport, Le Touquet 2.57 as F-BHVB; rest. 8.56 to Silver City; w.f.u. 1959

G-AGVC   (12732), Mk.I, 29.7.46, Bristol Co.; Silver City 7.48; Bristol Co. 8.49 and conv. to Mk.21 as G-18-2; Silver City 7.53; trooping 1955–56 as XF657; Manx Airlines 1.62; damaged beyond repair, Ronaldsway 30.6.62

G-AHJB   (12734), Mk.IIA, 27.6.46, Bristol Aeroplane Co. Ltd., Filton; ditched in South Atlantic 120 miles off Natal, Brazil 4.7.46

G-AHJC   (12735), Mk.IIA, 6.7.46, Bristol Aeroplane Co. Ltd.; conv. to Mk.21E; to Australian National Airways 9.49 as VH-INK 'Kiopana'; w.f.u. 10.60

G-AHJD   (12736), Mk.IIA, 2.8.46, Airwork Ltd.; conv. to Mk.21; Anglo Iranian Oil Co. Ltd. 7.50; West African A/W 4.52 as VR-NAK 'Rokel'; rest. 9.55 to Eagle Aviation Ltd.; B.K.S. A/T Ltd. 9.60; scrapped at Yeadon 1963

G-AHJE   (12737), Mk.IA, 15.10.46, Bristol Aeroplane Co. Ltd.; ferried to the Argentine 11.46 as LV-XII; to the Argentine Air Force as T-27

G-AHJF	(12738), Mk.II, 24.8.46, Bristol Aeroplane Co. Ltd.; conv. to Mk. 21; to Cie Air Transport 5.48 as F-BENF; crashed in the Sahara 29.7.50
G-AHJG	(12739), Mk.II, 6.9.46, Bristol Co.; to Suidair 4.47 as ZS-BOM 'Golden City'; converted to Mk.21; to Shell (Ecuador) Ltd. 8.48 as HC-SBU; crashed in the Eastern Cordilleras 6.8.49
G-AHJH	(12740), Mk.IIA, 4.10.46, Bristol Aeroplane Co. Ltd.; to R.E.A.L., Brazil ex Filton 5.10.46; became PP-YPD; scrapped at Sao Paulo 9.48
G-AHJI	(12741), Mk.IIA, 11.10.46, to Dalmia Jain A/W as VT-CHK; converted to Mk.21; to Aviacion y Comercio 4.50 as EC-AES; to Air Atlas 12.50 as F-DABI; rest. 12.55 to Silver City as 'City of Bath'; British United Air Ferries Ltd. Lydd 2.63; dismantled for spares at Lydd 1965
G-AHJJ	(12742), Mk.IIA, 29.10.46, to Dalmia Jain A/W as VT-CHL; converted to Mk.21; rest. 2.50 to Silver City; crashed near Cowbridge, Glam. 21.3.50
G-AHJK	(12743), Mk.IIA, 10.12.46, Bristol Aeroplane Co. Ltd.; to R.E.A.L., Brazil 12.46 as PP-YPE; scrapped at Sao Paulo 9.48
G-AHJL	(12744), Mk.IIC, to Indian National A/W 11.46 as VT-CGV; rest. 3.49 to Bristol Co.; conv. to Mk.21P; to Pakistan Air Force as G778
G-AHJM	(12745), Mk.IIC, to Indian National A/W 11.46 as VT-CGW; rest 3.49 to Airwork Ltd.; conv. Mk.21P; to Pakistan Air Force as G779
G-AHJN	(12746), Mk.IIA, 26.11.46, to Bharat A/W 12.46 as VT-CGX; rest. 10.50 to Bristol Co. as G-18-13; converted to Mk.21E; to Ministry of Supply 8.51 as WW378; to Royal Australian Air Force 1951 as A81-4
G-AHJO	(12747), Mk.IIA, 1.1.47, Bowmaker Ltd.; Bristol Aeroplane Co. Ltd. 8.49; converted to Mk.21P; to the Pakistan Air Force 11.49 as G781
G-AHJP	(12748), Mk.21E, Bristol Co.; to Cie Air Transport 4.48 as F-BENH; rest. 3.51 to Silver City; to Air Outremer 1.54 as F-DABJ, later F-OAUJ
G-AICF	(12749), Mk.IA, Bristol Aeroplane Co. Ltd.; ferried to the Argentine 1.47 as LV-XIJ; transferred to the Argentine Air Force as T-29
G-AICG	(12750), Mk.IA, Bristol Aeroplane Co. Ltd.; ferried to the Argentine 1.47 as LV-XIL; to the Argentine Air Force as T-28, crashed 8.7.49
G-AICH	(12751), Mk.IA, Bristol Co.; ferried to the Argentine 4.47 as LV-XIM; to the Argentine Air Force as T-30; to F.A.M.A. as LV-AEY
G-AICI	(12752), Mk.IA, Bristol Aeroplane Co. Ltd.; ferried to the Argentine 3.47 as LV-XIN; transferred to the Argentine Air Force as T-31
G-AICJ	(12753), Mk.IA, Bristol Co.; ferried to the Argentine 4.47 as LV-XIO; to the Argentine Air Force as T-32; to F.A.M.A. as LV-AEZ; w.f.u. 3.49
G-AICK	(12754), Mk.IA, Bristol Co.; ferried to the Argentine as LV-XIP; to the Argentine Air Force as T-33; to F.A.M.A. as LV-AEX; w.f.u. 3.49
G-AICL	(12755), Mk.21E, 11.11.48, Bristol Aeroplane Co. Ltd.; to Australian National Airways 3.49 as VH-INJ 'Pokana'; withdrawn from use 6.61
G-AICM	(12756), Mk.I, 8.12.47, leased Hunting Aerosurveys Ltd. for Iranian oilfield survey; converted to Mk.21; Silver City Airways Ltd. 4.51; crashed on railway outside Berlin on Berlin Airlift 19.1.53
G-AICN	(12757), Mk.21, Ministry of Civil Aviation; to Aviacion y Comercio, Bilbao 5.48 as EC-ADI; crashed at Barajas Airport, Madrid 9.5.57
G-AICO	(12758), Mk.IA, Bristol Aeroplane Co. Ltd.; ferried to the Argentine 4.47 as LV-XIQ; transferred to the Argentine Air Force as T-34
G-AICP	(12760), Mk.IA, Bristol Aeroplane Co. Ltd.; ferried to the Argentine 6.47 as LV-XIR; transferred to the Argentine Air Force as T-35

Freighter Mk. 21 EC-ADI, first registered as G-AICN, at Filton in April 1948 awaiting delivery to Aviacion y Comercio, Bilbao. (*Bristol Photo.*)

G-AICR   (12761), Mk.IA. 4.3.37, to Shell (Ecuador) Ltd. as HC-SBM; conv. to Mk.21E; to Australian Nat. A/W 10.49 as VH-INL 'Mannana'; w.f.u. 10.60

G-AICS   (12762), Mk.I, 26.3.47, to Shell (Ecuador) Ltd. as HC-SBN; rest. 1.49 to Airwork Ltd.; conv. to Mk.21; to Shell Refining Ltd. 10.49 as HC-SBZ; rest. 2.51 to B.E.A.; Silver City Airways 6.57; trooping 1956 as XF659; crashed Winter Hill, Horwich 27.2.58

G-AICT   (12763), Mk.IIA, 2.10.47, Bristol Co., leased to Airwork Ltd. in Sudan and Kenya; conv. to Mk.21E as G-18-40; to West African A/W 4.52 as VR-NAL 'Gambia'; rest. 9.57 to Channel A/W, Southend; scrapped 1966

G-AICU   (12764), Mk.IA, Bristol Aeroplane Co. Ltd.; ferried to the Argentine 5.47 as LV-XIS; transferred to the Argentine Air Force as T-36

G-AICW   (12765), Mk.IA, Bristol Aeroplane Co. Ltd.; ferried to the Argentine 6.47 as LV-XIT; to the Argentine Air Force as T-37; crashed 25.9.51

G-AIFF   (12766), Mk.XI, 5.9.47, Bristol Aeroplane Co. Ltd.; conv. to Mk.21 in 1948; conv. to Mk.31 in 1949; crashed in the English Channel 6.5.49

G-AIFG   (12767), Mk.21E, Ministry of Civil Aviation; to Saudi Arabian Airlines 8.49 as SA-AAD; re-registered 3.52 as HZ-AAD

G-AIFH   (12768), Mk.IA, Bristol Aeroplane Co. Ltd.; ferried to the Argentine 6.47 as LV-XIU; to the Argentine Air Force as T-38

G-AIFI   (12769), Mk.IA, as above 7.47 as LV-XIV; became T-39; crashed 31.8.49

G-AIFJ   (12770), Mk.IA, as above 7.47 as LV-XIW; became T-40

G-AIFK   (12771), Mk.IA, as above 8.47 as LV-XIX; became T-41; crashed 8.53

G-AIFL   (12772), Mk.21E, Ministry of Civil Aviation; to Saudi Arabian Airlines 8.49 as SA-AAC; re-registered 3.52 as HZ-AAC

G-AIFM   (12773), Mk.21, M.C.A. 'Giovanni Caboto'; to Cie Air Transport 5.48 as F-BEND; rest. 12.51 to Silver City; to Air Outremer 1.54 as F-DABK; rest. 2.56 to Air Kruise, later Silver City 'City of Carlisle'; B.U.A.F., Lydd 2.63; flown to Southend 15.5.64 and scrapped

G-AIFN   (12774), Mk.21, 6.7.48, to Cie Air Transport 8.48 as F-BENC; to Air Vietnam 1952 as F-VNAK; to Air Agriculture Pty. Ltd., Bankstown, Sydney 7.57 as VH-AAH; crashed 12.61

G-AIFO   (12775), Mk.21E, 1.9.48, to Central African A/W 9.48 as VP-YHZ; to West African A/W 9.49 as VR-NAA; rest. 4.57 to Channel A/W; w.f.u. 1966

G-AIFP   (12776), Mk.21, to Aviacion y Comercio 5.48 as EC-ADH; crashed on landing at Mahon Airport, Minorca 13.3.59

Freighter IA G-AIMC, with the square cut wing tips of the early marks, taking off from Sydney during the 1947 Australasian Tour. (*Bristol Photo*.)

G-AIFR   (12777), Mk.21E, to Aviacion y Comercio 7.48 as EC-ADK; crashed 28.2.50

G-AIFS   (12778), Mk.21E, to Aviacion y Comercio 7.48 as EC-ADL; rest. 2.66 to Autair International Airways Ltd., Luton; scrapped at Luton 1.68

G-AIFT   (12779), Mk.21E, to Central African A/W 6.48 as VP-YHW; to West African A/W 12.49 as VR-NAD; crashed 38 m. NW of Calabar, E. Nigeria 5.2.55

G-AIFU   (12780), Mk.21E, Bristol Aeroplane Co. Ltd.; to the Pakistan Air Force 8.48 as G775; crashed 21.8.49

G-AIFV   (12781), Mk.IIA, to Dalmia Jain A/W 12.46 as VT-CID; to Indian National A/W 5.47; rest. 3.50 to Silver City as Mk.21; w.f.u. at Lydd 10.61

G-AIFW   (12782), Mk.21, to Sté. Indochinoise de Transports Aériens, Saigon 10.48 as F-BECR; crashed en route Hue-Tourane, Fr. Indoch. 10.3.50

G-AIFX   (12783), Mk.21E, Ministry of Civil Aviation; to Saudi Arabian Airlines 6.49 as SA-AAB; re-registered 3.52 as HZ-AAB

G-AIFY   (12784), Mk.21, 17.1.49, Secy. of State for War; flown as G-18-62; to West African A/W 4.49 as VR-NAX; wrecked near Kaduna Airport 27.7.51

G-AILU   (12785), Mk.21, Ministry of Civil Aviation; to Pakistan Air Force 8.48 as G776

G-AILV   (12786), Mk.21, M.C.A.; to Aviacion y Comercio 12.48 as EC-AEH; converted 7.55 to Mk. 21E; written off 11.9.57

G-AILW   (12787), Mk.IA, to Cie des Transports Aériens Intern. 6.47 as F-BCJM; conv. 4.49 to Mk.21; rest. 1.57 to Independent Air Travel; leased to Tyne-Tees A/W, Woolsington 1.63; to Avions Fairey 11.63 as OO-FAH

G-AILX   (12788), Mk.I, to C.T.A.I. 5.47 as F-BCJN; crashed in the sea off Cartagena, Spain 16.10.47

G-AILY   (12789), Mk.II, Bristol Aeroplane Co. Ltd.; test vehicle flown 1948 in Class B marking R37; scrapped in 1950

G-AILZ   (12790), Mk.21, 21.12.48, Bristol demonstrator 'African Enterprise'; to Saudi Arabian Airlines 1.49 as SA-AAA; re-registered 3.52 as HZ-AAA

G-AIMA   (12791), Mk.21, 31.1.49, Secy. of State for War; to West African Airways 4.49 as VR-NAZ; rest. 9.55; Eagle Aviation Ltd. 9.56; to Lufttransport Union 5.57 as D-AHOI, later D-BODO; to Fairey 1962 as OO-FAG; to S.A.T.T. 1965 as I-SATC; withdrawn from use in 1966

G-AIMB   (12792), Mk.XI, to A.B. Trafik-Turist-Transportflyg 8.47 as SE-BNG; crashed at Santa Maria del Monte, Salerno, Italy 18.11.47

G-AIMC (12793), Mk.IA, 14.3.47, Bristol Aeroplane Co. Ltd.; written off after brakes failed on the ground at Wau, New Guinea 28.10.47

G-AIMD (12794), Mk.21E, M.C.A.; to Saudi Arabian Airlines 9.49 as SA-AAE; re-registered 3.52 as HZ-AAE

G-AIME (12795), Mk.XIA, 15.8.47, to Suidair 8.47 as ZS-BVI 'Golden City'; rest. 12.47 to Bristol Co. as R38; conv. to Mk.21; Silver City 1953; trooping 1953 as XF662; later 'City of Exeter'; withdrawn from use at Lydd 10.63

G-AIMF (12796), Mk.21P, Bristol Aeroplane Co. Ltd.; to Pakistan Air Force 7.50 as G789

G-AIMG (12797), Mk.21, M.C.A.; to Aviacion y Comercio, Bilbao 12.48 as EC-AEG; crashed in the Guadarrama Mts., 60 miles from Madrid 4.12.53

G-AIMH (12798), Mk.21, to Cie Air Transport 12.48 as F-BECT; rest. 4.52 to Silver City; trooping 1953 as XF663; later 'City of Birmingham'; w.f.u.

G-AIMI (12799), Mk.21, Ministry of Civil Aviation; to R.A.F. 3.49 as WB482; transferred to the R.A.A.F. as A81-1; to Jetair 2.70 as VH-SJG

G-AIMJ (12800), Mk.21P, Bristol Aeroplane Co. Ltd.; to Pakistan Air Force 7.50 as G790

G-AIMK (12801), Mk.21E, to S.I.T.A. 6.48 as F-BENX; to Air Vietnam 1952 as F-VNAJ; to Trans Gabon as F-OBDP; withdrawn from use 1965

G-AIMM (12803), Mk.21P, Bristol Aeroplane Co. Ltd.; to Pakistan Air Force 11.49 as G780; crashed 14.9.51

G-AIMN (12804), Mk.21P, Bristol Aeroplane Co. Ltd.; to Pakistan Air Force 12.49 as G782

G-AIMO (12805), Mk.21E, Ministry of Civil Aviation; to the R.A.F. 4.49 as WB483; transferred to the R.A.A.F. at Woomera as A81-2

G-AIMP (12806), Mk.21P, Ministry of Civil Aviation; to the Pakistan Air Force 11.49 as G777

G-AIMR (12807), Mk.21E, Ministry of Civil Aviation; to the R.A.F. 4.49 as WB484; transferred to the R.A.A.F. as A81-3; to Jetair 1.69 as VH-SJQ

G-AIMS (12808), Mk. 21P, Bristol Aeroplane Co. Ltd.; to the Pakistan Air Force 7.50 as G791

G-AIMT (12809), Mk.21E, to S.I.T.A. 4.48 as F-BENV; to Air Vietnam, Saigon 1952 as F-VNAI; crashed at Pakse, Laos 16.8.54

G-AIMU (12810), Mk.21P, Bristol Aeroplane Co. Ltd.; to the Pakistan Air Force 12.49 as G783; crashed 26.8.52

G-AIMV (12811), Mk. 21P, Bristol Aeroplane Co. Ltd.; to the Pakistan Air Force 12.49 as G784

G-AIMW (12812), Mk.I, 3.9.47, Bristol Co.; to Cie Air Transport 2.48 as F-BENG; crashed after taking off from Gibraltar 10.4.48

G-AIMX (12813), to G-AINJ (12825), Mk.21P, Bristol Aeroplane Co. Ltd.; to the Pakistan Air Force between 1.50 and 9.51 as G785–G788 and G792–G800. Crashes: G787 on 8.4.50; G792 on 24.11.51

G-AINK (12826), Mk.31, 6.4.51, Bristol Aeroplane Co. Ltd.; to the R.A.F. 1951 as WH575; to Straits Air Freight Express 4.51 as ZK-AYG 'Captain Cook'

G-AINL (12827), Mk.31, G-18-93, WJ320; rest. 6.51 to Bristol Co.; to Aer Lingus 3.52 as EI-AFP; to Min. of Supply 11.52 as WJ320; rest. 9.54 to Aviation Traders Ltd., Southend; Dan-Air Services Ltd., Lasham/Gatwick 8.57; to Lamb A/W, Manitoba via Prestwick 22.2.70 as CF-YDO

G-AINM (12828), Mk.31, Bristol Aeroplane Co. Ltd.; to Straits Air Freight Express 5.51 as ZK-AYH 'Endeavour'; crashed Christchurch 21.11.57

G-AINN (12829), Mk.31M, 9.11.51, Bristol Aeroplane Co. Ltd.; to the Royal Canadian Air Force 11.51 as 9697; crashed at Merville, France 31.12.63

G-AINO (12830), Mk.31M, 7.9.51, Bristol Aeroplane Co. Ltd.; to the Royal Canadian Air Force 11.51 as 9696; crashed in France 3.12.55

G-AINP (12831), Mk.31, 14.12.51, Bristol Aeroplane Co. Ltd.; to Associated Airways Ltd. 12.51 as CF-GBT; crashed at Abee, Alberta 17.9.55

G-AINR (12832), Mk.31M, Bristol Aeroplane Co. Ltd.; to the Royal New Zealand Air Force 12.51 as NZ5901; crashed in Malaya 10.12.56

G-AINS (12833) and G-AINT (12834), Mk.31M, as above; to R.N.Z.A.F. 11.51 and 2.52 as NZ5902 and NZ5903 respectively

G-ALSJ (12937), Mk.31E, Bristol Co.; to Aér Lingus 6.52 as EI-AFQ 'St. Finbarr'; to Straits Air Freight Express 11.55 as ZK-BMA 'Marlborough'

G-AMCR (12927), Mk.31M, Bristol Co.; to R.N.Z.A.F. 4.52 as NZ5904; loaned to Straits Air Freight Express 6.54 as ZK-BEV; reverted to NZ5904

G-AMLJ (13072), Mk.31E, Bristol Co.; to Aer Lingus 7.52 as EI-AFR 'St. Ronan'; rest. 11.55 to Skyways Ltd.; to Middle East Airlines 12.55 as OD-ACM 'Doha'; rest. to B.K.S. Air Transport Ltd. 10.58; to Aer Turas 3.66 as EI-APC

G-AMLK (13073), Mk.31, reg'n. not used; converted to Mk.32 prototype G-AMWA

G-AMLL (13074), Mk.31E, Bristol Aeroplane Co. Ltd.; to Aer Lingus 12.52 as EI-AFS 'St. Senan'; rest. 11.56 to Jersey Airlines Ltd.; Dan-Air Services Ltd. 9.59; Air Ferry Ltd. 1964; to Northcoast Air Services 5.66 as CF-UME

G-AMLM (13075), Mk.31E, Bristol Co.; to Aviacion y Comercio 12.52 as EC-AHN; rest. 1.65 to Aviation Traders Ltd.; to S.A.F.E. 10.66 as ZK-CQD

G-AMLN (13076), Mk. 31E, Bristol Co.; to Aer Lingus 1.53 as EI-AFT 'St. Flannan'; to Sté Comm. Aér. du Littorel 10.56 as F-BFUO; to Aer Turas 1966 as EI-APM; crashed at Dublin Airport 12.6.67

G-AMLO (13077), Mk.31E, Bristol Aeroplane Co. Ltd.; Aviacion y Comercio 2.53 as EC-AHO; disposed of to Air Fret (France) and scrapped 1964

G-AMLP (13078), Mk.31E, 20.2.53, Air Charter Ltd., Southend 'Vanguard'; conv. to Mk.32; British United Air Ferries 4.65; Midland Air Cargoes Ltd., Baginton 11.70; to Lambair Ltd., Canada 5.71 as CF-QWJ

G-AMLR (13079), Mk.31M, Bristol Aeroplane Co. Ltd.; to the Royal Canadian Air Force 2.53 as 9698; to Wardair 1968 as CF-WAC

G-AMLS (13080), Mk.31M, Bristol Aeroplane Co. Ltd.; to the Royal New Zealand Air Force 8.53 as NZ5909

G-AMLT (13081), Mk.31M, G-18-124, Bristol Aeroplane Co. Ltd.; to the Iraqi Air Force 4.53 as '330'

G-AMPE to G-AMPI, Mk.31, completed as Mk.32 aircraft G-AMWB to G-AMWF q.v.

G-AMRO (13124), Mk.31M, Bristol Aeroplane Co. Ltd.; to the Iraqi Air Force 4.53 as '331'; to Shannon 26.12.69; reduced to spares by Aer Turas

G-AMRP (13125), Mk.31E, Bristol Co.; to Iberia 3.53 as EC-AHH; rest. 1.65 to Aviation Traders Ltd.; to Straits Air Freight Express 9.65 as ZK-CPU; scrapped 6.68

G-AMRR (13126), Mk.31E, Bristol Aeroplane Co. Ltd.; to Iberia 3.53 as EC-AHI; rest. 1.65 to Aviation Traders Ltd.; to S.A.F.E. 9.65 as ZK-CPT

G-AMRS (13129), Mk.31E, Bristol Aeroplane Co. Ltd.; to Iberia 6.53 as EC-AHJ; withdrawn from use in 1962

G-AMRT (13130), Mk.31E, Bristol Aeroplane Co. Ltd.; to Iberia 7.53 as EC-AHK; withdrawn from use in 1961

Freighter Mk. 31E OD-ACM 'Doha' at Blackbushe in 1956 wearing the Cedar of Lebanon motif of Middle East Airlines. (*A. J. Jackson*)

G-AMRU (13136), Mk.31, Bristol Aeroplane Co. Ltd.; to Associated Airways via Prestwick 1.1.53 as CF-FZU; to Maritime Central A/W; crashed 13.2.56

G-AMRV (13137), Mk.31, Bristol Aeroplane Co. Ltd.; to Trans-Canada A/L 9.53 as CF-TFX; to Central Northern A/W 12.55; Wardair 1.57; w.f.u. 1968

G-AMRW (13138), Mk.31, Bristol Aeroplane Co. Ltd.; to Trans-Canada A/L 10.53 as CF-TFY; to Central Northern A/W 12.55; Trans-Air 1.56; w.f.u. 6.56

G-AMRX (13139), Mk.31, Bristol Aeroplane Co. Ltd.; to Trans-Canada A/L 10.53 as CF-TFZ; to Central Northern A/W 12.55; written off 5.56

G-AMRY (13140), Mk.31, Bristol Co.; to Air Vietnam, Saigon 10.53 as F-VNAR; to S.G.A.A. 8.57 as F-OBGF; to Air Fret as F-BBGF; to Corsair

G-AMRZ (13141), Mk.31, G-18-143, Bristol Co.; to Air Vietnam 11.53 as F-VNAS; to S.G.A.A. 8.57 as F-OBDR; to Air Fret as F-BCDR; to Corsair

G-AMSA (13142), Mk.31E, 9.2.54, Air Charter Ltd. 'Voyager'; trooping 1954 as XH385; converted to Mk.32 in 1958; scrapped at Lydd 1967

G-AMSB (13143), Mk.31M, Bristol Aeroplane Co. Ltd.; to Burmese Air Force 3.54 as UB721; sale to Trans-Australia Airlines 1966 as VH-TBC cancelled

G-AMWA (13073), Mk.32, 31.3.53, Silver City Airways Ltd. 'City of London'; crashed on take-off from Guernsey 24.9.63

G-AMWB (13127), Mk.32, 2.4.53, Silver City 'City of Salisbury'; w.f.u. 1967

G-AMWC (13128), Mk.32, 8.5.53, Silver City 'City of Durham'; w.f.u. 1967

G-AMWD (13131), Mk.32, 29.5.53, Silver City 'City of Leicester' (later 'City of Hereford'); to Cie Air Transport 5.61 as F-BKBD 'Quatorze Juillet'

G-AMWE (13132), Mk.32, 12.6.53, Silver City 'City of York'; scrapped 1967

G-AMWF (13133), Mk.32, 23.6.53, Silver City 'City of Edinburgh' (later 'City of Coventry'); scrapped at Lydd in 1968

G-ANMF (13216), Mk.31, 13.8.54, Air Charter Ltd., Southend 'Victory'; British United Air Ferries Ltd. 4.65; last flew 31.8.67; scrapped at Lydd 8.70

G-ANVR (13251), Mk.32, 24.3.55, Air Charter Ltd., Southend 'Valiant'; British United Air Ferries Ltd. 4.65; stored at Lydd 8.70

G-ANVS (13252), Mk.32, 4.4.55, Air Charter Ltd., Southend 'Vigilant'; British United Air Ferries Ltd. 4.65; last flew 28.11.67; scrapped at Lydd 8.70

G-ANWG (13211), Mk.32, 23.6.54, Silver City A/W, Lydd 'City of Winchester'; to Cie Air Transport 5.61 as F-BKBG 'Quatorze Juillet'; scrapped 1968

G-ANWH (13212), Mk.32, 7.7.54, Silver City A/W, Lydd 'City of Hereford'; to C.A.T. 1.63 as F-BLHH 'Dix-huit Juin'; d.b.r. at Le Touquet 11.6.69

G-ANWI (13213), Mk.32, 23.7.54, Silver City A/W, Lydd 'City of Glasgow'; to Cie Air Transport 5.61 as F-BKBI 'Onze Novembre'; scrapped 1968

G-ANWJ (13254), Mk. 32, 31.5.56, Silver City A/W 'City of Bristol'; British United Air Ferries Ltd. 4.65; last flew 3.3.68; scrapped at Lydd 8.70

G-ANWK (13259), Mk.32, 19.6.56, Silver City A/W, Lydd 'City of Leicester'; British United Air Ferries Ltd. 5.65; last flew 20.10.69, scrapped 8.70

G-ANWL (13260), Mk.32, 5.7.56, Silver City A/W, Lydd 'City of Worcester'; crashed at Les Provosts, St. Saviour, Guernsey 1.11.61

G-ANWM (13261), Mk.32, 19.7.56, Silver City A/W, Lydd 'City of Aberdeen'; to Cie Air Transport 2.68 as F-BPIM; rest. 12.69 to British Air Ferries Ltd.; scrapped at Lydd 8.70

G-ANWN (13262), Mk. 32, 31.7.56, Silver City A/W, Lydd 'City of Hull'; to Cie Air Transport 2.68 as F-BPIN; last flew 4.4.69; scrapped at Lydd 8.70

G-AOUU (13257), Mk.32, 18.12.56, Air Charter Ltd., Southend 'Venture'; scrapped at Lydd in 1967

G-AOUV (13258), Mk.32, 7.1.57, Air Charter Ltd., Southend 'Valour'; scrapped at Lydd in 1967

G-APAU (13256), Mk.32, 7.6.57, Air Charter Ltd., Southend 'City of Edinburgh'; British United Air Ferries Ltd. 4.65; Midland Air Cargo Ltd., Baginton 4.71

G-APAV (13263), Mk.32, 26.4.57, Air Charter Ltd., Southend 'Viceroy'; British United Air Ferries Ltd. 4.65; Midland Air Cargoes Ltd., Baginton 10.70

G-APLH (13250), Mk.31, 31.3.58, Dan-Air Services Ltd., Lasham/Gatwick; to Lamb Airways, Manitoba 10.68 as CF-YDP

G-ARSA (13169), Mk.31M, S4409, ferried Karachi–Southend, arrived 13.8.61 and dismantled for spares 1962

Bristol Type 171 Mks. 1 and 2

G-ALOU (12836), Mk.1, VL963, 25.4.49, Bristol Aeroplane Co. Ltd., Filton; to the R.A.F. 8.49 as VL963; crashed at Farnborough 8.9.53

G-AJGU (12869), Mk.2, VW905, Bristol Aeroplane Co. Ltd., Filton; to the R.A.F. as VW905, civil marks not carried; scrapped at Farnborough 12.62

Bristol Type 171 Mks. 3 and 3A*

G-ALSP (12900), completed as Sycamore Mk.12 WV783, converted to H.R. Mk.14, preserved by the R.A.F. Museum at Henlow as 7841M

G-ALSR (12886), 20.7.53, Bristol Aeroplane Co. Ltd.; leased to B.E.A., Heathrow as 'Sir Gareth' 1953–54; to the Ministry of Supply 7.54 as XH682

G-ALSS (12887), flown on development trials in the United Kingdom as WA576; relegated to instructional airframe as 7900M

G-ALST (12888), flown on development trials in the United Kingdom as WA577; relegated to instructional airframe 7718M at No. 4 S. of T.T., St. Athan

G-ALSU (12889), completed as Sycamore Mk.10 WA578 in 1951; left Filton 20.1.53 in Freighter WJ320/G-AINL for tropical trials in Malaya

G-ALSV (12890), completed as Sycamore Mk.11 WT923 for Metropolitan Communications Squadron, Northolt; scrapped 1963

G-ALSW (12891), completed as Sycamore WT933; tropical trials at Khartoum 1953; de-icing trials in Canada 10.56; to R.A.F. Halton 11.60 as 7709M

G-ALSX (12892), 3.5.51, Bristol Aeroplane Co. Ltd.; to Williamsons Diamonds Ltd. 2.58 as VR-TBS; rest. 3.60 to Bristol Aircraft Ltd.; became G-48-1

G-ALSY   (12893), completed as Sycamore Mk.11 WT924; scrapped 1963
G-ALSZ   (12894), completed as Sycamore WV695; to the R.A.A.F. as A91-1; to Rose
          Motors Ltd. 1965 as VH-GVR; crashed at Falls Creek, Victoria 25.1.67
G-ALTA   (12895), completed as Sycamore Mk.11 WT925; scrapped 1964
G-ALTB   (12896), Arctic trials in Canada 7.51; to R.A.F. 6.53 as WT939; to Canada
          10.53; naval trials 1.54
G-ALTC   (12897), civil marks daubed on one side only at 1951 S.B.A.C. Show,
          Farnborough; completed as Sycamore Mk.11 WT926; to spares 1953
G-ALTD   (12898), completed as Sycamore Mk.12 WV781 and based at Little
          Rissington; w.f.u. at Old Sarum 1964; to Henlow as instruct. airframe 7839M
G-ALTE   (12899), completed as Sycamore Mk.12 WV782 and based at Little
          Rissington; withdrawn from use at Old Sarum 1964; destroyed in accident
*G-AMWG (13068), 25.6.53, Bristol Co.; leased to B.E.A. 1954–56 as 'Sir Gawain'; to
          Ansett-A.N.A. 9.59 as VH-INQ; crashed at Glengyle, Queensland 4.9.61
*G-AMWH (13069), 30.6.53, British European Airways 'Sir Geraint'; damaged beyond
          repair landing at Cowes 15.8.64; wreck to Salfords, Redhill 9.64

Bristol Type 171 Mk. 4 Sycamore G-AMWI, showing the widened fuselage amidships.
(*Bristol Photo.*)

Bristol Type 171 Mk.4 Sycamore
G-AMWI   (13070), 7.9.53, Bristol Aeroplane Co. Ltd.; converted to Mk.51 for R.A.A.F.
          as XR592; to Rose Motors Ltd. 1965 as VH-BAW
G-AMWJ   (13171), completed as Sycamore Mk.51 for the R.A.A.F. as XD653
G-AMWK (13194) to G-AMWO (13198) completed as Sycamore Mk.14s XE313–
          XE317
G-AMWP (13199) to G-AMWS (13201), completed as Sycamore Mk.14B for the Belgian
          Air Force as B-1 (OT-ZKA) to B-3 (OT-ZKC)
G-AMWT (13202), completed as Sycamore Mk.14 for the R.A.A.F. as A91-2
G-AMWU (13203), completed 6.56 as Sycamore Mk.14 XJ361; relegated to instruct-
          ional airframe at Halton as 7852M
G-AOBM   (13270), 19.5.55, Bristol Co.; to Canada 5.55 as CF-HVX; converted to
          Mk.51 for R.A.A.F. as XN448; to Rose Motors Ltd. 1965 as VH-SYC
G-AODL   (13403), 19.9.55, Bristol Co.; to Australian National A/W 5.56 as VH-INO
          'Yarrana'; crashed in the Nundle State Forest, N.S.W. 11.1.60

Bristol Type 173 Mks. 1–3

G-ALBN   (12871), Mk.1, Ministry of Supply; naval trials 1953 as XF785; to R.A.F. Technical College, Henlow 1960 as 7648M

G-AMJI   (12872), Mk.2, Ministry of Supply; to R.A.F. 8.54 as XH379; leased to B.E.A. 8.56 as 'Sir Bors'; scrapped at Old Mixon 1958 after accident at air display at Filton 16.9.56

G-AMYF   (13204) to G-AMYH (13206), Mk.3, Ministry of Supply; completed as XE266–XE268. XE268 re-registered 7.56 as G-AORB

Bristol Type 175 Britannia Series 101

G-ALBO   (12873), f/f 16.8.52, C. of A. 22.9.54, Bristol Aircraft Ltd.; Ministry of Supply 8.52 (WB470 not used); to St. Athan 11.60 as 7708M

G-ALRX   (12874), f/f 23.12.53, Bristol Aircraft Ltd.; Ministry of Supply 8.52 (WB473 not used); d.b.r. at Littleton-upon-Severn 4.2.54

Bristol Type 175 Britannia Series 102

G-ANBA   (12902), f/f 5.9.54, C. of A. 8.8.57, British Overseas Airways Corp.; Britannia A/W, Luton 3.65; scrapped at Luton 1970

G-ANBB   (12903), f/f 18.1.55, C. of A. 18.6.57, B.O.A.C.; Britannia Airways Ltd., Luton 11.64; crashed on approach to Ljubljana Airport 1.9.66

G-ANBC   (12904), f/f 29.6.55, C. of A. 30.12.55, B.O.A.C.; beyond repair after casualty-free belly landing at Khartoum Airport 11.11.60

G-ANBD   (12905), f/f 14.11.55, C. of A. 30.12.55, B.O.A.C.; B.K.S. Air Transport Ltd. 1.65; scrapped at Woolsington 5.70

G-ANBE   (12906), f/f 17.1.56, C. of A. 2.3.56, B.O.A.C.; leased to Malayan A/W 1963; Britannia A/W, Luton 2.66; scrapped at Luton 1970

G-ANBF   (12907), f/f 23.2.56, C. of A. 13.3.56, B.O.A.C.; Britannia Airways Ltd., Luton 2.65; scrapped at Luton 2.70

G-ANBG* (12908), f/f 29.3.56, C. of A. 30.4.56, B.O.A.C.; B.K.S. Air Transport Ltd. 12.65; withdrawn from use 1970

G-ANBH   (12909), f/f 9.5.56, C. of A. 25.5.56, B.O.A.C., B.K.S. Air Transport Ltd. 3.65; withdrawn from use 1970

G-ANBI   (12910), f/f 24.5.56, C. of A. 28.6.56, B.O.A.C.; Britannia Airways Ltd., Luton 4.66; scrapped at Luton 8.69

G-ANBJ   (12911), f/f 5.8.56, C. of A. 10.8.56, B.O.A.C.; Britannia Airways Ltd., Luton 3.66; withdrawn from use at Luton 12.70

G-ANBK   (12912), f/f 14.9.56, C. of A. 12.2.57, B.O.A.C.; B.K.S. Air Transport Ltd. 3.64; Northeast Airlines Ltd. 1.71; w.f.u. at Woolsington 1.72

G-ANBL   (12913), f/f 24.2.57, C. of A. 1.3.57, B.O.A.C.; Britannia Airways Ltd., Luton 7.65

G-ANBM   (12914), f/f 6.3.57, C. of A. 11.3.57, B.O.A.C.; Laker A/W Ltd., Gatwick 3.66; leased Treffield 5–6.67; to Indonesian Angkasa 1.69 as PK-ICA

G-ANBN   (12915), f/f 11.4.57, C. of A. 3.5.57, B.O.A.C.; Laker A/W Ltd., Gatwick 4.66; leased Monarch Airlines 1968; Indonesian Angkasa 1.69 as PK-ICB

G-ANBO   (12916), f/f 17.5.57, C. of A. 31.3.57, B.O.A.C.; leased Cathay Pacific 1961; leased Malayan A/W 1962; Britannia A/W Ltd., Luton 1.65; withdrawn from use at Luton 12.70

* Re-registered as G-APLL in March 1958

528

Bristol Type 175 Britannia Series 252

G-APPE   (13450), f/f 13.10.58, C. of A. 10.11.58, Ministry of Supply; to No. 99 Sqn.,
          Lyneham 10.59 as C.Mk.2 XN392 'Acrux'
G-APPF   (13451), f/f 7.12.58, C. of A. 14.1.59, Ministry of Supply; to No. 99 Sqn.,
          Lyneham 3.59 as C.Mk.2 XN398 'Altair'
G-APPG   (13452), f/f 3.5.59, C. of A. 26.3.59, Ministry of Supply; to No. 99 Sqn.,
          Lyneham 4.59 as XN404 'Canopus'

Bristol Type 175 Britannia Series 301

G-ANCA   (12917), f/f 31.7.56, C. of A. 19.11.56, Bristol Aircraft Ltd.; Ministry of
          Supply 1957; crashed 3 miles south-east of Filton 6.11.57

Bristol Type 175 Britannia Series 302

G-ANCB   (12918), f/f 21.6.57 as G-18-1, C. of A. 30.10.57, Bristol Aircraft Ltd.; to
          Aeronaves de Mexico 11.57 as XA-MEC 'Tenochtitlan' later 'Acapulco'
G-ANCC   (12919), f/f 24.5.57 as G-18-2, C. of A. 15.12.57, Bristol Aircraft Ltd.; to
          Aeronaves de Mexico 12.57 as XA-MED 'Tzintzuntzan'; rest. 5.66 to
          Transglobe A/W Ltd., Gatwick; conv. to 308F; w.f.u. 10.70

G-ANCD, first Britannia 305 for Northeast Airlines, at Filton, January 1958. British
markings were allotted pending the issue of the American type certificate.

Bristol Type 175 Britannia Series 305-309

G-ANCD   (12920), 305, f/f 1.6.57 as G-18-3, C. of A. 25.3.58, Bristol Aircraft Ltd.; not
          d/d to Northeast A/L as N6595C; leased El Al 7.58 to 3.59 as Ser.306
          4X-AGE; rest. 3.59 to Air Charter Ltd. (later B.U.A.) as Ser.307; Lloyd
          International Airways Ltd., Stansted 6.69 as Ser.307F
G-ANCE   (12921), 305, f/f 3.9.58, C. of A. 12.9.58, Bristol Aircraft Ltd.; not d/d to
          Northeast A/L as N6596C; Air Charter Ltd. (later B.U.A.) 9.58; converted to
          Ser.307F; Lloyd International Airways Ltd., Stansted 6.69
G-ANCF   (12922), 305, f/f 19.11.58 as G-18-4, Bristol Aircraft Ltd.; not d/d to
          Northeast A/L as N6597C; conv. to Ser. 308 as G-14-1; to Transcontinental
          S.A. 12.59 as LV-PPJ, later LV-GJB; rest. 1.64 to British Eagle, C. of A.
          2.7.64 as Ser. 308F 'New Frontier'; Monarch Airlines Ltd., Luton 1.69
G-ANCG   (12923), 305, Bristol Aircraft Ltd.; not d/d to Northeast A/L as N6598C;
          conv. to Ser. 308; to Transcontinental S.A. 12.59 as LV-PPL, later LV-GJC;
          rest 2.64 to British Eagle, C. of A. 11.11.64 as Ser.308F 'Trojan'; d.b.r. in
          belly landing at Manston 20.4.67

G-ANCH (12924), 305, f/f 19.2.60, Bristol Aircraft Ltd.; not d/d to Northeast A/L as N6599C; converted to Ser.309; leased Ghana A/W 7.60 as 9G-AAG; rest. 6.65 to B.U.A. Ltd.; leased Ghana A/W 3.68; Monarch Airlines Ltd., Luton 6.68

Bristol Type 175 Britannia Series 312

G-AOVA (13207), 311, f/f 31.12.56, C. of A. 25.11.57, Bristol Aircraft Ltd.; to Ghana A/W 11.60 as Ser.319 9G-AAH 'Osagyefo'; rest. 3.64 to British Eagle as 'Justice'; Caledonian A/W Ltd., Gatwick 'County of Fife' 4.69; w.f.u. at Gatwick 5.70

G-AOVB (13230), f/f 5.7.57, C. of A. 30.8.57, B.O.A.C.; British Eagle 'Endeavour' 11.63; to A.E.R., Argentina 10.69 as LV-PNJ, later LV-JNL

G-AOVC (13231), f/f 22.10.57, C. of A. 15.11.57, B.O.A.C.; British Eagle 'Sovereign' 5.64; Donaldson International A/W Ltd. Gatwick 'Mikado' 5.69; last flight 16.11.70; to Stansted Fire School 12.70

G-AOVD (13235), f/f 13.11.57, C. of A. 3.12.57, B.O.A.C.; crashed near Hurn Airport 24.12.58 while on C. of A. test flight

G-AOVE (13236), f/f 8.12.57, 20.12.57, B.O.A.C.; leased B.U.A. 1961–64; leased Middle East A/L 1964; British Eagle 'Perseverance' 1964; to Air Spain 12.66 as EC-BFK 'Mediterraneo'

G-AOVF (13237), f/f 18.12.57, C. of A. 31.12.57, B.O.A.C.; British Eagle 'Friendship' 3.64; Donaldson International Airways Ltd., Gatwick 'Nike' 4.70; last flight 17.11.70; to Stansted Fire School 12.70

G-AOVG (13238), f/f 10.1.58, C. of A. 29.1.58, B.O.A.C.; British Eagle 'Bounteous' 3.64; Monarch Airlines Ltd., Luton 10.69

G-AOVH (12925), f/f 29.1.58, C. of A. 11.2.58, B.O.A.C.; British Eagle 'Crusader' 1964; Caledonian A/W Ltd. 3.65; Monarch Airlines Ltd. 1.68

G-AOVI (12926), f/f 15.2.58, C. of A. 25.2.58, B.O.A.C.; leased B.U.A. 1961–64; Caledonian A/W Ltd. 'County of Argyll' 12.64; Monarch A/L Ltd. 1.68; w.f.u. at Luton 2.72

G-AOVJ (13418), f/f 27.2.58, C. of A. 11.3.58, B.O.A.C.; Caledonian A/W Ltd. 'County of Aberdeen' 4.65; last flight 14.11.70; scrapped 12.70

G-AOVK (13419), f/f 18.3.58, C. of A. 2.4.58, B.O.A.C.; British Eagle 'Concord' 8.65; scrapped at Luton 8.69

G-AOVL (13420), f/f 9.4.58, C. of A. 18.4.58, B.O.A.C.; British Eagle 'Resolution' 3.64; Monarch Airlines Ltd. 1.68

G-AOVM (13421), f/f 29.4.58, C. of A. 13.5.58, B.O.A.C.; British Eagle 'Team Spirit' 3.64; converted to Ser.312F; to Air Spain 12.69 as EC-BSY

G-AOVN (13422), f/f 16.5.58, C. of A. 23.5.58, B.O.A.C.; British Eagle 'Prospect' 6.64; Monarch Airlines Ltd., Luton 9.69

G-AOVO (13423), f/f 3.7.58, C. of A. 11.7.58, B.O.A.C.; British Eagle 'Bonaventure' 1.64; crashed in the Austrian Alps near Innsbruck 29.2.64

G-AOVP (13424), f/f 22.7.58, C. of A. 29.7.58, B.O.A.C.; Lloyd International Airways Ltd., Stansted 4.65

G-AOVR (13429), f/f 4.8.58, C. of A. 26.8.58, B.O.A.C.; British Eagle 'Talisman' 3.65; to Air Spain 10.66 as EC-BFJ 'Atlantico', later 'Islas Canarias'

G-AOVS (13430), f/f 5.9.58, C. of A. 18.9.58, B.O.A.C.; Lloyd International Airways Ltd. 8.65; converted to Ser. 312F

G-AOVT (13427), f/f 17.12.58, C. of A. 30.12.58, B.O.A.C.; British Eagle 'Enterprise' 9.63, later 'Ajax'; Monarch Airlines Ltd., Luton 5.69

Bristol Type 175 Britannia Series 313

G-ARWZ (13233), f/f 2.9.57 as 4X-AGB, C. of A. 13.2.62 for British United Airways Ltd.; leased El Al 1965 as 4X-AGB; to Air Spain 1965 as EC-BFL

G-ARXA (13234), f/f 4.10.57 as 4X-AGC, C. of A. 12.3.62 for British United Airways Ltd.; leased El Al 1965 as 4X-AGC; British Eagle 'Talisman' 5.66, later 'Renown'; returned to El Al 4.69 as 4X-AGC

G-ASFU (13431), f/f 21.2.59 as 4X-AGD, operated by British United Airways Ltd. in British marks in March 1963 during an El Al strike; reverted to 4X-AGD; to Globe Air 1966 as HB-ITC; to Air Safari 1968 as 5X-UVH

G-ASFV (13232), f/f 28.7.57 as 4X-AGA, details as G-ASFU; to Globe Air 1966 as HB-ITB; crashed on approach to Nicosia, Cyprus 20.4.67

Bristol Type 175 Britannia Series 314

G-ASTF (13453), f/f 22.7.58 as CF-CZW, C. of A. 5.6.64 for British Eagle; to Canadian Pacific 10.64 as CF-CZW 'Toronto'; rest. 1.66 to Caledonian A/W as 'Flagship Bonnie Scotland', later 'County of Perth'; last flight 17.11.69; scrapped at Gatwick 10.70

G-ATGD (13393), f/f 11.1.58 as CF-CZA, C. of A. 9.7.65 for Air Links Ltd., Gatwick; Transglobe A/W Ltd. 12.65; to Air Safaris 9.69 as 5X-UVT

G-ATLE (13395), f/f 13.5.58 as CF-CZC, C. of A. 12.12.65 for Transglobe Airways Ltd., Gatwick; withdrawn from use at Gatwick 3.70

G-ATMA (13428), f/f 19.6.58 as CF-CZX, C. of A. 6.1.66 for Caledonian A/W Ltd. as 'County of Midlothian'; to African Safari Airways 5.71 as 5Y-ANS

G-ATNZ (13396), f/f 13.6.58 as CF-CZD, C. of A. 4.2.66 for Caledonian A/W Ltd. as 'County of Inverness'; withdrawn from use at Biggin Hill 4.71

Bristol Type 175 Britannia Series 317

G-APNA (13425), f/f 10.10.58, C. of A. 27.10.58, Hunting Clan Air Transport Ltd. (later B.U.A.); Donaldson International Airways Ltd. 'Juno' 1969; leased to Lloyd International Airways Ltd., Stansted 1969

G-APNB (13426), f/f 10.11.58, C. of A. 21.11.58, Hunting Clan Air Tranport Ltd. (later B.U.A.); Donaldson International Airways Ltd. 'Carillon' 1969

Bristol Type 175 Britannia Series 318

G-APYY (13432), f/f 24.11.58 as CU-T668, C. of A. 6.4.60 for Eagle Airways (later Cunard-Eagle); to Ceskoslovenske Aerolinie 10.61 as OK-MBA

Bristol Type 175 Britannia Series 324

G-ARKA (13516), f/f 9.10.59 as G-18-8/CF-CPD, C. of A. 9.3.61 for Cunard-Eagle Airways Ltd. (later British Eagle 'Good Fortune'); to Tellair 5.70 as HB-ITF, not delivered, scrapped at Baginton 7.71

G-ARKB (13517), f/f 4.11.59 as CF-CPE, C. of A. 2.5.61 for Cunard-Eagle Airways Ltd. (later British Eagle 'Endeavour', later 'Resolution'); to Tellair 5.70 as HB-ITG, not delivered, scrapped at Baginton 7.71

Bristol Type 175 Britannia Series 200, 300 and 250 prototypes

Construction of G-AMYK, Series 200 (13207); G-AMYL, Series 300 (13208); and G-ANGK, Series 250 (13234) was abandoned. Airframe 13207 completed later as Series 311 G-AOVA; and 13234 as Series 313 4X-AGC/G-ARXA

Britten-Norman BN-2 and BN-2A Islander

G-ATCT (1), f/f 13.6.65, C. of A. 16.6.65, Britten-Norman Ltd., Bembridge; crashed into Ringwiel Lake, near Leeuwarden, Holland 9.11.66

G-ATWU (2), f/f 20.8.66, C. of A. 4.10.66, Britten-Norman Ltd., Bembridge; converted 7.68 to stretched BN-2E; converted 8.70 to Trislander prototype; withdrawn from use at Bembridge 12.70 as static test airframe

G-AVCN (3), f/f 24.4.67, C. of A. 13.8.67, Glosair/Aurigny Air Services Ltd., Alderney

G-AVKC (4), f/f 21.6.67, C. of A. 10.8.67, Loganair Ltd., Kirkwall 'Capt. E. E. Fresson O.B.E.'

G-AVOS (5), f/f 9.9.67, C. of A. 27.9.67, d/d to Jonas via Shannon 28.9.67; became N584JA; mod. to F.A.A. standard; to Suburban A/L 6.68 as N589SA

G-AVRA (6), f/f 16.8.67, C. of A. 19.8.67, Loganair Ltd., Abbotsinch 'Capt. David Barclay M.B.E.'

G-AVRB (7), f/f 28.9.67, C. of A. 6.10.67, ferried to U.S.A. via Shannon 7.10.67; to Madriz Construcciones, Venezuela 20.12.67 as YV-T-MTM

G-AVRC (8), f/f 9.10.67, d/d to Aertirrana S.p.A., Florence, via Eastleigh 13.12.67 as I-TRAM

G-AVUB (9), f/f 24.10.67, C. of A. 10.11.67, Herts & Essex Aero Club; Rolls-Royce Ltd. 8.68; Miles Av. & Transport Ltd. 5.70; to Shoreham 10.71 as G-4-9

G-AVUC (10), f/f 27.11.67, d/d to Jonas via Shannon 20.12.67; sold to La Poseda A/W as N671JA (later N17UP); to Key Airlines, Utah 9.68 as N417UP

G-AVXO (11), f/f 4.12.67, d/d to Jonas via Shannon 23.12.67, became N672JA; to General A/L, Reading, Pa. 10.68; to Tri-State Av., W. Virginia 8.69

G-AVXP (12), f/f 29.12.67, d/d to Jonas via Shannon 29.1.68; sold to Viking Airways, Rhode Island N.Y. as N581JA

G-AVXR (13), f/f 2.1.68 as G-51-2, d/d to Transgabon Compagnie Aérienne, Libreville, Gabon, via Eastleigh–Le Bourget 30.1.68 as TR-LNG

G-AVXS (14), f/f 17.1.68, as G-51-3, test flown as G-AVXS 24.1.68–1.2.68; d/d to Aerovias del Valle, San Jose, Costa Rica via Eastleigh 13.2.68 as TI-1063C; crashed at Puerto Cortes, Costa Rica 8.10.68

G-AVXT (15), f/f 1.2.68, left Bembridge on delivery 16.2.68; handed over to Island Airways, Pialba Island, Great Barrier Reef 15.3.68 as VH-AIA

G-AVXU (16), f/f 18.2.68 as G-51-4, d/d to Air Gabon 6.3.68 as TR-LNF

G-AWBY (17), f/f 2.3.68, C. of A. 12.3.68, Glosair/Aurigny Air Services Ltd., Alderney

The development Islander G-ATWU in stretched form at Bembridge in September 1969.
(*M. J. Hooks*)

Islander I-TRAM in the snow at Bembridge in December 1967 ready for delivery to Aertirrana S.p.A., Florence.

G-AWBZ (18), f/f 13.3.68, C. of A. 21.3.68, Glosair/Aurigny Air Services Ltd., Alderney

G-AWCA (19), f/f 22.3.68, d/d to Jonas 8.4.68; sold to Viking A/W as N582JA; to Vaengiri, Reykjavik, Iceland 8.71

G-AWCB (20), f/f 11.4.68, d/d to Jonas 25.4.68; sold to Altus Airlines, Okla. 11.68 as N585JA; to Subsidiary Colony Airlines 8.69

G-AWCC (21), f/f 11.4.68, f/f as D-IOLT 14.4.68 and d/d to Ostfriesische Lufttaxi, Emden 17.4.68

G-AWHZ (22), f/f 23.4.68 as G-51-5, d/d to Ostfriesische Lufttaxi, Emden 25.4.68 as D-IJAN

G-AWIA (23), f/f 28.5.68, d/d to Jonas 31.5.68; sold to Lambair Ltd., La Paz, Manitoba as CF-XYK

G-AWIB (24), f/f 20.6.68, d/d to Jonas 1.7.68, became U.S. demonstrator N586JA

G-AWIC (25), f/f 14.7.68, delivered to Jonas 24.7.68; sold to Vieques Air Link, Puerto Rico as N589JA

G-AWID (26), f/f 27.7.68, C. of A. 9.8.68, Britten-Norman Ltd.; left for Thai Ministry of Agriculture, Bangkok 5.10.68; became Thai Air Force '501'

G-AWIE (27), f/f 27.8.68, d/d to Jonas 7.9.68; to Suburban A/L as N457SA

G-AWNR (30), f/f 14.10.68, C. of A. 22.10.68, Glosair/Aurigny Air Services Ltd., Alderney

G-AWNS (31), f/f 18.10.68 as G-51-6, delivered to Jonas 19.11.68 as N676SA; sold to Suburban Airlines, Fort Lauderdale, Florida

G-AWNT (32), f/f 7.9.68, C. of A. 20.9.68, Survey Flights Ltd., Yeadon

G-AWNU (33), f/f 2.10.68, C. of A. 10.10.68, Herts & Essex Aero Club, Stapleford

G-AWNV (34), f/f 27.10.68, C. of A. 4.11.68, Britten-Norman Ltd.; to the Abu Dhabi Defence Force and delivered via Hurn 11.68 as '201'

G-AWNW (35), f/f 11.11.68 as CF-RDI, delivered to Regent Drilling Ltd., Edmonton, Alberta 3.12.68

G-AWNX (36), f/f 8.11.68 as VH-ATS, delivered to Aerial Tours Pty. Ltd., Port Moresby, Papua via Eastleigh 25.11.68

G-AWNY (37), f/f 19.11.68, delivered to Jonas 15.1.69; later sold to SATAIR, Martinique, West Indies as F-OGDR

G-AWNZ (38), f/f 21.11.68 as G-51-7, delivered to Jonas 14.12.68 via Gatwick–Shannon; later sold to Suburban Airlines as N589SA

G-AWOD (39), f/f 12.12.68, as G-51-8, delivered to Jonas 24.12.68; later sold to Viking Airways, Rhode Island, N.Y. as N583JA

G-AWVX (47), f/f 24.1.69, C. of A. 11.2.69, Britten-Norman Ltd.; to the Abu Dhabi Defence Force 2.69 as '202'

G-AWVY (48), f/f 30.1.69, C. of A. 25.2.69, Glosair/Aurigny Air Services Ltd., Alderney

G-AWYA (54), f/f 25.2.69, delivered to Jonas 4.69; to Island Helicopters Ltd., Jamaica 5.69 as 6Y-JFL; later to Jamaican Transport Ltd. 8.69

G-AWYW (55), f/f 27.2.69, C. of A. 6.6.69, Britten-Norman Ltd.; d/d to the Kingdom of Libya Ministry of Petroleum Affairs 22.6.69 as 5A-BBA

G-AXBA (51), f/f 12.2.69 as G-51-15, C. of A. 14.3.69, Britten-Norman Ltd.; d/d to SATAIR, Martinique, West Indies via Eastleigh 29.3.69, re-registered F-OGEB on arrival

G-AXDH (70), f/f 20.4.69, C. of A. 22.4.69, Britten-Norman Ltd.; P. Cadbury, Lulsgate 6.70; Parachute Regt. Free Fall Club, Blackbushe 4.71

G-AXFC (76), f/f 22.5.69, C. of A. 19.6.69, Westward Airways Ltd., Roborough; Rent-a-Plane Ltd. 4.71

G-AXFL (73), f/f 12.5.69 as G-51-17, C. of A. 6.6.69, Britten-Norman Ltd.; to Malta–Gozo Air Services Ltd. 6.69 as 9H-AAB 'La Vallette'; rest. 9.70; to Macair Charters Pty. Ltd., Lae, N.G. 6.71 as VH-MKN

G-AXGB (75), f/f 17.6.69 as G-51-18, C. of A. 20.6.69, d/d to Airservices, Thailand 24.6.69; sold to Bangkok United Mechanical Co. as HS-SKA

G-AXHE (86), f/f 25.6.69, C. of A. 31.7.69, Westward Airways Ltd., Roborough; F. Hewitt, Shoreham 3.70

G-AXIN (79), f/f 6.6.69 as G-51-20, C. of A. 27.6.69, Britten-Norman Ltd.; flown to Australia 12.70

G-AXKB (95), f/f 17.7.69 as G-51-30, C. of A. 20.8.69, Loganair Ltd., Abbotsinch

G-AXKC (97), f/f 21.7.69 as G-51-32, delivered to Technicoimport, Bucharest 13.9.69 as YR-BNB

G-AXLY (91), f/f 9.7.69 as G-51-27, left on delivery to Ataka, Japan 15.8.69; later to Japan Sea Airlines, Nigata as JA-5175

G-AXMZ (105), f/f 25.8.69 as G-51-38, C. of A. 17.10.69, Britten-Norman Ltd.; left on delivery to Air Malawi 21.10.69; re-registered 7Q-YKC

G-AXNF (96), f/f 19.7.69 as G-51-31, registered 29.8.69 to Britten-Norman Ltd.; delivered to Aviron, Israel 24.12.69 as 4X-AYT

G-AXPE (117), f/f 1.10.69 as G-51-44, C. of A. 27.10.69, Britten-Norman Ltd.; delivered to the Abu Dhabi Defence Force 30.10.69 as '203'

G-AXPY (111), f/f 11.9.69 as G-51-41, C. of A. 13.2.70, Britten-Norman Ltd.; to N.V. National Vliegtuig Beheer-Seeprat Commuter 6.70 as PH-VNA

G-AXRJ (123), f/f 20.10.69 as G-51-49, N862JA ntu, C. of A. 6.11.69, Britten-Norman Ltd.; demonstrated in Greece, Pakistan, India, Nepal and Burma; destroyed landing at Rawalpindi, Pakistan 7.4.70

G-AXRM (128), f/f 5.11.69 as G-51-51, C. of A. 18.12.69, Humber Airways Ltd., Brough

G-AXRN (129), f/f 10.11.69 as G-51-52, C. of A. 31.12.69, Humber Airways Ltd., Brough

G-AXSN (81), f/f 11.6.69 as G-51-22, N870JA ntu, C. of A. 10.12.69, H. W. Astor and Sir W. S. Dugdale; 7th in London–Sydney Air Race 12.69; to Port Augusta Air Services Pty. Ltd. 3.70 as VH-ROB

G-AXUB   (121), f/f 13.10.69 as G-51-47, C. of A. 6.1.70, United Helicopters Ltd., Redhill; to Nigeria 3.70 and re-registered 5N-AIJ

G-AXUD   (132), f/f 20.11.69 as VH-ATZ, C. of A. 11.12.69, Britten-Norman Ltd.; first in Sydney Air Race 12.69; to Aerial Tours Pty. Ltd. as VH-ATZ

G-AXVP   (127), f/f 31.10.69 as G-51-50, C. of A. 4.3.70, Anglian Air Charter Ltd., North Denes

G-AXVR   (139), f/f 15.12.69 as G-51-65, C. of A. 2.2.70, Aurigny Air Services Ltd., Alderney

G-AXWG   (135), f/f 26.11.69 as G-51-55, C. of A. 22.1.70, United Helicopters Ltd., Redhill; to Nigeria 3.70 and re-registered 5N-AIK

G-AXWH   (137), f/f 9.12.69 as G-51-58, C. of A. 6.2.70, United Helicopters Ltd., Redhill, to Nigeria via Gatwick 10.3.70 and re-registered 5N-AIL

G-AXWK   (124), f/f 25.10.69 as VH-FLF, C. of A. 6.2.70, Britten-Norman Ltd.; to Vowell Air Services Ltd., Melbourne 2.70 as VH-EQT

G-AXWO   (140), f/f 15.12.69 as G-51-59, C. of A. 14.4.70, Britten-Norman Ltd.; built for the Honda Motor Co., Tokyo; to Shoreham 10.71 as G-4-10

G-AXWP   (147), f/f 14.1.70 as G-51-66, C. of A. 20.2.70, Aurigny Air Services Ltd., Alderney

G-AXWR   (149), f/f 12.1.70 as G-51-68, C. of A. 20.2.70, Aurigny Air Services Ltd., Alderney

G-AXWS   (152), f/f 22.1.70 as G-51-152, registered 26.1.70 to Britten-Norman Ltd.; left on delivery to Islander Aircraft Sales, Australia 13.2.70

G-AXXF   (134), f/f 25.11.69 as G-51-54, C. of A. 3.4.70, Douglas Arnold Aviation Ltd., Fairoaks; to Somerset Airways Ltd., Australia 6.70 as VH-BPV

G-AXXG   (143), f/f 1.1.70 as G-51-62, C. of A. 7.4.70, Douglas Arnold Aviation Ltd., Fairoaks; G.K.N. Birfield Transmissions Ltd., Elmdon 8.70

G-AXXH   (144), f/f 2.1.70 as G-51-64, C. of A. 24.4.70, Douglas Arnold Aviation Ltd., Fairoaks; Northern Executive Aviation Ltd., Ringway 11.71

G-AXXI   (148), f/f 24.1.70 as G-51-67, C. of A. 27.2.70, Douglas Arnold Aviation Ltd., Fairoaks; to Guyana Air Services Ltd. via Prestwick 11.6.70 as 8R-GDJ

Note: Islanders from c/n 150 onwards were first flown with constructor's numbers forming part of their Class B registrations.

G-AXXJ   (150), f/f 5.1.70 as G-51-150, C. of A. 27.2.70, Brymon Aviation Ltd., Fairoaks

G-AXXK   (151), f/f 27.1.70, C. of A. 26.2.70, Douglas Arnold Aviation Ltd., Fairoaks; to Ireland West Airways 4.70 as EI-AUF

G-AXYL   (155), f/f 10.2.70, C. of A. 20.3.70, Douglas Arnold Aviation Ltd., Fairoaks; P. E. Cadbury, Lulsgate 7.70

G-AXYM   (156), f/f 11.2.70, C. of A. 13.3.70, Douglas Arnold Aviation Ltd., Fairoaks; to Nigeria 12.70 as 5N-AIQ

G-AXYN   (157), f/f 11.2.70, C. of A. 3.4.70, Douglas Arnold Aviation Ltd., Fairoaks; to Kinshasa, Congo, via Gatwick 29.10.70 as 9Q-CRF

G-AXYP   (158), f/f 19.2.70, C. of A. 13.3.70, Douglas Arnold Aviation Ltd., Fairoaks; to R. & L. Holdings Pty. Ltd., Australia 10.70 as VH-FLD

G-AXYR   (159), f/f 19.2.70, C. of A. 23.3.70, Douglas Arnold Aviation Ltd., Fairoaks; to Preston Air Charter Pty. Ltd., Perth, W.A. 5.70 as VH-ISA

G-AXYS   (164), f/f 11.3.70, C. of A. 24.4.70, Britten-Norman Ltd.; to Australia 4.70 as VH-EQX; to Mt. Cook Airlines, Auckland 10.70 as ZK-DBV

G-AXYT (165), f/f 17.3.70, C. of A. 24.4.70, Britten-Norman Ltd.; to Union Air Pty. Ltd. t/a Richards Rent-a-Plane, Australia as VH-RUT

G-AXZK (153), f/f 31.1.70, C. of A. 23.3.70, Britten-Norman Ltd.; to Leeward Islands Air Transport Ltd. 3.70 as VP-LAD

G-AYBI (145), converted to 300 h.p. Lycomings, f/f 30.4.70 as G-51-63, C. of A. 4.6.70, Britten-Norman Ltd.; to I.A.S., Australia 2.71

G-AYBL (154), f/f 4.2.70, C. of A. 21.4.70, Britten-Norman Ltd.; delivered to Alar, Portugal 20.5.70; to Jet Sales, Münich 8.70 as D-INYL

G-AYBM (162), f/f 5.3.70, registered 15.4.70 to Britten-Norman Ltd.; delivered to Alar, Portugal 19.5.70; C. of A. 29.6.70, to Mozambique as CR-ALQ

G-AYBN (167), f/f 18.3.70, C. of A. 30.4.70, Britten-Norman Ltd., Bembridge; to Alar Ltda., Portugal 19.5.70; to Mozambique as CR-ALR

G-AYCD (168), f/f 31.3.70, C. of A. 28.4.70, Britten-Norman Ltd.; to Australia 5.70 as VH-EQY; d/d to Mt. Cook Airlines, Auckland 9.9.70 as ZK-DBW

G-AYCU (169), f/f 4.4.70, C. of A. 22.5.70, Britten-Norman Ltd., Bembridge; to GAR-X Surveys Ltd., Canada, via Shannon 10.10.70 as CF-CMY

G-AYCV (170), f/f 6.4.70, C. of A. 2.6.70, Island Air Charter Ltd., Fairoaks

G-AYCW (171), f/f 8.4.70, C. of A. 20.5.70, Britten-Norman Ltd., Bembridge (flown as G-51-171): sold in Israel 11.71

G-AYCX (172), f/f 9.4.70, C. of A. 21.5.70, Britten-Norman Ltd.; to Australia 6.70 as VH-EQV; to Air Melanesie as VP-PAS

G-AYCY (173), f/f 16.4.70, C. of A. 21.5.70, Britten-Norman Ltd.; to Australia 6.70 as VH-EQW; to Air Melanesie as VP-PAT

G-AYDL (174), f/f 20.5.70, C. of A. 30.5.70, Britten-Norman Ltd., Bembridge; delivered to Alar, Portugal 12.6.70 for Mozambique as CR-ALS

G-AYDM (179), f/f 12.6.70, C. of A. 19.6.70, Britten-Norman Ltd., Bembridge; delivered to Førde-Fly, Norway 10.7.70 as LN-VIW

G-AYGF (193), f/f 16.6.70, C. of A. 14.7.70, Fairoaks Aviation Services Ltd.; Imperial Tobacco Co. Ltd., Lulsgate 2.71; Berrico Advertising Co. Ltd., 6.71

G-AYGS (182), f/f 20.5.70, C. of A. 22.7.70, Britten-Norman Ltd., Bembridge; to Islander Aircraft Sales (South Africa) Pty. Ltd. 24.7.70 as ZS-IJA

G-AYGT (183), f/f 9.6.70, C. of A. 3.8.70, Britten-Norman Ltd., Bembridge; to H. J. Hughes, Huron Park, Ontario, Canada 6.71 as CF-ZUT

G-AYGU (190), f/f 6.6.70, C. of A. 1.8.70, Britten-Norman Ltd., Bembridge; to Air Cambodge, Cambodia, via Gatwick 17.12.70 as XU-BAE

G-AYGV (191), f/f 4.6.70, C. of A. 20.10.70, Britten-Norman Ltd.; parked at Fort Lauderdale, Florida 8.71

G-AYGW (192), f/f 15.6.70, C. of A. 25.9.70, Britten-Norman Ltd., Bembridge; to Islander Aircraft Sales (South Africa) Pty. Ltd. 25.9.70 as ZS-IJB

G-AYHK (194), f/f 17.6.70, C. of A. 31.7.70, Britten-Norman Ltd., Bembridge; to Murchison Air Charter Ltd., Perth, W.A. 7.70 as VH-RTK

G-AYHL (195), f/f 23.6.70, C. of A. 17.9.70, Britten-Norman Ltd., Bembridge; to Preston Air Charter Ltd., Jandakott 17.9.70 as VH-ISB; to Fiji as DQ-FBO

G-AYIS (205), f/f 16.7.70, C. of A. 28.8.70, Fairoaks Aviation Services Ltd.; to Brazil via Gatwick 27.10.71 as PT-DYL

G-AYIV (118), G-51-45, 8R-GDN ntu, f/f 6.10.69, C. of A. 6.10.70, Britten-Norman Ltd., Bembridge; to Alar Ltda., Portugal 10.70; to Mozambique as CR-AME

G-AYIW (125), G-51-49, 8R-GDQ ntu, f/f 27.10.69, C. of A. 6.10.70, Britten-Norman Ltd.; to Alar Ltda., Portugal 10.70 as CS-AJO

G-AYKP (207), BN-2A-3, f/f 12.10.70, C. of A. 30.10.70, Britten-Norman Ltd.; to
Islander Aircraft Sales Pty. Ltd., Australia 11.70 as VH-ISC

G-AYKR (217), BN-2A-3, f/f 19.10.70, C. of A. 29.10.70, Britten-Norman Ltd.; to
Carpentaria Exploration Pty. Ltd., Wewak, New Guinea, ex Bembridge
5.11.70; re-registered VH-MIB on arrival

G-AYLR (197), f/f 30.6.70, C. of A. 5.11.70, Britten-Norman Ltd.; to Wings Ltd., St.
Lucia via Shannon 17.11.70, re-registered VQ-LAQ on arrival

G-AYLS (227), BN-2A-3, f/f 13.11.70, C. of A. 27.11.70, Britten-Norman Ltd.,
Bembridge; to East Coast Aviation Services Ltd., Grafton, N.S.W. 1.71 as
VH-EDI

G-AYMB (200), f/f 3.7.70, C. of A. 17.12.70, Britten-Norman Ltd., Bembridge; to
Rousseau Aviation, Dinard 1.72 as F-BTGO

G-AYMC (204), N36JA, f/f 14.7.70, C. of A. 10.11.70, Britten-Norman Ltd.; delivered
to Virgin Islands Airmotive Corp. via Shannon 17.11.70; became HP-556

G-AYNH (213), N39JA, f/f 1.9.70, C. of A. 9.12.70, Britten-Norman Ltd.; delivered to
Islander Aircraft Sales (South Africa) Pty. Ltd. 9.1.71

G-AYNI (216), f/f 3.9.70, C. of A. 12.1.71, Fairoaks Aviation Services Ltd.; to Brazil
12.71 as PT-IAS

G-AYON (226), f/f 7.10.70, C. of A. 11.2.71, Britten-Norman Ltd., Bembridge; to
Alamo Aircraft via Shannon 11.2.71 en route to Panama; became HP-572

G-AYOO (247), BN-2A-3, f/f 19.12.70, C. of A. 22.3.71, Britten-Norman Ltd.,
Bembridge; to South Africa 1.71; later to Mozambique as CR-AMG

G-AYPL (253), BN-2A-3, f/f 16.1.71, C. of A. 19.5.70, Britten-Norman Ltd.;
to Islander Aircraft Sales (South Africa) Pty. Ltd. 20.2.71 as ZS-IJC

G-AYPX (271), BN-2A-3, 27.4.71, Britten-Norman Ltd., Bembridge

G-AYRU (181), OH-BNA, f/f 8.5.70, C. of A. 2.2.71, Britten-Norman Ltd., Bembridge

G-AYRV (233), f/f 28.10.70, registered 2.71 to Britten-Norman Ltd.; to A. Fecteau
Transport Ltd., Senneterre, Quebec 4.71 as CF-ZWF

G-AYRW (272), BN-2A-3, registered 2.71 to Britten-Norman Ltd., Bembridge

G-AYRX (273), BN-2A-3, 28.4.71, Britten-Norman Ltd.; to Iran 7.71 as EP-PAC

G-AYWJ (276), 21.5.71, Britten-Norman Ltd., Bembridge

G-AYYA (278), 27.8.70, Britten-Norman Ltd., Bembridge; sold in Australia 11.71

G-AYYB (281), 28.8.70, Britten-Norman Ltd., Bembridge

G-AYYP (246), f/f 18.11.70, C. of A. 3.6.71, Britten-Norman Ltd., Bembridge; flown to
U.S.A. via Shannon 17.6.71

G-AYYV (219), f/f 15.9.70, C. of A. 9.7.71, Britten-Norman Ltd., Bembridge; to
ETAPA, Nampula, Mozambique 7.71

G-AYYW (277), 27.5.71, Britten-Norman Ltd., Bembridge; to Ostfriesische Lufttaxi,
Emden 12.71 as D-IOLA

G-AZAX (241), 28.6.71, Britten-Norman Ltd., Bembridge; flown to Canada 7.71 as
competitor in London-Victoria Air Race; re-registered CF-QPM

G-AZBV (285), 11.8.71, Britten-Norman Ltd., Bembridge; Fairoaks Aviation Services
Ltd. 9.71

G-AZCG (288), 24.8.71, Britten-Norman Ltd., Bembridge; flown to South Africa 12.71;
became ZS-IJD

G-AZEH (289), 16.9.71, Fairoaks Aviation Services Ltd., Fairoaks

G-AZEI (291), 16.9.71, Fairoaks Aviation Services Ltd., Fairoaks

G-AZLI (297), registered 31.12.71 to Britten-Norman (Bembridge) Ltd.; for Pars Air,
Teheran

Britten-Norman BN-2A Islander (*erected in Rumania*)

G-AXHY (601, also 85 in the B-N series), f/f 4.8.69, C. of A. 20.9.69, d/d Bembridge 22.9.69; to Desert Locust Control, Nairobi 8.70 as 5Y-AMG

G-AXND (602), f/f 18.10.69, C. of A. 25.10.69, Britten-Norman Ltd., Bembridge; delivered to Malaysia-Singapore Airlines Ltd. 15.1.70 as 9M-APK

G-AXSS (603), f/f 3.12.69, C. of A. 1.6.70, Britten-Norman Ltd.; Loganair Ltd., Abbotsinch 11.71

G-AXST (604), f/f 6.12.69, d/d to Bembridge 6.2.70, C. of A. 10.6.70, Britten-Norman Ltd., Bembridge; to Air Malawi via Heathrow 4.9.70 as 7Q-YKD

G-AXSU (605), f/f 11.1.70, d/d to Bembridge 8.3.70, C. of A. 8.7.70, Britten-Norman Ltd.; d/d to I.A.S., Australia 9.7.70 as VH-EQZ; later to Air Melanesie as VP-PAU

G-AXUS (606), registered 12.12.69 to Britten-Norman Ltd., f/f 16.1.70, d/d Bembridge 13.2.70; to Indian Explosives Ltd., Calcutta 12.70 as VT-DYZ

G-AXUT (607), f/f 28.1.70, d/d Bembridge 12.3.70, C. of A. 18.3.70, Britten-Norman Ltd.; to Tramaco Services, Kinshasa, via Gatwick 6.6.70 as 9Q-CTS

G-AXUU (608), f/f 5.2.70, d/d to Bembridge 19.3.70, C. of A. 25.9.70, Britten-Norman Ltd.; to Bokara Steel Corp., India 23.12.70 as VT-EAN

G-AXWI (609), registered 16.1.70 to Britten-Norman Ltd., f/f 26.2.70, delivered to Bembridge 1.4.70; to Air Polynesie, Tahiti 10.70 as F-OCRA

G-AXWJ (610), registered 16.1.70 to Britten-Norman Ltd., f/f 22.3.70, d/d to Bembridge 6.4.70; to Guyana Air Services via Shannon 1.8.70 as 8R-GDS

G-AXZY (611), registered 23.3.70 to Britten-Norman Ltd., f/f 30.3.70, d/d to Bembridge 19.4.70; to U.T.A., Paris 23.10.70 for Air Polynesie as F-OCRB

G-AXZZ (612), registered 23.3.70 to Britten-Norman Ltd., Bembridge, f/f 30.4.70; to Guyana Air Services via Shannon 1.8.70 as 8R-GDT

G-AYAX (613), f/f 29.6.70, delivered to Bembridge 14.7.70, C. of A. 28.9.70, Britten-Norman Ltd.; to Solomon Islands Airways 30.9.70 as VP-PAM

G-AYAY (614), f/f 30.6.70, C. of A. 27.10.70, Britten-Norman Ltd., Bembridge; to Islander Aircraft Sales Pty. Ltd., Australia 30.10.70; to Fiji A/S as DQ-FBP

G-AYAZ (615), registered 6.4.70 to Britten-Norman Ltd., Bembridge, f/f 4.7.70, C. of A. 22.12.71; to Heli-Orient, Singapore 12.71, as 9V-BDW

G-AYBA (616), registered 6.4.70 to Britten-Norman Ltd., Bembridge, f/f 23.7.70; to Nativ Air Services Ltd., Israel 3.71 as 4X-AYN

G-AYBB (617), registered 6.4.70 to Britten-Norman Ltd., Bembridge, f/f 29.7.70; to Tramaco Air Services 3.71 as 9Q-CYA

G-AYGH (618), registered 9.7.70 to Britten-Norman Ltd., Bembridge, f/f 30.7.70, C. of A. 9.9.70; sold in Iran 1.72

G-AYGI (619), f/f 10.9.70, Britten-Norman Ltd., Bembridge; delivered to Botswana Airways Ltd. via Southend 8.5.71 as A2-ZFY

G-AYGJ (620), f/f 10.9.70, C. of A. 14.5.71, Britten-Norman Ltd., Bembridge; to Missionary Aviation Fellowship, Box Hill, Victoria 6.71 as VH-BAY

G-AYGK (621), f/f 26.9.70, delivered to Bembridge 25.11.70, C. of A. 28.5.71, Britten-Norman Ltd.; to Olympic Airways Ltd. 6.71 as SX-BBS

G-AYGL (622), f/f 27.10.70, C. of A. 27.11.70, Britten-Norman Ltd.

G-AYJE (623), f/f 12.12.70, C. of A. 27.12.70, delivered to Bembridge 2.2.71, Britten-Norman Ltd., Bembridge; to Cape Verde Islands 11.71 as CR-CAS

G-AYJF (624), f/f 11.11.70, delivered to Bembridge 6.12.70, Britten-Norman Ltd.

G-AYJG (625), f/f 11.11.70, Britten-Norman Ltd., Bembridge

Islander G-AYGK, delivered to Olympic Airways at the Paris Air Show, 29 May 1971, for scheduled services linking the islands of Rhodes and Scarpanto, a distance of 90 miles.

G-AYJH   (626), f/f 5.12.70, Britten-Norman Ltd., Bembridge; delivered to Air Caledonie 7.71 as F-OCQH

G-AYJI   (627), f/f 1.12.70, delivered to Bembridge 1.1.71, C. of A. 27.7.71, Britten-Norman Ltd., Bembridge; flown to Panama 10.71 as HP-566

G-AYJJ   (628), f/f 12.12.70, C. of A. 12.12.70, delivered to Bembridge 9.1.71, Britten-Norman Ltd.

G-AYJK   (629), f/f 1.2.71, delivered to Bembridge 11.2.71, Britten-Norman Ltd.

G-AYJL   (630), f/f 14.1.71, delivered to Bembridge 16.2.71, Britten-Norman Ltd.; to Ministry of Communications, Republic of Zaire 12.71 as 9Q-CYE

G-AYNT   (631), f/f 22.1.71, delivered to Bembridge 5.3.71, Britten-Norman Ltd.; to Flying Doctor Service, Republic of Zaire 3.72 as 9Q-CRP

G-AYNU   (632), registered 21.12.70 to Britten-Norman Ltd., delivered to Bembridge 19.3.71; to the Anrite Aviation Co. Ltd., Singapore 7.71 as 9V-BDH

G-AYNV   (633), f/f 22.1.71, delivered to Bembridge 2.3.71, Britten-Norman Ltd.; to Ministry of Communications, Republic of Zaire 9.71 as 9Q-CYB

G-AYNW   (634), f/f 15.1.71, delivered to Bembridge 24.2.71, C. of A. 27.7.71, Britten-Norman Ltd., Bembridge; to Singapore 10.71 as 9V-BEB

G-AYNX   (635), registered 21.12.70 to Britten-Norman Ltd., delivered to Bembridge 8.4.71; to Air British Virgin Islands Ltd. via Shannon 21.7.71 as VP-LVA

G-AYNY   (636), registered 21.12.70 to Britten-Norman Ltd., delivered to Bembridge 31.3.71; for TADT, Mozambique

G-AYNZ   (637), registered 21.12.70 to Britten-Norman Ltd., delivered to Bembridge 24.3.71

G-AYOA   (638), registered 21.12.70 to Britten-Norman Ltd., delivered to Bembridge 28.4.71; to Ministry of Communications, Republic of Zaire 9.71 as 9Q-CYC

G-AYOB   (639), registered 21.12.70 to Britten-Norman Ltd., delivered to Bembridge 5.5.71; to Heli-Orient, Singapore 12.71 as 9V-BEC

G-AYOC   (640), registered 21.12.70 to Britten-Norman Ltd., delivered to Bembridge 21.4.71

G-AYSM   (641), registered 16.2.71 to Britten-Norman Ltd.; remained in Rumania as YR-BNG, registration cancelled 7.71

G-AYSN   (642), registered 16.2.71 to Britten-Norman Ltd.

G-AYSO   (643), registered 16.2.71 to Britten-Norman Ltd., delivered to Bembridge 12.5.71

G-AYSP (644),
G-AYSR (645), registered 16.2.71 to Britten-Norman Ltd., Bembridge
G-AYSS (646),
G-AYST (647), registered 16.2.71 to Britten-Norman Ltd., delivered to Bembridge
4.8.71; to Interthon, Gabon 2.72 as F-OCSB
G-AYSU (648), registered 16.2.71 to Britten-Norman Ltd., delivered to Bembridge
7.8.71; to Govt. of Abu Dhabi 2.72 as '204'
G-AYSV (649), registered 16.2.71 to Britten-Norman Ltd., delivered to Bembridge
11.8.71; C. of A. 7.12.71
G-AYSW (650), registered 16.2.71 to Britten-Norman Ltd., delivered to Bembridge
14.8.71

Further batches of ten Rumanian-built Islanders were registered to Britten-Norman Ltd.
as under:

26.4.71	(c/n 651–660)	G-AYXC to G-AYXL	all delivered by 21.10.71
23.8.71	(c/n 661–670)	G-AZDL to G-AZDV	
11.10.71	(c/n 671–680)	G-AZGN to G-AZGX	

Britten-Norman BN-2A-7 Defender
G-AYTS (235), prototype, 21.5.71, Britten-Norman Ltd., Bembridge; to Singapore
12.71 as 9V-BDT for evaluation by the Royal Malaysian Air Force

G-AYTS, prototype Defender (military version of the Islander) taking off from Old
Warden with a full load of underwing stores, 29 August 1971. (*Air Portraits*)

Britten-Norman BN-2A Mk.3 Trislander
G-ATWU (2), prototype—see under Britten-Norman BN-2 Islander
G-AYTU (245), development prototype, 24.5.71, Britten-Norman Ltd.; to Air Gabon
2.72 as TR-LQL
G-AYWI (262), f/f 8.5.71, C. of A. 21.5.71, Brinsops Farms Ltd.; delivered to Staverton
29.6.71 for Aurigny Air Services Ltd., Alderney
G-AYZR (279), 28.6.71, Britten-Norman Ltd., Bembridge; delivered to Fort Lauderdale,
Florida as competitor in the London–Victoria Air Race 6.71; re-registered on
arrival as N85CA
G-AZFG (299), f/f 16.9.71, C. of A. 8.10.71, Britten-Norman (Bembridge) Ltd.; de-
livered to U.S.A. 2.72 as N60JA.

540

G-AZJA (305), 16.12.71, Brinsops Farms Ltd.; delivered to Staverton 17.12.71 for
Aurigny Air Services Ltd., Alderney
G-AZLJ (319), registered 31.12.71 to Britten-Norman (Bembridge) Ltd.; f/f 13.1.72;
delivered to Aurigny Air Services Ltd. 31.1.72

Broughton-Blayney Brawney
G-AENM (BB/50), 8.10.36, Broughton-Blayney Aircraft Co. Ltd., Hanworth; crashed in
the R.A.S.C. Depot, Feltham, and pilot Scaife killed 21.3.37
G-AERF (BB/51), 23.12.36, Broughton-Blayney Aircraft Co. Ltd., Hanworth; crashed
in Bromley Hill Cemetery, Kent, and pilot Bacon killed 6.6.37
G-AERG (BB/52), 23.12.36, Broughton-Blayney Aircraft Co. Ltd., Hanworth; withdrawn from use at A. to F. expiry 22.12.37

Brookland Mosquito Mk.1
G-ATSW (1), registered 5.4.66 to E. Brooks, Spennymoor, Co. Durham, P. to F.
21.5.68; converted to Mk.3 with 1,500 cc. Volkswagen; sold minus engine to
F. Gardiner, Ponteland, Newcastle in 1969

Brookland Mosquito Mk.2
G-AVHC (5), registered 16.2.67 to E. Brooks, P. to F. 28.4.67; Ryan Aviation Ltd.,
Acklington 1.70
G-AVYW (2), registered 27.11.67 to E. Brooks, P. to F. 27.4.68; crashed at Tees-side
Airport, Darlington and owner-designer killed 9.3.69
G-AWIF (3), supplied as a kit to L. Chiappi, Clitheroe, erected with c/n L.C.1 and
registered 17.4.68
G-AWJO (4), registered 17.5.68 to F. Fewsdale, Tees-side, P. to F. 30.7.69; c/n amended
to FT.7
G-AWLK (7), registered 5.7.68 to E. Brooks, P. to F. 31.7.68; sold in France 11.68

Brookland Mosquito Mk.3
G-AWTZ (8), registered 19.11.68 to E. Brooks, P. to F. 23.1.69; Brookland Rotorcraft
Ltd. 7.69; redesignated Gyroflight Hornet 1.70, P. to F. 3.2.70; fatal crash at
Woodford Aerodrome, Cheshire 27.6.70
G-AWVP (9), registered 6.12.68 to E. Brooks; completed as Brookland Hornet, P. to F.
29.5.70, Brookland Rotorcraft Ltd.
G-AWVU (10), registered 6.12.68 to E. Brooks; sold in France 5.70

Note: Total production amounted to 11 aircraft including (c/n 6) F-WMEF delivered to
France 8.68 and (c/n 11) completed to export order 3.10.69

Brookland Hornet
G-AYEU (12), registered 8.6.70 to Brookland Rotorcraft Ltd., Ferryhill, Co. Durham
G-AYFS (17), registered 25.6.70 to Brookland Rotorcraft Ltd., Ferryhill, Co. Durham

Bücker Bü 133C Jungmeister
G-AXIH (11), Swiss Air Force U-64, HB-MIP, A. to F. 10.7.69, R. E. Legg, Rochester
G-AXMT (46), U-99, HB-MIY, A. to F. 29.8.69, K. N. Rudd (Engineers) Ltd., Shoreham
G-AXNI (1001), U-51, HB-MIM, A. to F. 23.2.70, M. J. Coburn & C. C. G. Hughes,
Blackbushe, 'Bullfighter'
G-AYFO (4), U-57, HB-MIO, A. to F. 24.7.70, N. M. Browning, Stanford Rivers, Essex;
sold in Miami, U.S.A. 5.71 as N40BJ
G-AYSJ (38), U-91, HB-MIW, A. to F. 17.3.71, S. B. Riley, Sherburn-in-Elmet

Campbell-Bensen B-8 Gyrocopter

G-ASJN   (CA.1), B-8, A. to F. 14.4.65, P. M. Breton, Cirencester; J. C. Hoyland, Sherburn 1.66; to Rufforth 1968; blown over at Sherburn 28.9.69

G-ASNY   (CA.203), A. to F. 16.4.64, L. F. P. Walters, Navestock; D. L. Wallis, Chelmsford 8.67

G-ASPX   (CA.204), A. to F. 21.5.64, L. D. Goldsmith, Old Warden

G-ATCF   (CA.300), B-8S, Campbell Aircraft Ltd., built 2.66, cancelled 3.69

G-ATYG   (CA.304), registered 3.8.66 to Campbell Aircraft Ltd.; sold to Egelsbach, West Germany as D-HTYG

G-AVJP   (CA.305), A. to F. 12.10.67, G. R. Davies, Tewkesbury

G-AVOG   (CA.306), B-8M, registered 6.6.67 to J. T. K. Crossfield and taken to Spain; returned to Membury 1968; withdrawn from use at Membury 7.68

G-AWAS   (CA.307), B-8MC, registered 5.1.68 to Campbell Aircraft Ltd.; A. T. Scott, Egham 5.69

G-AWEH   (CA.308), B-8M, registered 1.3.68 to J. D. Taylor and shipped to Australia

G-AWIN   (CA.309), B-8MC, A. to F. 20.6.68, M. J. Cuttell & J. Deane, Staverton

G-AWJD   (CA.310), B-8M, registered 3.5.68 to Campbell Aircraft Ltd.

G-AWLM   (CA.311), B-8MS, A. to F. 30.4.69, Campbell Aircraft Ltd., Membury; to H. P. Goulding, Enniskerry, Ireland 8.69 as EI-ATE

G-AWMC   (CA.312), B-8MS, registered 18.7.68 to M. E. J. Hankinson, Wimborne

G-AWPY   (CA.314), B-8M, registered 20.9.68 to J. M. Deane, Staverton

G-AXLF   (CA.318), B-8, registered 23.7.69 to G. Rees, Cardiff, w.f.u. 7.70

G-AXLT   (CA.317), B-8MG, registered 31.7.69 to R. J. Gould, Cobham; A. to F. 16.1.70

Gyrocopter G-AWDW (see page 501) completed as the Campbell-Bensen CB-8S, forerunner of the Cricket, with fibreglass body, windscreen and new rudder unit.

Campbell Cricket

G-AXNU   (CA.319), 18.12.69, D. J. Green, Harleston, Norfolk

G-AXPZ   (CA.320), 8.2.70, P. F. Zimber, Bodmin, Cornwall

G-AXRA   (CA.321A), 10.2.70, Permit to Fly transferred to G-AYDJ, May 1970

G-AXRB   (CA.322), 10.2.70, J. C. Thomas, Falmouth, Cornwall

G-AXRC (CA.323), 10.2.70, Campbell Aircraft Ltd., Membury
G-AXRD (CA.324), 10.2.70, G. Rees, Rhoose
G-AXVH (CA.330), 16.6.70, Campbell Aircraft Ltd., Membury; to Norway 8.70 as
        LN-GGI
G-AXVI (CA.325), 25.2.70, Campbell Aircraft Ltd., Membury; sold in Malaysia 4.70
        to A. K. Nam Voon as 9M-APY
G-AXVJ (CA.326), 16.1.70, Campbell Aircraft Ltd., Membury; sold in Denmark 8.70
G-AXVK (CA.327), 12.6.70, Campbell Aircraft Ltd., Membury
G-AXVL (CA.328), 8.5.70, Campbell Aircraft Ltd., Membury; sold in Kuwait 8.70
G-AXVM (CA.329), 2.6.70, M. M. Cobbold and partners, Roborough
G-AYBX (CA.331), 14.7.70, Campbell Aircraft Ltd., Membury; sold in Kuwait 10.70
G-AYBY (CA.332), 14.7.70, Campbell Aircraft Ltd., Membury; sold in Kuwait 10.70
G-AYBZ (CA.333), 14.7.70, Campbell Aircraft Ltd., Membury; sold in Kuwait 10.70
G-AYCA (CA.334), 14.7.70, Campbell Aircraft Ltd., Membury; sold in Kuwait 10.70
G-AYCB (CA.335), 10.8.70, Campbell Aircraft Ltd., Membury; sold in Kuwait 10.70
G-AYCC (CA.336), 10.8.70, Campbell Aircraft Ltd., Membury; K. W. Deacon, Thame
        1.71
G-AYDJ (CA.321), 10.2.70, A. von Preussen, Enstoone
G-AYHE (CA.337), 7.10.70, Campbell Aircraft Ltd., Membury
G-AYHF (CA.338), 28.10.70, Campbell Aircraft Ltd., Membury
G-AYHG (CA.339), 18.12.70, Campbell Aircraft Ltd., Membury
G-AYHH (CA.340), 4.11.70, Campbell Aircraft Ltd., Membury
G-AYHI (CA.341), registered 21.7.70 to Campbell Aircraft Ltd., Membury
G-AYHJ (CA.342), registered 21.7.70 to Campbell Aircraft Ltd., Membury; sold in
        France 12.70
G-AYPZ (CA.343), registered 13.1.71 to Campbell Aircraft Ltd., Membury
G-AYRA (CA.344), 16.2.71, Campbell Aircraft Ltd., Membury
G-AYRB (CA.345), 16.2.71, Campbell Aircraft Ltd., Membury
G-AYRC (CA.346), 30.2.71, Campbell Aircraft Ltd., Membury
G-AYRD (CA.347), 16.2.71, Campbell Aircraft Ltd., Membury; sold in Morocco 7.71
G-AYRE (CA.348), registered 13.1.71 to Campbell Aircraft Ltd., Membury
G-AYXM (CA.349), registered 27.4.71 to Campbell Aircraft Ltd., Membury
G-AYXN (CA.350), registered 27.4.71 to Campbell Aircraft Ltd., Membury; C. of A.
        6.9.71, lo Chong Chin, Cirencester 10.71

Canadair C-4

G-ALHC (145), 26.3.49, B.O.A.C. 'Ariadne', to Royal Rhodesian Air Force 1.60 as
'180', later '601', rest. 8.64 to Air Links Ltd., scrapped at Redhill 7.65; G-ALHD (146),
11.4.49, B.O.A.C. 'Ajax', to East African Airways Corp. 2.59 as VP-KOY, rest. 1959
Overseas Aviation Ltd., Southend, to Flying Enterprise 5.61 as OY-AFC; G-ALHE (151),
15.6.49, B.O.A.C. 'Argo', crashed at Kano, Nigeria 24.6.56; G-ALHF (152), 25.6.49,
B.O.A.C. 'Atlas', to E.A.A.C. 8.57 as VP-KOI, to Air Links Ltd., Gatwick 5.64 as spares;
G-ALHG (153), 5.7.49, B.O.A.C. 'Aurora', Overseas Aviation Ltd., Southend 4.60, Derby
Aviation Ltd. 10.61, British Midland A/W Ltd. 12.64, crashed in Stockport 4.6.67;
G-ALHH (154), 15.7.49, B.O.A.C. 'Attica', to R.R.A.F. 2.60 as '181', later '602', rest.
8.64 to Air Links Ltd., scrapped at Redhill 7.65; G-ALHI (155), 21.7.49, B.O.A.C.
'Antares', to R.R.A.F. 3.60 as '182', later '603', rest. 6.64 to Air Links Ltd., Transglobe
A/W Ltd., Gatwick 10.65, Stansted Fire School 1.66

G-ALHJ (156), 27.7.49, B.O.A.C. 'Arcturus', to E.A.A.C. 8.57 as VP-KOT, to
B.O.A.C. Training School, Heathrow 1964, scrapped 1970; G-ALHK (157), 3.8.49,

Annular radiators fitted to the Merlins of the Canadair C-4, heightened its resemblance to the radial engined Douglas DC-4. (*B.O.A.C.*)

B.O.A.C. 'Atalanta', Overseas Aviation Ltd., Southend 2.59, to Flying Enterprise 1.61 as OY-AFB; G-ALHL (158), 8.8.49, B.O.A.C. 'Altair', crashed at Idris, Tripoli 21.9.55; G-ALHM (159), 12.8.49, B.O.A.C. 'Antaeus', to E.A.A.C. 8.57 as VP-KOJ, rest. 5.64 to Air Links Ltd., Transglobe A/W Ltd. 10.65, to spares at Castle Donington 3.66; G-ALHN (160), 17.8.49, B.O.A.C. 'Argosy', Overseas Aviation Ltd., Southend 2.60, to Flying Enterprise 6.60 as OY-AFA, rest. 10.61 to Derby Aviation Ltd., to spares at Burnaston 5.62; G-ALHO (161), 25.8.49, B.O.A.C. 'Amazon', to E.A.A.C. 8.57 as VP-KNY; G-ALHP (162), 31.8.49, B.O.A.C. 'Aethra', Overseas Aviation Ltd., Southend 6.59, Derby Aviation Ltd. 10.61, to spares at Burnaston 10.61; G-ALHR (163), 7.9.49, B.O.A.C. 'Antiope', to Aden A/W 2.60 as VR-AAR

G-ALHS (164), 14.9.49, B.O.A.C. 'Astra', Overseas Aviation Ltd., Southend 2.60, Derby Aviation Ltd. 10.61, British Midland A/W Ltd. 12.64, scrapped at Castle Donington 1970; G-ALHT (165), 19.9.49, B.O.A.C. 'Athena', Overseas Aviation Ltd., Southend 12.58, to Flying Enterprise 1.60 as OY-AAH, rest. 1.64 to Air Links Ltd., Transglobe A/W Ltd. 10.65, scrapped at Redhill 1.66; G-ALHU (166), 22.9.49, B.O.A.C. 'Artemis', Overseas Aviation Ltd., Southend 1.59, to Flying Enterprise 4.60 as OY-AAI; G-ALHV (167), 4.10.49, B.O.A.C. 'Adonis', to Aden A/W 6.60 as VR-AAT; G-ALHW (168), 13.10.49, B.O.A.C. 'Aeolus', to R.R.A.F. 11.59 as '179', later '600', rest. 7.64 to Air Links Ltd., Transglobe A/W Ltd. 10.65, to spares at Castle Donington 3.66; G-ALHX (169), 25.10.49, B.O.A.C. 'Astraea', to Aden A/W 4.60 as VR-AAS; G-ALHY (170), 8.11.49, B.O.A.C. 'Arion', Overseas Aviation Ltd., Southend 3.60, Derby Aviation Ltd. 10.61, British Midland Airways Ltd. 12.64, scrapped at Castle Donington in 1970

Canadair CL-44D-4

G-ATZH (21), N452T, registered 20.9.66 to Transglobe Airways Ltd., not imported, retained by Flying Tiger Line; G-ATZI (25), N455T, also retained by Flying-Tiger Line, rest. 4.70 to Transmeridian Air Cargo Ltd., Stansted, C. of A. 29.4.70; G-AWDK (23), N125SW, 8.4.68, Transglobe Airways Ltd., Gatwick, to Tradewinds Airways Ltd., Heathrow 3.69; G-AWGS (27), N127SW, 19.4.68, Transglobe Airways Ltd., Gatwick, to Tradewinds Airways Ltd., Heathrow 2.69; G-AWGT (30), N123SW, 24.5.68, Transglobe Airways Ltd., Gatwick, to Tradewinds Airways Ltd., Heathrow 2.69; G-AWOV (32), N229SW, 18.10.68, Transglobe Airways Ltd., Gatwick, reverted to Seaboard World

Airlines 2.69 as N429SW, rest. 7.70 to Tradewinds Airways Ltd., Stansted; G-AWSC (26), N126SW, registered 21.10.68 to Transglobe Airways Ltd., not imported, retained by Seaboard World Airlines, rest. 10.70 to Tradewinds Airways Ltd., Gatwick, C. of A. 30.10.70; G-AWUD (14), N124SW, registered 22.11.68, not imported as 'SC above; G-AWWB (17), N448T, 5.2.69, Transmeridian Air Cargo Ltd., Stansted 'African Trader'; G-AXAA (18), N449T, 7.3.69, Transmeridian Air Cargo Ltd., Stansted 'Pacific Trader'; G-AXUL (24), N454T, 14.12.69, Transmeridian Air Cargo Ltd., Stansted; G-AZIN (19), N450T, delivered to Transmeridian Air Cargo Ltd., Stansted 8.11.71; G-AZKJ (37), N1001T, delivered to Transmeridian Air Cargo Ltd., Stansted 24.11.71; G-AZML (38), N1002T, delivered to Transmeridian Air Cargo Ltd., Stansted 21.12.71

Cassutt 3M

G-AXDZ (PFA.1341), A. to F. 14.8.69, Airmark Ltd., Redhill 'Will o' Wisp'

G-AXEA (PFA.1342), A. to F. 2.10.69, Airmark Ltd., Redhill; F. S. Gathercole, Redhill 5.70 'Hopalong'

G-AXEB (PFA.1343), registered 21.4.69 to Airmark Ltd., Redhill, completed 7.72

G-AZHM (PFA.1379), registered 11.71 to M. S. Crossley, built at Wallington, Surrey, and first flown at Redhill 2.72

Caudron G.3

G-EACF (87/8271), K-115, 80 h.p. Gnome, registered 29.5.19 to the Cambridge School of Flying Ltd., Hardwick; registration lapsed 1920

G-EACH K-127, registered 29.5.19 to the Cheltenham Aviation Co.; cancelled 8.19

G-EACI K-128, registered 29.5.19 to the Cheltenham Aviation Co.; cancelled 8.19

G-EACK (3005), K-121, 70 h.p. Renault, built Cricklewood 1.17; registered 30.5.19 to L. C. G. M. Le Champion, Brooklands; registration lapsed 1920

G-EALV (1005), registered 29.8.19 to George Eyston, Brooklands; registration cancelled 9.20

G-EAON (3032), registered 15.10.19 to the Bournemouth Aviation Co. Ltd.; registration cancelled at census 10.1.23

G-EAOO (3030), registered 15.10.19 to the Bournemouth Aviation Co. Ltd.; registration cancelled at census 10.1.23

G-EAQK Registered 30.12.19 to H. T. Jakeman; registration not used and cancelled 12.19

G-AETA (7487), OO-ELA, 90 h.p. Anzani, registered 29.1.37 to K. H. F. Waller, Brooklands; registration cancelled 8.38; stored by the R.A.F. in 1972

Central Centaur IV, IVA and IVB

G-EABI (201), K-108, registered 7.5.19 to the Central Aircraft Co., Northolt; Gnat Aero & Motor Co., Shoreham 5.26; scrapped at Shoreham 4.30

G-EAHS (202), K-171, 4.3.20, Central Aircraft Co., Northolt; sold in Belgium 7.22

G-EALL (203), 8.3.20, Central Aircraft Co., Northolt; Gnat Aero & Motor Co., Shoreham 5.26; scrapped at Shoreham 4.30

G-EAOQ (204), 30.8.20, Central Aircraft Co., Northolt; sold in Belgium 10.21

G-EAOR (205), 30.6.20, Central Aircraft Co., Northolt; Mk.IVB converted to Mk.IVA; crashed 10.20

G-EAOS (206), 25.8.20, Central Aircraft Co., Northolt; sold in Belgium 10.22

G-EAQE (207), 15.10.21, Central Aircraft Co., Northolt; to Belgium 12.21 as O-BOTH

G-EAQF (208), Central Aircraft Co., Northolt; to Belgium 12.21 as O-BOTI; rebuilt 1925 as O-BOTH, later OO-OTH; destroyed by Germans 5.40

The third production Central Centaur IVA, showing the flat topped rudder.

Cessna 150 (*1958 model with 100 h.p. Continental A-200-A*)
G-APXY (17711), N7911E, 18.3.60; G-APZR (17861), N6461T, 24.8.60; G-ARAE (17885), N6485T, 25.7.60; G-ARAU (17894), N6494T, 3.8.60

Cessna 150A (*1960 model*)
G-ARFI (59100), N7000X, 21.3.61; G-ARFN (59172), N7072X, 29.3.61, crashed at Carlisle 23.9.67; G-ARFO (59174), N7074X, 29.3.61; G-ARRF (59297), N7197X, 19.10.61; G-ARSB (59337), N7237X, 9.10.61; G-ASMS (59204), N7104X, 22.11.63

Cessna 150B (*1961 model*)
G-ARTW (59471), N7371X, 9.4.62, w.f.u. at Perth 11.69; G-ARTX (59477), N7377X, 26.3.62; G-ARTY (59482), N7382X, 9.4.62, to instructional airframe at Perth 2.69; G-ARWC (59515), N1115Y, 24.5.62; G-ARWN (59523), N1123Y, 18.5.62, crashed near Swansea 2.5.70; G-ARZF (59610), N1210Y, 20.7.62; G-ARZX (59642), N1242Y, 26.7.62

Cessna 150C (*1963 model with additional seat for child*)
G-ASHF (59908), N7808Z, 3.7.63; G-ASLB (59971), N7871Z, 7.8.63

Cessna 150D (*1964 model with slim rear fuselage and wrap-around rear canopy*)
G-ASMU (60252), N4252U, 20.3.64; G-ASMW (60247), N4247U, 20.3.64; G-ASSO (60536), N4536U, 21.5.64; G-ASST (60630), N5930T, 23.7.64; G-ASTV (60705), N6005T, 9.9.64; G-ASUE (60718), N6018T, 15.9.64; G-AWAX (60153), N4153U, OY-TRJ, 6.5.68

Cessna 150E (*1965 model with bucket seats and redesigned instrument panel*)
G-ASVF (60799), N6099T, 20.11.64; G-ASYH (60987), N6087T, 24.3.65, crashed at Millom, Cumberland 22.2.66; G-ASYL (60795), N6095T, 17.12.64; G-ASYP (60794), N6094T, 27.11.64; G-ASZB (61113), N3013J, 2.4.65; G-ASZU (61152), N3052J,

2.4.65; G-ATAT (61141), N3041J, 22.5.65; G-ATEF (61378), N3978U, 26.5.65;
G-ATEG (61383), N3983U, 26.5.65; G-AWPX (60906), N6206T, 5N-AFR, 31.1.69

Cessna 150F (*1965 model with swept vertical tail surfaces*)
   G-ATHF (61592), N6292R, 26.8.65; G-ATHG (61719), 30.9.65; G-ATHV (62019),
N8719S, 7.12.65; G-ATHY (62059), not imported; G-ATHZ (61586), N6268R, EI-AOP
ntu, 27.8.65; G-ATIE (61591), N6291R, 14.9.65; G-ATJU (61865), N8265S, 12.11.65;
G-ATKD (62551), N8451G, 25.2.66; G-ATKE (62364), N3564L, 7.2.66; G-ATKF
(62386), N3586L, 16.3.66; G-ATKY (62613), N8513G, 1.4.66; G-ATLS (62954),
N8854G, 22.4.66, to France 4.70 as F-BSEP; G-ATMX (62372), N3572L, 2.1.66;
G-ATMY (62642), N8542G, 25.2.66

Cessna 150G (*1967 model with wider cabin and shorter nose leg*)
   G-AVMD (65504), N2404J, 4.8.67; G-AYWU (65352), N4052J, 23.6.71

Cessna 150H (*1968 model with revised flap system and increased leg room*)
   G-AWES (68626), N22933, 20.7.68

Cessna 150J (*1969 model*)
   G-AYRK (70856), 5N-AII, 27.11.71

Cessna 150L (*1971 model*)
   G-AZHF (72575), N1275Q, registered 18.11.71

Cessna F.150F (*built by Reims Aviation*)
   G-ATMB (F.0012), 23.3.66; G-ATMC (F.0020), 18.4.66; G-ATMK (F.0013),
28.3.66; G-ATML (F.0014), 28.3.66; G-ATMM (F.0016), 21.4.66; G-ATMN (F.0060),
14.6.66; G-ATNC (F.0055), 18.10.66; G-ATND (F.0041), 3.5.66; G-ATNE (F.0042),
2.6.66; G-ATNF (F.0061), not imported; G-ATNG (F.0062), ntu, imported later as
G-ATPM; G-ATNI (F.0058), 10.6.66; G-ATNJ (F.0059), 10.6.66; G-ATNK (F.0065),
15.7.66; G-ATNL (F.0066), 15.7.66; G-ATNW (F.0051), 2.6.66; G-ATNX (F.0052),
20.6.66; G-ATOD (F.0003), 31.3.66; G-ATOE (F.0031), 23.5.66; G-ATOF (F.0063),

G-APXY, first Cessna 150 on the British register, was typical of the type in its early form.
(*Richard Riding*)

27.6.66; G-ATOG (F.0064), 27.6.66; G-ATPM (F.0062), 18.10.66; G-ATRD (F.0043), 6.5.66; G-ATRJ (F.0044), 6.5.66, crashed at Honeydon, Beds. 25.7.67; G-ATRK (F.0049), 24.6.66; G-ATRL (F.0050), 7.6.66; G-ATRM (F.0053), 28.6.66; G-ATRN (F.0054), 7.6.66; G-ATSS (F.0017), 21.4.66, d.b.r. 8.70; G-ATUF (F.0040), 1.7.66; G-AWAV (F.0007), OY-DKL, 26.2.68; G-AWAW (F.0037), OY-DKJ, 22.1.68

Cessna F.150G (*built by Reims Aviation*)

G-ATYM (F.0074), 22.11.66; G-ATYN (F.0076), 22.11.66; G-ATZY (F.0135), 13.2.67; G-ATZZ (F.0136), 13.2.67; G-AVAA (F.0164), 17.3.67; G-AVAB (F.0165), 17.3.67; G-AVAC (F.0192), 31.5.67; G-AVAP (F.0107), 10.3.67; G-AVAR (F.0122), 20.1.67; G-AVCT (F.0128), 6.2.67; G-AVCU (F.0129), 6.2.67; G-AVEL (F.0176), 13.4.67, crashed at Fordoun 29.3.70; G-AVEM (F.0198), 31.5.67; G-AVEN (F.0202), 22.6.67; G-AVEO (F.0204), 22.6.67; G-AVEP (F.0205), 1.7.67; G-AVER (F.0206), 22.6.67

G-AVGL (F.0157), 11.3.67; G-AVGM (F.0158), 11.3.67; G-AVGU (F.0199), 15.6.67; G-AVGV (F.0149), 6.3.67; G-AVHM (F.0181), 1.5.67; G-AVHN (F.0182), 3.5.67; G-AVIA (F.0184), 15.4.67; G-AVIB (F.0180), 21.3.67; G-AVIT (F.0217), 10.7.67; G-AVJE (F.0219), 11.8.67; G-AVMF (F.0203), 3.7.67; G-AVMG (F.0068), d.b.f. at Reims before delivery; G-AVNB (F.0216), 4.7.67; G-AVNC (F.0200), 13.6.67; G-AVPG (F.0195), 4.7.67, crashed at Denham 19.12.68; G-AVPH (F.0197), 4.7.67

Cessna F.150H (*built by Reims Aviation*)

G-AVSS (F.0233), 4.11.67; G-AVTM (F.0238), 5.12.67; G-AVTN (F.0245), 29.11.67; G-AVTO (F.0252), 10.12.67; G-AVUG (F.0234), 24.9.67; G-AVUH (F.0244), 23.10.67; G-AVUI (F.0247), 18.11.67; G-AVVE (F.0230), 21.3.68; G-AVVL (F.0257), 21.11.67; G-AVVW (F.0258), 2.12.67; G-AVVX (F.0259), 29.12.67; G-AVVY (F.0264), 29.12.67; G-AVZU (F.0283), 16.2.68

G-AWBX (F.0286), 18.7.68; G-AWCJ (F.0314), 12.3.68; G-AWCK (F.0278), 19.2.68; G-AWCL (F.0276), 15.2.68; G-AWCM (F.0281), 15.2.68; G-AWCO (F.0338), 16.4.68; G-AWCP (F.0354), 3.7.68; G-AWEO (F.0342), 15.5.68; G-AWFF (F.0280), 8.4.68; G-AWFH (F.0274), 8.4.68; G-AWGK (F.0347), 8.7.68; G-AWGY (F.0306), 10.5.68; G-AWJZ (F.0356), 26.6.68

G-AWLA (F.0269), N13175, 19.7.68; G-AWLJ (F.0328), 5.8.68; G-AWLY (F.0364), 25.7.68; G-AWMT (F.0360), 23.9.68; G-AWOT (F.0389), 11.11.68; G-AWPJ (F.0376), 4.11.68; G-AWPP (F.0348), 16.11.68; G-AWUG (F.0299), 29.1.69; G-AWUH (F.0307), 4.9.69; G-AWUI (F.0318), 7.2.69; G-AWUJ (F.0332), 24.10.69; G-AWUK (F.0344), 4.9.69; G-AWUL (F.0346), 7.2.69; G-AWUM (F. 0362), 17.12.68; G-AWUN (F.0377), 28.3.69; G-AWUO (F.0380), 4.9.69; G-AWUP (F.0381), 17.12.68; G-AWXH (F.0353), 18.2.69

Cessna F.150J (*1969 model built by Reims Aviation*)

G-AWPU (F.0411), 11.3.69; G-AWRK (F.0410), 25.11.68; G-AWSD (F.0406), 18.4.69; G-AWTJ (F.0419), 28.1.69; G-AWTX (F.0404), 28.3.69; G-AWTY (F.0407), ntu, re-allotted as G-AXBL; G-AWUR (F.0390), 21.3.69; G-AWUS (F.0394), 21.3.69; G-AWUT (F.0405), 17.12.68; G-AWUU (F.0408), 3.6.69; G-AWUV (F.0409), 3.6.69; G-AWXU (F.0492), 22.9.69

G-AXBL (F.0407), G-AXBM (F.0425), G-AXBN (F.0430), G-AXBP (F.0434), G-AXBR (F.0443), G-AXBS (F.0445) not imported; G-AXDJ (F.0455), 4.7.69; G-AXGG (F.0440), 21.6.69; G-AXNK (F.0415), N13722, 19.6.69; G-AXUG (F.0497), F-BRBF, 14.1.70, to Switzerland 10.71 as HB-CVZ

Cessna F.150K (*1970 model built by Reims Aviation*)
G-AXPF (F.0543), 26.11.69; G-AXVW (F.0548), 12.6.70; G-AXWE (F.0530), 6.8.70; G-AYBC (F.0549), 15.7.70; G-AYBD (F.0583), 20.8.71; G-AYEY (F.0553), 3.7.70; G-AYGC (F.0556), 6.8.70

Cessna F.150L (*1971 model built by Reims Aviation*)
G-AYKL (F.0676), 2.2.71; G-AYRF (F.0665), 12.3.71; G-AYUC (F.0706), 4.5.71; G-AYYE (F.0715), 9.6.71; G-AYYF (F.0716), 9.6.71; G-AZJW (F.0752) registered 8.12.71; G-AZJX (F.0756), registered 8.12.71; G-AZKY (F.0804), registered 23.12.71; G-AZLH (F.0757), registered 31.12.71; G-AZLK (F.0743), registered 31.12.71; G-AZLY (F. 0771), registered 10.1.72; G-AZLZ (F.0772), registered 10.1.72

Cessna FA.150K (*1970 aerobatic two seater built by Reims Aviation*)
G-AXRT (FA.0018), 12.3.70; G-AXRU (FA..0020), 12.3.70; G-AXRZ (FA.0014), 14.5.70; G-AXSJ (FA.0029), 23.3.70; G-AXSK (FA.0051), 9.6.70, crashed at Goldhanger, Essex 17.8.71; G-AXSW (FA.0003), 20.2.70; G-AXUF (FA.0043), 26.5.70; G-AXUW (FA.0045), 23.5.70; G-AXVC (FA.0047), 16.7.70; G-AYBW (FA.0044), 17.6.70; G-AYCF (FA.0055), 12.6.70; G-AYJX (FA.0118), registered 23.9.70

Cessna FA.150L (*1971 model built by Reims Aviation*)
G-AYKM (FA.0084), 4.2.71; G-AYOV (FA.0104), 16.7.71; G-AYOZ (FA.0085), 1.3.71; G-AYPK (FA.0106), 12.3.71; G-AYRO (FA.0102), 1.3.71; G-AYRP (FA.0101), 14.5.71; G-AYSZ (FA.0092), 1.7.71; G-AYUY (FA.0081), 30.4.71; G-AYUZ (FA.0114), not imported; G-AYXV (F.0117), 25.6.71; G-AZBJ (F.0121), F-BSHP, returned to France 11.71; G-AZID (FA.0083), registered 11.71

G-APSZ, first British registered Cessna 172, was similar to the model 170 but with tricycle undercarriage and revised tail unit.

Cessna 172 (*1959 model with 145 h.p. Continental O-300-A*)
G-APSZ (46472), N6372E, 2.9.59; G-APYM (46690), N7090T, 24.3.60, crashed at Sarsden, Oxon. 11.8.62; G-AWRU (36788), N9188B, d.b.f. at Whatfield strip, Suffolk 29.12.68; G-AYOD (28379), F-OARV, 26.5.71

Cessna 172A (*1960 model with swept tail and 145 h.p. Continental O-300-C*)
G-ARAV (47571), N9771T, 5.8.60

Cessna 172B (*1961 model with shorter undercarriage*)

G-ARCM (47852), N6952X, 18.1.61; G-ARFJ (48306), N7806X, 17.4.61, crashed near Yeadon 30.7.64; G-ARFK (48211), N7711X, 24.3.61; G-ARID (48209), N7709X, 3.2.61; G-ARIU (48449), N7949X, 29.6.61; G-ARIV (48452), N7952X, 7.6.61; G-ARLT (48505), N8005X, 26.6.61; G-ARLU (48502), N8002X, 27.6.61; G-ARLV (48497), N7997X, 11.7.61; G-ARLW (48499), N7999X, 16.6.61; G-ARMO (48560), N8060X, 6.7.61; G-ARMP (48563), N8063X, 21.6.61; G-ARMR (48566), N8066X, 21.6.61; G-AROA (48628), N8128X, 28.9.61; G-AROB (48631), N8131X, 19.12.61, crashed at Barton 25.4.65

Cessna 172C Skyhawk (*1962 model with third seat and redesigned wing tips*)

G-ARWH (49166), N1466Y, 26.4.62; G-ARWO (49187), N1487Y, 4.5.62; G-ARWP (49192), N1492Y, 19.6.62, d.b.r. at Biggin Hill 23.7.67; G-ARWR (49172), N1472Y, 13.4.62; G-ARYI (49260), N1560Y, 9.3.63; G-ARYK (49288), N1588Y, 11.3.63; G-ARYS (49291), N1591Y, 26.2.63; G-ARZD (49389), N1689Y, 19.4.63; G-ARZE (49388), N1688Y, 19.3.63

Cessna 172D (*1963 model with wrap-around rear canopy; P.172D 'plush' interior*)

G-ASFA (50182), N2582U, 22.5.63; G-ASPT (49675), N2175Y, CF-OYN, 25.3.64; G-AXPI (57173), P.172D, 9M-AMR, 27.1.70

Cessna 172E (*1964 model*)

G-ASSS (51467), N5567T, 8.10.64; G-ASSX (51470), N5570T, 21.5.64

Cessna 172G (*1966 model with modified engine mountings and stall warning*)

G-AWEG (54322), N4253L, 16.7.68

Cessna 172K (*1968 model*)

G-AZDZ (58501), 5N-AIH, 2.9.71

Cessna F.172D (*built by Reims Aviation*)

G-ASHA (F.0008), 27.6.63; G-ASHE (F.0004), 21.7.63, crashed at Old Warden 26.6.66; G-ASIB (F.0006), 4.7.63

Cessna F.172E (*built by Reims Aviation*)

G-ASKU (F.0024), 24.10.63; G-ASLC (F.0028), 20.11.63, crashed near Henley-on-Thames 2.9.70; G-ASLY (F.0019), 2.10.63, crashed at Squires Gate 7.7.68; G-ASMJ (F.0029), 20.2.65; G-ASNW (F.0031), 24.4.65; G-ASOJ (F.0046), 24.9.64, crashed at Aldridge, Staffs. 16.4.66; G-ASOK (F.0057), 2.6.64; G-ASPI (F.0050), 29.3.64; G-ASUH (F.0070), 8.2.65; G-ASUP (F.0071), 11.8.64; G-ASVM (F.0077), 4.9.64; G-ASVU (F.0075), 4.9.64; G-ASWD (F.0089), 2.10.64, crashed on Berriew Mt., 15 miles west of Oswestry 7.9.68

Cessna F.172F (*built by Reims Aviation*)

G-ASWL (F.0087), 23.10.64; G-ASZW (F.0138), 18.6.65; G-ATAF (F.0135), 19.3.65; G-ATBK (F.0137), 22.3.65; G-ATBT (F.0119), 28.5.65, crashed on Winter Hill, Horwich 2.10.68; G-ATFL (F.0171), 22.7.65; G-ATWJ (F.0095), EI-ANS, 7.9.67

Cessna F.172G (*built by Reims Aviation*)

G-ATFX (F.0196), 5.10.65; G-ATFY (F.0199), 5.10.65; G-ATGO (F.0181), 1.10.65;

G-ATKS (F.0201), 15.12.65; G-ATKT (F.0206), 22.11.65; G-ATKU (F.0232), 30.3.66; G-ATLM (F.0252), 15.2.66; G-ATLN (F.0257), 6.5.66; G-ATLR (F.0204), 13.1.66; G-ATMO (F.0269), 28.3.66, crashed at Roborough 15.5.66; G-ATNH (F.0278), 27.4.66; G-ATRE (F.0288), 26.4.66; G-ATSL (F. 0260), 14.4.66; G-ATUN (F.0285), d.b.r. at North Denes 30.5.69; G-ATVV (F.0221), 18.10.66

Cessna F.172H (*1967 model with shorter nose leg, built by Reims Aviation*)

G-AVAS (F.0370), 20.1.67, d.b.r. at Squires Gate 23.1.70; G-AVBZ (F.0387), 13.9.67; G-AVCC (F.0365), 2.1.67; G-AVCD (F.0385), 30.8.67; G-AVCE (F.0389), 30.1.67; G-AVDC (F.0382), 14.2.67, d.b.r. at Manston 31.3.67; G-AVEC (F.0405), 24.2.67; G-AVHH (F.0337), 24.2.67; G-AVHI (F.0343), 24.2.67; G-AVIC (F.0320), N17011, 21.3.67; G-AVIE (F.0326), 21.3.67; G-AVIR (F.0423), 27.4.67; G-AVIS (F.0413), 15.6.67; G-AVJC (F.0363), 17.4.67, d.b.r. at Dinard, France 6.7.69; G-AVJF (F.0393), 12.5.67; G-AVJI (F.0442), 12.5.67; G-AVJM (F.0372), 17.4.67; G-AVKF (F.0366), 22.8.67; G-AVKG (F.0345), 15.5.67; G-AVPI (F.0409), 6.7.67

G-AVTP (F.0458), 28.9.67; G-AVTR (F.0470), 26.4.67, ditched in the Thames off Canvey Island 26.12.69; G-AVUA (F.0464), 8.11.67; G-AVUF (F.0477), 15.11.67; G-AVUL (F.0448), 30.10.67; G-AVUX (F.0476), 15.11.67; G-AVVC (F.0443), 28.3.68; G-AVVZ (F.0475), 18.12.67; G-AVZV (F.0511), 5.7.68

G-AWBW (F.0486), 18.7.68; G-AWCH (F.0522), 13.3.68; G-AWGC (F.0500), 30.4.68; G-AWGD (F.0503), 3.7.68; G-AWGE (F.0510), 3.7.68; G-AWGJ (F.0531), 9.4.70; G-AWGR (F.0484), 21.5.68; G-AWGW (F.0482), 10.5.68; G-AWGX (F.0492), 10.5.68; G-AWKA (F.0529), 26.6.68; G-AWLD (F.0517), 24.7.68; G-AWLE (F.0525), 24.7.68; G-AWLF (F.0536), 24.7.68; G-AWMJ (F.0550), 16.8.68; G-AWMP (F.0488), 23.8.68; G-AWMU (F.0487), 6.9.68; G-AWMZ (F.0554), 23.8.68

G-AWOJ (F.0535), 25.8.68; G-AWPV (F.0585), 3.4.68; G-AWRL (F.0581), 25.11.68; G-AWTH (F.0626), not imported; G-AWTI (F.0580), 10.1.69; G-AWUW (F.0576), 21.3.69; G-AWUX (F.0577), 17.4.69; G-AWUY (F.0578), 28.3.69; G-AWUZ (F.0587), 3.12.68; G-AWVA (F.0597), 13.6.69; G-AWXV (F.0619), 22.9.69

G-AXBH (F.0571), 10.10.69; G-AXBI (F.0572), not imported; G-AXBJ (F.0573), 18.7.69; G-AXBK (F.0579), 15.8.69, crashed at Mayenne, France 11.4.70; G-AXDI (F.0574), 4.7.69; G-AXFK (F.0613), 25.7.69; G-AXSI (F.0687), 18.9.70; G-AXSO (F.0570), 31.12.69; G-AXVB (F.0703), 21.4.70; G-AXVX (F.0664), 17.4.70; G-AXWF (F.0697), 3.6.70; G-AXZJ (F.0706), 3.4.70; G-AYAO (F.0695), 3.9.70; G-AYDC (F.0718), 5.3.71; G-AYSG (F.0758), 23.4.71; G-AYUV (F.0752), 17.6.71; G-AYXX (F.0656), N10656, 26.5.71

Cessna F.172K (*1969 model with restyled rudder, dorsal fin and larger windows*)

G-AXUV (F.0740), 9.7.70; G-AYCT (F.0724), 7.7.70; G-AYTI (F.0780), not imported, became D-ECMC; G-AYRG (F.0761), 33.5.71; G-AYRT (F.0777), 2.7.71; G-AYVB (F.0792), 8.10.71

Cessna F.172L (*1971 model built by Reims Aviation*)

G-AZJV (F.0810), registered 8.12.71; G-AZKG (F.0825), registered 8.12.71; G-AZKW (F.0836), registered 23.12.71; G-AZKZ (F.0814), registered 23.12.71; G-AZLM (F.0842), registered 31.12.71

Cessna FR.172E Reims Rocket (*1968 model built by Reims Aviation*)

G-AVXX (F.0013), 14.2.68; G-AVYI (F.0018), not imported; G-AVYJ (F.0017), not imported; G-AWCN (F.0020), 31.7.68; G-AWDR (F.0004), 23.3.69; G-AWFG

Air racing champion John Stewart-Wood's FR.172E Reims Rocket G-AWWU 'Snoopy V'. (*Air Portraits*)

(F.0028), not imported; G-AWWU (F.0111), 16.5.69; G-AWWV (F.0076), 7.5.70; G-AWYB (F.0075), 17.6.70; G-AWYC (F.0101), not imported; G-AYTH (F.0245), 14.10.70

Cessna FR.172F Reims Rocket (*1969 model built by Reims Aviation*)
  G-AWYK (F.0106), 27.8.69; G-AXBT (F.0062), not imported; G-AXBU (F.0073), 21.8.69; G-AXDA (F.0123), not imported

Cessna FR.172G Reims Rocket (*1970 model built by Reims Aviation*)
  G-AYGO (F.0146), N10146, 28.7.70; G-AYGX (F.0208), 14.8.70; G-AYJW (F.0225), 22.10.70; G-AZCD (F.0206), F-BRXE, 3.10.70

Cessna 175A Skylark (*1960 model with 175 h.p. Continental GO-300-E*)
  G-APYA (56444), N6944E, 18.3.60, to Ireland 9.63 as EI-AND; G-APZS (56677), N7977T, 21.6.60; G-ARCJ (56744), N8044T, 14.10.60, d.b.r. at Sibson 23.8.66; G-ARCK (56745), N8045T, 11.11.60; G-ARCL (56746), N8046T, 26.9.60; G-ARCV (56757), N8057T, 5.12.60; G-ARFG (56505), N7005E, 28.11.60; G-AYNL (56094), N6594E, 24.12.70, d.b.r. at Wilstead strip, Beds. 27.12.71

Cessna 175B Skylark (*1961 model*)
  G-AREB (56818), N8118T, 24.1.61; G-ARFL (56868), N8168T, 26.4.61; G-ARFM (56876), N8176T, 23.3.61; G-ARML (56995), N8295T, 3.8.61; G-ARMM (56996), N8296T, 4.8.61; G-ARMN (56994), N8294T, 12.9.61; G-AROC (56997), N8297T, 11.5.62; G-AROD (56998), N8298T, 1.2.62; G-ARRG (56999), N8299T, 5.3.62, d.b.r. at Great Yarmouth 3.11.70; G-ARRH (57000), N8300T, 13.3.62; G-ARRI (57001), N8301T, 11.5.62

Cessna 175C Skylark (*1962 model with third seat and redesigned wing tips*)
  G-ARUZ (57080), N8380T, 9.3.62; G-ARWM (57109), N8509X, 20.7.62; G-ARWS (57102), N8502X, 12.4.62

Cessna F.177 Cardinal RG (*built by Reims Aviation*)
  G-AYPF (F.0006), 11.5.71; G-AYPG (F.0007), 2.7.71; G-AYPH (F.0018), 10.9.71; G-AYPI (F.0025), 12.11.71; G-AYSK (F.0024), 3.9.71; G-AYSY (F.0026), registered

17.2.71; G-AYTG (F.0010), 22.2.71; G-AZFP (F.0031), registered 29.9.71; G-AZKH (F.0049), registered 8.12.71; G-AZKT (F.0039), registered 23.12.71; G-AZKU (F.0050), registered 23.12.71

Cessna 180 to Cessna 180H

(180) 1956 model with 225 h.p. Continental O-470-K; (180A) 1959 model with improved interior; (180C) 1960 model with increased headroom; (180D) 1961 model with improved equipment; (180H) 1964 model.

G-APYJ (50012), 180A, N9714B, N347TC, 5.5.60, to Ireland 7.60 as EI-ALO, rest. 5.61, to Australia 1.62 as VH-EDM; G-ARAT (50827), 180C, N9327T, 31.8.60; G-ARGC (50931), 180D, N6431X, 12.1.61; G-ARLC (50663), 180C, N9163T, 14.4.61, to Uganda 2.64 as VP-UBK; G-ASIT (32567), 180, N7670A, 12.6.63; G-ASYI (51485), 180H, N4785U, 25.6.65; G-AXWW (52109), 180H, sold in Angola 5.70; G-AXWX (52110), 180H, sold in Angola 5.70; G-AXZO (31137), 180, N3639C, 23.11.70; G-AYEZ (50695), 180C, TR-LLP, 29.10.70

Cessna 182 to Cessna 182G

(182) 1957 model with 230 h.p. Continental O-470-L; (182C) 1960 model with swept fin and rudder; (182D) 1961 model; (182E) 1962 model with slim rear fuselage and wrap-around rear canopy; (182F) 1963 model; (182G) 1964 model.

G-ARAA (52646), 182C, N8746T, 20.9.60, crashed at Blackgang, I.O.W. 5.5.61; G-ARAW (52843), 182C, N8943T, 27.7.60; G-ARGD (53088), 182D, N9088T, 2.3.61, sold in Angola 7.61; G-ARWL (53895), 182E, N2895Y, 13.4.62; G-ASHB (54633), 182F, N3233U, 3.5.63; G-ASHO (54832), 182F, 1.7.63; G-ASJR (54939), 182F, N3539U, 9.8.63; G-ASLH (54905), 182F, N3505U, 31.8.63; G-ASNN (55012), 182F, N3612U, 9.1.64; G-ASRR (55135), 182G, N3735U, to Ireland 3.70 as EI-ATF; G-ASSF (55593), 182G, 7.8.64; G-ASUL (55077), 182G, N3677U, 10.7.63; G-ASXZ (55738), 182G, N3238S, 6.11.64; G-ATNU (34078), 182, N6078B, EI-ANC, 22.4.66

Cessna 182H to Cessna 182N

(182H) 1965 model with modified engine cowlings and more pointed spinner; (182J) 1966 model with rear seat for two children; (182K) 1967 model with shorter nose-leg; (182L) 1968 model with revised aileron and flap controls; (182M) 1969 model with redesigned flap lever and instrument panel; (182N) 1970 model.   G-ATCW (56203), 182H, N3503S, 30.4.65, to Kenya 2.66 as 5Y-ADN; G-ATCX (55848), 182H, N3448S,

G-APYA, first British owned Cessna 175A, at Elstree in 1960. (*Richard Riding*)

G-ATNU was an early Cessna 182, built in 1957 and imported via Ireland in 1966.
(*A. J. Jackson*)

7.5.65; G-ATLA (56923), 182J, N2823F, 23.3.66; G-ATPT (57056), 182J, N2956F, 15.4.66; G-ATTD (57229), 182J, N3129F, 8.7.66; G-ATUT (57231), 182J, N3131F, 12.7.66, d.b.r. at Hoddesdon, Herts. 19.9.67; G-AVCV (57492), 182J, N3492F, 20.12.66; G-AVDA (57959), 182K, N27959, 19.5.67; G-AVGY (58112), 182K, 22.5.67; G-AVID (57734), 182K, N2534Q, 21.3.67; G-AWBP (58831), 182L, N3331R, 30.4.68; G-AWBV (58815), 182L, N3315R, 3.5.68; G-AWJA (58883), 182L, N1658C, 10.5.68; G-AWXA (59403), 182M, N70877, 20.3.69; G-AXEC (59491), 182M, N71088, 23.5.69; G-AXNX (59322), 182M, N70606, 2.10.69; G-AXZU (60104), 182N, N92233, 16.4.70; G-AYIB (60366), 182N, N92807, 14.8.70; G-AYIU (60411), 182N, N92885, 4.9.70; G-AYOW (60481), 182N, N8941G, 16.6.71; G-AYWD (60468), 182N, N8928G, 21.5.71; G-AZEA (60466), 182N, N8926G, 24.9.71

Cessna 205/206/207

(205) 1962 model with 260 h.p. Continental IO-470-S; (205A) 1964 model with internal improvements; (206) 1964 model with double cargo doors and 285 h.p. Continental IO-520-A; (P.206D) 1968 'plush' private owner variant with 6 seats; (U.206) 1965 utility model; (U.206A) 1966 utility model; (U.206D) 1969 utility model with cargo doors and 300 h.p. Continental IO-520-F; (TP.206D) as P.206D but with 285 h.p. Continental TSIO-520-C.

G-ASNK (205-0400), N8400Z, 21.12.63; G-ASOX (205A-0556), N4856U, 15.7.64; G-ASVN (206-0275), N5275U, 4.12.64; G-ATAN (U.206-0358), N2158F, 4.6.65, crashed at Bath Racecourse 23.5.69; G-ATCE (U.206-0380), N2180F, 25.6.65; G-ATLT (U.206A-0523), N4823F, 22.4.66; G-AVYH (206-0075), 5Y-KTT, not imported; G-AWUA (P.206D-0550), 23.5.68; G-AXJY (U.206D-0138), 19.9.69; G-AYCJ (TP.206D-0552), N8752Z, 4.6.70; G-AYJU (TP.206A-0241), N176WM, 3.11.70; G-AYTJ (207-00191), N1591U, 11.3.71

Cessna 210 to Cessna T.210K

(210) 1960 model with 260 h.p. Continental IO-470-E; (210D) 1964 model with 285 h.p. Continental IO-520-A; (210F) 1966 model; (T.210H) 1968 model with 300 h.p. Continental TSIO-520-C turbo-supercharged engine and cantilever mainplane; (210K) 1970 model; (T.210K) 1970 model with TSIO-520-L turbo-supercharged engine.

G-ARDC (57007), 210, N7307E, 14.7.60; G-ARGK (57427), 210, N9627T, 30.3.61; G-ASPO (58383), 210D, N3883Y, 13.8.64, crashed near Northampton 6.12.67;

G-ASWO (58502), 210D, N2302F, 18.12.64; G-ASXR (57592), 210, 5Y-KPW, 18.12.64; G-ATMP (58735), 210F, N1835F, 5.4.66; G-AWGI (59001), 210F, not imported; G-AWGP (T.210H-0337), 17.5.68; G-AXVE (59257), 210K, 31.7.70; G-AYCL (59306), N9406M, T.210K, 31.7.70; G-AYGM (59338), T.210K, 9.10.70; G-AYGN (59329), T.210K, 11.9.70; G-AYTZ (59360), T.210K, not imported; G-AYVI (T.210H-0351), N2201R, 14.5.71; G-AZCC, 210J, (59067), 5N-AIE, 25.8.71

Cessna 310 to Cessna 310C

(310) 1953 model with two 240 h.p. Continental O-470-M; (310B) 1957 model with detail improvements; (310C) 1959 model with two 260 h.p. Continental IO-470-D.

G-APNJ (35335), 310, N3635D, EI-AJY, 17.6.58; G-APTK (35453), 310, N5253A, OO-DST, 16.4.59; G-APUF (35960), 310C, N1860H, 4.8.59, crashed near Vieira do Minho, Portugal 18.11.70; G-APVC (35948), 310C, N1848H, 4.8.59, sold in U.S.A. 3.62; G-ARBI (35011), 310, N2611C, 27.5.60; G-ARGP (35260), 310, CF-ILF, N3060D, 7.4.61, to France 6.62 as F-BKBS; G-ARIG (35578), 310B, N5378A, EI-AOS, 29.3.61; G-AROX (35505), 310, N5305A, 10.6.61, to Sweden 12.65 as SE-ETU;

Three Cessna 310s—G-ARRR (illustrated), G-ASNS and 'SZ—imported by Keegan Aviation Ltd., Panshanger, 1961–64, were cleaned-up versions known as the Riley 65 Rocket. (*Flight Photo 43409S*)

G-ARRR (35416), 310, modified to Riley 65, N5216A, 8.9.61, to Switzerland 6.62 as HB-LBN; G-ARTK (35044), 310, N2644C, 11.11.61, to Southern Rhodesia 8.65 as VP-YYK; G-ASNS (35073), 310, modified to Riley 65, N2673C, LN-FAD, 18.2.64, d.b.r. at Marud, 150 miles south of Bombay, India 8.6.64; G-ASSZ (35407), 310, modified to Riley 65, N5207A, 15.5.64, to Denmark 2.69 as OY-DRH; G-ATCR (35311), 310, N3611D, SE-CXX, 4.10.64; G-ATSV (35795), 310C, N6695B, ZS-CKA, 9L-LAE, 18.4.66; G-AVZS (35660), 310B, N5460A, VP-YPT, ST-AAV, SE-ETW, 19.4.68

Cessna 310D to Cessna 310Q

(310D) 1960 model with swept fin and rudder; (310F) 1961 model with two additional cabin windows; (310G) 1962 model with 'stabila-tip' wings and wing tanks; (310I) 1964 model with baggage compartment in rear of nacelles; (310J) 1965 model; (310K) 1966 model with two 260 h.p. Continental IO-470-V; (310L) 1967 model with new main landing gear and one-piece windscreen; (310N) 1968 model with more fuel and better instrumentation; (310P) 1969 model with 5–6 seats; (310Q) 1970 model with increased all-up weight and revised panel.

G-ARAC (39154), 310D, N6854T, 6.7.60, crashed at Perth 24.6.64; G-ARBC (39234), 310D, N6934T, 6.9.60; G-ARCH (39253), 310D, N6953T, 9.11.60, crashed at Perth 16.2.70; G-ARCI (39266), 310D, N6966T, 21.11.60; G-ARMK (310F-0136), N5836X, 6.7.61, crashed near Capel Curig, North Wales 28.9.68; G-ARNU (310F-0142), N5842X, 19.7.61, crashed near Luxembourg 9.1.62; G-AROK (310F-0148), N5848X, 21.7.61; G-ARWF (310G-0050), N8950Z, 9.3.62, to Ireland 1.69 as EI-ATC; G-ASMD (39163), 310D, N6863T, 1.11.63, to France 10.69 as F-BRSE; G-ASVV (310I-0052), N8052M, 2.12.63; G-ASYV (310G-0048), N8948Z, HB-LBY, 17.2.65; G-ASZZ (310J-0077), N3077L, 23.4.65

G-ATCS (310J-0145), N3145L, 6.7.65; G-ATDL (310J-0146), N3146L, 29.7.65; G-ATLD (310K-0068), N6968L, 19.9.66; G-ATMR (310K-0098), N6998L, not imported; G-ATPS (310K-0090), N6990L, 2.11.66, to Finland 10.69 as OH-CDH; G-AVDB (310L-0079), 11.1.67; G-AVUV (310N-0013), 10.12.67; G-AVWX (310L-0186), N3336X, 24.11.67, to Australia 12.70 as VH-EDK; G-AWGH (310N-0141), to Italy 7.68 as I-ALCC; G-AWTA (310N-0054), N4154Q, EI-ATB, 25.11.68; G-AXLG (310K-0204), N3804X, 5.2.70; G-AXSL (310P-0167), N5867M, 10.12.69; G-AYGB (310Q-0111), N7611Q, 28.1.71; G-AYIN (310Q-0107), not imported, became D-ICAH; G-AYND (310Q-0110), N7610Q, 9.12.70; G-AZFJ (T.310Q-0234), N7734Q, 8.10.71; G-AZFL (310P-0221), N5921M, 24.9.71

Cessna 320 Skyknight

G-ARYU (320-0109), N5209X, 21.6.62; G-ASDJ (320A-0032), N3032R, 7.11.62, crashed in the North Sea off Arbroath 4.2.70; G-AZCI (320A-0021), CF-PKY, 13.5.71

The Cessna 336 G-ASLL (fixed undercarriage) operated in 1972 by Snowmountain Investments Ltd. of March, Cambs. (*Aviation Photo News*)

Cessna 336 Skymaster (*fixed undercarriage*)

G-ASKS (336-0070), N1770Z, 17.9.63; G-ASLL (336-0074), N1774Z, 29.9.63; G-ATAH (336-0007), N1707Z, 3.11.65

Cessna 337 Super Skymaster (*retractable undercarriage*)

(337) 1965 model with two 210 h.p. Continental IO-360-C and D; (337A) 1966 model; (337B) 1967 model; (337C) 1968 model with increased all-up weight; (337D) 1969 model; (337E) 1970 model

G-ASYC (337-033), N2133X, not imported; G-ATCU (337-0133), N2233X, 23.2.65; G-ATID (337-0239), N6239F, 20.10.65; G-ATJO (337A-0281), N6281F, 7.1.66, destroyed in air collision with Varsity WF334 near Immingham, Lincs. 14.6.66; G-ATNY (337-0364), N6364F, 24.3.66; G-ATPU (337A-0397), N6397F, 19.4.66, td the Lebanon

4.68 as F-OCLP, rest. 2.70; G-ATSM (337A-0434), 19.7.66; G-AVIX (337B-0554), N5454S, 21.3.67; G-AVJG (337B-0715), N5615S, 26.6.67; G-AWCI (337C-0863), 27.3.68; G-AWKE (337C-0939), N2639S, 24.6.68; G-AWKR (337C-0960), 24.9.68, to Israel 11.68 as 4X-AYD; G-AWVS (337D-0991), N2691S, 6.6.69; G-AWYD (337D-1076), not imported

G-AXBV (337D-1077), N86098, not imported; G-AXFG (337D-1070), N86081, 26.6.69; G-AXGI (337D-1095), N86141, 13.6.69, crashed near Dorchester 6.8.69; G-AXGJ (337D-1088), N86127, 19.9.69; G-AXHA (337A-0484), EI-ATH, 17.6.69; G-AXRX (337D-1077), N86098, G-AXBV ntu, 12.12.69; G-AZAV (337E-01388), N1788M, 28.6.71

Cessna F.337E Super Skymaster *(built by Reims Aviation)*

G-AXWN (F.0005), based at Cannes, France; G-AYFB (F.0009), 8.2.71; G-AYHW (F.0019), 16.10.70; G-AZKO (F.0041), registered 20.12.71; G-AZLO (F.0029), registered 4.1.72

Cessna 401, 411, 414 and 421

(401) 1966 model 6 seater for private owner with two 300 h.p. Continental TSIO-520-E; (401A) 1969 model with 'stabila-tip' wings and tip tanks; (411) 1964 model with 6–8 seats; (411A) 1967 model with double freight door and nose baggage compartment; (414) 1970 pressurised model with two 310 h.p. Continental TSIO-520 engines; (421) 1968 pressurised model with two 375 h.p. Continental GTSIO-520-D; (421A) 1969 model with flap pre-selector and increased all-up weight; (421B) 1970 model with GTSIO-520-H engines.

G-ATEY (411-0087), N7387U, 25.11.64; G-AVEK (411A-0274), N3274R, 14.7.67; G-AVKN (401-0082), N3282Q, 5.6.67; G-AWBK (421-0125), 30.1.69; G-AWDJ (411-0184), N4984T, 7.3.69; G-AWDM (401-0204), 21.3.69, d.b.r. at Bognor Regis 7.5.71; G-AWJU (421-0114), not imported; G-AWRJ (421-0192), 7.2.69; G-AWSF (401-0166), N4066Q, 28.10.69; G-AWVT (411A-0256), N3256R, 25.3.69; G-AWWW (401-0294), N8446F, 27.1.69; G-AWXM (401-0165), N4065Q, 9.9.69; G-AXAW (421A-0038), 12.5.69; G-AXBY (401A-0032), N6232Q, 17.3.69; G-AXVA (401B-0009), 25.3.70; G-AYDF (414-0091), N8191Q, not imported; G-AYMM (421B-0033), N8033Q, 15.2.71; G-AYOU (401B-0112), N79720, 23.4.71; G-AZFR (401B-0121), N7981Q, 5.10.71; G-AZFZ (414-0175), N8254Q, 2.11.71; G-AZHG (421B-0107), N8077Q, 1.12.71

Champion 7FC Tri-Traveller

G-APYS (386), dropped by crane at Ramsgate 7.60; G-APYT (387), 18.5.60; G-APYU (388), 25.5.60; G-APZW (393), 28.10.60; G-ARAP (394), 25.1.61; G-ARAR (395), 25.1.61, crashed at Sywell 27.3.70; G-ARAS (396), 18.10.60; G-AVJY (372), N8193R, 18.4.68

Chilton D.W.1 and D.W.1A

G-AESZ (D.W.1/1), 13.4.37, Hon. A. Dalrymple, Hungerford; subsequent owners are recorded on page 279; crashed at Felixstowe, Suffolk 24.5.53

G-AFGH (D.W.1/2), 20.5.38, Chilton Aircraft Ltd., High Trees, Marlborough; subsequent owners are recorded on page 279

G-AFGI (D.W.1/3), 20.10.38, owners as page 280; dismantled at Perth 1958; flown again 1960 by G. H. Baker; preserved at Staverton

G-AFSV (D.W.1A/1), 22.7.39, owners as page 280; to R. H. Fautley, Navestock 10.63; W. M. Hodgkins, Thetford 11.65; Sqn. Ldr. M. A. Kelly, Booker 11.69

G-AFSW (D.W.2/1), construction abandoned, components used as spares in 1951

APPENDIX F

Registrations not Issued

Registrations listed herein were not used because they represented international code signals; had been allotted to aircraft whose construction was abandoned; were likely to cause radio confusion by their similarity to another aircraft registration; or were considered offensive.

G-EBJI	G-AERD	G-AHAN	G-AMTN	G-ASSG	G-AXWC
G-AADR	G-AESB	G-AHEC	G-ANUS	G-ASVD	G-AXXX
G-AAMX	G-AEZX	G-AHIP	G-AOSG	G-ASWC	G-AYVD
G-AAMY	G-AFDO	G-AHOO	G-APAN	G-ATDI	G-AYWC
G-AAMZ	G-AFEL	G-AHRO	G-APGM	G-ATIT	G-AZBO
*G-AANF	G-AFFI	G-AHUF	G-APIS	G-ATPO	G-AZDG
to	G-AFGM	G-AHUN	G-APSG	G-ATSB	
G-AANZ	G-AFOH	G-AISS	G-ARCE	G-ATSG	
*G-AAOK	G-AFPV	G-AITP	G-ARIP	G-ATTT	
to	G-AFUC	G-AJAD	G-ARPV	G-ATVD	
G-AAOZ	G-AFUK	G-AJAO	G-ARSE	G-ATWC	
G-ABOX	G-AFUP	G-AJAP	G-ARSG	G-AVBF	
G-ABPO	G-AFWH	G-AJES	G-ARVD	G-AVBO	
G-ABUM	G-AFYD	G-AJON	G-ASBF	G-AVPO	
G-ABWC	G-AGAT	G-AKAZ	G-ASEX	G-AVVD	
G-ACAR	G-AGEG	G-AKIB	G-ASIC	G-AVWC	
G-ACFM	G-AGHY	G-AKRA	G-ASIK	G-AWBF	
G-ACNB	G-AGIV	G-AKUR	G-ASIN	G-AWOP	
G-ACOL	G-AGMI	G-ALEH	G-ASIS	G-AWPO	
*G-ADRA	*G-AGPK	G-ALIW	G-ASOD	G-AWRY	
to	to	G-ALOD	G-ASOP	G-AWVD	
G-ADRZ	G-AGPR	G-ALTO	G-ASOS	G-AWWC	
G-ADUD	G-AGVV	G-ALUL	G-ASOT	G-AXBF	
G-AENP	G-AGYY	G-AMEN	G-ASOW	G-AXBO	
G-AEOF	G-AGZZ	G-AMSG	G-ASPP	G-AXVD	

* Commencement of unused registration block.

In Volume 2 this appendix lists registrations allotted to gliders and in Volume 3 a number of airships, free balloons and miscellaneous craft.

INDEX

Index of Aeroplanes

564